First Printing, August 1950
Second Printing, July 1957
Third Printing, May 1959

NOTES

ON THE

OLD TESTAMEN

EXPLANATORY AND PRACTICAL

BY

ALBERT BARNES

ENLARGED TYPE EDITION

EDITED BY

ROBERT FREW, D.D.

DANIEL
VOL. II

BAKER BOOK HOUSE

GRAND RAPIDS, MICHIGAN

1959

THE BOOK OF DANIEL.

CHAPTER VI.

§ I.—AUTHENTICITY OF THE CHAPTER.

THIS chapter, like the previous ones, has not escaped serious objections as to its authenticity and credibility. The objections which have been made to it have been derived from what is regarded as incredible in its statements. It is important, as in the previous chapters, to inquire whether the objections are insuperable, or whether this is so free from reasonable objection as to be worthy to be received as a portion of Divine truth. The objections, as urged by Bertholdt (*Daniel aus dem Hebräisch-Aramäischen neu übersetzt*, &c., pp. 72–75, and pp. 357–364) and by Bleek, are capable of being reduced to the four following:—

I. That it is wholly improbable that a monarch, in the circumstances of Darius, would give an order so unreasonable and foolish as that no one of his subjects should present any petition for a month to any one, God or man, but to himself. It is alleged that no good end could have been proposed by it; that it would have perilled the peace of the empire; that among a people who worshipped many gods—who had gods in all their dwellings—it would have been vain to hope that the command could have been carried peaceably into execution; and that, whoever proposed this, it could not have been executed without shaking the stability of the throne. Bertholdt asks (p. 357, *seq.*), "Can one believe that, among a people so devoted to religion as the Babylonians were, it should have been forbidden them to address their gods for one single day? Is it credible that the counsellors of the king were so irreligious that, without fear of the avenging deities, they would endeavour to enforce such an order as that here referred to—that no petition should be addressed to God or man for a month, except to the king? And was Cyaxares so destitute of religion as not to refuse to sanction such a mandate? And does this agree with the fact that in the issue itself he showed so much respect to a foreign God—the God of the Jews? Under what pretence could the ministers of the king give him this counsel? Could it be under any purpose of deifying his own person? But it remains to be proved that either then, or soon after that time, it was customary in Asia to attribute Divine honours to a monarch, whether deceased or living."

To this objection, Hengstenberg (*Die Authentie des Daniel*, p. 125, *seq.*) replies, by an endeavour to show that it was a common opinion in Persia that the king was regarded "as a representative, and an incarnation of Ormuzd;" and that nothing is more probable than that such a monarch coming to the throne of Babylon would be willing to appear in that character, claiming Divine honours, and early testing the inclination of his new sub-

DANIEL II.   A

jects to receive him in that character in which he was recognized in his own land. In confirmation of this, he quotes two passages from Heeren (*Ideen 3te Ausg.* I. i. p. 446, 51) in proof that these ideas thus prevailed. "The person of the king," Heeren says, "is in Asiatic kingdoms the middle point around which all revolves. He is regarded, according to the Oriental notions, not so much the ruler as the actual owner of the people and land. All their arrangements are formed on this fundamental idea, and they are carried to an extent which to Europeans appears incredible and ridiculous." "The idea of citizenship, according to the European nations, is altogether a strange idea to them; all, without exception, from the highest to the lowest, are the servants of the king, and the right to rule over them, and to deal with them as he pleases, is a right which is never called in question." Hengstenberg then remarks, that it is capable of the clearest proof that *the kings of the Medes and Persians were regarded and honoured as the representatives and incarnations of Ormuzd.* In proof of this, he quotes the following passage from Heeren (p. 474), showing that this idea early prevailed among the followers of Zoroaster. "Zoroaster," says he, "saw the kingdom of light and of darkness both developed upon the earth; Iran, the Medo-Bactrish kingdom, under the sceptre of Gustasp, is to him the image of the kingdom of Ormuzd; *the king himself is an image of him;* Turan, the Northern Nomadland, when Afrasiab reigned, is the image of the kingdom of darkness, under the dominion of Ahriman." This idea, says Hengstenberg, the magi made use of when they wished to bring the king to their own interests, or to promote any favourite object of their own. The king was re-

garded as the representative, the visible manifestation of Ormuzd, ruling with power as uncircumscribed as his; the seven princes standing near him were representatives of the seven Amshaspands, who stood before the throne of Ormuzd. The evidence that the Persian kings were regarded as an embodiment of the deity, or that they represented him on earth, Hengstenberg remarks (p. 126), is clear in the classic writings, in the Scriptures, and in the Persian monuments. In proof of this, he appeals to the following authorities among the classic writers:—Plutarch (*Themistocl.* cap. 27); Xenophon (*Agesil.*); Isocrates (*Panegyri de Pers. princ.* p. 17); Arrian (6. 29); Curtius (8. 5). Curtius says, *Persas reges suos inter deos colere.* For the same purpose, Hengstenberg (pp. 128, 129) appeals to the following passage of Scripture, Esth. iii. 4, and the conduct of Mordecai in general, who refused, as he supposes, the respect which Haman demanded as the first minister of the king, on religious grounds, and because more was required and expected of him than mere civil respect—or that a degree of homage was required entirely inconsistent with that due to the true God. In proof of the same thing, Hengstenberg appeals to Persian monuments, pp. 129–132. The proof is too long to be inserted here. These monuments show that the Persian kings were regarded and adored as impersonations of Ormuzd. To this may be added many of their inscriptions. In the work by De Sacy, *Memoires s. divers. Antiq. de la Perse,* Pl. i. p. 27, 31, the Persian kings are mentioned as ἔκγονοι θεῶν, ἐκ γένους θεῶν, and θεοῖ—both as offsprings of the gods, as of the race of the gods, and as gods.

If this is correct, and the Persian kings were regarded as divine—as an impersonation or incarnation of the god that was worshipped—then there is no improbability in the supposition that it might be proposed to the king that for a given space of time he should allow no petition to be presented to any one else, god or man. It would be easy to persuade a monarch having such pretensions to issue such a decree, and especially when he had subjected a foreign people like the Babylonians to be willing thus to assert his authority over them, and show them what respect and homage he demanded. In judging also of the probability of what is here said, we are to remember the arbitrary character of Oriental monarchs, and of the Persian kings no less than others. Assuredly there were as strange things in the character and conduct of Xerxes, one of the successors of this same Darius, as any that are recorded in this chapter of the book of Daniel; and if the acts of folly which he perpetrated had been written in a book claiming to be Divinely inspired, they would have been liable to much greater objection than anything which is stated here. The mere fact that a thing is in itself foolish and unreasonable, and apparently absurd, is no conclusive evidence that a man clothed with absolute authority would not be guilty of it.

To all that has been said on this point, there should be added a remark made by Bertholdt himself (p. 357) respecting Darius, which will show that what is here said of him is really not at all inconsistent with his character, and not improbable. He says, speaking of Darius or Cyaxares, that "from his character, as given by Xenophon, a man of weak mind (*Cyrop.* i. 4, 22; iv. 1, 13); a man passionate and peevish (iii. 3, 29; iv. 5, 8; v. 5; i. 8); a man given to wine and women (iv. 5. 52; v. 5, 44), we are not to ex-pect much wisdom." There is nothing stated here by Daniel which is inconsistent with the character of such a man.

II. A second objection made to the probability of this statement is drawn from the character of the edict which Darius is said to have proclaimed, commanding that honour should be rendered to Jehovah, vers. 25–27. It is alleged that if such an edict had been published, it is incredible that no mention is made of it in history; that the thing was so remarkable that it must have been noticed by the writers who have referred to Darius or Cyaxares.

To this it may be replied, (1) that, for anything that appears to the contrary, Daniel may be as credible an historian as Xenophon or Herodotus. No one can demonstrate that the account here is not as worthy of belief as if it had appeared in a Greek or Latin classic author. When will the world get over the folly of supposing that what is found in a book claiming to be inspired, should be regarded as suspicious until it is confirmed by the authority of some heathen writer; that what is found in any other book should be regarded as necessarily true, however much it may conflict with the testimony of the sacred writers? Viewed in any light, Daniel is as worthy of confidence as any Greek or Latin historian; what he says is as credible as if it had been found in the works of Sanchoniathon or Berosus. (2.) There are, in fact, few things preserved in any history in regard to Darius the Mede. Comp. § II. The information given of him by Xenophon consists merely of a few detached and fragmentary notices, and it is not at all remarkable that the facts here mentioned, and the proclamation which he made, should be unnoticed by him. A proclamation respecting a foreign god, when it was customary to recognize so many gods, and indeed to regard all such gods as entitled to respect and honour, would not be likely to arrest the attention of a Greek historian even if he knew of it, and, for the same reason, it would be scarcely probable that he would know of it at all. Nothing would be more likely to pass away from the recollection of a people than such an edict, or less likely to be known to a foreigner. So far as the evidence goes, it would seem that the proclamation made no disturbance in the realm; the injunction appeared to be generally acquiesced in by all except Daniel; and it was soon forgotten. If it was understood, as it was not improbable, that this was designed as a sort of *test* to see whether the people would receive the commands of Darius as binding on them; that they would honour him, as the Persian monarch was honoured in his own proper kingdom, it would seem to have been entirely successful, and there was no occasion to refer to it again.

III. A third objection urged by Bertholdt (p. 361), is derived from the account respecting the lions in this chapter. It is alleged by him that the account is so full of improbabilities that it cannot be received as true; that though the fact that they did not fall on Daniel can be explained from the circumstance that they were not hungry, &c., yet that it is incredible that they should have fallen on the *enemies* of Daniel as soon as they were thrown into the den; that the king should expect to find Daniel alive after being thrown among them; that he should have called in this manner to Daniel, &c.

To all this it is sufficient to reply, that no one can suppose that the facts stated here can be explained by any natural causes. The whole representation is evidently designed to leave the impression that there was a special Divine interposition—a miracle—in the case, and the only explanation which is admissible here is that which would be proper in the case of any other miracle. The only questions which could be asked, or which would be proper, are these two; whether a miracle is possible; and whether this was a suitable occasion for the miraculous exertion of Divine power. As to the first of these questions, it is not necessary to argue that here—for the objection might lie with equal force against any other miracle referred to in the Bible. As to the second, it may be observed, that it is not easy to conceive of a case when a miracle would be *more* proper. If a miracle was ever proper to protect the innocent; or to vindicate the claims of the true God against all false gods: or to make a deep and lasting impression on the minds of men that Jehovah is the true God, it is not easy to conceive of a more appropriate occasion than this. No situation could be conceived to be more appropriate than when an impression was designed to be made on the mind of the sovereign of the most mighty empire on the earth; or that when, through a proclamation issued from the throne, the nations subject to his sceptre should be summoned to acknowledge him as the true God.

IV. A fourth objection urged by Bleek (*Theologische Zeitschrift*, pp. 262-264) is, substantially, the following: that it is remarkable that there is in this account no allusion to the three companions of Daniel; to those who had been trained with him at the Chaldean court, and had been admitted also to honour, and who had so abundantly shown that they were worshippers of the true God. The whole story, says Bleek, appears to have been designed to produce a moral effect on the mind of the Jews, by the unknown author, to persuade them in some period of persecution to adhere to the God of their fathers in the midst of all persecution and opposition.

To this objection it may be replied, (1.) That it is wholly probable that there were many other pious Jews in Babylon at this time beside Daniel— Jews who would, like him, adhere to the worship of the true God, regardless of the command of the king. We are not to suppose, by any means, that Daniel was the *only* conscientious Jew in Babylon. The narrative evidently does not require that we should come to such a conclusion, but that there was something *peculiar* in regard to Daniel. (2.) As to the three companions and friends of Daniel, it is possible, as Hengstenberg remarks (*Authentic*, &c. p. 135), that they may either have been dead, or may have been removed from office, and were leading private lives. (3.) This edict was evidently aimed at Daniel. The whole narrative supposes this. For some cause, according to the narrative —and there is no improbability that such an opposition *might* exist against a foreigner advanced to honour at court —there was some ground of jealousy against him, and a purpose formed to remove or disgrace him. There does not appear to have been any jealousy of others, or any purpose to disturb others in the free enjoyment of their religion. The aim was to humble Daniel; to secure his removal from office, and to degrade him; and for this purpose a plan was laid with consummate skill. He was known to be upright, and they who laid the plot felt assured that no charge of guilt, no accusation of crime, or unfaithfulness in his office, could be alleged against him. He was known to be a man who would not shrink from the avowal of his opinions, or from the performance of those duties which he owed to his God. He was known to be a man so much devoted to the worship of *Jehovah*, the God of his people, that no law whatever would prevent him from rendering to him the homage which was his due, and it was believed, therefore, that if a law were made, on any pretence, that no one in the realm should ask anything of either God or man, except the king, for a definite space of time, there would be a moral certainty that Daniel would be found to be a violator of that law, and his degradation and death would be certain. What was here proposed was a scheme worthy of crafty and jealous and wicked men; and the only difficulty, evidently, which would occur to their mind would be to persuade the king to enter into the measure so far as to promulgate such a law. As already observed, plausible pretences might be found for that; and when that was done, they would naturally conclude that their whole scheme was successful. (4.) There is no improbability, therefore, in supposing that, as the whole thing was aimed at Daniel, there might have been many pious Jews who still worshipped God in secret in Babylon, and that no one would give information against them. As the edict was not aimed at them, it is not surprising that we hear of no prosecution against them, and no complaint made of them for disregarding the law. If Daniel was found to violate the statute; if he was ensnared and entrapped by the cunning device; if he was humbled and punished, all the purposes contemplated by its authors would be accomplished, and we need not suppose that they would give themselves any trouble about others.

§ II.—THE QUESTION WHO WAS DARIUS THE MEDE.

Considerable importance is to be attached to the question who was "Darius the Mede," as it has been made a ground of objection to the Scripture narrative, that no person by that name is mentioned in the Greek writers.

There are three Medo-Persian kings of the name of Darius mentioned in the Old Testament. One occurs in the book of Ezra (iv. 5 ; vi. 1, 12, 15), in Haggai (i. 1 ; ii. 10), and in Zechariah (i. 7), as the king who, in the second year of his reign, effected the execution of those decrees of Cyrus which granted the Jews the liberty of rebuilding the temple, the fulfilment of which had been obstructed by the malicious representations which their enemies had made to his immediate successors. It is commonly agreed that this king was Darius Hystaspis, who succeeded the usurper Smerdis, B.C. 521, and reigned thirty-six years.

A second is mentioned as "Darius the Persian," in Nehe. xii. 22. All that is said of him is, that the succession of priests was registered up to his reign. This was either Darius Nothus, B.C. 423, or Darius Codomanus, B.C. 336. See Kitto's *Cyclop.*, art. *Darius.*

The remaining one is that mentioned in Daniel only as Darius the Median. In ch. ix. 1, he is mentioned as Darius the son of Ahasuerus, of the seed of the Medes. Much difference of opinion has prevailed as to the person here intended ; but a strict attention to what is actually expressed in, or fairly deduced from, the terms used in Daniel, tends to narrow the field of conjecture very considerably, if it does not decide the question. It appears from the passage in ch. v. 30, 31, and vi. 28, that Darius the Mede obtained the dominion over Babylon on the death of Belshazzar, who was the last Chaldean king, and that he was the immediate predecessor of Koresh (Cyrus) in the sovereignty. The historical juncture here defined belongs, therefore, to the period when the Medo-Persian army led by Cyrus took Babylon (B.C. 538), and Darius the Mede must denote the first king of a foreign dynasty who assumed the dominion over the Babylonian empire before Cyrus. These indications all concur in the person of Cyaxares the Second, the son and successor of Astyages [Ahasuerus], and the immediate predecessor of Cyrus.—Kitto's *Cyclop.*, art. *Darius.*

In reference to the question, who was Darius the Mede, Bertholdt has examined the different opinions which have been entertained in a manner that is satisfactory, and I cannot do better than to present his views on the subject. They are found in his *Vierter Excurs. uber den Darius Medus,* in his Commentary on Daniel, pp. 843–858. I will give the substance of the Excursus, in a free translation :—

" Who was Darius the Mede, the son of Ahasuerus, of whom mention is made in the sixth chapter of the book of Daniel, and again in ch. ix. 1, and xi. 1? It is agreed on all hands that he was the immediate successor of Belshazzar, the king of the Chaldeans (ch. v. 30). Comp. ch. vi. 1. But, notwithstanding this, there is uncertainty as to his person, since history makes no mention of a *Median* Darius. It is, therefore, not to be wondered at that various opinions have been entertained by commentators on the Scriptures, and by historical inquirers. Conring (*Advers. Chronol.* c. 13), whom many have followed, particularly Harenberg (*Aufklärung des Buchs Daniels,* s. 454, *seq.*), has endeavoured to show that Darius the Mede was the fourth Chaldean monarch, Neriglissar, and that Belshazzar, his predecessor, was Evil-Merodach. J. Scaliger (*De Emendat. Temporum*, p. 579, *seq.*) recognized in Darius the Mede the last Chaldean king in Babylon, Nabonned, and in Belshazzar, the one before the last, Laborosoarchod, which hypothesis also Calvisius, Petavius, and Buddeus adopted. On the other hand, Syncellus (*Chronogr.* p. 232), Cedrenus (*Chron.* p. 142), the Alexandrine Chronicle, Marsham (*Can. Chron.* p. 604, *seq.*), the two most recent editors of Æschylus, Schütz (in *zweiten Excurs. zu Æschylus's* σερσαι), and Bothe (*Æsch. dramata*, p. 671), held that Darius the Mede was the Median king Astyages, the maternal grandfather of Cyrus. Des Vignolles (*Chronologie*, t. 2. p. 495), and Schröer (*Regnum Babyl. Sect.* 6, § 12, *seq.*), held him to be a prince of Media, a younger brother of Astyages, whom Cyrus made king over Babylon. Another opinion, however, deserves more respect than this, which was advanced by Marianus Scotus, a Benedictine monk of the eleventh century, though this hypothesis is not tenable, which opinion has found, in modern times, a warm advocate in Beer (*Kings of Israel and Judah*, p. 22, *seq.*) According to this opinion, it was held that Darius the Mede is the same person as the third Persian king after Cyrus, Darius Hystaspis, and that Belshazzar was indeed the last Chaldean king, Nabonned, but that in the first capture of Babylon under Cyrus, according to the account of Berosus in (*Jos. c. Ap.* i. 20) and Megasthenes (in *Euseb. Præp. Evang.* ix. 44), he was not put to death, but was appointed by Cyrus as a vassal-king; and then in the second taking of Babylon under Darius Hystaspis (*Herod.* iii. 150, *seq.*), from whom he had sought to make himself independent, he was slain. This opinion has

this advantage, that it has in its favour the fact that it has the undoubted name of *Darius*, but it is not conformable to history to suppose that Darius Hystaspis was a son of Ahasuerus the Mede ; for his father, Hystaspis, was a native-born prince of Persia (Xenop. *Cyrop.* iv. 2, 46), of the family of the Achæmenides (*Herod.* i. 209, 210). Darius Hystaspis was indeed remotely related by means of the mother of Cyrus, Mandane, with the royal family ; but this relation could not entitle him to be called a Mede, for, since she was the mother of Cyrus, it is altogether inexplicable that since both were thus connected with each other, that Cyrus should be called *the Persian* (כַּרְסָיָא), and Darius *the Mede* (מָדְיָא), Dan. vi. 28, 29. The supposition, moreover, that Nabonned, after the taking of Babylon, was appointed as a tributary king by Cyrus, is wholly gratuitous ; since Nabonned, according to the express testimony of Xenophon (*Cyrop.* vii. 5, 26, *seq.*), was slain at the taking of Babylon.

"There is yet one other opinion respecting Darius the Mede, to which I will first prefix the following remarks : (1.) Darius the Mede is mentioned in ch. vi. 28 (29) as the immediate predecessor of Cyrus in Babylon. (2.) Belshazzar was the last Babylonish Chaldee king. (3.) The account of the violent death of Belshazzar, with which the fifth chapter closes, stands in direct historical connection with the statement in the beginning of the sixth chapter that Darius the Mede had the kingdom. (4.) Darius the Mede must, therefore, be the first foreign prince after the downfall of the Chaldean dynasty, which directly reigned over Babylon. (5.) The chronological point, therefore, where the history of Belshazzar and of Darius the Mede coincide, developes itself: the account falls in the time of the downfall of Babylon through the Medo-Persian army, and this must be the occasion as the connecting fact between the fifth and sixth chapters. According to this, Darius the Mede can be no other person than the Medish king Cyaxares II., the son and successor of Astyages, and the predecessor of Cyrus in the rule over Babylon; and Belshazzar is the last Chaldee monarch, Nabonned, or Labynet. With this agrees the account of Josephus (*Ant.* x. 11, 4); and later, this opinion found an advocate in Jerome.

"The existence of such a person as Cyaxares II. has been indeed denied, because, according to Herodotus (i. 109), and Justin (i. 4, 7), Astyages had no son. But it should be remarked, that the latter of these writers only copies from the former, and what Herodotus states respecting Astyages has so much the appearance of fable that no reliance is to be placed on it. It has been objected also that Dionysius of Halicarnassus (b. i. §. 1) says that the Medish kingdom continued only through four reigns, so that if we reckon the names of the reigning kings. Dejoces, Phraortes, Cyaxares (the contemporary of Nebuchadnezzar), and Astyages, there will be no place for a second Cyaxares. But is it not probable that Dionysius meant, by these words, only that the Median kingdom came to an end under the fourth dynasty? Finally, it has been objected that, according to Herodotus (i. 128, *seq.*), and Ctesias (Περσικ. 2 and 5), no Median prince sat upon the throne in Ecbatana after Astyages, but that with Astyages the kingdom of the Medes came to an end, and with Cyrus, his immediate successor, the Persian kingdom took its beginning. Therewith agree nearly all the historians of the following times, Diodorus (ii. 34),

Justin (i. 6, 16, 17, vii. 1), Strabo (ix. p. 735; xv. p. 1662), Polyän (vii. 7), and many others. But these writers only copy from Herodotus and Ctesias, and the whole rests only on their authority. But their credibility in this point must be regarded as doubtful, for it is not difficult to understand the reasons why they have omitted to make mention of Cyaxares II. They commenced the history of the reign of Cyrus with the beginning of his world-renowned celebrity, and hence it was natural to connect the beginning of his reign, and the beginning of the Persian reign, with the reign of his grandfather Astyages; for, so long as his uncle Cyaxares II. reigned, Cyrus alone acted, and he in fact was the regent. But if the silence of Herodotus and Ctesias is not to be regarded as proof that no such person as Cyaxares II. lived and reigned, there are in favour of that the following positive arguments:—

"(1.) The authority of Xenophon, who not only says that a Cyaxares ascended the throne after Astyages, but that he was a son of Astyages (*Cyr.* i. 5. 2), and besides relates so much of this Cyaxares (i. 4, 7; iii. 3, 20; viii. 5, 19) that his *Cyropædia* may be regarded as in a measure a history of him. Yea, Xenophon goes so far (viii. 7, 1) that he reckons the years of the reign of Cyrus from the death of Cyaxares II. Can any one conceive a reason why Xenophon had a motive to weave together such a tissue of falsehood as this, unless Cyaxares II. actually lived? If one should object, indeed, that he is so far to be reckoned among fictitious writers that he gives a moral character to the subjects on which he writes, and that he has passed over the difference between Cyrus and his grandfather Astyages, yet there is no reason why he should have brought upon the stage so important a person, wholly from fiction, as Cyaxares. What a degree of boldness it must have required, if he, who lived not much more than a century after the events recorded, had mentioned to his contemporaries so much respecting a prince of whom no one whatever had even heard. But the existence of Cyaxares II. may be proved,

"(2.) From a passage in Æschylus (Pers. ver. 762, seq.)—

Μῆδος·γὰρ ἦν ὁ πρῶτος ἡγεμὼν στρατοῦ
Ἀλλος δ' ἐκείνου παῖς τό δ' ἔργον ἤνυσε·
Τρίτος δ' ἀπ' αὐτοῦ Κῦρος, εὐδαίμων ἀνήρ,
κ.τ.λ.

The first who is here mentioned as the Mede (Μῆδος) is manifestly no other than Astyages, whom, before Cyrus, his son succeeded in the government, and who is the same whom we, after Xenophon, call Cyaxares. This testimony is the more important as Æschylus lived before Xenophon, in the time of Darius Hystaspis, and is free from all suspicions from this circumstance, that, according to the public relations which Æschylus sustained, no accounts of the former Persian history could be expected from any doubtful authorities to have been adduced by him. But the existence of Cyaxares II. does not depend solely on the authority of Xenophon, in his Cyropædia. For,

"(3.) Josephus (Ant. x. 11, 4), who speaks of this person under the name of Darius, adds, ᵛνῆ·ᵗἈστυάγους υἱὸς, ἕτερον δὲ παρὰ τοῖς Ἕλλησιν ἐκαλεῖτο ονομα—'he was the son of Astyages, but had another name among the Greeks.' This name, which he had among the Greeks, can be found only in their own Xenophon.

"(4.) To all this should be added, that many other data of history, especially those taken from the Hebrew writings, so set out the continuance

of the reign of the Medes over Upper Asia that it is necessary to suppose the existence of such a person as the Medish king, Cyaxares, after the reign of Astyages. Had Cyrus, after the death of Astyages, immediately assumed the government over Upper Asia, how happened it that until the downfall of the Babylonian-Chaldee kingdom mention is made almost always of the Medes, or at least of the Persians, of whom there is special mention? Whence is it that the passage of Abydenus, quoted from Megasthenes, p. 295, speaks of a Mede, who, in connection with a Persian, overthrew the Babylonish kingdom? Is not the Mede so represented as to show that he was a prominent and leading person? Is it not necessary to attribute to this fragment a higher authority, and to suppose that a Medish monarch, in connection with a Persian, brought the kingdom of Babylon to an end? Whence did Jeremiah, ch. l. and li., expressly threaten that the Jews would be punished by a Median king? Whence does the author of Isa. xiii. and xiv. mention that the destruction of the Chaldean monarchy would be effected by the Medes? The accession of Cyrus to the throne was no mere change of person in the authority, but it was a change of the reigning nation. So long as a Mede sat on the throne, the Persians, though they acted an important part in the affairs of the nation, yet occupied only the second place. The court was Medish, and the Medes were prominent in all the affairs of the government, as every page of the Cyropædia furnishes evidence. Upon the accession of Cyrus, the whole thing was changed. The Persians were now the predominant nation, and from that time onward, as has been remarked, the Persians are always mentioned as having the priority, though before they had but a secondary place. As the reign of Astyages, though he reigned thirty-five years (Herod. i. 130), could not have embraced the whole period mentioned to the accession of Cyrus, so the royal race of the Medes, and the kingdom of the Medes, could not have been extinguished with him, and it is necessary to suppose the existence of Cyaxares II. as his successor, and the predecessor of Cyrus."

These considerations, suggested by Bertholdt, are sufficient to demonstrate that such a person as Cyaxares II. lived between the reign of Astyages and Cyrus, and that, after the destruction of Babylon, he was the immediate successor of Belshazzar, or Nabonned, and was the predecessor of Cyrus. He was the first of the foreign princes who reigned over Babylon. It has been made a question why, in the book of Daniel, he is mentioned under the name of *Darius*, and not by his other name Cyaxares. It may be difficult to answer this question, but it will be sufficient to remark (a) that it was common for Oriental kings to have many names, and, as we have seen, in regard to the kings of Babylon, one writer might designate them by one name, and another by another. This is indeed the occasion of much confusion in ancient history, but it is inevitable. (b) As we have seen, Josephus (*Ant.* x. 11, 4) expressly says that this Darius had another name among the Greeks, and, as Bertholdt remarks, it is natural to seek that name in the writings of their own Xenophon. (c) Darius was a common name in Persia, and it may have been one of the names by which the princes of Persia and Media were commonly known. Three of that name are mentioned in the Scriptures, and three who were distinguished are mentioned in profane history—Darius Hystaspis, Darius

Ochus, or Darius Nothus, as he was known among the Greeks, and Darius Codomanus, who was overthrown by Alexander the Great.

An important statement is made by Xenophon respecting Cyaxares II., the son of Astyages, which may account for the fact that his name was omitted by Herodotus and Ctesias. He describes him as a prince given up to sensuality, and this fact explains the reason why he came to surrender all authority so entirely into the hands of his enterprising son-in-law and nephew Cyrus, and why his reign was naturally sunk in that of his distinguished successor.— *Cyrop.* i. 5, viii. 7.

§ III.—ANALYSIS OF THE CHAPTER.

This chapter contains the history of Daniel under the government, or during the reign of Darius the Mede, or Cyaxares II., from a period, it would seem, soon after the accession of Darius to the throne in Babylon, or the conquest of Babylon, till his death. It is not indeed said how soon after that event Daniel was exalted to the premiership in Babylon, but the narrative would lead us to suppose that it was soon after the conquest of Babylon by Cyrus, acting under the authority of Cyaxares. As Daniel, on account of the disclosure made to Belshazzar of the meaning of the handwriting on the wall, had been exalted to high honour at the close of the life of that monarch (ch. v.), it is probable that he would be called to a similar station under the reign of Darius, as it cannot be supposed that Darius would appoint Medes and Persians entirely to fill the high offices of the realm. The chapter contains a record of the following events: (1.) The arrangement of the government after the conquest of Babylon, consisting of one hundred and twenty officers over the kingdom, so divided as to be placed under the care of three superior officers, or "presidents," of whom Daniel held the first place (vers. 1–3). (2.) The dissatisfaction or envy of the officers so appointed against Daniel, for causes now unknown, and their conspiracy to remove him from office, or to bring him into disgrace with the king (ver. 4). (3.) The plan which they formed to secure this, derived from the known piety and integrity of Daniel, and their conviction that, at any hazard, he would remain firm to his religious principles, and would conscientiously maintain the worship of God. Convinced that they could find no fault in his administration; that he could not be convicted of malversation or infidelity in office; that there was nothing in his private or public character that was contrary to justice and integrity, they resolved to take advantage of his well-known piety, and to make that the occasion of his downfall and ruin (ver. 5). (4.) The plan that was artfully proposed was, to induce the king to sign a decree that if any one for thirty days should ask any petition for anything of God or man, he should be thrown into a den of lions—that is, should be, as they supposed, certainly put to death. This proposed decree they apprehended they could induce the king to sign, perhaps because it was flattering to the monarch, or perhaps because it would test the disposition of his new subjects to obey him, or perhaps because they knew he was a weak and effeminate prince, and that he was accustomed to sign papers presented to him by his counsellors without much reflection or hesitation (vers. 6–9). (5.) Daniel, when he was apprised of the contents of the decree, though he saw its bearing, and perhaps its design, yet continued his devotions as usual—praying, as he was known

to do, three times a-day, with his face toward Jerusalem, with his windows open. The case was one where he felt, undoubtedly, that it was a matter of principle that he should worship God in his usual manner, and not allow himself to be driven from the acknowledgment of his God by the fear of death (ver. 10). (6.) They who had laid the plan made report of this to the king, and demanded the execution of the decree. The case was a plain one, for though it had not been intended or expected by the king that Daniel would have been found a violator of the law, yet as the decree was positive, and there had been no concealment on the part of Daniel, the counsellors urged that it was necessary that the decree should be executed (vers. 11–13). (7.) The king, displeased with himself, and evidently enraged against these crafty counsellors, desirous of sparing Daniel, and yet feeling the necessity of maintaining a law positively enacted, sought some way by which Daniel might be saved, and the honour and majesty of the law preserved. No method, however, occurring to him of securing both objects, he was constrained to submit to the execution of the decree, and ordered Daniel to be cast into the den of lions (vers. 14–17). (8.) The king returned to his palace, and passed the night fasting, and overwhelmed with sadness (ver. 18). (9.) In the morning he came with deep anxiety to the place where Daniel had been thrown, and called to see if he were alive (vers. 19, 20). (10.) The reply of Daniel, that he had been preserved by the intervention of an angel, who had closed the mouths of the lions, and had kept him alive (vers. 21, 22). (11.) The release of Daniel from the den, and the command to cast those in who had thus accused Daniel, and who had sought his ruin (vers. 23, 24). (12.)

CHAPTER VI.

IT pleased Darius to set *a* over the kingdom an hundred and twenty *b* princes, which should be over the whole kingdom;

a 1 Pet. 2. 14.   b Esth. 1. 1.

2 And over these. three presidents, of whom Daniel *was* first; that the princes might give accounts unto them, and the *c* king should have no damage.

c Luke 19. 13, &c.; 1 Cor. 4. 2.

An appropriate proclamation from the king to all men to honour that God who had thus preserved his servant (vers. 25-27). (13.) A statement of the prosperity of Daniel, extending to the reign of Cyrus (ver. 28).

1. *It pleased Darius to set over the kingdom.* Evidently over the kingdom of Babylon, now united to that of Media and Persia. As this was now subject to him, and tributary to him, it would be natural to appoint persons over it in whom he could confide, for the administration of justice, for the collection of revenue, &c. Others, however, suppose that this relates to the whole kingdom of Persia, but as the reference here is mainly to what was the kingdom of Babylon, it is rather to be presumed that this is what is particularly alluded to. Besides, it is hardly probable that he would have exalted Daniel, a Jew, and a resident in Babylon, to so important a post as that of the premiership over the whole empire, though from his position and standing in Babylon there is no improbability in supposing that he might have occupied, under the reign of Darius, a place similar to that which he had occupied under Nebuchadnezzar and Belshazzar. In dividing the kingdom into provinces, and placing officers over each department, Darius followed the same plan which Xenophon tells us that Cyrus did over the nations conquered by him, *Cyrop.* viii.: Εδόκει αυτῷ σατράπας ήδη πέμπειν επι τα κατεστραμμένα έθνη — "It seemed good to him to appoint satraps over the conquered nations." Compare Esth. i. 1. Archbishop Usher (*Annal.*) thinks that the plan was first instituted by Cyrus, and was followed at his suggestion. It was a measure of obvious prudence in order to maintain so extended an empire in subjection. ¶ *An*

hundred and twenty princes. The word here rendered *princes* (אֲחַשְׁדַּרְפְּנַיָּא) occurs only in Daniel in the Chaldee form, though in the Hebrew form it is found in the book of Esther (iii. 12; viii. 9; ix. 3), and in Ezra (viii. 36); in Esther and Ezra uniformly rendered *lieutenants.* In Daniel (iii. 2, 3, 27; vi. 1-4, 6, 7) it is as uniformly rendered *princes.* It is a word of Persian origin, and is probably the Hebrew mode of pronouncing the Persian word *satrap,* or, as Gesenius supposes, the Persian word was pronounced *ksatrap.* For the etymology of the word, see Gesenius, *Lex.* The word undoubtedly refers to the Persian *satraps,* or governors, or viceroys in the large provinces of the empire, possessing both civil and military powers. They were officers high in rank, and being the representatives of the sovereign, they rivalled his state and splendour. Single parts, or subdivisions of these provinces, were under inferior officers; the satraps governed whole provinces. The word is rendered *satraps* in the Greek, and the Latin Vulgate.

2. *And over these, three presidents.* סָרְכִין. This word is found only in the plural. The etymology is uncertain, but its meaning is not doubtful. The word *president* expresses it with sufficient accuracy, denoting a high officer that presided over others. It is not improbable that these presided over distinct departments, corresponding somewhat to what are now called "secretaries"—as Secretaries of State, of the Treasury, of Foreign Affairs, &c., though this is not particularly specified. ¶ *Of whom Daniel was first.* First in rank. This office he probably held from the rank which he was known to have occupied under the kings of Babylon, and on account of his reputation for ability and integrity. ¶ *That the princes might give accounts unto*

3 Then this Daniel was preferred above the presidents and princes, because an excellent *a* spirit *was* in him : and the king thought to set him over the whole realm.

a ch. 5. 12; Prov. 17. 27.

4 ¶ Then *b* the presidents and princes sought *c* to find occasion against Daniel concerning the kingdom ; but they could find none occasion nor fault ; foras-

b Eccl. 4. 4.   *c* Ps. 37. 12, &c.

---

them. Be immediately responsible to them; the accounts of their own administration, and of the state of the empire. ¶ *And the king should have no damage.* Either in the loss of revenue, or in any maladministration of the affairs. Comp. Ezra iv. 13. "They pay not toll, tribute, and custom, and so thou shalt endamage the revenue of the kings." The king was regarded as the source of all power, and as in fact the supreme proprietor of the realm, and any malfeasance or malversation in office was regarded as an injury to him.

3. *Then this Daniel was preferred above the presidents and princes.* That is, he was at their head, or was placed in rank and office over them. ¶ *Because an excellent spirit was in him.* This may refer alike to his wisdom and his integrity—both of which would be necessary in such an office. It was an office of great difficulty and responsibility to manage the affairs of the empire in a proper manner, and required the talents of an accomplished statesman, and, at the same time, as it was an office where confidence was reposed by the sovereign, it demanded integrity. The word "excellent" (יַתִּירָא)

means, properly, that which hangs over, or which is abundant, or more than enough, and then anything that is very great, excellent, pre-eminent. Latin Vulgate, *Spiritus Dei amplior*—"the spirit of God more abundantly." Gr. πνεῦμα περισσόν. It is not said here to what trial of his abilities and integrity Daniel was subjected before he was thus exalted, but it is not necessary to suppose that any such trial occurred at once, or immediately on the accession of Darius. Probably, as he was found in office as appointed by Belshazzar, he was continued by Darius, and as a result of his tried integrity was in due time exalted to the premier-

ship. ¶ *And the king thought to set him over the whole realm.* The whole kingdom over which he presided, embracing Media, Persia, Babylonia, and all the dependent, conquered provinces. This shows that the princes referred to in ver. 1, were those which were appointed over Babylonia, since Daniel (ver. 2) was already placed at the head of all these princes. Yet, in consequence of his talents and fidelity the king was meditating the important measure of placing him over the whole united kingdom as premier. That he should form such a purpose in regard to an officer so talented and faithful as Daniel was, is by no means improbable. The Greek of Theodotion renders this as if it were actually done—καὶ ὁ βασιλεὺς κατέστησεν αὐτὸν, κ.τ.λ.—"And the king placed him over all his kingdom." But the Chaldee (עֲשִׁית) indicates rather a purpose or intention to do it; or rather, perhaps, that he was actually making arrangements to do this. Probably it was the fact that this design was perceived, and that the arrangements were actually commenced, that aroused the envy and the ill-will of his fellow-officers, and induced them to determine on his ruin.

4. *Then the presidents and princes sought to find occasion against Daniel.* The word rendered *occasion* (עִלָּה) means a pretext or pretence. "The Arabs use the word of any business or affair which serves as a cause or pretext for neglecting another business."—Gesenius, *Lex.* The meaning is, that they sought to find some plausible pretext or reason in respect to Daniel, by which the contemplated appointment might be prevented, and by which he might be effectually humbled. No one who is acquainted with the intrigues of cabinets and courts can have any doubts as to the probability of what is here stated. Nothing has been

much as he *was* faithful, neither was there any error or fault found in him.

more common in the world than intrigues of this kind to humble a rival, and to bring down those who are meritorious to a state of degradation. The *cause* of the plot here laid seems to have been mere envy and jealousy—and perhaps the consideration that Daniel was a foreigner, and was one of a despised people held in captivity. ¶ *Concerning the kingdom.* In respect to the administration of the kingdom. They sought to find evidence of malversation in office, or abuse of power, or attempts at personal aggrandizement, or inattention to the duties of the office. This is literally "from the side of the kingdom;" and the meaning is, that the accusation was sought in that quarter, or in that respect. No other charge would be likely to be effectual, except one which pertained to maladministration in office. ¶ *But they could find none occasion nor fault.* This is an honourable testimony to the fidelity of Daniel, and to the uprightness of his character. If there had been any malversation in office, it would have been detected by these men.

5. *We shall not find any occasion,* &c. We shall not find any pretext or any cause by which he may be humbled and degraded. They were satisfied of his integrity, and they saw it was vain to hope to accomplish their purposes by any attack on his moral character, or any charge against him in respect to the manner in which he had discharged the duties of his office. ¶ *Except we find it against him concerning the law of his God.* Unless it be in respect to his religion; unless we can so construe his known conscientiousness in regard to his religion as to make *that* a proof of his unwillingness to obey the king. It occurred to them that such was his well-understood faithfulness in his religious duties, and his conscientiousness, that they might expect that, whatever should occur, he would be found true to his God, and that this might be a basis of calculation in any measure they might propose for his downfall. His habits seem to have

5 Then said these men, We shall not find any occasion against this Daniel, except we find *it* against

been well understood, and his character was so fixed that they could proceed on this as a settled matter in their plans against him. The only question was, *how* to construe his conduct in this respect as criminal, or *how* to make the king listen to any accusation against him on this account, for his religious views were well known when he was appointed to office; the worship of the God of Daniel was not prohibited by the laws of the realm, and it would not be easy to procure a law directly and avowedly prohibiting that. It is not probable that the king would have consented to pass such a law directly proposed—a law which would have been so likely to produce disturbance, and when no plausible ground could have been alleged for it. There was another method, however, which suggested itself to these crafty counsellors—which was, while they did not seem to aim absolutely and directly to have that worship prohibited, to approach the king with a proposal that would be flattering to his vanity, and that, perhaps, might be suggested as a *test* question, showing the degree of esteem in which he was held in the empire, and the willingness of his subjects to obey him. By proposing a law that, for a limited period, no one should be allowed to present a petition of any kind to any one except to the king himself, the object would be accomplished. A vain monarch could be prevailed on to pass such a law, and this could be represented to him as a measure not improper in order to *test* his subjects as to their willingness to show him respect and obedience; and at the same time it would be certain to effect the purpose against Daniel—for they had no doubt that he would adhere steadfastly to the principles of his religion, and to his well-known habits of worship. This plan was, therefore, crafty in the extreme, and was the highest tribute that could be paid to Daniel. It would be well if the religious character and the fixed habits of all who profess religion were so well understood that it was abso-

him concerning the law of his
God.

6 Then these presidents and
princes ¹assembled together to the
king, and said thus unto him, King
Darius, live ᵃ for ever.

1 or, *came tumultuously.*　　a ver. 21; Neh. 2. 3.

7 All the presidents of the
kingdom, the governors, and the
princes, the counsellors, and the
captains, have consulted ᵇ together
to establish a royal statute, and to
make a firm ²decree, that whoso-

b Ps. 2. 2.　　2 or, *interdict.*

lutely certain that no accusation could
lie against them on any other ground,
but that their adherence to their religious principles could be calculated on
as a basis of action, whatever might
be the consequences.

6. *Then these presidents and princes
assembled together.* Marg., *came tumultuously.* The margin expresses the
proper meaning of the original word—

רְגַשׁ—*to run together with tumult.* Why
they came together in that manner is
not stated. Bertholdt suggests that it
means that they came in a procession,
or in a body, to the king; but there is
undoubtedly the idea of their doing it
with haste, or with an appearance of
great earnestness or excitement. Perhaps they imagined that they would be
more likely to carry the measure if proposed as something that demanded immediate action, or something wherein
it appeared that the very safety of the
king was involved, than if it were proposed in a sedate and calm manner.
If it were suggested in such a way as
to seem to admit of deliberation, perhaps the suspicion of the king might
be aroused, or he might have asked
questions as to the ground of the necessity of such a law, which it might
not have been easy to answer. ¶ *King
Darius, live for ever.* The usual way
of saluting a monarch. See Notes on
ch. ii. 4.

7. *All the presidents of the kingdom,
the governors,* &c. Several function-
aries are enumerated here who are not
in the previous verses, as having entered into the conspiracy. It is possible, indeed, that all these different
classes of officers had been consulted,
and had concurred in asking the enactment of the proposed law; but it is
much more probable that the leaders
merely represented or affirmed what is
here said in order to be more certain

of the enactment of the law. If represented as proposed by all the officers
of the realm, they appear to have conceived that there would be no hesitation
on the part of Darius in granting the
request. They could not but be conscious that it was an unusual request,
and that it might appear unreasonable,
and hence they seem to have used
every precaution to make the passing
of the law certain. ¶ *Have consulted
together to establish a royal statute.* Or,
that such a statute might be established. They knew that it could be
established only by the king himself,
but they were in the habit, doubtless,
of recommending such laws as they
supposed would be for the good of the
realm. ¶ *And to make a firm decree.*
Marg., *interdict.* The word used (אֱסָר
—from אָסַר—to bind, make fast) means,
properly, *a binding;* then anything
which is binding or obligatory—as a
prohibition, an interdict, a law. ¶ *That
whosoever shall ask.* Any one of any
rank. The real purpose was to involve
Daniel in disgrace, but in order to do
this it was necessary to make the prohibition universal—as Herod, in order
to be sure that he had cut off the infant
king of the Jews, was under a necessity of destroying all the children in
the place. ¶ *Of any god or man.*
This would include all the gods acknowledged in Babylon, and all foreign
divinities. ¶ *For thirty days.* The
object of this limitation of time was
perhaps twofold: (1) they would be
sure to accomplish their purpose in regard to Daniel, for they understood
his principles and habits so well that
they had no doubt that within that
time he would be found engaged in the
worship of his God; and (2) it would
not do to make the law perpetual, and
to make it binding longer than thirty
days might expose them to the danger

ever shall ask a petition of any god or man for thirty days, save of

thee, O king, he shall be cast into the den of lions.

of popular tumults. It was easy enough to see that such a law could not be long enforced, yet they seem to have supposed that the people would acquiesce in it for so brief a period as one month. Unreasonable though it might be regarded, yet for so short a space of time it might be expected that it would be patiently submitted to. ¶ *Save of thee, O king.* Perhaps either directly, or through some minister of the realm. ¶ *He shall be cast into the den of lions.* The word *den* (גֹּב) means, properly, a pit, or cistern; and the idea is that the den was underground, probably a cave constructed for that purpose. It was made with so narrow an entrance that it could be covered with a stone, and made perfectly secure, ver. 17. "The inclosures of wild beasts," says Bertholdt, pp. 397, 398, "especially of lions, which the kings of Asia and of North-western Africa formerly had, as they have at the present day, were generally constructed underground, but were ordinarily caves which had been excavated for the purpose, walled up at the sides, inclosed within a wall through which a door led from the outer wall to the space lying between the walls, within which persons could pass round and contemplate the wild beasts." "The emperor of Morocco," says Höst (*Beschreibung von Marokos und Fess*, p. 290, as quoted in Rosenmüller's *Morgenland, in loc.*), "has a cave for lions—Löwengrube— into which men sometimes, and especially Jews, are cast; but they commonly came up again uninjured, for the overseers of the lions are commonly Jews, and they have a sharp instrument in their hands, and with this they can pass among them, if they are careful to keep their faces towards the lions, for a lion will not allow one to turn his back to him. The other Jews will not allow their brethren to remain longer in such a cave than one night, for the lions would be too hungry, but they redeem their brethren out of the cave by the payment of money—which, in fact, is the object of the emperor." In another place (p. 77), he describes one

of these caves. "In one end of the inclosure is a place for ostriches and their young ones, and at the other end towards the mountain is a cave for lions, which stands in a large cavern in the earth that has a division wall, in the midst of which is a door, which the Jews who have the charge of the lions can open and close from above, and, by means of food, they entice the lions from one room into another, that they may have the opportunity of cleaning the cage. It is all under the open sky." Under what pretext the crafty counsellors induced the king to ratify this statute is not stated. Some one or all of the following things may have induced the monarch to sign the decree: (1.) The law proposed was in a high degree flattering to the king, and he may have been ready at once to sign a decree which for the time gave him a supremacy over gods and men. If Alexander the Great desired to be adored as a god, then it is not improbable that a proud and weak Persian monarch would be willing to receive a similar tribute. Xerxes did things more foolish than what is here attributed to Darius. Instances of this are not wanting. Of Holofernes, in Judith iii. 8, it is said that he "had decreed to destroy all the gods of the land, that all nations should worship Nabuchodonosor only, and that all tongues and tribes should call upon him as god." (2.) It may have occurred to him, or may have been suggested, that this was an effectual way to test the readiness of his subjects to obey and honour him. Some such test, it may have been urged, was not improper, and this would determine what was the spirit of obedience as well as any other. (3.) More probably, however, it may have been represented that there was some danger of insubordination, or some conspiracy among the people, and that it was necessary that the sovereign should issue some mandate which would at once and effectually quell it. It may have been urged that there was danger of a revolt, and that it would be an effectual way

8 Now, O king, establish the decree, and sign the writing, that it be not changed, according to the

a Esth. 1. 19; 8. 8.　　1 *passeth.*

law *a* of the Medes and Persians, which 1 altereth not.

9 Wherefore king Darius signed the writing and the decree.

of preventing it to order that whoever should solicit any favour of any one but the king should be punished, for this would bring all matters at once before him, and secure order. The haste and earnestness with which they urged their request would rather seem to imply that there was a representation that some *sudden* occasion had arisen which made the enactment of such a statute proper. (4.) Or the king may have been in the habit of signing the decrees proposed by his counsellors with little hesitation, and, lost in ease and sensuality, and perceiving only that this proposed law was flattering to himself, and not deliberating on what might be its possible result, he may have signed it at once.

8, 9. *Now, O king, establish the decree.* Ordain, enact, confirm it. ¶ *And sign the writing.* An act necessary to make it the law of the realm. ¶ *That it be not changed.* That, having the sign-manual of the sovereign, it might be so confirmed that it could not be changed. With that sign it became so established, it seems, that even the sovereign himself could not change it. ¶ *According to the law of the Medes and Persians, which altereth not.* Marg., *passeth.* Which does not *pass away;* which is not abrogated. A similar fact in regard to a law of the Medes and Persians is mentioned in Esther viii., in which the king was unable to recal an order which had been given for the massacre of the Jews, and in which he attempted only to counteract it as far as possible by putting the Jews on their guard, and allowing them to defend themselves. Diodorus Siculus (lib. iv.) refers to this custom where he says that Darius, the last king of Persia, would have pardoned Charidemus after he was condemned to death, but could not reverse what the law had passed against him.—Lowth. "When the king of Persia," says Montesquieu (*Spirit of Laws,* as quoted by Rosenmüller, *Morgenland, in loc.*), "has condemned any one to

death, no one dares speak to him to make intercession for him. Were he even drunk when the crime was committed, or were he insane, the command must nevertheless be executed, for the law cannot be countermanded, and the laws cannot contradict themselves. This sentiment prevails throughout Persia." It may seem singular that such a custom prevailed, and that the king, who was the fountain of law, and whose will was law, could not change a statute at his pleasure. But this custom grew out of the opinions which prevailed in the East in regard to the monarch. His will was absolute, and it was a part of the system which prevailed then to exalt the monarch, and leave the impression on the mind of the people that he was more than a man—that he was infallible, and could not err. Nothing was better adapted to keep up that impression than an established principle of this kind—that a law once ordained could not be repealed or changed. To do this would be a practical acknowledgment that there was a defect in the law; that there was a want of wisdom in ordaining it; that all the circumstances were not foreseen ; and that the king was liable to be deceived and to err. With all the disadvantages attending such a custom, it was judged better to maintain it than to allow that the monarch could err, and hence when a law was ordained it became fixed and unchanging. Even the king himself could not alter it, and, whatever might be the consequences, it was to be executed. It is evident, however, that such a custom might have *some* advantages. It would serve to prevent hasty legislation, and to give stability to the government by its being known what the laws were, thus avoiding the evils which result when they are frequently changed. It is often preferable to have permanent laws, though not the best that could be framed, than those which would be better, if there were no stability. There is only one Being, how-

10 ¶ Now when Daniel *a* knew that the writing was signed, he went into his house; and his win-

a Luke 14. 26; Acts 4. 17–19.

dows being open in his chamber toward *b* Jerusalem, he kneeled upon his knees three *c* times a day,

b 1 Kings 8. 44, 48; Ps. 5. 7; Jon. 2. 4.
c ver. 13; Ps. 55. 17; Acts 2. 15; 3. 1; 10. 9.

ever, whose laws can be safely unchanging—and that is God, for his laws are formed with a full knowledge of all the relations of things, and of their bearing on all future circumstances and times. It serves to confirm the statement here made respecting the ancient custom in Media and Persia, that the same idea of the inviolability of the royal word has remained, in a mitigated form, to modern times. A remarkable example of this is related by Sir John Malcolm, of Aga Mohammed Khan, the last but one of the Persian kings. After alluding to the present case, and that in Esther, he observes, "The character of the power of the king of Persia has undergone no change. The late king, Aga Mohammed Khan, when encamped near Shiraz, said that he would not move till the snow was off the mountains in the vicinity of his camp. The season proved severe, and the snow remained longer than was expected ; the army began to suffer distress and sickness, but the king said while the snow remained upon the mountain, he would not move; and his word was as law, and could not be broken. A multitude of labourers were collected and sent to remove the snow; their efforts, and a few fine days, cleared the mountains, and Aga Mohammed Khan marched."—*History of Persia*, i. 268, quoted in the *Pict. Bible, in loc.*

10. *Now when Daniel knew that the writing was signed.* Probably there was some proclamation made in regard to that decree. ¶ *He went into his house.* That is, he went in in his usual manner. He made no change in his habits on account of the decree. ¶ *And his windows being open in his chamber.* Open in the usual manner. It does not mean that he took pains to open them for the purpose of ostentation, or to show that he disregarded the decree, but that he took no care to close them with any view to avoid the consequences. In the warm climate of Babylon, the windows probably were

commonly open. Houses among the Jews in later times, if not in the time of the exile, were usually constructed with an upper chamber— ὑπερῷον — which was a room not in common use, but employed as a guest chamber, where they received company and held feasts, and where at other times they retired for prayer and meditation. See Notes on Matt. ix. 2. Those "upper rooms" are often the most pleasant and airy part of the house. Dr. Robinson (*Researches*, vol. iii. p. 417), describing the house of the American consular-agent in Sidon, says, "His house was a large one, built upon the eastern wall of the city ; the rooms were spacious, and furnished with more appearance of wealth than any I saw in the country. An upper parlour with many windows, on the roof of the proper house, resembled a summer palace ; and commanded a delightful view of the country towards the east, full of trees and gardens, and country-houses, quite to the foot of the mountains." ¶ *Toward Jerusalem.* It is not improbable that the windows were open on each side of the chamber, but this is particularly mentioned, because he turned his face toward Jerusalem when he prayed. This was natural to an exile Hebrew in prayer, because the temple of God had stood at Jerusalem, and that was the place where he abode by a visible symbol. It is probable that the Jews in their own country always in their prayers turned the face toward Jerusalem, and it was anticipated when the temple was dedicated, that this would be the case in whatever lands they might be. Thus in the prayer of Solomon, at the dedication, he says, "If thy people go out to battle against their enemy, whithersoever thou shalt send them, and shall pray unto the Lord toward the city which thou hast chosen, and toward the house which I have built for thy name,"&c., 1 Ki. viii. 44. And again (vers. 46–49), "If they sin against thee, and thou be angry with

and prayed, and gave *a* thanks

a Phil. 4. 6.

them, and deliver them to the enemy, so that they carry them away captives unto the land of the enemy, far or near; if they shall bethink themselves in the land whither they were carried captives, and repent—and pray unto thee toward their land which thou gavest unto their fathers, the city which thou hast chosen, and the house which I have built for thy name, then hear thou their prayer," &c. Comp. vers. 33, 35, 38. So in Psa. v. 7: "As for me, I will come into thy house in the multitude of thy mercy: and in thy fear will I worship toward thy holy temple." So Jonah ii. 4: "Then I said, I am cast out of thy sight; yet I will look again toward thy holy temple." So in the first book of Esdras (Apocrypha), iv. 58: "Now when this young man was gone forth, he lifted up his face to heaven, toward Jerusalem, and praised the King of heaven." Comp. Intro. § II. V. C. Daniel, therefore, in turning his face toward Jerusalem when he prayed, was acting in accordance with what Solomon had anticipated as proper in just such a supposed case, and with the prevailing habit of his people when abroad. This was not, indeed, particularly prescribed as a duty, but it was recognized as proper; and it was not only in accordance with the instinctive feelings of love to his country and the temple, but a foundation was laid for this in the fact that Jerusalem was regarded as the peculiar dwelling-place of God on earth. In the Koran it *is* enjoined as a duty on all Mussulmen, in whatever part of the earth they may be, to turn their faces towards the Caaba at Mecca when they pray: "The foolish men will say, What hath turned them from their Keblah toward which they formerly prayed? Say, Unto God belongeth the East and the West; he directeth whom he pleaseth in the right way. Thus have we placed you, O Arabians, an intermediate nation, that ye may be witnesses against the rest of mankind, and that the apostle may be a witness against you. We appointed the Keblah, towards which

before his God, as he did aforetime.

thou didst formerly pray, only that we might know him who followeth the apostle from him that turneth back on his heels: though this change seem a great matter, unless unto those whom God hath directed. But God will not render your faith of none effect; for God is gracious and merciful unto man. We have seen thee turn about thy face towards heaven with uncertainty, but we will cause thee to turn thyself toward a Keblah that will please thee. Turn, therefore, thy face towards the holy temple of Mecca; and wherever ye be, turn your faces towards that place."—Sale's *Koran*, ch. ii. Wherever Mussulmen are, therefore, they turn their faces towards the temple at Mecca when they pray. Daniel complied with what was probably the general custom of his countrymen, and what was natural in his case, for there was, in the nature of the case, a *reason* why he should turn his face towards the place where God had been accustomed to manifest himself. It served to keep up in his mind the remembrance of his beloved country, and in his case could be attended with no evil. As all visible symbols of the Divine Being are now, however, withdrawn from any particular place on the earth, there is no propriety in imitating his example, and when we pray it is wholly immaterial in what direction the face is turned. ¶ *He kneeled upon his knees three times a day.* In accordance, doubtless, with his usual custom. The amount of the statement is, that he did not vary his habit on account of the command. He evidently neither assumed a posture of ostentation, nor did he abstain from what he was accustomed to do. To have departed from his usual habit in any way would have been a yielding of principle in the case. It is not mentioned at what time in the day Daniel thus kneeled and prayed, but we may presume that it was evening, and morning, and noon. Thus the Psalmist says: "Evening, and morning, and at noon, will I pray, and cry aloud; and he shall hear my voice" (Psa. lv. 17). No one can doubt

11 Then these men assembled, and found Daniel praying and making supplication before his God.

12 Then they came near,[a] and spake before the king concerning the king's decree; Hast thou not signed a decree, that every man that shall ask *a petition* of any god or man within thirty days, save of thee, O king, shall be cast into the den of lions? The king answered

a ch. 3. 8.   *b* ver. 8.

c ch. 5. 13.   *d* ch. 3. 12; Acts 5. 29.

and said, The thing *is* true, according to the law of the Medes and Persians, which altereth [b] not.

13 Then answered they, and said before the king, That Daniel, [c]which *is* of the children of the captivity of Judah, regardeth [d] not thee, O king, nor the decree that thou hast signed, but maketh his petition three times a day.

14 Then the king, when he heard *these* words, was sore [e] displeased

e Mar. 6. 26.

the propriety of thus praying to God; and it would be well for all thus to call upon their God. ¶ *As he did aforetime.* Without making any change. He neither increased nor diminished the number of times each day in which he called upon God; nor did he make any change in the manner of doing it. He did not seek ostentatiously to show that he was a worshipper of God, nor was he deterred by the fear of punishment from doing as he had been accustomed to do. If it should be said that Daniel's habit of worship was ostentatious ; that his praying with his windows open was contrary to the true spirit of retiring devotion, and especially contrary to the spirit required of worshippers in the New Testament, where the Saviour commands us when we pray to "enter into the closet, and to shut the door" (Matt. vi. 6), it may be replied, (1) that there is no *evidence* that Daniel did this for the purpose of ostentation, and the supposition that he did it for that purpose is contrary to all that we know of his character ; (2) as we have seen, this was the customary place for prayer, and the manner of the prayer was that which was usual ; (3) the chamber, or upper part of the house, was in fact the most retired part, and was a place where one would be least *likely* to be heard or seen ; and (4) there is no evidence that it would not have been quite private and unobserved if these men had not gone to his house and listened for the very purpose of detecting him at his devotions. No one could well guard against such a purpose.

11. *Then these men assembled.* &c.

Evidently with a *design* of finding him at his devotions.

12. *Then they came near.* That is, they came near to the king. They had detected Daniel, as they expected and desired to do, in a palpable violation of the law, and they lost no time in apprising the king of it, and in reminding him of the law which he had established. Informers are not apt to lose time. ¶ *The king answered and said, The thing is true,* &c. It is undeniable, whatever may be the consequences. There is no reason to suppose that he as yet had any suspicion of their design in asking this question. It is not improbable that he apprehended there had been some violation of the law, but it does not appear that his suspicions rested on Daniel.

13. *Then answered they — That Daniel, which is of the children of the captivity of Judah.* Who is one of the captive Jews. There was art in thus referring to Daniel, instead of mentioning him as sustaining an exalted office. It would serve to aggravate his guilt to remind the king that one who was in fact a foreigner, and a captive, had thus disregarded his solemn commandment. If he had been mentioned as the prime minister, there was at least a possibility that the king would be less disposed to deal with him according to the letter of the statute than if he were mentioned as a captive Jew. ¶ *Regardeth not thee,* &c. Shows open disregard and contempt for the royal authority by making a petition to his God three times a-day.

14. *Then the king, when he heard*

with himself, and set *his* heart on Daniel to deliver him; and he

these *words, was sore displeased with himself.* That is, for having consented to such a decree without deliberation, or with so much haste—or for having consented to it at all. It is remarkable that it is not said that he was displeased with *them* for having proposed it; but it is clear that he saw that the guilt was his own for having given his assent to it, and that he had acted foolishly. There is no evidence as yet that he saw that the decree had been proposed for the purpose of securing the degradation and ruin of Daniel— though he ultimately perceived it (ver. 24); or if he did perceive it, there was no way of preventing the consequences from coming on Daniel—and that was the point that now engrossed his attention. He was doubtless displeased with himself, (1) because he saw that he had done wrong in confirming such a decree, which interfered with what had been tolerated—the free exercise of religion by his subjects; (2) because he now saw that it was foolish, and unworthy of a king, thus to assent to a law for which there was no good reason, and the consequences of which he had not foreseen; and (3) because he now saw that he had involved the first officer of the realm, and a man of unsullied character, in ruin, unless some way could be devised by which the consequences of the statute could be averted. It is no uncommon thing for men to be displeased *with themselves* when they experience the unexpected consequences of their follies and their sins. An instance strongly resembling that here stated, in its main features, occurred at a later period in the history of Persia—an instance showing how the innocent may be involved in a general law, and how much perplexity and regret may be caused by the enactment of such a law. It occurred in Persia, in the persecution of Christians, A.D. 344. "An edict appeared, which commanded that all Christians should be thrown into chains and executed. Many belonging to every rank died as martyrs. Among these was an eunuch of the palace, named Azades,

laboured till the going down of the sun to deliver him.

a man greatly prized by the king. So much was the latter affected by his death, that he commanded the punishment of death should be inflicted from thenceforth only on the leaders of the Christian sect; that is, only on persons of the clerical order."—Neander's *Church History,* Torrey's Translation, vol. iii. p. 146. ¶ *And set* his *heart on Daniel to deliver him.* In what *way* he sought to deliver him is not said. It would seem probable from the representation in the following verse, that it was by an inquiry whether the statute might not properly be changed or cancelled, or whether the penalty might not be commuted—for it is said that his counsellors urged as a reason for the strict infliction of the punishment the absolute unchangeableness of the statute. Perhaps he inquired whether a precedent might not be found for the abrogation of a law enacted by a king by the same authority that enacted it; or whether it did not come within the king's prerogative to change it; or whether the punishment might not be commuted without injury; or whether the evidence of the guilt was perfectly clear; or whether he might not be pardoned without anything being done to maintain the honour of the law. This is one of the most remarkable instances on record of the case of a monarch seeking to deliver a subject from punishment when the monarch had absolute power, and is a striking illustration of the difficulties which often arise in the administration of justice, where the law is absolute, and where justice seems to demand the infliction of the penalty, and yet where there are strong reasons why the penalty should *not* be inflicted; that is, why an offender should be pardoned. And yet there is no improbability in this statement about the perplexity of the king; for (1) there were strong reasons, easily conceivable, why the penalty should *not* be inflicted in this case, because (*a*) the law had been evidently devised by the crafty enemies of Daniel to secure just such a result; (*b*) Daniel had been guilty of

15 Then these men assembled unto the king, and said unto the king, Know, O king, that the law of the Medes and Persians *is*, That no decree nor statute which the king establisheth may be changed.

no *crime*—no moral wrong, but had done only that which should commend him more to favour and confidence ; (*c*) his character was every way upright and pure ; (*d*) the very worship which he had been detected in had been up to that period allowed, and there was no reason why it should now be punished, and (*e*) the infliction of the penalty, though strictly according to the letter of the law, would be manifestly a violation of justice and equity ; or, in other words, it was every way desirable that it should not be inflicted. (2.) Yet there was great difficulty in pardoning him who had offended, for (*a*) the law was absolute in the case ; (*b*) the evidence was clear that Daniel had done what the law forbade ; (*c*) the law of the realm prohibited any change; (*d*) the character and government of the king were involved in the matter. If he interposed and saved Daniel, and thus suffered the law to be violated with impunity, the result would be that there would be a want of stability in his administration, and any other subject could hope that he might violate the law with the same impunity. Justice, and the honour of the government, therefore, seemed to demand that the law should be enforced, and the penalty inflicted. (3.) It may be added, that cases of this kind are frequently occurring in the administration of law— cases where there is a conflict between justice and mercy, and where one must be sacrificed to the other. There are numerous instances in which there can be no doubt that the law has been violated, and yet in which strong reasons exist why the offender should be pardoned. Yet there are great difficulties in the whole subject of *pardon*, and there are more embarrassments in regard to this than anything else pertaining to the administration of the laws. If an offence is *never* pardoned, then the government is stern and inexorable, and its administration violates some of the finest and most tender feelings of our nature—for there *are* cases when all the benevolent feelings of our nature demand that there should be the remission of a penalty— cases, modified by youth, or age, or sex, or temptation, or previous character, or former service rendered to one's country. And yet pardon in any instance always does just so much to weaken the strong arm of the law. It is a proclamation that in some cases crime may be committed with impunity. If *often* exercised, law loses its force, and men are little deterred from crime by fear of it. If it were *always* exercised, and a proclamation were sent forth that *any one* who committed an offence might be pardoned, the authority of government would be at an end. Those, therefore, who are intrusted with the administration of the laws, are often substantially in the same perplexity in which Darius was in respect to Daniel—all whose *feelings* incline them to mercy, and who yet see no way in which it can be exercised consistently with the administration of justice and the prevention of crime. ¶ *And he laboured.* He sought to devise some way in which it might be done. ¶ *Till the going down of the sun.* Houbigant understands this, "Till the sun arose ;" but the common rendering is probably the correct one. *Why* that hour is mentioned is not known. It would seem from the following verse that the king was pressed by his counsellors to carry the decree into execution, and it is probable that the king saw that the case was a perfectly clear one, and that nothing could be hoped for from delay. The law was clear, and it was equally clear that it had been violated. There was no way, then, but to suffer it to take its course.

15. *Then these men assembled unto the king.* The Chaldee here is the same as in ver. 6, "they came tumultuously." They were earnest that the law should be executed, and they probably apprehended that if the king were allowed to dwell upon it, the firmness of his own mind would give way, and that he would release Daniel.

16 Then the king commanded, and they brought ^{a} Daniel, and

a Jer. 26.14; Acts 25.11.

cast *him* into the den of lions. *Now* the king spake and said unto Daniel, Thy God, whom thou

Perhaps they dreaded the effect of the compunctious visitings which he might have during the silence of the night, and they, therefore, came tumultuously to hasten his decision. ¶ *Know, O king, that the law,* &c. That is a settled matter about which there can be no debate or difference of opinion. It would seem that this was a point so well settled that no question could be raised in regard to it, and, to their minds, it was equally clear that if this were so, it was necessary that the sentence should be executed without delay.

16. *Then the king commanded,* &c. See Notes on ver. 7. Some recent discoveries among the ruins of Babylon have shown that the mode of punishment by throwing offenders against the laws to lions was actually practised there, and these discoveries may be classed among the numerous instances in which modern investigations have tended to confirm the statements in the Bible. Three interesting figures illustrating this fact may be seen in the *Pictorial Bible*, vol. iii. p. 232. The first of those figures, from a block of stone, was found at Babylon near the great mass of ruin that is supposed to mark the site of the grand western palace. It represents a lion standing over the body of a prostrate man, extended on a pedestal which measures nine feet in length by three in breadth. The head has been lately knocked off; but when Mr. Rich saw it, the statue was in a perfect state, and he remarks that "the mouth had a circular aperture into which a man might introduce his fist." The second is from an engraved gem, dug from the ruins of Babylon by

Captain Mignan. It exhibits a man standing on two sphinxes, and engaged with two fierce animals, possibly intended for lions. The third is from a

servest continually, he will *a* deliver thee.

17 And a stone *b* was brought,

a ch. 3. 17; Ps. 37. 39, 40.   *b* Lam. 3. 53.

and laid upon the mouth of the den; and the king sealed *c* it with his own signet, and with the signet

c Matt. 27. 66.

block of white marble found near the tomb of Daniel at Susa, and thus described by Sir Robert Ker Porter in his *Travels* (vol. ii. p. 416): "It does not exceed ten inches in width and depth, measures twenty in length, and is hollow within, as if to receive some deposit. Three of its sides are cut in bass-relief, two of them with similar representations of a man apparently naked, except a sash round his waist, and a sort of cap on his head. His hands are bound behind him. The corner of the stone forms the neck of the figure, so that its head forms one of its ends. Two lions in sitting postures appear on either side at the top, each having a paw on the head of the man." See *Pict. Bible, in loc.* ¶ Now *the king spake and said unto Daniel, Thy God,* &c. What is here stated is in accordance with what is said in ver. 14, that the king sought earnestly to deliver Daniel from the punishment. He had entire confidence in him, and he expressed that to the last. As to the question of *probability* whether Darius, a heathen, would attempt to comfort Daniel with the hope that he would be delivered, and would express the belief that this would be done by that God whom he served, and in whose cause he was about to be exposed to peril, it may be remarked, (1.) That it was a common thing among the heathen to believe in the interposition of the gods in favour of the righteous, and particularly in favour of their worshippers. See Homer, *passim.* Hence it was that they called on them ; that they committed themselves to them in battle and in peril ; that they sought their aid by sacrifices and by prayers. No one can doubt that such a belief prevailed, and that the mind of Darius, in accordance with the prevalent custom, might be under its influence. (2.) Darius, undoubtedly, in accordance with the prevailing belief, regarded the God whom Daniel worshipped as *a* god, though not as exclusively *the* true God. He had the

same kind of confidence in him that he had in any god worshipped by foreigners—and probably regarded him as the tutelary divinity of the land of Palestine, and of the Hebrew people. As he might consistently express this belief in reference to *any* foreign divinity, there is no improbability that he would in reference to the God worshipped by Daniel. (3.) He had the utmost confidence both in the integrity and the piety of Daniel ; and as he believed that the gods interposed in human affairs, and as he saw in Daniel an eminent instance of devotedness to *his* God, he did not doubt that in such a case it might be hoped that he would save him.

17. *And a stone was brought, and laid upon the mouth of the den.* Probably a large flat stone sufficient to cover the mouth of the cave, and so heavy that Daniel could not remove it from within and escape. It was usual then, as it is now, to close up the entrance to sepulchres with a large stone. See John xi. 38 ; Matt. xxvii. 60. It would be natural to endeavour to secure this vault or den in the same way —on the one hand so that Daniel could not escape from within, and on the other so that none of his friends could come and rescue him from without. ¶ *And the king sealed it with his own signet.* With his own *seal.* That is, he affixed to the stone, probably by means of clay or wax, his seal in such a way that it could not be removed by any one without breaking it, and consequently without the perpetration of a crime of the highest kind—for no greater offence could be committed against his authority than thus to break his seal, and there could be no greater security that the stone would not be removed. On the manner of sealing a stone in such circumstances, comp. Notes on Matt. xxvii. 66. ¶*And with the signet of his lords.* That it might have all the security which there could be. Perhaps this was at the suggestion of his lords, and the design,

net of his lords, that the purpose might not be changed concerning Daniel.

18 ¶ Then the king went to his palace, and passed the night fast-

ing: neither were [1] instruments of music brought before him; and his sleep went from him.

19 Then the king arose very

1 or, *table.*

on their part, may have been so to guard the den that the king should not release Daniel.

[In a chamber, or passage, in the south-west corner of the palace of Kouyunjik, Layard discovered " a large number of pieces of fine clay, bearing the impressions of seals, which, there is no doubt, had been affixed, like modern official seals of wax, to documents written on leather, papyrus, or parchment. Such documents, with seals in clay still attached, have been discovered in Egypt, and specimens are preserved in the British Museum. The writings themselves had been consumed by the fire

which destroyed the building, or had perished from decay."—"The seals most remarkable for beauty of design and skilful execution re-

present horsemen, one, at full speed, raising a spear, the other hunting a stag." But the most noticeable and important are two impressions of a royal signet; the one of Egyptian character, and the other representing a priest ministering before the Assyrian king. An engraved cylinder of translucent green felspar, found near the entrance of the palace, is conjectured to be the signet or amulet of Sennacherib, the presumed builder of the structure. The king stands in an arched frame, with his face to the sacred tree, which is surmounted by the symbol of Baal; and opposite to him is a eunuch. A goat, standing upon the lotus flower, occupies the rest of the cylinder.—*See annexed engravings.*]

¶ *That the purpose might not be changed concerning Daniel.* By the king. Probably they feared that if there was not this security, the king might release him; but they presumed that he would not violate the seal of the great officers of the realm. It would seem that some sort of *concurrence* between the king and his nobles was required in making and executing the laws.

18. *Then the king went to his palace, and passed the night fasting.* Daniel was probably cast into the den soon after the going down of the sun, ver. 14. It was not unusual to have *suppers* then late at night, as it is now in many places. The great anxiety of the king, however, on account of what had occurred, prevented him from participating in the usual evening meal. As to the *probability* of what is here affirmed, no one can have any doubt who credits the previous statements. In the consciousness of wrong done to a worthy officer of the government; in the deep anxiety which he had to deliver him; in the excitement which must have existed against the cunning and wicked authors of the plot to deceive the king and to ruin Daniel; and in his solicitude and hope that after all Daniel might escape, there is a satisfactory reason for the facts stated that he had no desire for food; that instruments of music were not brought before him;

early in the morning, and went in
haste unto the den of lions.
20 And when he came to the
den, he cried with a lamentable
voice unto Daniel; and the king
spake and said to Daniel, O Daniel,
servant of the living God, is thy

God, whom thou servest continually, able to deliver thee from the
lions?
21 Then said Daniel unto the
king, O king, live for ever.
22 My God hath sent his *angel,

a ch. 3. 28.

---

and that he passed a sleepless night.
¶ *Neither were instruments of music
brought before him.* It was usual
among the ancients to have music at
their meals. This custom prevailed
among the Greeks and Romans, and
doubtless was common in the Oriental
world. It should be observed, however, that there is considerable variety
in the interpretation of the word here
rendered *instruments of music*—דחון.
The margin is *table.* The Latin Vulgate, "He slept supperless, neither
was food brought before him." The
Greek renders it *food,* ἐδέσματα. So
the Syriac. Bertholdt and Gesenius
render it *concubines,* and Saadias *danc-
ing girls.* Any of these significations
would be appropriate; but it is impossible to determine which is the most
correct. The word does not occur
elsewhere in the Scriptures.
19. *Then the king arose very early in
the morning,* &c. No one can doubt the
probability of what is here said, if the
previous account be true. His deep
anxiety; his wakeful night; the remorse
which he endured, and his hope that
Daniel would be after all preserved, all
would prompt to an early visit to the
place of his confinement, and to his
earnestness in ascertaining whether he
were still alive.
20. *He cried with a lamentable voice.*
A voice full of anxious solicitude. Literally, " a voice of grief." Such a cry
would be natural on such an occasion.
¶ *O Daniel, servant of the living God.*
The God who has life; who imparts
life; and who can preserve life. This
was the appellation, probably, which
he had heard Daniel use in regard to
God, and it is one which he would
naturally employ on such an occasion
as this; feeling that the question of *life*
was entirely in his hands. ¶ *Whom
thou servest continually.* At all times,

and in all circumstances: as a captive
in a distant land; in places of honour and
power; when surrounded by the great
who worship other gods; and when
threatened with death for your devotion to the service of God. This had
been the character of Daniel, and it
was natural to refer to it now.
21. *Then said Daniel unto the king, O
king, live for ever.* The common form
of salutation in addressing the king.
See Notes on ch. ii. 4. There might
be more than mere *form* in this, for
Daniel may have been aware of the
true source of the calamities that had
come upon him, and of the innocence
of the king in the matter; and he doubtless recalled the interest which the king
had shown in him when about to be
cast into the den of lions, and his expression of confidence that his God
would be able to deliver him (ver. 16),
and he could not but have been favourably impressed by the solicitude which
the monarch now showed for his welfare in thus early visiting him, and by
his anxiety to know whether he were
still alive.
22. *My God hath sent his angel.* It
was common among the Hebrews to
attribute any remarkable preservation
from danger to the intervention of an
angel sent from God, and no one can
demonstrate that it did not occur as
they supposed. There is no more absurdity in supposing that God employs
an angelic being to defend his people,
or to impart blessings to them, than
there is in supposing that he employs
one human being to render important
aid, and to convey important blessings,
to another. As a matter of fact, few
of the favours which God bestows upon
men are conveyed to them directly from
himself, but they are mostly imparted
by the instrumentality of others. So
it is in the blessings of liberty, in deliverance from bondage, in the provision

and hath shut *a* the lions' mouths, that they have not hurt me: forasmuch as before him *b* innocency was found in me; and also before thee, O king, have I done no hurt. 23 Then was the king exceeding glad for him, and commanded that they should take Daniel up out of

a Heb. 11. 33.   *b* Ps. 18. 20, 24; 26. 6.

the den. So Daniel was taken up out of the den, and no manner of hurt was found upon him, because he believed in his God.

24 ¶ And the king commanded, and they brought those men *c* which had accused Daniel, and they cast *them* into the den of lions, them,

c Deut. 19. 19.

made for our wants, in the favour bestowed on us in infancy and childhood. As this principle prevails everywhere on the earth, it is not absurd to suppose that it may prevail elsewhere, and that on important occasions, and in instances above the rank of human intervention, God may employ the instrumentality of higher beings to defend his people in trouble, and rescue them from danger. Comp. Psa. xxxiv. 7; xci. 11; Dan. ix. 21; Matt. xviii. 10; Luke xvi. 22; Heb. i. 14. Daniel does not say whether the angel was *visible* or not, but it is rather to be presumed that he was, as in this way it would be more certainly known to him that he owed his deliverance to the intervention of an angel, and as this would be to him a manifest token of the favour and protection of God. ¶ *And hath shut the lions' mouths.* It is clear that Daniel supposed that this was accomplished by a miracle; and this is the only satisfactory solution of what had occurred. There is, moreover, no more objection to the supposition that this was a miracle than there is to any miracle whatever, for (*a*) there is no more fitting occasion for the Divine intervention than when a good man is in danger, and (*b*) the object to be accomplished on the mind of the king, and through him on the minds of the people at large, was worthy of such an interposition. The design was evidently to impress the mind of the monarch with the belief of the existence of the true God, and to furnish in the court of Babylon proof that should be convincing that he is the *only* God. ¶ *Forasmuch as before him innocency was found in me.* (1.) Absolute innocency in reference to the question of guilt on the point in which he had been condemned—he having done only that which God ap-

proved; and (2) general integrity and uprightness of character. We need not suppose that Daniel claimed to be absolutely perfect (comp. ch. ix.), but we may suppose that he means to say that God saw that he was what he professed to be, and that his life was such as he approved. ¶ *And also before thee, O king, have I done no hurt.* That is, he had in no manner violated his duty to the king; he had done nothing that tended to overthrow his government, or to spread disaffection among his subjects. 23. *Then was the king exceeding glad for him.* On account of Daniel. That is, he was rejoiced for the sake of Daniel that he had received no hurt, and that he might be restored to his place, and be useful again in the government. 24. *And the king commanded, and they brought those men which had accused Daniel,* &c. It would seem probable that the king had been aware of their wicked designs against Daniel, and had been satisfied that the whole was the result of a conspiracy, but he felt himself under a necessity of allowing the law to take its course on him whom he believed to be really innocent. That had been done. All that the law could be construed as requiring had been accomplished. It could not be pretended that the law required that any *other* punishment should be inflicted on Daniel, and the way was now clear to deal with the authors of the malicious plot as they deserved. No one can reasonably doubt the *probability* of what is here said in regard to the conspirators against Daniel. The king had arbitrary power. He was convinced of their guilt. His wrath had been with difficulty restrained when he understood the nature of the plot against Daniel. Nothing, there-their children,[a] and their wives; and the lions had the mastery[b] of them, and brake all their bones in

a Deut. 24. 16; 2 Kings 14. 6; Esth. 9. 10.

fore, was more natural than that he should subject the guilty to the same punishment which they had sought to bring upon the innocent; nothing more natural than that a proud despot, who saw that, by the force of a law which he could not control, he had been made a tool in subjecting the highest officer of the realm, and the best man in it, to peril of death, should, without any delay, wreak his vengeance on those who had thus made use of him to gratify their own malignant passions. ¶ *Them, their children, and their wives.* This was in accordance with Oriental notions of justice, and was often done. It is said expressly by Ammianus Marcellinus (23, 6, 81), to have been a custom among the Persians: "The laws among them (the Persians) are formidable; among which those which are enacted against the ungrateful and deserters, and similar abominable crimes, surpass others in cruelty, by which, on account of the guilt of one, all the kindred perish"—per quas ob noxam unius omnis propinquitas perit. So Curtius says of the Macedonians: "It is enacted by law that the kindred of those who conspire against the king shall be put to death with them." Instances of this kind of punishment are found among the Hebrews (Josh. vii. 24; 2 Sam. xxi. 5, *seq.*), though it was forbidden by the law of Moses, in judicial transactions, Deut. xxiv. 16. Compare also Ezek. xviii.; Maurer, *in loc.* In regard to this transaction we may observe (*a*) that nothing is more probable than that this would occur, since, as appears from the above quotations, it was often done, and there was nothing in the character of Darius that would prevent it, though it seems to us to be so unjust. (*b*) It was the act of a heathen monarch, and it is not necessary, in order to defend the Scripture narrative, to vindicate the justice of the transaction. The record may be true, though the thing itself was evil and wrong. (*c*) Yet the same thing substantially occurs in the course of

pieces or ever they came at the bottom of the den.

25 ¶ Then[c] king Darius wrote

b Ps. 54. 5.   c ch. 4. 1.

Providence, or the administration of justice now. Nothing is more common than that the wife and children of a guilty man should suffer on account of the sin of the husband and father. Who can recount the woes that come upon a family through the intemperance of a father? And in cases where a man is condemned for crime, the consequences are not confined to himself. In shame and mortification, and disgrace; in the anguish experienced when he dies on a gibbet; in the sad remembrance of that disgraceful death; in the loss of one who might have provided for their wants, and been their protector and counsellor, the wife and children *always* suffer; and, though this took another form in ancient times, and when adopted as a principle of punishment is not in accordance with our sense of justice in administering laws, yet it is a principle which pervades the world—for the effects of crime cannot and do not terminate on the guilty individual himself. ¶ *And the lions had the mastery of them.* As the Divine restraint furnished for the protection of Daniel was withdrawn, they acted out their proper nature. ¶ *And brake all their bones in pieces or ever,* &c. Literally "they did not come to the bottom of the den until the lions had the mastery of them, and brake all their bones." They seized upon them as they fell, and destroyed them.

25. *Then king Darius wrote unto all people,* &c. Comp. Notes on ch. ii. 47; iii. 29; iv. 1. If there is a probability that Nebuchadnezzar would make such a proclamation as he did, there is no less probability that the same thing would be done by Darius. Indeed, it is manifest on the face of the whole narrative that one great design of all that occurred was to proclaim the knowledge of the true God, and to secure his recognition. That object was *worthy* of the Divine interposition, and the facts in the case show that God has *power* to induce princes and rulers to

unto all people, nations, and languages, that dwell in all the earth; Peace be multiplied unto you.

26 I make a decree, That in every dominion of my kingdom men*a* tremble and fear before the God of Daniel; for he *b is* the living God, and stedfast for ever, and his kingdom *c that* which shall not be

a Ps. 99.1.   *b* ch. 4. 34.   *c* ch. 2. 44.
d Ps. 18. 50; 32. 7.   *e* ch. 4. 3.   1 hand.

destroyed, and his dominion *shall be even* unto the end.

27 He delivereth*d* and rescueth, and he worketh signs *e* and wonders in heaven and in earth, who hath delivered Daniel from the power 1 of the lions.

28 So this Daniel prospered in the reign of Darius, and in the reign of Cyrus *f* the Persian.

f ch. 1. 21; Ezra 1. 1, 2.

recognize his existence and perfections, and his government over the earth.

26. *I make a decree.* Comp. ch. iii. 29. ¶ *That in every dominion of my kingdom.* Every department or province. The entire kingdom or empire was made up of several kingdoms, as Media, Persia, Babylonia, &c. The meaning is, that he wished the God of Daniel to be honoured and reverenced throughout the whole empire. ¶ *Men tremble and fear before the God of Daniel.* That they honour and reverence him as God. There is no certain evidence that he meant that he should be honoured as the *only* God; but the probability is, that he meant that he should be recognized as a God of great power and glory, and as worthy of universal reverence. How far this heathen monarch might still regard the other deities worshipped in the empire as gods, or how far his own heart might be disposed to honour the God of Daniel, there are no means of ascertaining. It was much, however, that so great a monarch should be led to make a proclamation acknowledging the God of Daniel as having a real existence, and as entitled to universal reverence. ¶ *For he is the living God.* An appellation often given to God in the Scriptures, and probably learned by Darius from Daniel. It is not, however, absolutely certain that Darius would attach *all* the ideas to these phrases which Daniel did, or which we would. The attributes here ascribed to God are correct, and the views expressed are far beyond any that prevailed among the heathen; but still it would not be proper to suppose that Darius certainly had all the views of God which these words would convey

to us now. ¶ *And stedfast for ever.* That is, he is always the same. He ever lives; he has power over all; his kingdom is on an immovable foundation. He is not, in his government, to cease to exist, and to be succeeded by another who shall occupy his throne. ¶ *And his kingdom that which shall not be destroyed,* &c. See Notes on ch. iv. 3, 34. The similarity between the language used here, and that employed by Nebuchadnezzar, shows that it was probably derived from the same source. It is to be presumed that both monarchs expressed the views which they had learned from Daniel.

27. *He delivereth and rescueth.* As in the case of Daniel. This attribute would of course be prominent in the view of Darius, since so remarkable an instance of his power had been recently manifested in rescuing Daniel. ¶ *And he worketh signs and wonders,* &c. Performs miracles far above all human power. If he had done it on earth in the case of Daniel, it was fair to infer that he did it also in heaven. Comp. Notes, ch. iv. 2, 3. ¶ *The power of the lions.* Marg., *hand.* The hand is the instrument of power. The word *paw* would express the idea here, and would accord with the meaning, as it is usually with the paw that the lion strikes down his prey before he devours it.

28. *So this Daniel prospered in the reign of Darius.* That is, to the end of his reign. It is fairly implied here that he was restored to his honours. ¶ *And in the reign of Cyrus the Persian.* Cyrus the Great, the nephew and successor of Darius. For an account of Cyrus, see Notes on Isa. xli. 2. How *long* during the reign of Cyrus

Daniel "prospered" or lived is not
said. During a part of the reign of
Darius or Cyaxares, he was occupied
busily in securing by his influence the
welfare of his own people, and making
arrangements for their return to their
land; and his high post in the nation
to which, under Divine Providence, he
had doubtless been raised for this purpose, enabled him to render essential
and invaluable service at the court.
In the third year of Cyrus, we are informed (ch. x.–xii.), he had a series
of visions respecting the future history
and sufferings of his nation to the period
of their true redemption through the
Messiah, as also a consolatory direction to himself to proceed calmly and
peaceably to the end of his days, and
then await patiently the resurrection
of the dead, ch. xii. 12, 13. From
that period the accounts respecting
him are vague, confused, and even
strange, and little or nothing is known
of the time or circumstances of his
death. Comp. Intro. § 1.
From this chapter we may derive
the following instructive

PRACTICAL LESSONS.

(1.) We have an instance of what
often occurs in the world—of *envy* on
account of the excellency of others,
and of the honours which they obtain
by their talent and their worth, vers.
1–4. Nothing is more frequent than
such envy, and nothing more common,
as a consequence, than a determination
to degrade those who are the subjects
of it. Envy always seeks in some way
to humble and mortify those who are
distinguished. It is the pain, mortification, chagrin, and regret which we
have at their superior excellence or
prosperity, and this prompts us to endeavour to bring them down to our
own level, or below it; to calumniate
their characters; to hinder their prosperity; to embarrass them in their
plans; to take up and circulate rumours
to their disadvantage; to magnify their
faults, or to fasten upon them the suspicion of crime. In the instance be-

fore us, we see the effect in a most guilty
conspiracy against a man of incorrupti-
ble character; a man full in the confidence of his sovereign; a man eminently the friend of virtue and of God.

" Envy will merit, as its shade, pursue;
But, like a shadow, proves the substance
    true."
        —Pope's *Essay on Criticism*
" Base envy withers at another's joy,
And hates that excellence it cannot reach."
        —Thomson's *Seasons.*
" Be thou as chaste as ice, as pure as snow,
Thou shalt not escape calumny."
                —Shakspeare.
" That thou art blamed shall not be thy defect,
For slander's mark was ever yet the fair:
So thou be good, slander doth yet approve
Thy worth the greater."
                —Shakspeare.

(2.) We have in this chapter (vers.
4–9) a striking illustration of the nature and the evils of a *conspiracy* to
ruin others. The plan here was deliberately formed to ruin Daniel—the
best man in the realm—a man against
whom no charge of guilt could be alleged, who had done the conspirators
no wrong; who had rendered himself
in no way amenable to the laws. A
"conspiracy" is a combination of men
for evil purposes; an agreement between two or more persons to commit some crime in concert, usually
treason, or an insurrection against a
government or state. In this case, it
was a plot growing wholly out of envy
or jealousy; a concerted agreement to
ruin a good man, where no wrong had
been done or could be pretended, and
no crime had been committed. The
essential things in this conspiracy, as
in all other cases of conspiracy, were
two: (*a*) that the purpose was *evil;*
and (*b*) that it was to be accomplished
by the combined influences of *numbers.*
The means on which they relied, or
the grounds of calculation on the success of their plot, were the following:
(1) that they could calculate on the
unwavering integrity of Daniel—on
his firm and faithful adherence to the

principles of his religion in all circumstances, and in all times of temptation and trial; and (2) that they could induce the king to pass a law, irrepealable from the nature of the case, which Daniel would be certain to violate, and to the penalty of which, therefore, he would be certainly exposed. Now in this purpose there was every element of iniquity, and the grossest conceivable wrong. There were combined all the evils of envy and malice; of perverting and abusing their influence over the king; of secresy in taking advantage of one who did not suspect any such design; and of involving the king himself in the necessity of exposing the best man in his realm, and the highest officer of state, to the certain danger of death. The result, however, showed, as is often the case, that the evil recoiled on themselves, and that the very calamity overwhelmed them and their families which they had designed for another.

(3.) We have here a striking instance of what often occurs, and what should always occur, among the friends of religion, that "no occasion can be found against them except in regard to the law of their God"—on the score of their religion, ver. 5. Daniel was known to be upright. His character for integrity was above suspicion. It was certain that there was no hope of bringing any charge against him that would lie, for any want of uprightness or honesty; for any failure in the discharge of the duties of his office; for any malversation in administering the affairs of the government; for any embezzlement of the public funds, or for any act of injustice towards his fellow-men. It was certain that his character was irreproachable on all these points; and it was equally certain that he did and would maintain unwavering fidelity in the duties of religion. Whatever consequences might follow from it, it was clear that they could calculate on his maintaining with faithfulness the duties of piety. Whatever plot, therefore, could be formed against him on the basis either of his moral integrity or his piety, it was certain would be successful. But there was no hope in regard to the former, for no law could have been carried prohibiting his doing what was right on the subject of morals. The only hope, therefore, was in respect to his religion; and the main idea in their plot—the thing which constituted the basis of their plan was, *that it was certain that Daniel would maintain his fidelity to his God irrespective of any consequences whatever.* This certainty ought to exist in regard to every good man; every man professing religion. His character ought to be so well understood; his piety ought to be so firm, unwavering, and consistent, that it could be calculated on just as certainly as we calculate on the stability of the laws of nature, that he will be found faithful to his religious duties and obligations. There *are* such men, and the character of every man *should be* such. Then indeed we should know what to depend on in the world; then religion would be respected as it should be.

(4.) We may learn what is our *duty* when we are opposed in the exercise of our religion, or when we are in any way threatened with loss of office, or of property, on account of our religion, ver. 10. *We are to persevere in the discharge of our religious duties, whatever may be the consequences.* So far as the example of Daniel goes, this would involve two things: (*a*) not to swerve from the faithful performance of duty, or not to be deterred from it; and (*b*) not to change our course from any desire of display. These two things were manifested by Daniel. He kept steadily on his way. He did **not** abridge the number of times of his daily devotion; nor, as far as appears, did he change the form or the length. He did not cease to pray in an audible voice; he did not give up prayer in the daytime, and pray only at night; he did not even close his windows; he did not take any precautions to pray when none were near; he did not withdraw into an inner chamber. At the same time, he made no changes in his devotion for the sake of ostentation. He did not open his windows before closed; he did not go into the street; he did not call around him his friends or foes to witness his devotions; he did not, as far as appears, either elevate his voice, or prolong his prayers, in order to attract attention, or to invite persecution. In all this he manifested the true spirit of religion, and set an example to men to be followed in all ages. Not by the loss of fame or money; by the dread of persecution, or contempt of death; by the threatenings of law or the fear of shame, are we to be deterred from the proper and the usual performance of our religious duties; nor by a desire to provoke persecution, and to win the crown of martyrdom, and to elicit applause, and to have our names blazoned abroad, are we to multiply our religious acts, or make an ostentatious display of them, when we are threatened, or when we know that our conduct will excite opposition. We are to ascertain what is right and proper; and then we are modestly and firmly to do it, no matter what may be the consequences. Comp. Matt. v. 16; Acts iv. 16–20; ʋ. 29.

(5.) We have, in the case of Darius, an instance of what often happens, the regret and anguish which the mind experiences in consequence of a rash act, when it cannot be repaired, ver. 14. The act of Darius in making the de-

cree was eminently a rash one. It was done without deliberation at the suggestion of others, and probably under the influence of some very improper feeling—the desire of being esteemed as a god. But it had consequences which he did not foresee, consequences which, if he had foreseen them, would doubtless have prevented his giving a sanction to this iniquitous law. The state of mind which he experienced when he saw how the act involved the best officer in his government, and the best man in his realm, was just what might have been expected, and is an illustration of what often occurs. It was too late now to prevent the effects of the act; and his mind was overwhelmed with remorse and sorrow. He blamed himself for his folly; and he sought in vain for some way to turn aside the consequences which he now deplored. Such instances often occur. (a) Many of our acts are rash. They are performed without deliberation; under the influence of improper passions; at the suggestion of others who would be thought to be our friends; and without any clear view of the consequences, or any concern as to what the result may be. (b) As an effect, they often have consequences which we did not anticipate, and which would have deterred us in each instance had we foreseen them. (c) They often produce regret and anguish when too late, and when we cannot prevent the evil. The train of evils which has been commenced it is now too late to retard or prevent, and they now inevitably come upon us. We can only stand and weep over the effects of our rashness and folly; and must now feel that if the evil is averted, it will be by the interposition of God alone.

(6.) We have in this chapter an affecting instance of the evils which often arise in a human government from the want of something like an atonement, ver. 14, *seq.* As has been remarked in the Notes, cases often arise when it is desirable that pardon should be extended to the violators of law. See Notes on ver. 14. In such cases, some such arrangement as that of an atonement, by which the honour of the law might be maintained, and at the same time the merciful feelings of an executive might be indulged, and the benevolent wishes of a community gratified, would remove difficulties which are now felt in every administration. The difficulties in the case, and the advantage which would arise from an atonement, may be seen by a brief reference to the circumstances of the case before us : (*a*) the law was inexorable. It demanded punishment, as all law does ; for no law in itself makes any provision for pardon. If it did, it would be a burlesque on all legislation. Law denounces penalty ; it does not pardon or show mercy. It has become necessary indeed to lodge a pardoning power with some *man* intrusted with the administration of the laws, but the pardon is not extended by the law itself. (*b*) The anxiety of the king in the case is an illustration of what often occurs in the administration of law ; for, as above observed, there *are* cases where, on many accounts, it would seem to be desirable that the penalty of the law should not be inflicted. Such a case was that of Dr. Dodd, in London, in which a petition, signed by thirty thousand names, was presented, praying for the remission of the penalty of death. Such a case was that of Major Andrè, when Washington shed tears at the necessity of signing the death-warrant of so young and so accomplished an officer. Such cases often occur, in which there is the deepest anxiety in the bosom of

DANIEL II.

an executive to see if there is not some way by which the infliction of the penalty of the law may be avoided. (*c*) Yet there was in the case of Darius no possibility of a change, and this too is an illustration of what often occurs. The law was inexorable. It could not be repealed. So now there are instances where the penalty of law *cannot* be avoided consistently with the welfare of a community. Punishment *must* be inflicted, or all law become a nullity. An instance of this kind was that of Dr. Dodd. He was convicted of forgery. So important had it been deemed for the welfare of a commercial community that *that* crime should be prevented, that no one ever had been pardoned for it, and it was felt that no one should be. Such an instance was that of Major Andrè. The safety and welfare of the whole army, and the success of the cause, seemed to demand that the offence should not go unpunished. (*d*) Yet there are difficulties in extending pardon to the guilty ; (1) if it *is done at all*, it always does so much to weaken the strong arm of the law, and if *often* done, it makes law a nullity ; and (2) if it is *never* done, the law seems stern and inexorable, and the finer feelings of our nature, and the benevolent wishes of the community, are disregarded. (*e*) These difficulties are obviated by an atonement. The things which are accomplished in the atonement made under the Divine government, we think, so far as this point is concerned, and which distinguishes pardon in the Divine administration from pardon everywhere else, relieving it from all the embarrassments felt in other governments, are the following : (1.) There is the utmost respect paid to the *law*. It is honoured (*a*) in the personal obedience of the Lord Jesus, and (*b*) in the sacrifice which

c

he made on the cross to maintain its dignity, and to show that it could not be violated with impunity — *more* honoured by far than it would be by the perfect obedience of man himself, or by its penalty being borne by the sinner. (2.) Pardon can be offered to any extent, or to any number of offenders. All the feelings of benevolence and mercy can be indulged and gratified in the most free manner ; for now that an atonement is made, all proper honour has been shown to the law and to the claims of justice, and no interest will suffer though the most ample proclamation of pardon is issued. There is but one government in the universe that can safely to itself make an unlimited offer of pardon—that is, the government of God. There is not a human government that could safely make the offer which we meet everywhere in the Bible, that *all* offences may be forgiven : that *all* violators of law may be pardoned. If such a proclamation were made, there is no earthly administration that could hope to stand ; no community which would not soon become the prey of lawless plunder and robbery. The reason, and the sole reason, why it can be done in the Divine administration is, that an atonement has been made by which the honour of the law has been secured, and by which it is shown that, while pardon is extended to all, the law is to be honoured, and can never be violated with impunity. (3) The plan of pardon by the atonement secures the observance of the law on the part of those who are pardoned. This can never be depended on when an offender against human laws is pardoned, and when a convict is discharged from the penitentiary. So far as the effect of punishment, or any influence from the act of pardon is concerned, there is no security that the pardoned convict will

not, as his first act, force a dwelling or commit murder. But in the case of *all* who are pardoned through the atonement, it is made certain that they *will be* obedient to the laws of God, and that their lives will be changed from sin to holiness, from disobedience to obedience. This has been secured by incorporating into the plan a provision by which the heart shall be changed *before* pardon is granted : not as the *ground* or *reason* of pardon, but as essential to it. The heart of the sinner is renewed by the Holy Ghost, and he becomes in fact obedient, and is disposed to lead a life of holiness. Thus every hinderance which exists in a human government to pardon is removed in the Divine administration ; the honour of law is secured ; the feelings of benevolence are gratified, and the sinner becomes obedient and holy.

(7.) We have in this chapter (ver. 16) an instance of the confidence which wicked men are constrained to express in the true God. Darius had no doubt that the God whom Daniel served was able to protect and deliver him. The same may be said now. Wicked men know that it is safe to trust in God ; that he is able to save his friends ; that there is more security in the ways of virtue than in the ways of sin ; and that when human help fails, it is proper to repose on the Almighty arm. There is a feeling in the human heart that they who confide in God are safe, and that it is proper to rely on his arm ; and even a wicked father will not hesitate to exhort a Christian son or daughter to serve their God faithfully, and to confide in him in the trials and temptations of life. Ethan Allen, of Vermont, distinguished in the American revolution, was an infidel. His wife was an eminent Christian. When he was about to die, he was asked which of the two he wished his son to imitate in his religious views—his father or his mother. He replied, " His mother."

(8.) The righteous may look for the Divine protection and favour (ver. 22) ; that is, it is an advantage in this world of danger, and temptation, and trial, to be truly religious ; or, in other words, those who are righteous may confidently expect the Divine interposition in their behalf. It is, indeed, a question of some difficulty, but of much importance, to what extent, and in what forms we are authorized now to look for the Divine interposition in our behalf, or what is the real benefit of religion in this world, so far as the Divine protection is concerned; and on this point it seems not inappropriate to lay down a few principles that may be of use, and that may be a proper application of the passage before us to our own circumstances:

(A) There is then a class of Scripture promises that refer to such protection, and that lead us to believe that we may look for the Divine interference in favour of the righteous, or that there is, in this respect, an advantage in true religion. In support of this, reference may be made to the following, among other passages of Scripture :— Psa. xxxiv. 7, 17–22 ; lv. 22 ; xci. 1–8 ; Isa. xliii. 1, 2 ; Luke xii. 6, 7 ; Heb. i. 14 ; xiii. 5, 6.

(B) In regard to the proper interpretation of these passages, or to the nature and extent of the Divine interposition, which we may expect in behalf of the righteous, it may be remarked.

I. That we are *not* to expect now the following things :—

(a) The Divine interposition by miracle. It is the common opinion of the Christian world that the age of miracles is past ; and certainly there is nothing in the Bible that authorizes us to expect that God will *now* interpose for us in that manner. It would be a wholly illogical inference, however, to maintain that there never *has* been any such interposition in behalf of the righteous ; since a reason may have existed for such an interposition in former times which may not exist now.

(b) We are not authorized to expect that God will interpose by sending his angels visibly to protect and deliver us in the day of peril. The fair interpretation of those passages of Scripture which refer to that subject, as Psa. xxxiv. 7; Heb. i. 14, does not require us to believe that there will be such interposition, and there is no evidence that such interposition takes place. *This* fact, however, should not be regarded as proof, either (1) that no such visible interposition has ever occurred in former times—since it in no way demonstrates that point; or (2) that the angels may not interpose in our behalf now, though to us invisible. For anything that can be proved to the contrary, it may still be true that the angels may be, invisibly, "ministering spirits to those who shall be heirs of salvation," and that they may be sent to accompany the souls of the righteous on their way to heaven, as they were to conduct Lazarus to Abraham's bosom, Luke xvi. 22.

(c) We are not authorized to expect that God will set aside the regular laws of nature in our behalf—that he will thus interpose for us in regard to diseases, to pestilence, to storms, to mildew, to the ravages of the locust or the caterpillar—for this would be a miracle, and all the interposition which we are entitled to expect must be consistent with the belief that the laws of nature will be regarded.

(d) We are not authorized to expect that the righteous will never be overwhelmed with the wicked in calamity—that in an explosion on a steam-boat, in a shipwreck, in fire or flood, in an earthquake or in the pestilence, they will not be cut down together. To suppose that God would directly interpose in behalf of his people in such cases, would be to suppose that there would be miracles still, and there is nothing in the Bible, or in the facts that occur, to justify such an expectation.

II. The Divine interposition which we *are* authorized to expect, may be referred to under the following particulars :—

(*a*) All events, great and small, are under the control of the God who loves righteousness—the God of the righteous. Not a sparrow falls to the ground without his notice ; not an event happens without his permission. If, therefore, calamity comes upon the righteous, it is not because the world is without control ; it is not because God could not prevent it ; it must be because he sees it best that it should be so.

(*b*) There is a general course of events that is favourable to virtue and religion ; that is, there is a state of things on earth which demonstrates that there is a moral government over men. The essence of such a government, as Bishop Butler (*Analogy*) has shown, is, that virtue, in the course of things, is rewarded as virtue, and that vice is punished as vice. This course of things is so settled and clear as to show that God is the friend of virtue and religion, and the enemy of vice and irreligion—that is, that under his administration, the one, as a great law, has a tendency to promote happiness ; the other to produce misery. But if so, there is an advantage in being righteous; or there is a Divine interposition in behalf of the righteous.

(*c*) There are large classes of evils

which a man will certainly avoid by virtue and religion, and those evils are among the most severe that afflict mankind. A course of virtue and religion will make it certain that *those* evils will never come upon him or his family. Thus, for example, by so simple a thing as total abstinence from intoxicating drinks, a man will certainly avoid all the evils that afflict the drunkard—the poverty, disease, disgrace, wretchedness, and ruin of body and soul which are certain to follow from intemperance. By chastity, a man will avoid the woes that come, in the righteous visitation of God, on the debauchee, in the form of the most painful and loathsome of the diseases that afflict our race. By integrity a man will avoid the evils of imprisonment for crime, and the disgrace which attaches to its committal. And by religion—pure religion—by the calmness of mind which it produces—the confidence in God ; the cheerful submission to his will ; the contentment which it causes, and the hopes of a better world which it inspires, a man will certainly avoid a large class of evils which unsettle the mind, and which fill with wretched victims the asylums for the insane. Let a man take up the report of an insane asylum, and ask what proportion of its inmates would have been saved from so fearful a malady by true religion; by the calmness which it produces in trouble ; by its influence in moderating the passions and restraining the desires ; by the acquiescence in the will of God which it produces, and he will be surprised at the number which would have been saved by it from the dreadful evils of insanity. As an illustration of this, I took up the *Report of the Pennsylvania Hospital for the Insane*, for the year 1850, which happened to be lying before me, and looked to see what were the *causes* of insanity in regard to the inmates of the asylum, with a view to the inquiry what proportion of them would probably have been saved from it by the proper influence of religion. Of 1599 patients whose cases were referred to, I found the following, a large part of whom, it may be supposed, would have been saved from insanity if their minds had been under the proper influence of the gospel of Christ, restraining them from sin, moderating their passions, checking their desires, and giving them calmness and submission in the midst of trouble :—

Intemperance	95
Loss of property	72
Dread of poverty	2
Intense study	19
Domestic difficulties	48
Grief for the loss of friends	77
Intense application to business	13
Religious excitement	61
Want of employment	24
Mortified pride	3
Use of opium and tobacco	10
Mental anxiety	77

(*d*) There are cases where God *seems* to interpose in behalf of the righteous directly, in answer to prayer, in times of sickness, poverty, and danger—raising them up from the borders of the grave ; providing for their wants in a manner which appears to be as providential as when the ravens fed Elijah, and rescuing them from danger. There are numerous such cases which cannot be well accounted for on any other supposition than that God does directly interpose in their behalf, and show them these mercies because they are his friends. These are not miracles. The purpose to do this was a part of the original plan when the world was made, and the prayer and the interposition are only the fulfilling of the eternal decree.

(*e*) God *does* interpose in behalf of his children in giving them support and consolation ; in sustaining them in the time of trial ; in upholding them in bereavement and sorrow, and in granting them peace as they go into the valley of the shadow of death. The evidence here is clear, that there *is* a degree of comfort and peace given to true Christians in such seasons, and given in consequence of their religion, which is not granted to the wicked, and to which the devotees of the world are strangers. And if these things are so, then it is clear that there *is* an advantage in this life in being righteous, and that God does now interpose in the course of events, and in the day of trouble, in behalf of his friends.

(9.) God often overrules the malice of men to make himself known, and constrains the wicked to acknowledge him, vers. 25–27. Darius, like Nebuchadnezzar, was constrained to acknowledge him as the true God, and to make proclamation of this throughout his vast empire. So often, by his providence, God constrains the wicked to acknowledge him as the true God, and as ruling in the affairs of men. His interpositions are so apparent ; his works are so vast ; the proofs of his administration are so clear ; and he so defeats the counsels of the wicked, that they cannot but feel that he rules, and they cannot but acknowledge and proclaim it. It is in this way that from age to age God is raising up a great number of witnesses even among the wicked to acknowledge his existence, and to proclaim the great truths of his government ; and it is in this way, among others, that he is constraining the intellect of the world to bow before him. Ultimately all this will be so clear, that the intellect of the world will acknowledge it, and all kings and people will see, as Darius did, that "he is the living God, and steadfast for ever, and his kingdom that which shall not be destroyed, and his dominion shall be unto the end."

CHAPTER VII.

§ I.—ANALYSIS OF THE CHAPTER.

This chapter contains an account of a remarkable prophetic dream which Daniel had in the first year of the reign of Belshazzar, and of the interpretation of the dream. After a brief statement of the contents of the chapter, it will be proper, in order to its more clear exposition, to state the different methods which have been proposed for interpreting it, or the different views of its application which have been adopted. The chapter comprises the following main points : the vision, vers. 1–14 ; and the explanation, vers. 15–28.

I. The vision, vers. 1–14. The dream occurred in the first year of the reign of Belshazzar, and was immediately written out. Daniel is represented as standing near the sea, and a violent wind rages upon the sea, tossing the waves in wild commotion. Suddenly he sees four monsters emerge from the agitated waves, each one apparently remaining for a little time, and then disappearing. The first, in its general form, resembled a lion, but had wings like an eagle. On this he attentively gazed, until the wings were plucked away, and the beast was made to stand upright as a man, and the heart of a man was given to it.

Nothing is said as to what became of the beast after this. Then there appeared a second beast, resembling a bear, raising itself up on one side, and having three ribs in its mouth, and a command was given to it to arise and devour much flesh. Nothing is said further of what became of this beast. Then there arose another beast like a leopard, with four wings, and four heads, and to this beast was given wide dominion. Nothing is said as to what became of this animal. Then there arose a fourth beast more remarkable

still. Its form is not mentioned, but it was fierce and strong. It had great iron teeth. It trampled down everything before it, and devoured and brake in pieces. This beast had at first ten horns, but soon there sprang up in the midst of them another—a smaller horn at first, but as this increased three of the ten horns were plucked up by the roots—apparently either *by* this, or in order to give place to it. What was more remarkable still, in this smaller horn there appeared the eyes of a man —emblematic of intelligence and vigilance ; and a mouth speaking great things—indicative of pride and arrogance. Daniel looked on this singular vision till a throne was set up or established, and then the Ancient of days did sit—till the old forms of dominations ceased, and the reign of God was introduced and established. He contemplated it till, on account of the great words which the "horn spake," the beast was slain, and his body was destroyed, and given to the burning flame. In the meantime the dominion was taken away from the other beasts ; though their existence was prolonged for a little time. Then appeared in vision one in the form of man, who came to the Ancient of days, and there was given to him universal dominion over all people—a kingdom that should never be destroyed.

II. The interpretation of the vision (verses 15–28). Daniel was greatly troubled at the vision which he had seen, and he approached one who stood near, and asked him the meaning of it, vers. 15, 16. The explanation with which he was favoured was, in general, the following :—That those four beasts which he had seen represented four kings or kingdoms which would exist on the earth, and that the great design of the vision was to state the fact that the saints of the Most High would ultimately possess the kingdom, and would reign for ever, vers. 17, 18. The grand purpose of the vision was to represent the succession of dynasties, and the particular character of each one, until the government over the world should pass into the hands of the people of God, or until the actual rule on the earth should be in the hands of the righteous. The ultimate object, the thing to which all revolutions tended, and which was designed to be indicated in the vision, was the final reign of the saints on the earth. There was to be a time when the kingdom under the whole heaven was to be given to the people of the saints of the Most High; or, in other words, there would be a state of things on the earth, when "all dominions," or all "rulers" (margin, ver. 27), would obey him. This general announcement in reference to the ultimate thing contemplated, and to the three first kingdoms, represented by the three first beasts, was satisfactory to Daniel, but he was still perplexed in regard to the particular thing designed to be represented by the *fourth* beast, so remarkable in its structure, so unlike all the others, and undergoing so surprising a transformation, vers. 19-22. The sum of what was stated to him, in regard to the events represented by the fourth beast, is as follows: (1.) That this was designed to represent a fourth kingdom or dynasty which would arise upon the earth, in many respects, different from the three which would precede it. It was to be a kingdom which would be distinguished for oppressive conquests. It would subdue the whole earth, and it would crush, and prostrate, and trample down those whom it invaded. The description would characterize a dominion that would be stern, and mighty, and cruel, and successful; that would keep the nations which it subdued under its control by the terror of arms rather than by the administration of just laws, ver. 23. (2.) The ten horns that Daniel saw spring out of its head denoted ten kings that would arise, or a succession of rulers that would sway the authority of the kingdom, ver. 24. (3.) The other horn that sprang up among the ten, and after them, denoted another dynasty that would arise, and this would have peculiar characteristics. It would so far have connection with the former that it would spring out of them. But in most important respects it would differ from them. Its characteristics may be summed up as follows: (*a*) It would spring from their midst, or be somehow attached, or connected with them—as the horn sprang from the head of the beast—and this would properly denote that the new power somehow sprang from the dynasty denoted by the fourth beast—as the horn sprang from the head of that beast; (*b*) though springing from that, it would be "diverse" from it, having a character to be determined, not from the mere fact of its origin, but from something else. (*c*) It would "subdue three of these kings;" that is, it would overcome and prostrate a certain portion of the power and authority denoted by the ten horns—perhaps meaning that it would usurp something like one-third of the power of the kingdom denoted by the fourth beast. (*d*) It would be characterized by arrogance and haughtiness—so much so that the fair construction of its claims would be that of "speaking against the Most High." (*e*) It would "wear out the saints of the Most High"—evidently referring to persecution. (*f*) It would claim legislative authority so as to "change times and laws"—clearly referring to some claim set up over established laws, or to unusual authority, vers. 24, 25. (4.) Into the hand of this new power, all these things would be given for "a time, and times, and half a time:" implying that it would not be permanent, but would come to an end, ver. 25. (5.) After that there would be a judgment—a judicial determination in regard to this new power, and the dominion would be taken away, to be utterly destroyed, ver. 26. (6.) There would come a period when the whole dominion of the earth would pass into the hands of the saints; or, in other words, there would be a universal reign of the principles of truth and righteousness, ver. 27.

In the conclusion of the chapter (ver. 28), Daniel says that these communications deeply affected his heart. He had been permitted to look far into futurity, and to contemplate vast changes in the progress of human affairs, and even to look forward to a period when all the nations would be brought under the dominion of the law of God, and the friends of the Most High would be put in possession of all power. Such events were fitted to fill the mind with solemn thought, and it is not wonderful that he contemplated them with deep emotion.

§ II.—VARIOUS METHODS OF INTERPRETING THIS CHAPTER.

It is hardly necessary to say that there have been very different methods of interpreting this chapter, and that the views of its proper interpretation are by no means agreed on by expositors. It may be useful to refer to some of those methods before we advance to its exposition, that they may be before the mind in its consideration. We shall be the better able to ascertain what is the true interpretation by inquiring which of them, if any, accords with the *fair* exposition of the language employed by the sacred writer. The opinions entertained may be reduced to the following classes :—

I. Hardt supposes that the four beasts here denote four particular kings —Nebuchadnezzar, Evil-Merodach, Belshazzar, and Cyrus.

II. Ephræm, who is followed by Eichhorn, supposes that the first beast referred to the Babylonish-Chaldean kingdom; the second, the Medish empire under Cyaxares II., the three "ribs" of which denote the Medish, Persian, and Chaldean portions of that empire; the third, the Persian empire, the four heads and wings of which denote the spread of the Persian empire towards the four regions under heaven, or to all parts of the world; the fourth, to the Grecian empire under Alexander and his successors, the ten horns of which denote ten eminent kings among the successors of Alexander, and the "little horn," that sprang up among them, Antiochus Epiphanes. The succeeding state of things, according to Ephræm and Eichhorn, refers to the kingdom of the Messiah.

III. Grotius, representing another class of interpreters, whom Hetzel follows, supposes that the succession of the kingdoms here referred to is the Babylonish-Chaldean; the Persian; the kingdom of Alexander, and his successors. The fifth is the Roman empire.

IV. The most common interpretation which has prevailed in the church is that which supposes that the first beast denotes the Chaldean kingdom; the second, the Medo-Persian; the third, the Greek empire under Alexander and his successors; the fourth, the Roman empire. The dominion of the saints is the reign of the Messiah and his laws. But this opinion, particularly as far as pertains to the fourth and fifth of these kingdoms, has had a great variety of modifications, especially in reference to the signification of the ten horns, and the little horn that sprang up among them. Some who, under the fifth kingdom, suppose that the reign of Christ is referred to, regard the fourth kingdom as relating to Rome under the Cæsars, and that the ten horns refer to a succession of ten regents, and the little horn to Julius Cæsar. Others, who refer the last empire to the personal reign of Christ on the earth, and the kingdom which he would set up, suppose that the ten horns refer to ten kings or dynasties that sprang out of the Roman power—either a succession of the emperors, or those who came in after the invasion of the northern hordes, or certain kingdoms of Europe which succeeded the Roman power after it fell; and by the little horn, they suppose that either the Turkish power with its various branches is designated, or Mahomet, or the Papacy, or Antichrist.

V. The Jews, in general, suppose that the fifth kingdom refers to the reign of the Messiah; but still there has been great diversity of views among them in regard to the application of particular parts of the prophecy. Many of the older interpreters among them supposed that the ten horns denoted ten Roman Cæsars, and that the last horn referred to Titus Vespasian. Most of the later Jewish interpreters refer this to their fabulous Gog and Magog.

VI. Another interpretation which has had its advocates is that which supposes that the first kingdom was the Chaldean; the second, the Persian; the third, that of Alexander; the fourth, that of his successors; and the fifth, that of the Asmonean princes who rose up to deliver the Jewish nation from the despotism of the Syrian kings.

VII. As a specimen of one mode of interpretation which has prevailed to some extent in the church, the opinion of Cocceius may be referred to. He supposes that the first beast, with the eagle's wings, denoted the reign of the Christian emperors in Rome, and the spread of Christianity under them into remote regions of the East and West; the second, with the three ribs in his mouth, the Arian Goths, Vandals, and Lombards; the third, with the four heads and four wings, the Mahometan kingdom with the four Caliphates; the fourth, the kingdom of Charlemagne, and the ten horns in this kingdom, the Carlovingians, Saxons, Salic, Swedish, Hollandish, English, &c., princes and dynasties or people; and the little horn, the Papacy as the actual Antichrist.

The statement of these various opinions, and methods of interpretation, I have translated from Bertholdt, *Daniel*, pp. 419–426. To these should be added the opinion which Bertholdt himself maintains, and which has been held by many others, and which Bertholdt has explained and defended at length, pp. 426–446. That opinion is, substantially, that the first kingdom is the Babylonish kingdom under Nebuchadnezzar, and that the wings of the first beast denote the extended spread of that empire. The second beast, with the three "ribs," or *fangs*, denotes the Median, Lydian, and Babylonish kingdoms, which were erected under one sceptre, the Persian. The third beast, with the four wings and four heads, denotes the Grecian dynasty under Alexander, and the spread of that kingdom throughout the four parts of the world. The fourth beast denotes the kingdom of the Lagidæ and Seleucidæ, under which the Hebrews suffered so much. The statement respecting this kingdom (ver. 7), that "it was diverse from all that went before it," refers to the "plurality of the fourth kingdom," or the fact

CHAPTER VII.

IN the first year of Belshazzar king of Babylon, Daniel [1]had a dream,[a] and visions of his head

[1] saw.

upon his bed: then he wrote the dream, *and* told the sum of the matters.[2]

a ch. 2. 28; Numb. 12. 6; Amos 3. 7.
[2] or, *words.*

that it was an *aggregate* made up of many others—a kingdom in a *collective* sense. The "ten horns" denote ten successive princes or kings in that kingdom, and Bertholdt enumerates them in the following order:—1, Seleucus Nicator ; 2, Antiochus Soter ; 3, Antiochus Theos ; 4, Seleucus Kallinicus ; 5, Seleucus Keraunus ; 6, Antiochus the Great ; 7, Seleucus Philopater ; 8, Heliodorus ; 9, Ptolemy Philometer ; 10, Demetrius. The eleventh—denoted by the little horn —was Antiochus Epiphanes, who brought so many calamities upon the Hebrew people. His reign lasted, according to Bertholdt, "a time, and times, and half a time"—or three years and a half; and then the kingdom was restored to the people of God to be a permanent reign, and, ultimately, under the Messiah, to fill the world and endure to the end of time.

The interpretation thus stated, supposing that the "little horn" refers to Antiochus Epiphanes, is also maintained by Prof. Stuart.—*Hints on Prophecy,* 2nd ed., pp. 85–98. Compare also *Commentary on Daniel,* pp. 173–194, and 205–211.

Amidst such a variety of views, the only hope of arriving at any satisfactory conclusion respecting the meaning of this chapter is by a careful examination of the text, and the fair meaning of the symbols employed by Daniel.

1. *In the first year of Belshazzar king of Babylon.* On the character and reign of Belshazzar, see Intro. to ch. v. § II. He was the last of the kings of Babylon, and this fact may cast some light on the disclosures made in the dream. ¶ *Daniel had a dream.*

Marg., as in Heb., *saw.* He saw a series of events in vision when he was asleep. The dream refers to that representation, and was of such a nature that it was proper to speak of it as if he saw it. Comp. Notes on ch. ii. 1. ¶ *And visions of his head upon his bed.* Notes on ch. iv. 5. ¶ *Then he wrote the dream.* He made a record of it at the time. He did not commit it to tradition, or wait for its fulfilment before it was recorded, but long before the events referred to occurred he committed the prediction to writing, that when the prophecy was fulfilled they might be compared with it. It was customary among the prophets to record their predictions, whether communicated in a dream, in a vision, or by words to them, that there might be no doubt when the event occurred that there had been an inspired prediction of it, and that there might be an opportunity of a careful comparison of the prediction with the event. Often the prophets were *commanded* to record their predictions. See Isa. viii. 1, 16 ; xxx. 8 ; Hab. ii. 2. Comp. Rev. i. 19 ; xiv. 13 ; xxi. 5. In many instances, as in the case before us, the record was made hundreds of years before the event occurred, and as there is all the evidence that there could be in a case that the record has not been altered to adapt it to the event, the highest proof is thus furnished of the inspiration of the prophets. The meaning here is, that Daniel *wrote out* the dream as soon as it occurred. ¶ And *told the sum of the matters.* Chald., "And spake the head of the words." That is, he spake or told them *by writing.* He made a communication of them in this manner to the world. It is not implied that he made any *oral* communication of them to any one, but that he *communicated* them— to wit, in the way specified. The word *sum* here—רֵאשׁ—means *head ;* and would properly denote such a record

2 Daniel spake and said, I saw in my vision by night, and, be- | hold, the four winds of the heaven strove upon the great sea.

as would be a *heading up,* or a *summary*—as stating in a brief way the contents of a book, or the chief points of a thing without going into detail. The meaning here seems to be that he did not go into detail—as by writing names, and dates, and places ; or, perhaps, that he did not enter into a minute description of *all* that he saw in regard to the beasts that came up from the sea, but that he recorded what might be considered as peculiar, and as having special significancy. The *Codex Chis.* renders this, έγραψεν εἰς κεφάλαια λόγων—"He wrote in heads of words," that is, he reduced it to a summary description. It is well remarked by Lengerke, on this place, that the prophets, when they described what was to occur to tyrants in future times, conveyed their oracles in a comparatively dark and obscure manner, yet so as to be clear when the events should occur. The reason of this is obvious. If the meaning of many of the predictions had been understood by those to whom they referred, that fact would have been a motive to them to induce them to defeat them ; and as the fulfilment depended on their voluntary agency, the prophecy would have been void. It was necessary, therefore, in general, to avoid *direct* predictions, and the mention of names, dates, and places, and to make use of *symbols* whose meaning would be obscure at the time when the prediction was made, but which would be plain when the event should occur. A comparison of vers. 4, 9, 11, 14, will show that only a *summary* of what was to occur was recorded. ¶ *Matters.* Marg., as in Chald., *words.* The term *words,* however, is often used to denote *things.*

2. *Daniel spake and said.* That is, he spake and said in the manner intimated in the previous verse. It was by a *record* made at the time, and thus he might be said to *speak* to his own generation and to all future times. ¶ *I saw in my vision by night.* I beheld in the vision ; that is, he saw represented to him the scene which he

proceeds to describe. He seemed to see the sea in a tempest, and these monsters come up from it, and the strange succession of events which followed. ¶ *And, behold, the four winds of the heaven.* The winds that blow under the heaven, or that seem to come from the heaven—or the air. Comp. Jer. xlix. 36. The number of the winds is here referred to as *four* as they are now, as blowing mainly from the four quarters of the earth. Nothing is more common now than to designate them in this manner—as the east, the south, the west, the north wind. So the Latins—Eurus, Auster, Zephyrus, Boreas. ¶ *Strove.* מְגִיחָן. Burst, or rushed forth ; seemed to conflict together. The winds burst, rushed from all quarters, and seemed to meet on the sea, throwing it into wild commotion. The Hebrew word (גִּיחַ) means to break or burst forth, as a fountain or stream of waters, Job xl. 23 ; an infant breaking forth from the womb, Job xxxviii. 8 ; a warrior rushing forth to battle, Ezek. xxxii. 2. Hence the Chaldean to break forth ; to rush forth as the winds. The symbol here would naturally denote some wild commotion among the nations, as if the winds of heaven should rush together in confusion. ¶ *Upon the great sea.* This expression would properly apply to *any* great sea or ocean, but it is probable that the one that would occur to Daniel would be the Mediterranean Sea, as that was best known to him and his contemporaries. A heaving ocean—or an ocean tossed with storms—would be a natural emblem to denote a nation, or nations, agitated with internal conflicts, or nations in the midst of revolutions. Among the sacred poets and the prophets, hosts of armies invading a land are compared to overflowing waters, and mighty changes among the nations to the heaving billows of the ocean in a storm. Comp. Jer. xlvi. 7, 8 ; xlvii. 2 ; Isa. viii. 7, 8 ; xvii. 12 ; lix. 19 ; Dan. xi. 40 ; Rev. xiii. 1. The classic reader will be reminded in the description here of

3 And four great beasts *a* came up from the sea, diverse one from another.

a Rev. 13. 1.

the words of Virgil, *Æn.* I. 82, *seq :*—

"Ac venti, velut agmine facto
Qua data porta ruunt, et terras turbine perflant.
Incubuere mari, totumque a sedibus imis
Una Eurusque, Notusque ruunt, creberque pro-
    cellis.
Africus, et vastos volvunt ad littora fluctus."

Comp. also Ovid, *Trist.* I. 2, 25, *seq.* It was from this agitated sea that the beasts that Daniel saw, representing successive kingdoms, seemed to rise; and the fair interpretation of this part of the symbol is, that there was, or would be, as it appeared in vision to Daniel, commotions among the nations resembling the sea driven by storms, and that from these commotions there would arise successive kingdoms having the characteristics specified by the appearance of the four beasts. We naturally look, in the fulfilment of this, to some state of things in which the nations were agitated and convulsed; in which they struggled against each other, as the winds strove upon the sea ; a state of things which *preceded* the rise of these four successive kingdoms. Without now pretending to determine whether that was the time denoted by this, it is certain that all that is here said would find a counterpart in the period which immediately preceded the reign of Nebuchadnezzar, or the kingdom which he founded and adorned. His rapid and extensive conquests; the agitation of the nations in self-defence, and their wars against one another, would be well denoted by the agitation of the ocean as seen in vision by Daniel. It is true that there have been many other periods of the world to which the image would be applicable, but no one can doubt that it was applicable to *this* period, and that would be all that would be necessary if the design was to represent a series of kingdoms commencing with that of Nebuchadnezzar.

3. *And four great beasts came up from the sea.* Not at once, but in succession. See the following verses. Their particular form is described in the subsequent verses. The design of mentioning them here, as coming up *from the sea,* seems to have been to show that this succession of kingdoms sprang from the agitations and commotions among the nations represented by the heaving ocean. It is not uncommon for the prophets to make use of animals to represent or symbolize kingdoms and nations — usually by some animal which was in a manner peculiar to the land that was symbolized, or which abounded there. Thus in Isa. xxvii. 1, leviathan, or the dragon, or crocodile, is used to represent Babylon. See Notes on that passage. In Ezek. xxix. 3–5, the dragon or the crocodile of the Nile is put for Pharaoh; in Ezek. xxxii. 2, Pharaoh is compared to a young lion, and to a whale in the seas. In Psal. lxxiv. 13, 14, the kingdom of Egypt is compared to the dragon and the leviathan. So on ancient coins, animals are often used as emblems of kingdoms, as it may be added, the lion and the unicorn represent Great Britain now, and the eagle the United States. It is well remarked by Lengerke (*in loc.*), that when the prophets design to represent kingdoms that are made up of other kingdoms, or that are combined by being brought by conquest under the power of others, they do this, not by any single animal as actually found in nature, but by monsters — fabulous beings that are compounded of others, in which the peculiar qualities of different animals are brought together—as in the case of the lion with eagle's wings. Thus in Rev. xiii. 1, the Romish power is represented by a beast coming out of the sea, having seven heads and ten horns. Comp. ii. Ezra (Apocry.) xi. 1, where an eagle is represented as coming from the sea with twelve feathered wings and three heads. As an illustration of the attempts made in the apocryphal writings to imitate the prophets, the whole of ch. xi. and ch. xii. of the second book of Ezra may be referred to. ¶ *Diverse one from another.* Though they all came up from the same abyss, yet they differed from each other —denoting, doubtless, that though the successive kingdoms referred to would all rise out of the nations represented

by the agitated sea, yet that in important respects they would differ from each other.

[We present some illustrations from Assyrian sculptures. They are undoubtedly examples of the symbolical style of representation common in the East; to which Daniel, or the Spirit of God by Daniel, has accommodated himself. See a very full explanation of the subject under Rev. iv. 7, p. 123, where the author has availed himself of the observations of the indefatigable Layard. The reader will recognize as much resemblance between the figures described in the text, and those presented in the illustrations, as will lead him to ascribe both to one and the same principle or style of instruction, which, being common in the time of Daniel, would, therefore, be well understood. The winged and human-headed lion, shown in the

first engraving, is one of a pair which stood at the entrance to the principal hall at Nimroud.

The first beast of the vision "was like a lion, and had eagle's wings," as in the figure before

us; and when the wings were plucked, " and it was lifted up from the earth, and made stand

4 The first *was* like a lion, *a* and had eagle's *b* wings: I beheld till the wings thereof were plucked, and[1] it was lifted up from the earth, and made stand upon the feet as a man, and a man's heart was given to it.

a Jer.4.7.   *b* Deut.28.49; Ezek.17.3; Hab.1.8.
1 or, *wherewith.*

upon the feet as a man," it takes a form like that in the second engraving, which represents a lion-headed human figure, also from Nimroud. We need not seek the perfect counterpart of every prophetic beast named by Daniel, and, therefore, leave the remaining four engravings as examples of conventional forms that may be recognized, more or less distinctly, either in Daniel, Ezekiel, or the Apocalypse.]

4. *The first* was *like a lion.* It is to be assumed, in explaining and applying these symbols, that they are *significant* —that is, that there was some adaptedness or propriety in using these symbols to denote the kingdoms referred to; or that in each case there was a *reason* why the particular animal was selected for a symbol rather than one of the others; that is, there was something in the *lion* that was better fitted to symbolize the kingdom referred to than there was in the bear or the leopard, and this was the reason why this particular symbol was chosen in the case. It is to be further assumed that all the characteristics in the symbol were significant, and we are to expect to find them *all* in the kingdom which they were designed to represent; nor can the symbol be fairly applied to any kingdom, unless something shall be found in its character or history that shall correspond alike to the particular circumstances referred to in the symbol, and to the grouping or succession. In regard to the first beast, there were five things that entered into the symbol, all of which it is to be presumed were significant: the lion, the eagle's wings—the fact that the wings were plucked—the fact that the beast was lifted up so as to stand up as a man—and the fact that the heart of a man was given to it. It is proper to consider these in their order, and then to inquire whether they found a fulfilment in any known state of things.

(*a*) The animal that was seen:—*the lion.* The lion, "the king of beasts," is the symbol of strength and courage, and becomes the proper emblem of a king—as when the Mussulmans call Ali, Mahomet's son-in-law, "The Lion of God, always victorious." Thus it is often used in the Scriptures. Gen. xlix. 9, "Judah is a lion's whelp: from the prey, my son, thou art gone up: he stooped down, he couched as a lion, and as an old lion; who shall rouse him up?" The warlike character, the conquest, the supremacy of that tribe are here undoubtedly denoted. So in Ezek. xix. 2, 3. "What is thy mother? A lioness: she lay down among lions, she nourished her whelps among young lions." Here is an allusion, says Grotius, to Gen. xlix. 9. Judea was among the nations like a lioness among the beasts of the forest; she had strength and sovereignty. The lion is an emblem of a hero: 2 Sam. xxiii. 20, "He slew two lion-like men of Moab." Comp. Gesenius *zu Isa.* i. 851. So Hercules and Achilles are called by Homer θυμολέοντα, or λεοντόθυμον —*lion-hearted.—Il.* *s.* 639, *η.* 228, *Odys.* λ. 766. See the character, the intrepidity, and the habits of the lion fully illustrated in Bochart, *Hieroz.* lib. iii. c. 2, pp. 723–745.—Credner, *der Prophet Joel,* s. 100. f. Compare also the following places in Scripture: Psal. vii. 2; xxii. 21; lvii. 4; lviii. 6; lxxiv. 4; 1 Sam. xvii. 37; Job iv. 10; Jer. iv. 7; xlix. 19; Joel i. 6; Isa. xxix. 1, 2. The *proper* notion here, so far as the emblem of *a lion* is concerned, is that of a king or kingdom that would be distinguished for power, conquest, dominion; that would be in relation to other kings and kingdoms as the lion is among the beasts of the forest—keeping them in awe, and maintaining dominion over them—marching where he pleases, with none to cope with him or to resist him.

(*b*) The eagle's wings: — *and had eagle's wings.* Here appears one peculiarity of the emblem—the union of things which are not found joined together in nature—the representation of things or qualities which no one animal would represent. The lion would denote *one* thing, or *one* quality in the kingdom referred to—power, dominion, sovereignty—but there would be some characteristic in that king or kingdom which nothing in the lion would properly represent, and which could be symbolized only by attaching to him qualities to be found in some other animal. The lion, distinguished for his power, his dominion, his keeping other animals in awe—his spring, and the severity of his blow—is not remarkable for his speed, nor for *going forth* to conquest. He does not range far to accomplish his purpose, nor are his movements eminent for fleetness. Hence there were attached to the lion the wings of an eagle. The proper notion, therefore, of this symbol, would be that of a dominion or conquest *rapidly* secured, *as if* a lion, the king of beasts, should move, not as he commonly does, with a spring or bound, confining himself to a certain space or range, but should move as the eagle does, with rapid and prolonged flight, extending his conquests afar. The meaning of the symbol may be seen by comparing this passage with Isa. xlvi. 11, where Cyrus is compared to "a ravenous bird"—"calling a ravenous bird from the east, the man that executeth my counsels from a far country." The eagle is an emblem of *swiftness:* Jer. iv. 13, "His horses are swifter than eagles;" xlviii. 40, "Behold, he shall fly as an eagle, and shall spread his wings over Moab." See also ch. xlix. 22; Lam. iv. 19; Hab. i. 8.

(c) The clipping of the wings :—*I beheld till the wings thereof were plucked.* The word used (מְרַט) means, to pluck or pull, as to pull out the beard (comp. Neh. xiii. 25; Isa. l. 6), and would here be properly applied to some process of pulling out the feathers or quills from the wings of the eagle. The obvious and proper meaning of this symbol is, that there was some *check* put to the progress of the conqueror—as there would be to an eagle by plucking off the feathers from his wings; that is, the *rapidity* of his conquests would cease. The prophet says, that he looked on until this was done, imply-

ing that it was not accomplished at once, but leaving the impression that these conquests were extended far. They were, however, checked, and we see the lion again without the wings; the sovereign who has ceased to spread his triumphs over the earth.

(d) The lifting up from the earth :—*and it was lifted up from the earth, and made to stand upon the feet as a man.* That is, the lion, with the wings thus plucked off, was made to stand upright on his hind feet—an unusual position, but the meaning of the symbol is not difficult. It was still the lion—the monarch—but changed *as if* the lion was changed to a man; that is, as if the ferocity, and the power, and the energy of the lion had given place to the comparative weakness of a man. There would be as much difference in the case referred to as there would be if a lion so fierce and powerful should be made so far to change his nature as to stand upright, and to walk as a man. This would evidently denote some remarkable change —something that would be unusual— something where there would be a diminution of ferocity, and yet perhaps a change to comparative weakness—as a man is feebler than a lion.

(e) The giving to it of a man's heart: —*and a man's heart was given to it.* The word *heart* in the Scriptures often has a closer relation to the intellect or the understanding than it now has commonly with us; and here perhaps it is a general term to denote something like *human nature* — that is, there would be as great a change in the case as if the nature of the lion should be transformed to that of a man ; or, the meaning may be, that this mighty empire, carrying its arms with the rapidity of an eagle, and the fierceness of a lion, through the world, would be checked in its career ; its ferocity would be tamed, and it would be characterized by comparative moderation and humanity. In ch. iv. 16, it is said of Nebuchadnezzar, "Let his heart be changed from man's, and let a beast's heart be given unto him ;" here, if the symbol refers to him, it does not refer to that scene of humiliation when he was compelled to eat grass like a beast, but to the fact that he was brought to look at things as a man should do; he ceased to act like a ravenous beast, and was led to calm reflection, and to think and speak like a man—a rational being. Or, if it refers to the empire of Babylon, instead of the monarch, it would mean that a change had come over the nation under the succession of princes, so that the fierceness and ferocity of the first princes of the empire had ceased, and the nation had not only closed its conquests, but had actually become, to some extent, moderate and rational.

Now, in regard to the application of *this* symbol, there can be but little difficulty, and there is almost no difference of opinion among expositors. All, or nearly all, agree that it refers to the kingdom of Babylon, of which Nebuchadnezzar was the head, and to the gradual diminution of the ferocity of conquest under a succession of comparatively weak princes. Whatever view may be taken of the book of Daniel—whether it be regarded as inspired prophecy composed by Daniel himself, and written at the time when it professes to have been, or whether it be supposed to have been written long after his time by some one who forged it in his name, there can be no doubt that it relates to the head of the Babylonian empire, or to that which the "head of gold," in the image referred to in ch. ii., represents. The circumstances all so well agree with that application, that, although in the explication of the dream (vers. 16-27) this part of it is not explained—for the perplexity of Daniel related particularly to the fourth beast (ver. 19), yet there can be no reasonable doubt as to what was intended. For (*a*) the lion—the king of beasts—would accurately symbolize that kingdom in the days of Nebuchadnezzar—a kingdom occupying the same position among other kingdoms which the lion does among other beasts, and well represented in its power and ferocity by the lion. See the character and position of this kingdom fully illustrated in the Notes on ch. ii. 37, 38. (*b*) The eagle's wings would accurately denote the rapid conquests of that kingdom—its leaving, as it were, its own native domain, and flying abroad. The lion alone would have represented the character of the kingdom considered as already having spread itself, or as being at the head of other kingdoms; the wings of the eagle, the rapidity with which the arms of the Babylonians were carried into Palestine, Egypt, Assyria, &c. It is true that *this* symbol alone would not designate Babylon any more than it would the conquests of Cyrus, or Alexander, or Cæsar, but it is to be taken in the connection in which it is here found, and no one can doubt that it has a striking applicability to Babylon. (*c*) The clipping or plucking of these wings would denote the cessation of conquest—as if it would extend no farther; that is, we see a nation once distinguished for the invasion of other nations now ceasing its conquests; and remarkable, not for its victories, but as standing at the head of all other nations, as the lion stands among the beasts of the forest. All who are acquainted with history know that, after the conquests of that kingdom under Nebuchadnezzar, it ceased characteristically to be a kingdom distinguished for conquest, but that, though under his successors, it held a pre-eminence or headship among the nations, yet its victories were extended no further. The successors of Nebuchadnezzar were comparatively weak and indolent princes—as if the wings of the monster had been plucked. (*d*) The rising up of the lion on the feet, and standing on the feet as a man, would denote, not inappropriately, the change of the kingdom under the successors of Nebuchadnezzar. See above in the explanation of the symbol. (*e*) The giving of a man's heart to it would not be inapplicable to the change produced in the empire after the time of Nebuchadnezzar, and under a succession of comparatively weak and inefficient princes. Instead of the heart of the lion—of being "lion-hearted"—it had the heart of a man; that is,—the character of wildness and fierceness denoted by an untamed beast was succeeded by that which would be better represented by a human being. It is not the character of the lion changed to that of the bear, or the panther, **or**

5 And, behold, another *a* beast, a second, like to a bear, and it raised up ¹itself on one side, and

a ch. 2. 39.　　1 or, *one dominion.*

the leopard; nor is it man considered as a warrior or conqueror, but man as he is distinguished from the wild and ferocious beast of the desert. The change in the character of the empire, until it ceased under the feeble reign of Belshazzar, would be well denoted by this symbol.

5. *And, behold, another beast, a second, like to a bear.* That is, *after* the lion had appeared, and he had watched it until it had undergone these surprising transformations. There are several circumstances, also, in regard to this symbol, all of which, it is to be supposed, were significant, and all of which demand explication before it is attempted to apply them.

(*a*) The animal seen:—*the bear.* For a full description of the bear, see Bochart, *Hieroz.* lib. iii. c. ix. The animal is well known, and has properties quite distinct from the lion and other animals. There was doubtless some reason why this symbol was employed to denote a particular kingdom, and there was something in the kingdom that corresponded with these peculiar properties, as there was in the case of the lion. The bear might, in some respects, have been a proper representative of Babylon, but it would not in all nor in the main respects. According to Bochart (*Hieroz.* vol. i. p. 812), the bear is distinguished mainly for two things, cunning and ferocity. Aristotle says that the bear is greedy as well as silly and foolhardy. (Wemyss, *Key to the Symbolic Language of Scripture.*) The *name* in Hebrew is taken from his grumbling or growling. Comp. Isa. lix. 11:—

"We roar all like bears."

Comp. Horace, *Epod.* 16, 51 :—

"Nec vespertinus circumgemit ursus ovile."

Virgil mentions their ferocity:—

"Atque in præsepibus ursi Sævire."
—*Æn.* vii. 17.

The bear is noted as especially fierce when hungry, or when robbed of its whelps. Jerome (on Hos. xiii. 8) remarks, "It is said by those who have

studied the nature of wild beasts, that none among them is more ferocious than the bear when deprived of its young, or when hungry." Compare 2 Sam. xvii. 8; Prov. xvii. 12; Hos. xiii. 8. The characteristics of the kingdom, therefore, that would be denoted by the bear would be ferocity, roughness, fierceness in war, especially when provoked; a spirit less manly and noble than that denoted by the lion; severe in its treatment of enemies, with a mixture of fierce and savage cunning.

(*b*) Its rising up on one of its sides: —*and it raised up itself on one side.* The Chaldee word here used (שְׁטַר) occurs nowhere else. It means *side* (Gesenius), and would be applied here to the side of an animal, as if he lifted up one side before the other when he rose. The Latin Vulgate renders it, *in parte stetit.* The Greek (Walton), εἰς μέρος ἓν ἐστάθη—"it stood on one part;" or, as Thompson renders it, "he stood half erect." The *Codex. Chis.,* ἐπὶ τοῦ ἑνὸς πλευροῦ ἐστάθη—"it stood upon one side." Maurer renders this, "on one of its forefeet it was recumbent, and stood on the other," and says that this is the figure exhibited on one of the stones found in Babylon, an engraving of which may be seen in Munter, *Religion d. Babyl.* p. 112. The animal referred to here, as found in Babylon, says Lengerke, "lies kneeling on the right forefoot, and is in the act of rising on the left foot." Bertholdt and Hävernick understand this as meaning that the animal stood on the hindfeet, with the forepart raised, as the bear is said to do; but probably the true position is that referred to by Maurer and Lengerke, that the animal was in the act of raising itself up from a recumbent posture, and rested on one of its forefeet while the other was reached out, and the body on that side was partially raised. This *position* would naturally denote a kingdom that had been quiet and at rest, but that was now rousing itself deliberately for some purpose, as of conquest or war— as the bear that had been couching

it had three ribs in the mouth of it between the teeth of it: and

they said thus unto it, Arise, devour much flesh.

down would rise when hungry, or when going forth for prey.

(c) The ribs in its mouth:—*and it had three ribs in the mouth of it between the teeth of it.* Bertholdt understands this of fangs or tusks—or fangs crooked or bent like ribs, p. 451. But the proper meaning of the Chaldee עֲלַע is the same as the Hebrew צֵלָע—*a rib.*— Gesenius. The Latin Vulgate is, *tres ordines*—three rows; the Syriac and the Greek, *three ribs.* This would be sufficiently characteristic of a bear, and the attitude of the animal here seems to be that it had killed some other animal, and had, in devouring it, torn out three ribs from its side, and now held them in its mouth. It was slowly rising from a recumbent posture, with these ribs in its mouth, and about to receive a command to go forth and devour much flesh. The number *three,* in this place, Lengerke supposes to be a round number, without any special significancy; others suppose that it denotes the number of nations or kingdoms which the people here represented by the bear had overcome. Perhaps this latter would be the more obvious idea as suggested by the symbol, but it is not necessary, in order to a proper understanding of a symbol, to press such a point too closely. The natural idea which would be suggested by this part of the symbol would be that of a kingdom or people of a fierce and rough character having already subdued some, and then, after reposing, rising up with the trophies of its former conquests to go forth to new victories, or to overcome others. The symbol would be a very striking one to represent a conquering nation in such a posture.

(d) The command given to this beast: —*and they said thus unto it, Arise, devour much flesh.* That is, it was said to it; or some one having authority said it. A voice was heard commanding it to go forth and devour. This command is wholly in accordance with the nature of the bear. The bear is called by Aristotle σαρκοφαγῶν, *flesh-eater,* and ξῶον πάμφαγον, *a beast devour-*

ing everything (*Hist. Nat.* viii. 5), and no better description could be given of it. As a symbol, this would properly be applicable to a nation about receiving, as it were, a command from God to go forth to wider conquests than it had already made; to arouse itself from its repose and to achieve new triumphs.

The application of this symbol was not explained by the angel to Daniel; but if the former appertained to Babylon, there can be little difficulty in understanding to what this is to be applied. It is evidently to that which succeeded the Babylonian—the Medo-Persian, the kingdom ruled successively by Cyrus, Cambyses, Smerdis, Darius, Xerxes, Artaxerxes, and Darius Nothus, until it was overthrown by Alexander the Great. The only inquiry now is as to the pertinency of the symbol here employed to represent this kingdom.

(a) The symbol of the bear. As already seen, the bear would denote any fierce, rough, overbearing, and arbitrary kingdom, and it is clear that while it *might* have applicability to any such kingdom, it would *better* represent that of Medo-Persia than the *lion* would; for while, in some respects, either symbol would be applicable to either nation, the Medo-Persian did not stand so decidedly at the head of nations as the Babylonian. As to its *character,* however, the bear was not an inappropriate symbol. Taking the whole nation together, it was fierce and rough, and unpolished, little disposed to friendliness with the nations, and dissatisfied while any around it had peace or prosperity. In the image seen in ch. ii., this kingdom, denoted by the breast and arms of silver (ver. 32), is described in the explanation (ver. 39) as "inferior to thee;" that is, to Nebuchadnezzar. For a sufficiently full account of this kingdom—of the mad projects of Cambyses, and his savage rage against the Ethiopians— well represented by the ferocity of the bear; of the ill-starred expedition to Greece under Xerxes—an expedition in its fierceness and folly well represented by the bear, and of the degeneracy of the national character after Xerxes—well represented by the bear as compared with the lion, see Notes on ch. ii. 39. No one acquainted with the history of that nation can doubt the propriety and applicability of the emblem.

(*b*) The rising up on its side, or from a recumbent posture, as if it had been in a state of repose, and was now arousing itself for action. Different interpretations have been adopted of this emblem as applicable to the Medo-Persians. The ancient Hebrew interpreters, as Jerome remarks, explain it as meaning that that kingdom was "on one side" in the sense of *separate;* that is, that this kingdom kept itself aloof from Judea, or did not inflict injury on it. Thus also Grotius explains it as meaning that it did not injure Judea —"Judea nihil nocuit." Ephræm the Syrian, and Theodoret, explain it as meaning that the empire of the Medo-Persians was situated *on the side* of Judea, or held itself within its proper bounds, in the sense that it never extended its dominion, like Babylon, over the whole earth. Rosenmüller explains it as meaning that in relation to the kingdom represented by the lion, it was *at its side*, both occupying the regions of the East. J. D. Michaelis understands it as denoting that, as the bear was raising itself up, one part being more raised than the other, the Medo-Persian empire was composed of two kingdoms, one of which was more exalted or advanced than the other. Comp. Lengerke. The true meaning however is, that, as seen by Daniel, the nation that had been in a state of repose was now preparing itself for new conquests—a state descriptive of, and in every way quite applicable to the condition of the Medo-Persian empire, after the conquests by Cyrus, as he overran the kingdom of Lydia, &c., then reposing, and *now* about arousing to the conquest and subjugation of Babylon. The precise time, therefore, indicated would be about B.C. 544 (Calmet), when, having overcome the Medes, and having secured the conquest of Lydia, and the dethronement of Crœsus, he is meditating the destruction of Babylon. This interval of re-

pose lasted about a year, and it is at this time that the united empire is seen, under the image of the bear rising on its side, arousing itself to go forth to new conquests.

(*c*) The ribs in the mouth of the beast. This, as above remarked, would properly refer to some previous conquest —as a bear appearing in that manner would indicate that some other animal had been overcome and slain by him, and torn in pieces. The emblem would be fulfilled if the power here symbolized had been successful in former wars, and had rent kingdoms or people asunder. That this description would apply to the Medo-Persian power before its attack on Babylon, or before extending its dominion over Babylon, and its establishment *as* the Medo-Persian kingdoms, no one can doubt. Compare the Notes on ch. ii. 39. It has been commonly supposed that Cyrus succeeded to the throne of Media without war. But this is far from being the case— though so represented in what may be regarded as the romance of the *Cyropœdia*. In the *Anabasis* of Xenophon, however, the fact of his having subdued Media by arms is distinctly admitted, iii. 4, 7, 12. Herodotus, Ctesias, Isocrates, and Strabo, all agree also in the fact that it was so. The Upper Tigris was the seat of one campaign, where the cities of Larissa and Mespila were taken by Cyrus. From Strabo we learn that the decisive battle was fought on the spot where Cyrus afterwards built Pasargardæ, in Persia, for his capital. See Kitto, *Cyclo.*, art. "Cyrus." In addition to this, we are to remember the well-known conquests of Cyrus in Lydia and elsewhere, and the propriety of the emblem will be apparent. It may not be certain that the *number* three is significant in the emblem, but it is *possible* that there may have been reference to the three kingdoms of Persia, Media, and Lydia, that were actually under the dominion of Cyrus when the aggressive movement was made on Babylon.

(*d*) The command to "arise and devour much flesh." No one can fail to see the appropriateness of this, considered as addressed to the Medo-Persian power—that power which subdued

6 After this I beheld, and, lo, another, like a leopard, which had upon the back of it four wings of a fowl; the beast had also four heads; and *a* dominion was given to it.

Babylon; which brought under its dominion a considerable part of the world, and which, under Darius and Xerxes, poured its millions on Greece. The emblem here used is, therefore, one of the most striking and appropriate that could be employed, and it cannot be doubted that it had reference to this kingdom, and that, in all the particulars, there was a clear fulfilment.

6. *After this I beheld, and, lo, another, like a leopard.* That is, as before, after the bear had appeared—indicating that this was to be a succeeding kingdom or power. The beast which now appeared was a monster, and, as in the former cases, so in regard to this, there are several circumstances which demand explanation in order to understand the symbol. It may assist us, perhaps, in forming a correct idea of the symbol here introduced to have before us a representation of the animal as it appeared to Daniel.

(*a*) The animal itself:—*a leopard.* The word here used—נְמַר—or in Heb. נָמֵר—denotes a panther or leopard, so called from his spots. This is a well-known beast of prey, distinguished for blood-thirstiness and cruelty, and these characteristics are especially applicable to the female panther. The animal is referred to in the Scriptures as emblematic of the following things, or as having the following characteristics: (1.) As next in dignity to the lion—of the same general nature. Compare Bochart, *Hieroz.* P. I. lib. iii. c. vii. Thus the lion and the panther, or leopard, are often united in the Scriptures. Comp. Jer. v. 6; Hos. xiii. 7. See also in the Apocrypha, Ecclesias. xxviii. 23. So also they are united in Homer, *Il. ρ*:—

"Ουτε ουν παρδαλιος τοσσον μενος, ουτε λεοντος.

"Neither had the leopard nor the lion such strength." (2.) As distinguished for cruelty, or a fierce nature, as contrasted with the gentle and tame animals. Isa. xi. 6, "And the leopard shall lie down with the kid." In Jer. v. 6, it is compared with the lion and the wolf: "A lion out of the forest shall slay them, and a wolf of the evenings shall spoil them, a leopard shall watch over their cities." Comp. Hos. xiii. 7. (3.) As distinguished for swiftness or fleetness. Habak. i. 8: "Their horses are swifter than the leopards." Comp. also the quotations from the classics in Bochart as above, p. 788. His fleetness is often referred to—the celerity of his *spring* or *bound* especially—by the Greek and Roman writers. (4.) As insidious, or as lying in wait, and springing unexpectedly upon the unwary traveller. Compare Hos. xiii. 7: "As a leopard by the way will I observe them;" that is, I will *watch* (אָשׁוּר) them. So Pliny says of leopards: *Insidunt pardi condensa arborum, occultatique earum ramis in prætereuntia desiliunt.* (5.) They are characterized by their spots. In the general nature of the animal there is a strong resemblance to the lion. Thus, an Arabic writer quoted by Bochart, *defines* the leopard to be "an animal resembling the lion, except that it is smaller, and has a skin marked by black spots." The proper idea in this representation, when used as a symbol, would be of a nation or kingdom that would have more nobleness than the one represented by the bear, but a less decisive headship over others than that represented by the lion; a nation that was addicted to conquest, or that preyed upon others; a nation rapid in its movements, and springing upon others unawares, and *perhaps* in its spots denoting a nation or people made up, not of homogeneous elements, but of various different people. See below in the application of this.

(*b*) The four wings:—*which had upon the back of it four wings of a fowl.* The first beast was seen with the wings of an eagle, but without any specified number; this appears with wings, but without specifying any particular *kind* of wings, though the *number* is mentioned. In both of them celerity of movement is undoubtedly intended—celerity beyond what would be properly denoted by the animal itself—the lion or the leopard. If there is a difference in the design of the representation, as there would seem to be by mentioning the *kind* of wings in the one case, and the *number* in the other, it is probable that the former would denote a more bold and extended flight; the latter a flight more rapid, denoted by the *four* wings. We should look for the fulfilment of the former in a nation that extended its conquests over a broader space; in the latter, to a nation that moved with more celerity. But there is some danger of pressing these similitudes too far. Nothing is said in the passage about the arrangement of the wings, except that they were on the back of the animal. It is to be supposed that there were two on each side.

(*c*) The four heads:—*the beast had also four heads*. This representation must have been designed to signify either that the one power or kingdom denoted by the leopard was composed of *four* separate powers or nations now united in one; or that there were four successive kings or dynasties that made up its history; or that the power or kingdom actually appeared, as seen in its prevailing characteristic, *as a* distinct dominion, as having four heads, or as being divided into so many separate sovereignties. It seems to me that either one of these would be a proper and natural fulfilment of the design of the image, though the second suggested would be less proper than either of the others, as the heads appeared on the animal not in succession—as the little horn sprung up in the midst of the other ten, as represented in the fourth beast—but existed simultaneously. The general idea would be, that in some way the one particular sovereignty had four sources of power blended into one, or actually exerted the same kind of dominion, and constituted, in fact, the one kingdom as distinguished from the others.

(*d*) The dominion given to it:—*and dominion was given to it*. That is, it was appointed to rule where the former had ruled, and until it should be suc-

ceeded by another—the beast with the ten horns.

In regard to the application of this, though the angel did not explain it to Daniel, except in general that a kingdom was represented by it (ver. 17), it would seem that there could be little difficulty, though there has been some variety in the views entertained. Maurer, Lengerke, and some others, refer it to the Medo-Persian empire—supposing that the second symbol referred to the kingdom of Media. But the objections to this are so obvious, and so numerous, that it seems to me the opinion cannot be entertained; for (1) the kingdom of Media did not, in any proper sense, *succeed* that of Babylon; (2) the representation of the bear with three ribs has no proper application to Media; (3) the whole description, as we have seen above, of the second beast, accords entirely with the history of the Medo-Persian empire. If this be so, then we naturally look for the fulfilment of this symbol—the third head—in the kingdom or dynasty that followed directly that of Medo-Persia—the Macedonian dynasty or kingdom founded by Alexander the Great, extending over the same countries before occupied by Babylon and the Medo-Persian empire, and continuing till it was swallowed up in the conquests of Rome. We shall find that all the circumstances agree with this supposition:—

(*a*) The animal—the leopard. The comparative nobleness of the animal; a beast of prey; the celerity of its movements; the spring or bound with which it leaps upon its prey—all agree well with the kingdom of which Alexander was the founder. Indeed there was no other kingdom among the ancients to which it could be better applied; and it will be admitted that, on the supposition that it was the design of Daniel to choose a symbol that would represent the Macedonian empire, he could not have selected one that was better adapted to it than the leopard. All the characteristics of the animal that have been noticed—(1) as next in dignity to the lion: (2) as distinguished for a fierce nature; (3) as characterized by fleetness; (4) as

7 After this I saw in the night visions, and, behold, a fourth *a* beast,

a ver. 19, 23; ch. 2. 40.

dreadful and terrible, and strong exceedingly; and it had great iron teeth: it devoured and brake in

---

known for lying in wait, and springing suddenly upon its prey; and (5) in the point to be noticed soon—their spots —all agree with the characteristics of Alexander, and his movements among the nations, and with the kingdom that was founded by him in the East. (*b*) The four wings. These represent well the rapidity of the conquests of Alexander, for no more rapid conquests were ever made than were his in the East. It was noticed that the leopard had *four* wings, as contrasted with the first beast, in reference to which the *number* is not mentioned: the one denoting a broader flight, and the other a more rapid one; and the one agrees well with the conquests of Nebuchadnezzar, and the other with those of Alexander. (*c*) The four heads united to one body. It is well known that when Alexander died, his empire was left to four of his generals, and that they came to be at the head of as many distinct dominions, yet all springing from the same source, and all, in fact, out of the Macedonian empire. This fact would not be *so well* represented by four distinct and separate animals, as by *one* animal with four heads; that is, as the head represents authority or dominion, one empire, in fact, now ruling by four distinct authorities. The *one* empire, considered as *Macedonian*, continued its sway till it was swallowed up by the Romans; that is, the Macedonian power or dominion as *distinct* from that of Babylon or Medo-Persia; as having characteristics *unlike* these; as introducing a new order of things, continued, though that power was broken up and exercised under distinct manifestations of sovereignty. The fact was, that, at the death of Alexander, to whom the founding of this empire was owing, "Philip Aridæus, brother of Alexander, and his infant son by Roxana, were appointed by the generals of the army to succeed, and Perdiccas was made regent. The empire was divided into thirty-three governments, distri-

buted among as many general officers. Hence arose a series of bloody, desolating wars, and a period of confusion, anarchy, and crime ensued, that is almost without a parallel in the history of the world. After the battle of Ipsus, 301 B.C., in which Antigonus was defeated, the empire was divided into four kingdoms—Thrace and Bithynia under Lysimachus; Syria and the East under Seleucus; Egypt, under Ptolemy Soter; and Macedonia under Cassander."— Lyman, *Hist. Chart.* It was these four powers, thus springing out of the one empire founded by Alexander, that was clearly represented by the four heads. (*d*) The dominion given to it. No one can doubt that a dominion was given to Alexander and the Macedonian dynasty, which would fully correspond with this. In fact the dominion of the world was practically conceded to that kingdom. (*e*) There is only one other circumstance to be noticed, though perhaps we are not to seek an exact accomplishment for that in any specific events. It is the fact that the leopard is marked by *spots*— a circumstance which many have supposed had a fulfilment in the fact that numerous nations, not homogeneous, were found in the empire of Alexander. So Bochart, *Hieroz.* P. I. lib. iii. c. vii. p. 789, says: "The spots of the leopard refer to the different customs of the nations over which he ruled. Among these, besides the Macedonians, Greeks, Thracians, and Illyrians, in Europe, there were in Africa the Libyans, Egyptians, and Troglodites; in Asia, almost all the nations to the Ganges." But, without insisting on this, no one can compare the *other* particulars which were clearly designed to be symbolical, without perceiving that they had a full accomplishment in the Macedonian empire.

7, 8. *After this I saw in the night visions.* The other beasts were seen also in a dream (ver. 1), and this probably in the same night, though as

pieces, and stamped the residue with the feet of it: and it *was* diverse from all the beasts that *were* before it; and it had ten horns.[a]

a subsequent part of the dream, for the whole vision evidently passed before the prophet in a single dream. The succession, or the fact that he saw one after the other, indicates a sucession in the kingdoms. They were not to be at the same time upon the earth, but one was to arise after another in the order here indicated, though they were in some respects to occupy the same territory. The singular character of the beast that now appears; the number of the horns; the springing up of a new horn; the might and terror of the beast, and the long duration of its dominion upon the earth, attracted and fixed the attention of Daniel, led him into a more minute description of the appearance of the animal, and induced him particularly to ask an explanation of the angel of the meaning of this part of the vision, ver. 19. ¶ *And, behold, a fourth beast.* This beast had peculiar characteristics, all of which were regarded as symbolical, and all of which demand explanation in order that we may have a just view of the nature and design of the symbol.

As in reference to the three former beasts, so also in regard to this, it will be proper to explain first the significance of the different parts of the symbol, and then in the exposition (ver. 19, *seq.*) to inquire into the application. The particulars of this symbol are more numerous, more striking, and more important than in either of the previous ones. These particulars are the following (vers. 7–11):—

(*a*) The animal itself (v. 7):—*a fourth beast, dreadful and terrible, and strong exceedingly.* The form or nature of the beast is not given as in the preceding cases—the lion, the bear, and the leopard—but it is left for the imagination to fill up. It was a beast more terrific in its appearance than either of the others, and was evidently a monster such as could not be designated by a single name. The *terms* which are used here in describing the beast— *dreadful, terrible, exceedingly strong,*

are nearly synonymous, and are heaped together in order to give an impressive view of the terror inspired by the beast. There can be no doubt as to the general *meaning* of this, for it is explained (ver. 23) as denoting a kingdom that "should devour the whole earth, and tread it down, and break it in pieces." As a symbol, it would denote some power much more fearful and much more to be dreaded; having a wider dominion; and more stern, more oppressive in its character, more severe in its exactions, and more entirely destroying the liberty of others; advancing more by power and terror, and less by art and cunning, than either. This characteristic is manifest throughout the symbol.

(*b*) The teeth (ver. 7):—*and it had great iron teeth.* Not only teeth or tusks, such as other animals may have, but teeth made of *iron.* This is characteristic of a monster, and shows that there was to be something very peculiar in the dominion that was here symbolized. The teeth are of use to eat or devour; and the symbol here is that of devouring or rending—as a fierce monster with such teeth might be supposed to rend or devour all that was before it. *This,* too, would denote a nation exceedingly fierce; a nation of savage ferocity; a nation that would be signally formidable to all others. For illustration, comp. Jer. xv. 12; Mic. iv. 13. As explained in ver. 23, it is said that the kingdom denoted by this would "*devour* the whole earth." Teeth—great teeth, are often used as the symbols of cruelty, or of a devouring enemy. Thus in Prov. xxx. 14: "There is a generation whose teeth are as swords, and their jaw teeth are as knives, to devour the poor from off the earth, and the needy from among men." So David uses the word to denote the cruelty of tyrants: Ps. iii. 7, "Thou hast broken the teeth of the ungodly;" lvii. 4, "whose teeth are spears and arrows;" lviii. 6, "break their teeth in their mouth; break out the great teeth of the young lions."

(c) The stamping with the feet (ver. 7):—*it devoured and brake in pieces, and stamped the residue with the feet of it.* That is, like a fierce monster, whatever it could not devour it stamped down and crushed in the earth. This indicates a disposition or purpose to destroy, *for the sake of destroying,* or where no other purpose could be gained. It denotes rage, wrath, a determination to crush all in its way, to have universal dominion; and would be applicable to a nation that subdued and crushed others *for the mere sake of doing it,* or because it was unwilling that any other should exist and enjoy liberty—even where itself could not hope for any advantage.

(d) The fact that it was different from all that went before it (ver. 7): —*and it* was *diverse from all the beasts that* were *before it.* The prophet does not specify particularly in what respects it was different, for he does not attempt to give its appearance. It was not a lion, a bear, or a leopard, but he does not say precisely what it was. Probably it was such a monster that there were no animals with which it could be compared. He states some circumstances, however, in which it was different—as in regard to the ten horns, the little horn, the iron teeth, &c., but still the imagination is left to fill up the picture in general. The meaning of this must be, that the fourth kingdom, represented by this beast, would be materially different from those which preceded it, and we must look for the fulfilment in some features that would characterize it by which it would be unlike the others. There must be something *marked* in the difference—something that would be more than the common difference between nations.

(e) The ten horns (ver. 7):—*and it had ten horns.* That is, the prophet saw on it ten horns as characterizing the beast. The *horn* is a symbol of power, and is frequently so used as an emblem or symbol in Daniel (vii. 7, 8, 20, 24; viii. 3–9, 20–22) and Revelation (v. 6; xiii. 1, 11; xvii. 3, 12, 16). It is used as a symbol because the

great strength of horned animals is found there. Thus in Amos vi. 13, it is said:—

" Ye that rejoice in a thing of nought,
That say, Have we not taken *dominion* to ourselves by our own strength?"
(Heb. *horns.*)

So in Deut. xxxiii. 17:—
" His beauty shall be that of a young bull,
And his horns shall be the horns of a rhinoceros:
With these he shall push the people to the extremities of the land:
Such are the ten thousands of Ephraim,
Such the thousands of Manasseh."
—Wemyss.

So in 1 Kings xxii. 11, we find horns used in a symbolical action on the part of the false prophet Zedekiah. "He made him horns of iron, and said, Thus saith Jehovah, With these shalt thou push the Syrians, until thou have consumed them." In Zech. i. 18, the four horns that are seen by the prophet are said to be the four great powers which had scattered and wasted the Jews. Compare Wemyss on the *Symbolic Language of Scripture,* art. "Horns." There can be no doubt as to the meaning of the symbol here, for it is explained in a subsequent part of the chapter (ver. 24), "the ten horns are the ten kings that shall arise." It would seem also, from that explanation, that they were to be ten kings that would "arise" or spring out of that kingdom at some period of its history. "And the ten horns out of this kingdom are ten kings that shall arise;" that is, not that the kingdom itself would spring out of ten others that would be amalgamated or consolidated into one, but that out of that one kingdom there would spring up *ten* that would exercise dominion, or in which the power of the one kingdom would be ultimately lodged. Though Daniel appears to have seen these horns as appertaining to the beast when he first saw him, yet the subsequent explanation is, that these horns were emblems of the manner in which the power of that one kingdom would be finally exerted; or that ten kings or dynasties would spring out of it. We are, then, naturally to look for the fulfilment of this in some one great kingdom of huge power that would crush the nations, and from which,

8 I considered the horns, and, behold, there came up among them another little horn,[a] before whom there were three of the first horns plucked up by the roots: and, behold, in this horn *were* eyes like the eyes of man, [b] and a [c] mouth speaking great things.

a vers. 20, 21, 24.   *b* Rev. 9. 7.   *c* Rev. 13. 5.

while the same general characteristic would remain, there would spring up *ten* kings, or dynasties, or kingdoms, in which the power would be concentrated.

(*f*) The springing up of the little horn (ver. 8):—*I considered the horns, and, behold, there came up among them another little horn.* There are several points to be noticed in regard to this: (1.) The fact that he "considered the horns;" that is, he looked on them until another sprang up among them. This implies that when he first saw the monster, it had no such horn, and that the horn sprang up a considerable time after he first saw it—intimating that it would occur, perhaps, far on in the history of the kingdom that was symbolized. It is implied that it was not an event which would *soon* occur. (2.) It sprang up "among" the others (בֵּינֵיהֶן) — starting from the same source, and appertaining to the same animal, and therefore a development or putting forth of the same power. The language here used does not designate, with any degree of certainty, the precise place which it occupied, but it would seem that the others stood close together, and that this sprang out of the centre, or *from the very midst* of them—implying that the new dominion symbolized would not be a *foreign* dominion, but one that would spring out of the kingdom itself, or that would seem to grow up *in* the kingdom. (3.) It was a little horn; that is, it was small at first, though subsequently it grew so as to be emblematic of great power. This would denote that the power symbolized would be *small* at first—springing up gradually. The fulfilment of this would be found, neither in conquest nor in revolution, nor in a change of dynasty, nor in a sudden change of a constitution, but in some power that had an obscure origin, and that was feeble

and small at the beginning, yet gradually increasing, till, by its own growth, it put aside a portion of the power before exercised and occupied its place. We should naturally look for the fulfilment of this in the increase of some power within the state that had a humble origin, and that slowly developed itself until it absorbed a considerable portion of the authority that essentially resided in the kingdom represented by the monster. (4.) In the growth of that "horn," three of the others were plucked up by the roots. The proper meaning of the word used to express this (אֶתְעֲקַרוּ) is, that they were *rooted out*—as a tree is overturned by the roots, or the roots are turned out from the earth. The process by which this was done seems to have been by *growth*. The gradual increase of the horn so crowded on the others that a portion of them was forced out, and fell. What is fairly indicated by this was not any act of violence, or any sudden convulsion or revolution, but such a gradual *growth* of power that a portion of the original power was removed, and this new power occupied its place. There was no *revolution*, properly so called; no change of the whole dynasty, for a large portion of the horns remained, but the gradual rise of a new power that would wield a portion of that formerly wielded by others, and that would now wield the power in its place. The number *three* would either indicate that three parts out of the ten were absorbed in this way, or that a considerable, though an indefinite portion, was thus absorbed. (5.) The eyes:—*and behold, in this horn* were *eyes like the eyes of a man.* Eyes denote intelligence, as we see objects by their aid. The rims of the wheels in Ezekiel's vision were full of eyes (Ezek. i. 18), as symbolic of intelligence. This would denote that the

9 ¶ I beheld till the thrones were cast down,*a* and the *b*Ancient

a ch. 2. 44; 1 Cor. 15. 24, 25.

of days did sit, whose *c*garment was *d* white as snow, and the hair

b ver. 22; Isa. 9. 6.   *c* Psa. 45. 8.   *d* Rev. 1. 14.

power here referred to would be remarkably sagacious. We should naturally look for the fulfilment of this in a power that laid its plans wisely and intelligently; that had large and clear views of policy; that was shrewd and far-seeing in its counsels and purposes; that was skilled in diplomacy; or, that was eminent for statesmanlike plans. This part of the symbol, if it stood alone, would find its fulfilment in *any* wise and shrewd administration; as it stands here, surrounded by others, it would seem that this, as contrasted with them, was characteristically shrewd and far-seeing in its policy. Lengerke, following Jerome, supposes that this means that the object referred to would be a *man*, "as the eyes of men are keener and sharper than those of other animals." But the more correct interpretation is that above referred to—that it denotes intelligence, shrewdness, sagacity. (6.) The mouth:—*and a mouth speaking great things.* A mouth indicating pride and arrogance. This is explained in ver. 25, as meaning that he to whom it refers would "speak great words against the Most High;" that is, would be guilty of blasphemy. There would be such arrogance, and such claims set up, and such a spirit evinced, that it would be in fact a speaking against God. We naturally look for the fulfilment of this to some haughty and blaspheming power; some power that would really blaspheme religion, and that would be opposed to its progress and prosperity in the world. The Sept., in the *Cod. Chis.*, adds here, "and shall make war against the saints;" but these words are not found in the original Chaldee. They accord, however, well with the explanation in ver. 25. What has been here considered embraces all that pertains properly to this symbol—the symbol of the fourth beast—except the fact stated in ver. 11, that the beast was slain, and that his body was given to the burning flame. The inquiry as to the fulfilment will be ap-

propriate when we come to consider the explanation given at the request of Daniel, by the angel, in ver. 19–25.

9. *I beheld.* "I continued looking on these strange sights, and contemplating these transformations." This implies that some time elapsed before all these things had occurred. He looked on till he saw a solemn judgment passed on this fourth beast particularly, *as if* God had come forth in his majesty and glory to pronounce that judgment, and to bring the power and arrogance of the beast to an end. ¶ *Till the thrones were cast down.* The Chaldee word (כָּרְסָוָן) means, properly, *thrones*—seats on which monarchs sit. So far as the *word* is concerned, it would apply either to a throne occupied by an earthly monarch, or to the throne of God. The use of the *plural* here would seem to imply, at least, that the reference is not to the throne of God, but to some other throne. Maurer and Lengerke suppose that the allusion is to the thrones on which the celestial beings sat in the solemn judgment that was to be pronounced—the throne of God, and the thrones or seats of the attending inhabitants of heaven, coming with him to the solemn judgment. Lengerke refers for illustration to 1 Kings xxii. 19; Isa. vi. 1; Job i. 6, and Rev. v. 11, 12. But the word itself might be properly applied to the thrones of earthly monarchs as well as to the throne of God. The phrase "were cast down" (רְמִיו), in our translation, would seem to suppose that there was some throwing down, or overturning of thrones, at this period, and that the solemn judgment would follow this, or be consequent on this. The Chaldee word (רְמָא) means, as explained by Gesenius, to *cast*, to *throw* (Dan. iii. 21, 24; vi. 16, 17); to *set*, to *place*, e.g., thrones; to *impose* tribute (Ezra vii. 24). The passage is rendered by the Latin Vulgate, *throni positi sunt*—"thrones were placed;" by the

of his head like the pure wool: his

a Acts 2, 30, 33.　　b Ezek. 1. 15, 16.

throne _a was like_ the fiery flame, _and_ his wheels _b as_ burning fire.

Greek, ἐτέθησαν—"were placed." So Luther, _stühle gesetzt;_ and so Lengerke, _stühle aufgestellt_ — the thrones were placed, or set up. The proper meaning, therefore, of the phrase would seem to be—not, as in our translation, that the "thrones would be _cast down_"—as if there was to be an overturning of thrones on the earth to mark this particular period of history—but that there was, in the vision, a setting up, or a placing of thrones for the purpose of administering judgment, &c., on the beast. The use of the plural is, doubtless, in accordance with the language elsewhere employed, to denote the fact that the great Judge would be surrounded with others who would be, as it were, associated in administering justice—either angels or redeemed spirits. Nothing is more common in the Scripture than to represent others as thus associated with God in pronouncing judgment on men. Comp. Matt. xix. 28; Lu. xxii. 30; 1 Cor. vi. 2, 3; 1 Ti. v. 21; Rev. ii. 26; iv. 4. The era, or period, therefore, marked here, would be when a solemn Divine judgment was to be passed on the "beast," or when some events were to take place, _as if_ such a judgment were pronounced. The events pertaining to the fourth beast were to be the last in the series preparatory to the reign of the saints, or the setting up of the kingdom of the Messiah, and therefore it is introduced in this manner, _as if_ a solemn judgment scene were to occur. ¶ _And the Ancient of days did sit._ Was seated for the purposes of judgment. The phrase "Ancient of days"—עַתִּיק יוֹמִין —is one that denotes an elderly or old person; meaning, _he who is most ancient as to days,_ and is equivalent to the French _L'Eternel,_ or English, _The Eternal._ It occurs only in this chapter (vers. 9, 13, 22), and is a representation of one venerable in years, sitting down for the purposes of judgment. The appellation does not of itself denote _eternity,_ but it is employed, probably, with reference to the fact that God is eternal. God is often repre-

sented under some such appellation, as he that is "from everlasting to everlasting" (Psal. xc. 2), "the first and the last" (Isa. xliv. 6), &c. There can be no doubt that the reference here is to God as a Judge, or as about to pronounce judgment, though there is no necessity for supposing that it will be in a visible and literal form, any more than there is for supposing that all that is here represented by symbols will _literally_ take place. If it should be insisted on that the proper interpretation demands that there will be a literal and visible judgment, such as is here described, it may be replied that the same rigid interpretation would demand that there will be a _literal_ "slaying of the beast, and a giving of his body to the flame" (ver. 11), and more generally still, that _all_ that is here referred to by symbols will literally occur. The fact, however, is, that all these events are referred to by symbols —symbols which have an expressive meaning, but which, by their very nature and design, are not to be literally understood. All that is fairly implied here is, that events would occur in regard to this fourth beast _as if_ God should sit in solemn judgment on it, and should condemn it in the manner here referred to. We are, doubtless, in the fulfilment of this, to look for some event that will be of so decisive and marked a character, that it may be regarded _as_ a Divine judgment in the case, or that will show the strongly-marked Divine disapprobation — as really _as if_ the judgment-seat were formally set, and God should appear in majesty to give sentence. _Sitting_ was the usual posture among the ancients, as it is among the moderns, in pronouncing judgment. Among the ancients the judge sat on a throne or bench while the parties stood before him (comp. Zech. iv. 13), and with the Greeks and Romans so essential was the sitting posture for a judge, that a sentence pronounced in any other posture was not valid. — Lengerke. It was a maxim, _Animus sedendo magis sapit;_ or, as Servius on the _Æn._ i. 56,

10 A fiery *a* stream issued and came forth from before him: thousand thousands ministered unto him, and ten thousand times ten

a Psa. 50. 3; Isa. 66. 15, 16.

thousand stood *b* before him: the judgment *c* was set, and the books were opened.

b 1 Kings 22. 19; Psa. 68. 17; Heb. 12. 22.
c Rev. 20. 4, 12.

remarks, *Est enim curantis et solliciti sedere.* ¶ *Whose garment* was *white as snow.* Whose robe. The reference here is to the long flowing robe that was worn by ancient princes, noblemen, or priests. See Notes on Isa. vi. 1. Comp. Notes on Rev. i. 13. White was an emblem of purity and honour, and was not an improper symbol of the purity of the judge, and of the justness of the sentence which he would pronounce. So the elder Pitt, in his celebrated speech against employing Indians in the war with the American people, besought the bishops to "interpose the unsullied purity of their lawn." Lengerke supposes, as Prof. Stuart does on Rev. i. 13, that the whiteness here referred to was not the mere colour of the material of which the robe was made, but was a celestial splendour or brightness, as if it were lightning or fire—such as is appropriate to the Divine Majesty. Lengerke refers here to Exod. xix. 18–24; Dan. ii. 22; Matt. xvii. 2; 1 Ti. vi. 16; 2 Esdras vii. 55; *Ascension of Isa.* viii. 21–25; Rev. i. 13, 14; iv. 2–4. But the more correct interpretation is to suppose that this refers to a pure white robe, such as judges might wear, and which would not be an improper symbol of their office. ¶ *And the hair of his head like the pure wool.* That is, for whiteness—a characteristic of venerable age. Compare Notes on Rev. i. 14. The image here set before us is that of one venerable by years and wisdom. ¶ *His throne* was like *the fiery flame.* The seat on which he sat seemed to be fire. That is, it was brilliant and splendid, as if it were a mass of flame. ¶ And *his wheels* as *burning fire.* The wheels of his throne—for, as in Ezek. i., x., the throne on which Jehovah sat appeared to be on wheels. In Ezekiel (i. 16; x. 9), the wheels of the throne appeared to be of the colour of beryl; that is, they were like precious stones. Here, perhaps, they had only the *appearance* of a flame—as such wheels would *seem* to flash flames. So

Milton, in describing the chariot of the Son of God:—

"Forth rush'd with whirlwind sound
The chariot of Paternal Deity,
Flashing thick flames, wheel within wheel undrawn,
Itself instinct with spirit, but convoyed
By four cherubic shapes; four faces each
Had wondrous; as with stars their bodies all,
And wings were set with eyes; with eyes the wheels
Of beryl, *and careering fires between.*"
                              —*Par. Lost,* b. vi.

10. *A fiery stream issued and came forth from before him.* Streams of fire seemed to burst forth from his throne. Representations of this kind abound in the Scriptures to illustrate the majesty and glory of God. Comp. Rev. iv. 5, "And out of the throne proceeded lightnings, and thunderings, and voices." Exod. xix. 16; Hab. iii. 4; Psal. xviii. 8. ¶ *Thousand thousands ministered unto him.* "A thousand of thousands;" that is, thousands multiplied a thousand times. The mind is struck with the fact that there are *thousands* present—and then the number seems as great as if those thousands were multiplied a thousand times. The idea is that there was an immense—a countless host. The reference here is to the angels, and God is often represented as attended with great numbers of these celestial beings when he comes down to our world. Deut. xxxiii. 2, "He came with ten thousands of saints;" that is, of holy ones. Psal. lxviii. 17, "The chariots of God are twenty thousand, even thousands of angels." Comp. Jude, ver. 14. The word "ministered" means that they attended on him. ¶ *And ten thousand times ten thousand stood before him.* An innumerable host. These were not to be judged, but were attendants on him as he pronounced sentence. The judgment here referred to was not on the world at large, but on the beast, preparatory to giving the kingdom to the one who was like the Son of man (vers. 13, 14). ¶ *The judgment was set.* That is, all the arrangements for

11 I beheld then, because of the voice of the great words which the horn spake; I beheld, *even* till the beast was slain, [a] and his body destroyed and given to the burning flame.　　　*a* Rev. 19. 20.

a solemn act of judgment were made, and the process of the judgment commenced. ¶ *And the books were opened.* As containing the record of the deeds of those who were to be judged. Comp. Rev. xx. 12. The great Judge is represented as having before him the record of all the deeds on which judgment was to be pronounced, and to be about to pronounce sentence according to those deeds. The judgment here referred to seems to have been some solemn act on the part of God transferring the power over the world, from that which had long swayed it, to the saints. As already remarked, the necessary interpretation of the passage does not require us to understand this of a literal and visible judgment—of a personal appearing of the "Ancient of days"—of a formal application to him by "one like the Son of man" (ver. 13) —or of a public and visible making over to him of a kingdom upon the earth. It is to be remembered that all this passed in vision before the mind of the prophet; that it is a symbolical representation; and that we are to find the fulfilment of this in some event changing the course of empire—putting a period to the power represented by the "beast" and the "horn," and causing that power to pass into other hands—producing a change as great on the earth *as if* such a solemn act of judgment were passed. The nature of the representation requires that we should look for the fulfilment of this in some great and momentous change in human affairs — some events that would take away the power of the "beast," and that would cause the dominion to pass into other hands. On the fulfilment, see the Notes on ver. 26.

11. *I beheld then, because of the voice of the great words which the horn spake.* I was attracted by these words —by their arrogance, and haughtiness, and pride ; and I saw that it was on account of these mainly that the solemn judgment proceeded against the beast. The attitude of the seer here is this—he heard arrogant and proud words uttered by the "horn," and he waited in deep attention, and in earnest expectation, to learn what judgment would be pronounced. He had seen (ver. 8) that horn spring up and grow to great power, and utter great things ; he had then seen, immediately on this, a solemn and sublime preparation for judgment, and he now waited anxiously to learn what sentence would be pronounced. The result is stated in the subsequent part of the verse. ¶ *I beheld.* I continued beholding. This would seem to imply that it was not done at once, but that some time intervened. ¶ Even *till the beast was slain.* The fourth beast : that which had the ten horns, and on which the little horn had sprung up. This was the result of the judgment. It is evidently implied here that the beast was slain *on account* of the words uttered by the horn that sprang up, or that the pride and arrogance denoted by that symbol were the cause of the fact that the beast was put to death. It is not said *by whom* the beast would be slain ; but the fair meaning is, that the procuring cause of that death would be the Divine judgment, on account of the pride and arrogancy of the "horn" that sprang up in the midst of the others. If the "beast" represents a mighty monarchy that would exist on the earth, and the "little horn" a new power that would spring out of that, then the fulfilment is to be found in such a fact as this— that this power, so mighty and terrible formerly, and that crushed down the nations, would, under the Divine judgment, be ultimately destroyed, on account of the nature of the authority claimed. We are to look for the accomplishment of this in some such state of things as that of a new power springing out of an existing dominion, that the existing dominion still remains, but was so much controlled by the new power, that it would be necessary to destroy the former on account of the arrogance and pride of that which sprang from it. In other words,

12 As concerning the rest of the beasts, they had their dominion taken away: yet [1] their lives were prolonged for a season and time.

1 *a prolonging in life was given them.*

the destruction of the kingdom represented by the fourth beast would be, as a Divine judgment, on account of the arrogancy of that represented by the little horn. ¶ *And his body destroyed.* That is, there would be a destruction of the kingdom here represented as much as there would be of the beast if his body was destroyed. The power of that kingdom, as such, is to come to an end. ¶ *And given to the burning flame.* Consumed. This would represent, in strong terms, that the power here symbolized by the beast would be utterly destroyed. It is not, however, necessary to suppose that this is to be the *mode* in which it would be done, or that it would be by fire. It is to be remembered that all this is *symbol*, and no one part of the symbol should be taken literally more than another, nor is it congruous to suppose there would be a literal consuming *fire* in the case any more than that there would be literally a *beast*, or ten horns, or a little horn. The fair meaning is, that there would be as real a destruction *as if* it were accomplished by fire; or a destruction of which fire would be the proper emblem. The allusion is here, probably, to the fact that the dead bodies of animals were often consumed by fire.

12. *As concerning the rest of the beasts.* They had been superseded, but not destroyed. It would seem that they were still represented in vision to Daniel, as retaining their existence, though their power was taken away, and their fierceness subdued, or that they still seemed to remain alive for a time, or while the vision was passing. They were not cut down, destroyed, and consumed as the fourth beast was. ¶ *They had their dominion taken away.* They were superseded, or they no longer exercised power. They no more appeared exerting a control over the nations. They still existed, but they were subdued and quiet. It was possible to discern them, but they no

longer acted the conspicuous part which they had done in the days of their greatness and grandeur. Their power had passed away. This cannot be difficult of interpretation. We should naturally look for the fulfilment of this in the fact that the nations referred to by these first three beasts were still in being, and could be recognized as nations, in their boundaries, or customs, or languages; but that the *power* which they had wielded had passed into other hands. ¶ *Yet their lives were prolonged.* Marg., as in Chaldee, "a prolonging in life was given them." That is, they were not utterly destroyed and consumed as the power of the fourth beast was after the solemn judgment. The meaning is, that in these kingdoms there would be energy for a time. They had life still; and the difference between them and the kingdom represented by the fourth beast was that which would exist between wild animals subdued but still living, and a wild animal killed and burned. We should look for the fulfilment of this in some state of things where the kingdoms referred to by the three beasts were subdued and succeeded by others, though they still retained something of their national character; while the other kingdom had no successor of a civil kind, but where its power wholly ceased, and the dominion went wholly into other hands—so that it might be said that that kingdom, as such, had *wholly* ceased to be. ¶ *For a season and time.* Comp. Notes on ver. 25. The time mentioned here is not definite.

The phrase used (עַד־זְמַן וְעִדָּן) refers to a definite period, both the words in the original referring to a *designated* or *appointed* time, though neither of them indicates anything about the *length* of the time, any more than our word *time* does. Luther renders this, "For there was a time and an hour appointed to them how long each one should continue." Grotius explains this as meaning, "Beyond the time

13 I saw in the night visions, and, behold, *one* like the Son of man *a* came with the clouds of heaven, and came to the *b* Ancient of days, and they brought him near before him.

a Matt.24.30; 25.31; 26.64; Rev.1.7,13; 14.14.

b ver. 9.

fixed by God they could not continue." The true meaning of the Chaldee is probably this: "For a time, even a definite time." The mind of the prophet is at first fixed upon the fact that they continue to live; then upon the fact, somehow apparent, that it is for a definite period. Perhaps in the vision he saw them one after another die or disappear. In the words here used, however, there is nothing by which we can determine *how long* they were to continue. The time that the power represented by the little horn is to continue *is* explained in ver. 25, but there is no clue by which we can ascertain how long the existence of the power represented by the first three beasts was to continue. All that is clear is, that it was to be lengthened out for some period, but that that was a definite and fixed period.

13. *I saw in the night visions.* Evidently in the same night visions, or on the same occasion, for the visions are connected. See vers. 1, 7. The meaning is, that he continued beholding, or that a new vision passed before him. ¶ *And, behold, one like the Son of man,* &c. It is remarkable that Daniel does not attempt to represent this by any symbol. The representation by symbols ceases with the fourth beast; and now the description assumes a literal form—the setting up of the kingdom of the Messiah and of the saints. *Why* this change of form occurs is not stated or known, but the sacred writers seem carefully to have avoided any representation of the Messiah by symbols. The phrase "The Son of Man"—אֱנָשׁ בַּר—does not occur elsewhere in the Old Testament in such a connection, and with such a reference as it has here, though it is often found in the New, and is, in fact, the favourite term by which the Saviour designates himself. In Dan. iii. 25, we have the phrase "the Son of God" (see Notes on that passage), as applicable to one who appeared with the three "children"

that were cast into the burning furnace; and in Ezekiel, the phrase "son of man" often occurs as applicable to himself as a prophet, being found more than eighty times in his prophecies, but the expression here used does not elsewhere occur in the Old Testament as applicable to the personage intended. As occurring here, it is important to explain it, not only in view of the events connected with it in the prophecy, but as having done much to mould the language of the New Testament. There are three questions in regard to its meaning: What does it signify? To whom does it refer? And what would be its proper fulfilment? (1.) The phrase is more than a mere Hebrew or Chaldee expression to denote *man,* but is always used with some peculiar significancy, and with relation to some peculiar characteristic of the person to whom it is applied, or with some special design. To ascertain this design, regard should be had to the expression of the original. "While the words אִישׁ and אִישָּׁה are used simply as designations of sex, אֱנוֹשׁ, which is etymologically akin to אִישׁ, is employed with constant reference to its original meaning, *to be weak, sick;* it is the ethical designation of man, but אָדָם denotes man as to his physical, natural condition—whence the use of the word in such passages as Psa. viii. 4; Job xxv. 6, and also its connection with בֵּן, are satisfactorily explained, The emphatic address בֶּן אָדָם—*Son of man*—is therefore [in Ezekiel] a continued admonition to the prophet to remember that he is a man like all the rest."—Hävernick, *Com. on Ezek.* ii. 1, 2, quoted in the *Bibliotheca Sacra,* v. 718. The expression here used is בַּר אֱנוֹשׁ, and would *properly* refer to man as weak and feeble, and as liable to be sick, &c. Applied to any one as "*a* Son of man," it would be used to denote that he partook of the weakness and infirmities of the race; and, as the phrase "*the* Son of man" is used in the New Testament when applied by the Saviour to himself, there is an undoubted reference to this fact —that he sustained a peculiar relation to our race ; that he was in all respects a man ; that he was one of us ; that he had so taken our nature on himself that there was a peculiar propriety that a term which would at once designate this should be given to him. The phrase here used by Daniel would denote some one (*a*) in the human form ; (*b*) some one sustaining a peculiar relation to man—as if human nature were embodied in him. (2.) The next inquiry here is, *to whom* this refers ? Who, in fact, was the one that was thus seen in vision by the prophet ? Or who was designed to be set forth by this ? This inquiry is not so much, Whom did Daniel suppose or understand this to be ? as, Who was in fact designed to be represented ; or in whom would the fulfilment be found ? For, on the supposition that this was a heavenly vision, it is clear that it was intended to designate some one in whom the complete fulfilment was to be found. Now, admitting that this was a heavenly vision, and that it was intended to represent what would occur in future times, there are the clearest reasons for supposing that the Messiah was referred to ; and indeed this is so plain, that it may be assumed as one of the indisputable things by which to determine the character and design of the prophecy. Among these reasons are the following : (*a*) The name itself, as a name assumed by the Lord Jesus—the favourite name by which he chose to designate himself when on the earth. This name he used technically ; he used it as one that would be understood to denote the Messiah ; he used it as if it needed no explanation as having a reference to the Messiah. But this usage could have been derived only from this passage in Daniel ; for there is no other place in the Old Testament where the name could refer with propriety to the Messiah, or would be understood to be applicable to him. (*b*) This interpretation has been given to it by the Jewish writers in general, in all ages.

I refer to this, n**o**t to say that their explanation is authoritative, but to show that it is the natural and obvious meaning; and because, as we shall see, it is that which has given shape and form to the language of the New Testament, and is fully sanctioned there. Thus, in the ancient book of Zohar it is said, " In the times of the Messiah, Israel shall be one people to the Lord, and he shall make them one nation in the earth, and they shall rule above and below; as it is written, *Behold, one like the Son of man came with the clouds of heaven ;* this is the King Messiah, of whom it is written, *And in the days of these kings shall the God of heaven set up a kingdom which shall never be destroyed,"* &c. So in the Talmud, and so the majority of the ancient Jewish Rabbins. See Gill, *Com. in loc.* It is true that this interpretation has not been uniform among the Jewish Rabbins, but still it has prevailed among them, as it has among Christian interpreters. (*c*) A sanction seems to be given to this interpretation by the adoption of the title "Son of man" by the Lord Jesus, as that by which he chose to designate himself. That title was such as would constantly suggest this place in Daniel as referring to himself, and especially as he connected with it the declaration that "the Son of man would come in the clouds of heaven," &c. It was hardly possible that he should use the title in such a connection without suggesting this place in Daniel, or without leaving the impression on the minds of his hearers that he meant to be understood as applying this to himself. (*d*) It may be added, that it cannot with propriety be applied to any other. Porphyry, indeed, supposed that Judas Maccabeus was intended ; Grotius that it referred to the Roman people; Aben Ezra to the people of Israel ; and Cocceius to the people of the Most High (Gill) ; but all these are unnatural interpretations, and are contrary to that which one would obtain by allowing the language of the New Testament to influence his mind. The title—so often used by the Saviour himself ; the attending circumstances of the clouds of heaven ; the *place* which the vision occupies—so immediately preceding the setting up of the kingdom of the saints ; and the fact that that kingdom can be set up only under the Messiah, all point to him as the personage represented in the vision. (3.) But if it refers to the Messiah, the next inquiry is, What is to be regarded as the proper fulfilment of the vision ? To what precisely does it relate ? Are we to suppose that there will be a literal appearing of the Son of man—the Messiah—in the clouds of heaven, and a passing over of the kingdom in a public and solemn manner into the hands of the saints ? In reply to these questions, it may be remarked (*a*), that this cannot be understood as relating to the last judgment ; for it is not introduced with reference to that at all. The "Son of man" is not here represented as coming with a view to judge the world at the winding-up of human affairs, but for the purpose of setting up a kingdom, or procuring a kingdom for his saints. There is no assembling of the people of the world together ; no act of judging the righteous and the wicked ; no pronouncing of a sentence on either. It is evident that the world is to continue much longer under the dominion of the saints. (*b*) It is not to be taken literally ; that is, we are not, from this passage, to expect a literal appearance of the Son of man in the clouds of heaven, preparatory to the setting up of the kingdom of the saints. For if one portion is to be taken literally, there is no reason why all should not be. Then we are to expect, not merely the appearing of the Son of man in the clouds, but also the following things, as a part of the fulfilment of the vision, to wit : the literal placing of a throne, or seat ; the literal streaming forth of flame from his throne ; the literal appearing of the "Ancient of days," with a garment of white, and hair as wool ; a literal approach of the Son of man to him as seated on his throne to ask of him a kingdom, &c. But no one can believe that all this is to occur ; no one does believe that it will. (*c*) The proper interpretation is to regard this, as it was seen by Daniel, as a vision—a representation of a state of things in the

world *as . if* what is here described would occur. That is, great events were to take place, of which this would be a proper symbolical representation —or *as if* the Son of man, the Messiah, would thus appear ; would approach the "Ancient of days ;" would receive a kingdom, and would make it over to the saints. Now, there is no real difficulty in understanding what is here meant to be taught, and what we are to expect ; and these points of *fact* are the following, viz. :—1. That he who is here called the "Ancient of days " is the source of power and dominion. 2. That there would be some severe adjudication of the power here represented by the *beast* and the *horn*. 3. That the kingdom or dominion of the world is to be in fact given to him who is here called "the Son of man" —the Messiah—a fact represented here by his approaching the "Ancient of days " who is the source of all power. 4. That there is to be some passing over of the kingdom or power into the hands of the saints ; or some setting up of a kingdom on the earth, of which he is to be the head, and in which the dominion over the world shall be in fact in the hands of his people, and the laws of the Messiah everywhere prevail. What will be the essential characteristics of that kingdom we may learn by the exposition of ver. 14, compared with ver. 27. ¶ *Came with the clouds of heaven.* That is, he seemed to come down from the sky encompassed with clouds. So the Saviour, probably intending to refer to this language, speaks of himself, when he shall come to judge the world, as coming in clouds, or encompassed by clouds, Matt. xxiv. 30 ; xxvi. 64 ; Mark xiii. 26 ; xiv. 62. Comp. Rev. i. 7. Clouds are an appropriate symbol of the Divinity. See Psa. xcvii. 2 ; civ. 3. The same symbol was employed by the heathen, representing their deities as appearing covered with a cloud :—

    " Tandem venias, precamur,
Nube candentes humeros amictus,
      Augur Apollo !"—Horace, *Lyr.* I. 2.

The allusion in the place before us is not to the last judgment, but to the fact that a kingdom on the earth would

14 And ^athere was given him dominion, and glory, and a king-dom, that all people, nations, and

a Psa. 2. 6-8; Matt. 28. 18; John 3. 35; 1 Cor. 15. 27; Eph. 1. 20, 22.

be passed over into the hands of the Messiah. He is represented as coming sublimely to the world, and as receiving a kingdom that would *succeed* those represented by the beasts. ¶ *And came to the Ancient of days.* Ver. 9. This shows that the passage cannot refer to the final judgment. He comes to the "Ancient of days"—to God as the source of power—as if to ask a petition for a kingdom ; not to pronounce a judgment on mankind. The act here appropriately denotes that God is the source of all power; that all who reign derive their authority from him, and that even the Messiah, in setting up his kingdom in the world, receives it at the hand of the Father. This is in accordance with all the representations in the New Testament. We are not to suppose that this will occur literally. There is to be no such literal sitting of one with the appearance of age—denoted by the "Ancient of days"—on a throne ; nor is there to be any such literal approaching him by one in the form of a man to receive a kingdom. Such passages show the absurdity of the attempts to interpret the language of the Scriptures literally. All that this symbol fairly means must be, that the kingdom that was to be set up under the Messiah on the earth was received from God. ¶ *And they brought him near before him.* That is, he was brought near before him. Or, it may mean that his attendants brought him near. All that the language necessarily implies is, that he came near to his seat, and received from him a kingdom.

14. *And there was given him dominion.* That is, by him who is represented as the "Ancient of days." The fair interpretation of this is, that he received the dominion from him. This is the uniform representation in the New Testament. Comp. Matt. xxviii. 18 ; John iii. 35 ; 1 Cor. xv. 27. The word *dominion* here means *rule* or *authority*—such as a prince exercises. He was set over a kingdom as a prince or ruler. ¶ *And glory.* That is, the

glory or honour appropriate to one at the head of such an empire. ¶ *And a kingdom.* That is, he would reign. He would have sovereignty. The nature and the extent of this kingdom is immediately designated as one that would be universal and perpetual. What is properly implied in this language as to the question whether it will be literal and visible, will be appropriately considered at the close of the verse. All that is necessary to be noticed here is, that it is everywhere promised in the Old Testament that the Messiah would be a king, and have a kingdom. Comp. Psal. ii. ; Isa. ix. 6, 7. ¶ *That all people, nations, and languages should serve him.* It would be universal; would embrace all nations. The language here is such as would emphatically denote universality. See Notes on ch. iii. 4; iv. 1. It implies that that kingdom would extend over all the nations of the earth, and we are to look for the fulfilment of this only in such a universal reign of the Messiah. ¶ *His dominion is an everlasting dominion,* &c. The others, represented by the four beasts, would all pass away, but this would be permanent and eternal. Nothing would destroy it. It would not have, as most kingdoms of the earth have had, any such internal weakness or source of discord as would be the cause of its destruction, nor would there be any external power that would invade or overthrow it. This declaration affirms nothing as to the *form* in which the kingdom would exist, but merely asserts the *fact* that it would do so. Respecting the kingdom of the Messiah, to which this undoubtedly alludes, the same thing is repeatedly and uniformly affirmed in the New Testament. Compare Matt. xvi. 18 ; Heb. xii. 28 ; Rev. xi. 15. The form and manner in which this will occur is more fully developed in the New Testament; in the vision seen by Daniel the fact only is stated.

The question now arises, What would be a fulfilment of this prediction respecting the kingdom that will be

languages should serve him: his dominion *is* an everlasting *a* dominion, which shall not pass away, and his kingdom *that* which shall not *b* be destroyed.

15 ¶ I Daniel was grieved in my spirit in the midst of *my* [1] body, and the visions of my head troubled me.

a Psa.145.13. *b* Heb.12.28. 1 *sheath,* 2 Pet.1.14.

given to the saints? What, from the language used in the vision, should we be legitimately authorized to expect to take place on the earth? In regard to these questions, there are but two views which can be taken, and the interpretation of the passage must sustain the one or the other. (*a*) One is that which supposes that this will be literally fulfilled in the sense that the Son of God, the Messiah, will reign personally on earth. According to this, he will come to set up a visible and glorious kingdom, making Jerusalem his capital, and swaying his sceptre over the world. All nations and people will be subject to him; all authority will be wielded by his people under him. (*b*) According to the other view, there will be a spiritual reign of the Son of God over the earth; that is, the principles of his religion will everywhere prevail, and the righteous will rule, and the laws of the Redeemer will be obeyed everywhere. There will be such a prevalence of his gospel on the hearts of all—rulers and people; the gospel will so modify all laws, and control all customs, and remove all abuses, and all the forms of evil; men will be so generally under the influence of that gospel, that it may be said that *He* reigns on the earth, or that the government actually administered is *his.*

In regard to these different views, and to the true interpretation of the passage, it may be remarked, (1.) That we are not to look for the *literal* fulfilment of this; we are not to expect that what is here described will literally occur. The whole is evidently a symbolical representation, and the fulfilment is to be found in something that the symbol would properly denote. No one can pretend that there is to be an actual sitting on the throne, by one in the form of an old man—"the Ancient of days"—or that there is to be a literal coming to him by one "like the Son of man," to receive a kingdom. But if one part of the re-

presentation is not to be literally interpreted, why should the other be? It may be added, that it is nowhere *said* that this would literally occur. (2.) All that is fairly implied here is found in the latter interpretation. Such a prevalence of the principles of the gospel would meet the force of the language, and every part of the vision would find a *real* fulfilment in that. (*a*) The fact that it proceeds from God —represented as "the Ancient of days." (*b*) The fact that it is given by him, or that the kingdom is made over by him to the Messiah. (*c*) The fact that the Messiah would have such a kingdom; that is, that he would reign on the earth, in the hearts and lives of men. (*d*) The fact that that kingdom would be universal—extending over all people. (*e*) And the fact that it would be perpetual; that is, that it would extend down to the end of time, or the consummation of all things here, and that it would be then eternal in the heavens. For a very full and ample illustration of this passage—so full and ample as to supersede the necessity of any additional illustration here, see the Notes on ch. ii. 44, 45.

15. *I Daniel was grieved in my spirit.* That is, I was *troubled;* or my heart was made heavy and sad. This was probably in part because he did not fully understand the meaning of the vision, and partly on account of the fearful and momentous nature of that which was indicated by it. So the apostle John (Rev. v. 4) says, "And I wept much because no man was found worthy to open and to read the book." ¶ *In the midst of* my *body.* Marg., as in the Chald., *sheath.* The body is undoubtedly referred to, and is so called as the envelope of the mind —or as that in which the soul is *inserted,* as the sword is in the sheath, and from which it is drawn out by death. The same metaphor is employed by Pliny: *Donec cremato eo inimici remeanti animæ velut vaginam*

16 I came near unto one of them that stood by, and asked him the truth of all this. So he told me, and made me know the interpretation of the things.

17 These great beasts, which are

four, *are* four kings, *which* shall arise out of the earth.

18 But the saints of the [1]Most High shall take the kingdom, and possess the kingdom *a* for ever, even for ever and ever.

1 *high ones, i.e., things or places,* Eph.1.3; 6.12.

a Rev. 3. 21.

---

ademerint. So, too, a certain philosopher, who was slighted by Alexander the Great on account of his ugly face, is said to have replied, *Corpus hominis nil est nisi vagina gladii in qua anima reconditur.*—Gesenius. Comp. Lengerke, *in loc.* See also Job xxvii. 8, "When God *taketh away* his soul;" or rather *draws out* his soul, as a sword is drawn out of the sheath. Comp. Notes on that place. See also Buxtorf's *Lex. Tal.* p. 1307. The meaning here is plain—that Daniel felt sad and troubled in mind, and that this produced a sensible effect on his body. ¶ *And the visions of my head troubled me.* The head is here regarded as the seat of the intellect, and he speaks of these visions as if they were seen by the head. That is, they seemed to pass before his eyes.

16. *I came near unto one of them that stood by.* That is, to one of the angels who appeared to stand near the throne. ver. 10. Comp. ch. viii. 13 ; Zech. iv. 4, 5 ; Rev. vii. 13. It was natural for Daniel to suppose that the angels who were seen encircling the throne would be able to give him information on the subject, and the answers which Daniel received show that he was not mistaken in his expectation. God has often employed angels to communicate important truths to men, or has made them the medium of communicating his will. Comp. Rev. i. 1 ; Acts vii. 53 ; Heb. ii. 2. ¶ *So he told me, and made me know the interpretation of the things.* He explained the meaning of the symbols, so that Daniel understood them. It would seem probable that Daniel has not recorded *all* that the angel communicated respecting the vision, but he has preserved so much that we may understand its general signification.

17. *These great beasts, which are four, are four kings.* Four kings or four

dynasties. There is no reason for supposing that they refer to individual *kings*, but the obvious meaning is, that they refer to four *dominions* or *empires* that would succeed one another on the earth. So the whole representation leads us to suppose, and so the passage has been always interpreted. The Latin Vulgate renders it *regna ;* the Sept. βασιλεῖαι; Luther, *Reiche;* Lengerke, *Königreiche.* This interpretation is confirmed, also, by ver. 23, where it is expressly said that "the fourth beast shall be the fourth *kingdom* upon earth." See also ver. 24. ¶ *Which shall arise out of the earth.* In ver. 2 the beasts are represented as coming up from the *sea*—the emblem of agitated nations. Here the same idea is presented more literally—that they would seem to spring up out of the earth, thus thrown into wild commotion. These dynasties were to be upon the earth, and they were in all things to indicate their earthly origin. Perhaps, also, it is designed by these words to denote a marked contrast between these four dynasties and the one that would follow—which would be of heavenly origin. This was the *general* intimation which was given to the meaning of the vision, and he was satisfied at once as to the explanation, so far as the first three were concerned; but the fourth seemed to indicate more mysterious and important events, and respecting this he was induced to ask a more particular explanation.

18. *But the saints of the Most High shall take the kingdom.* That is, they shall ultimately take possession of the rule over all the world, and shall control it from that time onward to the end. This is the grand thing which the vision is designed to disclose, and on this it was evidently the intention to fix the mind. Everything before was preparatory and subordinate to

19 Then I would know the truth of the fourth beast, which was diverse from all [1] the others, exceeding dreadful, whose teeth *were* of iron, and his nails *of* brass;

1 *those.*

which devoured, brake in pieces, and stamped the residue with his feet;

20 And of the ten horns that *were* in his head, and *of* the other which came up, and before whom

---

this, and to this all things tended. The phrase rendered *the Most High*—in the margin "*high ones, i.e., things or places*"—עֶלְיוֹנִין—is in the plural number, and means literally *high ones;* but there can be no doubt that it refers here to God, and is given to him as the word *Elohim* is (Gen. i. 1, *et sæpe*), to denote majesty or honour—*pluralis excellentiæ.* The word rendered *saints* means *the holy,* and the reference is undoubtedly to the people of God on the earth, meaning here that they would take possession of the kingdom, or that they would rule. When true religion shall everywhere prevail, and when all offices shall be in the hands of good men—of men that fear God and that keep his commandments—instead of being in the hands of bad men, as they generally have been, then this prediction will be accomplished in respect to all that is fairly implied in it. ¶ *And possess the kingdom for ever, even for ever and ever.* This is a strong and emphatic declaration, affirming that this dominion will be perpetual. It will not pass away, like the other kingdoms, to be succeeded by another one. What is here affirmed, as above remarked, will be true if such a reign should continue on earth to the winding up of all things, and should then be succeeded by an eternal reign of holiness in the heavens. It is not necessary to interpret this as meaning that there would be literally an eternal kingdom on this earth, for it is everywhere taught in the Scriptures that the present order of things will come to a close. But it does seem necessary to understand this as teaching that there will be a state of prevalent righteousness on the earth hereafter, and that when that is introduced it will continue to the end of time.

19. *Then I would know the truth of the fourth beast.* I desired to know

particularly what was symbolized by that. He appears to have been satisfied with the most general intimations in regard to the first three beasts, for the kingdoms represented by them seemed to have nothing very remarkable. But it was different in regard to the fourth. The beast itself was so remarkable—so fierce and terrific; the number of the horns was so great; the springing up of the little horn was so surprising; the character of that horn was so unusual; the judgment passed on it was so solemn; and the vision of one like the Son of man coming to take possession of the kingdom—all these things were of so fearful and so uncommon a character, that the mind of Daniel was peculiarly affected in view of them, and he sought earnestly for a further explanation. In the description that Daniel here gives of the beast and the horns, he refers in the main to the same circumstances which he had before described; but he adds a few which he had before omitted, all tending to impress the mind more deeply with the fearful character and the momentous import of the vision; as, for instance, the fact that it had nails of brass, and made war with the saints. ¶ *Which was diverse from all the others.* Different in its form and character;—so different as to attract particular attention, and to leave the impression that something very peculiar and remarkable was denoted by it. Notes, ver. 7. ¶ *Exceeding dreadful.* Notes, ver. 7. ¶ *And his nails* of *brass.* This circumstance is not mentioned in the first statement, ver. 7. It accords well with the other part of the description, that his teeth were of iron, and is designed to denote the fearful and terrific character of the kingdom, symbolized by the beast. ¶ Which *devoured,* &c. See Notes on ver. 7.

20. *And of the ten horns,* &c. See

three fell; even *of* that horn that had eyes, and a mouth that spake very great things, whose look *was* more stout than his fellows.

21 I beheld, and *a* the same horn

a Rev. 13. 7, &c.

made war with the saints, and prevailed against them;

22 Until the Ancient of days came, and judgment was given to the saints of the Most High; and the time came that the saints possessed the kingdom.

Notes on vers. 7, 8. ¶ *Whose look* was *more stout than his fellows.* Literally, "whose aspect was *greater* than that of its companions." This does not mean that its *look* or aspect was more *fierce* or *severe* than that of the others, but that the appearance of the horn was *greater*—רב. In ver. 8, this is described as a "little horn;" and to understand this, and reconcile the two, we must suppose that the seer watched this as it grew until it became the largest of the number. Three fell before it, and it outgrew in size all the others until it became the most prominent. This would clearly denote that the kingdom or the authority referred to by this eleventh horn would be more distinct and prominent than either of the others—would become so conspicuous and important as in fact to concentrate and embody all the power of the beast.

21. *I beheld, and the same horn made war with the saints.* I continued to look on this until I saw war made by this horn with the people of God. This circumstance, also, is not referred to in the first description, and the order of time in the description would seem to imply that the war with the saints would be at a considerable period *after* the first appearance of the horn, or would be only when it had grown to its great size and power. This *"war"* might refer to open hostilities, carried on in the usual manner of war; or to persecution, or to any invasion of the rights and privileges of others. As it is a "war with the *saints,*" it would be most natural to refer it to persecution. ¶ *And prevailed against them.* That is, he overcame and subdued them. He was stronger than they were, and they were not able to resist him. The same events are evidently referred to and in almost similar language—borrowed probably from Daniel—in Rev.

xiii. 5–7: "And there was given him a mouth speaking great things and blasphemies, and power was given unto him to continue forty and two months. And he opened his mouth in blasphemy against God, to blaspheme his name, and his tabernacle, and them that dwell in heaven. And it was given him to make war with the saints, and to overcome them; and power was given him over all kindreds, and tongues, and nations."

22. *Until the Ancient of days came.* Notes, ver. 9. That is, this was to occur *after* the horn grew to its full size, and *after* the war was made with the saints, and they had been overcome. It does not affirm that this would occur *immediately*, but that at some subsequent period the Ancient of days would come, and would set up a kingdom on the earth, or would make over the kingdom to the saints. There would be as real a transfer and as actual a setting up of a peculiar kingdom, *as if* God himself should appear on the earth, and should publicly make over the dominion to them. ¶ *And judgment was given to the saints of the Most High.* That is, there was a solemn act of judgment in the case by which the kingdom was given to their hands. It was as real a transfer as if there had been a judgment pronounced on the beast, and he had been condemned and overthrown, and as if the dominion which he once had should be made over to the servants of the Most High. ¶ *And the time came that the saints possessed the kingdom.* That they ruled on the earth; that good men made and administered the laws; that the principles of religion prevailed, influencing the hearts of all men, and causing righteousness and justice to be done. The universal prevalence of true religion, in controlling the hearts and lives of men, and disposing them to do what in all circumstances *ought*

23 Thus he said, The fourth beast shall be the fourth kingdom upon earth, which shall be diverse from all kingdoms, and shall devour the whole earth, and shall tread it down, and break it in pieces.

---

to be done, would be a complete fulfilment of all that is here said. Thus far the description of what Daniel saw, of which he was so desirous to obtain an explanation. The explanation follows, and embraces the remainder of the chapter.

23-27. *Thus he said,* &c. That is, in explanation of the fourth symbol which appeared—the fourth beast, and of the events connected with his appearing. This explanation embraces the remainder of the chapter; and as the whole subject appeared difficult and momentous to Daniel before the explanation, so it may be said to be in many respects difficult, and in all respects momentous still. It is a question on which expositors of the Scriptures are by no means agreed, to what it refers, and whether it has been already accomplished, or whether it extends still into the future ; and it is of importance, therefore, to determine, if possible, what is its true meaning. The two points of inquiry which are properly before us are, first, What do the words of explanation as used by the angel fairly imply—that is, what, according to the fair interpretation of these words, would be the course of events referred to, or what should we naturally expect to find as actually occurring on the earth in the fulfilment of this ? and, secondly, To what events the prophecy is actually to be applied—whether to what has already occurred, or what is yet to occur; whether we can find anything in what is now past which would be an accomplishment of this, or whether it is to be applied to events a part of which are yet future ? This will lead us into a statement of the *points* which it is affirmed would occur in regard to this kingdom: and then into an inquiry respecting the application.

What is fairly implied in the explanation of the angel ? This would embrace the following points :—

(1.) There was to be a fourth kingdom on the earth :—*the fourth beast*

shall be the fourth kingdom upon earth, ver. 23. This was to succeed the other three, symbolized by the lion, the bear, and the leopard. No further reference is made to them, but the characteristics of this are fully stated. Those characteristics, which have been explained in the Notes on ver. 7, are, as here repeated, (*a*) that it would be in important respects different from the others ; (*b*) that it would devour or subdue the whole earth ; (*c*) that it would tread it down and break it in pieces ; that is, it would be a universal dynasty, of a fierce and warlike character, that would keep the whole world subdued and subject by power.

(2.) Out of this sovereignty or dominion, ten powers would arise (ver. 24) :—*and the ten horns out of this kingdom* are *ten kings* that *shall arise.* Comp. Notes on ver. 7. That is, they would spring out of this one dominion, or it would be broken up into these minor sovereignties, yet all manifestly springing from the one kingdom, and wielding the same power. We should not naturally look for the fulfilment of this in a *succession* of kings ; for that would have been symbolized by the beast itself representing the entire dominion or dynasty, but rather to a number of contemporaneous powers that had somehow sprung out of the one power, or that now possessed and wielded the power of that one dominion. If the kingdom here referred to should be broken up into such a number of powers, or if in any way these powers became possessed of this authority, and wielded it, such a fact would express what we are to expect to find in this kingdom.

(3.) From the midst of these sovereignties or kingdoms there was to spring up another one of peculiar characteristics, vers. 24, 25. These characteristics are the following : (*a*) That it would spring out of the others, or be, as it were, one form of the administration of the same power—as the eleventh horn sprang from the same source as

24 And the ten horns out of this kingdom *are* ten kings *that* shall arise : and another shall rise after them ; and he shall be diverse from the first, and he shall subdue three kings.

the ten, and we are, therefore, to look for the exercise of this power somehow in connection with the same kingdom or dynasty. (*b*) This would not spring up contemporaneously with the ten, but would arise "after them"—and we are to look for this power as in some sense *succeeding* them. (*c*.) It would be small at first—as was the horn (ver. 8), and we are to look for the fulfilment in some power that would be feeble at first. (*d*) It would grow to be a mighty power—for the little horn became so powerful as to pluck up three of the others (ver. 8), and it is said in the explanation (ver. 24), that he would subdue three of the kings. (*e*) It would subdue "three kings;" that is, three of the ten, and we are to look for the fulfilment in some manifestation of that power by which, either literally three of them were overthrown, or by which about one-third of their power was taken away. The mention of the exact number of "three," however, would rather seem to imply that we are to expect some such exact fulfilment, or some prostration of three sovereignties by the new power that would arise. (*f*) It would be proud, and ambitious, and particularly arrogant against God:—"*and he shall speak great words against the Most High*," ver. 25. The Chaldee here rendered *against*—ˈ:ˈ—means, literally, *at*, or *against the part of it*, and then *against*. Vulg. *contra;* Gr. πρὸς. This would be fulfilled in one who would blaspheme God directly; or who would be rebellious against his government and authority; or who would complain of his administration and laws; or who would give utterance to harsh and reproachful words against his real claims. It would find a fulfilment obviously in an open opposer of the claims and the authority of the true God; or in one the whole spirit and bearing of whose pretensions might be fairly construed as in fact an utterance of great words against him. (*g*) This

would be a persecuting power :—"*and shall wear out the saints of the Most High*," ver. 25. That is, it would be characterized by a persecution of the real saints—of those who were truly the friends of God, and who served him. (*h*) It would claim legislative power, the power of changing established customs and laws : — "*and think to change times and laws*," ver. 25. The word rendered *think* (סְבַר)

means, more properly, to *hope;* and the idea here is, that he hopes and trusts to be able to change times and laws. Vulg., *Putabit quòd possit mutare tempora*, &c. The state of mind here referred to would be that of one who would *desire* to produce changes in regard to the times and laws referred to, and who would hope that he would be able to effect it. If there was a strong wish to do this, and if there was a belief that in any way he could bring it about, it would meet what is implied in the use of the word here. There would be the exercise of some kind of authority in regard to existing times for festivals, or other occasions, and to existing laws, and there would be a purpose so to change them as to accomplish his own ends.

The word *times*—זִמְנִין—would seem

to refer properly to some stated or designated times—as times appointed for festivals, &c. Gesenius, "*time*, specially *an appointed time, season:*" Eccles. iii. 1 ; Neh. ii. 6 ; Esth. ix. 27, 31. Lengerke renders the word *Fest-Zeiten*—"festival times," and explains it as meaning *the holy times, festival days*, Lev. xxiii. 2, 4, 37, 44. The allusion is, undoubtedly, to such periods set apart as festivals or fasts—seasons consecrated to the services of religion; and the kind of jurisdiction which the power here referred to would hope and desire to set up would be to have control of these periods, and so to change and alter them as to accomplish his own purposes—either by abolishing

25 And he shall speak *great* words against the Most High, and shall wear out the saints of the | Most High, and think to change times and laws: and they shall be given into his hand, until a time

those in existence, or by substituting others in their place. At all times these seasons have had a direct connection with the state and progress of religion; and he who has power over them, either to abolish existing festivals, or to substitute others in their places, or to appoint new festivals, has an important control over the whole subject of religion, and over a nation. The word rendered *laws* here—דָּת—while it might refer to any law, would more properly designate laws pertaining to religion. See Dan. vi. 5, 7, 12 (6, 9, 13); Ezra vii. 12, 21. So Lengerke explains it as referring to the laws of religion, or to religion. The kind of jurisdiction, therefore, referred to in this place would be that which would pertain to the laws and institutions of religion; it would be a purpose to obtain the control of these; it would be a claim of right to abolish such as existed, and to institute new ones; it would be a determination to exert this power in such a way as to promote its own ends. (*i*) It would continue for a definite period:—*and they shall be given into his hands until a time and times and the dividing of time*, ver. 25. *They;* that is, either those laws, or the people, the powers referred to. Maurer refers this to the "saints of the Most High," as meaning that *they* would be delivered into his hands. Though this is not designated expressly, yet perhaps it is the most natural construction, as meaning that he would have jurisdiction over the saints during this period; and if so, then the meaning is, that he would have absolute control over them, or set up a dominion over them, for the time specified—the time, and times, &c. In regard to this expression "a time and times," &c., it is unnecessary to say that there has been great diversity of opinion among expositors, and that many of the controversies in respect to future events turn on the sense attached to this and to the similar expressions which occur in the book of Revelation. The first and main

inquiry pertains, of course, to its literal and proper signification. The word used here rendered *time, times, time*—עִדָּנִין עִדָּן—is a word which in itself would no more designate any definite and fixed period than our word *time* does. See ch. ii. 8, 9, 21; iii. 5, 15; iv. 16, 23, 25, 32; vii. 12. In some of these instances, the period *actually referred to* was a year (ch. iv. 16, 23), but this is not necessarily implied in the word used, but the limitation is demanded by the circumstances of the case. So far as the *word* is concerned, it would denote a day, a week, a month, a year, or a larger or smaller division of time, and the period actually intended to be designated must be determined from the connection. The Latin Vulgate is indefinite—*ad tempus;* so the Greek—ἕως καιροῦ; so the Syriac, and so Luther—*eine Zeit;* and so Lengerke—*eine Zeit.* The phrase "for a time" expresses accurately the meaning of the original word. The word rendered "*times*" is the same word in the plural, though evidently with a dual signification.—Gesenius, *Lex.*; Lengerke, *in loc.* The obvious meaning is two such times as is designated by the former "time." The phrase "and the dividing of a time" means clearly *half* of such a period. Thus, if the period denoted by a "time" here be a year, the whole period would be three years and a half. Designations of time like this, or of this same period, occur several times in the prophecies (Daniel and Revelation), and on their meaning much depends in regard to the interpretation of the prophecies pertaining to the future. This period of three years and a half equals forty-two months, or twelve hundred and sixty days—the periods mentioned in Rev. xi. 2; xii. 6, and on which so much depends in the interpretation of that book. The only question of importance in regard to the period of time here designated is, whether this is to be taken literally to denote three years and a half, or whether a symbo-

and times and the dividing of time.

26 But the judgment shall sit, and they shall take away his dominion, to consume and to destroy *it* unto the end.

lical method is to be adopted, by making each one of the days represent a year, thus making the time referred to, in fact, twelve hundred and sixty years. On this question expositors are divided, and probably will continue to be, and according as one or the other view is adopted, they refer the events here to Antiochus Epiphanes, or to the Papal power ; or perhaps it should be said more accurately, according as they are disposed to refer the events here to Antiochus or to the Papacy, do they embrace one or the other method of interpretation in regard to the meaning of the days. At this point in the examination of the passage, the only object is to look at it *exegetically ;* to examine it *as language* apart from the application, or unbiassed by any purpose of application ; and though absolute certainty cannot perhaps be obtained, yet the following may be regarded as exegetically probable :— (1.) The word *time* may be viewed as denoting *a year :* I mean a year rather than a week, a month, or any other period — because a year is a more marked and important portion of time, and because a day, a week, a month, is so short that it cannot be reasonably supposed that it is intended. As there is no *larger* natural period than a year—no cycle in nature that is so marked and obvious as to be properly suggested by the word *time*, it cannot be supposed that any such cycle is intended. And as there is so much *particularity* in the language used here, "a time, and times, and half a time," it is to be presumed that some definite and marked period is intended, and that it is not time in general. It may be presumed, therefore, that in some sense of the term the period of a *year* is referred to. (2.) The language does not forbid the application to a literal year, and then the actual time designated would be three years and a half. No laws of exegesis, nothing in the language itself, could be regarded as violated, if such an interpretation were given to the language, and so far as this point is concerned, there would be no room for debate. (3.) The same remark may be made as to the symbolical application of the language—taking it for a much longer period than literally three years and a half; that is, regarding each day as standing for a year, and thus considering it as denoting twelve hundred and sixty years. This could not be shown to be a violation of prophetic usage, or to be forbidden by the nature of prophetic language, because nothing is more common than symbols, and because there are actual instances in which such an interpretation must be understood. Thus in Ezek. iv. 6, where the prophet was commanded to lie upon his right side forty days, it is expressly said that it was symbolical or emblematical : "I have appointed thee each day for a year." No one can doubt that it would be strictly consistent with prophetic usage to suppose that the time here *might* be symbolical, and that a longer time might be referred to than the literal interpretation would require. (4.) It may be added, that there are some circumstances, even considering the passage with reference only to the interpretation of the language, and with no view to the question of its application, which would make this appear *probable*. Among these circumstances are the following : (*a*) The fact that, in the prophecies, it is unusual to designate the *time* literally. Very few instances can be referred to in which this is done. It is commonly by some symbol ; some mark ; some peculiarity of the time or age referred to, that the designation is made, or by some symbol that may be understood when the event has occurred. (*b*) *This* designation of time occurs in the midst of symbols—where all is symbol—the beasts, the horns, the little horn, &c. ; and it would seem to be much more probable that such a method would be adopted as designating the time referred to than a *literal* method. (*c*) It is quite apparent on the mere perusal of the passage here

27 And the kingdom and dominion, and the greatness of the kingdom under the whole heaven, shall be given to the people of the saints of the Most High, whose kingdom *is* an everlasting kingdom, and all

1 or, *rulers.*

dominions¹ shall serve and obey him.

28 Hitherto *is* the end of the matter. As for me Daniel, my cogitations much troubled me, and my countenance changed in me: but I kept the matter in my heart.

that the events do actually extend far into the future—far beyond what would be denoted by the brief period of three and a half years. This will be considered more fully in another place in the inquiry as to the meaning of these prophecies. (See also Editor's Preface to volume on Revelation.)

(4.) A fourth point in the explanation given by the interpreter to Daniel is, that there would be a solemn judgment in regard to this power, and that the dominion conceded to it over the saints for a time would be utterly taken away, and the power itself destroyed :—*but the judgment shall sit, and they shall take away his dominion, to consume, and to destroy* it *unto the end,* ver. 26. That is, it *shall be* taken away ; it shall come entirely to an end. The interpreter does not say *by whom* this would be done, but he asserts the fact, and that the destruction of the dominion would be final. That is, it would entirely and forever cease. This would be done by an act of Divine judgment, or as if a solemn judgment should be held, and a sentence pronounced. It would be *as* manifestly an act of God as if he should sit as a judge, and pronounce sentence. See Notes on vers. 9–11.

(5.) And a fifth point in the explanation of the interpreter is, that the dominion under the whole heaven would be given to the saints of the Most High, and that all nations should serve him ; that is, that there would be a universal prevalence of righteousness on the earth, and that God would reign in the hearts and lives of men, ver. 27. See Notes on vers. 13, 14.

28. *Hitherto* is *the end of the matter.* That is, the end of what I saw and heard. This is the sum of what was disclosed to the prophet, but he still says that he meditated on it with profound interest, and that he had much

solicitude in regard to these great events. The words rendered *hitherto,* mean, *so far,* or *thus far.* The phrase "end of the matter," means "the close of the saying a thing ;" that is, this was all the revelation which was made to him, and he was left to his own meditations respecting it. ¶ *As for me Daniel.* So far as I was concerned ; or so far as this had any effect on me. It was not unnatural, at the close of this remarkable vision, to state the effect that it had on himself. ¶ *My cogitations much troubled me.* My thoughts in regard to it. It was a subject which he could not avoid reflecting on, and which could not but produce deep solicitude in regard to the events which were to occur. Who could look into the future without anxious and agitating thought? These events were such as to engage the profoundest attention ; such as to fix the mind in solemn thought. Compare Notes on Rev. v. 4. ¶ *And my countenance changed in me.* The effect of these revelations depicted themselves on my countenance. The prophet does not say in what way—whether by making him pale, or careworn, or anxious, but merely that it produced a change in his appearance. The Chaldee is *brightness -* זִיו and the meaning would seem to be, that his bright and cheerful countenance was changed ; that is, that his bright looks were changed ; either by becoming pale (Gesenius, Lengerke), or by becoming serious and thoughtful. ¶ *But I kept the matter in my heart.* I communicated to no one the cause of my deep and anxious thoughts. He hid the whole subject in his own mind, until he thought proper to make this record of what he had seen and heard. Perhaps there was no one to whom he could communicate the matter who would credit it ; perhaps there was no one at court who would sympathize with him; perhaps he thought that it might savour of vanity if it were known; perhaps he felt that as no one could throw any new light on the subject, there would be no use in making it a subject of conversation; perhaps he felt so overpowered that he could not readily converse on it.

We are prepared now, having gone through with an exposition of this chapter, as to the meaning of the symbols, the words, and the phrases, to endeavour to ascertain what events are referred to in this remarkable prophecy, and to ask what events it was designed should be pourtrayed. And in reference to this there are but two opinions, or two classes of interpretations, that require notice: that which refers it primarily and exclusively to Antiochus Epiphanes, and that which refers it to the rise and character of the Papal power; that which regards the fourth beast as referring to the empire of Alexander, and the little horn to Antiochus, and that which regards the fourth beast as referring to the Roman empire, and the little horn to the Papal dominion. In inquiring which of these is the true interpretation, it will be proper, first, to consider whether it is applicable to Antiochus Epiphanes; secondly, whether it in fact finds a fulfilment in the Roman empire and the Papacy; and, thirdly, if such is the proper application, what are we to look for in the future in what remains unfulfilled in regard to the prophecy.

I. The question whether it is applicable to the case of Antiochus Epiphanes. A large class of interpreters, of the most respectable character, among whom are Lengerke, Maurer, Prof. Stuart (*Hints on the Interpretation of Prophecy*, p. 86, *seq.;* also *Com. on Daniel*, pp. 205–211), Eichhorn, Bertholdt, Bleek, and many

others, suppose that the allusion to Antiochus is clear, and that the primary, if not the exclusive, reference to the prophecy is to him. Professor Stuart (*Hints*, p. 86) says, "The passage in Daniel vii. 25 is so clear as to leave no reasonable room for doubt." "In vers. 8, 20, 24, the rise of Antiochus Epiphanes is described; for the fourth beast is, beyond all reasonable doubt, the divided Grecian dominion which succeeded the reign of Alexander the Great. From this dynasty springs Antiochus, vers. 8, 20, who is most graphically described in ver. 25 'as one who shall speak great words against the Most High,' &c."

The *facts* in regard to Antiochus, so far as they are necessary to be known in the inquiry, are briefly these:—Antiochus Epiphanes (*the Illustrious,* a name taken on himself, Prideaux, iii. 213), was the son of Antiochus the Great, but succeeded his brother, Seleucus Philopator, who died B.C. 176. Antiochus reigned over Syria, the capital of which was Antioch, on the Orontes, from B.C. 176 to B.C. 164. His character, as that of a cruel tyrant, and a most bloodthirsty and bitter enemy of the Jews, is fully detailed in the first and second book of Maccabees. Comp. also Prideaux, *Con.* vol. iii. 213–234. The facts in the case of Antiochus, so far as they are supposed to bear on the application of the prophecy before us, are thus stated by Prof. Stuart (*Hints on the Interpretation of Prophecy*, pp. 89, 90): "In the year 168 before Christ, in the month of May, Antiochus Epiphanes was on his way to attack Egypt, and he detached Apollonius, one of his military confidants, with 22,000 soldiers, in order to subdue and plunder Jerusalem. The mission was executed with entire success. A horrible slaughter was made of the men at Jerusalem, and a large portion of the women and children, being made captives, were sold and treated as slaves. The services of the temple were interrupted, and its joyful feasts were turned into mourning, 1 Mac. i. 37–39. Soon after this the Jews in general were compelled to eat swine's flesh, and to sacrifice to idols. In December of that same year, the temple was profaned by introducing the statue of Jupiter Olympius ; and on the 25th of that month sacrifices were offered to that idol on the altar of Jehovah. Just three years after this last event, viz., December 25, 165 B.C., the temple was expurgated by Judas Maccabeus, and the worship of Jehovah restored. Thus, *three years and a half*, or almost exactly this period, passed away, while Antiochus had complete possession and control of everything in and around Jerusalem and the temple. It may be noted, also, that just three years passed, from the time when the profanation of the temple was carried to its greatest height —viz., by sacrificing to the statue of Jupiter Olympius on the altar of Jehovah, down to the time when Judas renewed the regular worship. I mention this last circumstance in order to account for the *three years* of Antiochus' profanations, which are named as the period of them in Josephus, *Ant.* xii. 7, § 6. This period tallies exactly with the time during which the profanation as consummated was carried on, if we reckon down to the period when the temple worship was restored by Judas Maccabeus. But in *Prœm. ad Bell. Jud.* § 7, and *Bell. Jud.* l. 1, § 1, Josephus reckons three years and a half as the period during which Antiochus ravaged Jerusalem and Judea."

In regard to this statement, while the general facts are correct, there are some additional statements which should be made, to determine as to its real bearing on the case. The act of detaching Apollonius to attack Jerusalem was not, as is stated in this extract, when Antiochus was on his way to Egypt, but was on his return from Egypt, and was just two years after Jerusalem had been taken by Antiochus.—Prideaux, iii. 239. The *occasion* of his detaching Apollonius, was that Antiochus was enraged because he had been defeated in Egypt by the Romans, and resolved to vent all his wrath upon the Jews, who at that time had given him no particular offence. When, two years before, Antiochus had himself taken Jerusalem, he slew forty thousand persons ; he took as many captives, and sold them for slaves ; he forced himself into the temple, and entered the most holy place ; he caused a great sow to be offered on the altar of burnt-offering, to show his contempt for the temple and the Jewish religion ; he sprinkled the broth over every part of the temple for the purpose of polluting it ; he plundered the temple of the altar of incense, the shew-bread table, and the golden candlestick, and then returned to Antioch, having appointed Philip, a Phrygian, a man of a cruel and barbarous temper, to be governor of the Jews.—Prideaux, iii. 231. When Apollonius again attacked the city, two years afterwards, he waited quietly until the Sabbath, and then made his assault. He filled the city with blood, set it on fire, demolished the houses, pulled down the walls, built a strong fortress over against the temple, from which the garrison could fall on all who should attempt to go to worship. From this time, "the temple became deserted, and the daily sacrifices were omitted," until the service was restored by Judas Maccabeus, three years and a half after. The *time* during which this continued was, in fact, just three years and a half, until Judas Maccabeus succeeded in expelling the heathen from the temple and from Jerusalem, when the temple was purified, and was solemnly reconsecrated to the worship of God. See Prideaux, *Con.* iii. 240, 241, and the authorities there cited.

Now, in reference to this interpretation, supposing that the prophecy relates to Antiochus, it must be admitted that there are coincidences which are remarkable, and it is on the ground of these coincidences that the prophecy has been applied to him. These circumstances are such as the following : (*a*) The general character of the authority that would exist as denoted by the "little horn," as that of severity and cruelty. None could be better fitted to represent that than the character of Antiochus Epiphanes. Comp. Prideaux, *Con.* iii. 213, 214. (*b*) His arrogance and blasphemy— "speaking great words against the Most High." Nothing is easier than to find what would be a fulfilment of this in the character of Antiochus— in his sacrilegious entrance into the most holy places ; in his setting up the statue of Jupiter ; in his offering a sow as a sacrifice on the great altar ; in his sprinkling the broth of swine on the temple in contempt of the Hebrews and their worship, and in his causing the daily sacrifice at the temple to cease. (*c*) His making war with the "saints," and "wearing out the saints of the Most High"—all this could be found accomplished in the wars which Antiochus waged against the Jews in the slaughter of so many thousands, and in sending so many into hopeless slavery. (*d*) His attempt to "change times and laws"—this could be found to have been fulfilled in the case of Antiochus—in his arbitrary character, and in his interference with the laws of the Hebrews. (*e*) The *time*, as above stated, is the most remarkable coincidence. If this is *not* to be regarded as referring exclusively to Antiochus, it must be explained on one of two suppositions—either that it is one of those coincidences which *will* be found to happen in history, as coincidences happen in dreams ; or as having a double reference, intended to refer primarily to Antiochus, but in a secondary and more important sense referring also to other events having a strong resemblance to this ; or, in other words, that the language was designedly so couched as to relate to two similar classes of events. It is not to be regarded as very remarkable, however, that it is possible to find a fulfilment of these predictions in Antiochus, though it be supposed that the design was to describe the Papacy, for some of the expressions are of so general a character that they could be applied to many events which have occurred, and, from the nature of the case, there were strong points of resemblance between Antiochus and the Papal power. It is not absolutely necessary, therefore, to suppose that this had reference to Antiochus Epiphanes ; and there are so many *objections* to this view as to make it, it seems to me, morally impossible that it should have had such a reference. Among these objections are the following :—

(1.) This interpretation makes it necessary to divide the kingdom of the Medes and Persians, and to consider them two kingdoms, as Eichhorn, Jahn, Dereser, De Wette, and Bleek do. In order to this interpretation, the following are the kingdoms denoted by the four beasts—by the first, the Chaldee ; by the second, the Medish ; by the third, the Persian ; and by the fourth, the Macedonian, or the Macedonian-Asiatic kingdom under Alexander the Great. But to say nothing now of any other difficulties, it is an insuperable objection to this, that so far as the kingdoms of the Medes and Persians are mentioned in Scripture, and so far as they play any part in the fulfilment of prophecy, they are always mentioned as *one*. They appear as one; they act as one; they are regarded as one. The kingdom of the Medes does not appear until it is united with that of the Persians, and this remark is of special importance when they are spoken of as *succeeding* the kingdom of Babylon. The kingdom of the Medes was contemporaneous with that of Babylon; it was the Medo-Persian kingdom that was in any proper sense the successor of that of Babylon, as described in these symbols. The kingdom of the Medes, as Hengstenberg well remarks, could in no sense be said to have succeeded that of Babylon any longer than during the reign of Cyaxares II., after the taking of Babylon: and even during that short period of two years, the government was in fact in the hands of Cyrus.—*Die Authentie des Daniel*, p. 200. Schlosser (p. 243) says, " the kingdom of the Medes and Persians is to be regarded as in fact one and the same kingdom, only that in the change of the dynasty another branch obtained the authority." See particularly, Rosenmüller, *Alterthumskunde*, i. 290, 291. These two kingdoms are in fact always blended—their laws, their customs, their religion, and they are mentioned as one. Comp. Esth. i. 3, 18, 19; x. 2; Dan. v. 28; vi. 8, 12, 15.

(2.) In order to this interpretation, it is necessary to divide the empire founded by Alexander, and instead of regarding it as one, to consider that which existed when he reigned as one, and that of Antiochus, one of the successors of Alexander, as another. This opinion is maintained by Bertholdt, who supposes that the first beast represented the Babylonian kingdom; the second, the kingdom of the Medes and Persians; the third, that of Alexander; and the fourth the kingdoms that sprang out of that. In order to this, it is necessary to suppose that the four heads and wings, and the ten horns, equally represent that kingdom, or sprang from it—the four heads, the kingdom when divided at the death of Alexander, and the ten horns, powers that ultimately sprang up from the same dominion. But this is contrary to the whole representation in regard to the Asiatic-Macedonian empire. In ch. viii. 8, 9, where there is an undoubted reference to that empire, it is said " the he-goat waxed very great: and when he was strong, the great horn was broken; and for it came up four notable ones toward the four winds of heaven. And out of one of them came forth a little horn, which waxed exceeding great, toward the south," &c. Here is an undoubted allusion to Alexander, and to his followers, and particularly to Antiochus, but no mention of any such division as is necessary to be supposed if the fourth beast represents the power that succeeded Alexander in the East. In no place is the kingdom of the successors of Alexander divided from his in the same sense in which the kingdom of the Medes and Persians is from that of Babylon, or the kingdom of Alexander from that of the Persians. Comp. Hengstenberg, as above, pp. 203–205.

(3.) The supposition that the fourth beast represents either the kingdom of Alexander, or, according to Bertholdt and others, the successors of Alexander, by no means agrees with the character of that beast as compared with the others. That beast was far more formidable, and more to be dreaded, than either of the others. It had iron teeth and brazen claws; it stamped down all before it, and broke all to pieces, and manifestly represented a far more fearful dominion than either of the others. The same is true in regard to the parallel representation in ch. ii. 33, 40, of the fourth kingdom represented by the legs and feet of iron, as more terrific than either of those denoted by the gold, the silver, or the brass. But this representation by no means agrees with the character of the kingdom of either Alexander or his successors, and in fact would not be true of them. It would agree well, as we shall see, with the Roman power, even as contrasted with that of Babylon, Persia, or Macedon; but it is not the representation which would, with propriety, be given of the empire of Alexander, or his successors, as contrasted with those which preceded them. Comp. Hengstenberg, as above, pp. 205-207. Moreover, this does not agree with what is expressly said of this power that should succeed that of Alexander, in a passage undoubtedly referring to it, in ch. viii. 22, where it is said, "Now that being broken, whereas four stood up for it, four kingdoms shall stand up out of the nation, *but not in his power.*"

(4.) On this supposition it is impossible to determine who are meant by the "ten horns" of the fourth beast (ver. 7), and the "ten kings" (ver. 24) that are represented by these. All the statements in Daniel that refer to the Macedonian kingdom (ch. vii. 6; viii. 8, 22) imply that the Macedonian empire in the East, when the founder died, would be divided into four great powers or monarchies — in accordance with what is well known to have been the fact. But who are the ten kings or sovereignties that were to exist under this general Macedonian power, on the supposition that the fourth beast re-

presents this? Bertholdt supposes that the ten horns are "ten Syrian kings," and that the eleventh little horn is Antiochus Epiphanes. The *names* of these kings, according to Bertholdt (pp. 432, 433), are Seleucus Nicator, Antiochus Soter, Antiochus Theos, Seleucus Callinicus, Seleucus Ceraunus, Antiochus the Great, Seleucus Philopator, Heliodorus, Ptolemy Philometor, and Demetrius. So also Prof. Stuart, *Com. on Dan.* p. 208. But it is impossible to make out this exact number of *Syrian* kings from history, to say nothing now of the improbability of supposing that their power was represented by the fourth beast. These kings were not of the same dynasty, of Syria, of Macedonia, or of Egypt, but the list is made up of different kingdoms. Grotius (*in loc.*) forms the catalogue of ten kings out of the lists of the kings of Syria and Egypt—five out of one, and five out of the other; but this is manifestly contrary to the intention of the prophecy, which is to represent them as springing out of one and the same power. It is a further objection to this view, that these are lists of *successive* kings—rising up one after the other; whereas the representation of the ten horns would lead us to suppose that they existed *simultaneously;* or that somehow there were ten powers that sprang out of the one great power represented by the fourth beast.

(5.) Equally difficult is it, on this supposition, to know who are intended by the "three horns" that were plucked up by the little horn that sprang up among the ten, ver. 8. Grotius, who regards the "little horn" as representing Antiochus Epiphanes, supposes that the three horns were his elder brothers, Seleucus, Demetrius, the son of Seleucus, and Ptolemy Philopator, king of Egypt. But it is an insuperable objection to this that the three kings mentioned by Grotius are not all in his list of ten kings, neither Ptolemy Philometor (if Philometor he meant), nor Demetrius being of the number.— Newton *on the Proph.* p. 211. Neither were they plucked up by the roots by Antiochus, or by his order. Seleucus was poisoned by his treasurer, Heliodorus, whose aim it was to usurp the crown for himself, before Antiochus came from Rome, where he had been detained as a hostage for several years. Demetrius lived to dethrone and murder the son of Antiochus, and succeeded him in the kingdom of Syria. Ptolemy Philopator died king of Egypt almost thirty years before Antiochus came to the throne of Syria; or if Ptolemy Philometor, as is most probable, was meant by Grotius, though he suffered much in the wars with Antiochus, yet he survived him about eighteen years, and died in possession of the crown of Egypt.—Newton, *ut supra.* Bertholdt supposes that the three kings were Heliodorus, who poisoned Seleucus Philopator, and sought, by the help of a party, to obtain the throne; Ptolemy Philometor, king of Egypt, who, as sister's son to the king, laid claim to the throne; and Demetrius, who, as son of the former king, was legitimate heir to the throne. But there are two objections to this view; (*a*) that the representation by the prophet is of *actual* kings—which these were not; and (*b*) that Antiochus ascended the throne *peaceably;* Demetrius, who would have been regarded as the king of Syria, not being able to make his title good, was detained as a hostage at Rome. Hengstenberg, pp. 207, 208. Prof. Stuart, *Com. on Dan.,* pp. 208, 209, supposes that the three kings referred to were Heliodorus, Ptolemy Philometor, and Demetrius I.; but in

DANIEL II.

regard to these it should be observed, that they were mere *pretenders* to the throne, whereas the text in Daniel supposes that they would be *actual* kings. Comp. Hengstenberg, p. 208.

(6.) The *time* here mentioned, on the supposition that literally three years and a half (ver. 25) are intended, does not agree with the actual dominion of Antiochus. In an undoubted reference to him in ch. viii. 13, 14, it is said that "the vision concerning the daily sacrifice, and the transgression of desolation," would be "unto two thousand and three hundred days; then shall the sanctuary be cleansed;" that is, one thousand and forty days, or some two years and ten months more than the time mentioned here. I am aware of the difficulty of explaining this (see Prof. Stuart, *Hints on the Interpretation of Prophecy,* p. 98, *seq.*), and the exact meaning of the passage in ch. viii. 13, 14, will come up for consideration hereafter; but it is an objection of some force to the application of the "time, and times, and dividing of a time" (ver. 25) to Antiochus, that it is not the *same* time which is applied to him elsewhere.

(7.) And one more objection to this application is, that, in the prophecy, it is said that he who was represented by the "little horn" would continue till "the Ancient of days should sit," and evidently till the kingdom should be taken by the one in the likeness of the Son of man, vers. 9, 10, 13, 14, 21, 22, 26. But if this refers to Antiochus, then these events must refer to the coming of the Messiah, and to the setting up of his kingdom in the world. Yet, as a matter of fact, Antiochus died about 164 years before the Saviour came, and there is no way of showing that he *continued* until the Messiah came in the flesh.

F

These objections to the opinion that this refers to Antiochus Epiphanes seem to me to be insuperable.

II. The question whether it refers to the Roman empire and the Papal power. The fair inquiry is, whether the things referred to in the vision actually find such a correspondence in the Roman empire and the Papacy, that they would fairly represent them if the symbols had been made use of *after* the events occurred. Are they such as we might properly use now as describing the portions of those events that are *past*, on the supposition that the reference was to those events? To determine this, it will be proper to refer to the things in the symbol, and to inquire whether events corresponding to them have actually occurred in the Roman empire and the Papacy. Recalling the exposition which has been above given of the explanation furnished by the angel to Daniel, the things there referred to will find an ample and a striking fulfilment in the Roman empire and the Papal power.

(1.) The fourth kingdom, symbolized by the fourth beast, is accurately represented by the Roman power. This is true in regard to the *place* which that power would occupy in the history of the world, on the supposition that the first three referred to the Babylonian, the Medo-Persian, and the Macedonian. On this supposition there is no need of regarding the Medo-Persian empire as divided into two, represented by two symbols; or the kingdom founded by Alexander—the Asiatic-Macedonian—as distinct from that of his successors. As the Medo-Persian was in fact one dominion, so was the Macedonian under Alexander, and in the form of the four dynasties into which it was divided on his death, and down to the time when the whole was subverted by the Roman conquests. On this supposition, also, everything in the symbol is fulfilled. The fourth beast —so mighty, so terrific, so powerful, so unlike all the others, armed with iron teeth, and with claws of brass, trampling down and stamping on all the earth—well represents the Roman dominion. The symbol is such a one as we should now use appropriately to represent that power, and in every respect that empire was well represented by the symbol. It may be added, also, that this supposition corresponds with the obvious interpretation of the parallel place in chapter ii. 33, 40, where the same empire is referred to in the image by the legs and feet of iron. See Notes on that passage. It should be added, that this fourth kingdom is to be considered as prolonged through the entire continuance of the *Roman* power, in the various forms in which that power has been kept up on the earth—alike under the empire, and when broken up into separate sovereignties, and when again concentrated and embodied under the Papacy. That *fourth* power or dominion was to be continued, according to the prediction here, until the establishment of the kingdom of the saints. Either, then, that kingdom of the saints has come, or has been set up, or the fourth kingdom, in some form, still remains. The truth is, that in prophecy the entire Roman dominion seems to be contemplated as *one*—one mighty and formidable power trampling down the liberties of the world; oppressing and persecuting the people of God—the true church; and maintaining an absolute and arbitrary dominion over the souls of men—as a mighty domination standing in the way of the progress of truth, and keeping back the reign of the saints on the earth. In these respects the Papal dominion is, and has been, but a prolongation, in another form, of the influence of heathen Rome, and the entire domination may be represented as one, and might be symbolized by the fourth beast in the vision of Daniel. When that power shall cease, we may, according to the prophecy, look for the time when the "kingdom shall be given to the saints," or when the true kingdom of God shall be set up all over the world.

(2.) Out of this one sovereignty, represented by the fourth beast, ten powers or sovereignties, represented by the ten horns, were to arise. It was shown in the exposition, that these would all spring out of that one dominion, and would wield the power that was wielded by that; that is, that the one great power would be broken up and distributed into the number represented by ten. As the horns all appeared at the same time on the beast, and did not spring up after one another, so these powers would be simultaneous, and would not be a mere succession; and as the horns all sprang from the beast, so these powers would all have the same origin, and be a portion of the same one power now divided into many. The question then is, whether the Roman power was in fact distributed into so many sovereignties at any period such as would be represented by the springing up of the little horn—if that refers to the Papacy. Now, one has only to look into any historical work, to see how in fact the Roman power became distributed and broken up in this way into a large number of kingdoms, or comparatively petty sovereignties, occupying the portions of the world once governed by Rome. In the decline of the empire, and as the new power represented by the "little horn" arose, there was a complete breaking up of the one power that was formerly wielded, and a large number of states and kingdoms sprang out of it. To see that there is no difficulty

in making out the number *ten*, or that some such distribution and breaking up of the one power is naturally suggested, I cast my eye on the historical chart of Lyman, and found the following kingdoms or sovereignties specified as occupying the same territory which was possessed by the Roman empire, and springing from that—viz., the Vandals, Alans, Suevi, Heruli, Franks, Visigoths, Ostrogoths, Burgundians, Lombards, Britons. The Roman empire as such had ceased, and the power was distributed into a large number of comparatively petty sovereignties— well represented at this period by the ten horns on the head of the beast. Even the Romanists themselves admit that the Roman empire was, by means of the incursions of the northern nations, dismembered into ten kingdoms (Calmet on Rev. xiii. 1; and he refers likewise to Berengaud, Bossuet, and Dupin. See Newton, p. 209); and Machiaveli (*Hist. of Flor.* l. i.), with no design of furnishing an illustration of this prophecy, and probably with no recollection of it, has mentioned these names:—1, the Ostrogoths in Mœsia; 2, the Visigoths in Pannonia; 3, the Sueves and Alans in Gascoign and Spain; 4, the Vandals in Africa; 5, the Franks in France; 6, the Burgundians in Burgundy; 7, the Heruli and Turingi in Italy; 8, the Saxons and Angles in Britain; 9, the Huns in Hungary; 10, the Lombards at first upon the Danube, afterwards in Italy. The arrangement proposed by Sir Isaac Newton is the following:—1, The kingdom of the Vandals and Alans in Spain and Africa; 2, the kingdom of the Suevians in Spain; 3, the kingdom of the Visigoths; 4, the kingdom of the Alans in Gallia; 5, the kingdom of the Burgundians; 6, the kingdom of the Franks; 7, the kingdom of the Britons; 8, the kingdom of the Huns;

9, the kingdom of the Lombards; 10, the kingdom of Ravenna. Comp. also Duffield *on the Prophecies*, pp. 279, 280. For other arrangements constituting the number *ten*, as embracing the ancient power of the Roman empire, see Newton *on the Prophecies*, pp. 209, 210. There is some slight variation in the arrangements proposed by Mr. Mede, Bishop Lloyd, and Sir Isaac Newton; but still it is remarkable that it is easy to make out that number with so good a degree of certainty, and particularly so, that it should have been suggested by a Romanist himself. Even if it is not practicable to make out the number with strict exactness, or if all writers do not agree in regard to the dynasties constituting the number *ten*, we should bear in remembrance the fact that these powers arose in the midst of great confusion; that one kingdom arose and another fell in rapid succession; and that there was not that entire certainty of location and boundary which there is in old and established states. One thing is certain, that there never has been a case in which an empire of vast power has been broken up into small sovereignties, to which this description would so well apply as to the rise of the numerous dynasties in the breaking up of the vast Roman power; and another thing is equally certain, that if we were now to seek an appropriate symbol of the mighty Roman power—of its conquests, and of the extent of its dominion, and of the condition of that empire, about the time that the Papacy arose, we could not find a more striking or appropriate symbol than that of the terrible fourth beast with iron teeth and brazen claws—stamping the earth beneath his feet, and with ten horns springing out of his head.

(3.) In the midst of these there sprang up a little horn that had re-markable characteristics. The inquiry now is, if this does not represent Antiochus, whether it finds a proper fulfilment in the Papacy. Now, in regard to this inquiry, the slightest acquaintance with the history and claims of the Papal power will show that there was a striking appropriateness in the symbol—such an appropriateness, that if we desired *now* to find a symbol that would represent this, we could find no one better adapted to it than that employed by Daniel. (*a*) The little horn would spring up among the others, and stand among them—as dividing the power with them, or sharing or wielding that power. That is, on the supposition that it refers to the Papacy, the Papal power would spring out of the Roman empire; would be one of the sovereignties among which that vast power would be divided, and share with the other ten in wielding authority. It would be an eleventh power added to the ten. And who can be ignorant that the Papal power at the beginning, when it first asserted civil authority, sustained just such a relation to the crumbled and divided Roman empire as this? It was just one of the powers into which that vast sovereignty passed. (*b*) It would not spring up contemporaneously with them, but would arise in their midst, when they already existed. *They* are seen in vision as actually existing together, and this new power starts up among them. What could be more strikingly descriptive of the Papacy—as a power arising when the great Roman authority was broken to fragments, and distributed into a large number of sovereignties? Then this new power was seen to rise—small at first, but gradually gaining strength, until it surpassed any one of them in strength, and assumed a position in the world which no one of them had.

The representation is exact. It is not a foreign power that invaded them; it starts up in the midst of them—springing out of the head of the same beast, and constituting a part of the same mighty domination that ruled the world. (c) It would be small at first, but would soon become so powerful as to pluck up and displace three of .the others. And could any symbol have been better chosen to describe the Papal power than this? Could we find any *now* that would better describe it? Any one needs to have but the slightest acquaintance with the history of the Papal power to know that it was small at its beginnings, and that its ascendency over the world was the consequence of slow but steady growth. Indeed, so feeble was it at its commencement, so undefined were its first appearance and form, that one of the most difficult things in history is to know exactly when it *did* begin, or to determine the exact date of its origin as a distinct power. Different schemes in the interpretation of prophecy turn wholly on this. We see, indeed, that power subsequently strongly marked in its character, and exerting a mighty influence in the world—having subjugated nations to its control; we see causes for a long time at work tending to this, and can trace their gradual operation in producing it, but the exact period when its dominion began, what was the first characteristic act of the Papacy as such, what constituted its precise beginning as a peculiar power blending and combining a peculiar civil and ecclesiastical authority, no one is able with absolute certainty to determine. Who can fix the exact date? Who can tell precisely when it was? It is true that there were several distinct acts, or the exercise of civil authority, in the early history of the Papacy, but what was the precise *beginning* of that power no

one has been able to determine with so much certainty as to leave no room for doubt. Any one can see with what propriety the commencement of such a power would be designated by a little horn springing up among others. (d) It would grow to be mighty, for the "little horn" thus grew to be so powerful as to pluck up three of the horns of the beast. Of the growth of the power of the Papacy no one can be ignorant who has any acquaintance with history. It held nations in subjection, and claimed and exercised the right of displacing and distributing crowns as it pleased. (e) It would subdue "three kings;" that is, three of the ten represented by the ten horns. The prophet saw this at some point in its progress when *three* fell before it, or were overthrown by it. There might have been also other points in its history when it might have been seen as having overthrown more of them—perhaps the whole ten, but the attention was arrested by the fact that, soon after its rise, three of the ten were seen to fall before it. Now, in regard to the application of this, it may be remarked, (1.) That it does *not* apply, as already shown, to Antiochus Epiphanes—there being no sense in which he overthrew three of the princes that occupied the throne in the succession from Alexander, to say nothing of the fact that these were contemporaneous kings or kingdoms. (2.) There is no other period in history, and there are no other events to which it could be applied except either to Antiochus or the Papacy. (3.) In the confusion that existed on the breaking up of the Roman empire, and the imperfect accounts of the transactions which occurred in the rise of the Papal power, it would not be wonderful if it should be difficult to find events *distinctly* recorded that would be in all respects an accurate and absolute fulfilment of the vision. (4.) Yet it is possible to make out the fulfilment of this with a good degree of certainty in the history of the Papacy. If applicable to the Papal power, what seems to be demanded is, that three of these ten kingdoms, or sovereignties should be rooted up by that power; that they should cease to exist as separate sovereignties; that they should be added to the sovereignty that should spring up; and that, as distinct kingdoms, they should cease to play a part in the history of the world. The three sovereignties thus transplanted, or rooted up, are supposed by Mr. Mede to have been the Greeks, the Longobards, and the Franks. Sir Isaac Newton supposes they were the Exarchate of Ravenna, the Lombards, and the senate and dukedom of Rome. The *objections* which may be made to these suppositions may be seen in Newton *on the Prophecies*, pp. 216, 217. The kingdoms which he supposes are to be referred to were the following:—*First.* The Exarchate of Ravenna. This of right belonged to the Greek emperors. This was the capital of their dominions in Italy. It revolted at the instigation of the Pope, and was seized by Astolphus, king of the Lombards, who thought to make himself master of Italy. The Pope in his exigency applied for aid to Pepin, king of France, who marched into Italy, besieged the Lombards in Pavia, and forced them to surrender the Exarchate and other territories in Italy. These were not restored to the Greek emperor, as they in justice should have been, but, at the solicitation of the Pope, were given to St. Peter and his successors for perpetual possession. "And so," says Platina, "the name of the Exarchate, which had continued from the time of Narses to the taking of Ravenna, one

hundred and seventy years, was extinguished."—*Lives of the Popes*. This, according to Sigonius, was effected in the year 755. See Gibbon, *Dec. and Fall*, vol. ii. 224, iii. 332, 334, 338. From this period, says Bp. Newton, the Popes being now become temporal princes, no longer date their epistles and bulls by the years of the emperor's reign, but by the years of their own advancement to the Papal chair. *Secondly*. The kingdom of the Lombards. This kingdom was troublesome to the Popes. The dominions of the Pope were invaded by Desiderius, in the time of Pope Adrian I. Application was again made to the king of France, and Charles the Great, the son and successor of Pepin, invaded the Lombards; and desirous of enlarging his own dominions, conquered the Lombards, put an end to their kingdom, and gave a great part of their territory to the Pope. This was the end of the kingdom of the Lombards, in the 206th year after their obtaining possessions in Italy, and in the year of our Lord 774. See Gibbon, *Dec. and Fall*, vol. iii. 335. *Thirdly*. The Roman States subjected to the Popes in a civil sense. Though subjected to the Pope spiritually, yet for a long time the Roman people were governed by a senate, and retained many of their old privileges, and elected both the Western Emperors and the Popes. This power, however, as is well known, passed into the hands of the Popes, and has been retained by them to the present time, the Pope having continued to be the civil as well as the ecclesiastical head. See Bp. Newton, pp. 319, 320. All semblance of the freedom of ancient Rome passed away, and this Roman dominion, as such, ceased to be, being completely absorbed in the Papacy. The Saxons, the Franks, &c., continued *their* independence as civil powers; these states passed entirely into the dominion of the Pope, and as independent kingdoms or sovereignties ceased to be. This is the solution in regard to the "three horns" that were to be plucked up, as given by Bp. Newton. Absolute certainty in a case of this kind is not to be expected in the confusion and indefiniteness of that portion of history, nor can it be reasonably demanded. If there were three of these powers planted in regions that became subject to the Papal power, and that disappeared or were absorbed in that one dominion constituting the peculiarity of the Papal dominion, or which entered into the Roman Papal state, considered as a sovereignty by itself among the nations of the earth, this is all that is required. Mr. Faber supposes the three to have been these: the Herulo-Turingic, the Ostrogothic, and the Lombardic, and says of them, that they "were necessarily eradicated in the immediate presence of the Papacy, before which they were geographically standing — and that the temporal principality which bears the name of St. Peter's patrimony, was carved out of the mass of their subjugated dominions."—*Sacred Calendar*, vol. ii. p. 102. Prof. Gaussen (*Discourse on Popery:* Geneva, 1844) supposes that the three kings or kingdoms here referred to were the Heruli, the Ostrogoths, and the Lombards. According to Bower (*Lives of the Popes*, vol. ii. 108, Dr. Cox's edition, note), the temporal dominions granted by Pepin to the Pope, or of which the Pope became possessed in consequence of the intervention of the kings of France, were the following: (1) The Exarchate of Ravenna, which comprised, according to Sigonius, the following cities : — Ravenna, Bologna, Imola, Fienza, Forlimpoli, Forli, Cesena, Bobbio, Ferrara, Commachio,

Adria, Servia, and Secchia. (2.) The Pentapolis, comprehending Rimini, Pesaro, Concha, Fano, Sinigalia, Ancono, Osimo, Umono, Jesi, Fossombrone, Monteferetro, Urbino, Cagli, Lucoli, and Eugubio. (3.) The city and dukedom of Rome, containing several cities of note, which had withdrawn themselves from all subjection to the emperor, had submitted to St. Peter ever since the time of Pope Gregory II. See also Bower, ii. 134, where he says, "The Pope had, by Charlemagne, been put in possession of the Exarchate, the Pentapolis, and the dukedom of Spoleti" [embracing the city and dukedom of Rome]. And again, on the same page (note): "The Pope possessed the Exarchate, the Pentapolis, and the dukedom of Spoleti, with the city and dukedom of Rome." It should be remembered that these statements are made by historians with no reference to any supposed fulfilment of this prophecy, and no allusion to it, but as matters of simple historical fact, occurring in the regular course of history. The *material* fact to be made out in order to show that this description of the "little horn" is applicable to the Papacy is, that at the *commencement* of what was properly the *Papacy* —that is, as I suppose, the *union* of the spiritual and temporal power, or the *assumption* of temporal authority by him who was Bishop of Rome, and who had been before regarded as a mere spiritual or ecclesiastical ruler, there was a *triple* jurisdiction assumed or conceded, a threefold domination ; or a union under himself of what had been three sovereignties, that now disappeared as independent administrations, and whose distinct governments were now merged in the *one* single sovereignty of the Pope. Now, that there was, just at this time, or at the *beginning* of the Papacy, or when it had so increased that it could be recognized as having a place among the temporal sovereignties of the earth, such a united domination, or such a union of three separate powers under one, will be apparent from an extract from Mr. Gibbon. He is speaking of the rewards conferred on the Pope by the Carlovingian race of kings, on account of the favour shown to them in his conferring the crown of France on Pepin, the mayor of the palace—directing in his favour over Childeric, the descendant of Clovis. Of this transaction, Mr. Gibbon observes, in general (iij. 336), that "the mutual obligations of the Popes and the Carlovingian family form the important link of ancient and modern, of civil and ecclesiastical history." He then proceeds (1) to specify the gifts or favours which the Popes conferred on the Carlovingian race; and (2) those which, in return, Pepin and Charlemagne bestowed on the Popes. In reference to the latter, he makes the following statement (iii. 338) :—"The gratitude of the Carlovingians was adequate to these obligations, and their names are consecrated as the saviours and benefactors of the Roman church. Her ancient patrimony of farms and houses was transformed by their bounty *into the temporal dominion of cities and provinces, and the donation of the Exarchate was the first-fruits of the conquests of Pepin.* Astolphus [king of the Lombards] with a sigh relinquished his prey; the keys and the hostages of the principal cities were delivered to the French ambassador; and in his master's name *he presented them before the tomb of St. Peter.* The ample measure of the Exarchate might comprise all the provinces of Italy which had obeyed the emperor or his vicegerent; but its strict and proper limits were included in the territories of Ravenna, Bologna, and Ferrara; its inseparable dependency

was the Pentapolis, which stretched along the Adriatic from Rimini to Ancona, and advanced into the midland country as far as the ridge of the Apennines. In this transaction, the ambition and avarice of the Popes have been severely condemned. Perhaps the humility of a Christian priest should have rejected an earthly kingdom, which it was not easy for him to govern without renouncing the virtues of his profession. Perhaps a faithful subject, or even a generous enemy, would have been less impatient to divide the spoils of the barbarian; and if the emperor had intrusted Stephen to solicit in his name the restitution of the Exarchate, I will not absolve the Pope from the reproach of treachery and falsehood. But, in the rigid interpretation of the laws, every one may accept, without inquiry, whatever his benefactor may bestow without injustice. The Greek emperor had abdicated or forfeited his right to the Exarchate; and the sword of Astolphus was broken by the stronger sword of the Carlovingian. It was not in the cause of the Iconoclast that Pepin had exposed his person and army in a double expedition beyond the Alps; he possessed, and he might lawfully alienate his conquests: and to the importunities of the Greeks he piously replied, that no human consideration should tempt him to resume the gift which he had conferred on the Roman pontiff for the remission of his sins and the salvation of his soul. The splendid donation was granted in supreme and absolute dominion, *and the world beheld for the first time a Christian bishop invested with the prerogatives of a temporal prince,* the choice of magistrates, the exercise of justice, the imposition of taxes, and the wealth of the palace of Ravenna. In the dissolution of the Lombard kingdom, the inhabitants of the duchy of Spoleti sought a refuge from the storm, shaved their heads after the Ravenna fashion, declared themselves the servants and subjects of St. Peter, *and completed, by this voluntary surrender, the present circle of the Ecclesiastical State.*" The following things are apparent from this extract:—(*a*) That here, according to Mr. Gibbon, was the beginning of the temporal power of the Pope. (*b*) That this was properly, in the view above taken, the commencement of the Papacy as a distinct and peculiar dominion. (*c*) That in this there was a threefold government, or three *temporal* sovereignties united under him, and constituting at that time, in the language of Mr. Gibbon, "the present circle of the ecclesiastical state." There was, *first*, the Exarchate of Ravenna; *secondly*, the Pentapolis, "which," he says, was its "inseparable dependency;" and, *thirdly*, the "duchy of Spoleti," which, he says, "completed the present circle of the ecclesiastical state." This was afterwards, Mr. Gibbon goes on to say, greatly "enlarged;" but this was the form in which the Papal power first made its appearance among the temporal sovereignties of Europe. I do not find, indeed, that the kingdom of the *Lombards* was, as is commonly stated, among the number of the temporal sovereignties that became subject to the authority of the Popes, but I *do* find that there *were* three distinct temporal sovereignties that lost their independent existence, and that were united under that one temporal authority—constituting by the union of the spiritual and temporal power that one peculiar kingdom. In Lombardy the power remained in the possession of the kings of the Lombards themselves, until that kingdom was subdued by the arms of Pepin and Charlemagne, and then it became subject to the crown of France, though for a time under the

nominal reign of its own kings. See Gibbon, iii. 334, 335, 338. If it should be said, that in the interpretation of this passage respecting the "three horns" that were plucked up, or the three kingdoms that were thus destroyed, it would be proper to look for them among the *ten* into which the one great kingdom was divided, and that the three above referred to—the Exarchate of Ravenna, the Pentapolis, and the dukedom of Spoleti and Rome—were *not* properly of that number, according to the list above given, it is necessary, in reply to this, to advert only to the two main facts in the case: (1) that the great Roman power was actually divided into a large number of sovereignties that sprang up on its ruins—usually, but not in fact exactly, represented by *ten;* and (2) that the Papacy began its career with a conceded dominion over the three territories above referred to—a part, in fact, of the one great dominion constituting the Roman power, and in the same territory. It is a remarkable fact that the popes to this day wear a triple crown—a fact that exists in regard to no other monarchs—*as if* they had absorbed under themselves three separate and distinct sovereignties; or *as if* they represented three separate forms of dominion. The sum of what is said in the exposition of these verses may be thus expressed:— (1.) That there was originally *one* great sovereignty represented here by the "fourth beast"—the Roman empire. (2.) That, in fact, as is abundantly confirmed by history, this one great and united power was broken up into a large number of separate and independent sovereignties—most naturally and obviously described by *ten*, or such as would appear in a prophetic vision to be *ten*, and such as is actually so represented by historians having no interest in the fulfilment of the prophecy, and no designed reference to what may be symbolized by the "ten horns." (3.) That there was another peculiar and distinct power that sprang out of them, and that grew to be mighty—a power unlike the others, and unlike anything that had before appeared in the world —combining qualities to be found in no other sovereignty—having a peculiar relation at the same time to the *one* original sovereignty, and to the *ten* into which that was divided—the prolongation, in an important sense, of the power of the one, and springing up in a peculiar manner among the others —that peculiar ecclesiastical and civil power—the Papacy—well represented by the "little horn." (4.) That, in fact, this one power absorbed into itself *three* of these sovereignties — annihilating them as independent powers, and combining them into one most peculiar dominion — properly represented by "plucking them up." (5.) That as a proper symbol, or emblem of some such domination, a crown or diadem is still worn, most naturally and obviously *suggesting* such a threefold absorption of dominion. (6.) That all this is actually prefigured by the symbols employed by the prophet, or that the symbols are such as would be naturally employed on the supposition that these events were designed to be referred to. (7.) And that there have been *no other* historical events to which these remarkable symbols could be naturally and obviously applied. And if these things are so, how are they to be explained except on the supposition that Daniel was inspired? Has man any natural sagacity by which such symbols representing the future could be suggested? (*f*) It would be arrogant and proud, "speaking great words against the Most High." No *Protestant* will doubt that this is true of the Papacy; no one acquainted with history will presume to call it in question. The arrogant pretensions of the Papacy have been manifested in all the history of that power, and no one can doubt that its assumptions have been, in fact, by fair construction, "a speaking of great words against God." The Pope has claimed, or allowed to be conferred on him, names and prerogatives which can belong only to God. See this fully shown in the Notes on 2 Thess. ii. 4. The facts there referred to are all that is necessary to illustrate this passage, on the supposition that it refers to the Papacy. Comp. also the *Literalist*, vol. i. pp. 24–27. (*g*) This would be a persecuting power—"making war with the saints," and "wearing out the saints of the Most High." Can any one doubt that this is true of the Papacy? The Inquisition; the "persecutions of the Waldenses;" the ravages of the Duke of Alva; the fires of Smithfield; the tortures at Goa— indeed, the whole history of the Papacy may be appealed to in proof that this is applicable to that power. If anything *could* have "worn out the saints of the Most High"—could have cut them off from the earth so that evangelical religion would have become extinct, it would have been the persecutions of the Papal power. In the year 1208, a crusade was proclaimed by Pope Innocent III. against the Waldenses and Albigenses, in which a million of men perished. From the beginning of the order of the Jesuits, in the year 1540 to 1580, nine hundred thousand were destroyed. One hundred and fifty thousand perished by the Inquisition in thirty years. In the Low Countries fifty thousand persons were hanged, beheaded, burned, or buried alive, for the crime of heresy, within the space of thirty-eight years from the edict of Charles V., against the Protestants, to the peace of Chateau Cambresis in 1559. Eighteen thousand suffered by the hands of the executioner, in the space of five years and a half, during the administration of the Duke of Alva. Indeed, the slightest acquaintance with the history of the Papacy, will convince any one that what is here said of "making war with the saints" (ver. 21), and "wearing out the saints of the Most High" (ver. 25), is strictly applicable to that power, and will accurately describe its history. There have been, indeed, other persecuting powers, but none to which this language would be so applicable, and none which it would so naturally suggest. In proof of this, it is only necessary to refer to the history of the Papacy, and to what it has done to extirpate those who have professed a different faith. Let any one recal (1) the persecution of the Waldenses; (2) the acts of the Duke of Alva in the Low Countries; (3) the persecution in England under Mary; (4) the Inquisition; (5) the attempts, too successful, to extinguish all the efforts at reformation in Italy and Spain in the time of Luther and Calvin (see M'Crie), and (6) the attempts to put down the Reformation in Germany and Switzerland—all which were either directly originated or sanctioned by the Papacy, and all for the same end, and he will see no reason to doubt that the language here is *strictly* applicable to that power, and that there has been no government on earth which would be so naturally suggested by it. — Cunninghame, in the *Literalist*, i. 27, 28. Indeed, who can number up all that have perished in the Inquisition alone? (*h*) It would claim legislative power— "thinking to change times and laws." The original Chaldee here may be rendered, as is done by Gesenius and De Wette, *set times, stated times*, or *festival seasons*. The word here, says Gesenius (*Lex.*), is "spoken of sacred

seasons, festivals," and there can be no doubt that in this place it refers to religious institutions. The meaning is, that he would claim control over such institutions or festivals, and that he would appoint or change them at his pleasure. He would abolish or modify existing institutions of that kind, or he would institute new ones, as should seem good to him. This would be applicable, then, to some power that should claim authority to prescribe religious institutions, and to change the laws of God. No one, also, can fail to see a fulfilment of this in the claims of the Papacy, in setting up a jurisdiction over seasons of festival and fast; and in demanding that the laws of kingdoms should be so modelled as to sustain its claims, and modifying the laws of God as revealed in the Bible. The right of deposing and setting up kings; of fixing the boundaries of nations; of giving away crowns and sceptres; and of exercising dominion over the sacred seasons, the customs, the amusements of nations—all these, as illustrated under the Papacy, will leave no doubt that all this would find an ample fulfilment in the history of that power. The Pope has claimed to be the head of the church, and has asserted and exercised the right of appointing sacred seasons; of abolishing ancient institutions; of introducing numberless new festival occasions, practically abrogating the laws of God on a great variety of subjects. We need only refer, in illustration of this, (*a*) to the claim of infallibility, by which an absolute jurisdiction is asserted that covers the whole ground; (*b*) to all the laws pertaining to image-worship, so directly in the face of the laws of God; (*c*) to the celibacy of the clergy, rendering void one of the laws of heaven in relation to marriage; (*d*) to the whole doctrine respecting purgatory;

(e) to the doctrine of transubstantia-tion; (f) to the practical abolition of the Christian Sabbath by appointing numerous saints' days to be observed as equally sacred ; (g) to the law withholding the cup from the laity—contrary to the commandment of the Saviour ; and (h) in general to the ab-solute control claimed by the Papacy over the whole subject of religion. In-deed, nothing would better characterize this power than to say that it asserted the right to "change times and laws." And to all this should be added another characteristic (ver. 8), that "it would have the eyes of a man ;" that is, would be distinguished for a far-seeing saga-city. Could this be so appropriately applied to anything else as to the deep, the artful, and the far-reaching diplo-macy of the court of Rome; to the saga-city of the Jesuit ; to the skilful policy which subdued the world to itself ?

These illustrations will leave no doubt, it seems to me, that all that is here said will find an ample fulfilment in the Papacy, and that it is to be re-garded as having a reference to that power. If so, it only remains,

III. To inquire what, according to this interpretation, we are to expect will yet occur, or what light this pas-sage throws on events that are yet fu-ture. The origin, the growth, the general character and influence of this power up to a distant period are illus-trated by this interpretation. What remains is the inquiry, from the pas-sage before us, how long this is to con-tinue, and what we are to anticipate in regard to its fall. The following points, then, would seem to be clear, on the supposition that this refers to the Papal power:—

It is to continue a definite period from its establishment, ver. 25. This duration is mentioned as "a time, and times, and the dividing of a time"—

three years and a half—twelve hundred and sixty days—twelve hundred and sixty years. See the Notes on that verse. The only *difficulty* in regard to this, if that interpretation is correct, is to determine the time when the Papacy actually *began*—the *terminus a quo*—and this has given rise to all the diver-sity of explanation among Protestants. Assuming any one time as the period when the Papal power *arose*, as a date from which to calculate, it is easy to compute *from* that date, and to fix some period—*terminus ad quem*—to which this refers, and which may be looked to as the time of the overthrow of that power. But there is nothing more difficult in history than the determina-tion of the exact time when the *Papacy* properly began : — that is, when the peculiar domination which is fairly un-derstood by that system commenced in the world; or what were its first dis-tinguishing acts. History has not so marked that period that there is no room for doubt. It has not affixed definite dates to it; and to this day it is not easy to make out the *time* when that power commenced, or to designate any one event at a certain period that will surely mark it. It *seems* to have been a gradual growth, and its com-mencement has not been so definitely characterized as to enable us to demon-strate with absolute certainty the time to which the twelve hundred and sixty years will extend.

Different writers have assigned dif-ferent periods for the rise of the Pa-pacy, and different acts as the first act of that power; and all the prophecies as to its termination depend on the period which is fixed on as the time of its rise. It is this which has led to so much that is conjectural, and which has been the occasion of so much dis-appointment, and which throws so much obscurity now over all calculations as to the termination of that power. In nothing is the Scripture more clear than that that power shall be destroyed; and if we could ascertain with exactness the date of its origin, there would be little danger of erring in regard to its close. The different *periods* which have been fixed on as the date of its rise have been principally the following: (1.) An edict published by Justinian (A.D. 533), and a letter addressed by him at the same time to the Pope, in which he acknowledged him to be the head of the churches, thus conferring on him a title belonging only to the Saviour, and putting himself and empire under the dominion of the bishop of Rome.—Duffield *on the Prophecies*, p. 281. (2.) The decree of the emperor Phocas (A.D. 606), confirming what had been done by Justinian, and giving his sanction to the code of laws promulgated by him; a code of laws based on the acknowledged supremacy of the Pope, and which became the basis of European legislation for centuries; and conferring on him the title of "Universal Bishop." (3.) The act of Pope Stephen, by which, when appealed to by the claimant to the crown of France, he confirmed Pepin in the kingdom, and set aside Childeric III., and, in return, received from Pepin the Exarchate of Ravenna and the Pentapolis. See Ranke's *Hist. of the Papacy*, vol. i. 23. This occurred about A.D. 752. (4.) The opinion of Mr. Gibbon (IV. 363), that Gregory VII. was the true founder of the Papal power. "Gregory VII.," says he, "who may be adored or detested *as the founder of the Papal monarchy*, was driven from Rome, and died in exile at Salerno." Gregory became Pope A.D. 1073. These different dates, if assumed as the foundation of the Papal power, would, by the addition to each of the period of 1260 years, lead respectively to the years 1793, 1866, 2012, and 2333, as the period of the termination of the Papal dominion. As this is a point of great importance in the explanation of the prophecies, it may be proper to examine these opinions a little more in detail. But in order to this, it is necessary to have a clear conception of what the *Papacy* as a distinct domination is, or what constitutes its peculiarity, as seen by the sacred writers, and as it has in fact existed, and does exist in the world; and in regard to this there can be little difference of opinion. It is not a mere ecclesiastical power—not a mere spiritual domination—not the control of a bishop as such over a church or a diocese—nor is it a mere temporal dominion, but it is manifestly the *union of the two:* that peculiar domination which the bishop of Rome has claimed, as growing out of his primacy as the head of the church, and of a temporal power also, asserted at first over a limited jurisdiction, but ultimately, and as a natural consequence, over all other sovereignties, and claiming universal dominion. We shall not find the Papacy, or the Papal dominion as such, clearly, in the mere spiritual rule of the first bishop of Rome, nor in that mere spiritual dominion, however enlarged, but in that junction of the two, when, in virtue of a pretended Divine right, a temporal dominion grew up that ultimately extended itself over Europe, claiming the authority to dispose of crowns; to lay kingdoms under interdict, and to absolve subjects from their allegiance. If we can find the beginning of this claim—the germ of this peculiar kind of domination—we shall doubtless have found the commencement of the Papacy—the *terminus a quo*—as it was seen by the prophets—the point from which we are to reckon in determining the question of its duration.

With this view, then, of the nature of the Papacy, it is proper to inquire *when* it commenced, or which of the periods referred to, if either, can be properly regarded as the commencement.

I. The edict of Justinian, and the letter to the bishop of Rome, in which he acknowledged him to be the head of the church, A.D. 533. This occurred under John II., reckoned as the fifty-fifth bishop of Rome. The nature of this application of Justinian to the Pope, and the honour conferred on him, was this: On an occasion of a controversy in the church, on the question whether "one person of the Trinity suffered in the flesh," the monks of Constantinople, fearful of being condemned under an edict of Justinian for heresy in denying this, applied to the Pope to decide the point. Justinian, who took great delight in inquiries of that nature, and who maintained the opposite opinion on that subject, also made his appeal to the Pope. Having, therefore, drawn up a long creed, containing the disputed article among the rest, he despatched two bishops with it to Rome, and laid the whole matter before the Pope. At the same time he wrote a letter to the Pope, congratulating him on his election, assuring him that the faith contained in the confession which he sent him was the faith of the whole Eastern church, and entreating him to declare in his answer that he received to his communion all who professed that faith, and none who did not. To add weight to the letter, he accompanied it with a present to St. Peter, consisting of several chalices and other vessels of gold, enriched with precious stones. From this deference to the Pope, on the part of the emperor, and this submitting to him, as the head of the whole church, of an important question to be determined, it has been argued that this was properly the beginning of the Papacy, and that the twelve hundred and sixty years are to be reckoned from that. But against this opinion the objections are insuperable; for (*a*) there was here nothing of that which *properly* constitutes the Papacy—the peculiar union of the temporal and spiritual power; or the peculiar domination which that power has exerted over the world. All that occurred was the mere deference which an emperor showed to one who claimed to be the *spiritual* head of the church, and who had long before claimed that. There was no *change*—no *beginning*, properly so called—no commencement of a new form of domination over mankind, such as the Papacy has been. (*b*) But, as a matter of fact, there was, after all, little real deference to the Pope in this case. "Little or no account," says Bower, "ought to be made of that extraordinary deference [the deference shown by carrying this question before the Pope]. Justinian paid great deference to the Pope, as well as to all other bishops, when they agreed with him; but none at all when they did not—thinking himself at least as well qualified as the best of them— and so he certainly was—to decide controversies concerning the faith; and we shall soon see him entering the lists with his holiness himself."—*Lives of the Popes,* i. 336.

II. The second date which has been assigned to the origin of the Papacy is the decree made by the emperor Phocas (A.D. 606), by which, it is said, he confirmed the grant made by Justinian. This act was the following:—Boniface III., when he had been made bishop of Rome, relying on the favour and partiality which Phocas had shown him, prevailed on him to revoke the decree settling the title of "Universal

Bishop" on the bishop of Constantinople, and obtained another settling that title on himself and his successors. The decree of Phocas, conferring this title, has not indeed come down to us; but it has been the common testimony of historians that such title was conferred. See Mosheim, i. 513 ; Bower, i. 426. The fact asserted here has been doubted, and Mosheim supposes that it rests on the authority of Baronius. "Still," says he, "it is certain that something of this kind occurred." But there are serious objections to our regarding this as properly the commencement of the Papacy as such. For (*a*) this was not the beginning of that peculiar domination, or form of power, which the Pope has asserted and maintained. If this title were conferred, it imparted no new power ; it did not change the nature of this domination ; it did not, in fact, make the Roman bishop different from what he was before. He was still, in all respects, subject to the civil power of the emperors, and had no control beyond that which he exercised in the church. (*b*) And even *this* little was withdrawn by the same authority which granted it—the authority of the emperor of Constantinople—though it has always since been claimed and asserted by the Pope himself. See Bower, i. 427. It is true that, as a consequence of the fact that this title was conferred on the Popes, they began to *grasp* at power, and aspire to temporal dominion ; but still there was no formal grasp of such power growing out of the assumption of this title, nor was any such temporal dominion set up as the immediate result of such a title. The act, therefore, was not sufficiently marked, distinct, and decisive, to constitute an epoch, or the beginning of an era, in the history of the world, and the rise of the Papacy cannot with any

propriety be dated from that. This was undoubtedly one of the *steps* by which that peculiar power rose to its greatness, or which contributed to lay the foundation of its subsequent claims, its arrogance, and its pride ; but it is doubtful whether it was so important an event characterizing the Papacy as to be regarded as the origin, or the *terminus a quo* in ascertaining the time of its continuance.* It was, however, in view of this, and with this considered as properly the origin of the Papacy, that the Rev. Robert Fleming, in his work on the *Rise and Fall of the Papacy*, first published in 1701, uttered the following remarkable language, as based on his calculations respecting the continuance of that power :—"If we may suppose that Antichrist began his reign in the year 606, the additional one thousand two hundred and sixty years of his duration, were they *Julian* or ordinary years, would lead down to the year 1866, as the last period of the seven-headed monster. But seeing

* Mr. Hallam (*Middle Ages*, i. 420, note) urges the following arguments substantially against the supposition that the Papal supremacy had its rise from this epoch, and is to be dated from the concession of the title of Universal Bishop made by Phocas to Boniface III., viz.: (1.) Its truth, as commonly stated, appears more than questionable. (2.) "But if the strongest proof could be advanced for the authenticity of this circumstance, we may well deny its importance. The concession of Phocas could have been of no validity in Lombardy, France, and other western countries, where, nevertheless, the Papal supremacy was incomparably more established than in the east." (3.) "Even within the empire it could have had no efficacy after the violent death of that usurper, which occurred soon afterwards." (4.) "The title of Universal Bishop is not very intelligible, but whatever it means the patriarchs of Constantinople had borne it before, and continued to bear it afterwards." (5.) "The preceding Popes, Pelagius II. and Gregory I., had constantly disclaimed the appellation; nor does it appear to have been claimed by the successors of Boniface, at least for some centuries." (6.) "The Popes had undoubtedly exercised a species of supremacy for more than two centuries before this time, which had lately reached a high point of authority under Gregory I." (7.) "There are no sensible marks of this supremacy making a more rapid progress for a century and a half after the pretended grant of this emperor."

they are prophetical years only [of 360 days], we must cast away eighteen years in order to bring them to the exact measure of time that the Spirit of God designs in this book. *And thus the final period of the Papal usurpations* (*supposing that he did indeed rise in the year* 606) *must conclude with the year* 1848."—[Cobbin's Edition, p. 32.] Whether this be considered as merely a *happy conjecture*— the one successful one among thousands that have failed, or as the result of a proper calculation respecting the future, no one in comparing it with the events of the year 1848, when the Pope was driven from Rome, and when a popular government was established in the very seat of the Papal power, can fail to see that it is remarkable considered as having been uttered a century and a half ago. Whether it is the correct calculation, and that temporary downfall of the Papal government is to be regarded as the first in a series of events that will ultimately end in its destruction, time must determine. The reasons mentioned above, however, and those which will be suggested in favour of a different beginning of that power, make it, at present, more probable that a different period is to be assigned as its close.

III. The third date which has been assigned as the beginning of the Papacy is the grant of Pepin above referred to, A.D. 752. This grant conferred by Pepin was confirmed also by Charlemagne and his successors, and it was undoubtedly at this period that the Papacy began to assume its place among the sovereignties of Europe. In favour of this opinion—that this was properly the rise of the Papacy—the *terminus a quo* of prophecy, the following considerations may be urged: (*a*) We have here a definite act—an act which is palpable and apparent, as characterizing the progress of this domination over men. (*b*) We have here properly the *beginning* of the temporal dominion, or the first acknowledged exercise of that power in acts of temporal sovereignty —in giving laws, asserting dominion, swaying a temporal sceptre, and wearing a temporal crown. All the acts before had been of a spiritual character, and all the deference to the Bishop of Rome had been of a spiritual nature. Henceforward, however, he was acknowledged as a temporal prince, and took his place as such among the crowned heads of Europe. (*c*) This is properly the beginning of that mighty domination which the Pope wielded over Europe—a beginning, which, however small at first, ultimately became so powerful and so arrogant as to claim jurisdiction over all the kingdoms of the earth, and the right to absolve subjects from their allegiance, to lay kingdoms under interdict, to dispose of crowns, to order the succession of princes, to tax all people, and to dispose of all newly-discovered countries. (*d*) This accords better with the prophecies than any other one event which has occurred in the world—especially with the prophecy of Daniel, of the springing up of the little horn, and the fact that that little horn plucked up three others of the ten into which the fourth kingdom was divided. (*e*) And it should be added that this agrees with the idea all along held up in the prophecies, that this would be properly *the fourth empire prolonged.* The fifth empire or kingdom is to be the reign of the saints, or the reign of righteousness on the earth; the fourth extends down in its influences and power to that. As a matter of fact, this *Roman* power was thus concentrated in the Papacy. The form was changed, but it was the *Roman* power that was in the eye of the prophets, and this was contemplated under its various phases, as heathen and nominally Christian, until the reign of the saints should commence, or the kingdom of God should be set up. But it was only in the time of Stephen, and by the act of Pepin and Charlemagne, that this change occurred, or that this dominion of a temporal character was settled in the Papacy—and that the Pope was acknowledged as having this temporal power. This was *consummated* indeed in Hildebrand, or Gregory VII. (Gibbon, iii. 353, iv. 363), but *this* mighty power properly had its *origin* in the time of Pepin.

IV. The fourth date assigned for the origin of the Papacy is the time of Hildebrand, or Gregory VII. This is the period assigned by Mr. Gibbon. Respecting this, he remarks (vol. iv. p. 363), "Gregory the Seventh, who may be adored or detested *as the founder of the Papal monarchy*, was driven from Rome, and died in exile at Salerno." And again (vol. iii. p. 353), he says of Gregory, "After a long series of scandal, the apostolic see was reformed and exalted, by the austerity and zeal of Gregory VII. That ambitious monk devoted his life to the execution of two projects: I. To fix in the college of Cardinals the freedom and independence of election, and forever to abolish the right or usurpation of the emperors and the Roman people. II. To bestow and resume the Western Empire as a fief or benefice of the church, and to extend his temporal dominion over the kings and kingdoms of the earth. After a contest of fifty years, the first of these designs was accomplished by the firm support of the ecclesiastical order, whose liberty was connected with that of the chief. But the second attempt, though it was crowned with some apparent and partial success, has been vigorously resisted

DANIEL II.

by the secular power, and finally extinguished by the improvement of human reason."

If the views above suggested, however, are correct; or if we look at the Papacy as it was in the time of Hildebrand, it must be apparent that this was not the *rise* or *origin* of that peculiar domination, but was only the carrying out and completing of the plan laid long before to set up a temporal dominion over mankind.

It should be added, that whichever of the three first periods referred to be regarded as the time of the rise of the Papacy, if we add to them the prophetic period of 1260 years, we are *now* in the midst of scenes on which the prophetic eye rested, and we cannot, as fair interpreters of prophecy, but regard this mighty domination as hastening to its fall. It would seem probable, then, that according to the most obvious explanation of the subject, we are at present not far from the termination and fall of that great power, and that events may be expected to occur at about this period of the world, which will be connected with its fall.

(B.) Its power is to be taken away as by a solemn judgment—*as if* the throne was set, and God was to come forth to pronounce judgment on this power to overthrow it, verses 10, 11, 26. This destruction of the power referred to is to be absolute and entire —*as if* the "beast were slain, and the body given to the burning flame"— "and they shall take away his dominion, to consume and destroy it unto the end." This would denote the absolute destruction of this peculiar power—its entire cessation in the world; that is, the absolute destruction of that which had constituted its *peculiarity*—the prolonged power of

G

the beast of the fourth kingdom—concentrated and embodied in that represented by the little horn. If applied
to the Roman power, or the fourth
kingdom, it means that *that* power
which would have been prolonged
under the dominion of that represented
by the little horn, would wholly cease
—as if the body of the beast had been
burned. If applied to the power represented by the "little horn"—the
Papacy—it means that *that* power
which sprang up amidst the others,
and which became so mighty—em-
bodying so much of the power of the
beast, would wholly pass away *as* an
ecclesiastico-civil power. It would
cease its dominion, and as one of the
ruling powers of the earth would disappear. This would be accomplished
by some remarkable Divine manifestation—*as if* God should come in
majesty and power to judgment, and
should pronounce a sentence; that is,
the overthrow would be decisive, and
as manifestly the result of the Divine
interposition *as if* God should do it by
a formal act of judgment. In the
overthrow of that power, whenever it
occurs, it would be natural, from this
prophecy, to anticipate that there
would be some scenes of commotion
and revolution bearing directly on it,
as if God were pronouncing sentence
on it; some important changes in the
nations that had acknowledged its
authority, *as if* the great Judge of
nations were coming forth to assert his
own power and his own right to rule,
and to dispose of the kingdoms of the
earth as he pleased.

(C.) It is to be anticipated that the
power referred to will be destroyed on
account of its pride and arrogance.
See Notes on ver. 11. That is, whatever power there is upon the earth at
the time referred to that shall be
properly that of the fourth beast or

kingdom, will be taken away on account of the claims set up and maintained by the "little horn:" "I beheld
because of the voice of the great words
which the horn spake; I beheld till
the beast was slain," &c., verse 11.
On the supposition that this refers to
the Papacy, what is to be expected
would be, that the pride and arrogance
of that power as such—that is, as an
ecclesiastical power claiming dominion
over civil things, and wielding civil
authority, would be such that the
Roman power—the lingering power
of the fourth kingdom—would be
taken away, and its dominion over the
world would cease. That vast Roman
domination that once trod down the
earth, and that crushed and oppressed
the nations, would still linger, like the
prolonged life of the beast, until, on
account of the arrogance and pride of
the Papacy, it would be wholly taken
away. If one were to judge of the
meaning of this prophecy without attempting to apply it to particular passing events, he would say that it would
be fulfilled by some such events as
these :—if the people over whom the
prolonged Roman civil power would
be extended, and over whom the ecclesiastical or papal sceptre would be
swayed, should, on account of the
pride and arrogance of the Papacy,
rise in their might, and demand liberty—*that* would be in fact an end of
the prolonged power of the fourth
beast ; and it would be on account of
the " great words which the horn
spake," and would be in all respects a
fulfilment of the language of this prophecy. Whether such an end of this
power is to occur, time is to determine.

(D.) Simultaneously with this event,
as the result of this, we are to anticipate such a spread of truth and righteousness, and such a reign of the
saints on the earth, as would be pro-

perly symbolized by the coming of the Son of man to the Ancient of days to receive the kingdom, vers. 13, 14. As shown in the interpretation of those verses, this does not necessarily imply that there would be any visible appearing of the Son of man, or any personal reign (see the Notes on these verses), but there would be such a making over of the kingdom to the Son of man and to the saints as would be properly symbolized by such a representation. That is, there would be great changes; there would be a rapid progress of the truth; there would be a spread of the gospel; there would be a change in the governments of the world, so that the power would pass into the hands of the righteous, and they would in fact rule. From that time the "saints" would receive the kingdom, and the affairs of the world would be put on a new footing. From that period it might be said that the reign of the saints would *commence;* that is, there would be such changes in this respect that *that* would constitute an epoch in the history of the world—the proper beginning of the reign of the saints on the earth—the setting up of the new and final dominion in the world. If there should be such changes—such marked progress—such facilities for the spread of truth—such new methods of propagating it—and such certain success attending it, all opposition giving way, and persecution ceasing, as would properly constitute an *epoch* or *era* in the world's history, which would be connected with the conversion of the world to God, this would fairly meet the interpretation of this prophecy; this occurring, all would have taken place which could be fairly shown to be implied in the vision.

(E.) We are to expect a reign of righteousness on the earth. On the character of what we are fairly to expect from the words of the prophecy, see Notes on ver. 14. The prophecy authorizes us to anticipate a time when there shall be a general prevalence of true religion; when the power in the world shall be in the hands of good men—of men fearing God; when the Divine laws shall be obeyed—being acknowledged as the laws that are to control men; when the civil institutions of the world shall be pervaded by religion, and moulded by it; when there shall be no hinderance to the free exercise of religion, and when in fact the reigning power on the earth shall be the kingdom which the Messiah shall set up. There is nothing more certain in the future than such a period, and to that all things are tending. *Such* a period would fulfil all that is fairly implied in this wonderful prophecy, and *to* that faith and hope should calmly and confidently look forward. For that they who love their God and their race should labour and pray; and by the certain assurance that such a period will come, we should be cheered amidst all the moral darkness that exists in the world, and in all that now discourages us in our endeavours to do good.

CHAPTER VIII.

ANALYSIS OF THE CHAPTER.

This chapter contains an account of a vision seen by the prophet in the third year of the reign of Belshazzar. The prophet either was, or appeared to be, in the city of Shushan—afterwards the capital of the Persian empire, in the province of Elam. To that place —then an important town—there is no improbability in supposing that he had gone, as he was then unconnected with the government, or not employed by the government (ch. v.), and as it is not unreasonable to suppose that he would be at liberty to visit other parts of the empire than Babylon. Possibly there may have been Jews at that place, and he may have gone on a visit to them. Or perhaps the scene of the vision may have been laid in Shushan, by the river Ulai, and that the prophet means to represent himself *as if* he had been there, and the vision had seemed to pass there before his mind. But there is no valid objection to the supposition that he was actually there; and this seems to be affirmed in ver. 2. While there, he saw a ram with two horns, one higher than the other, pushing westward, and northward, and southward, so powerful that nothing could oppose him. As he was looking on this, he saw a he-goat come from the west, bounding along, and scarcely touching the ground, with a single remarkable horn between his eyes. This he-goat attacked the ram, broke his two horns, and overcame him entirely. The he-goat became very strong, but at length the horn was broken, and there came up four in its place. From one of these there sprang up a little horn that became exceeding great and mighty, extending itself toward the south, and the east, and the pleasant land—the land of Palestine. This horn became so mighty that it seemed to attack "the host of heaven"—the stars; it cast some of them down to the ground; it magnified itself against the Prince of the host; it caused the daily sacrifice in the temple to cease, and the sanctuary of the Prince of the host was cast down. An earnest inquiry was made by one saint to another how long this was to continue, and the answer was, unto two thousand and three hundred days, and that then the sanctuary would be cleansed. Gabriel is then sent to explain the vision to the prophet, and he announces that the ram with the two horns repre-

sented the kings of Media and Persia; the goat, the king of Greece; the great horn between his eyes, the first king; the four horns that sprang up after that was broken, the four dynasties into which the kingdom would be divided; and the little horn, a king of fierce countenance, and understanding dark sentences, and that would stand up against the Prince of princes, and that would ultimately be destroyed. The effect of this was, that Daniel was overcome by the vision for a certain time; afterward he revived, and attended to the business of the king, but none understood the vision.

This is one of the few prophecies in the Scriptures that are explained to the prophets themselves, and it becomes, therefore, important as a key to explain other prophecies of a similar character. Of the reference to the kingdom of Media and Persia, and to the kingdom of Greece, there is an express statement. The application of a portion of the prophecy to Alexander the Great, and to the four monarchies into which his kingdom was divided at his death, is equally certain. And there can be as little doubt of the application of the remainder to Antiochus Epiphanes, and in this nearly all expositors are agreed. Indeed, so striking and clear is the application to this series of historical events, that Porphyry maintained that this, as well as other portions of Daniel, were written *after* the events occurred. One of two things, indeed, is certain—either that this *was* written after the events here referred to occurred, or that Daniel was inspired. No man by any natural sagacity could have predicted these events with so much accuracy and particularity.

The portion of Daniel which follows is in pure Hebrew. The portion of the book from the fourth verse of the

CHAPTER VIII.

IN the third year of the reign of king Belshazzar a vision appeared unto me, *even unto* me

Daniel, after that which appeared unto me at the first.

2 And I saw in a vision; and it came to pass, when I saw, that I

---

second chapter to the end of the seventh chapter was written in Chaldee. On this point, see Intro. § IV. III. (1).

1. *In the third year of the reign of king Belshazzar.* In regard to Belshazzar, see Intro. to ch. v. § II. ¶ *A vision appeared unto me.* This vision appears to have occurred to him when awake, or in an ecstasy; the former one occurred when he was asleep, ch. vii. 1. Comp. vers. 17, 18 of this chap., where the prophet represents himself as overpowered, and as falling down to the earth on account of the vision. The representation would seem to have been made to pass before his mind in open day, and when he was fully awake. Comp. the case of Balaam, Num. xxiv. 4: "Which saw the vision of the Almighty, falling into a trance, but having his eyes open." ¶ *After that which appeared unto me at the first.* That occurred in the first year of Belshazzar, ch. vii. 1.

2. *And I saw in a vision.* I looked as the vision appeared to me; or I saw certain things represented to me in a vision. On the word *vision*, see Notes on ch. i. 17. The meaning here would seem to be that a vision appeared to Daniel, and that he contemplated it with earnestness, to understand what it meant. ¶ *That I was at Shushan.* As remarked in the introduction to this chapter, this might mean that he *seemed* to be there, or that the vision was represented to him as being there; but the most natural construction is to suppose that Daniel was actually there himself. *Why* he was there he has not informed us directly—whether he was on public business, or on his own. From ver. 27, however—"Afterward I rose up, and did the king's business"—it would seem most probable that he was then in the service of the king. This supposition will not conflict with the statement in ch. v. 10, 11, in which the queen-mother, when the handwriting appeared on the wall of the palace, informs Belshazzar that there

was "a man in his kingdom in whom was the spirit of the holy gods," &c.—from which it might be objected that Daniel was at that time unknown to the king, and could not have been in his employ; for it might have been a fact that he was in the employ of the king as an officer of the government, and yet it may have been forgotten that he had this power of disclosing the meaning of visions. He may have been employed in the public service, but his services to the father of the king, and his extraordinary skill in interpreting dreams and visions may not at once have occurred to the affrighted monarch and his courtiers. Shushan, or Susa, the chief town of Susiana, was the capital of Persia after the time of Cyrus, in which the kings of Persia had their principal residence, Nehem. i. 1; Esther i. 2–5. It was situated on the Eulæus or Choaspes, probably on the spot now occupied by the village Shus.—Rennel, *Geog. of Herodotus;* Kinneir, *Mem. Pers. Emp.;* K. Porter's *Travels,* ii. 4, 11; Ritter, *Erdkunde, Asien,* ix. 294; *Pict. Bib. in loc.* At Shus there are extensive ruins, stretching perhaps twelve miles from one extremity to the other, and consisting, like the other ruins in that country, of hillocks of earth, and rubbish, covered with broken pieces of brick and coloured tile. At the foot of these mounds is the so-called tomb of Daniel, a small building erected on the spot where the remains of Daniel are believed in that region to rest. It is apparently modern, but nothing but the belief that this was the site of the prophet's sepulchre could have led to its being built in the place where it stands.—Malcolm, *Hist. of Persia,* i. 255, 256. The city of Shus is now a gloomy wilderness, inhabited by lions, hyenas, and other beasts of prey.—Kitto's *Cyclo.,* art. "Shushan." Sir John Kinneir says that the dread of these animals compelled Mr. Monteith and himself to take shelter for the night within the walls that encompass

was at Shushan *a in* the palace, which *is* in the province of Elam; and I saw in a vision, and I was by the river of Ulai.

3 Then I lifted up mine eyes,

and saw, and, behold, there stood before the river a ram, which had *two* horns, and the *two* horns *were* high; but one *was* higher than the other [1] and the higher came up last.

---

a Esth. 1. 2.

[1] *second.*

Daniel's tomb. Of that tomb Sir John Malcolm says, "It is a small building, but sufficient to shelter some dervishes who watch the remains of the prophet, and are supported by the alms of pious pilgrims, who visit the holy sepulchre. The dervishes are now the only inhabitants of Susa; and every species of wild beast roams at large over the spot on which some of the proudest palaces ever raised by human art once stood." —Vol. i. pp. 255, 256. For a description of the ruins of Susa, see *Pict. Bib. in loc.* This city was about 450 Roman miles from Seleucia, and was built, according to Pliny, 6, 27, in a square of about 120 stadia. It was the summer residence of the Persian kings (*Cyrop.* 8, 6, 10), as they passed the spring in Ecbatana, and the autumn and winter in Babylon. See Lengerke, *in loc.* It was in this city that Alexander the Great married Stateira, daughter of Darius Codomanus. The *name* means a *lily*, and was probably given to it on account of its beauty.— Lengerke. Rosenmüller supposes that the vision here is represented to have appeared to Daniel in this city because it would be the future capital of Persia, and because so much of the vision pertained to Persia. See Maurer, *in loc.* ¶ *In the palace.* This word

(בִּירָה) means a fortress, a castle, a fortified palace.—Gesenius. See Neh. i. 1; Esth. i. 5; ii. 5; viii. 14; ix. 6, 11, 12. It would seem to have been given to the city because it was a fortified place. The word applied not only to the *palace* proper, a royal residence, but to the whole adjacent city. It is not necessary to suppose that Daniel was in the palace proper, but only that he was in the city to which the name was given. ¶ *Which is in the province of Elam.* See Notes on Isa. xi. 11. This province was bounded on the east by Persia Proper, on the

west by Babylonia, on the north by Media, and on the south by the Persian Gulf. It was about half as large as Persia, and not quite as large as England.—Kitto's *Cyclo.* It was probably conquered by Nebuchadnezzar, and in the time of Belshazzar was subject to the Babylonian dominion, Shushan had been doubtless the capital of the kingdom of Elam while it continued a separate kingdom, and remained the capital of the province while it was under the Babylonian yoke, and until it was subdued as a part of the empire by Cyrus. It was then made one of the capitals of the united Medo-Persian empire. It was when it was the capital of a province that it was visited by Daniel, and that he saw the vision there. Possibly he may have dwelt there subsequently, and died there. ¶ *And I was by the river of Ulai.* This river flowed by the city of Shushan, or Susa, and fell into the united stream of the Tigris and the Euphrates. It is called by Pliny (*Nat. Hist.* vi. 81) Eulæus; but it is described by Greek writers generally under the name of Choaspes.— Herod. v. 49; Strabo, xv. p. 728. It is now known by the name Kerah, called by the Turks Karasu. It passes on the west of the ruins of Shus (Susa), and enters the Shat-ul-Arab about twenty miles below Korna.—Kinneir, *Geog. Mem. of the Persian Empire,* pp. 96, 97. See Kitto's *Cyclo.,* art. "Ulai."

3. *Then I lifted up mine eyes and saw.* And saw in vision, or there seemed to be before me. ¶ *There stood before the river.* On the bank of the river. ¶ *A ram, which had* two *horns.* There can be no error in explaining the design of this symbol, for in ver. 20 it is expressly said that it denoted the two kings of Media and Persia. The united power of the kingdom was denoted by the ram itself; the fact that

4 I saw the ram pushing westward, and northward, and southward ; so that no beasts might
stand before him, neither *was there
any* that could deliver out of his
_a ch. 5. 19; 11. 3, 16; Isa. 10. 13, 14.

hand ; but he did according to his
will, ^a and became great.

5 And as I was considering, be-
hold, an he-goat ^b came from the
west, on the face of the whole earth,
_b ver. 21.

there were two powers or kingdoms
combined, by the two horns of the ram.
¶ *And the* two *horns* were *high*. Both
indicating great power.   ¶ *But one*
was *higher than the other, and the
higher came up last.* The higher horn
springing up last denotes Persia, that
became the more mighty power of the
two, so that the name *Media* became
finally almost dropped, and the united
kingdom was known in Grecian history as the *Persian*. The Median or
Assyrian power was the older, but the
Persian became the most mighty.

4. *I saw the ram pushing westward,
and northward, and southward.* Denoting the conquests of the united
kingdom. The *east* is not mentioned,
for none of the conquests of the Medo-
Persian empire extended in that direction. Yet nothing could better express
the conquests actually made by the
Medo-Persian empire than this representation. On the west the conquests
embraced Babylonia, Mesopotamia,
Syria, and Asia Minor ; on the north,
Colchis, Armenia, Iberia, and the regions around the Caspian Sea ; and on
the south, Palestine, Ethiopia, Egypt,
and Lybia.—Lengerke. This Medo-
Persian power is represented as coming
from the east. Isa. xli. 2 : " Who
raised up the righteous man *from the
east*," &c. Isa. xlvi. 11 : " Calling a
ravenous bird *from the east*," &c.
¶ *He did according to his will, and
became great.* This expresses well also
the character of the Medo-Persian empire. It extended over a great part of
the known world, subduing to itself a
large portion of the earth. In its early
conquests it met with no successful
opposition, nor was it stayed until it
was subdued by Greece—as at Leuctra
and Marathon, and then as it was
finally overthrown by Alexander the
Great.

5. *And as I was considering.* As I
was looking on this vision. It was a
vision which would naturally attract

attention, and one which would not be
readily understood. It evidently denoted some combined power that was
attempting conquest, but we are not
to suppose that Daniel would readily
understand what was meant by it. The
whole scene was future—for the Medo-
Persian power was not yet consolidated
in the time of Belshazzar, and the conquests represented by the ram continued through many years, and those
denoted by the he-goat extended still
much further into futurity. ¶ *Behold,
an he-goat came from the west.* In ver.
21, this is called the " rough-goat."
There can be no doubt as to the application of this, for in ver. 21 it is
expressly said that it was "the king
of Grecia." The power represented
is that of Greece when it was consolidated under Alexander the Great, and
when he went forth to the subjugation
of this vast Persian empire. It may
serve to illustrate this, and to show
the propriety of representing the Macedonian power by the symbol of a
goat, to remark that this symbol is
often found, in various ways, in connection with Macedon, and that, for
some reason, the goat was used as
emblematic of that power. A few
facts, furnished to the editor of Calmet's *Dictionary*, by Taylor Combe,
Esq., will show the propriety of this
allusion to Macedonia under the emblem of a goat, and that the allusion
would be readily understood in after-
times. They are condensed here from
his account in Taylor's *Calmet*, v.
410–412. (1.) Caranus, the first king
of the Macedonians, commenced his
reign 814 years before the Christian
era. The circumstance of his being
led by goats to the city of Edessa, the
name of which, when he established
there the seat of his kingdom, he converted into *Ægæ*, is well worthy of
remark : *Urbem Edessam, ob memoriam
muneris Ægas, populum Ægeadas.*—
Justin, lib. vii. c. 1. The adoption of

and [1] touched not the ground : and the goat *had* [2] a notable horn between his eyes.

1 or, *none touched* him *in the earth.*
2 *a horn of sight.*

---

the *goat* as an emblem of Macedon would have been early suggested by an important event in their history. (2.) Bronze figures of a goat have been found as the symbol of Macedon. Mr. Combe says, "I have lately had an opportunity of procuring an ancient bronze figure of a goat with one horn, which was the old symbol of Macedon. As figures representing the types of ancient countries are extremely rare, and as neither a bronze nor marble symbol of Macedon has been hitherto noticed, I beg leave to trouble you with the few following observations," &c. He then says, "The goat which is sent for your inspection was dug up in Asia Minor, and was brought, together with other antiquities, into this country by a poor Turk." The annexed engraving is a representation of this figure.

The slightest inspection of this figure will show the propriety of the representation before us. Mr. Combe then says, "Not only many of the individual towns in Macedon and Thrace employed this type, but the kingdom itself of Macedon, which is the oldest in Europe of which we have any regular and connected history, was represented also by a goat, with this peculiarity, that it had but one horn." (3.) In the reign of Amyntas the First,

nearly 300 years after Caranus, and about 547 years before Christ, the Macedonians, upon being threatened with an invasion, became tributary to the Persians. In one of the pilasters of Persepolis, this very event seems to be recorded in a manner that throws considerable light on this subject. A goat is represented with an immense horn growing out of the middle of his forehead, and a man in a Persian dress is seen by his side, holding the horn with his left hand, by which is signified the subjection of Macedon. The subjoined is the figure referred to, and it

strikingly shows how early this symbol was used. (4.) In the reign of Archelaus of Macedon, B.C. 413, there occurs on the reverse of a coin of that king the head of a goat having only one horn. Of this coin, so remarkable for the single horn, there are two varieties, one (No. 1) engraved by Pellerin, and the other (No. 2) preserved in the cabinet of the late Dr. W. Hunter.

(No. 1.)

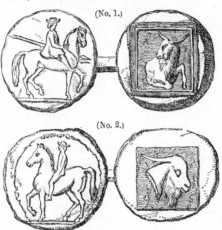

(No. 2.)

(5.) "There is a gem," says Mr. Combe, "engraved in the Florentine collection, which, as it confirms what has been already said, and has not hitherto been understood, I think worthy of mention. It will be seen by the drawing of this gem that nothing

more or less is meant by the ram's head with two horns, and the goat's head with one, than the kingdoms of Persia and Macedon, represented under their appropriate symbols. From the circumstance, however, of these characteristic types being united, it is extremely probable that the gem was engraved after the conquest of Persia by Alexander the Great." These remarks and illustrations will show the pro-priety of the symbol used here, and show also how readily it would be understood in after-times. There is no evidence that Daniel understood that this ever had been a symbol of Macedonia, or that, if he had, he could have conjectured, by any natural sagacity, that a power represented by that symbol would have become the conqueror of Media and Persia, and every circumstance, therefore, connected with this only shows the more clearly that he was under the influence of inspiration. It is affirmed by Josephus (*Ant.* b. xi. ch. viii.) that when Alexander was at Jerusalem, the prophecies of Daniel respecting him were shown to him by the high-priest, and that this fact was the means of his conferring important favours on the Jews. If such an event occurred, the circumstances here alluded to show how readily Alexander would recognize the reference to his own country, and to himself, and how probable the account of Josephus is, that this was the means of conciliating him towards the Jewish people. The credibilty of the account, which has been called in question, is examined in Newton *on the Prophecies*, pp. 241–246. ¶ *On the face of*

6 And he came to the ram that had *two* horns, which I had seen standing before the river, and ran unto him in the fury of his power.

7 And I saw him come close unto the ram, and he was moved with choler against him, and smote the ram, and brake his two horns;

the whole earth. He seemed to move over the whole world—well representing the movements of Alexander, who conquered the known world, and who is said to have wept because there were no other worlds to conquer. ¶ *And touched not the ground.* Marg., *none touched* him *in the earth.* The translation in the text, however, is more correct than that in the margin. He seemed to bound along as if he did not touch the ground—denoting the rapidity of his movements and conquests. A similar description of great beauty occurs in Virgil, *Æn.* vii. 806, seq. of Camilla :—

"Cursu pedum prævertere ventos.
Illa vel intactæ segetis per summia volaret
Gramina, nec teneras cursu læsisset aristas,
Vel mare per medium fluctu suspensa tumenti
Ferret iter, celeres nec tingeret æquore plantas."

Nothing would better express the rapid conquests of Alexander the Great than the language employed by Daniel. He died at the early age of thirty-three, and having been chosen generalissimo of the Greeks against the Persians at the age of twenty-one, the whole period occupied by him in his conquests, and in his public life, was but twelve years; yet in that time he brought the world in subjection to his arms. A single glance at his rapid movements will show the propriety of the description here. In the year 334 B.C., he invaded Persia, and defeated the Persians in the battle of the Granicus; in the year 333, he again defeated them at the battle of Issus, and conquered Parthia, Bactria, Hyrcania, Sogdiana, and Asia Minor. In the year 332, he conquered Tyre and Egypt, and built Alexandria. In the year 331, he defeated Darius Codomanus, and in 330 completed the conquest of the Persian empire. In the year 328, he defeated Porus, king of India, and pursued his march to the Ganges. In these few years, therefore, he had overrun nearly all the then known world, in conquests more rapid and more decisive than had ever before been made. ¶ *And the goat*

had *a notable horn between his eyes.* The goat represented the Macedonian power, and all this power was concentrated in the person of Alexander—undoubtedly denoted by the single horn —as if all the power of Greece was concentrated in him. The margin is, *a horn of sight.* This corresponds with the Hebrew—the word rendered *notable* (חָזוּת) meaning, properly, *look, appearance,* and then something *conspicuous* or *remarkable.* The literal translation would be, *a horn of appearance;* that is, conspicuous, large.—Gesenius, *Lex.*

6. *And he came to the ram,* &c. Representing the Medo-Persian power. ¶ *And ran unto him in the fury of his power.* Representing the fierceness and fury with which Alexander attacked the Persians at the Granicus, at Issus, and at Arbela, with which he invaded and overthrew them in their own country. Nothing would better express this than to say that it was done in " the fury of power."

[The following is from a medallion of Alexander the Great, in which the ram's horn is allusive to his boast that he was the son of Jupiter-Ammon.]

7. *And I saw him come close unto the ram.* The ram standing on the banks of the Ulai, and in the very heart of the empire. This representa-

and there was no power in the ram to stand before him, but he cast him down to the ground, and stamped upon him : and there was

none that could deliver the ram out of his hand.

8 Therefore the he-goat waxed very great : and when he was

---

tion is designed undoubtedly to denote that the Grecian power would attack the Persian in its own dominions. Perhaps the vision was represented at the place which would be the capital of the empire in order to denote this. ¶ *And he was moved with choler against him* [*i.e., the ram*]. With wrath or anger. That is, he acted as if he were furiously enraged. This is not an improper representation. Alexander, though spurred on by ambition as his ruling motive, yet might be supposed without impropriety to represent the concentrated wrath of all Greece on account of the repeated Persian invasions. It is true the Persians had been defeated at Leuctra, at Marathon, and at Salamis, that their hosts had been held in check at Thermopylæ, that they had never succeeded in subduing Greece, and that the Grecians in defending their country had covered themselves with glory. But it is true, also, that the wrongs inflicted or attempted on the Greeks had never been forgotten, and it cannot be doubted that the remembrance of these wrongs was a motive that influenced many a Greek at the battle of the Granicus and Issus, and at Arbela. It would be one of the most powerful motives to which Alexander could appeal in stimulating his army. ¶ *And brake his two horns.* Completely prostrated his power—as Alexander did when he overthrew Darius Codomanus, and subjugated to himself the Medo-Persian empire. That empire ceased at that time, and was merged in that of the son of Philip. ¶ *And there was no power in the ram to stand before him.* To resist him. ¶ *But he cast him down to the ground, and stamped upon him.* An act strikingly expressive of the conduct of Alexander. The empire was crushed beneath his power, and, as it were, trampled to the earth. ¶ *And there was none that could deliver the ram out of his hand.* No auxiliaries that the Persian empire could

call to its aid that could save it from the Grecian conqueror.

8. *Therefore the he-goat waxed very great.* The Macedonian power, especially under the reign of Alexander. ¶ *And when he was strong, the great horn was broken.* In the time, or at the period of its greatest strength. Then an event occurred which broke the horn in which was concentrated its power. It is easy to see the application of this to the Macedonian power. At no time was the empire so strong as at the death of Alexander. Its power did not pine away; it was not enfeebled, as monarchies are often, by age, and luxury, and corruption; it was most flourishing and prosperous just at the period when broken by the death of Alexander. Never afterwards did it recover its vigour; never was it consolidated again. From that time this mighty empire, broken into separate kingdoms, lost its influence in the world. ¶ *And for it came up four notable ones.* In the place of this one horn in which all the power was concentrated, there sprang up four others that were distinguished and remarkable. On the word *notable*, see Notes on ver. 5. This representation would lead us to suppose that the power which had thus been concentrated in one monarchy would be divided and distributed into four, and that instead of that one power there would be four kingdoms that would fill up about the same space in the world, occupy about the same territory, and have about the same characteristics— so that they might be regarded as the succession to the one dynasty. The same representation we have of this one power in ch. vii. 6 :—" The beast had also four heads." See also ch. xi. 4: " His kingdom shall be broken, and shall be divided toward the four winds of heaven." This accords with the accounts in history of the effect of Alexander's death, for though the kingdom was not by him divided into

strong, the great horn was broken;
and for it came up four ^a notable

four parts, yet, from the confusion and
conflicts that arose, the power was ultimately concentrated into four dynasties.
At his death, his brother Aridæus was
declared king in his stead, and Perdiccas regent. But the unity of the Macedonian power was gone, and disorder
and confusion, and a struggle for empire,
immediately succeeded. The author of
the books of Maccabees (1 Macc. i. 7–9)
says: " So Alexander reigned twelve
years, and then died. And his servants bare rule every one in his place.
And after his death, they all put crowns
upon themselves; so did their sons
after them many years; and evils were
multiplied in the earth." Alexander
died B.C. 323; Antipater succeeded
Perdiccas, B.C. 321; Ptolemy Lagus
the same year took possession of Egypt;
Cassander assumed the government of
Macedon, B.C. 317; Seleucus Nicator
took possession of Syria, B.C. 311; in
305 B.C. the successors of Alexander
took the title of kings, and in 301 B.C.
there occurred the battle of Ipsus, in
which Antigonus, who reigned in Asia
Minor, was killed, and then followed
in that year a formal division of Alexander's empire between the four victorious princes, Ptolemy, Seleucus,
Cassander, and Lysimachus. This
great battle of Ipsus, a city of Phrygia,
was fought between Antigonus and his
son Demetrius on the one side, and
the combined forces of these princes
on the other. Antigonus had aimed
at universal sovereignty; he had taken
and plundered the island of Cyprus;
had destroyed the fleet of Ptolemy
Lagus, and had assumed the crown.
Against him and his usurpations,
Ptolemy, Cassander, and Lysimachus,
combined their forces, and the result
was his complete overthrow at the
battle of Ipsus. — Lengerke, *in loc.*
In this battle, Antigonus lost all his
conquests and his life. In the division
of the empire, Seleucus Nicator obtained Syria, Babylonia, Media, and
Susiana, Armenia, a part of Cappadocia, Cilicia, and his kingdom, in name
at least, extended from the Hellespont

ones, toward the four winds of
heaven.

9 And ^b out of one of them came

to the Indies. The kingdom of Lysimachus extended over a part of Thrace,
Asia Minor, part of Cappadocia, and
the countries within the limits of
Mount Taurus. Cassander possessed
Macedonia, Thessaly, and a part of
Greece. Ptolemy obtained Egypt,
Cyprus, and Cyrene, and ultimately
Cœlo-Syria, Phœnicia, Judea, and a
part of Asia Minor and Thrace.—
Lengerke, *in loc.* ¶ *Toward the four
winds of heaven.* Towards the four
quarters of the world. Thus the dominions of Seleucus were in the east;
those of Cassander in the west; those
of Ptolemy in the south, and those of
Lysimachus in the north.

9. *And out of one of them came
forth a little horn.* Emblematic of a
new power that should spring up.
Comp. Notes on ch. vii. 8. This little
horn sprang up out of one of the
others; it did not spring up in the
midst of the others as the little horn,
in ch. vii. 8, did among the ten others.
This seemed to grow out of one of the
four, and the meaning cannot be mis-
understood. From one of the four
powers or kingdoms into which the
empire of Alexander would be divided,
there would spring up this ambitious
and persecuting power. ¶ *Which waxed
exceeding great.* Which became exceedingly powerful. It was comparatively small at first, but ultimately became mighty. There can be no doubt
that Antiochus Epiphanes is denoted
here. All the circumstances of the
prediction find a fulfilment in him;
and if it were supposed that this was
written *after* he had lived, and that it
was the design of the writer to describe
him by this symbol, he could not have
found a symbol that would have been
more striking or appropriate than this.
The Syriac version has inserted here,
in the Syriac text, the words " Antiochus Epiphanes," and almost without
exception expositors have been agreed
in the opinion that he is referred to.
For a general account of him, see Notes
on ch. vii. 24, *seq.* The author of the
book of Maccabees, after noticing, in

forth a little horn, which waxed exceeding great, toward the south, and toward the east, and toward the pleasant *a land*.

a Psa. 48. 2; Ezek. 20. 15.

the passage above quoted, the death of Alexander, and the distractions that followed his death, says, "And there came out of them a wicked root, Antiochus, surnamed Epiphanes, son of Antiochus the king, who had been a hostage at Rome, and he reigned in the hundred and thirty and seventh year of the kingdom of the Greeks," 1 Macc. i. 10. A few expositors have supposed that this passage refers to Antichrist—what will not expositors of the Bible suppose? But the great body of interpreters have understood it to refer to Antiochus. This prince was a successor of Seleucus Nicator, who, in the division of the empire of Alexander, obtained Syria, Babylonia, Media, &c. (see above on ver. 8), and whose capital was Antioch. The succession of princes who reigned in Antioch, from Seleucus to Antiochus Epiphanes, were as follows :—

(1.) Seleucus Nicator, B.C. 312–280.

(2.) Antiochus Soter, his son, 280–261.

(3.) Antiochus Theos, his son, 261–247.

(4.) Seleucus Callinicus, his son, 247–226.

(5.) (Alexander), or Seleucus Ceraunus, his son, 226–223.

(6.) Antiochus the Great, his brother, 223–187.

(7.) Seleucus Philopator, his son, 187–176.

(8.) Antiochus Epiphanes, his brother, 176–164. —Clinton's *Fasti Hellenici*, vol. iii. Appendix, ch. iii.

The succession of the Syrian kings reigning in Antioch was continued until Syria was reduced to the form of a Roman province by Pompey, B.C. 63. Seleucus Philopator, the immediate predecessor of Antiochus, having been assassinated by one of his courtiers, his brother Antiochus hastened to occupy the vacant throne, although the natural heir, Demetrius, son of Seleucus, was yet alive, but a hostage at Rome. Antiochus assumed the name of Epiphanes, or *Illustrious*. In Dan. xi. 21, it is intimated that he gained the kingdom *by flatteries;* and there can be no doubt that bribery, and the promise of reward to others, was made use of to secure his power. See Kitto's *Cyclo.*, i. 168–170. Of the acts of this prince there will be occasion for a fuller detail in the Notes on the remainder of this chapter, and ch. xi. ¶ *Toward the south.* Toward the country of Egypt, &c. In the year B.C. 171, he declared war against Ptolemy Philometor, and in the year 170 he conquered Egypt, and plundered Jerusalem. 1 Macc. i. 16–19: "Now when the kingdom was established before Antiochus, he thought to reign over Egypt, that he might have the dominion of two realms. Wherefore he entered Egypt with a great multitude, with chariots, and elephants, and horsemen, and a great navy. And made war against Ptolemee king of Egypt: but Ptolemee was afraid of him, and fled; and many were wounded to death. Thus they got the strong cities in the land of Egypt, and he took the spoils thereof." ¶ *And toward the east.* Toward Persia and the countries of the East. He went there—these countries being nominally subject to him—according to the author of the book of Maccabees (1 Macc. iii. 21–37), in order to replenish his exhausted treasury, that he might carry on his wars with the Jews, and that he might keep up the splendour and liberality of his court: "He saw that the money of his treasures failed, and that the tributes in the country were small, because of the dissension and plague which he had brought upon the land, and he feared that he should not be able to bear the charges any longer, nor to have such gifts to give so liberally as he did before ; wherefore, being greatly perplexed in his mind, he determined to go into Persia, there to take the tributes of the countries, and to gather much money. So the king departed from Antioch, his royal city, the hundred forty and seventh year; and having passed the river Euphrates, he went through the high countries."

10 And it waxed great, *even* [1] to the *a* host of heaven; and it cast down *b some* of the host and of the

1 or, *against*.   *a* Isa. 14. 13.

stars to the ground, and stamped upon them.

11 Yea, he *c* magnified *himself*

b Rev. 12. 4.   *c* ver. 25.

¶ *And toward the pleasant* land. The word here used (צְבִי) means, properly, *splendour, beauty*, Isa. iv. 2; xxiv. 16; xxviii. 1, 4, 5. It is applied, in Isa. xiii. 19, to Babylon—"the *glory* of kingdoms." Here it evidently denotes the land of the Israelites, or Palestine —so often described as a land of beauty, as flowing with milk and honey, &c. This is such language as a pious Hebrew would naturally use of his own country, and especially if he was an exile from it, as Daniel was. Nothing more would be necessary to designate the land so as to be understood than such an appellation—as nothing more would be necessary to designate his country to an exile from China than to speak of "the flowery land." Antiochus, on his return from Egypt, turned aside and invaded Judea, and ultimately robbed the temple, destroyed Jerusalem, and spread desolation through the land. See 1 Macc. i.

10. *And it waxed great.* It became very powerful. This was eminently true of Antiochus, after having subdued Egypt, &c.   ¶ *Even to the host of heaven.* Marg., *against*. The Hebrew word (עַד) means *to* or *unto*, and the natural idea would seem to be that he wished to place himself among the stars, or to exalt himself above all that was earthly. Comp. Notes on Isa. xiv. 13: "For thou hast said in thine heart, I will ascend into heaven, I will exalt my throne above the stars of God." Lengerke supposes that the meaning here is, that he not only carried his conquests to Egypt and to the East, and to the Holy Land in general, but that he made war on the holy army of God—the priests and worshippers of Jehovah, here spoken of as the host of heaven. So Maurer understands it. In 2 Macc. ix. 10, Antiochus is described in this language: "And the man that thought a little afore he could reach the stars of heaven," &c. The *connection* would

seem to demand the interpretation proposed by Lengerke and Maurer, for it is immediately said that he cast down some of the host and the stars to the ground. And such an interpretation accords with the language elsewhere used, of the priests and rulers of the Hebrew people. Thus, in Isa. xxiv. 21, they are called "the host of the high ones that are on high." See Notes on that passage. This language is by no means uncommon in the Scriptures. It is usual to compare princes and rulers, and especially ecclesiastical rulers, with the sun, moon, and stars. Undoubtedly it is the design here to describe the pride and ambition of Antiochus, and to show that he did not think anything too exalted for his aspiration. None were too high or too sacred to be secure from his attempts to overthrow them, and even those who, by their position and character, seemed to deserve to be spoken of as suns and stars, as "the host of heaven," were not secure.   ¶ *And it cast down* some *of the host and of the stars to the ground.* The horn seemed to grow up to the stars, and to wrest them from their places, and to cast them to the earth. Antiochus, in the fulfilment of this, cast down and trampled on the princes, and rulers, and people, of the holy host or army of God. All that is implied in this was abundantly fulfilled in what he did to the Jewish people. Comp. 1 Macc. i., and 2 Macc. viii. 2. ¶ *And stamped upon them.* With indignation and contempt. Nothing could better express the conduct of Antiochus towards the Jews.

11. *Yea, he magnified* himself *even to the prince of the host.* Grotius, Ephræm the Syrian, and others, understand this of Onias the high-priest, as the chief officer of the holy people. Lengerke supposes that it means God himself. This interpretation is the more probable; and the idea in the phrase "prince of the host" is, that as God is the ruler of the host of

even ¹ to the prince of the host, and by ² him the daily *ᵃ sacrifice* was taken away, and the place of his sanctuary was cast down.

12 And an ³ host was given *him*

1 or, *against.*   2 or, *from.*   a Exod. 29. 38.
3 or, *the host was given over for the transgression against the daily sacrifice.*

heaven—leading on the constellations, and marshalling the stars, so he may be regarded as the ruler of the holy army here below—the ministers of religion, and his people. Against him *as* the Ruler and Leader of his people Antiochus exalted himself, particularly by attempting to change his laws, and to cause his worship to cease. ¶ *And by him.* Marg., *"from him."* The meaning is, that the command or authority to do this proceeded from him. ¶ *The daily* sacrifice *was taken away.* The sacrifice that was offered daily in the temple, morning and evening, was suspended. A full account of this may be found in 1 Macc. i. 20-24, 29-32, 44-50. In the execution of the purposes of Antiochus, he "entered the sanctuary, and took away the golden altar, and the candlestick, and all the vessels thereof; and the table of shew-bread, the pouring vessels, &c., and stripped the temple of all the ornaments of gold." After two years he again visited the city, and "smote it very sore, and destroyed much people of Israel, and when he had taken the spoils of the city he set it on fire, and pulled down the walls thereof on every side." Everything in Jerusalem was made desolate. "Her sanctuary was laid waste like a wilderness, her feasts were turned into mourning, her Sabbaths into reproach, her honour into contempt." Subsequently, by a solemn edict, and by more decisive acts, he put a period to the worship of God in the temple, and polluted and defiled every part of it. "For the king had sent letters by messengers unto Jerusalem and the cities of Judah, that they should follow the strange laws of the land, and forbid burnt-offerings, and sacrifices, and drink-offerings in the temple; and that they should profane the Sabbaths and festival days, and pollute the sanctuary and holy people; set up altars, and groves, and chapels of idols, and sacrifice swine's flesh, and unclean beasts; that they

should also leave their children uncircumcised, and make their souls abominable with all manner of uncleanness and profanation; to the end they might forget the laws, and change all the ordinances," 1 Macc. i. 44-49. It was undoubtedly to these acts of Antiochus that the passage before us refers, and the event accords with the words of the prediction as clearly as if what is a prediction had been written afterwards, and had been designed to represent what actually occurred as a matter of historical record. The word which is rendered "*daily* sacrifice"—the word "sacrifice" being supplied by the translators — תָּמִיד — means, properly, *continuance, perpetuity,* and then that which is continuous or constant—as a sacrifice or service daily occurring. The word *sacrifice* is properly inserted here.—Gesenius, *Lex.* The meaning of the word rendered "was taken away"—

הֻרָם (Hophal from רוּם—to exalt, to lift up)—here is, that it was *lifted up,* and then was taken away; that is, it was made to cease—*as if* it had been carried away.—Gesenius. ¶ *And the place of his sanctuary.* Of the sanctuary or holy place of the "Prince of the host," that is, of God. The reference is to the temple. ¶ *Was cast down.* The temple was not entirely destroyed by Antiochus, but it was robbed and rifled, and its holy vessels were carried away. The walls indeed remained, but it was desolate, and the whole service then was abandoned. See the passages quoted above from 1 Macc.

12. *And a host was given* him. The Vulgate renders this, "and *strength—robur*—was given him," &c. Theodotion, "and sin was permitted—ἐδόθη—against the sacrifice; and this righteousness was cast on the ground; so he acted and was prospered." Luther renders it, "and such might (or power, *macht*) was given him." The Syriac

against the daily *sacrifice* by reason of transgression, and it cast down the truth to the ground; and it practised, and prospered.

13 ¶ Then I heard one *a* saint

a 1 Pet. 1. 12.

speaking, and another saint [1] said unto that certain *saint* which spake, How long *shall be* the vision *concerning* the daily *sacrifice*, and the

1 *Palmoni*, or, *the numberer of secrets*, or, *the wonderful numberer.*

---

renders it, "and strength was given him," &c. Bertholdt renders it, *Statt jenes stellte man den Greuel auf*, "instead of this [the temple] there was set up an abomination." Dathe, "and the stars were delivered to him"—*tradita ei fuerunt astra, seu populus Judaicus.* Maurer understands it also of the Jewish people, and interprets it, "and an army—*exercitus*—the people of the Jews was delivered to destruction, at the same time with the perpetual sacrifice, on account of wickedness, that is, for a wicked thing, or for impure sacrifices." Lengerke renders it, as in our translation, "an host—*ein Heer*—was given up to him at the same time with the daily offering, on account of evil."

The word *host* (צָבָא) is doubtless to be taken here in the same sense as in ver. 10, where it is connected with *heaven* —"the host of heaven." If it refers there to the Jewish people, it doubtless does here, and the appellation is such a one as would not unnaturally be used. It is equivalent to saying "the army of the Lord," or "the people of the Lord," and it should have been rendered here "and *the* host was given up to him;" that is, the people of God, or the holy people were given into his hands. ¶ *Against the daily* sacrifice. This does not convey any clear idea. Lengerke renders it, *sammt den beständigen opfer*—"at the same time with the permanent sacrifice." He remarks that the preposition עַל (rendered in our version *against*), like the Greek ἐπὶ, may denote a connection with anything, or a being with a thing —*Zusammenseyn*—and thus it would denote a union of time, or that the things occurred together, Gen. xxxii. 11 (12); Hos. x. 14; Amos iii. 15. Comp. Gesenius (*Lex.*) on the word עַל,

3. According to this, the meaning is,

that the "host," or the Jewish people, were given to him *at the same time*, or in connection with the daily sacrifice. The conquest over the people, and the command respecting the daily sacrifice, were simultaneous. Both passed into his hands, and he exercised jurisdiction over them both. ¶ *By reason of transgression*—בְּפֶשַׁע. That is, all this was on account of the transgression of the people, or on account of abounding iniquity. God gave up the people, and their temple, and their sacrifices, into the hands of Antiochus, on account of the prevailing impiety. Comp. 1 Macc. i. 11–16. The author of that book traces all these calamities to the acts of certain wicked men, who obtained permission of Antiochus to introduce heathen customs into Jerusalem, and who actually established many of those customs there. ¶ *And it cast down the truth to the ground*. The true system of religion, or the true method of worshipping God—represented here as truth in the abstract. So in Isa. lix. 14, it is said : "Truth is fallen in the street, and equity cannot enter." The meaning here is, that the institutions of the true religion would be utterly prostrate. This was fully accomplished by Antiochus. See 1 Macc. i. ¶ *And it practised*. Hebrew, "it did," or it acted. That is, it undertook a work, and was successful. So in Psa. i. 3, where the same expression occurs : "And whatsoever he doeth shall prosper." This was fully accomplished in Antiochus, who was entirely successful in all his enterprises against Jerusalem. See 1 Macc. i.

13. *Then I heard one saint speaking*. One holy one. The vision was now ended, and the prophet represents himself now as hearing earnest inquiries as to the length of time during which this desolation was to continue. This conversation, or these inquiries, he repre-

transgression[1] of desolation, to give both the sanctuary and the host to be trodden under foot?

1 or, *making desolate;* ch. 11. 31; 12. 11.

sents himself as hearing among those whom he calls "saints"—or holy ones —קְדוֹשׁ. This *word* might refer to a saint on earth, or to an angel—to any holy being. As one of these, however, was able to explain the vision, and to tell how long the desolation was to continue, it is more natural to refer it to angels. So Lengerke understands it. The representation is, that one holy one, or angel, was heard by Daniel speaking on this subject, but nothing is recorded of what he said. It is implied only that he was conversing about the desolations that were to come upon the holy city and the people of God. To him thus speaking, and who is introduced as having power to explain it, another holy one approaches, and asks how long this state of things was to continue. The answer to this question (ver. 14) is made, not to the one who made the inquiry, but to Daniel, evidently that it might be recorded. Daniel does not say *where* this vision occurred—whether in heaven or on earth. It was so near to him, however, that he could hear what was said. ¶ *And another saint.* Another holy one—probably an angel. If so, we may conclude, what is in itself every way probable, that one angel has more knowledge than another, or that things are communicated to some which are not to others. ¶ *Unto that certain saint which spake.* Marg., *Palmoni,* or, *the numberer of secrets,* or, *the wonderful numberer.* The Hebrew word, פַּלְמוֹנִי *palmoni,* occurs nowhere else in the Scriptures. The similar form, פְּלֹנִי *peloni,* occurs in Ruth iv. 1, " *Ho, such* a one, turn aside;" in 1 Sam. xxi. 2, "appointed my servants to *such* and such a place;" and 2 Kings vi. 8, " In *such* and such a place." The Italic words denote the corresponding Hebrew word. The word, according to Gesenius, means *some one, a certain one;* in Arabic, one who is distinct or definite, whom one points out as with the finger, and not by name. It is

derived from an obsolete noun, פָּלוֹן *palon,* from the verb פָּלָה *palá,* to distinguish, and is united commonly with the word אַלְמֹנִי—meaning, properly, one concealed or unknown. It is language, therefore, which would be properly addressed to an unknown person with whom we would desire to speak, or whom we would designate by the finger, or in some such way, without being able to call the name. Thus applied in the passage here, it means that Daniel did not know the names of the persons thus speaking, but simply saw that one was speaking to another. He had no other way of designating or distinguishing them than by applying a term which was commonly used of a stranger when one wished to address him, or to point him out, or to call him to him. There is no foundation in the word for the meaning suggested in the margin. Theodotion does not attempt to translate the word, but retains it— φελμουνὶ—Phelmouni. The Latin Vulgate well expresses the meaning, *dixit unus sanctus alteri nescio cui loquenti.* The full sense is undoubtedly conveyed by the two ideas, (*a*) that the one referred to was unknown by name, and (*b*) that he wished to designate him in some way, or to point him out. ¶ *How long* shall be *the vision* concerning *the daily* sacrifice? How long is that which is designed to be represented by the vision to continue; that is, how long in fact will the offering of the daily sacrifice in the temple be suspended? ¶ *And the transgression of desolation.* Marg., *making desolate.* That is, the act of iniquity on the part of Antiochus producing such desolation in the holy city and the temple—how long is that to continue? ¶ *To give both the sanctuary.* The temple; the holy place where God dwelt by a visible symbol, and where he was worshipped. ¶ *And the host.* The people of God—the Jewish people. ¶ *To be trodden under foot.* To be utterly despised and prostrated—as anything which is trodden under our feet.

DANIEL II.

H

14 And he said unto me, Unto two thousand and three hundred

1 *evening, morning.*

days ;[1] then shall the sanctuary be [2] cleansed.

2 *justified.*

14. *And he said unto me.* Instead of answering the one who made the inquiry, the answer is made to Daniel, doubtless that he might make a record of it, or communicate it to others. If it had been made to the inquirer, the answer would have remained with him, and could have been of no use to the world. For the encouragement, however, of the Hebrew people, when their sanctuary and city would be thus desolate, and in order to furnish an instance of the clear fulfilment of a prediction, it was important that it should be recorded, and hence it was made to Daniel. ¶ *Unto two thousand and three hundred days.* Marg., *evening, morning.* So the Hebrew,

עֶרֶב בֹּקֶר. So the Latin Vulgate, *ad vesperam et mane.* And so Theodotion—ἕως ἑσπέρας καὶ πρωΐ—"to the evening and morning." The *language* here is evidently that which was derived from Gen. i., or which was common among the Hebrews, to speak of the "evening and the morning" as constituting a day. There can be no doubt, however, that a *day* is intended by this, for this is the fair and obvious interpretation. The Greeks were accustomed to denote the period of a day in the same manner by the word νυχθήμερον (see 2 Cor. xi. 25), in order more emphatically to designate one complete day. See Prof. Stuart's *Hints on Prophecy,* pp. 99, 100. The time then specified by this would be six years and a hundred and ten days. Much difficulty has been felt by expositors in reconciling this statement with the other designations of time in the book of Daniel, supposed to refer to the same event, and with the account furnished by Josephus in regard to the period which elapsed during which the sanctuary was desolate, and the daily sacrifice suspended. The other designations of time which have been *supposed* to refer to the same event in Daniel, are ch. vii. 25, where the time mentioned is three years and a half, or twelve hundred and sixty

days; and ch. xii. 7, where the same time is mentioned, "a time, times, and an half," or three years and an half, or, as before, twelve hundred and sixty days; and ch. xii. 11, where the period mentioned is "a thousand two hundred and ninety days;" and ch. xii. 12, where the time mentioned is "a thousand three hundred and thirty-five days." The time mentioned by Josephus is three years exactly from the time when "their Divine worship was fallen off, and was reduced to a profane and common use," till the time when the lamps were lighted again, and the worship restored, for he says that the one event happened precisely three years after the other, on the same day of the month.—*Ant.* b. xii. ch. vii. § 6. In his *Jewish Wars,* however, b. i. ch. i. § 1, he says that Antiochus "spoiled the temple, and put a stop to the constant practice of offering a daily sacrifice of expiation for three years and six months." Now, in order to explain the passage before us, and to reconcile the accounts, or to show that there is no contradiction between them, the following remarks may be made: (1.) We may lay out of view the passage in ch. vii. 25. See Notes on that passage. If the reasoning there be sound, then that passage had no reference to Antiochus, and though, according to Josephus, there is a remarkable coincidence between the time mentioned there and the time during which the daily sacrifice was suspended, yet that does not demonstrate that the reference there is to Antiochus. (2.) We may lay out of view, also, for the present, the passages in ch. xii. 11, 12. Those will be the subject of consideration hereafter, and for the present ought not to be allowed to embarrass us in ascertaining the meaning of the passage before us. (3.) On the assumption, however, that those passages refer to Antiochus, and that the accounts in Josephus above referred to are correct — though *he* mentions different times, and though different periods are referred to by Daniel, the *variety* may be accounted for by the supposition that separate epochs are referred to at the *starting point* in the calculation—the *terminus a quo*. The truth was, there were several decisive acts in the history of Antiochus that led to the ultimate desolation of Jerusalem, and at one time a writer may have contemplated one, and at another time another. Thus, there was the act by which Jason, made high-priest by Antiochus, was permitted to set up a gymnasium in Jerusalem after the manner of the heathen (Prideaux, iii. 216; 1 Macc. i. 11–15); the act by which he assaulted and took Jerusalem, entering the most holy place, stripping the temple of its treasures, defiling the temple, and offering a great sow on the altar of burnt-offerings (Prideaux, iii. 230, 231; 1 Macc. i. 20–28); the act, just two years after this, by which, having been defeated in his expedition to Egypt, he resolved to vent all his wrath on the Jews, and, on his return, sent Apollonius with a great army to ravage and destroy Jerusalem—when Apollonius, having plundered the city, set it on fire, demolished the houses, pulled down the walls, and with the ruins of the demolished city built a strong fortress on Mount Acra, which overlooked the temple, and from which he could attack all who went to the temple to worship (Prideaux, iii. 239, 240; 1 Macc. i. 29–40); and the act by which Antiochus solemnly forbade all burnt-offerings, and sacrifices, and drink-offerings in the temple— (Prideaux, iii. 241, 242; 1 Macc. i. 44–51). Now, it is evident that one writing of these calamitous events, and mentioning *how long* they would continue, might at one time contemplate one of these events as the beginning, the *terminus a quo*, and at another time, another of these events might be in his eye. Each one of them was a strongly marked and decisive event, and each one might be contemplated as a period which, in an important sense, determined the destiny of the city, and put an end to the worship of God there. (4.) It seems probable that the time mentioned in the passage before us is designed to take in the whole series of disastrous events, from the first decisive act which led to the suspending of the daily sacrifice, or the termination of the worship of God there, to the time when the "sanctuary was cleansed." That this is so would seem to be probable from the series of visions presented to Daniel in the chapter before us. The acts of the "little horn" representing Antiochus, as seen in vision, began with his attack on the "pleasant land" (ver. 9), and the things which attracted the attention of Daniel were, that he "waxed great," and made war on "the host of heaven," and "cast some of the host and of the stars to the ground" (ver. 10), and "magnified himself against the prince of the host" (ver. 11)—acts which refer manifestly to his attack on the people of God, and the priests or ministers of religion, and on God himself as the "prince of the host"—unless this phrase should be understood as referring rather to the high-priest. We are then rather to look to the whole series of events as included within the two thousand and three hundred days, than the period in which literally the daily sacrifice was *forbidden* by a solemn statute. It was practically suspended, and the worship of God interrupted during all that time. (5.) The *terminus ad quem*—the conclusion of the period is marked and settled. This was the "cleansing of the sanctuary." This took place, under Judas Maccabeus, Dec. 25, 165 B.C.—Prideaux, iii. 265–268. Now, reckoning *back* from this period, two thousand and three hundred days, we come to August 5, 171 B.C. The question is, whether there were in this year, and at about this time, any events in the series of sufficient importance to constitute *a period* from which to reckon; events answering to what Daniel saw as the commencement of the vision, when "some of the host and the stars were cast down and stamped upon." Now, as a matter of fact, there commenced in the year 171 B.C. a series of aggressions upon the priesthood, and temple, and city of the Jews on the part of Antiochus, which terminated only with his death. Up to this year, the relations of Antiochus and the Jewish people were peaceful and cordial. In the year 175 B.C. he granted to the Jewish people, who desired it, permission to erect a gymnasium in Jerusalem, as above stated. In the year 173 B.C. demand was made of Antiochus of the provinces of Cœlo-Syria and Palestine by the young Philometor of Egypt, who had just come to the throne, and by his mother—a demand which was the origin of the war between Antiochus and the king of Egypt, and the beginning of all the disturbances.—Prideaux, iii. 218. In the year 172 B.C., Antiochus bestowed the office of high-priest on Menelaus, who was the brother of Jason the high-priest. Jason had sent Menelaus to Antioch to pay the king his tribute-money, and while there Menelaus conceived the design of supplanting his brother, and by offering for it more than Jason had, he procured the appointment and returned to Jerusalem.—Prideaux, iii. 220–222. Up to this time all the intercourse of Antiochus with the Jews had been of a peaceful character, and nothing of a hostile nature had occurred. In 171 B.C. began the series of events which finally resulted in the invasion and destruction of the city, and in the cessation of the public worship of God. Menelaus, having procured the high-priesthood, refused to pay the tribute-money which he had promised for it, and was summoned to Antioch. Antiochus being then absent, Menelaus took advantage of his absence, and having, by means of Lysimachus, whom he had left at Jerusalem, procured the vessels out of the temple, he sold them at Tyre, and thus raised money to pay the king. In the meantime, Onias III., the lawful high-priest, who had fled to Antioch, sternly rebuked Menelaus for his sacrilege, and soon after, at the instigation of Menelaus, was allured from his retreat at Daphné, where he had sought an asylum, and was murdered by Andronicus, the vicegerent of Antiochus. At the same time, the Jews in Jerusalem, highly indignant at the profanation by Menelaus, and the sacrilege in robbing the temple, rose in rebellion against Lysimachus and the Syrian forces who defended him, and both cut

off this "sacrilegious robber" (Prideaux), and the guards by whom he was surrounded. This assault on the officer of Antiochus, and rebellion against him, was the commencement of the hostilities which resulted in the ruin of the city, and the closing of the worship of God.—Prideaux, iii. 224–226; Stuart's *Hints on Prophecy*, p. 102. Here commenced a series of aggressions upon the priesthood, and the temple, and the city of the Jews, which, with occasional interruption, continued to the death of Antiochus, and which led to all that was done in profaning the temple, and in suspending the public worship of God, and it is doubtless to this time that the prophet here refers. This is the natural period in describing the series of events which were so disastrous to the Jewish people; this is the period at which one who should now describe them as *history*, would begin. It may not, indeed, be practicable to make out the precise number of *days*, for the exact dates are not preserved in history, but the calculation brings it into the year 171 B.C., the year which is necessary to be supposed in order that the two thousand and three hundred days should be completed. Comp. Lengerke, *in loc.*, p. 388. Various attempts have been made to determine the exact number of the days by historic records. Bertholdt, whom Lengerke follows, determines it in this manner. He regards the time referred to as that from the command to set up heathen altars to the victory over Nicanor, and the solemn celebration of that victory, as referred to in 1 Macc. vii. 48, 49. According to this reckoning, the time is as follows :—The command to set up idol altars was issued in the year 145, on the 15th of the month Kisleu. There remained of that year, after the command was given—

Half of the month Kisleu			15 days.	
The month Thebet			30	„
„	Shebath		29	„
„	Adar		30	„
The Year	146		354	„
„	147		354	„
„	148		354	„
„	149		354	„
„	150		354	„

Carry forward, 1874 days.

15 ¶ And it came to pass, when I, *even* I Daniel, had seen the vision, and sought for the meaning, then, behold, there stood before me as the appearance of a man.

16 And I heard a man's voice

between *the banks of* Ulai, which called, and said, Gabriel, [a] make this *man* to understand the vision.

17 So he came near where I stood; and when he came, I was

a Luke 1. 19, 26.

Brought over,	1874 days.

The year 151 to the 13th day of the month Adar, when the victory over Nicanor was achieved..................... 337 „

Two intercalary months during this time, according to the Jewish reckoning... 60 „

2271 days.

This would leave but twenty-nine days of the 2300 to be accounted for, and this would be required to go from the place of the battle—between Beth-Horon and Adasa (1 Macc. vii. 39, 40) to Jerusalem, and to make arrangements to celebrate the victory. See Bertholdt, pp. 501–503. The reckoning here is from the time of founding the kingdom of the Seleucidæ, or the era of the Seleucidæ. ¶ *Then shall the sanctuary be cleansed.* Marg., *justified.* The Hebrew word (צָדַק) means, to be right or straight, and then to be just or righteous ; then to vindicate or justify. In the form here used (Niphal), it means to be declared just ; to be justified or vindicated, and, as applied to the temple or sanctuary, to be vindicated from violence or injury ; that is, to be cleansed. See Gesenius, *Lex.* There is undoubtedly reference here to the act of Judas Maccabeus, in solemnly purifying the temple, and repairing it, and re-dedicating it, after the pollutions brought upon it by Antiochus. For a description of this, see Prideaux's *Connexions,* iii. 265–269. Judas designated a priesthood again to serve in the temple ; pulled down the altars which the heathen had erected ; bore out all the defiled stones into an unclean place ; built a new altar in place of the old altar of burnt-offerings which they had defiled ; hallowed the courts ; made a new altar of incense, table of shew-bread, golden candlestick, &c., and solemnly re-consecrated the whole to the service of God. This act occurred on the twenty-fifth day of the ninth month (Kisleu), and the solemnity

continued for eight days. This is the festival which is called "the feast of dedication" in the New Testament (John x. 22), and which our Saviour honoured with his presence. See 1 Macc. iv. 41–58 ; 2 Macc. x. 1–7 ; Josephus, *Ant.* b. xii. ch. vii. § 6, 7.

15. *And it came to pass,* &c. Daniel saw the vision, but was unable to explain it. ¶ *And sought for the meaning.* Evidently by meditating on it, or endeavouring in his own mind to make it out. ¶ *There stood before me as the appearance of a man.* One having the appearance of a man. This was evidently Gabriel (ver. 16), who now assumed a human form, and who was addressed by the voice from between the banks of the Ulai, and commenced to make known the meaning of the vision.

16. *And I heard a man's voice between* the banks of *Ulai.* Notes on ver. 2. The voice seemed to come from the river, as if it were that of the Genius of the river, and to address Gabriel, who stood near to Daniel on the shore. This was doubtless the voice of God. The speaker was invisible, and this method of explaining the vision was adopted, probably to make the whole scene more impressive. ¶ *Which called, and said, Gabriel.* Gabriel is mentioned in the Scriptures only in Dan. viii. 16 ; ix. 21 ; Luke i. 19, 26. In Luke i. 19, he is mentioned as saying of himself, "I am Gabriel, that stand in the presence of God." The word means, properly, "man of God." Nothing more is known of him, and he is mentioned only as bearing messages to Daniel, to Zacharias the father of John the Baptist, and to Mary. ¶ *Make this* man *to understand the vision.* Explain it to him so that he will understand its meaning.

17. *So he came near where I stood.* He had seen him, evidently, at first in

afraid, and fell upon my face : but he said unto me, Understand, O son of man; for at the time of the end *shall be* the vision.

a ch. 10. 9, 10.

18 Now, as he was speaking with me, I was in a deep sleep *a* on my face toward the ground : but he touched me, and [1] set me upright.

1 *made me stand upon my standing.*

the distance. He now drew near to Daniel, that he might communicate with him the more readily. ¶ *And when he came, I was afraid, and fell upon my face.* Doubtless perceiving that he was a celestial being. See Notes on Rev. i. 17. Comp. Ezek. i. 28, and Dan. x. 8, 9. He was completely overpowered by the presence of the celestial stranger, and sank to the ground. ¶ *But he said unto me, Understand, O son of man.* Give attention, that you may understand the vision. On the phrase "son of man," see Notes on ch. vii. 13. It is here simply an address to him as a man. ¶ *For at the time of the end* shall be *the vision.* The *design* of this expression is undoubtedly to cheer and comfort the prophet with some assurance of what was to occur in future times. In what way this was done, or what was the precise idea indicated by these words, interpreters have not been agreed. Maurer explains it, "for this vision looks to the last time ; that is, the time which would immediately precede the coming of the Messiah, which would be a time of calamity, in which the guilt of the wicked would be punished, and the virtue of the saints would be tried, to wit, the time of Antiochus Epiphanes." Lengerke supposes that the end of the existing calamities—the sufferings of the Jews—is referred to; and that the meaning is, that in the time of the Messiah, to which the vision is extended, there would be an end of their sufferings and trials. The design of the angel, says he, is to support and comfort the troubled seer, as if he should not be anxious that these troubles were to occur, since they would have an end, or, as Michaelis observes, that the seer should not suppose that the calamities indicated by the vision would have no end. Perhaps the meaning may be this: "The vision is for the time of the end ;" that is, it has respect

to the closing period of the world, under which the Messiah is to come, and necessarily precedes that, and leads on to that. It pertains to a series of events which are to introduce the latter times, when the kingdom of God shall be set up on the earth. In justification of this view of the passage, it may be remarked that this is not only the most obvious view, but is sustained by all those passages which speak of the coming of the Messiah as "the end," the "last days," &c. Thus 1 Cor. x. 11: "upon whom the ends of the world are come." Comp. Notes on Isa. ii. 2. According to this interpretation, the meaning is, "the vision pertains to the end, or the closing dispensation of things ;" that is, it has a bearing on the period when the end will come, or will introduce that period. It looks on to future times, even to those times, though now remote (comp. ver. 26), when a new order of things will exist, under which the affairs of the world will be wound up. Comp. Notes on Heb. i. 2.

18. *Now, as he was speaking with me, I was in a deep sleep on my face toward the ground.* Overcome and prostrate with the vision. That is, he had sunk down stupified or senseless. See ch. x. 9. His strength had been entirely taken away by the vision. There is nothing improbable in this, that the sudden appearance of a celestial vision, or a heavenly being, should take away the strength. Compare Gen. xv. 12; Job iv. 13, *seq.; Judg.* vi. 22; xiii. 20, 22; Isa. vi. 5; Luke i. 12, 29.; ii. 9; Acts ix. 3, 8. ¶ *But he touched me, and set me upright.* Marg., as in Heb., "made me stand upon my standing." He raised me up on my feet. So the Saviour addressed Saul of Tarsus, when he had been suddenly smitten to the earth, by his appearing to him on the way to Damascus: "Rise, and stand upon thy feet," &c., Acts xxvi. 16.

19 And he said, Behold, I will make thee know what shall be in the last end of the indignation : for at the time appointed *a* the end *shall be.*

20 The ram *b* which thou sawest having *two* horns *are* the kings of Media and Persia.

21 And the rough goat *is* the king of Grecia: and the great horn

that *is* between his eyes *is* the first king.

22 Now that being broken, whereas four stood up for it, four kingdoms shall stand up out of the nation, but not in his power.

23 And in the latter time of their kingdom, when the transgressors are ¹ come to the full, a king of fierce countenance, and un-

a Hab. 2. 3; Rev. 10. 7.　　*b* ver. 3.

1 *accomplished.*

19. *And he said, Behold, I will make thee know what shall be in the last end of the indignation.* In the future time when the Divine indignation shall be manifest toward the Hebrew people ; to wit, by suffering the evils to come upon them which Antiochus would inflict. It is everywhere represented that these calamities would occur as a proof of the Divine displeasure on account of their sins. Comp. ch. ix. 24; xi. 35; 2 Macc. vii. 33. ¶ *For at the time appointed the end shall be.* It shall not always continue. There is a definite period marked out in the Divine purpose, and when that period shall arrive, the end of all this will take place. See Notes on ver. 17.

20. *The ram which thou sawest,* &c. See Notes on ver. 3. This is one of the instances in the Scriptures in which symbols are explained. There can be no doubt, therefore, as to the meaning.

21. *And the rough goat.* Notes on ver. 5. In ver. 5 he is called a *he-goat.* Here the word *rough* or *hairy—*שָׂעִיר*—* is applied to it. This appellation is often given to a goat (Lev. iv. 24 ; xvi. 9 ; Gen. xxxvii. 31). It would seem that *either* term—a *he-goat,* or a *hairy-goat*—would serve to designate the animal, and it is probable that the terms were used indiscriminately. ¶ *Is the king of Grecia.* Represents the king of Greece. The word here rendered *Grecia* (יָוָן *Javan*) denotes usually and properly *Ionia,* the western part of Asia Minor ; but this name was extended so as to embrace the whole of Greece. See Aristoph. *Acharn.* 504, *ibique Schol.; Æschyl. Pers.* 176, 561; Gesenius, *Lex.* Latin Vulgate and

Theodotion, here render it "the king of the Grecians," and there can be no doubt that the royal power among the Greeks is here referred to. See Notes on ver. 5. ¶ *And the great horn that is between his eyes* is *the first king.* Alexander the Great. The first that consolidated the whole power, and that was known in the East as the king of Greece. So he is expressly called in 1 Macc. i. 1: "The first over Greece." Philip, his father, was opposed in his attempts to conquer Greece, and was defeated. Alexander invaded Greece, burned Thebes, compelled the Athenians to submit, and was declared generalissimo of the Grecian forces against the Persians.

22. *Now that being broken.* By the death of Alexander. ¶ *Whereas four stood up for it.* Stood up in its place. ¶ *Four kingdoms shall stand up.* Ultimately. It is not necessary to suppose that this would be immediately. If four such should in fact spring out of this one kingdom, all that is implied in the prophecy would be fulfilled. On the fulfilment of this, see Notes on ver. 8. ¶ *But not in his power.* No one of these four dynasties had at any time the power which was wielded by Alexander the Great.

23. *And in the latter time of their kingdom.* When it shall be drawing to an end. All these powers were ultimately absorbed in the Roman power ; and the meaning here is, that taking the time from the period of their formation — the division of the empire after the battle of Ipsus (see Notes on ver. 8), till the time when all would be swallowed up in the Roman dominion, what is here stated—to wit, the rise of Antiochus — would be in

derstanding dark sentences, shall stand up.

24 And his power shall be mighty, *a* but not by his own

a Rev. 17. 13, 17.   *b* vers. 10, 12, &c.

power: and he shall destroy wonderfully, and shall prosper, and practise, and *b* shall destroy the mighty and the 1 holy people.

1 *people of the holy ones.*

the latter portion of that period. The battle of Ipsus was fought 301 B.C., and the Roman power was extended over all those regions gradually from 168 B.C.—the battle of Pydna, when Perseus was defeated, and Macedonia was reduced to a Roman province, to 30 B.C., when Egypt was subjected—the last of these kingdoms that submitted to the Roman arms. Antiochus began to reign, 175 B.C.—so that it was in the latter part of this period. ¶ *When the transgressors are come to the full.* Marg., *accomplished.* That is, when the state of things—the prevalence of wickedness and irreligion in Judea—shall have been allowed to continue as long as it can be—or so that the cup shall be full—then shall appear this formidable power to inflict deserved punishment on the guilty nation. The sacred writers often speak of iniquity as being *full*—of the cup of iniquity as being full—as if there was a certain limit or capacity beyond which it could not be allowed to go. When that arrives, God interposes, and cuts off the guilty by some heavy judgment. Comp. Gen. xv. 16: "The iniquity of the Amorites is not yet full." Matt. xxiii. 32: "Fill ye up then the measure of your fathers." 1 Thess. ii. 16: "To fill up their sins alway." The idea is, that there is a certain measure or amount of sin which can be tolerated, but beyond that the Divine compassion cannot go with safety to the universe, or consistently with the honour of God, and then the punishment may be expected; then punishment must come. This is true, doubtless, of individuals and nations, and this period had arrived in regard to the Jews when Antiochus was permitted to lay their temple, city, and country waste. ¶ *A king of fierce countenance.* Stern and severe. This expression would be applicable to many who have held the kingly office, and no one can doubt that it may be ap-

plied with strict propriety to Antiochus. ¶ *And understanding dark sentences.* Gesenius (*Lex.*) explains the word here rendered "dark sentences" to mean *artifice, trick, stratagem.* This will better agree with the character of Antiochus, who was more distinguished for craft and policy than he was for wisdom, or for explaining enigmas. The meaning seems to be that he would be politic and crafty, seeking to make his way, and to accomplish his purpose, not only by the terror that he inspired, but by deceit and cunning. That this was his character is well known. Comp. Notes on ver. 25. ¶ *Shall stand up.* Shall succeed, or there shall be such a king.

24. *And his power shall be mighty.* He shall be a powerful monarch. Though not *as* mighty as Alexander, yet his conquests of Egypt and other places show that he deserved to be numbered among the mighty kings of the earth. ¶ *But not by his own power.* That is, it shall not be by any strength of his own, but by the power which God gives him. This is true of all kings and princes (comp. John xix. 11; Isa. x. 5, *seq.*), but it seems to be referred to here particularly to show that the calamities which he was about to bring upon the Hebrew people were by Divine direction and appointment. This great power was given him in order that he might be an instrument in the Divine hand of inflicting deserved punishment on them for their sins. ¶ *And he shall destroy wonderfully.* In a wonderful or extraordinary manner shall he spread desolation. This refers particularly to the manner in which he would lay waste the holy city, and the land of Judea. The history in the books of Maccabees shows that this was literally fulfilled. ¶ *And shall prosper.* Antiochus was among the most successful kings in his various expeditions. Particularly was he successful in his enterprises against the

25 And through his policy also he shall cause craft to prosper in his hand; and he shall magnify *himself* in his heart, and by [1] peace shall destroy many: he shall also

1 or, *prosperity.*

holy land. ¶ *And practise.* Heb., *do.* That is, he shall be distinguished not only for *forming* plans, but for *executing* them; not merely for *purposing*, but for *doing*. ¶ *And shall destroy the mighty and the holy people.* The people of God—the Jewish nation. See Notes on vers. 9–12.

25. *And through his policy.* The word rendered *policy* here (שֵׂכֶל) means, properly, intelligence, understanding, wisdom; and then, in a bad sense, craft, cunning. So it is rendered here by Gesenius, and the meaning is, that he would owe his success in a great measure to craft and subtilty. ¶ *He shall cause craft to prosper in his hand.* He shall owe his success in a great measure to a crafty policy, to intrigue, and to cunning. This was true in an eminent sense, of Antiochus. See his history in Prideaux, above referred to, and the books of Maccabees. Comp. Notes on ch. xi. 21. The same character is given of him by Polybius, *Relig.* lib. xxxi. c. 5, tom. iv. p. 501, ed. Schweighäuser; Appian, *de reb. Syr.* xlv. t. 1, p. 604, ed. Schweigh. Comp. 2 Macc. v. 24–26. He came to the kingdom by deceit (Prideaux, iii. 212), and a great part of his success was owing to craft and policy. ¶ *And he shall magnify* himself *in his heart.* Shall be lifted up with pride, or esteem himself of great consequence. ¶ *And by peace shall destroy many.* Marg., *prosperity.*

The Hebrew word (שַׁלְוָה) means, properly, tranquillity, security, ease, carelessness. Here the phrase seems to mean "in the midst of security" (Gesenius, *Lex.*); that is, while they were at ease, and regarded themselves as in a state of safety, he would come suddenly and unexpectedly upon them, and destroy them. He would make sudden war on them, invading their territories, so that they would have no opportunity to make preparation to meet him. Comp. ch. xi. 21, 24. It would seem to mean that he would endeavour to produce the impression that he was coming in peace; that he pretended friendship, and designed to keep those whom he meant to invade and destroy in a state of false security, so that he might descend upon them unawares. This was his policy rather than to declare war openly, and so give his enemies fair warning of what he intended to do. This description agrees every way with the character of Antiochus, a leading part of whose policy always was to preserve the appearance of friendship, that he might accomplish his purpose while his enemies were off their guard. ¶ *He shall also stand up against the Prince of princes.* Notes, ver. 11. Against God, the ruler over the kings of the earth. ¶ *But he shall be broken without hand.* That is, without the hand of man, or by no visible cause. He shall be overcome by a Divine, invisible power. According to the author of the first book of Maccabees (ch. vi. 8–16), he died of grief and remorse in Babylon. He was on an expedition to Persia, and there laid siege to Elymais, and was defeated, and fled to Babylon, when, learning that his forces in Palestine had been repulsed, penetrated with grief and remorse, he sickened and died. According to the account in the second book of Maccabees (ix.), his death was most distressing and horrible. Comp. Prideaux, iii. 272–275. All the statements given of his death, by the authors of the books of Maccabees, by Josephus, by Polybius, by Q. Curtius, and by Arrian (see the quotations in Prideaux), agree in representing it as attended with every circumstance of horror that can be well supposed to accompany a departure from this world, and as having every mark of the just judgment of God. The Divine prediction in Daniel was fully accomplished, that his death would be "without hand," in the sense that it would not be by human instrumentality; but that it would be by a direct Divine infliction. When Antiochus died, the

stand up against the Prince of
princes; but he shall be broken
without hand.

26 And the vision of the evening
and the morning which was told

is true: wherefore shut *a* thou up
the vision; for it *shall be* for many
days.

27 And I Daniel fainted, and

opposition to the Jews ceased, and
their land again had peace and rest.

26. *And the vision of the evening and
the morning.* That is, of the two thousand three hundred days. See ver. 14,
and the margin on that verse. The
meaning here is, "the vision pertaining to that succession of evenings and
mornings." Perhaps this appellation
was given to it particularly because it
pertained so much to the evening and
morning sacrifice. ¶ Is *true.* Shall
be certainly accomplished. This was
said by the angel, giving thus to Daniel
the assurance that what he had seen
(vers. 9–14) was no illusion, but would
certainly come to pass. ¶ *Wherefore
shut thou up the vision.* Seal it up.
Make a record of it, that it may be
preserved, and that its fulfilment may
be marked. See Notes on Isa. viii. 16.
¶ *For it* shall be *for many days.*
That is, many days will elapse before
it will be accomplished. Let a fair
record, therefore, be made of it, and
let it be sealed up, that it may be preserved to prepare the people for these
events. *When* these things would come
thus fearfully upon the people of Judea,
they would be the better able to bear
these trials, knowing the period when
they would terminate.

27. *And I Daniel fainted.* Heb.,
"I was "—נִהְיֵיתִי. Comp. Dan. ii. 1.

The meaning, according to Gesenius
(*Lex.*), is, "I was done up, and was
sick:"—I was done over, &c. Perhaps the *reason* of his using this verb
here is, that he represents himself
as *having been sick,* and then as faint-
ing away, as if his life had departed.
The Latin Vulgate renders it *langui.*
Theodotion, ἐκοιμήθην — "was laid in
my bed." The general idea is plain,
that he was overcome and prostrate
at the effect of the vision. He had
been permitted to look into the future, and the scenes were so appal-
ling—the changes that were to occur
were so great—the calamities were so

fearful in their character—and, above
all, his mind was so affected that the
daily sacrifice was to cease, and the
worship of God be suspended, that he
was entirely overcome. And who of
us, probably, could *bear* a revelation
of what is to occur hereafter? Where
is there strength that could endure the
disclosure of what may happen even
in a few years? ¶ *And was sick* certain *days.* The exact time is not specified. The natural interpretation is,
that it was for a considerable period.
¶ *Afterwards I rose up, and did the
king's business.* Compare Notes on
ver. 2. From this it would appear
that he had been sent to Shushan on
some business pertaining to the government. What it was we are not informed. As a matter of fact, he was
sent there for a more important purpose than any which pertained to the
government at Babylon—to receive a
disclosure of most momentous events
that were to occur in distant times.
Yet this did not prevent him from
attending faithfully to the business
intrusted to him—as no views which
we take of heavenly things, and no
disclosures made to our souls, and no
absorption in the duties and enjoy-
ments of religion, should prevent us
from attending with fidelity to whatever secular duties may be intrusted
to us. Sickness justifies us, of course,
in not attending to them; the highest
views which we may have of God and
of religious truth should only make us
more faithful in the discharge of our
duties to our fellow-men, to our country, and in all the relations of life. He
who has been favoured with the clearest
views of Divine things will be none the
less prepared to discharge with faithfulness the duties of this life; he who
is permitted and enabled to look far
into the future will be none the less
likely to be diligent, faithful, and la-
borious in meeting the responsibilities
of the present moment. If a man could
see all that there is in heaven, it would

was sick *certain* days : afterward
I rose up, and did the king's busi-

only serve to impress him with a deeper
conviction of his obligations in every
relation ; if he could see all that there
is to come in the vast eternity before
him, it would only impress him with
a profounder sense of the consequences
which may follow from the discharge
of the present duty.   ¶ *And I was
astonished at the vision.* He was stupified—he was overcome—at the splendid appearance, and the momentous
nature of the disclosures. Compare
Notes on ch. iv. 19.   ¶ *But none understood* it. It would seem probable
from this, that he communicated it to
others, but no one was able to explain
it. Its general features were plain,
but no one could follow out the details, and tell *precisely* what would
occur, before the vision was fulfilled.
This is the general nature of prophecy ;
and if neither Daniel nor any of his
friends could explain this vision in detail, are we to hope that we shall be
successful in disclosing the full meaning of those which are not yet fulfilled ?
The truth is, that in all such revelations of the future, there must be much
in detail which is not now fully understood. The general features may be
plain—as, in this case, it was clear
that a mighty king would rise ; that
he would be a tyrant ; that he would
oppress the people of God ; that he
would invade the holy land ; that he
would for a time put a period to the
offering of the daily sacrifice ; and that
this would continue for a definite period ; and that then he would be cut
off without human instrumentality :
but who from this would have been
able to draw out, in detail, all the
events which in fact occurred ? Who
could have told precisely how these
things would come to pass ? Who
could have ventured on a biography
of Antiochus Epiphanes ? Yet these
three things are true in regard to this :
(1) that no one by human sagacity
could have foreseen these events so
as to have been able to furnish these
sketches of what was to be ; (2) that
these were sufficient to apprise those
who were interested particularly of

ness ; and I was astonished at the
vision, but none understood *it.*

what would occur ;̣ and (3) that when
these events occurred, it was plain to
all persons that the prophecy had reference to them.   So plain is this—so
clear is the application of the predictions in this book, that Porphyry
maintained that it was written after
the events had occurred, and that the
book must have been forged.

CHAPTER IX.

ANALYSIS OF THE CHAPTER.

This chapter is properly divided into
three parts, or comprises three things :

I. The inquiry of Daniel into the
time that the desolations of Jerusalem
were to continue, and his determination to seek the Lord, to pray that his
purpose in regard to the restoration of
the city and temple might be speedily
accomplished, vers. 1–3.   Daniel says
(ver. 1), that this occurred in the first
year of Darius of the seed of the Medes.
He was engaged in the study of the
books of Jeremiah.   He learned from
these books that seventy years were to
elapse during which the temple, the
city, and the land were to be desolate.
By a calculation as to the time when
this commenced, he was enabled to
ascertain the period when it would
close, and he found that that period
was near, and that, according to the
prediction, it might be expected that
the time of the restoration was at
hand.   His mind was, of course, filled
with the deepest solicitude.   It would
seem not improbable that he did not
perceive any preparation for this, or
any tendency to it, and it could not
but be that he would be filled with
anxiety in regard to it.   He does not
appear to have entertained any doubt
that the predictions would be fulfilled,
and the fact that they were so clear
and so positive was a strong reason
why he should pray, and was *the* rea-

son why he prayed so earnestly at this time. The prayer which he offered is an illustration of the truth that men will pray more earnestly when they have reason to suppose that God intends to impart a blessing, and that an assurance that an event is to occur is one of the strongest encouragements and incitements to prayer. So men will pray with more faith when they see that God is blessing the means of restoration to health, or when they see indications of an abundant harvest; so they will pray with the more fervour for God to bless his Word when they see evidences of a revival of religion, or that the time has come when God is about to display his power in the conversion of sinners; and so undoubtedly they will pray with the more earnestness as the proofs shall be multiplied that God is about to fulfil all his ancient predictions in the conversion of the whole world to himself. A belief that God intends to do a thing is never any hinderance to real prayer; a belief that he is in fact about to do it does more than anything else can do to arouse the soul to call with earnestness on his name.

II. The prayer of Daniel, vers. 4–19. This prayer is remarkable for its simplicity, its fervour, its appropriateness, its earnestness. It is a frank confession that the Hebrew people, in whose name it was offered, had deserved all the calamities which had come upon them, accompanied with earnest intercession that God would now hear this prayer, and remove the judgments from the people, and accomplish his purpose of mercy towards the city and temple. The long captivity of nearly seventy years; the utter desolation of the city and temple during that time; the numberless privations and evils to which during that period they had been exposed, had demonstrated the greatness of the sins for which these calamities had come upon the nation, and Daniel now, in the name, and uttering the sentiments, of the captive people, confessed their guilt, and the justness of the Divine dealings with them. Never has there been an instance in which punishment has had more of its designed and appropriate effect than in prompting to the sentiments which are uttered in this prayer: and the prayer, therefore, is just the expression of what we *should* feel when the hand of the Lord has been long and severely laid upon us on account of our sins. The burden of the prayer is confession; the object which he who offers it seeks is, that God would cause the severity of his judgments to cease, and the city and temple to be restored. The particular points in the prayer will be more appropriately elucidated in the exposition of this part of the chapter.

III. The answer to the prayer, vers. 20–27. The principal difficulty in the exposition of the chapter is in this portion; and indeed there is perhaps no part of the prophecies of the Old Testament that is, on some accounts, more difficult of exposition, as there is, in some respects, none more clear, and none more important. It is remarkable, among other things, as not being a direct answer to the prayer, and as seeming to have no bearing on the subject of the petition—that the city of Jerusalem might be rebuilt, and the temple restored; but it directs the mind onward to another and more important event — the coming of the Messiah, and the final closing of sacrifice and oblation, and a more entire and enduring destruction of the temple and city, after it should have been rebuilt, than had yet occurred. To give this information, an angel—the same one whom Daniel had seen before—

was sent forth from heaven, and came near to him and touched him, and said that he was commissioned to impart to him skill and understanding, vers. 20-23. "The speediness of his coming indicates a joyful messenger. The substance of that message is as follows: As a compensation for the seventy years in which the people, the city, and the temple had been entirely prostrate, seventy weeks of years, seven times seventy years of a renewed existence would be secured to them by the Lord; and the end of this period, far from bringing the mercies of God to a close, would for the first time bestow them on the Theocracy in their complete and full measure." — Hengstenberg, *Christology*, ii. 293. The *points* of information which the angel gives in regard to the future condition of the city are these :—

(*a*) That the whole period determined in respect to the holy city, to finish transgression, and to make an end of sins, and to make reconciliation for the people, and to bring in everlasting righteousness, and to seal up the vision and prophecy, and to anoint the Most Holy, was seventy weeks— evidently seventy prophetic weeks, that is, regarding each day as a year, four hundred and ninety years, ver. 24. The time when this period would *commence*—the *terminus a quo*—is not indeed distinctly specified, but the fair interpretation is, from that time when the vision appeared to Daniel, the first year of Darius, ver. 1. The literal meaning of the phrase "seventy weeks," according to Prof. Stuart (*Hints on the Interpretation of Prophecy*, p. 82), is *seventy sevens*, that is, seventy sevens of years, or four hundred and ninety years. "Daniel," says he, "had been meditating on the accomplishment of the seventy years of exile for the Jews, which Jeremiah had pre-

dicted. At the close of the fervent supplication for the people which he makes, in connection with his meditation, Gabriel appears, and announces to him that '*seventy sevens* are appointed for his people,' as it respects the time then future, in which very serious and very important events are to take place. Daniel had been meditating on the close of the seventy years of Hebrew exile, and the angel now discloses to him a new period of seventy times seven, in which still more important events are to take place."

(*b*) This period of seventy sevens, or four hundred and ninety years, is divided by the angel into smaller portions, each of them determining some important event in the future. He says, therefore (ver. 25), that from the going forth of the command to rebuild the temple, until the time when the Messiah should appear, the whole period might be divided into two portions—one of *seven sevens*, or forty-nine years, and the other of *threescore and two sevens*—sixty-two sevens, or four hundred and thirty-four years, making together four hundred and eighty-three years. This statement is accompanied with the assurance that the "street would be built again, and the wall, even in troublous times." Of these periods of seven weeks, sixty-two weeks, and one week, the close of the first is distinguished by the completion of the rebuilding of the city ; that of the second by the appearing of the Anointed One, or the Messiah, the Prince ; that of the third by the finished confirmation of the covenant with the many for whom the saving blessings designated in ver. 24, as belonging to the end of the whole period, are designed. The last period of one week is again divided into two halves. While the confirmation of the covenant extends through it, from beginning to end, the cessation of the sacrifice and meat-offering, and the death of the Anointed One, on which this depends, take place in the middle of it.

(c) The Messiah would appear after the seven weeks—reaching to the time of completing the rebuilding of the city—and the sixty-two weeks following that (that is, sixty-nine weeks altogether) would have been finished. Throughout half of the other week, after his appearing, he would labour to confirm the covenant with many, and then die a violent death, by which the sacrifices would be made to cease, while the confirmation of the covenant would continue even after his death.

(d) A people of a foreign prince would come and destroy the city and the sanctuary. The end of all would be a "flood"—an overflowing calamity, till the end of the desolations should be determined, vers. 26, 27. This fearful desolation is all that the prophet sees in the end, except that there is an obscure intimation that there would be a termination of that. But the design of the vision evidently did not reach thus far. It was to show the series of events *after* the rebuilding of the city and temple up to the time when the Messiah would come; when the great atonement would be made for sin, and when the oblations and sacrifices of the temple would finally cease ; cease in fact and naturally, for the one great sacrifice, superseding them all, would have been offered, and because the people of a foreign prince would come and sweep the temple and the altar away.

The design of the whole annunciation is, evidently, to produce consolation in the mind of the prophet. He was engaged in profound meditation on the present state, and the long-continued desolations of the city and temple. He gave his mind to the study of the prophecies to learn whether these desolations were not soon to end. He ascertained beyond a doubt that the period drew near. He devoted himself to earnest prayer that the desolation might not longer continue ; that God, provoked by the sins of the nation, would no longer execute his fearful judgments, but would graciously interpose, and restore the city and temple. He confessed ingenuously and humbly the sins of his people ; acknowledged that the judgments of God were just, but pleaded earnestly, in view of his former mercies to the same people, that he would now have compassion, and fulfil his promises that the city and temple should be restored. An answer is not given *directly*, and in the exact form in which it might have been hoped for; but an answer *is* given, in which it is *implied* that these blessings so earnestly sought would be bestowed, and in which it is *promised* that there would be far greater blessings. It is *assumed* in the answer (ver. 25) that the city would be rebuilt, and then the mind is directed onward to the assurance that it would stand through seven times seventy years— seven times as long as it had now been desolate, and that *then* that which had been the object of the desire of the people of God would be accomplished ; that for which the city and temple had been built would be fulfilled—the Messiah would come, the great sacrifice for sin would be made, and all the typical arrangements of the temple would come to an end. Thus, in fact, though not in form, the communication of the angel was an answer to prayer, and that occurred to Daniel which often occurs to those who pray—that the direct prayer which is offered receives a gracious answer, and that there accompanies the answer numberless other mercies which are drawn along in the

CHAPTER IX.

IN the first year of Darius, *a* the son of Ahasuerus, of the seed of the Medes, ¹ which was made king over the realm of the Chaldeans;

2 In the first year of his reign, I Daniel understood by books the

a ch. 5. 31.

¹ or, *in which he.*

---

train; or, in other words, that God gives us many more blessings than we ask of him.

1. *In the first year of Darius.* See Notes on ch. v. 31, and Intro. to ch. vi. § II. The king here referred to under this name was Cyaxares II., who lived between Astyages and Cyrus, and in whom was the title of king. He was the immediate successor of Belshazzar, and was the predecessor of Cyrus, and was the first of the foreign princes that reigned over Babylon. On the reasons why he is called in Daniel Darius, and not Cyaxares, see the Intro. to ch. vi. § II. Of course, as he preceded Cyrus, who gave the order to rebuild the temple (Ezra i. 1), this occurred before the close of the seventy years of the captivity. ¶ *The son of Ahasuerus.* Or the son of Astyages. See Intro. to ch. vi. § II. It was no unusual thing for the kings of the East to have several names, and one writer might refer to them under one name, and another under another. ¶ *Of the seed of the Medes.* See as above. ¶ *Which was made king over the realm of the Chaldeans.* By conquest. He succeeded Belshazzar, and was the immediate predecessor of Cyrus. Cyaxares II. ascended the throne of Media, according to the common chronology, B.C. 561. Babylon was taken by Cyrus, acting under the authority of Cyaxares, B.C. 538, and, of course, the reign of Cyaxares, or Darius, over Babylon commenced at that point, and that would be reckoned as the "first year" of his reign. He died B.C. 536, and Cyrus succeeded him; and as the order to rebuild the temple was in the first year of Cyrus, the time referred to in this chapter, when Daniel represents himself as meditating on the close of the captivity, and offering this prayer, cannot long have preceded that order. He had ascertained that the period of

the captivity was near its close, and he naturally inquired in what way the restoration of the Jews to their own land was to be effected, and by what means the temple was to be rebuilt.

2. *I Daniel understood by books.* By the sacred books, and especially by the writings of Jeremiah. It has been made a ground of objection to the genuineness of Daniel that he mentions "books" in this place (סְפָרִים) as if there were at that time a collection of the sacred books, or as if they had been enrolled together in a volume. The objection is, that the writer speaks as if the canon of the Scriptures was completed, or that he uses such language as the Hebrews did when the canon of the Scriptures was finished, and thus betrays himself. See Bertholdt, *Comm.* p. 78. Comp. De Wette, *Einl.* § 13. This objection has been examined by Hengstenberg, *Beitrag.* pp. 32–35. It is sufficient to reply to it, that there is every probability that the Jews in Babylon would be in possession of the sacred books of their nation, and that, though the canon of the Scriptures was not yet completed, there would exist private collections of those writings. The word here used by Daniel is just such as he would employ on the supposition that he referred to a private collection of the writings of the prophets. Comp. Lengerke, *in loc.* See the Intro., where the objection is examined. ¶ *The number of the years, whereof the word of the Lord came to Jeremiah.* The number of the years in respect to which the word of the Lord came to Jeremiah; that is, which he had revealed to Jeremiah. The *books* referred to, therefore, were evidently a collection of the writings of Jeremiah, or a collection which embraced his writings. ¶ *That he would accomplish seventy years in the desolations of Jerusalem.* That Jerusalem would so long lie waste. This was

number of the years, whereof the word of the LORD came to Jeremiah the *a* prophet, that he would accomplish seventy years in the desolations of Jerusalem.

3 ¶ And *b* I set my face unto the Lord God, to seek by prayer and supplications, with fasting, and sackcloth, and ashes :

a Jer. 25. 11, 12.
b Neh. 1. 4, &c.; Jer. 29. 10-13.

expressly declared by Jeremiah (ch. xxv. 11, 12): "And this whole land shall be a desolation and an astonishment; and these nations shall serve the king of Babylon seventy years. And it shall come to pass, when seventy years are accomplished, that I will punish the king of Babylon, and that nation, saith the Lord, for their iniquity," &c. So also Jer. xxix. 10: "For thus saith the Lord, That after seventy years be accomplished at Babylon, I will visit you, and perform my good word toward you, in causing you to return to this place." The time of the desolation and of the captivity, therefore, was fixed and positive, and the only difficulty in determining when it would *close*, was in ascertaining the exact year when it *commenced*. There were several occurrences which might, perhaps, be regarded as the beginning of the desolations and the captivity— the *terminus a quo*—and, according as one or another of them was fixed on, the close would be regarded as nearer or more remote. Daniel, it seems, by close study, had satisfied his own mind on that subject, and had been able to fix upon some period that was undoubtedly the proper beginning, and hence compute the time when it would close. The result showed that his calculation was correct, for, at the time he expected, the order was given by Cyrus to rebuild the city and temple. When he instituted this inquiry, and engaged in this solemn act of prayer, it would have been impossible to have conjectured in what way this could be brought about. The reigning monarch was Cyaxares II., or, as he is here called, Darius, and there was nothing in his character, or in anything that he had done, that could have been a basis of calculation that he would favour the return of the Jews and the rebuilding of the city, and there was then no probability that Cyrus would so soon come

to the throne, and nothing in *his* character, as known, that could be a ground of hope that he would voluntarily interpose, and accomplish the Divine purposes and promises in regard to the holy city. It was probably such circumstances as these which produced the anxiety in the mind of Daniel, and which led him to offer this fervent prayer; and his fervent supplications should lead us to trust in God that he will accomplish his purposes, and should induce us to pray with fervour and with faith when we see no way in which he will do it. In all cases he can as easily devise a way in answer to prayer, as he could remove Cyaxares from the throne, and incline the heart of Cyrus to undertake the rebuilding of Jerusalem and the temple.

3. *And I set my face unto the Lord God.* Probably the meaning is, that he turned his face toward Jerusalem, the place where God had dwelt; the place of his holy abode on earth. See Notes on ch. vi. 10. The language, however, would not be inappropriate to denote prayer without such a supposition. We turn to one whom we address, and so prayer may be described by "setting the face toward God." The essential idea here is, that he engaged in a set and formal prayer; he engaged in earnest devotion. He evidently set apart a time for this, for he prepared himself by fasting, and by putting on sackcloth and ashes. ¶ *To seek by prayer and supplications.* To seek his favour; to pray that he would accomplish his purposes. The words "prayer and supplications," which are often found united, would seem to denote *earnest* prayer, or prayer when *mercy* was implored—the notion of *mercy* or *favour* implored entering into the meaning of the Hebrew word rendered *supplications.* ¶ *With fasting.* In view of the desolations of the city and temple;

4 And I prayed unto the LORD my God, and made my confession, and said, O Lord, the great *a* and dreadful God, keeping *b* the cove-nant and mercy to them that love him, and to them that keep his commandments:

a Neh. 9. 32, &c.   *b* Exod. 20. 6.

the calamities that had come upon the people; their sins, &c.; and in order also that the mind might be prepared for earnest and fervent prayer. The occasion was one of great importance, and it was proper that the mind should be prepared for it by fasting. It was the purpose of Daniel to humble himself before God, and to recal the sins of the nation for which they now suffered, and fasting was an appropriate means of doing that. ¶ *And sackcloth.* Sackcloth was a coarse kind of cloth, usually made of hair, and employed for the purpose of making sacks, bags, &c. As it was dark, and coarse, and rough, it was regarded as a proper badge of mourning and humiliation, and was worn as such usually by passing or girding it around the loins. See Notes on Isa. iii. 24; Job xvi. 15. ¶ *And ashes.* It was customary to cast ashes on the head in a time of great grief and sorrow. The principles on which this was done seem to have been, (*a*) that the external appearance should correspond with the state of the mind and the heart, and (*b*) that such external circumstances would have a tendency to produce a state of heart corresponding to them—or would produce true humiliation and repentance for sin. Comp. Notes on Job ii. 8. The practical truth taught in this verse, in connection with the preceding, is, that the fact that a thing is certainly predicted, and that God means to accomplish it, is an encouragement to prayer, and will lead to prayer. We could have no encouragement to pray except in the purposes and promises of God, for we have no power ourselves to accomplish the things for which we pray, and all must depend on his will. When that will is known it is the very thing to encourage us in our approaches to him, and is all the assurance that we need to induce us to pray.

4. *And I prayed unto the Lord my God.* Evidently a set and formal prayer. It would seem probable that he offered this prayer, and then recorded the substance of it afterwards. We have no reason to suppose that we have the whole of it, but we have doubtless its principal topics. ¶ *And made my confession.* Not as an individual, or not of his own sins only, but a confession in behalf of the people, and in their name. There is no reason to suppose that what he here says did *not* express their feelings. They had been long in captivity—far away from their desolate city and temple. They could not but be sensible that these calamities had come upon them on account of their sins; and they could not but feel that the calamities could not be expected to be removed but by confession of their sins, and by acknowledging the justice of the Divine dealings towards them. When we have been afflicted—when we are called to pass through severe trials—and when, borne down by trial, we go to God, and pray that the evil may be removed, the first thing that is demanded is, that we should confess our sins, and acknowledge the justice of God in the judgments that have come upon us. If we attempt to vindicate and justify ourselves, we can have no hope that the judgment will be averted. Daniel, therefore, in the name of the people, began his prayer with the humble and penitent acknowledgment that all that they had suffered was deserved. ¶ *O Lord, the great and dreadful God.* A God great,

and to be feared or venerated—הַנּוֹרָא.

This does not mean *dreadful* in the sense that there is anything stern or unamiable in his character, but mainly that he is to be regarded with veneration. ¶ *Keeping the covenant and mercy.* Keeping his covenant and showing mercy. This is often ascribed to God, that he is faithful to his covenant; that is, that he is faithful to his promises to his people, or to those who

DANIEL II.   I

5 We *a* have sinned, and have committed iniquity, and have done wickedly, and have rebelled, even by departing from thy precepts, and from thy judgments:

6 Neither *b* have we hearkened unto thy servants the prophets, which spake in thy name to our kings, our princes, and our fathers, and to all the people of the land.

7 O Lord, righteousness 1 *belongeth* unto thee, *c* but unto us

a Ps. 106. 6; Isa. 64. 6, 7.   *b* 2 Chron. 36. 15, 16.

1 or, *thou hast.*   *c* Psa. 51. 4.

sustain a certain relation to him, and who are faithful to *their* covenant vows. If there is alienation and estrangement, and want of faithfulness on either side, it does not begin with him. He is faithful to all his promises, and his fidelity may always be assumed as a basis of calculation in all our intercourse with him. See the word "Covenant," in Cruden's *Concordance.* The word *mercy* seems to be added here to denote that *mercy* enters into his dealings with us even in keeping the covenant. We are so sinful and so unfaithful ourselves, that if *he* is faithful to his covenant, it must be by showing mercy to us. ¶ *To them that love him,* &c. The conditions of the covenant extend no farther than this, since, in a compact of any kind, one is bound to be faithful only while the terms are maintained by the other party. So God binds himself to show favour only while we are obedient, and we can plead his covenant only when we are obedient, when we confess our sins and plead his promises in this sense—that he has assured us that he will restore and receive us if we are penitent. It was this which Daniel pleaded on this occasion. He could not plead that his people had been obedient, and had thus any claims to the Divine favour; but he could cast himself and them on the mercy of a covenant-keeping God, who would remember his covenant with them if they were penitent, and who would graciously pardon.

5. *We have sinned.* Though Daniel was alone, he spake in the name of the people in general—doubtless recounting the long series of crimes in the nation which had preceded the captivity, and which were the cause of the ruin of the city and temple. ¶ *And have committed iniquity,* &c. These varied forms of expression are designed to give *intensity* to what he says. It

is equivalent to saying that they had sinned in every way possible. The mind, in a state of true repentance, dwells on its sins, and recounts the various forms in which iniquity has been done, and multiplies expressions of regret and sorrow on account of transgression. ¶ *From thy precepts.* Thy commands; thy laws. ¶ *Thy judgments.* Thy laws—the word *judgments* in the Scripture denoting what God judges to be right for us to *do,* as well as what it is right for him to *inflict.*

6. *Neither have we hearkened unto thy servants the prophets.* Who called upon us to turn from our sins; who made known the will of God, and who proclaimed that these judgments would come upon us if we did not repent. ¶ *Which spake in thy name to our kings,* &c. To all classes of the people, calling on kings and rulers to turn from their idolatry, and the people to forsake their sins, and to seek the Lord. It was a characteristic of the prophets that they spared no classes of the nation, but faithfully uttered all the word of God. Their admonitions had been unheeded, and the people now saw clearly that these calamities had come upon them because they had *not* hearkened to their voice.

7. *O Lord, righteousness* belongeth *unto thee.* Marg., "or, *thou hast.*" The Hebrew is, "to thee is righteousness, to us shame," &c. The state of mind in him who makes the prayer is that of ascribing righteousness or justice to God. Daniel feels and admits that God has been right in his dealings. He is not disposed to blame him, but to take all the shame and blame to the people. There is no murmuring or complaining on his part as if God had done wrong in any way, but there is the utmost confidence in him, and in his government. This is the true feel-

confusion of faces, as at this day: to the men of Judah, and to the inhabitants of Jerusalem, and unto all Israel, *that are* near, and *that are* far off, through all the countries whither *a* thou hast driven them, because of their trespass that they have trespassed against thee.

8 O Lord, to us *belongeth b* confusion of face, to our kings, to our princes, and to our fathers, because we have sinned against thee.

9 To the Lord our God *c belong* mercies and forgivenesses, though we have rebelled against him;

a Lev.26.33,34.　*b* Ezek.16.63.　*c* Psa. 130.4,7.

ing with which to come before God when we are afflicted, and when we plead for his mercy and favour. God should be regarded as righteous in all that he has done, and holy in all his judgments and claims, and there should be a willingness to address him as holy, and just, and true, and to take shame and confusion of face to ourselves. Comp. Psa. li. 4. ¶ *But unto us confusion of faces.* Heb., "shame of faces;" that is, that kind of shame which we have when we feel that we are guilty, and which commonly shows itself in the countenance. ¶ *As at this day.* As we actually are at this time. That is, he felt that at that time they were a down-trodden, an humbled, a contemned people. Their country was in ruins; they were captives in a far distant land, and all on which they had prided themselves was laid waste. All these judgments and humiliating things he says they had deserved, for they had grievously sinned against God. ¶ *To the men of Judah.* Not merely to the *tribe* of Judah, but to the kingdom of that name. After the revolt of the ten tribes—which became known as the kingdom of Ephraim, because Ephraim was the largest tribe, or as the kingdom of Israel—the other portion of the people, the tribes of Judah and Benjamin were known as the kingdom of Judah, since Judah was by far the larger tribe of the two. This kingdom is referred to here, because Daniel belonged to it, and because the ten tribes had been carried away long before and scattered in the countries of the East. The ten tribes had been carried to Assyria. Jerusalem always remained as the capital of the kingdom of Judah, and it is to this portion of the Hebrew people that the prayer of Daniel more

especially appertains. ¶ *And to the inhabitants of Jerusalem.* Particularly to them, as the heaviest calamities had come upon them, and as they had been prominent in the sins for which these judgments had come upon the people. ¶ *And unto all Israel.* All the people who are descendants of Israel or Jacob, wherever they may be, embracing not only those of the kingdom of Judah properly so called, but all who appertain to the nation. They were all of one blood. They had had a common country. They had all revolted, and a succession of heavy judgments had come upon the nation as such, and all had occasion for shame and confusion of face. ¶ *That are near, and that are far off.* Whether in Babylon, in Assyria, or in more remote countries. The ten tribes had been carried away some two hundred years before this prayer was offered by Daniel, and they were scattered in far distant lands. ¶ *Through all the countries whither thou hast driven them,* &c. In Babylonia, in Assyria, in Egypt, or in other lands. They were scattered everywhere, and wherever they were they had common cause for humiliation and shame.

8. *O Lord, to us* belongeth *confusion,* &c. To all of us; to the whole people, high and low, rich and poor, the rulers and the ruled. All had been partakers of the guilt; all were involved in the calamities consequent on the guilt. As all had sinned, the judgments had come upon all, and it was proper that the confession should be made in the name of all.

9. *To the Lord our God* belong *mercies and forgivenesses.* Not only does righteousness belong to him in the sense that he has done right, and that he cannot be blamed for what he has done, but mercy and forgiveness be-

10 Neither have we obeyed the voice of the Lord our God, to walk in his laws which he set before us by his servants the prophets.

11 Yea, all *a* Israel have transgressed thy law, even by departing, that they might not obey thy voice; therefore the curse is poured upon us, and the oath that *is* written in

a Isa. 1. 4–6.

the law of Moses the servant of God, because we have sinned against him.

12 And he hath confirmed his words, which he spake against us, and against our judges that judged us, by bringing upon us a great evil: for under the whole heaven hath not been done as hath been done upon Jerusalem.

---

long to him in the sense that he only can pardon, and that these are attributes of his nature. ¶ *Though we have rebelled against him.* The word here used and rendered *though* (כִּי) may mean either *though* or *for.* That is, the passage may mean that mercy belongs to God, and we may hope that he will show it, *although* we have been so evil and rebellious; or it may mean that it belongs to him, and he only can show it, *for* we have rebelled against him; that is, our only hope now is in his mercy, *for* we have sinned, and forfeited all claims to his favour. Either of these interpretations makes good sense, but the latter would seem to be most in accordance with the general strain of this part of the prayer, which is to make humble and penitent confession. So the Latin Vulgate *quia.* So Theodotion, ὅτι. So Luther and Lengerke, *denn.* In the same way, the passage in Psa. xxv. 11 is rendered, "For thy name's sake, O Lord, pardon mine iniquity, for (כִּי) it is great"—though this passage will admit of the other interpretation, "*although* it is great."

10. *Neither have we obeyed the voice of the Lord.* The commands of God as made known by the prophets, ver. 6.

11. *Yea, all Israel have transgressed,* &c. Embracing not only the tribe and the kingdom of Judah, but the whole nation. The calamity, therefore, had come upon them all. ¶ *Even by departing.* By departing from thy commandments; or by rebellion against thee. ¶ *That they might not obey thy voice.* By refusing to obey thy voice, or thy commands. ¶ *Therefore the curse is poured upon us.* As rain de-

scends, or as water is poured out. The *curse* here refers to that which was so solemnly threatened by Moses in case the nation did not obey God. See Deut. xxviii. 15–68. ¶ *And the oath that is written in the law of Moses,* &c. The word here rendered *oath* (שְׁבֻעָה) means, properly, a *swearing,* or *an oath;* and hence, either an oath of promise as in a covenant, or an oath of cursing or imprecation—that is, a curse. It is evidently used in the latter sense here. See Gesenius, *Lex.* Daniel saw clearly that the evils which had been threatened by Moses (Deut. xxviii.) had actually come upon the nation, and he as clearly saw that the cause of all these calamities was that which Moses had specified. He, therefore, frankly and penitently confessed these sins in the name of the whole people, and earnestly supplicated for mercy.

12. *And he hath confirmed his words,* &c. By bringing upon the people all that he had threatened in case of their disobedience. Daniel saw that there was a complete fulfilment of all that he had said would come upon them. As all this had been threatened, he could not complain; and as he had confirmed his words in regard to the threatening, he had the same reason to think that he would in regard to his promises. What Daniel here says was true in his time, and in reference to his people will be found to be true at all times, and in reference to all people. Nothing is more certain than that God will "confirm" all the words that he has ever spoken, and that no sinner can hope to escape on the ground that God will be found to be false to his threatenings, or that he has forgotten

13 As *it is* written *a* in the law of Moses, all this evil is come upon us: yet ¹ made we not our prayer before the LORD our God, that we might turn from our iniquities, and understand thy truth.

14 Therefore hath the LORD

watched upon the evil, and brought it upon us: for the LORD our God *is* righteous *b* in all his works which he doeth: for we obeyed not his voice.

15 And now, O Lord our God, that hast brought thy people forth

a Lev.26.14, &c.; Deut.28.15,&c.; Lam.2.15–17.　　1 *entreated we not the face of.*　*b* Neh. 9. 33.

them, or that he is indifferent to them. ¶ *Against our judges that judged us.* Our magistrates or rulers. ¶ *For under the whole heaven.* In all the world. ¶ *Hath not been done as hath been done upon Jerusalem.* In respect to the slaughter, and the captivity, and the complete desolation. No one can show that at that time this was not literally true. The city was in a state of complete desolation; its temple was in ruins; its people had been slain or borne into captivity.

13. *As* it is *written in the law of Moses.* The word *law* was given to all the writings of Moses. See Notes on Luke xxiv. 44. ¶ *Yet made we not our prayer before the Lord our God.* Marg., *entreated we not the face of.* The Hebrew word here used (חִלָּה) means, properly, *to be polished;* then to be worn down in strength, to be weak; then to be sick, or diseased; then in Piel (the form used here), to rub or stroke the face of any one, to soothe or caress, and hence to beseech, or supplicate. See Gesenius, *Lex.* Here it means, that, as a people, they had failed, when they had sinned, to call upon God for pardon; to confess their sins; to implore his mercy; to deprecate his wrath. It would have been easy to turn aside his threatened judgments if they had been penitent, and had sought his mercy, but they had not done it. What is here said of them can and will be said of all sinners when the Divine judgment comes upon them. ¶ *That we might turn from our iniquities.* That we might seek grace to turn from our transgressions. ¶ *And understand thy truth.* The truth which God had revealed; equivalent to saying that they might be righteous.

14. *Therefore hath the Lord watched upon the evil.* The word here used

and rendered *watched*—שָׁקַד—means, properly, *to wake; to be sleepless; to watch.* Then it means to watch over anything, or to be attentive to it. Jer. i. 12; xxxi. 28; xliv. 27.—Gesenius, *Lex.* The meaning here is, that the Lord had not been inattentive to the progress of things, nor unmindful of his threatening. He had never slumbered, but had carefully observed the course of events, and had been attentive to all that they had done, and to all that he had threatened to do. The practical *truth* taught here—and it is one of great importance to sinners—is, that God is not inattentive to their conduct, though he may seem to be, and that in due time he will show that he has kept an unslumbering eye upon them. See Notes on Isa. xviii. 4. ¶ *For the Lord our God* is *righteous in all his works,* &c. This is the language of a true penitent; language which is always used by one who has right feelings when he reflects on the Divine dealings towards him. God is seen to be righteous in his law and in his dealings, and the only reason why we suffer is that we have sinned. This will be found to be true always; and whatever calamities we suffer, it should be a fixed principle with us to "ascribe righteousness to our Maker," Job xxxvi. 3.

15. *And now, O Lord our God, that hast brought thy people forth out of the land of Egypt.* In former days. The reference to this shows that it is proper to use *arguments* before God when we plead with him (comp. Notes on Job xxiii. 4); that is, to suggest considerations or reasons why the prayer should be granted. Those reasons must be, of course, such as will occur to our own minds as sufficient to make it proper for God to bestow the blessing, and when they are presented before him, it

out of the land of Egypt with a mighty hand, and hast [1] gotten thee renown, as at this day; we have sinned, we have done wickedly.

16 ¶ O Lord, according to all thy righteousness, I beseech thee,

1 *made thee a name.*

let thine anger and thy fury be turned away from thy city Jerusalem, thy holy mountain; because for our sins, and for the iniquities of our fathers, Jerusalem and thy people *are become* a reproach to all *that are* about us.

---

must be with submission to his higher view of the subject. The arguments which it is proper to urge are those derived from the Divine mercy and faithfulness; from the promises of God; from his former dealings with his people; from our sins and misery; from the great sacrifice made for sin; from the desirableness that his name should be glorified. Here Daniel properly refers to the former Divine interposition in favour of the Hebrew people, and he pleads the fact that God had delivered them from Egypt as a reason why he should now interpose and save them. The strength of this argument may be supposed to consist in such things as the following: (*a*) in the fact that there was as much reason for interposing now as there was then; (*b*) in the fact that his interposing then might be considered as a proof that he intended to be regarded as their protector, and to defend them as his people; (*c*) in the fact that he who evinced such mighty power at that time must be able to interpose and save them now, &c. ¶ *And hast gotten thee renown.* Marg., *made thee a name.* So the Hebrew. The idea is, that that great event had been the means of making him known as a faithful God, and a God able to deliver. As he was thus known, Daniel prayed that he would again interpose, and would now show that he was *as* able to deliver his people as in former times. ¶ *As at this day.* That is, as God was then regarded. The remembrance of his interposition had been diffused abroad, and had been transmitted from age to age. ¶ *We have sinned,* &c. This turn in the thought shows how deeply the idea of their sinfulness pressed upon the mind of Daniel. The natural and obvious course of thought would have been, that, as God had interposed when his people were de-

livered from Egyptian bondage, he would now again interpose; but instead of that, the mind of Daniel is overwhelmed with the thought that they had sinned grievously against one who had shown that he was a God so great and glorious, and who had laid them under such obligations to love and serve him.

16. *O Lord, according to all thy righteousness.* The word *righteousness* here seems to refer to all that was excellent and glorious in the character of God. The eye of Daniel is fixed upon what he had formerly done; upon his character of justice, and mercy, and goodness; upon the faithfulness of God to his people, and, in view of all that was excellent and lovely in his character, he pleaded that he would interpose and turn away his anger from his people now. It is the character of God that is the ground of his plea—and what else is there that can give us encouragement when we come before him in prayer. ¶ *Let thine anger and thy fury be turned away,* &c. The anger which had come upon the city, and which appeared to rest upon it. Jerusalem was in ruins, and it seemed still to be lying under the wrath of God. The word rendered *fury* is the common one to denote wrath or indignation. It implies no more than anger or indignation, and refers here to the Divine displeasure against their sins, manifested in the destruction of their city. ¶ *Thy holy mountain.* Jerusalem was built on hills, and the city in general might be designated by this phrase. Or, more probably, there is allusion either to Mount Zion, or to Mount Moriah. ¶ *Because for our sins,* &c. There is, on the part of Daniel, no disposition to blame God for what he had done. There is no murmuring or complaining, as if he had been unjust or severe in his dealings with his people.

17 Now, therefore, O our God, hear the prayer of thy servant, and his supplications, and cause thy face to shine upon thy sanctuary that is desolate, for the Lord's sake.

18 O my God, incline thine ear, and hear; open thine eyes, and behold our desolations, and the city which[1] is called by thy name: for

we do not [2] present our supplications before thee for our righteousnesses, but for thy great mercies.

19 O Lord, hear; O Lord, forgive; O Lord, hearken, and do; defer not, for thine own sake, O my God; for thy city and thy people are called by thy name.

1 *whereupon thy name is called.* 2 *cause to fall.*

Jerusalem was indeed in ruins, and the people were captives in a distant land, but he felt and admitted that God was just in all that he had done. It was too manifest to be denied that all these calamities had come upon them on account of their sins, and this Daniel, in the name of the people, humbly and penitently acknowledged. ¶ *A reproach to all* that are *about us.* All the surrounding nations. They reproach us with our sins, and with the judgments that have come upon us, as if we were peculiarly wicked, and were forsaken of heaven.

17. *Now, therefore, O our God, hear the prayer of thy servant.* In behalf of the people. He pleaded for his people and country, and earnestly entreated the Lord to be merciful. His argument is based on the confession of sin; on the character of God; on the condition of the city and temple; on the former Divine interpositions in behalf of the people; and by all these considerations, he pleads with God to have mercy upon his people and land. ¶ *And cause thy face to shine upon thy sanctuary.* Upon the temple. That is, that he would look upon it benignly and favourably. The language is common in the Scriptures, when favour and kindness are denoted by lifting up the light of the countenance, and by similar phrases. The allusion is originally, perhaps, to the sun, which, when it shines brightly, is an emblem of favour and mercy; when it is overclouded, is an emblem of wrath. ¶ *For the Lord's sake.* That is, that he would be propitious for his own sake; to wit, that his glory might be promoted; that his excellent character might be displayed; that his mercy and compassion might be shown. All true prayer has its seat in a desire that the glory of God may

be promoted, and the excellence of his character displayed. That is of more consequence than *our* welfare, and the gratification of *our* wishes, and that should be uppermost in our hearts when we approach the throne of grace.

18. *O my God, incline thine ear, and hear.* Pleading earnestly for his attention and his favour, as one does to a man. ¶ *Open thine eyes.* As if his eyes had been closed upon the condition of the city, and he did not see it. Of course, all this is figurative, and is the language of strong and earnest pleading when the heart is greatly interested. ¶ *And the city which is called by thy name.* Marg., *whereupon thy name is called.* The margin expresses the sense more literally; but the meaning is, that the city had been consecrated to God, and was called his—the city of Jehovah. It was known as the place of his sanctuary—the city where his worship was celebrated, and which was regarded as his peculiar dwelling-place on the earth. Comp. Psa. xlviii. 1–3; lxxxvii. 3. This is a new ground of entreaty, that the city belonged to God, and that he would remember the close connection between the prosperity of that city and the glory of his own name.

19. *O Lord, hear,* &c. The language in this verse does not require any particular explanation. The repetition—the varied forms of expression—indicate a mind intent on the object; a heart greatly interested; an earnestness that cannot be denied. It is language that is respectful, solemn, devout, but deeply earnest. It is not vain repetition, for its force is not in the *words* employed, but in the manifest fervour, earnestness, and sincerity of spirit which pervade the pleading. It is earnest intercession and supplica-

20 ¶ And whiles I was speaking, and praying, and confessing my sin and the sin of my people Israel, and presenting my supplica-

tion that God would hear—that he would forgive, that he would hearken and do, that he would not defer his gracious interposition. The sins of the people; the desolation of the city; the promises of God; the reproach that the nation was suffering—all these come rushing over the soul, and prompt to the most earnest pleading that perhaps ever proceeded from human lips. And these things justified that earnest pleading—for the prayer was that of a prophet, a man of God, a man that loved his country, a man that was intent on the promotion of the Divine glory as the supreme object of his life. Such earnest intercession; such confession of sin; such a dwelling on arguments why a prayer should be heard, is at all times acceptable to God; and though it cannot be supposed that the Divine Mind needs to be instructed, or that our arguments will convince God or influence him as arguments do men, yet it is undoubtedly proper to urge them as if they would, for it may be only in this way that our own minds can be brought into a proper state. The great argument which *we* are to urge why our prayers should be heard is the sacrifice which has been made for sin by the Redeemer, and the fact that he has purchased for us the blessings which we need; but in connection with that it is proper to urge our own sins and necessities; the wants of our friends or our country; our own danger and that of others; the interposition of God in times past in behalf of his people, and his own gracious promises and purposes. If we have the spirit, the faith, the penitence, the earnestness of Daniel, we may be sure that our prayers will be heard as his was.

20. *And whiles I was speaking,* &c. In the very time when I was thus pleading. ¶ *For the holy mountain of my God.* Notes on ver. 16.

21. *Yea, whiles I* was *speaking in prayer.* How *long* the prayer continued we are not informed. It is probable that we have only the substance

before the LORD my God for the holy mountain of my God;

21 Yea, whiles I *was* speaking in prayer, even the man Gabriel,

of it, and that Daniel has recorded only the topics on which he dwelt more at length. The subject was of great importance, and it is reasonable to suppose that a day had been devoted to an examination of the prophecies, and to solemn prayer. ¶ *Even the man Gabriel.* Who had the appearance of a man, and hence so called. ¶ *Whom I had seen in the vision at the beginning.* That is, in a *former* vision. See Notes on ch. viii. 16. It cannot refer to what is mentioned in this (the ninth) chapter, for (*a*) he had as yet had no *vision*, but all that is recorded is a prayer; (*b*) there is no intimation that Gabriel had appeared to him at the beginning of the prayer; and (*c*) it is declared that at the beginning of the prayer, Gabriel, then evidently in heaven, had received commandment to go to Daniel, and to communicate the message to him, ver. 23. The meaning undoubtedly is, that the personage who now appeared to him he recognized to be the same who had appeared in a former vision on the banks of the Ulai. The proper meaning of the Hebrew here is, " in a vision at the beginning," as in our translation. So the Vulgate, *à principio;* and so Theodotion— ἐν τῇ ἀρχῇ. The Hebrew word תְּחִלָּה means, properly, *beginning,* Hos. i. 2; Prov. ix. 10; but, in connection with the preposition, as here—בַּתְּחִלָּה—it means also, *before, formerly,* Gen. xiii. 3; xli. 21; xliii. 18, 20; Isa. i. 26. ¶ *Being caused to fly swiftly.* Marg., *with weariness,* or *flight.* On the difficult Hebrew expression here—מֻעָף בִּיעָף— Lengerke may be consulted, *in loc.* The words, according to Gesenius, are derived from יָעַף, to go swiftly, and then, to be wearied, to faint, either with running, Jer. ii. 24, or with severe labour, Isa. xl. 28, or with sorrows, Isa. l. 4. If derived from this word, the meaning in Hophal, the form here used, would be, *wearied with swift running,* and the sense is, that Gabriel had borne the message swiftly to him, and ap-

whom I had seen in the vision at the beginning, being caused to fly swiftly,[1] touched me about the time of the evening oblation.

22 And he informed *me*, and

1 *with weariness,* or, *flight.*

peared before him as one does who is wearied with a rapid course. If this be the idea, there is no direct allusion to his *flying,* but the reference is to the rapidity with which he had come on the long journey, as if exhausted by his journey. The Latin Vulgate renders it *cito volans—quickly flying;* Theodotion, *πετόμενος* — flying; the *Codex Chis.,* *τάχει φερόμενος — borne swiftly.* The Syriac, "with a swift flying he flew and came from heaven." It cannot be determined with certainty, from the words used here, that the coming of Gabriel was by an act of *flying* as with wings. The common representation of the angels in the Old Testament is not with wings, though the Cherubim and Seraphim (Isa. vi. 2, *seq.*) are represented with wings ; and in Rev. xiv. 6, we have a representation of an angel flying. Probably the more exact idea here is that of a rapid course, so as to produce weariness, or such as would naturally produce fatigue. ¶ *Touched me.* Daniel was doubtless at this time engaged in prayer. ¶ *About the time of the evening oblation.* The evening sacrifice. This was at the ninth hour of the day, or about three o'clock in the afternoon.

22. *And he informed* me. Heb., Gave me intelligence or understanding. That is, about the design of his visit, and about what would be hereafter. ¶ *And talked with me.* Spake unto me. ¶ *O Daniel, I am now come forth to give thee skill.* Marg., *make thee skilful of.* The Hebrew is, literally, "to make thee skilful, or wise, in understanding." The design was to give him information as to what was to occur.

23. *At the beginning of thy supplications.* We are not informed at what time Daniel began to pray, but as remarked above, it is most natural to suppose that he devoted the day to prayer, and had commenced these solemn acts of devotion in the morning.

talked with me, and said, O Daniel, I am now come forth to [2] give thee skill and understanding.

23 At the beginning of thy supplications the [3] commandment came

2 *make thee skilful of.* 3 *word.*

¶ *The commandment came forth.* Marg., *word.* That is, the word of God. This evidently means, in heaven; and the idea is, that as soon as he began to pray a command was issued from God to Gabriel that he should visit Daniel, and convey to him the important message respecting future events. It is fair to conclude that he had at once left heaven in obedience to the order, and on this high embassage, and that he had passed over the amazing distance between heaven and earth in the short time during which Daniel was engaged in prayer. If so, and if heaven—the peculiar seat of God, the dwelling-place of angels and of the just—is beyond the region of the fixed stars, some central place in this vast universe, then this may give us some idea of the amazing rapidity with which celestial beings may move. It is calculated that there are stars so remote from our earth, that their light would not travel down to us for many thousand years. If so, how much more rapid may be the movements of celestial beings than even light; perhaps more than that of the lightning's flash—than the electric fluid on telegraphic wires—though *that* moves at the rate of more than 200,000 miles in a second. Compare Dick's *Philosophy of a Future State,* p. 220. "During the few minutes employed in uttering this prayer," says Dr. Dick, "this angelic messenger descended from the celestial regions to the country of Babylonia. This was a rapidity of motion surpassing the comprehension of the most vigorous imagination, and far exceeding even the amazing velocity of light." With such a rapidity it *may be* our privilege yet to pass from world to world on errands of mercy and love, or to survey in distant parts of the universe the wonderful works of God. ¶ *And I am come to show thee.* To make thee acquainted with

forth, and I am come to shew *thee;* for thou *art*[1] greatly beloved: therefore understand the matter, and consider the vision.

what will yet be. ¶ *For thou* art *greatly beloved.* Marg., as in Heb., "a man *of desires.*" That is, he was one whose happiness was greatly desired by God; or, a man of God's delight; that is, as in our version, greatly beloved. It was on this account that his prayer was heard, and that God sent to him this important message respecting what was to come. ¶ *Therefore understand the matter.* The matter respecting what was yet to occur in regard to his people. ¶ *And consider the vision.* This vision —the vision of future things which he was now about to present to his view. From this passage, describing the appearance of Gabriel to Daniel, we may learn, (*a*) That our prayers, if sincere, are heard in heaven *as soon* as they are offered. They enter at once into the ears of God, and he regards them at the instant. (*b*) A command, as it were, may be at once issued to answer them—*as if* he directed an angel to bear the answer at once. (*c*) The angels are ready to hasten down to men, to communicate the will of God. Gabriel came evidently with pleasure on his embassage, and to a benevolent being anywhere there is nothing more grateful than to be commissioned to bear glad tidings to others. Possibly that may be a part of the employment of the righteous for ever. (*d*) The thought is an interesting one, if we are permitted to entertain it, that good angels may be constantly employed as Gabriel was ; that whenever prayer is offered on earth they may be commissioned to bring answers of peace and mercy, or despatched to render aid, and that thus the universe may be constantly traversed by these holy beings ministering to those who are "heirs of salvation," Heb. i. 1, 4.

24. *Seventy weeks are determined.* Here commences the celebrated prophecy of the SEVENTY WEEKS—a portion of Scripture which has excited as

24 Seventy weeks *a* are determined upon thy people, and upon thy holy city, to [2] finish the transgression, and to [3] make an end of

much attention, and led to as great a variety of interpretation, as perhaps any other. Of this passage, Professor Stuart (*Hints on the Interpretation of Prophecy,* p. 104) remarks, "It would require a volume of considerable magnitude even to give a history of the ever-varying and contradictory opinions of critics respecting this *locus vexatissimus;* and perhaps a still larger one to establish an exegesis which would stand. I am fully of opinion, that no interpretation as yet published will stand the test of thorough grammatico-historical criticism ; and that a candid, and searching, and thorough *critique* here is still a *desideratum.* May some expositor, fully adequate to the task, speedily appear !" After these remarks of this eminent Biblical scholar, it is with no great confidence of success that I enter on the exposition of the passage. Yet, perhaps, though *all* difficulties may not be removed, and though I cannot hope to contribute anything *new* in the exposition of the passage, something may be written which may relieve it of some of the perplexities attending it, and which may tend to show that its author was under the influence of Divine inspiration. The passage may be properly divided into two parts. The first, in ver. 24, contains a *general* statement of what would occur in the time specified—the seventy weeks ; the second, vers. 25–27, contains a *particular* statement of the manner in which that would be accomplished. In this statement, the whole time of the seventy weeks is broken up into three smaller portions of seven, sixty-two, and one— designating evidently some important epochs or periods (ver. 25), and the last one week is again subdivided in such a way, that, while it is said that the whole work of the Messiah in confirming the covenant would occupy the entire week, yet that he would be cut off in the middle of the week, verse 27.

sins, and to make reconciliation for iniquity, and to bring in everlasting *a* righteousness, and to seal

up the vision and [1] prophecy, and to anoint the Most Holy.

a Heb 9. 12.   1 *prophet.*

In the *general* statement (ver. 24) it is said that there was a definite time—seventy weeks—during which the subject of the prediction would be accomplished; that is, during which all that was to be done in reference to the holy city, or in the holy city, to finish the transgression, to make an end of sin, &c., would be effected. The things specified in this verse are *what was to be done*, as detailed more particularly in the subsequent verses. The design in this verse seems to have been to furnish a *general* statement of what was to occur in regard to the holy city—of that city which had been selected for the peculiar purpose of being a place where an atonement was to be made for human transgression. It is quite clear that when Daniel set apart this period for prayer, and engaged in this solemn act of devotion, his design was not to inquire into the ultimate events which would occur in Jerusalem, but merely to pray that the purpose of God, as predicted by Jeremiah, respecting the captivity of the nation, and the rebuilding of the city and temple, might be accomplished. God took occasion from this, however, not only to give an implied assurance about the accomplishment of these purposes, but also to state in a remarkable manner the *whole* ultimate design respecting the holy city, and the great event which was ever onward to characterize it among the cities of the world. In the consideration of the whole passage (vers. 24–27), it will be proper, first, to examine into the literal meaning of the words and phrases, and then to inquire into the fulfilment. ¶ *Seventy weeks.* שָׁבֻעִים שִׁבְעִים. Vulg., *Septuaginta hebdomades.* So Theodotion, Ἑβδομήκοντα ἑβδομάδες. Prof. Stuart (*Hints,* p. 82) renders this " *seventy sevens;*" that is, seventy times seven years: on the ground that the word denoting *weeks* in the Hebrew is not שָׁבֻעִים, but שְׁבֻעוֹת. "The form which is used here," says he, "which is a regular masculine plural, is no doubt

purposely chosen to designate the plural of seven; and with great propriety here, inasmuch as there are many sevens which are to be joined together in one common sum. Daniel had been meditating on the close of the seventy *years* of Hebrew exile, and the angel now discloses to him a new period of *seventy times seven,* in which still more important events are to take place. Seventy sevens, or (to use the Greek phraseology), *seventy heptades,* are determined upon thy people. Heptades of what? Of days, or of years? No one can doubt what the answer is. Daniel had been making diligent search respecting the seventy *years;* and, in such a connection, nothing but seventy heptades of years could be reasonably supposed to be meant by the angel." The inquiry about the *gender* of the word, of which so much has been said (Hengstenberg, *Chris.* ii. 297), does not seem to be very important, since the same result is reached whether it be rendered *seventy sevens,* or *seventy weeks.* In the former case, as proposed by Prof. Stuart, it means seventy sevens of *years,* or 490 years; in the other, seventy *weeks* of years; that is, as a *week of years* is seven years, seventy such weeks, or as before, 490 years. The usual and proper meaning of the word here used, however—שָׁבוּעַ is *a seven,* ἑβδομάς, *hebdomad, i.e., a week.* — Gesenius, *Lex.* From the *examples* where the word occurs it would seem that the masculine or the feminine forms were used indiscriminately. The word occurs only in the following passages, in all of which it is rendered *week,* or *weeks,* except in Ezek. xlv. 21, where it is rendered *seven,* to wit, days. In the following passages the word occurs in the masculine form plural, Dan. ix. 24–26; x. 2, 3; in the following in the feminine form plural, Exod. xxxiv. 22; Numb. xxviii. 26; Deut. xvi. 9, 10, 16; 2 Chron. viii. 13; Jer. v. 24; Ezek. xlv. 21; and in the following in the singular number, common gender, rendered *week*, Gen. xxix. 27, 28, and in the dual masculine in Lev. xii. 5, rendered *two weeks*. From these passages it is evident that nothing certain can be determined about the meaning of the word from its gender. It would seem to denote *weeks*, periods of seven days—*hebdomads*—in either form, and is doubtless so used here. The fair translation would be, weeks seventy are determined; that is, seventy times seven days, or four hundred and ninety *days*. But it may be asked here, whether this is to be taken literally, as denoting four hundred and ninety days? If not, in what sense is it to be understood? and why do we understand it in a different sense? It is clear that it must be explained literally as denoting four hundred and ninety *days*, or that these days must stand for years, and that the period is four hundred and ninety *years*. That this latter is the true interpretation, as it has been held by all commentators, is apparent from the following considerations: (*a*) This is not uncommon in the prophetic writings. See Notes on ch. vii. 24–28. (See also Editor's Preface to volume on Revelation.) (*b*) Daniel had been making inquiry respecting the seventy *years*, and it is natural to suppose that the answer of the angel would have respect to *years* also; and, thus understood, the answer would have met the inquiry pertinently —"not *seventy* years, but a week of years — seven times seventy years." Comp. Matt. xviii. 21, 22. "In such a connection, nothing but seventy heptades of years could be reasonably supposed to be meant by the angel." — Prof. Stuart's *Hints*, &c., p. 82. (*c*) Years, as Prof. Stuart remarks, are the measure of all considerable periods of time. When the angel speaks, then, in reference to certain events, and declares that they are to take place during *seventy heptades*, it is a matter of course to suppose that he means years. (*d*) The circumstances of the case demand this interpretation. Daniel was seeking comfort in view of the fact that the city and temple had been desolate now for a period of seventy years. The angel comes to bring him consolation, and to give him assurances about the rebuilding of the

city, and the great events that were to occur there. But what consolation would it be to be told that the city would indeed be rebuilt, and that it would continue seventy ordinary weeks —that is, a little more than a year, before a new destruction would come upon it? It cannot well be doubted, then, that by the time here designated, the angel meant to refer to a period of four hundred and ninety years; and if it be asked why this number was not literally and exactly specified in so many words, instead of choosing a mode of designation comparatively so obscure, it may be replied, (1) that the number *seventy* was employed by Daniel as the time respecting which he was making inquiry, and that there was a propriety that there should be a reference to that fact in the reply of the angel—*one* number seventy had been fulfilled in the desolations of the city, there would be *another* number seventy in the events yet to occur; (2) this is in the usual prophetic style, where there is, as Hengstenberg remarks (*Chris.* ii. 299), often a "*concealed* definiteness." It is usual to designate numbers in this way. (3.) The term was sufficiently clear to be understood, or is, at all events, made clear by the result. There is no reason to doubt that Daniel would so understand it, or that it would be so interpreted, as fixing in the minds of the Jewish people the period when the Messiah was about to appear. The meaning then is, that there would be a period of four hundred and ninety years, during which the city, after the order of the rebuilding should go forth (ver. 25), until the entire consummation of the great object for which it should be rebuilt, and that then the purpose would be accomplished, and it would be given up to a greater ruin. There was to be this long period in which the most important transactions were to occur in the city. ¶ *Are determined*. The word here used (נֶחְתַּךְ from חָתַךְ) occurs nowhere else in the Scriptures. It properly means, according to Gesenius, to cut off, to divide; and hence, to determine, to destine, to appoint. Theodotion renders it, συνετμήθησαν—are cut off, decided, defined. The Vulgate renders it, *abbreviatæ sunt.* Luther, *Sind bestimmet* — are determined. The meaning would seem to be, that this portion of time—the seventy weeks—was *cut off* from the whole of duration, or cut out of it, as it were, and set by itself for a definite purpose. It does not mean that it was cut off from the time which the city would naturally stand, or that this time was *abbreviated,* but that a portion of time—to wit, four hundred and ninety years—was designated or appointed with reference to the city, to accomplish the great and important object which is immediately specified. A certain, definite period was fixed on, and when this was past, the promised Messiah would come. In regard to the construction here—the singular verb with a plural noun, see Hengstenberg, *Christ. in loc.* The true meaning seems to be, that the seventy weeks are spoken of *collectively,* as denoting a period of time; that is, a period of seventy weeks is determined. The prophet, in the use of the singular verb, seems to have contemplated the time, not as separate weeks, or as particular portions, but as one period. ¶ *Upon thy people.* The Jewish people; the nation to which Daniel belonged. This allusion is made because he was inquiring about the close of their exile, and their restoration to their own land. ¶ *And upon thy holy city.* Jerusalem, usually called the holy city, because it was the place where the worship of God was celebrated, Isa. lii. 1; Neh. xi. 1, 18; Matt. xxvii. 53. It is called *"thy holy city"*—the city of Daniel, because he was here making especial inquiry respecting it, and because he was one of the Hebrew people, and the city was the capital of their nation. As one of that nation, it could be called *his.* It was then, indeed, in ruins, but it was to be rebuilt, and it was proper to speak of it as if it were then a city. The meaning of "*upon* thy people and city" (עַל) is, *respecting* or *concerning.* The purpose respecting the seventy weeks *pertains* to thy people and city;

or there is an important period of four hundred and seventy years determined on, or designated, respecting that people and city. ¶ *To finish the transgression.* The angel proceeds to state what was the object to be accomplished in this purpose, or what would occur during that period. The first thing, *to finish the transgression.* The margin is, *restrain.* The Vulgate renders it, *ut consummetur prævaricatio.* Theodotion, τοῦ συντελεσθῆναι ἁμαρτίαν —to finish sin. Thompson renders this, "to finish sin-offerings." The difference between the marginal reading (*restrain*) and the text (*finish*) arises from a doubt as to the meaning of the original word. The common reading of the text is כַּלֵּא, but in 39 Codices examined by Kennicott, it is כלה. The reading in the text is undoubtedly the correct one, but still there is not absolute certainty as to the signification of the word, whether it means to *finish* or to *restrain.* The proper meaning of the word in the common reading of the text (כָּלֵא) is, to shut up, confine, restrain—as it is rendered in the margin. The meaning of the other word found in many MSS. (כָּלָה) is, to be completed, finished, closed—and in Piel, the form used here, to complete, to finish—as it is translated in the common version. Gesenius (*Lex.*) supposes that the word here is *for*—כַּלֵּה—meaning to finish or complete. Hengstenberg, who is followed in this view by Lengerke, supposes that the meaning is to *"shut up* transgression," and that the true reading is that in the text—כלא—though as that word is not used in Piel, and as the Masorites had some doubts as to the derivation of the word, they gave to it not its appropriate *pointing* in this place—which would have been כְּלֹא— but the pointing of the other word (כָּלָה) in the margin. According to Hengstenberg, the sense here of *shutting up* is derived from the general notion of *restraining* or *hindering,* belonging to the word; and he supposes that this will best accord with the other words in this member of the verse—

to cover, and *to seal up.* The idea according to him is, that "sin, which hitherto lay naked and open before the eyes of a righteous God, is now by his mercy *shut up, sealed*, and *covered*, so that it can no more be regarded as existing—a figurative description of the forgiveness of sin." So Lengerke renders it, *Um einzuschliessen [den] Abfall.* Bertholdt, *Bis der Frevel vollbracht.* It seems most probable that the true idea here is that denoted in the margin, and that the sense is not that of *finishing*, but that of *restraining, closing, shutting up*, &c. So it is rendered by Prof. Stuart—"to *restrain* transgression."—*Com. on Daniel, in loc.* The word is used in this sense of *shutting up*, or *restraining*, in several places in the Bible: 1 Sam. vi. 10, " *and shut up* their calves at home ;" Jer. xxxii. 3, " Zedekiah *had shut him up ;*" Psa. lxxxviii. 8, " I am *shut up*, and I cannot come forth ;" Jer. xxxii. 2, " Jeremiah the prophet was *shut up*." The sense of shutting up, or *restraining*, accords better with the connection than that of *finishing.* The reference of the whole passage is undoubtedly to the Messiah, and to what would be done sometime during the " seventy weeks ;" and the meaning here is, not that he would " finish transgression" —which would not be true in any proper sense, but that he would do a work which would *restrain* iniquity in the world, or, more strictly, which would *shut it up*—inclose it—as in a prison, so that it would no more go forth and prevail. The effect would be that which occurs when one is shut up in prison, and no longer goes at large. There would be a restraining power and influence which would check the progress of sin. This does not, I apprehend, refer to the particular transgressions for which the Jewish people had suffered in their long captivity, but sin (הַפֶּשַׁע) in general—the sin of the world. There would be an influence which would restrain and curb it, or which would shut it up so that it would no longer reign and roam at large over the earth. It is true that this might not have been so understood by Daniel at the time,

for the *language* is so general that it *might* have suggested the idea that it referred to the sins of the Jewish people. This language, if there had been no farther explanation of it, might have suggested the idea that in the time specified—seventy weeks— there would be some process—some punishment—some Divine discipline —by which the iniquities of that people, or their propensity to sin, for which this long captivity had come upon them, would be cohibited, or restrained. But the language is not such as necessarily to confine the interpretation to that, and the subsequent statements, and the actual fulfilment in the work of the Messiah, lead us to understand this in a much higher sense, as having reference to sin in general, and as designed to refer to some work that would ultimately be an effectual check on sin, and which would tend to cohibit, or restrain it altogether in the world. Thus understood, the language will well describe the work of the Redeemer—that work which, through the sacrifice made on the cross, is adapted and designed to restrain sin altogether. ¶ *And to make an end of sins.* Marg., *to seal up.* The difference here in the text and the margin arises from a difference in the readings in the Hebrew. The common reading in the text is חָתַם —from חָתַם—*to seal, to seal up.* But the Hebrew marginal reading is a different word—הָתֵם, from תָּמַם—*to complete, to perfect, to finish.* The *pointing* in the text in the word חָתֵם is not the proper pointing of that word, which would have been הָתֵם, but the Masorites, as is not unfrequently the case, gave to the word in the text the pointing of another word which they placed in the margin. The marginal reading is found in fifty-five MSS. (Lengerke), but the weight of authority is decidedly in favour of the common reading in the Hebrew text— *to seal*, and not *to finish*, as it is in our translation. The marginal reading, *to finish*, was doubtless substituted by some transcribers, or rather *suggested* by the Masorites, because it seemed to convey a better signification to say that " sin would be *finished*," than to say that it would be *sealed*. The Vulgate has followed the reading in the margin—*et finem accipiat peccatum;* Theodotion has followed the other reading, σφραγίσαι άμαρτίας. Luther also has it, *to seal*. Coverdale, " that sin may have an end." The true rendering is, doubtless, " to seal sin;" and the idea is that of removing it from sight; to remove it from view. " The expression is taken," says Lengerke, " from the custom of sealing up those things which one lays aside and conceals." Thus in Job ix. 7, " And sealeth up the stars;" that is, he so shuts them up in the heavens as to prevent their shining—so as to hide them from the view. They are concealed, hidden, made close—as the contents of a letter or package are sealed, indicating that no one is to examine them. See Notes on that passage. So also in Job xxxvii. 7, referring to winter, it is said, " He sealeth up the hand of every man, that all men may know his work." That is, in the winter, when the snow is on the ground, when the streams are frozen, the labours of the husbandman must cease. The hands can no more be used in ordinary toil. Every man is prevented from going abroad to his accustomed labour, and is, as it were, *scaled up* in his dwelling. Comp. Jer. xxxii. 11, 14; Isa. xxix. 11; Cant. iv. 12. The idea in the passage before us is, that the sins of our nature will, as it were, be sealed up, or closed, or hidden, so that they will not be seen, or will not develop themselves; that is, " they will be inert, inefficient, powerless."—Prof. Stuart. The language is applicable to anything that would hide them from view, or remove them from sight—as a book whose writing is so sealed that we cannot read it; a tomb that is so closed that we cannot enter it and see its contents; a package that is so sealed that we do not know what is within it; a room that is so shut up that we may not enter it, and see what is within. It is not to be supposed that Daniel would see clearly how this was to be done; but we, who have now a full revelation of the method by which God can re-

move sin, can understand the method in which this is accomplished by the blood of the atonement, to wit, that *by* that atonement sin is now forgiven, or is treated *as if* it were hidden from the view, and a seal, which may not be broken, placed on that which covers it. The language thus used, as we are now able to interpret it, is strikingly applicable to the work of the Redeemer, and to the method by which God removes sin. In not a few MSS. and editions the word rendered *sins* is in the singular number. The amount of authority is in favour of the common reading—sins—though the sense is not materially varied. The work would have reference to *sin*, and the effect would be to seal it, and hide it from the view. ¶ *And to make reconciliation for iniquity.* More literally, "and to cover iniquity." The word which is rendered to "make reconciliation "—כָּפַר *kâphăr*,—properly means *to cover* (whence our English word *cover*); to cover over, to overlay, as with pitch (Gen. vi. 14); and hence to cover over sin; that is, to atone for it, pardon it, forgive it. It is the word which is commonly used with reference to atonement or expiation, and seems to have been so understood by our translators. It does not necessarily refer to the means by which sin is covered over, &c., by an atonement, but is often used in the general sense of *to pardon* or *forgive*. Comp. Notes on Isa. vi. 7, and more fully, Notes on Isa. xliii. 3. Here there is no necessary allusion to the atonement which the Messiah would make in order to cover over sin; that is, the word is of so general a character in its signification that it does not necessarily imply this, but it is the word which would naturally be used on the supposition that it had such a reference. As a matter of fact, undoubtedly, the means by which this was to be done was by the atonement, and that was referred to by the Spirit of inspiration, but this is not essentially implied in the meaning of the word. In whatever way that should be done, this word would be properly used as expressing it. The Latin Vulgate renders thus, *et delcatur iniquitas.* Theodotion, ἀπαλεῖψαι τὰς ἀδικίας — "to wipe out iniquities." Luther, "to reconcile for transgression." Here are three things specified, therefore, in regard to sin, which would be done. Sin would be

Restrained,
Sealed up,
Covered over.

These expressions, though not of the nature of a climax, are intensive, and show that the great work referred to pertained to sin, and would be designed to remove it. Its bearing would be on human transgression ; on the way by which it might be pardoned ; on the methods by which it would be removed from the view, and be kept from rising up to condemn and destroy. Such expressions would undoubtedly lead the mind to look forward to some method which was to be disclosed by which sin could be consistently pardoned and removed. In the remainder of the verse, there are three additional things which would be done as necessary to complete the work :—

To bring in everlasting righteousness ; To seal up the vision and prophecy ; and *To anoint the Most Holy.*

¶ *And to bring in everlasting righteousness.* The phrase "to bring in" —literally, "to cause to come"—refers to some direct agency by which that righteousness would be introduced into the world. It would be such an agency as would cause it to exist; or as would establish it in the world. The *mode* of doing this is not indeed here specified, and, so far as the *word* here used is concerned, it would be applicable to any method by which this would be done—whether by making an atonement; or by setting an example; or by persuasion ; or by placing the subject of morals on a better foundation ; or by the administration of a just government ; or in any other way. The term is of the most general character, and its exact force here can be learned only by the subsequently revealed facts as to the way by which this would be accomplished. The essential idea in the language is, that this would be *introduced* by the Messiah ; that is, that he would be its author. The word *righteousness* here

also (צֶדֶק) is of a general character. The fair meaning would be, that some method would be introduced by which men would become *righteous*. In the former part of the verse, the reference was to *sin*—to the fact of its existence —to the manner in which it would be disposed of—to the truth that it would be coerced, sealed up, covered over. Here the statement is, that, in contradistinction from that, a method would be introduced by which man would become, in fact, righteous and holy. But the *word* implies nothing as to the method by which this would be done. Whether it would be by a new mode of justification, or by an influence that would make men personally holy— whether this was to be as the result of example, or instruction, or an atoning sacrifice—is not necessarily implied in the use of this word. That, as in the cases already referred to, could be learned only by subsequent developments. It would be, doubtless, understood that there was a reference to the Messiah—for that is specified in the next verse ; and it would be inferred from this word that, under him, righteousness would reign, or that men would be righteous, but nothing could be argued from it as to the methods by which it would be done. It is hardly necessary to add, that, in the prophets, it is constantly said that righteousness would characterize the Messiah and his times ; that he would come to make men righteous, and to set up a kingdom of righteousness in the earth. Yet the exact mode in which it was to be done would be, of course, more fully explained when the Messiah should himself actually appear. The word "*everlasting*" is used here to denote that the righteousness would be permanent and perpetual. In reference to the method of becoming righteous, it would be unchanging—the standing method ever onward by which men would become holy ; in reference to the individuals who should become righteous under this system, it would be a righteousness which would continue for ever. This is the characteristic which is everywhere given of the righteousness which would be introduced by the Messiah. Thus in Isa.

li. 6–8 : "Lift up your eyes to the heavens, and look upon the earth beneath : for the heavens shall vanish away like smoke, and the earth shall wax old like a garment, and they that dwell therein shall die in like manner : but my salvation shall be for ever, and my righteousness shall not be abolished. Hearken unto me, ye that know righteousness, the people in whose heart is my law ; fear ye not the reproach of men, neither be ye afraid of their revilings. For the moth shall eat them up like a garment, and the worm shall eat them like wool : but my righteousness shall be for ever, and my salvation from generation to generation." So Isa. xlv. 17 : "But Israel shall be saved in the Lord with an everlasting salvation ; ye shall not be ashamed nor confounded, world without end." Compare Jer. xxxi. 3. The language used in the passage before us, moreover, is such as could not properly be applied to anything but that righteousness which the Messiah would introduce. It could not be used in reference to the temporal prosperity of the Jews on their return to the holy land, nor to such righteousness as the nation had in former times. The fair and proper meaning of the term is, that it would be *eternal*—that which would *endure for ever*—יְמִים־עֹלָם צֶדֶק. It would place righteousness on a permanent and enduring foundation ; introduce that which would endure through all changes, and exist when the heavens would be no more. In the plan itself there would be no change ; in the righteousness which any one would possess under that system there would be perpetual duration—it would exist for ever and ever. This is the nature of that righteousness by which men are now justified ; this is that which all who are interested in the scheme of redemption actually possess. The *way* in which this "everlasting righteousness" would be introduced is not stated here, but is reserved for future revelations. Probably all that the words would convey to Daniel would be, that there would be some method disclosed by which men would become righteous, and that this would not be temporary or changing,

but would be permanent and eternal. It is not improper that *we* should understand it, as it is explained by the subsequent revelations in the New Testament, as to the method by which sinners are justified before God. ¶ *And to seal up the vision and prophecy.* Marg., as in the Heb., *prophet.* The evident meaning, however, here is *prophecy.* The word *seal* is found, as already explained, in the former part of the verse—"to seal up sins." The word *vision* (for its meaning, see Notes on Isaiah i. 1) need not be understood as referring particularly to the visions seen by Daniel, but should be understood, like the word *prophecy* or *prophet* here, in a general sense—as denoting all the visions seen by the prophets—the series of visions relating to the future, which had been made known to the prophets. The idea seems to be that they would at that time be all *sealed*, in the sense that they would be closed or shut up—no longer open matters—but that the fulfilment would, as it were, close them up for ever. Till that time they would be open for perusal and study ; then they would be closed up as a sealed volume which one does not read, but which contains matter hidden from the view. Comp. Notes on Isa. viii. 16 : "Bind up the testimony ; seal the law among my disciples." See also Dan. viii. 26 ; xii. 4. In Isaiah (viii. 16) the meaning is, that the prophecy was complete, and the direction was given to bind it up, or roll it up like a volume, and to seal it. In Dan. viii. 26, the meaning is, seal up the prophecy, or make a permanent record of it, that, when it is fulfilled, the event may be compared with the prophecy, and it may be seen that the one corresponds with the other. In the passage before us, Gesenius (*Lex.*) renders it, "to complete, to finish"—meaning that the prophecies would be fulfilled. Hengstenberg supposes that it means, that "as soon as the fulfilment takes place, the prophecy, although it retains, in other respects, its great importance, reaches the end of its destination, in so far as the view of believers, who stand in need of consolation and encouragement, is no longer directed to it, to the future prosperity, but to that which has appeared." Lengerke supposes that it means to confirm, corroborate, ratify—*bekräftigen, bestätigen;* that is, "the eternal righteousness will be given to the pious, and the predictions of the prophets will be confirmed and fulfilled." To seal, says he, has also the idea of confirming, since the contents of a writing are secured or made fast by a seal. After all, perhaps, the very idea here is, that of *making fast,* as a lock or seal does—for, as is well known, a seal was often used by the ancients where a lock is with us; and the sense may be, that, as a seal or lock made fast and secure the contents of a writing or a book, so the *event,* when the prophecy was fulfilled, would make it *fast* and *secure.* It would be, as it were, locking it up, or sealing it, forever. It would determine all that seemed to be undetermined about it; settle all that seemed to be indefinite, and leave it no longer uncertain what was meant. According to this interpretation the meaning would be, that the prophecies would be sealed up or settled by the coming of the Messiah. The prophecies terminated on him (comp. Rev. xix. 10); they would find their fulfilment in him; they would be completed in him—and might then be regarded as closed and consummated—as a book that is fully written and is sealed up. All the prophecies, and all the visions, had a reference more or less direct to the coming of the Messiah, and when he should appear they might be regarded as complete. The spirit of prophecy would cease, and the facts would confirm and seal all that had been written. ¶ *And to anoint the Most Holy.* There has been great variety in the interpretation of this expression. The word rendered *anoint*—

מָשַׁח —infinitive from מָשַׁח (whence the word Messiah, ver. 25), means, properly, to strike or draw the hand over anything; to spread over with anything, to smear, to paint, to anoint. It is commonly used with reference to a sacred rite, to anoint, or consecrate by unction, or anointing to any office or use; as, *e.g.,* a priest, Exod. xxviii. 41; xl. 15; a prophet, 1 Kings xix.

16; Isa. lxi. 1; a king, 1 Sam. x. 1; xv. 1; 2 Sam. ii. 4; 1 Kings i. 34. So it is used to denote the consecration of a stone or column as a future sacred place, Gen. xxxi. 13; or vases and vessels as consecrated to God, Exod. xl. 9, 11; Lev. viii. 11; Numb. vii. 1. The word would then denote a setting apart to a sacred use, or consecrating a person or place as holy. Oil, or an unguent, prepared according to a specified rule, was commonly employed for this purpose, but the word may be used in a figurative sense—as denoting to set apart or consecrate in any way *without* the use of oil—as in the case of the Messiah. So far as this *word,* therefore, is concerned, what is here referred to may have occurred without the literal use of oil, by any act of consecration or dedication to a holy use. The phrase, "the· Most Holy" (קֹדֶשׁ קָדָשִׁים) has been very variously interpreted. By some it has been understood to apply literally to the most holy place—the holy of holies, in the temple; by others to the whole temple, regarded as holy; by others to Jerusalem at large as a holy place; and by others, as Hengstenberg, to the Christian church as *a* holy place. By some the thing here referred to is supposed to have been the consecration of the most holy place after the rebuilding of the temple; by others the consecration of the whole temple; by others the consecration of the temple and city by the presence of the Messiah, and by others the consecration of the Christian church, by his presence. The phrase properly means "holy of holies," or most holy. It is applied often in the Scriptures to the *inner sanctuary,* or the portion of the tabernacle and temple containing the ark of the covenant, the two tables of stone, &c. See Notes on Matt. xxi. 12. The phrase occurs in the following places in the Scripture: Exod. xxvi. 33, 34; xxix. 37; xxx. 29, 36; xl. 10; Lev. ii. 3, 10, *et al.*—in all, in about twenty-eight places. See the *Englishman's Hebrew Concordance.* It is not necessarily limited to the inner sanctuary of the temple, but may be applied to the whole house, or to anything that was consecrated to

God in a manner peculiarly sacred. In a large sense, possibly it might apply to Jerusalem, though I am not aware that it ever occurs in this sense in the Scriptures, and in a figurative sense it might be applied undoubtedly, as Hengstenberg supposes, to the Christian church, though it is certain that it is not elsewhere thus used. In regard to the meaning of the expression—an important and difficult one, as is admitted by all—there are five principal opinions which it may be well to notice. The truth will be found in one of them. (1.) That it refers to the consecration by oil or anointing of the temple, that would be rebuilt after the captivity, by Zerubbabel and Joshua. This was the opinion of Michaelis and Jahn. But to this opinion there are insuperable objections: (*a*) that, according to the uniform tradition of the Jews, the holy oil was wanting in the second temple. In the case of the first temple there might have been a literal anointing, though there is no evidence of that, as there was of the anointing of the vessels of the tabernacle, Exod. xxx. 22, &c. But in the second temple there is every evidence that there can be, that there was no literal anointing. (*b*) The *time* here referred to is a fatal objection to this opinion. The period is seventy weeks of years, or four hundred and ninety years. This cannot be doubted (see Notes on the first part of the verse) to be the period referred to; but it is absurd to suppose that the consecration of the new temple would be deferred for so long a time, and there is not the slightest evidence that it was. This opinion, therefore, cannot be entertained. (2.) The second opinion is, that it refers to the re-consecration and cleansing of the temple after the abominations of Antiochus Epiphanes. See Notes on ch. viii. 14. But this opinion is liable substantially to the same objections as the other. The cleansing of the temple, or of the sanctuary, as it is said in ch. viii. 14, did *not* occur four hundred and ninety years after the order to rebuild the temple (ver. 25), but at a much earlier period. By no art of construction, if the period here referred to is four hundred and ninety years,

can it be made to apply to the re-dedication of the temple after Antiochus had defiled it. (3.) Others have supposed that this refers to the Messiah himself, and that the meaning is, that he, who was most holy, would then be consecrated or anointed as the Messiah. It is probable, as Hengstenberg (*Christ.* ii. 321, 322) has shown, that the Greek translators thus understood it, but it is a sufficient objection to this that the phrase, though occurring many times in the Scriptures, is never applied to *persons*, unless this be an instance. Its uniform and proper application is to *things*, or *places*, and it is undoubtedly so to be understood in this place. (4.) Hengstenberg supposes (pp. 325–328) that it refers to the Christian church as *a* holy place, or "the New Temple of the Lord," "the Church of the New Covenant," as consecrated and supplied with the gifts of the Spirit. But it is a sufficient refutation of this opinion that the phrase is nowhere else so used; that it has in the Old Testament a settled meaning as referring to the tabernacle or the temple; that it is nowhere employed to denote a collection of *people*, any more than an individual person—an idea which Hengstenberg himself expressly rejects (p. 322); and that there is no proper sense in which it can be said that the Christian church is *anointed*. The language is undoubtedly to be understood as referring to some *place* that was to be thus consecrated, and the uniform Hebrew usage would lead to the supposition that there is reference, in some sense, to the temple at Jerusalem. (5.) It seems to me, therefore, that the obvious and fair interpretation is, to refer it to the temple—as the holy place of God; his peculiar abode on earth. Strictly and properly speaking, the phrase would apply to the inner room of the temple—the sanctuary properly so called (see Notes on Heb. ix. 2); but it might be applied to the whole temple as consecrated to the service of God. If it be asked, then, what anointing or consecration is referred to here, the reply, as it seems to me, is, not that it was then to be set apart anew, or to be dedicated; not that it was literally to be anointed with the consecrating oil, but

25 Know, therefore, and understand, *that* from the going forth of
the commandment to ¹ restore and

to build Jerusalem, unto the Messiah the Prince, *shall be* seven weeks

1 or, *build again.*

that it was to be consecrated in the
highest and best sense by the presence
of the Messiah—that by his coming
there was to be a higher and more solemn consecration of the temple to the
real purpose for which it was erected
than had occurred at any time.   It
was reared as a holy place ; it would
become eminently holy by the presence
of him who would come as the anointed
of God, and his coming to it would accomplish the purpose for which it was
erected, and with reference to which
all the rites observed there had been
ordained, and then, this work having
been accomplished, the temple, and all
the rites appertaining to it, would pass
away.   In confirmation of this view,
it may be remarked, that there are repeated allusions to the coming of the
Messiah to the second temple, reared
after the return from the captivity—
as that which would give a peculiar
sacredness to the temple, and which
would cause it to surpass in glory all
its ancient splendour.   So in Hag. ii.
7, 9 : "And I will shake all nations,
and the desire of all nations shall
come : and I will fill this house with
glory, saith the Lord of hosts.—The
glory of this latter house shall be
greater than of the former, saith the
Lord of hosts : and in this place will I
give peace, saith the Lord of hosts."
So Mal. iii. 1, 2 : "The Lord, whom
ye seek, shall suddenly come to his
temple, even the messenger of the
covenant whom ye delight in : behold,
he shall come, saith the Lord of hosts.
But who may abide the day of his
coming ? and who shall stand when he
appeareth ? for he is like a refiner's
fire, and like fullers' soap," &c.   Comp.
Matt. xii. 6 : "But I say unto you,
That in this place is one greater than
the temple."   Using the word *anoint*,
therefore, as denoting to consecrate, to
render holy, to set apart to a sacred
use, and the phrase *holy of holies* to
designate the temple as such, it seems
to me most probable that the reference
here is to the highest consecration
which could be made of the temple in

the estimation of a Hebrew, or, in
fact, the presence of the Messiah, as
giving a sacredness to that edifice
which nothing else did give or could
give, and, therefore, as meeting all the
proper force of the language used here.
On the supposition that it was designed
that there should be a reference to this
event, this would be such language as
would have been not unnaturally employed by a Hebrew prophet.   And if
it be so, this may be regarded as the
probable meaning of the passage.   In
this sense, the temple which was to be
reared again, and about which Daniel
felt so solicitous, would receive its
highest, its truest consecration, as connected with an event which was to
bring in everlasting righteousness, and
to seal up the vision and the prophecy.
    25.   *Know, therefore, and under-*
stand.   Hengstenberg renders this,
"and thou wilt know and understand ;"
and supposes that the design of Gabriel
is to awaken the attention and interest
of Daniel by the assurance that, if he
would give attention, he would understand the subject by the explanation
which he was about to give.   So also
Theodotion renders it in the future
tense.   The Hebrew is in the future
tense, and would probably convey the
idea that he might or would know and
understand the matter.   So Lengerke
renders it, *Und so mögest du wissen,*
&c.   The object is doubtless to call
the attention of Daniel to the subject,
with the assurance that he might comprehend the great points of the communication which he was about to
make respecting the seventy weeks.
In the previous verse, the statement
was a general one ; in this, the angel
states the time when the period of the
seventy weeks was to commence, and
then that the whole period was to be
broken up or divided into three smaller
portions or epochs, each evidently
marking some important event, or
constituting an important era.   The
first period of seven weeks was evidently to be characterized by something
in which it would be different from

| and threescore and two weeks: the street shall ¹ be built again, | and the ²wall, even *a* in ³ troublous times. |
| 1 *return and be builded.* 2 *or, breach,* or, *ditch.* | *a* Neh. 4. 8, &c.; 6. 15.   3 *strait of.* |

that which would follow, or it would reach to some important epoch, and then would follow a continuous period of sixty-two weeks, after which, during the remaining one week, to complete the whole number of seventy, the Messiah would come and would be cut off, and the series of desolations would commence which would result in the entire destruction of the city. ¶ That *from the going forth of the command-ment.* Heb., "of the word"—דָּבָר. It is used, however, as in ver. 23, in the sense of commandment or order. The expression "gone forth" (מֹצָא) would properly apply to the *issuing* of an order or decree. So in ver. 23— יָצָא דָבָר—"the commandment went forth." The word properly means a going forth, and is applied to the rising sun, that goes forth from the east, Psa. xix. 6 (7); then a *place* of going forth, as a gate, a fountain of waters, the east, &c., Ezek. xlii. 11; Isa. xli. 18; Psa. lxxv. 6 (7). The word here has undoubted reference to the promulgation of a decree or com-mand, but there is nothing in the words to determine *by whom* the command was to be issued. So far as the *lan-guage* is concerned, it would apply equally well to a command issued by God, or by the Persian king, and no-thing but the circumstances can deter-mine which is referred to. Hengsten-berg supposes that it is the former, and that the reference is to the Divine pur-pose, or the command issued from the "heavenly council" to rebuild Jerusa-lem. But the more natural and obvious meaning is, to understand it of the command actually issued by the Persian monarch to restore and build the city of Jerusalem. This has been the in-terpretation given by the great body of expositors, and the reasons for it seem to be perfectly clear: (*a*) This would be the interpretation affixed to it natur-ally, if there were no theory to support, or if it did not open a chronological difficulty not easy to settle. (*b*) This is the only interpretation which can

give anything like definiteness to the passage. Its purpose is to designate some fixed and certain period from which a reckoning could be made as to the time when the Messiah would come. But, so far as appears, there was no such definite and marked command on the part of God; no period which can be fixed upon when *he* gave command-ment to restore and build Jerusalem; no exact and settled point from which one could reckon as to the period when the Messiah would come. It seems to me, therefore, to be clear, that the al-lusion is to some order to rebuild the city, and as this order could come only from one who had at that time juris-diction over Jerusalem and Judea, and who could command the resources ne-cessary to rebuild the ruined city, that order must be one that would emanate from the reigning power; that is, in fact, the Persian power,—for that was the power that had jurisdiction at the close of the seventy years' exile. But, as there were several orders or com-mands in regard to the restoration of the city and the temple, and as there has been much difficulty in ascertaining the exact chronology of the events of that remote period, it has not been easy to determine the precise order referred to, or to relieve the whole subject from perplexity and difficulty. Lengerke supposes that the reference here is the same as in ver. 2, to the promise made to Jeremiah, and that this is the true point from which the reckoning is to be made. The exact edict referred to will be more properly considered at the close of the verse. All that is neces-sarily implied here is, that the time from which the reckoning is to be com-menced is some command or order issued to restore and build Jerusalem. ¶ *To restore.* Marg., *build again.* The Hebrew is, properly, *to cause to* *return—* לְהָשִׁיב. The word might be applied to the return of the captives to their own land, but it is evidently here used with reference to the city of Jeru-salem, and the meaning must be, *to restore it to its former condition.* It was evidently the purpose to cause it to return, as it were, to its former splendour; to reinstate it in its former condition as a holy city—the city where the worship of God would be celebrated, and it is this purpose which is referred to here. The word, in Hiphil, is used in this sense of restoring to a former state, or to renew, in the following places: Psa. lxxx. 3, *" Turn us again* —הֲשִׁיבֵנוּ—and cause thy face to shine."

So vers. 7, 19, of the same Psalm. Isa. i. 26, "And I will *restore* thy judges as at the first," &c. The meaning here would be met by the supposition that Jerusalem was to be put into its former condition. ¶ *And to build Jerusalem.* It was then in ruins. The command, which is referred to here, must be one to build it up again—its houses, temple, walls; and the fair sense is, that some such *order* would be issued, and the reckoning of the seventy weeks must *begin* at the issuing of this command. The proper interpretation of the prophecy demands that *that* time shall be assumed in endeavouring to ascertain when the seventy weeks would terminate. In doing this, it is evidently required in all fairness that we should not take the time when the Messiah *did* appear— or the birth of the Lord Jesus, assuming that to be the *terminus ad quem*— the point to which the seventy weeks were to extend—and then reckon *backward* for a space of four hundred and ninety years, to see whether we cannot find some event which by a possible construction would bear to be applied as the *terminus a quo,* the point from which we are to begin to reckon; but we are to ascertain when, in fact, the order was given to rebuild Jerusalem, and to make *that* the *terminus a quo*— the starting point in the reckoning. The consideration of the fulfilment of this may with propriety be reserved to the close of the verse. ¶ *Unto the Messiah.* The word *Messiah* occurs but four times in the common version of the Scriptures: Dan. ix. 25, 26: John i. 41; iv. 25. It is synonymous in meaning with the word *Christ,* the Anointed. See Notes on Matt. i. 1.

Messiah is the Hebrew word; Christ the Greek. The Hebrew word (מָשִׁיחַ) occurs frequently in the Old Testament, and, with the exception of these two places in Daniel, it is uniformly translated *anointed,* and is applied to priests, to prophets, and to kings, as being originally set apart to their offices by solemn acts of anointing. So far as the *language* is concerned here, it might be applied to any one who sustained these offices, and the proper application is to be determined from the connection. Our translators have introduced the article — " unto *the* Messiah." This is wanting in the Hebrew, and should not have been introduced, as it gives a definiteness to the prophecy which the original language does not necessarily demand. Our translators undoubtedly understood it as referring to him who is known as the Messiah, but this is not necessarily implied in the original. All that the language fairly conveys is, " until an anointed one." Who *that* was to be is to be determined from other circumstances than the mere use of the language, and in the interpretation of the language it should not be assumed that the reference is to any particular individual. That some eminent personage is designated; some one who by way of eminence would be properly regarded as anointed of God; some one who would act so important a part as to characterize the age, or determine the epoch in which he should live; some one so prominent that he could be referred to as " *anointed,*" with no more definite appellation; some one who would be understood to be referred to by the mere use of this language, may be fairly concluded from the expression used—for the angel clearly meant to imply this, and to direct the mind forward to some one who would have such a prominence in the history of the world. The object now is merely to ascertain the meaning of the *language.* All that is fairly implied is, that it refers to some one who would have such a prominence as anointed, or set apart to the office of prophet, priest, or king, that it could be understood that he was referred to by the use of this language. The reference is not to *the* anointed one, as of one who was already known or looked forward to as such—for then the article would have been used; but to some one who, when he appeared, would have such marked characteristics that there would be no difficulty in determining that he was the one intended. Hengstenberg well remarks, "We must, therefore, translate *an anointed one, a prince*, and assume that the prophet, in accordance with the uniform character of his prophecy, chose the more indefinite, instead of the more definite designation, and spoke only of *an* anointed one, *a* prince, instead of *the* anointed one, *the* prince—κατ᾽ ἐξοχήν—and left his hearers to draw a deeper knowledge respecting him, from the prevailing expectations, grounded on earlier prophecies of a future great King, from the remaining declarations of the context, and from the fulfilment, the coincidence of which with the prophecy must here be the more obvious, since an accurate date had been given."—*Christol.* ii. 334, 335. The Vulgate renders this, *Usque ad Christum ducem* — "even to Christ the leader," or ruler. The Syriac, "to the advent of Christ the king." Theodotion, ἕως Χριστοῦ ἡγουμένου — " to Christ the leader," or ruler. The question whether this refers to Christ will be more appropriately considered at the close of the verse. The inquiry will then occur, also, whether this refers to his birth, or to his appearance *as* the anointed one—his taking upon himself publicly the office. The language would apply to either, though it would perhaps more properly refer to the latter—to the time when he should *appear* as such—or should be anointed, crowned, or set apart to the office, and be fully instituted in it. It could not be demonstrated that *either* of these applications would be a departure from the fair interpretation of the words, and the application must be determined by some other circumstances, if any are expressed. What those are in the case will be considered at the close of the verse. ¶ *The Prince.* נָגִיד. This word properly means a leader, a prefect, a prince. It is a

word of very general character, and might be applied to *any* leader or ruler. It is applied to an overseer, or, as we should say, a *secretary* of the treasury, 1 Chron. xxvi. 24 ; 2 Chron. xxxi. 12 ; an overseer of the temple, 1 Chron. ix. 11 ; 2 Chron. xxxi. 13 ; of the palace, 2 Chron. xxviii. 7 ; and of military affairs, 1 Chron. xiii. 1 ; 2 Chron. xxxii. 21. It is also used absolutely to denote a prince of a people, any one of royal dignity, 1 Sam. ix. 16 ; x. 1 ; xiii. 14.—Gesenius. So far as this *word*, therefore, is concerned, it would apply to *any* prince or leader, civil or military; any one of royal dignity, or who should distinguish himself, or make himself a leader in civil, ecclesiastical, or military affairs, or who should receive an appointment to any such station. It is a word which would be as applicable to the Messiah as to any other leader, but which has nothing in itself to make it necessary to apply it to him. All that can be fairly deduced from its use here is, that it would be some prominent leader; some one that would be known without any more definite designation ; some one on whom the mind would naturally rest, and some one to whom when he appeared it would be applied without hesitation and without difficulty. There can be no doubt that a Hebrew, in the circumstances of Daniel, and with the known views and expectations of the Hebrew people, *would* apply such a phrase to the Messiah. ¶ Shall be *seven weeks*. See Notes on ver. 24. The *reason* for dividing the whole period into seven weeks, sixty-two weeks, and one week, is not formally stated, and will be considered at the close of the verse. All that is necessary here in order to an explanation of the language, and of what is to be anticipated in the fulfilment, is this: (*a*) That, according to the above interpretation (ver. 24), the period would be forty-nine years. (*b*) That this was to be the *first* portion of the whole time, not time that would be properly taken out of *any* part of the whole period. (*c*) That there was to be some event at the end of the forty-nine years which would designate a period, or a natural division of the time, or that the portion which was designated by the forty-nine years was to be distinctly characterized from the next period referred to as sixty-two weeks, and the next period as one week. (*d*) No intimation is given in the words as to the nature of this period, or as to what would distinguish one portion from the others, and *what* that was to be is to be learned from subsequent explanations, or from the actual course of events. If one period was characterized by war, and another by peace; one in building the city and the walls, and the other by quiet prosperity; one by abundance, and the other by famine; one by sickness, and the other by health—all that is fairly implied by the *words* would be met. It is foretold only that there would be *something* that would designate these periods, and serve to distinguish the one from the other. ¶ *And threescore and two weeks.* Sixty-two weeks; that is, as above explained (ver. 24), four hundred and thirty-four years. The fair meaning is, that there would be something which would characterize that long period, and serve to distinguish it from that which preceded it. It is not indeed intimated what that would be, and the nature of the case seems to require that we should look *to* the events—to the facts in the course of the history to determine what that was. Whether it was peace, prosperity, quiet, order, or the prevalence of religion as contrasted with the former period, all that the words fairly imply would be fulfilled in either of them. ¶ *The street shall be built again.* This is a general assertion or prediction, which does not seem to have any special reference to the *time* when it would be done. The fair interpretation of the expression does not require us to understand that it should be *after* the united period of the seven weeks and the sixty-two weeks, nor during either one of those periods; that is, the language is not such that we are necessarily required to affix it to any one period. It seems to be a general assurance designed to comfort Daniel with the promise that the walls and streets of Jerusalem, now desolate, would be built again, and that this

would occur some time during this period. His mind was particularly anxious respecting the desolate condition of the city, and the declaration is here made that it would be restored. So far as the language—the grammatical construction is concerned, it seems to me that this would be fulfilled if it were done either at the time of the going forth of the commandment, or during either of the periods designated, or even after these periods. It is, however, most natural, in the connection, to understand it of the *first* period—the seven weeks, or the forty-nine years—since it is said that "the commandment would go forth to restore, and to build Jerusalem;" and since, as the whole subsequent period is divided into three portions, it may be presumed that the thing that would characterize the first portion, or that which would first be done, would be to execute the commandment—that is, to restore and build the city. These considerations would lead us, therefore, to suppose that the thing which would characterize the first period—the forty-nine years—would be the rebuilding of the city; and *the time*—a time which, considering the extent and entireness of the ruins, the nature of the opposition that might be encountered, the difficulty of collecting enough from among the exiles to return and do it, the want of means, and the embarrassments which such an undertaking might be supposed to involve, cannot, probably, be regarded as too long.

The word rendered *street* — רְחֹב —

means a *street*, so called from its *breadth*, and would properly, therefore, be applied to a *wide* street. Then it denotes a market-place, or a forum —the broad open place at the gates of Oriental cities where public trials were held, and things exposed for sale, 2 Chron. xxxii. 6. In Ezra x. 9, the word refers to the area or court before the temple: "And all the people sat in the street (בִּרְחוֹב) of the house of God," &c. Comp. Nehe. viii. 1, 3, 16. The reference in this place, therefore, may be to that area or court; or it may be to any place of concourse, or any thoroughfare. It is such language as would be naturally used to denote that the city would be restored to its former condition. The phrase "shall be built again" is, in the margin, *return and be builded.* This is in accordance with the Hebrew. That is, it would be restored to its former state; it would, as it were, come back and be built up again. Hengstenberg renders it "a street is restored and built." The phrase properly implies that it would assume its former condition, the word *built* here being used in the sense of *made,* as we speak of *making a road.* Lengerke renders it, *wird wieder hergestellt* — "shall be again restored." Theodotion renders it, ἐπιστρέψει — "it shall return," understanding it as meaning that there would be a return, to wit, from the exile. But the more correct meaning undoubtedly is, that *the street* would return to its former state, and be rebuilt. ¶ *And the wall.* Marg., *ditch.* Hengstenberg renders this, "and firmly is it determined;" maintaining that the word חָרוּץ here means fixed, determined,

resolved on, and that the idea is, the purpose that the city should be rebuilt was firmly resolved on in the Divine mind, and that the *design* of what is here said was to comfort and animate the returned Hebrews in their efforts to rebuild the city, in all the discouragements and troubles which would attend such an undertaking. The common interpretation, however, has been that it refers to a ditch, trench, or wall, that would be constructed at the time of the rebuilding of the city. So the Vulgate, *muri, walls.* So Theodotion, τεῖχος — *wall.* The Syriac renders it, "Jerusalem, and the *villages,* and the streets." Luther, *Mauren, walls.* Lengerke renders it, as Hengstenberg does, "and it is determined." Maurer understands the two expressions, *street* and *wall,* to be equivalent to *within* and *without* — meaning that the city would be thoroughly and entirely rebuilt. The Hebrew word חָרוּץ means, properly, that which

is cut in, or dug out, from חָרַץ — to cut in. The word is translated *sharp-pointed things* in Job xli. 30; *gold, fine gold, choice gold,* in Psa. lxviii. 13; Prov. iii. 14; viii. 10, 19; xvi. 16; Zech. ix. 3; *a threshing instrument,* Isa. xxviii. 27; Amos i. 3; *sharp* (referring to a threshing instrument), Isa. xli. 15; *wall,* Dan. ix. 25; and *decision,* Joel iii. 14. It does not elsewhere occur in the Scriptures. The notion of *gold* as connected with the word is probably derived from the fact of its being dug for, or eagerly sought by men. That idea is, of course, not applicable here. Gesenius supposes that it here means a *ditch* or *trench* of a fortified city. This seems to me to be the probable signification. At all events, this has the concurrence of the great body of interpreters; and this accords well with the connection. The word does not properly mean *wall,* and it is never elsewhere so used. It need not be said that it was common, if not universal, in walled cities to make a deep ditch or trench around them to prevent the approach of an enemy, and such *language* would naturally be employed in speaking of the rebuilding of a city. Prof. Stuart renders it, "with broad spaces, and *narrow limits.*" ¶ *Even in troublous times.* Marg., *strait of.* Hengstenberg, "in a time of distress." Lengerke, *Im Druck der Zeiten* — "in a pressure of times." Vulg., *In angustia temporum.* Theodotion, in the Septuagint, renders it, "And these times shall be emptied out" (Thompson) — καὶ ἐκκενωθήσονται οἱ καιροί. The proper meaning of the Hebrew word (צוֹק) is, distress, trouble, anguish; and the reference is, doubtless, to times that would be characterized by trouble, perplexity, and distress. The allusion is clearly to the rebuilding of the city, and the use of this language would lead us to anticipate that such an enterprise would meet with opposition or embarrassment; that there would be difficulty in accomplishing it; that the work would not be carried on easily, and that a considerable time would be necessary to finish it.

Having gone through with an investigation of the meaning of the words and phrases of this verse, we are now prepared to inquire more particularly what things are referred to, and whether the predictions have been fulfilled. The points which it is necessary to examine are the following:—To whom reference is made by the Messiah the Prince; the time designated by the going forth of the commandment—or the *terminus a quo;* the question whether the whole period extends to the *birth* of him here referred to as the Messiah the Prince, or to his assuming the office or appearing as such; the time embraced in the first seven weeks—and the fulfilment —or the question whether, from the time of the going forth of the commandment to the appearing of the Messiah, the period of the four hundred and ninety years can be fairly made out. These are evidently important points, and it need not be said that a great variety of opinions has prevailed in regard to them, and that they are attended with no little difficulty.

I. To whom reference is made as the Messiah the Prince. In the exposition of the meaning of the words, we have seen that there is nothing in the language itself to determine this. It is applicable to *any* one who should be set apart as a ruler or prince, and might be applied to Cyrus, to any anointed king, or to him who is properly designated now as the Messiah —the Lord Jesus. Comp. Notes on Isa. xlv. 1. It is unnecessary to show that a great variety of opinions has been entertained, both among the Jewish Rabbins and among Christian commentators, respecting the question to whom this refers. Among the Jews, Jarchi and Jacchiades supposed that it referred to Cyrus; Ben Gersom, and others, to Zerubbabel; Aben Ezra to Nehemiah; Rabbi Azariah to Artaxerxes. Bertholdt, Lengerke, Maurer, and this class of expositors generally, suppose that the reference is to Cyrus, who is *called* the Messiah, or the "Anointed," in Isa. xlv. 1. According to this interpretation, it is supposed that the reference is to the

seventy years of Jeremiah, and that the meaning is, that "seven weeks," or forty-nine years, would elapse from the desolation of the city till the time of Cyrus. See Maurer, *in loc.* Comp. also Lengerke, pp. 444, 445. As specimens of the views entertained by those who deny the reference of the passage to the Messiah, and of the difficulties and absurdities of those views, we may notice those of Eichhorn and Bertholdt. Eichhorn maintains that the numbers referred to are *round* numbers, and that we are not to expect to be able to make out an exact conformity between those numbers and the events. The "commandment" mentioned in ver. 25 he supposes refers to the order of Cyrus to restore and rebuild the city, which order was given, according to Usher, A.M. 3468. From this point of time must the "seven weeks," or the forty-nine years, be reckoned; but, according to his view, the reckoning must be "backwards and forwards;" that is, it is seven weeks, or forty-nine years, *backward* to Nebuchadnezzar, who is here called "Messiah the Prince," who destroyed the temple and city, A.M. 3416—or about fifty-two years before the going forth of the edict of Cyrus. From that time, the reckoning of the sixty-two weeks must be commenced. But again, this is not to be computed literally from the time of Nebuchadnezzar; but since the Jews, in accordance with Jeremiah xxv. 11, 12, reckoned *seventy* years, instead of the true time, the point from which the estimate is to begin is the fourth year of the reign of Jehoiakim, and this occurred, according to Usher, A.M. 3397. Reckoning from this point onward, the sixty-two weeks, or 434 years, would bring us to the time of Antiochus Epiphanes (A.M. 3829). At the end of the sixty-two weeks, in the first year of Antiochus Epiphanes, the high-priest, Onias III. (the Messiah of ver. 26), was displaced—"cut off"— וְיִבְרַת—and Jason was appointed in his place, and Menelaus the year after removed him. Thus Onias had properly no successor, &c. This absurd opinion Bertholdt (p. 605, *seq.*) attempts to set aside—a task which is very easily performed, and then proposes his own —a hypothesis not less absurd and improbable. According to his theory (p. 613, *seq.*), the seventy years have indeed a historical basis, and the time embraced in them extends from the destruction of Jerusalem by Nebuchadnezzar to the death of Antiochus Epiphanes. It is divided into three periods: (*a*) The seven first hebdomads extend from the destruction of Jerusalem by Nebuchadnezzar to king Cyrus, who gave the exiles permission to return to their land. This is the period during which Jerusalem must lie waste (ver. 2); and after the close of this, by the favour of Cyrus (ver. 25), the promise of Jeremiah (ver. 25 — ‎דָּבָר—"commandment"), that Jerusalem shall be rebuilt, goes forth. (*b*) The following sixty-two weeks extend from the return of the exiles to the beginning of the troubles and persecutions under Antiochus. This is the period of the rebuilding of Jerusalem (ver. 25). (*c*) The last period of one week extends from the time of the oppressions and wrongs commenced under Antiochus, to the death of Antiochus. See this view fully explained and illustrated in Bertholdt, *ut supra*. The great mass of Christian interpreters, however, have supposed that the reference is to the Messiah properly so called—the promised Saviour of the world—the Lord Jesus. In support of this opinion, the following considerations may be suggested, which seem to me to be conclusive: (1.) The language itself is such as is properly applicable to him, and such as would naturally suggest him. It is true, as we see in Isa. xlv. 1, that the term Messiah *may* be applied to another, as it is there to Cyrus (see the Notes on the meaning of the word in that place, and in the exposition of this verse), but it is also true that if the term stands by itself, and with no explanation, it would naturally suggest him who, by way of eminence, is known as *the* Messiah. In Isa. xlv. 1, it is expressly limited to Cyrus, and there can be no danger of mistake. Here there is no such limitation, and it is natural, therefore, to apply it in the sense in which among

the Hebrews it would be obviously understood. Even Bertholdt admits the force of this. Thus (p. 563) he says: "That at the words ‎מָשִׁיחַ נָגִיד [Messiah the Prince] we should be led to think of the Messiah, Jesus, and at those, ver. 26, ‎יִכָּרֵת מָשִׁיחַ וְאֵין לֹו [shall be cut off but not for himself], of his crucifixion, though not absolutely necessary, is still very natural." (2.) This would be the interpretation which would be given to the words by the Jews. They were so much accustomed to look forward to a great prince and deliverer, who would be by way of eminence the Anointed of the Lord, that, unless there was some special limitation or designation in the language, they would naturally apply it to the Messiah, properly so called. Comp. Isa. ix. 6, 7. Early in the history of the Jews, the nation had become accustomed to the expectation that such a deliverer would come, and its hopes were centred on him. In all times of national trouble and calamity; in all their brightest visions of the future, they were accustomed to look to him as one who would deliver them from their troubles, and who would exalt their people to a pitch of glory and of honour, such as they had never known before. Unless, therefore, there was something in the connection which would demand a different interpretation, the language would be of course applied to the Messiah. But it cannot be pretended that there is anything in the connection that demands such a limitation, nor which forbids such an application. (3.) So far as the ancient versions throw any light on the subject, they show that this is the correct interpretation. So the Latin Vulgate, *usque ad Christum ducem.* So the Syriac, "unto Messiah, the most holy" —literally, "*holy* of holies." So Theodotion—ἕως Χριστοῦ—where there can be little doubt that the Messiah was understood to be referred to. The same is found in the Arabic. The *Codex Chis.* is in utter confusion on this whole passage, and nothing can be made of it. (4.) All the circumstances referred to in connection with him who is here called "Messiah the Prince" are such as to be properly applicable to the work which the Lord Jesus came to do, and *not* to Cyrus, or Antiochus, or any other leader or ruler. See the Notes on ver. 24. To no other one, according to the interpretation which the passage in that verse seems to demand, can the expressions there used be applied. In that exposition it was shown that the verse is designed to give a *general* view of what would be accomplished, or of what is expressed more in detail in the remaining verses of the vision, and that the language there used can be applied properly to the work which the Lord Jesus came to accomplish. Assuredly to no one else can the phrases "to restrain transgression," "to seal up sins," "to cover over iniquity," "to bring in everlasting righteousness," "to seal up the vision and prophecy," and "to consecrate the most holy place," be so well applied. The same is true of the language in the subsequent part of the prophecy, "Messiah shall be cut off," "not for himself," "shall confirm the covenant," "cause the oblation to cease." Any one may see the perplexities in which they are involved by adopting another interpretation, by consulting Bertholdt, or Lengerke on the passage. (5.) The expression here used ("prince"—נָגִיד)—is applied to the Messiah beyond all question in Isa. lv. 4: "I have given him for a witness to the people, a *leader*—נָגִיד—and a commander to the people." (6.) The perplexity attending any other interpretation is an additional proof of this point. In full illustration of this, it is necessary only to refer to the views of Bertholdt and Eichhorn as above exhibited. Whatever may be said about the difficulties on the supposition that it refers to the Lord Jesus—the true Messiah—no one can undertake to reconcile the applications which they have proposed with any belief of the inspiration of the passage. These considerations seem to me to make it clear that the prophecy had reference to the Messiah properly so called—the hope and the expectation of the Jewish people. There can be no doubt that Daniel would so understand it; there

can be no doubt that it would be so applied by the Jews.

II. The next question is, From what point are we to reckon in computing the time when the Messiah would appear—the *terminus a quo?* It is important to fix this, for the whole question of the fulfilment depends on it, and *honesty* requires that it should be determined without reference to the time to which four hundred and ninety years would reach—or the *terminus ad quem.* It is clearly not proper to do as Prideaux does, to *assume* that it refers to the birth of Christ, and then to reckon backward *to* a time which may be made to mean the "going forth of the commandment." The true method, undoubtedly, would be to fix on a time which would accord with the expression here, with no reference to the question of the fulfilment—for in that way only can it be determined to be a true *prophecy*, and in that way only would it be of any use to Daniel, or to those who succeeded him. It need hardly be said, that a great variety of opinions have been maintained in regard to the time designated by the "going forth of the commandment." Bertholdt (pp. 567, 568) mentions no less than *thirteen* opinions which have been entertained on this point, and in such a variety of sentiment, it *seems* almost hopeless to be able to ascertain the truth with certainty. Now, in determining this, there are a few points which may be regarded as certain. They are such as these: (*a*) That the commandment referred to is one that is issued by some prince or king having authority, and not the purpose of God. See Notes above on the first part of the verse. (*b*) That the distinct command would be to "restore and build *Jerusalem.*" This is specified, and therefore would seem to be distinguished from a command to build the *temple*, or to restore that from its state of ruin. It is true that the one might appear to be implied in the other, and yet this does not necessarily follow. For various causes it might be permitted to the Jews to rebuild their *temple*, and there might be a royal ordinance commanding that, while there was no purpose to restore the *city* to its former power and splendour, and even while there might be strong objections to it. For the use of the Jews who still resided in Palestine, and for those who were about to return, it might be a matter of policy to permit them to rebuild their temple, and even to aid them in it, while yet it might be regarded as perilous to allow them to rebuild the city, and to place it in its former condition of strength and power. It was a place easily fortified; it had cost the Babylonian monarch much time, and had occasioned him many losses, before he had been able to conquer and subdue it, and, even to Cyrus, it might be a matter of very questionable policy to allow it to be built and fortified again. Accordingly we find that, as a matter of fact, the permission to rebuild the *temple*, and the permission to rebuild the *city*, were quite different things, and were separately granted by different sovereigns, and that the work was executed by different persons. The former might, without impropriety, be regarded as the close of the captivity —or the end of the "seventy years" of Jeremiah—for a permission to rebuild the *temple* was, in fact, a permission to return to their own country, and an implied purpose to aid them in it, while a considerable interval might, and probably would elapse, before a distinct command was issued to restore and rebuild the city itself, and even then a long period might intervene before it would be completed. Accordingly, in the edict published by Cyrus, the permission to rebuild the *temple* is the one that is carefully specified: "Thus saith Cyrus, king of Persia, The Lord God of heaven hath given me all the kingdoms of the earth; and he hath charged me *to build him an house* at Jerusalem, which is in Judah. Who is there among you of all his people? his God be with him, and let him go up to Jerusalem, which is in Judah, and *build the house of the Lord God of Israel* (he is the God), which is in Jerusalem," Ezra i. 2, 3. In this order there is nothing said of the restoration of the *city*, and that in fact occurred at a different time, and under the direction of different leaders. The first

enterprise was to rebuild the *temple;* it was still a question whether it would be a matter of policy to allow the *city* to be rebuilt, and that was in fact accomplished at a different time. These considerations seem to make it certain that the edict referred to here was not that which was issued by *Cyrus*, but must have been a subsequent decree bearing particularly on the rebuilding of the city itself. It is true that the command to rebuild *the temple* would imply that either there were persons residing amidst the ruins of Jerusalem, or in the land of Palestine, who were to worship there, and that there would be inhabitants in Jerusalem, probably those who would go from Babylon— for otherwise the temple would be of no service, but still this might be, and there be no permission to rebuild the city with any degree of its ancient strength and splendour, and none *to surround it with walls*—a very material thing in the structure of an ancient city. (*c*) This interpretation is confirmed by the latter part of the verse: "the street shall be built again, and the wall, even in troublous times." If the word rendered *wall* means *trench* or *ditch*, as I have supposed, still it was a trench or ditch which was designed as a *defence* of a city, or which was excavated for making a wall, for the purpose of fortifying a walled city in order to make it stronger, and the expression is one which would not be applied to the mere purpose of rebuilding the *temple*, nor would it be used except in a command to restore the city itself. We are, then, in the fair interpretation of the passage, required now to show that such a command went forth from the Persian king to "restore and rebuild" *the city itself*— that is, a permission to put it into such a condition of strength as it was before.

In order to see how this interpretation accords with the facts in the case, and to determine whether such a period can be found as shall properly correspond with this interpretation, and enable us to ascertain the point of time here referred to—the *terminus a quo*—it is proper to inquire what are the *facts* which history has preserved.

For this purpose, I' looked at this point of the investigation into Jahn's *Hebrew Commonwealth*, (pp. 160–177), a work not written with any reference to the fulfilment of this prophecy, and which, indeed, in the portion relating to this period of the world, makes no allusion whatever to Daniel. The inquiry which it was necessary to settle was, whether under any of the Persian kings there was any order or command which would properly correspond with what we have ascertained to be the fair meaning of the passage. A very brief synopsis of the principal events recorded by Jahn as bearing on the restoration of the Jews to their own country, will be all that is needful to add to determine the question before us.

The kings of the Persian universal monarchy, according to Ptolemy, were ten, and the whole sum of their reign two hundred and seven years—from the time of Cyaxares II. to the time of Alexander the Great. But Ptolemy's specific object being chronology, he omitted those who continued not on the throne a full year, and referred the months of their reign, partly to the preceding, and partly to the succeeding monarch. The whole number of sovereigns was in reality fourteen, as appears by the following table :—

B.C.		YEARS.	MONTHS.
538.	Cyaxares II. reigned...	2	—
536.	Cyrus.......................	7	—
529.	Cambyses.................	7	5
522.	Smerdis....................	—	7
521.	Darius Hystaspis.......	36	—
485.	Xerxes I...................	21	—
464.	Artaxerxes Longimanus	40	3
424.	Xerxes II.	—	2
424.	Sogdianus.................	—	7
423.	Darius Nothus..........	19	—
404.	Artaxerxes Mnemon...	46	—
358.	Darius Ochus............	21	—
337.	Arses......................	—	2
335.	Darius Codomanus. ...	—	4

Under the reign of this last prince, B.C. 331, the kingdom was entirely subdued by Alexander the Great.

In respect to the question whether any order or command was issued pertaining to the rebuilding of the city of Jerusalem that corresponds with the meaning of the prediction as above explained, the following facts will probably furnish all the knowledge which can be obtained :—

(*a*) *Cyaxares* II. Of course there was nothing in the time of Cyaxares II., the Darius of Daniel (vi. 1; ix. 1), as it was under him that Babylon was conquered, and there was no movement towards a restoration of the Jews to their own land commenced by him, the first movement of that kind being under Cyrus.

(*b*) *Cyrus.* What was the nature of the order issued by *him* we have seen above. It was a command to build the *temple*, and was limited to that, and involved no reference to the city. The command, as we have seen above, did not extend to that, and there were probably good reasons why it was not contemplated that it should be rebuilt in its former strength, and fortified as it was before. The purpose to fortify the city, or to encompass it by a wall or ditch, or even to build it at all, could not have been brought within the order of Cyrus, as recorded in Ezra, and that is the only form of the order which we have. The language of Daniel, therefore, seems to have been chosen of design when he says that the command would be issued to rebuild the *city*, not the *temple*. At any rate, such *is* the language, and such was *not* the order of Cyrus.

(*c*) *Cambyses.* After the death of Cyrus the Samaritans wrote to Cambyses (called, by Ezra, Ahasuerus) against the Jews. We are not informed what effect this letter produced, but we can easily judge from the character of this degenerate son of Cyrus, as it is represented in history. He was a "thoughtless, gluttonous, furious warrior, who was considered as raving mad even by his own subjects."—Jahn. He madly invaded Egypt, and on his return learned that Smerdis, his brother, had usurped the throne in his absence ; and died of a wound received from the falling of his sword from its sheath, as he was mounting his horse. No order is mentioned during his reign pertaining to the rebuilding either of the city or the temple.

(*d*) *Smerdis.* He retained the throne about seven months. In the Bible he has the name of Artaxerxes. Comp., respecting him, Ctesias, x. ; Justin, i. 9 ; Herod. iii. 61–67. "To this monarch the Samaritans again addressed themselves, complaining that the Jews were building (that is, *fortifying*) the city of Jerusalem, which they had never thought of doing; and in consequence of this false accusation, Smerdis issued a positive prohibition of their work."—Jahn. Two things, therefore, may be remarked respecting this reign: —(1) the order or commandment referred to by Daniel could not have been issued during *this* reign, since there was an express "prohibition" against the work of building and fortifying the city; and (2) this confirms what is said above about the improbability that any order would have been issued by Cyrus to rebuild and fortify the city itself. It could not but have been foreseen that such an order would be likely to excite opposition from the Samaritans, and to cause internal dissensions and difficulties in Palestine, and it is not probable that the Persian government would allow the rebuilding of a city that would lead to such collisions.

(e) *Darius Hystaspis.* He reigned thirty-six years. He was a mild and benevolent ruler. "As Smerdis was a mere usurper, his prohibition of rebuilding the temple was of no authority."—Jahn. In the second year of his reign, Haggai and Zechariah appeared, who plied the governor Zerubbabel, the high-priest Joshua, and the whole people, with such powerful appeals to the Divine commands, that the building of the house of God was once more resumed. Upon this, Tatnai, the Persian governor on the west side of the Euphrates, came with his officers to call the Jews to an account, who referred him to the permission of Cyrus, and the Jews were suffered to proceed. The whole matter was, however, made known to Darius, and he caused search to be made among the archives of the state in reference to the alleged decree of Cyrus. The edict of Cyrus was found, which directed that a temple should be built at Jerusalem at the royal expense, and of much larger dimensions than the former. A copy of this was sent to Tatnai, and he was commanded to see that the work should be forwarded, and that the expenses should

be defrayed from the royal treasury, and that the priests should be supplied with whatever was necessary to keep up the daily sacrifice. The work was, therefore, pressed on with renewed vigour, and in the sixth year of his reign the temple was completed and consecrated. The remainder of his reign was spent in unnecessary wars with Scythia, Thrace, India, and Greece. He suffered an overthrow at Marathon, and was preparing for a more energetic campaign in Greece when he died, and left his dominion and his wars to Xerxes. No order was issued during his reign for the rebuilding of the *city* of Jerusalem. All his edicts pertain to the original grant of Cyrus—the permission to build the *temple.*

(f) *Xerxes I.* The career of Xerxes is well known. He was distinguished for gluttony, voluptuousness, and cruelty. He is celebrated for his invasion of Greece, for the check which he met at Thermopylæ, and for the overthrow of his naval forces at Salamis by Themistocles. In the twenty-first year of his reign he was murdered by Artabanus, commander of his life-guard. He died in the year 464 B.C. According to Jahn, it is probable that "the Artaxerxes of Ezra, who is mentioned next after Darius Hystaspis, and the Ahasuerus of Esther, are names of Xerxes I." If so, it was under him that the second caravan of Jews went to Judea, under the direction of Ezra (Ezra vii.) Xerxes, if he was the prince referred to, gave Ezra an ample commission in regard to the temple at Jerusalem, granting him full power to do all that was necessary to maintain public worship there, and committing to him the vessels of gold and silver in Babylon, pertaining to the temple, &c. The decree may be found in Ezra vii. 13–26. This decree, however, relates wholly to the temple—the "house of God." There was no order for rebuilding the city, and there is no evidence that anything material was done *in* building the city, or the walls. Respecting this reign, Jahn remarks, "The Hebrew colony in Judea seems never to have been in a very flourishing condition. The administration of justice was particularly defective, and neither civil nor religious institutions were firmly established. Accordingly, the king gave permission anew for all Hebrews to emigrate to Judea," p. 172. Ezra made the journey with the caravan in three months; deposited the precious gifts in the temple, caused the Scriptures to be read and explained; commenced a moral reformation, but did nothing, so far as appears, in reconstructing the city—for his commission did not extend to that.

(g) *Artaxerxes Longimanus.* According to Jahn, he began to reign B.C. 464, and reigned forty years and three months. It was during his reign that Nehemiah lived, and that he acted as governor of Judea. The colony in Judea, says Jahn, which had been so flourishing in the time of Ezra, had greatly declined, in consequence of the fact that Syria and Phœnicia had been the rendezvous of the armies of Artaxerxes. "Nehemiah, the cup-bearer of Artaxerxes, learned the unhappy state of the Hebrews, B.C. 444, from a certain Jew named Hanani, who had come from Judea to Shushan with a caravan. Of the regulations introduced by Esra 478 B.C. there was little remaining, and, amid the confusions of war, the condition of the Jews continually grew worse. This information so affected Nehemiah that the king observed his melancholy, and inquiring its cause, he appointed him governor of Judea, *with full power to fortify Jerusalem*, and thus to secure it from the disasters to which unprotected places are always exposed in time of war. Orders were sent to the royal officers west of the Euphrates *to assist in the fortification of the city*, and to furnish the requisite timber from the king's forest; probably on Mount Libanus, near the sources of the river Kadisha, as that was the place celebrated for its cedars. Thus commissioned, Nehemiah journeyed to Judea, accompanied by military officers and cavalry," pp. 175, 176. Jahn further adds, "as soon as Nehemiah, on his arrival in Palestine, had been acknowledged governor of Judea by the royal officers, he made known his preparations for fortifying Jerusalem to the

elders who composed the Jewish council. All the heads of houses, and the high-priest Eliashib, engaged zealously in the work. The chiefs of the Samaritans, Sanballat, Tobiah, and Geshem, endeavoured to thwart their undertaking by insults, by malicious insinuations that it was a preparation for revolt, by plots, and by threats of a hostile attack. The Jews, notwithstanding, proceeded earnestly in their business, armed the labourers, protected them still further by a guard of armed citizens, and at length happily completed the walls of their city." We have reached a point, then, in the history of the kings of Persia, when there was a distinct order to restore and fortify Jerusalem, and when there was an express expedition undertaken to accomplish this result. In the history of these kings, as reported by Jahn, this is the *first* order that would seem to correspond with the language of Daniel—"the commandment to restore and rebuild Jerusalem," and the assertion that "the street should be built again, and the wall, even in troublous times." It may be well, therefore, to pause here, and to look more distinctly at this order of Artaxerxes Longimanus, and inquire into its conformity with the language of Daniel. The circumstances, then, as stated in the book of Nehemiah, are these: (a) Nehemiah learned from Hanani the state of his brethren in Judea, and the fact that the "walls of the city were broken down, and that the gates were burned with fire," and that the people who were at Jerusalem were in a state of "great affliction and reproach," and gave himself to weeping, and fasting, and prayer, on that account, Neh. i. (b) On coming into the presence of Artaxerxes, to perform the usual duty of presenting the wine to the king, the king saw the sadness and distress of Nehemiah, and inquired the cause, Neh. ii. 1, 2. This, Nehemiah (ii. 1) is careful to remark occurred in the twentieth year of his reign. (c) He states distinctly, that it was because Jerusalem was still in ruins: "Why should not my countenance be sad, when *the city*, the place of my fathers' sepulchres, *lieth waste*, and the gates thereof are consumed with fire ?" Neh. ii. 3. (d) The *request* of Nehemiah, in accordance with the language in Daniel, was, that he might be permitted to go to Jerusalem and *rebuild the city:* "And I said unto the king, If it please the king, and if thy servant have found favour in thy sight, that thou wouldst send me unto Judah, *unto the city of my fathers' sepulchres, that I may build it,*" Neh. ii. 5. (e) The edict of Artaxerxes contemplated the same thing which is foretold by the angel to Daniel: "And a letter unto Asaph the keeper of the king's forest, that he may give me timber to make beams for the gates of the palace which appertained to the house, and *for the wall of the city,*" &c., Neh. ii. 8. (f) The work which Nehemiah did, under this edict, was that which is supposed in the prediction in Daniel. His first work was to go forth by night to survey *the state of the city:* "And I went out by night by the gate of the valley, &c., and viewed the walls of Jerusalem, which were broken down, and the gates thereof were consumed with fire," Neh. ii. 13. His next work was to propose to rebuild these walls again: "Then said I unto them, Ye see the distress that we are in, how Jerusalem lieth waste, and the gates thereof are burned with fire: come, and let us build up the wall of Jerusalem, that we be no more a reproach," ver. 17. The next work was to rebuild those walls, a full description of which we have in the third chapter of Nehemiah, vers. 1–32, and in ch. iv. 1–23. The city was thus fortified. It was built again according to the purpose of Nehemiah, and according to the decree of Artaxerxes. It took its place again *as* a fortified city, and the promised work of restoring and rebuilding it was complete. (g) The building of the city and the walls under Nehemiah occurred in just such circumstances as are predicted by Daniel. The angel says, "The wall shall be built again, *even in troublous times.*" Let any one read the account of the rebuilding in Nehemiah — the description of the "troubles" which were produced by the opposition of Sanballat and those associated with him (Neh. iv.), and he will see the

striking accuracy of this expression— an accuracy as entire *as if* it had been employed *after* the event in describing it, instead of having been used *before* in predicting it.

It may confirm this interpretation to make three remarks: (1.) *After* this decree of Artaxerxes there was no order issued by Persian kings pertaining to the restoration and rebuilding of the city. Neither Xerxes II., nor Sogdianus, nor Darius Nothus, nor Artaxerxes Mnemon, nor Darius Ochus, nor Arses, nor Darius Codomanus, issued any decree that corresponded at all with this prediction, or any that related to the rebuilding of Jerusalem. There was no occasion for any, for the work was *done.* (2.) A second remark is, that, in the language of Hengstenberg, "Until the twentieth year of Artaxerxes, the new city of Jerusalem was an open, thinly inhabited village, exposed to all aggressions from its neighbours, sustaining the same relation to the former and the latter city as the huts erected after the burning of a city for the first protection from rain and wind do to those which are still uninjured, or which have been rebuilt."—*Christ.* ii. 381. This is quite apparent from the remarks which have been already made respecting the state of the city. The want of any permission to rebuild the city and the walls; the fact that the permission to return extended only to a right to rebuild the temple; the improbabilities above stated, that the rebuilding of the city in its strength would be allowed when they first returned, and the account which Nehemiah gives of the condition of Jerusalem at the time when he asked leave to go and "build" it, all tend to confirm this supposition. See Hengstenberg, as above, pp. 381–386. (3.) A third remark is, that a confirmation of this may be found in the book of Ecclesiasticus, showing how Nehemiah was regarded in respect to the rebuilding of the city: "And among the elect was Neemias, whose renown is great, who raised up for us the walls that were fallen, and set up the gates and the bars, and raised up our ruins again," ch. xlix. 13. On the other hand, Joshua and Zerubbabel are ex-

DANIEL II..   L

tolled only as rebuilders of the *temple:*
"How shall we magnify Zorobabel?
even he was as a signet on the right
hand:" "so was Jesus the son of Jose-
dec: who in their time builded *the
house* and set up *a holy temple* to the
Lord," vers. 11, 12. These considerations make the case•clear, it seems
to me, that the time referred to—the
terminus a quo—according to the fair
interpretation, was the twentieth year
of Artaxerxes. To this we are conducted by the proper and necessary
exposition of the *language*, and by the
orders actually issued from the Persian court in regard to the temple and
city.

If it should be objected—the only
objection of importance that has been
alleged against it—that this would not
meet the inquiry of Daniel; that he
was seeking for the time when the
captivity would cease, and looking for
its termination as predicted by Jeremiah; that it would not console him
to be referred to a period so remote as
is here supposed—the time of the rebuilding of the city; and, still more,
that, not knowing that time, the prophecy would afford *him* no basis of calculation as to the appearing of the
Messiah, it may be replied: (*a*) That
the prediction contained all the consolation and assurance which Daniel
sought—the assurance that the city
would be rebuilt, and that an order *would
go forth* for its restoration. (*b*) That
the angel does not *profess* to answer
the precise point of the inquiry which
Daniel had suggested. The prayer of
Daniel was the *occasion* of uttering a
higher prophecy than the one which
he had been contemplating. (*c*) It is
not necessary to suppose that the design was that *Daniel* should be able to
compute the exact time when the
Messiah would appear. It was sufficient for him if he had the assurance
that he *would* appear, and if he were
furnished with a basis by which it
might be calculated when he would
appear, after the order to rebuild the
city had gone forth. (*d*) At any rate,
the prophecy must have appeared to
Daniel to have a much more important
meaning than would be implied merely
by a direct answer to his prayer—per-

taining to the close of the exile. The
prophecy indubitably stretched far into
future years. Daniel must have seen
at once that it contained an important
disclosure respecting future events,
and, as it implied that the exile *would*
close, and that the city would be rebuilt, and as he had already a sufficient intimation *when* the exile would
close, from the prophecies of Jeremiah,
we may suppose that the mind of
Daniel would rest on this as more than
he had desired to know—a revelation
far beyond what he anticipated when
he set apart this day for special prayer.

The only remaining difficulty as to
the time referred to as the beginning
of the seventy weeks—the *terminus a
quo*—is that of determining the exact
chronology of the twentieth year of
Artaxerxes—the point from which we
are to reckon. The time, however,
varies only a few years according to
the different estimates of chronology,
and not so as materially to affect the
result. The following are the principal
estimates:—

Jahn	444 B.C.
Hengstenberg	454 „
Hales	414 „
Calmet	449 „
Usher	454 „

It will be seen from this, that the difference in the chronology is, at the
greatest, but ten years, and in such a
matter, where the ancient records are
so indefinite, and so little pains were
taken to make exact dates, it cannot
perhaps be expected that the time could
be determined with exact accuracy.
Nor, since the numbers used by the
angel are in a sense *round* numbers—
"seventy weeks," "sixty-two weeks,"
"one week," is it necessary to suppose that the time could be made out
with the exactness of a year, or a
month—though this has been often
attempted. It is sufficient if the prediction were *so* accurate and determi-
nate that there could be no doubt, in
general, as to the time of the appearing of the Messiah, and so that when
he appeared it should be manifest that
he was referred to. Hengstenberg,
however, supposes that the chronology can be made out with literal accuracy. See *Christ.* ii. 394–408.

Taking the dates above given as the *terminus a quo* of the prophecy—the time from which to reckon the beginning of the sixty-nine weeks to the "Messiah the Prince"—or the four hundred and eighty-three years, we obtain, respectively, the following results:—

The period of 414 B.C., the period of Jahn and Hales, would extend to A.D. 39.

That of 454 B.C., the period of Hengstenberg and Usher, to A.D. 29.

That of 449 B.C., the period of Calmet, to A.D. 34.

It is remarkable how all these periods terminate at *about* the time when the Lord Jesus entered on his work, or assumed, at his baptism, the public office of the Messiah—when he was thirty years of age. It is undeniable that, whichever reckoning be correct, or whatever computation we may suppose to have been employed by the Jews, the expectation would have been excited in the public mind that the Messiah was about to appear at that time. Perhaps the real truth may be seen in a stronger light still by supposing that if a sagacious impostor had resolved to take upon himself the office of the Messiah, and had so shaped his plans as to meet the national expectations growing out of this prediction of Daniel, he would have undoubtedly set up his claims at *about* the time when the Lord Jesus publicly appeared as the Messiah. According to the common chronologies, there would not have been a variance of more than nine years in the calculation, and, perhaps, after all, when we consider how little the chronology of ancient times has been regarded or settled, it is much more to be wondered at that there should be so great accuracy than that the time is not more certainly determined. If, notwithstanding the confusion of ancient dates, the time is so *nearly* determined with accuracy, is it not rather to be presumed that if the facts of ancient history could be ascertained, the exact period would be found to have been predicted by the angel?

III. The next point properly is, what is the time referred to by the phrase "*unto* the Messiah the Prince" —the *terminus ad quem*. Here there can be but two opinions—that which refers it to his birth, and that which refers it to his public manifestation as the Messiah, or his taking the office upon himself. The remarks under the last head have conducted us to the probability that the latter is intended. Indeed, it is morally certain that this is so, if we have ascertained the *terminus a quo* with accuracy. The only question then is, whether this is the fair construction, or whether the language can properly be so applied. We have seen, in the interpretation of the phrase above, that the grammatical construction of the *language* is such as might, without impropriety, be applied to either event. It remains only to look at the probabilities that the latter was the design. It may be admitted, perhaps, that *before* the event occurred, there might have been some uncertainty on the subject, and that with many, on reading the prophecy, the supposition would be that it referred to the birth of the Messiah. But a careful consideration of all the circumstances of the passage might even then have led to different expectation, and might have shown that the probabilities were that it was the public manifestation of the Messiah that was intended. Those may be regarded as stronger now, and may be such as to leave no reasonable doubt on the mind; that is, we may now see what would not be likely to have been seen then— as in the case of all the prophecies. Among these considerations are the following :—(*a*) Such an interpretation may be, after all, the most probable. If we conceive of one who should have predicted the appearance or coming of Jenghis Khan, or Alaric, or Attila, as conquerors, it would not be unnatural to refer this to their public appearing in that character, as to the time when they became known as such, and still more true would this be of one who should be inaugurated or set apart to a public office. If, for example, there had been a prophecy of Gregory the Great, or Leo X., as *Popes*, it would be most natural, unless there was a distinct reference to their birth, to refer this to their election and consecration *as* Popes, for that would in fact be the period when they appeared as such. (*b*) In the case of this prophecy, there is no allusion to *the birth* of the Messiah. It is not "to his birth," or "to his incarnation," but "unto the Messiah the Prince;" that is, most manifestly, when he appeared *as* such, and was in fact such. In many instances in the prophecies there are allusions to *the birth* of the Messiah; and so numerous and accurate had they become, that there was a general expectation of the event at about the time when he was actually born. But, in the passage before us, the language is that which would be used on the supposition that the designed reference was to his entering as Messiah on the functions of his office, and *not* such as would have been so naturally employed if the reference had been to his birth. (*c*) His taking upon himself the office of the Messiah by baptism and by the descent of the Holy Spirit on him was, in fact, the most prominent event in his work. Before that, he had passed his life in obscurity. The work which he did *as* Messiah was commenced at that time, and was to be dated from that period. In fact, he was not the Messiah, as such, till he was set apart to the office —any more than an heir to a crown is king until he is crowned, or an elected chief-magistrate is president before he has taken the oath of office. The position which he occupied was, that he was designated or destined for the office of the Messiah, but had not, in fact, entered on it, and could not as yet be spoken of as such. (*d*) This is the usual method of recording the reign of a king—not from his birth, but from his coronation. Thus, in the table above, respecting the Persian kings, the periods included are those from the beginning of the reign, not from the birth to the decease. So in all statutes and laws, as when we say the first of George III., or the second of Victoria, &c. (*e*) To these considerations may be added an argument stated by Hengstenberg, which seems to make the proof irrefragable. It is in the following words:—"After the course of seventy weeks shall the whole work of salvation, to be performed by the Mes-

siah, be completed; after sixty-nine weeks, and, as it appears from the more accurate determination in ver. 27, in the middle of the seventieth, he shall be cut off. As now, according to the passage before us, sixty-nine weeks shall elapse before the Messiah, there remains from that event to the completion of salvation only a period of seven, until his violent death, of three and a half years; a certain proof that 'unto the Messiah' must refer, not to his birth, but to the appearance of the Messiah as such."—*Christ*. ii. 337.

IV. The next question then is, whether, according to this estimate, the time can be made out with any degree of accuracy. The date of the decrees of Artaxerxes are found to be, according to the common reckoning of chronologists, either 444, or 454, or 449 B.C. The addition of 483 years to them we found also to reach, respectively, to A.D. 39, to A.D. 29, and to A.D. 34. One of these (29) varies scarcely at all from the time when the Saviour was baptized, at thirty years of age; another (34) varies scarcely at all from the time when he was put to death; and either of them is so accurate that the mind of any one who should have made the estimate when the command to build the city went forth, would have been directed with great precision to the expectation of the true time of his appearance; and to those who lived when he *did* appear, the time was so accurate that, in the reckoning of any of the prevailing methods of chronology, it would have been sufficiently clear to lead them to the expectation that he was about to come. Two or three remarks, however, may be made in regard to this point. (*a*) One is, that it is now, perhaps, impossible to determine with *precise* accuracy the historical period of events so remote. Time was not then measured as accurately as it is now; current events were not as distinctly recorded; chronological tables were not kept as they are now; there was no uniform method of determining the length of the year, and the records were much less safely kept. This is manifest, because, even in so important an event as the issuing of the command to rebuild the city in the time of Artaxerxes—an event which it would be supposed was one of sufficient moment to have merited an exact record, at least among the Jews. There is now, among the best chronologists, a difference of ten years as to the computation of the time. (*b*) There is a variation arising from the difference of the lunar or the solar year—some nations reckoning by the one, and some by the other—and the difference between them, in the period now under consideration, would be greater than that which now occurs in the ordinary reckonings of chronology. (*c*) Till the exact length of the *year*, as then understood, is ascertained, there can be no hope of fixing the time with the exactness of a month or a day ; and if the usual and general understanding of the length of the year be adopted, then the time here referred to would be so intelligible that there would be no difficulty in ascertaining at about what time the Messiah was to appear, or when he did appear in determining that it was he. This was all that was really necessary in regard to the prophecy. (*d*) Yet it has been supposed that the time can be made out, even under these disadvantages, with almost entire accuracy. The examination in the case may be seen at length in Hengstenberg, *Chris.* ii. 394–408. It is agreed on all hands that the commencement of the reign of Xerxes occurred in the year 485 before Christ, and that Artaxerxes died in 423. The difference concerns only the beginning of the reign of Artaxerxes. If that occurred in the year 464 B.C., then the problem is solved, for then the decree of the twentieth year of Artaxerxes would occur 444 B.C. ; and if 483 be added to that, the result is A.D. 29—a difference, then, even in reckoning whole years and round numbers, of only one year between that and the time when Jesus was baptized by John. The full proof of this point, about the beginning of the reign of Artaxerxes, may be seen in Hengstenberg, as above. The argument, though long, is so important, and so clear, that it may without impropriety be inserted in this place :—

" According to the prophecy, the *terminus a quo*, the twentieth year of Artaxerxes, is separated from the *terminus ad quem*, the public appearance of Christ, by a period of sixty-nine weeks of years, or four hundred and eighty-three years. If, now, we compare history with this, it must appear, even to the most prejudiced, in the highest degree remarkable, that, among all the current chronological determinations of this period, not one differs over ten years from the testimony of the prophecy. This wonder must rise to the highest pitch, when it appears from an accurate examination of these determinations, that the only one among them which is correct makes the prophecy and history correspond with each other even to a year.

"Happily, to attain this end, we are not compelled to involve ourselves in a labyrinth of chronological inquiries. We find ourselves, in the main, on sure ground. All chronologists agree, that the commencement of the reign of Xerxes falls in the year 485 before Christ, the death of Artaxerxes, in the year 423. The difference concerns only the year of the commencement of the reign of Artaxerxes. Our problem is completely solved, when we have shown that this falls in the year 474 before Christ. For then the twentieth year of Artaxerxes is the year 455 before Christ, according to the usual reckoning.*　　　 = 299 U.C.
Add to this, 483 years.

782 U.C.
"We should probably have been saved the trouble of this investigation, had not the error of an acute man, and the want of independence in his successors, darkened what was in itself clear. According to Thucydides, Artaxerxes began to reign shortly before the flight of Themistocles to Asia. Deceived by certain specious arguments, hereafter to be examined, Dodwell, in the *Annall. Thucyd.*, placed both

* The intelligent reader will perceive that the author has intentionally made his investigation entirely independent of the difficult inquiries respecting the year of the birth of Christ, which, in his judgment, have in recent times, by the introduction of uncertain astronomical combinations, particularly by Munter and Ideler, been led far astray.

events in the year 465 before Christ. The thorough refutation of Vitringa, in the cited treatise, remained, strange as it may appear, unknown to the philologians and historians, even as it seems to those of Holland, as Wesseling. The view of Dodwell, adopted also by Corsini in the *Fasta Attica*, became the prevailing one, at which we cannot wonder, when we consider how seldom, in modern times, chronological investigations in general have been fundamental and independent; when *e.g.*, we observe that Poppo, a generally esteemed recent editor of Thucydides, in a thick volume, entitled, *In Thucydidem Commentarii politici, geograph., chronologici*, furnishes, in reference to the last, nothing more than a reprint of the school edition of the chronological tables collected from Dodwell, excusing himself with an *odio quodam, inveterato totius hujus disciplinæ!* Clinton also (*Fasti Hellenici, lat. vert. Krüger*, Leipz., 1830), though he clearly perceives that Dodwell has confused the whole chronology of this period (comp., *e.g.*, p. 248–253), has not been able to free himself from him in the most important points, though he successfully opposed him in several; and thus the confusion only becomes still greater, since now neither the actual chronological succession of events, nor the one ingeniously invented by Dodwell, any longer remains. Nevertheless, the truth is advanced by this increased confusion. For now the harmony introduced by Dodwell into the fictitious history is destroyed. The honour, however, of having again discovered the true path, belongs to Krüger alone, who, after more than a hundred years, as an entirely independent inquirer, coincides with Vitringa, in the same result, and in part in the employment of the same arguments. In the acute treatise, *Ueber den Cimonischen Frieden* (in the *Archiv f. Philologie und Pädagog. von Seebode*, I. 2, p. 205, ff.) he places the death of Xerxes in the year 474 or 473, and the flight of Themistocles a year later. This treatise may serve to shame those who reject in the mass the grounds of our opinion (to the establishment of which we now proceed), with the re-

mark, that the author has only found what he sought. Whoever does not feel capable of entering independently upon the investigation, should at least be prevented from condemning, by the circumstance, that a learned man, who has no other design in view than to elucidate a chronologically confused period of Grecian history, gives, for the event which serves to determine the *terminus a quo* of our prophecy, the precise year, which places prophecy and fulfilment in the most exact harmony.

"We examine first the grounds which seem to favour the opinion, that the reign of Artaxerxes commenced in the year 465. (1.) 'The flight of Themistocles must precede the transfer of the dominion of Greece from Athens to Sparta by several years. For this happened during the siege of Byzantium, when the treasonable efforts of Pausanias first commenced; the flight of Themistocles, however, was a consequence of the complaint, which was raised against him, out of the documents found after the death of Pausanias. But Isocrates says, in the *Panathenaikos*, that the dominion of the Lacedemonians had endured ten years. The expedition of Xerxes, taken as the *terminus a quo*, this transfer falls in the year 470.' But we may spare ourselves the labour which Vitringa takes to invalidate this alleged testimony of Isocrates, since all recent scholars, in part independent of one another, agree that Isocrates speaks of a ten years' dominion, not before, but after that of the Athenians; compare Coray on *Pan.* c. 19; Dahlmann, *Forschungen*, I. p. 45; Krüger, p. 221; Clinton, p. 250, ff. (2.) That Themistocles in the year 472 was still in Athens, Corsini infers (*Fasti Att.* III. p. 180) from *Æl.* lib. 9, c. 5. According to this, Themistocles sent back Hiero, who was coming to the Olympic games, asserting that, whoever had not taken part in the greatest danger, could not be a sharer of the joy. (The fact is also related by Plutarch.) Now as Hiero, Ol. 75, 3 (478), began to reign, only the Ol. 77 (472) could be intended. But who does not at once perceive that the reference to the games of the Ol. 76 (476) was far more obvious, since the occurrence pre-supposed that the μέγιστος τῶν κ.νδύνων was still fresh in remembrance? (3.) According to this supposition, Xerxes would reign only eleven years; Artaxerxes, on the contrary, fifty-one. This is in opposition to the testimony of the *Can. Ptolem.* (comp. thereon Ideler, I. p. 109, ff.), which gives to Xerxes twenty-one, and to Artaxerxes forty-one years, and of Ctesias, who gives to Artaxerxes forty-two years, and of some other writers; comp. the passages in Bähr on Ctesias, p. 184. *Ceteris paribus,* this argument would be wholly decisive. But when other weighty authorities are opposed to it, it is not of itself sufficient to outweigh them. The canon has high authority, only where it rests on astronomical observations, which is here not the case. Otherwise it stands on the same ground as all other historical sources. The whole error was committed, as soon as only an *ιά* in an ancient authority was confounded with a *κά*; for when a reign of twenty-one years had thus been attributed to Xerxes, the shortening of the reign of Artaxerxes to forty-one years necessarily followed. Wesseling (on Diod. 12, 64) attributes forty-five years to Artaxerxes, thus without hesitation rejecting the authority of the canon. To these arguments, already adduced by others, we subjoin the following. (4.) It seems to be evident from Ctesias, ch. 20, that Artaxerxes was born a considerable time after the commencement of the reign of Xerxes. Ctesias, after relating it, proceeds— γαμεῖ δὲ Ξέρξης Ὀνόφα ἐυγατέρα "Αμιστριν καὶ γίνεται αὐτῷ παῖς Δαρειαῖος, καὶ ἕτερος μετὰ δύο ἔτη Ὑστασπης, καὶ ἔτι Ἀρταξέρξης. If he relates the events in their true chronological order, Artaxerxes in the year 474 could at most have been seven years old. On the contrary, however, all accounts agree, that at the death of Xerxes, although still young (comp. Justin, 3, 1), he was yet of a sufficient age to be capable of reigning himself. We must not be satisfied with the answer that it is very improbable that Xerxes, who was born at the beginning of the thirty-sixth year of the reign of Darius (comp. Herod. 7, 2), and was already thirty-four or thirty-five years old at his death, was

not married until so late a period. Ctesias himself frees us from the embarrassment into which we were thrown by his inaccuracy. According to chap. 22, Megabyzus was already married, before the expedition against Greece, with a daughter of Xerxes, who, already mentioned (ch. 20), if Ctesias is there chronologically accurate, could not have been born before that time. According to ch. 28, Megabyzus, immediately after the return of Xerxes from Greece, complained to him of the shameful conduct of this wife of his. (5.) There can be no doubt that the Ahasuerus of the book of Esther is the same as Xerxes. But the twelfth year of this king is there expressly mentioned, ch. iii. 7, and the events related in the following context fall, in part, about the end of the same year. But this difficulty vanishes, as soon as we include the years of the co-regency of Xerxes with Darius. According to the full account in Herodot. 7, ch. 2–4, Xerxes, two years before the death of Darius, was established by him as king: comp. e.g. ch. 4— ἀπέδεξε δὲ βασιλῆα Πέρσησι Δαρεῖος Ξέρξεα. Of the custom of the Hebrew writers to include the years of a co-regency, where it existed, we have a remarkable example in the account concerning Nebuchadnezzar (comp. Bietr. I. p. 63). But we find even in the book of Esther itself plain indications of this mode of reckoning. The account of the great feast (ch. i.) is placed in its true light by this supposition. The occasion of it was the *actual* commencement of the reign of Xerxes, though we need not on this account exclude, what has hitherto been regarded as the exclusive object, consultations with the nobles respecting the expeditions about to be undertaken. What is related (ch. ii. 16) then falls precisely in the time of the return of Xerxes from Greece, while otherwise, and this is attended with difficulty, about two years after that event.

"We now proceed to lay down the positive grounds for our view; and in the first place, the immediate, and then the mediate proofs, which latter are far more numerous and strong, since they show that the flight of Themistocles, which must precede the reign of Artaxerxes, cannot possibly be placed later than 473 before Christ.

"To the first class belong the following :—1. It must appear very strange to those who assume a twenty-one years' reign of Xerxes, that the whole period from the eleventh year is a complete *tabula rasa*. The Biblical accounts stop short at the close of the tenth year. Ctesias relates only one inconsiderable event after the Grecian war (ch. 28), which occurred immediately after its termination. No later writer has ventured to introduce anything into the ten years, which, according to our view, the permutation of an *c* and *z* adds to his age.

"2. We possess a twofold testimony, which places the return of Xerxes from Greece, and his death, in so close connection, that, without rejecting it, we cannot possibly assume a fifteen years' reign after this return, but are rather compelled to place his death not beyond the year 474. The first is that of Ælian, *Var. Hist.* 13, 3 : εἶτα ἐπανελθὼν, αἰσχιστα ἀνθρώπων ἀπέθανεν, ἀποσφαγεὶς νύκτωρ ἐν τῇ εὐνῇ ὑπὸ τοῦ υἱοῦ. The second, that of Justin, 3, 1 : '*Xerxes rex Persarum, terror antea gentium, bello in Grœciam infeliciter gesto, etiam suis contemtui esse cœpit. Quippe Artabanus prœfectus ejus, deficiente quotidie regis majestate, in spem regni adductus, cum septem robustissimis filiis,'* &c.

"3. The testimonies of Justin, 1. c., respecting the age of his sons at his death, are not reconcilable with the twenty-one years' reign of Xerxes : '*Securior de Artaxerxe, puero admodum, fingit regem a Dario, qui erat adolescens, quo maturius regno potiretur, occisum.*' If Xerxes reigned twenty-one years, his firstborn, Darius, according to a comparison of Ctesias (ch. 22), could not at his death have been an *adolescens*, but at least thirty-one years old. On the contrary, if eleven years' reign be assumed, these determinations are entirely suitable. Darius was then towards twenty-one years old ; Artaxerxes, according to Ctesias (ch. 20), near four years younger than Darius, about seventeen. This determination shows also that it cannot be objected against a fifty-one

years' reign of Artaxerxes that it would give him too great an age. The suggestion can be refuted by the simple remark, that the length of his life remains exactly the same, whether he reigned fifty-one or forty-one years. If he ascended the throne at seventeen, his life terminated at sixty-eight.

"4. According to the most numerous and weighty testimonies, the peace of Cimon was probably concluded after the battle of the Eurymedon (before Christ 470). Now, as all agree that this peace was concluded with Artaxerxes, the commencement of his reign must, in any event, be placed before 470. Comp. Krüger, l. c., p. 218.

"5. The history of Nehemiah is scarcely reconcilable with the supposition that Artaxerxes reigned only forty-seven years. After Nehemiah had accomplished all that is related in ch. i.–xii. of his book, he returned to Persia to discharge the duties of his office, at court. This happened, according to xiii. 6, in the thirty-second year of Artaxerxes. The time of his return is not accurately determined. It says merely, after a considerable time, the לְקֵץ יָמִים. That his absence, however, must have continued a whole series of years, appears from the relation of that which took place in the mean time. The law against marriage with foreign women, to the observance of which the people had bound themselves anew, ch. x. 30, was first violated during his absence ; then again, by a decree of the people, executed in all severity, xiii. 1–3 ; and then again broken, as appears from the fact that Nehemiah, at his return, according to ver. 23, found a great many foreign women in the colony. That these marriages had already existed for some time appears from ver. 24, where it is said that the children of them had spoken half in the language of Ashdod, and could not speak Hebrew. A long absence is also implied in the other abuses which Nehemiah, according to ch. xiii. 10, *seq.*, found on his return. He saw the fruits of the former labours almost destroyed. The same is also evident from the prophecies of Malachi, which were delivered exactly in the time between the two periods of Nehemiah's presence at Jerusalem: comp. Vitringa's excellent *Dissert. de Ætate Mal.*, in his *Obss. ss.* vi. 7, t. 2, p. 353, *seq.* The condition of the people appears here, as it could have been only after they had already been deprived, for a considerable time, of their two faithful leaders, Ezra, who, having arrived thirteen years earlier, had co-operated for a considerable time with Nehemiah, and Nehemiah himself. But, if we consider barely the first-mentioned fact, the marriages with foreign women, it will be evident that a longer period than nine years would be required. For each change there will then only three years be allowed; and as this is undeniably too little for the third, according to ver. 24, the two first must be still more shortened, which is inadmissible. Besides, we do not even have nine years for these events, if the reign of Artaxerxes is fixed at forty-one years. For the relation of Nehemiah pre-supposes that Artaxerxes was yet living at the time of its composition. This, however, cannot be placed in the time immediately after the return of Nehemiah, since it must have been preceded by the abolition of all these abuses. If, however, we are conducted by the authority of Nehemiah, which is liable to no exception, since he was contemporary and closely connected with Artaxerxes, a few years over forty-one, we have gained much. For then the only objection to our determination, the testimony of the canon, is completely set aside.

"We must premise a remark, before we bring forward our indirect proofs, in order to justify the connection in which we place the commencement of the reign of Artaxerxes with the flight of Themistocles. This connection has not, indeed, the unanimous testimony of the ancient writers in its favour. The vouchers for it are, Thucydides (ch. 137), where it is said of Themistocles, who had come into Asia, ἐπέμπει γράμματα ἐς βασιλέα Ἀρταξέρξην τὸν Ξέρξου, νεωστὶ βασιλεύοντα, and Charon of Lampsacus, who, according to Plutarch (*Them.* ch. 27), makes him in like manner fly to Artaxerxes. On the contrary, others, as Ephorus, Di-

non, Klitarch, and Heraclides (comp. Plut. l. c.), represent him as going to Xerxes. If, now, we examine these testimonies, according to the authorities of the witnesses the decision will unquestionably be in favour of that of Thucydides and Charon. Thucydides was contemporary with Artaxerxes, and was born about the time of the flight of Themistocles. This prince of Greek historians gives (ch. 97) as the cause why he relates the events between the Median and Peloponnesian war, that all his predecessors had passed over these events in silence, and that the only one who touched upon them, Hellanicus, βραχέως τε καὶ τοῖς χρόνοις οὐκ ἀκριβῶς ἐπεμνήσθη them, from which it is evident, first, how little certain are the accounts of this period in later authors, because they can have no credible contemporary voucher, since he could not have been unknown to Thucydides; and, secondly, that Thucydides himself claims to be regarded as a careful and accurate historian of this period, and therefore must be esteemed such, because so honest a man would assume nothing to himself which did not belong to him. The other witness, Charon, was the less liable to err, since, at the very time of this event, he was a writer of history, and even lived in Asia. On the other hand, the oldest witnesses for the opposite supposition lived more than a century after the event. Ephorus (see on his *Akrisic*, Dahlmann) outlived the dominion of Alexander in Asia; Dinon was father of Klitarch, who accompanied Alexander.

"In weighing these grounds, the authority of Thucydides and Charon was unhesitatingly followed in ancient times. Plutarch (l. c.) does this, with the remark, that the testimony of Thucydides agrees better with the chronological works. Nepos says: '*Scio plerosque ita scripsisse, Themistoclem Xerxe regnante in Asiam transiisse: sed ego potissimum Thucydidi credo, quod ætate proximus de his, qui illorum temporum historias reliquerunt et ejusdem civitatis fuit.*' Suidas, and the Scholiast on *Aristoph. Equites*, from which the former borrowed *verbatim* his second article on Themistocles, makes him flee, πρὸς τὸν ᾿Αρταξέρξην, τὸν Ξέρξου τοῦ Πέρσου παῖδα, without even mentioning the other supposition. And in this respect, we have the less fear of contradiction, since, as far as we know, all modern critics, without exception, follow Thucydides and Charon. We only still remark that the opposite view can the more easily be rejected, since its origin can so readily be explained, either from the fact that this event fell on the border of the reign of Xerxes and of Artaxerxes, or from a simple confounding of the two names, the assumption of which is more easy the more frequently it occurs; we find it even in Aristotle, the contemporary of those writers, *Pol.* 5, 8, and twice in Ctesias, ch. 35, where Bähr would make a change in opposition to all the manuscripts, and chap. 44. Comp. Bähr on the passage, and Reimarus on *Dio Cass.* II. p. 1370. Finally, the error might arise also from the circumstance that the flight of Themistocles was placed in the right year; but twenty-one years were attributed to Xerxes, from which it necessarily follows that he took refuge with Xerxes. This last opinion is favoured by the coincidence of several contemporary writers in the same error, which presupposes some plausible reason for it.

"We now proceed to lay down our indirect proofs. (1.) We begin with the testimony which gives precisely the year of the flight of Themistocles, that of Cicero, *Lœl.* ch. 12. It is true, Corsini, l. c. 3, p. 180, asserts, that Cicero speaks of the year in which Themistocles was banished from Athens; but we need only examine the passage to be convinced of the contrary: '*Themistocles—fecit idem, quod viginti annis ante apud nos fecerat Coriolanus.*' The flight of Coriolanus to the Volci falls in the year 263 U.C., B.C. 492. The flight of Themistocles is accordingly placed by Cicero in the year 472, a year later than by us, which is of no importance, since the round number twenty was the more suitable to the object of Cicero, as the more accurate nineteen, for the chronologists. If Dodwell's view were correct, there would be the space of twenty-seven years between the two events.

"2. Diodorus Siculus, who (11, 55) places the flight of Themistocles in Ol. 77, 2 (B.C. 471), in any event favours our determination, which ascends only two years higher, far more than the opposite one. We remark, however, that he also places in the same year the residence of Themistocles at Magnesia, and his death; and thus it is evident that, whether by mistake or design, he compresses the events in the life of Themistocles, which filled up some years, into the year of his death. If this took place in the year 471, the flight must be dated at least as far back as 473. Our determination differs only a single year from that of Eusebius, who relates the flight of Themistocles in Ol. 77, 1.

"3. But that which forms the chief argument, the whole series of transactions, as they have been recorded in accurate order, especially by Thucydides, compels us without reserve to place the flight of Themistocles not below the year 473. That the expedition of the allied Greeks under the direction of Pausanias, against Cyprus and Byzantium, the capture of the latter city, and the transfer of the supremacy from the Lacedemonians to the Athenians, occasioned by the insolence of Pausanias, fall in the year 477, we may regard as established beyond dispute by Clinton, p. 270, *seq.** The view of O. Müller (*Dorier,* ii. p. 498), who distributes these events into a period of five years, is contradicted by the expression ἐν τῇδε τῇ ἡγεμονίᾳ of Thucydides, ch. 94, whereby the capture of Byzantium is brought into the same year with the expedition against Cyprus. That these words cannot be connected with what follows, without a change of the text in opposition to all critical authority, is shown by Poppo. Moreover, the very last of these events is placed, by the unanimous testimony of antiquity, in the year 477.

* The grounds are thus briefly summed up by Win., p. 252: "Dodwelli rationi neutiquam favet Isocratis auctoritas. Repugnat rerum gestarum series, repugnat quod Thucyd. significat, Plutarchus et Aristides diserte tradunt, repugnat demique temporis spatium, quod Atheniensium imperio assignant Lysias, Isocrates ipse, Plato, Demosthenes, Aristides, quibus fortasse addendus est Lycurgus."

Clinton shows, p. 249, that all reckonings of the time of the supremacy of the Athenians, setting out from this year, differ from one another only in reference to the assumed termination. Also, Thucyd. ch. 128, the expedition against Cyprus, and that against Byzantium, are connected as immediately succeeding each other. If, however, Dodwell were compelled by the force of the arguments to acknowledge that these events, which he compresses into one year, do not, as he assumes (p. 61), belong to the year 470, but to the year 477, he would surely be compelled, perceiving it to be impossible to lengthen out the thread of the events until the year 465, to give up the whole hypothesis. The dissatisfaction of the allies was followed by the recal of Pausanias. That this belongs still to the same year plainly appears, partly from the nature of the case itself, since it pre-supposes a continuance of supremacy, partly from Thucydides, ch. 95: ἐν τούτῳ δὲ οἱ Λακεδαιμόνιοι μετιπέμποντο Παυσανίαν ἀνακρινοῦντες ὧν περὶ ἐπυνθάνοντο. Pausanias having come to Sparta, and been there set at liberty, now betook himself privately in a galley to Byzantium. This cannot have happened long afterwards, for Thucydides, ch. 128, immediately subjoins it, and what is of the most importance, Pausanias finds the fleet still at Byzantium. That his residence there did not long continue appears from the account of Thucydides, ch. 131, that he was forcibly expelled thence by the Athenians. He now retired to the colony in Troas; from there he was recalled to Sparta, after it had been reported that he kept up an understanding with the barbarians. The Ephori threw him into prison, but soon after released him. At this time his intercourse with Themistocles took place, who, being at the time already expelled from Athens, resided at Argos, and thence made excursions into the rest of the Peloponnesus. That Pausanias then for the first time drew Themistocles into his plan, when the latter had been driven from Athens, is asserted by Plutarch, and a personal intercourse between them is rendered certain by all accounts. That there was no considerable period

between this release of Pausanias and his death is clear. Pausanias was not condemned, because there was no certain proof against him. It is, however, psychologically improbable that he did not soon afford it, that he prudently kept himself from giving open offence for a series of years, when we consider that he was deprived of all prudence by his haughtiness, arising to madness; that he himself rendered the execution of his treasonable plan impossible; that, according to Thucydides, ch. 130, he went about in a Median dress, and caused himself to be accompanied on a journey through Thrace with Median and Egyptian satellites, spread a Persian table, made difficult the access to his person, gave free course to his passions, of whom Thucydides himself very significantly remarks, καὶ κατίχειν τὴν διάνοιαν οὐκ ἠδύνατο ἀλλ᾽ ἔργοις βραχίσι προυδήλου, ἃ τῇ γνώμῃ μειζόνως ἐρέπειτα ἔμελλε πράξειν, and of whose senseless arrogance the same historian, ch. 132, gives an example, even out of the time immediately after the battle of Platea. The discovery was effected by him who was to bring to Artabazus the last letters to the king. With what haste the transactions were carried on, and that by no means a space of four years was consumed, is evident from the fact that the king, in order to accelerate them, had expressly sent Artabazus to Asia Minor. His death immediately followed the discovery (comp. Thucyd. 133). We surely do not assume too little when we give to these events a period of three years. That we need not go beyond this is shown by Diodorus, who compresses all these events into the year 477 (Ol. 75, 4). How could he have done this, or how could such an error have arisen, if the beginning and end had been separated from each other by a period of eight or nine years? How impossible it was for him, with his sources, to place the destruction of Pausanias far beyond this time appears from his fiction, which can in no other way be explained, of a twofold accusation of Themistocles. If, now, we must place the death of Pausanias about the year 474, and in no event later, the flight of Themistocles cannot be placed farther back than the year 473. For Themistocles, at the death of Pausanias, had already been a considerable time in the Peloponnesus. His accusation followed immediately after the event (comp. Thucydides, I. 135); and the combined interests of the Lacedemonians, to whom nothing could be more desirable than to have the Athenians share their disgrace, and of the enemies of Themistocles at Athens (Plut. *Them.* c. 23: κατεβόων μὲν αὐτοῦ Λακεδαιμόνιοι, κατηγόρουν δ' οἱ φθονοῦντες τῶν πολιτῶν), would cause the decision to be hastened as much as possible. Themistocles, persecuted both by the Athenians and Lacedemonians, now flees from the Peloponnesus to Corcyra. Being denied a residence there, he retires to the opposite continent. In danger of being overtaken by his persecutors (Thucyd. ch. 136: καὶ διωκόμενος ὑπὸ τῶν προστεταγμένων κατὰ πύστιν ᾗ χωροίη), he sees himself compelled to flee to Admetus, the king of the Molossians. Nor can he have long resided there, for, according to Thucydides, ch. 137, he was sent forward by Admetus, as soon as his persecutors came. And how can we suppose that they would have been long behind him? How long could his place of residence have remained a secret? It is expressly said by Thucydides, that the coming of his persecutors, and the flight of Themistocles to Asia, very soon happened (ὕστερον οὐ πολλῷ). It is true, that if we could credit the account of Stesimbrotus, in Plut. ch. 24, we must assume that the residence of Themistocles with Admetus continued some months; for he related that his friends brought to him there his wife and children, whom they had secretly conducted out of Athens. But that no dependence is to be placed upon this is evident from the absurd fiction of Stesimbrotus that immediately follows, which, to the surprise even of Plutarch (εἶτ' οὐκ οἶδ' ὅπως ἐπιλαθόμενος τούτων, ἢ τὸν Θεμιστοκλέα ποιῶν ἐπιλαθόμενον, πλεῖσαί φησιν, κ. τ. λ.), he brings forward, without observing that the one fable does away the other —viz., that Themistocles was sent by Admetus to Sicily, and had desired of

Hiero his daughter in marriage, with the promise to bring Greece under subjection to him. Plutarch designates Stesimbrotus as a shameless liar, Pericles, ch. 13. That the sons of Themistocles remained in Athens is manifest from a relation in Suidas, and the testimony of Thucydides, ch. 137, and of Plutarch, that the gold was first sent to Themistocles by his friends after his arrival in Asia, to enable him to reward the service of the captain who brought him to Asia, shows at the same time the incorrectness of the assertion of Stesimbrotus, and confirms the opinion that Themistocles remained in no one place of his flight long enough for his friends to send to him there the necessary gold. Themistocles was conducted by Admetus to Pidna, and from there he betook himself in a boat directly to Asia. This, accordingly, since between the death of Pausanias, and the coming of Themistocles into Asia there could at most be only a year, can at latest have happened in the year 473, perhaps in 474; and even in the former case we are completely justified in placing the beginning of the reign of Artaxerxes, which still cannot have immediately coincided with the coming of Themistocles, in the year 474.

"4. On the supposition that the commencement of the reign of Artaxerxes, and the flight of Themistocles, fall in 465, an extravagant old age must be attributed to Charon of Lampsacus. According to Suidas, he was still flourishing under the first Darius, Ol. 69, 504 B.C. Since now, in his history, he mentions the flight of Themistocles to Artaxerxes, this being placed in 465, he must have been employed in writing history at least forty years. This is not, indeed, absolutely impossible; but, in a doubtful case, it must be rejected as the more improbable alternative. '*Historiæ enim non sunt explicandæ*—says Vitringa (*Proll. in Zach.* p. 29)—*ex raris et insolentibus exemplis, sed ex communi vivendi lege et ordine. Si res secus se habeat, in ipsa historia ascribitur ne fallat incautos.*' Compare his farther excellent remarks on this subject. That this argument is not without force, is evident even from the efforts of some advocates of the false chronology to set it aside by cutting the knot. Suidas, after he has cited the above-mentioned determination of the time of Charon, as he found it in his more ancient authorities, subjoins, μᾶλλον δὲ ἦν ἐπὶ τῶν Περσικῶν. Creuzer, on the *Fragm. Historr. Græc.*, p.95, rejects this date without farther examination, because it gives too great an age to Charon.

"5. According to Thucyd. 1, 136, Themistocles, on his passage to Asia, fell in with the Athenian fleet, which was besieging Naxos. This siege of Naxos, however, according to the testimony of Thucydides, ch. 100, which makes all other arguments superfluous, happened before the great victory of the Athenians on the Eurymedon, which, according to Diodorus, belongs to the year 470, and cannot be placed later, because this was the first considerable undertaking of the Athenians against the Persians, the war with whom formed the only ground for the important requisitions which they made upon their allies. Comp. Thucyd. i. 94. Hitherto, since the supremacy had passed over to the Athenians, scarcely anything had been done against the Persians, except the taking of the unimportant Ægon. Thucydides also leads us to about the same year as that given by Diodorus, who connects the defection of Thasos (467) with χρόνῳ ὕστερον, which cannot stand where events immediately succeed each other. Even for these reasons, the siege of Naxos and the flight of Themistocles, do not fall after 471. If, however, we consider that Naxos was the first confederate city with which the Athenians were involved in discord (comp. Thucyd., p. 1, 98)—which, from the nature of the case, as is rendered especially clear by the remarks of Thucydides and a comparison of the later historians, could scarcely have first happened after seven years—and if we farther consider the way in which Thucydides (ch. 98) connects the events, from the transfer of the supremacy until the capture of Naxos, with one another, we shall, without hesitation, place the latter some years earlier, in the year 474 or 473.

"6. The flight of Themistocles falls at least three years earlier than the battle on the Eurymedon, because in all probability he was dead before the latter event. His death, however, must have been some years subsequent to his coming into Asia (comp. Thucyd. ch. 138). One year passed in learning the language, and some time, in any event, was required for what is implied in ταύτης ἔρχε τῆς χώρας, δόντος, κ. τ. λ. Thucydides relates that, according to the account of some, Themistocles took poison. ἀδύνατον νομίσαντα εἶναι ἐπιτελέσαι βασιλεῖ ἃ ὑπέσχετο. This pre-supposes that Themistocles was compelled to fulfil his promises; and had this not been the case at his death, the report that Thucydides only in this instance relied upon himself could not have arisen. Plutarch expressly connects the death of Themistocles with the expedition of Cimon. This is done by several writers, with the mention of the most special circumstances (compare the passages in Staveren on *Nep. Them.* 10) all of which may be regarded, as they are by Cicero (*Brut.* ch. 11) and Nepos, as fictitious, and yet the historical basis on which alone everything depends, *the fact* that Thucydides died before the battle on the Eurymedon is firmly established.

"7. Krüger (l. c. p. 218) has shown that the account of Plutarch, that Themistocles reached an age of sixty-five years, forbids us to place his death beyond the year 470, and therefore his flight beyond the year 473. According to an account which has internal evidence of credibility, in Ælian, *Var. Hist.* iii. 21, Themistocles, as a small boy coming from school, declined going out of the way of the tyrant Pisistratus. Assuming that this happened in the last year of Pisistratus, B.C. 529, and that Themistocles was at that time six years old, he must have been born in 535, and died in 70. Nor is it a valid objection that, according to Plutarch, Themistocles was still living at the time of the Cyprian expedition of Cimon (449 B.C.), and was still young at the battle of Marathon. For the former rests on a manifest confounding of the former event with the victory over the Persian fleet at Cyprus, which is supposed to have immediately preceded the victory on the Eurymedon (comp. Diodor. 11, 60; Dahlmann, *Forschungen*, i. p. 69), and the latter merely on a conclusion drawn from this error. 'Whoever,' remarks Dahlmann, p. 71, 'reads without prejudice the passage, Thucyd. 1, 138, will perceive that the death of Themistocles followed pretty soon after his settlement in Persia; probably in the second year, if Thucydides is worthy of credit.'

"Until all these arguments are refuted, it remains true that the Messianic interpretation of the prophecy is the only correct one, and that the alleged pseudo-Daniel, as well as the real Daniel, possessed an insight into the future, which could have been given only by the Spirit of God; and hence, as this favour could have been shown to no deceiver, the genuineness of the book necessarily follows, and the futility of all objections against it is already manifest." *

V. The only remaining point of inquiry on this verse is, as to the division of the whole period of sixty-nine weeks into two smaller portions of seven weeks and sixty-two weeks; that is, of the four hundred and eighty-three years into one period of four hundred and thirty-four years, and one of forty-nine years. This inquiry resolves itself into another, Whether, after the issuing of the command in the twentieth year of Artaxerxes, there was a period of forty-nine years that was in any manner distinguished from that which followed, or any *reason* why an epoch should be made there? If the command in the twentieth of Artaxerxes was in the year B.C. 454, then the subtraction of forty-nine years from this would make the year 405 B.C. the marked period; that is, about that time some important change would occur, or a new series of affairs would commence which would properly separate the previous period from that which followed. Now, the fair interpretation of this passage respecting the seven weeks, or forty-nine years, undoubtedly is, that that time would be required in rebuilding the city, and in settling its affairs on a

permanent foundation, and that, from the close of that time, another period of sixty-two weeks, or four hundred and thirty-four years, would elapse to the appearing of the Messiah. It is true that this is not distinctly specified in the text, and true that in the text the phrase "the street shall be built again, and the wall, even in troublous times," is not limited expressly to either period, but it is also said in the next verse, that the period of sixty-two weeks would be terminated by the appearing of the Messiah, or by his being cut off, and, therefore, it is fair to presume that the previous period of seven weeks was to be characterized particularly as the "troublous times" in which the street and the wall were to be built again. The inquiry now is, Whether that time was actually occupied in rebuilding and restoring the city? In regard to this, it may be remarked, (1.) That there is a strong *probability* that a considerable time would be necessary to rebuild the walls of the city, and to restore Jerusalem to a condition like that in which it was before the captivity. We are to remember that it had been long lying in ruins; that the land was desolate; that Jerusalem had no commercial importance to make its growth rapid; that there were few in the city on whom reliance could be placed in rebuilding it; that a large portion of the materials for rebuilding it was to be brought from a distance; that the work was opposed with much determination by the Samaritans; that it was necessary, as Nehemiah informs us, in building the walls, that the workmen should have a weapon of defence in one hand whilst they laboured with the other, and that those who were engaged on it were mostly poor. When these things are considered, it is at least not *improbable* that the period of forty-nine years would be required before it could be said that the work was fully completed. (2.) A more material question, however, is, whether the *facts* in the case confirm this, or whether there was such a termination of the rebuilding of the city at about that period, that it could be said that the time occupied was *seven* weeks rather than, for ex-

* *Christ.* ii. 391-408.

ample, six, or five, or nine. It may not be necessary so to make this out as to determine the precise year, or the termination of forty-nine years, but in a general division of the time, it *is* necessary, undoubtedly, so to determine it as to see that *that* time should have been designated, rather than one equally general at the close of *one* week, or two, or six, or nine, or any other number. Now that that *was* the period of the completion of the work contemplated by the decree issued under Artaxerxes, and the work undertaken by Nehemiah, it is not difficult to show: (*a*) It is reasonable to presume that the time referred to in the seven weeks would be the rebuilding of the city, and the restoration of its affairs to its former state—or the completion of the arrangements to restore the nation from the effects of the captivity, and to put it on its former footing. This was the main inquiry by Daniel; this would be a marked period; this would be that for which the "commandment would go forth;" and this would constitute a natural division of the time. (*b*) As a matter of fact, the completion of the work undertaken by Nehemiah, under the command of the Persian kings, reached to the period here designated; and his last act as governor of Judea, in restoring the people, and placing the affairs of the nation on its former basis, occurred at just about the period of the forty-nine years after the issuing of the command by Artaxerxes Longimanus. That event, as is supposed above, occurred B.C. 454. The close of the seven weeks, or of the forty-nine years, would therefore be B.C. 405. This would be about the last year of the reign of Darius Nothus. See the table above. Nehemiah was twice governor of Judea, and the work of restoration which he undertook was not completed until his being the second time in that office. The first time he remained twelve years in office, for he received his commission in the twentieth year of Artaxerxes, and in the thirty-second year he returned again to him, Neh. xiii. 6. This, according to the computation above, would bring it down to B.C. 442. How long he then remained with

the king of Persia he does not definitely state himself, but says it was "certain days," Neh. xiii. 6. After this, he again obtained permission of the king to return to Jerusalem, and went back the second time as governor of Judea, Neh. xiii. 6, 7. The time from his first return to Persia, after the twelve years that he spent in Judea to the year 405 B.C., would be thirty-seven years. According to this, the close of the "seven weeks," and the completion of the enterprise of "rebuilding and restoring" the city, must have been at the end of that thirty-seven years. In reference to this, it may be remarked, (1.) That Nehemiah is known to have lived to a great age (Josephus); yet, supposing he was thirty years old when he was first appointed governor of Judea, and that the time referred to at the close of the "seven weeks," or forty-nine years, was the completion of his work in the restoration of the affairs of Jerusalem, the whole period would only reach to the seventy-ninth year of his age. (2.) The last act of Nehemiah in restoring the city occurred in the fifteenth year of the reign of Darius Nothus—according to Prideaux (*Con.* II. 206, *seq.*)—that is, 408 B.C. This would make, according to the common computation of chronology, a difference from the estimate above of only three years, and, perhaps, considering that the time of "seven weeks" is a reckoning in round numbers, this would be an estimate of sufficient accuracy. But, besides this, it is to be remembered that the exact chronology to a year or a month cannot be made out with absolute certainty; and taking all the circumstances into consideration, it is remarkable that the period designated in the prophecy coincides so nearly with the historical record. The only remaining inquiries, therefore, are, whether the last act of Nehemiah referred to occurred *at* the time mentioned—the 15th of Darius Nothus, or 408 B.C. — and whether that was of sufficient prominence and importance to divide the two periods of the prophecies, or to be a proper closing up of the work of restoring and rebuilding Jerusalem. What he

26 And after threescore and two weeks shall Messiah *a* be cut off, but [1] not for himself: and [2] the

a Luke 24. 26, 46.
1 or, *and shall have nothing.* John 14. 30.

people of the prince that shall come shall destroy the city and the sanc-

2 or, *and they (the Jews) shall be no more his people, Hos.* 1. 9; *or, the prince's (Messiah's,* ver. 25) *future people.*

did in his office as governor of Judea, at his second visitation to Jerusalem, is recorded in Neh. xiii. 7–31. The particular acts which he performed consisted in removing certain abuses which had been suffered to grow up in his absence respecting the temple service, by which the temple had become greatly polluted (ch. xiii. 7–14); in restoring the Sabbath to its proper observance, which had become greatly disregarded (ch. xiii. 15–22); and in constraining those Jews who had contracted unlawful marriages to separate themselves from their wives (ch. xiii. 23–31). These acts were necessary to put the affairs of the temple, and the condition of the city, on their former basis. The *last* of these acts—the separation of those who had contracted unlawful marriages from their wives, is that which designates the close of the "seven weeks," and respecting which the date is to be sought. This is stated in the book of Nehemiah (xiii. 28) to have occurred in the time of "one of the sons of Joiada, the son of Eliashib the high-priest, son-in-law to Sanballat the Horonite." That is, it occurred when Joiada was high-priest. But, according to the *Chron. Alexandrinum,* Joiada succeeded his father in the office in the eleventh year of Darius Nothus, and Prideaux supposes, without improbability, that this event may have occurred as long as four years after he entered on the office of high-priest, which would bring it to the fifteenth of Darius Nothus, or 408 B.C. Comp. Jahn, *Heb. Com.* pp. 179–182; and Prideaux, *Con.* ii. 206–210. The *time,* then, if this be the event referred to, is sufficiently accurate to make it coincide with the prophecy—sufficiently so to divide the previous period from that which succeeded it. The event itself was of sufficient *importance* to have a place here. It was, in fact, *finishing* what was necessary to be done in order to a completion of the purpose to "restore and

rebuild Jerusalem." It was in fact *the restoration of Jewish affairs under the Persian edict,* or what was accomplished in fact under that edict in placing the Jewish affairs on the proper basis—the basis on which they were substantially before the captivity. This was the termination of that captivity in the fullest sense, and divided the past from the future—or constituted a *period* or *epoch* in the history of the Jewish people. It remains only to add, on this verse—and the remark will be equally applicable to the exposition of the two remaining verses of the chapter—that on the supposition that this had been written *after* the coming of the Messiah, and it had been designed to frame what would *seem* to be a prophecy or prediction of these events, the language here would be such as would have been appropriately employed. From the time of the going forth of the command to rebuild the city, the whole duration would have been accurately divided into two great portions—that requisite for the completion of the work of restoring the city, and that extending to the coming of the Messiah, and the former would have been made to terminate where it is now supposed the period of "seven weeks," or forty-nine years, did actually terminate. If this would have been the correct apportionment in a *historic* review, it is correct as *a prophetic* review.

26. *And after threescore and two weeks.* After the completion of the last period of four hundred and thirty-four years. The angel had shown in the previous verse what would be the characteristic of the first period of "seven weeks"—that during that time the wall and the street would be built in circumstances of general distress and anxiety, and he now proceeds to state what would occur in relation to the remaining sixty-two weeks. The particular thing which would characterize that period would

tuary; and the end thereof *shall be*

1 or, *it shall be cut off by desolations.*

with a flood, and unto the end of the war [1] desolations are determined.

be, that the Messiah would be cut off, and that the series of events would commence which would terminate in the destruction of the city and the temple. He does not say that this would be *immediately* on the termination of the sixty-two weeks, but he says that it would be "*after*"—אַחֲרֵי —*subsequent* to the close of that period. The word does not mean necessarily *immediately*, but it denotes that which is to succeed—to follow—and would be well expressed by the word *afterwards:* Gen. xv. 14 ; xxiii. 19 ; xxv. 26, *et al.* See Gesenius, *Lex.* The natural meaning here would be, that this would be the *next event* in the order of events to be reckoned; it would be that on which the prophetic eye would rest subsequent to the close of the period of sixty-two weeks. There are two circumstances in the prophecy itself which go to show that it is not meant that this would *immediately* follow :—(*a*) One is, that in the previous verse it is said that the "sixty-two weeks" would extend "*unto* the Messiah;" that is, either to his birth or to his manifestation as such; and it is not implied anywhere that he would be "cut off" *at once* on his appearing, nor is such a supposition reasonable, or one that would have been embraced by an ancient student of the prophecies; (*b*) the other is, that, in the subsequent verse, it is expressly said that what he would accomplish in causing the oblation to cease would occur "in the midst of the week;" that is, of the remaining one week that would complete the seventy. This could not occur if he were to be "cut off" immediately at the close of the sixty-two weeks. The careful student of this prophecy, therefore, would anticipate that the Messiah would appear at the close of the sixty-two weeks, and that he would continue during a part, at least, of the remaining one week before he would be cut off. This point could have been clearly made out from the prophecy before the Messiah came. ¶ *Shall Messiah.*

Notes, ver. 25. ¶ *Be cut off.* The word here used (כָּרַת) means, properly, to cut, to cut off, as a part of a garment, 1 Sa. xxiv. 5 (6), 11 (12); a branch of a tree, Numb. xiii. 23 ; the prepuce, Exod. iv. 25 ; the head, 1 Sa. xvii. 51 ; v. 4 ; to cut down trees, Deut. xix. 5 ; Isa. xiv. 8 ; xliv. 14 ; Jer. x. 3 ; xxii. 7. Then it means to cut off persons, to destroy, Deut. xx. 20 ; Jer. xi. 19 ; Gen. ix. 11 ; Psa. xxxvii. 9 ; Prov. ii. 22 ; x. 31, *et al. sæpe.* The phrase, "that soul shall be cut off from his people," "from the midst of the people," "from Israel," "from the congregation," &c., occurs frequently in the Scriptures (compare Gen. xvii. 14 ; Lev. vii. 20, 21 ; Num. xv. 30 ; xix. 13, 20 ; Exod. xii. 19, *et al.*), and denotes the punishment of *death* in general, without defining the manner. "It is never the punishment of *exile.*"—Gesenius, *Lex.* The proper notion or meaning here is, undoubtedly, that of being cut off by death, and would suggest the idea of a *violent* death, or a death by the agency of others. It would apply to one who was assassinated, or murdered by a mob, or who was appointed to death by a judicial decree; or it might be applied to one who was cut down in battle, or by the pestilence, or by lightning, or by shipwreck, but it would not naturally or properly be applied to one who had lived out his days, and died a peaceful death. We always now connect with the word the idea of some unusual interposition, as when we speak of one who is cut down in middle life. The ancient translators understood it of a violent death. So the Latin Vulgate, *occidetur Christus;* Syriac, "the Messiah shall be slain," or put to death. It need not be here said that this phrase would find a complete fulfilment in the manner in which the Lord Jesus was put to death, nor that this is the very language in which it is proper now to describe the manner in which he was removed. He was cut off by violence ; by a judicial decree : by a

M

mob; in the midst of his way, &c. If it should be admitted that the angel *meant* to describe the manner of his death, he could not have found a single word that would have better expressed it. ¶ *But not for himself.* Marg., *and shall have nothing.* This phrase has given rise to not a little discussion, and not a little diversity of opinion. The Latin Vulgate is, *et non erit ejus populus, qui eum negaturus est*—" and they shall not be his people who shall deny him." Theodotion (in the Sept.), καὶ κρίμα οὐκ ἔστιν ἐν αὐτῷ—" and there is no crime in him." Syriac, " And it is not with him." The Hebrew is וְאֵין לֹו—and the interpretation turns on the meaning of the word אֵין. Hengstenberg maintains that it is never used in the sense of לֹא (not), but that it always conveys the idea of *nothing*, or *non-existence*, and that the meaning here is, that, then, "there was nothing to him ;" that is, that he ceased to have authority and power, as in the cutting off of a prince or ruler whose power comes to an end. Accordingly he renders it, " and is not to him ;" that is, his dominion, authority, or power over the covenant people as an anointed prince, would cease when he was cut off, and another one would come and desolate the sanctuary, and take possession. Bertholdt renders it, *Ohne Nachfolger von den Seinigen zu haben*—" without any successors of his own "—meaning that his family, or that the dynasty would be cut off, or would end with him. He maintains that the whole phrase denotes " a sudden and an unexpected death," and that it here means that he would have no successor of his own family. He applies it to Alexander the Great. Lengerke renders it, *Und nicht ist vorhanden, der ihm angehöret*—and explains the whole to mean, " The anointed one [as the lawful king] shall be cut off, but it shall not then be one who belongs to his family [to wit, upon the throne], but a Prince shall come to whom the crown did not belong, to whom the name *anointed* could not properly belong." Maurer explains it, " There shall be to him no successor or lawful heir." Prof. Stuart renders

it, " One shall be cut off, and there shall be none for it" (the people). C. B. Michaelis, " and not to be will be his lot." Jacch. and Hitzig, " and no one remained to him." Rosch, " and no one was present for him." Our translation—*but not for himself*—was undoubtedly adopted from the common view of the atonement—that the Messiah did not die for himself, but that his life was given as a ransom for others. There can be no doubt of that fact to those who hold the common doctrine of the atonement, and yet it may be doubted whether the translators did not undesignedly allow their views of the atonement to shape the interpretation of this passage, and whether it can be fairly made out from the Hebrew. The ordinary meaning of the Hebrew word אֵין is, undoubtedly, *nothing, emptiness*—in the sense of there being nothing (see Gesenius, *Lex.*); and, thus applied, the sense here would be, that after he was cut off, or in consequence of his being cut off, that which he before possessed would cease, or there would be " nothing" to him ; that is, either his life would cease, or his dominion would cease, or he would be cut off as the Prince—the Messiah. This interpretation appears to be confirmed by what is immediately said, that *another* would come and would destroy the city and the sanctuary, or that the possession would pass into his hands. It seems probable to me that this is the fair interpretation. The Messiah would come as a "Prince." It might be expected that he would come to rule—to set up a kingdom. But he would be suddenly cut off by a violent death. The anticipated dominion over the people as a prince would not be set up. It would not pertain to him. Thus suddenly cut off, the expectations of such a rule would be disappointed and blasted. He would in fact set up no such dominion as might naturally be expected of an anointed prince; he would have no successor ; the dynasty would not remain in his hands or his family, and soon the people of a foreign prince would come and would sweep all away. This interpretation does not suppose that the *real* object of his coming would be thwarted, or that he would not set up a kingdom in accordance with the prediction properly explained, but that such a kingdom as would be expected by the people would not be set up. He would be cut off soon after he came, and the anticipated dominion would not pertain to him, or there would be "nothing" of it found in him, and soon after a foreign prince would come and destroy the city and the sanctuary. This interpretation, indeed, will take this passage away as a proof-text of the doctrine of the atonement, or as affirming the design of the death of the Messiah, but it furnishes a meaning as much in accordance with the general strain of the prophecy, and with the facts in the work of the Messiah. For it was a natural expectation that when he came he would set up a kingdom—a temporal reign—and this expectation was extensively cherished among the people. He was, however, soon cut off, and all such hopes at once perished in the minds of his true followers (comp. Luke xxiv. 21), and in the minds of the multitudes who, though not his true followers, began to inquire whether he might not be the predicted Messiah— the Prince to sit on the throne of David. But of such an anticipated dominion or rule, there was "nothing" to him. All these expectations were blighted by his sudden death, and soon, instead of his delivering the nation from bondage and setting up a visible kingdom, a foreign prince would come with his forces and would sweep away everything. Whether this would be the interpretation affixed to these words *before* the advent of the Messiah cannot now be determined. We have few remains of the methods in which the Hebrews interpreted the ancient prophecies, and we may readily suppose that they would not be *disposed* to embrace an exposition which would show them that the reign of the Messiah, as they anticipated it, would not occur, but that almost as soon as he appeared, he would be put to death, and the dominion pass away, and the nation be subjected to the ravages of a foreign power. ¶ *And the people of the prince that shall come.*

Marg., "And they (the Jews) shall be no more his people; or, the Prince's (Messiah's) future people." This seems to be rather an *explanation* of the meaning, than a translation of the Hebrew. The literal rendering would be, "and the city, and the sanctuary, the people of a prince that comes, shall lay waste." On the general supposition that this whole passage refers to the Messiah and his time, the language here used is not difficult of interpretation, and denotes with undoubted accuracy the events that soon followed the "cutting off" of the Messiah.

The word *people* (עַם) is a word that may well be applied to subjects or armies—such a people as an invading prince or warrior would lead with him for purposes of conquest. It denotes properly (*a*) a people, or tribe, or race in general; and then (*b*) the people as opposed to kings, princes, rulers (comp. λαός, the people as opposed to chiefs in Homer, *Il.* ii. 365, xiii. 108, xxiv. 28): and then as soldiers, Judg. v. 2. Hence it may be applied, as it would be understood to be here, to the soldiers of the prince that should come. ¶ *Of the prince that shall come.* The word *prince* here (נָגִיד) is the same which occurs in ver. 25, "Messiah *the* *prince*." It is clear, however, that another prince is meant here, for (*a*) it is just said that that prince—the Messiah—would be "*cut off*," and this clearly refers to one that was to follow; (*b*) the phrase "that is to come" (הַבָּא) would also imply this. It would naturally suggest the idea that he would come from abroad, or that he would be a foreign prince—for he would "come" for the purposes of destruction. No one can fail to see the applicability of this to the destruction of Jerusalem by the Roman power, after the Lord Jesus was put to death. If that was the design of the prophecy, or if it be admitted that the prophecy contemplated that, the language could not have been better chosen, or the prediction more exact. No one can reasonably doubt that, if the ancient Hebrews had understood the former part of the prophecy, as meaning that the true Messiah would be put to death soon after his appearing, they could not fail to anticipate that a foreign prince would soon come and lay waste their city and sanctuary. ¶ *Shall destroy the city and the sanctuary.* The "holy place" —the temple. This is the termination of the prophecy. It begins with the command to "rebuild and restore" the city, and ends with its destruction. The *time* is not fixed, nor is there in the prophecy any direct intimation when it would occur, unless it be found in the general declaration in ver. 24, that "seventy weeks were determined upon the people and the city." The whole scope of the prophecy, however, would lead to the supposition that this was *soon* to occur after the Messiah should be "cut off." The series of events under the Romans which led to the destruction of the city and temple, in fact, began very soon after the death of the Lord Jesus, and ceased only when the temple was wholly demolished, and the city was rased to its foundations. ¶ *And the end thereof.* Heb., "its end," or "his end"—וְקִצּוֹ. It is not certain as to what the word *it* (וֹ) here refers. It may be either the end of the city, or of the prince, or of the prophecy, so far as the grammatical construction is concerned. As the principal and immediate subject of the prophecy, however, is the city, it is more natural to refer it to that. Hengstenberg renders it, "it will end," supposing, with Vitringa, that it refers to the subject of the discourse : "the thing —the whole affair—all that is here predicted in this series of events— will end with a flood." This accords well with the whole design of the prophecy. ¶ *With a flood.* בַּשֶּׁטֶף. That is, it shall be *like* an overflowing flood. The word here used means a *gushing, outpouring,* as of rain, Job xxxviii. 25 ; of a torrent, Prov. xxvii. 4 ; an overflowing, inundation, flood, Psa. xxxii. 6 ; Nah. i. 8. Hence it would appropriately denote the ravages of an army, sweeping everything away. It would be like a sudden inundation, carrying everything before it. No one can

doubt that this language is applicable in every respect to the desolations brought upon Jerusalem by the Roman armies. ¶ *And unto the end of the war desolations are determined.* Marg., "it shall be cut off by desolations." Hengstenberg renders this, "and unto the end is war, a decree of ruins." So Lengerke—*und bis aufs Ende Krieg und Beschluss der Wüsten.* Bertholdt renders it, "and the great desolations shall continue unto the end of the war." The Latin Vulgate renders it, *et post finem belli statuta desolatio*—"and after the end of the war desolation is determined." Prof. Stuart translates it, "and unto the end shall be war, a decreed measure of desolations." The *literal* meaning of the passage is, "and unto the end of the war desolations are decreed," or determined. The word rendered "determined" (הֶּחֱרָץ) means, properly, to cut, cut in, engrave ; then to decide, to determine, to decree, to pass sentence. See Notes on ver. 24. Here the meaning naturally is, that such desolations were settled or determined as by a decree or purpose. There was something which made them certain ; that is, it was a part of the great plan here referred to in the vision of the seventy weeks, that there should be such desolations extending through the war. The things which would, therefore, be anticipated from this passage would be, (*a*) that there would be war. This is implied also in the assurance that the people of a foreign prince would come and take the city. (*b*) That this war would be of a *desolating* character, or that it would in a remarkable manner extend and spread ruin over the land. All wars are thus characterized ; but it would seem that this would do it in a remarkable manner. (*c*) That these desolations would extend *through* the war, or to its close. There would be no intermission ; no cessation. It is hardly necessary to say that this was, in fact, precisely the character of the war which the Romans waged with the Jews after the death of the Saviour, and which ended in the destruction of the city and temple ; the overthrow of the whole Hebrew polity ; and the re-

27 And he shall confirm [1] the covenant with many for one week: and in the midst of the week he

1 or, *a*.

moval of great numbers of the people to a distant and perpetual captivity. No war, perhaps, has been in its progress more marked by desolation; in none has the purpose of destruction been more perseveringly manifested to its very close. The *language* here, indeed, might apply to many wars—in a certain sense to all wars; to none, however, would it be more appropriate than to the wars of the Romans with the Jews.

27. *And he shall confirm the covenant.* Literally, "he shall make strong"—וְהִגְבִּיר. The idea is that of giving strength, or stability; of making firm and sure. The Hebrew word here evidently refers to the "covenant" which God is said to establish with his people—so often referred to in the Scriptures as expressing the relation between Him and them, and hence used, in general, to denote the laws and institutions of the true religion—the laws which God has made for his church; his promises to be their protector, &c., and the institutions which grow out of that relation. The margin reads it, more in accordance with the Hebrew, "*a*," meaning that he would confirm or establish "*a* covenant" with the many. According to this, it is not necessary to suppose that it was any existing covenant that it referred to, but that he would ratify what was understood by the word "covenant;" that is, that he would lead many to enter into a true and real covenant with God. This would be fulfilled if he should perform such a work as would bring the "many" into a relation to God corresponding to that which was sustained to him by his ancient people; that is, bring them to be his true friends and worshippers. The meaning of the expression here cannot be mistaken, that during the time specified, "he" (whoever may be referred to) would, for "one week"—pursue such a course as would tend to establish the true religion; to render it more stable and firm; to give it higher sanctions in the approbation of the "many,"

and to bring it to bear more decidedly and powerfully on the heart. Whether this would be by some law enacted in its favour; or by protection extended over the nation; or by present example; or by instruction; or by some work of a new kind, and new influences which he would set forth, is not mentioned, and beforehand perhaps it could not have been well anticipated in what way this would be. There has been a difference of opinion, however, as to the proper nominative to the verb *confirm*—הִגְבִּיר—whether it is the Messiah, or the foreign prince, or the "one week." Hengstenberg prefers the latter, and renders it, "And one week shall confirm the covenant with many." So also Lengerke renders it. Bertholdt renders it "he," that is, "he shall unite himself firmly with many for one week"—or, a period of seven years, *ein Jahrsiebend lang*. It seems to me that it is an unnatural construction to make the word "week" the nominative to the verb, and that the more obvious interpretation is to refer it to some *person* to whom the whole subject relates. It is not usual to represent *time* as an agent in accomplishing a work. In poetic and metaphorical language, indeed, we personate time as cutting down men, as a destroyer, &c., but this usage would not justify the expression that "time would confirm a covenant with many." That is, evidently, the work of a conscious, intelligent agent; and it is most natural, therefore, to understand this as of one of the two agents who are spoken of in the passage. These two agents are the "Messiah," and the "prince that should come." But it is not reasonable to suppose that the latter is referred to, because it is said (ver. 26) that the effect and the purpose of his coming would be to "destroy the city and the sanctuary." He was to come "with a flood," and the effect of his coming would be only desolation. The more correct interpretation, therefore, is to refer it to the Messiah, who is the principal subject of the prophecy;

shall cause the sacrifice and the oblation to cease, and ¹ for the over-

spreading of abominations he shall

1 or, *upon the battlements shall be the idols of the desolator.*

and the work which, according to this, he was to perform was, during that "one week," to exert such an influence as would tend to establish a covenant between the people and God. The effect of his work during that one week would be to secure their adhesion to the *true religion;* to confirm to them the Divine promises, and to establish the principles of that religion which would lead them to God. Nothing is said of the *mode* by which that would be done; and anything, therefore, which would secure this would be a fulfilment of the prophecy. As a matter of fact, if it refers to the Lord Jesus, this was done by his personal instructions, his example, his sufferings and death, and the arrangements which he made to secure the proper effect of his work on the minds of the people — all designed to procure for them the friendship and favour of God, and to unite them to him in the bonds of an enduring covenant. ¶ *With many.*

לָרַבִּים. Or, *for* many; or, *unto* many.

He would perform a work which would pertain to many, or which would bear on many, leading them to God. There is nothing in the word here which would indicate *who* they were, whether his own immediate followers, or those who already were *in* the covenant. The simple idea is, that this would pertain to *many* persons, and it would be fulfilled if the effect of his work were to confirm *many* who were already in the covenant, or if he should bring *many* others into a covenant relation with God. Nothing could be determined from the meaning of the word used here as to which of these things was designed, and consequently a fair fulfilment would be found if *either* of them occurred. If it refers to the Messiah, it would be fulfilled if in fact the effect of his coming should be either by statute or by instructions to confirm and establish those who already sustained this relation to God, or if he gathered other followers, and confirmed them in their allegiance to God. ¶ *For*

one week. The fair interpretation of this, according to the principles adopted throughout this exposition, is, that this includes the space of seven years. See Notes on ver. 24. This is the one week that makes up the seventy — seven of them, or forty-nine years, embracing the period from the command to rebuild the city and temple to its completion under Nehemiah; sixty-two, or four hundred and thirty-four years, to the public appearing of the Messiah, and this one week to complete the whole seventy, or four hundred and ninety years "to finish the transgression, and to make an end of sins, and to make reconciliation for iniquity, and to bring in everlasting righteousness," &c., ver. 24. It is essential, therefore, to find something done, occupying these seven years, that would go to "confirm the covenant" in the sense above explained. In the consideration of this, the attention is arrested by the announcement of an important event which was to occur "in the midst of the week," to wit, in causing the sacrifice and the oblation to cease, showing that there was to be an important change occurring during the "week," or that while he would be, in fact, confirming the covenant through the week in some proper sense, the sacrifice and oblation would cease, and *therefore* the confirming of the many in the covenant must depend on something else than the continuation of the sacrifice and oblation. In regard to this language, as in respect to all the rest of the prophecy, there are, in fact, just two questions: one is, what is *fairly* to be understood by the words, or what is the proper interpretation, independent of anything in the result; the other is, whether anything occurred in that which is regarded as the fulfilment which corresponds with the language so interpreted. (1.) The first inquiry then, is, What is the fair meaning of the language? Or what would one who had a correct knowledge of the proper principles of interpretation understand by this? Now,

make *it* desolate, even until the consummation, and that deter- | mined shall be poured upon [1] the desolate.   1 or, *desolator.*

in regard to this, while it may be admitted, perhaps, that there would be some liability to a difference of view in interpreting it with no reference to the event, or no shaping of its meaning *by* the event, the following things seem to be clear: (*a*) that the "one week," would comprise seven years, immediately succeeding the appearance of the Messiah, or the sixty-two weeks, and that there was something which he would do in "confirming the covenant," or in establishing the principles of religion, which would extend through that period of seven years, or that that would be, in some proper sense, a *period* of time, having a beginning—to wit, his appearing, and some proper close or termination at the end of the seven years: that is, that there would be some reason why that should be a marked period, or why the whole should terminate *there*, and not at some other time. (*b*) That in the middle of that period of seven years, *another* important event would occur, serving to divide *that* time into two portions, and especially to be known as causing the sacrifice and oblation to cease; in some way affecting the public offering of sacrifice, so that from that time there would be in fact a cessation. (*c*) And that this would be succeeded by the consummation of the whole matter expressed in the words, "and for the overspreading of abomination he shall make it desolate," &c. It is not said, however, that this latter would *immediately* occur, but this would be one of the events that would appertain to the fulfilment of the prophecy. There is nothing, indeed, in the prediction to *forbid* the expectation that this would occur at once, nor is there anything in the words which makes it imperative that we *should* so understand it. It may be admitted that this would be the most *natural* interpretation, but it cannot be shown that that is required. It may be added, also, that this may not have appertained to the direct design of the prophecy—which was to foretell the coming of the Messiah,—but that this was *appended* to show the end

of the whole thing. When the Messiah should have come, and should have made an atonement for sin, the great design of rebuilding Jerusalem and the temple would have been accomplished, and both might pass away. Whether that would occur *immediately* or not might be in itself a matter of indifference; but it was important to state here that it would occur, for that was properly a completion of the design of rebuilding the city, and of the purpose for which it had ever been set apart as a holy city. (2.) The other inquiry is, whether there was that in what is regarded as the fulfilment of this, which *fairly* corresponds with the prediction. I have attempted above (on ver. 25) to show that this refers to the Messiah properly so called—the Lord Jesus Christ. The inquiry now is, therefore, whether we can find in his life and death what is a fair fulfilment of these reasonable expectations. In order to see this, it is proper to review these points in their order: (*a*) The period, then, which is embraced in the prophecy, is seven years, and it is necessary to find in his life and work something which would be accomplished during these seven years which could be properly referred to as "confirming the covenant with many." The main difficulty in the case is on this point, and I acknowledge that this seems to me to be the most embarrassing portion of the prophecy, and that the solutions which can be given of this are less satisfactory than those that pertain to any other part. Were it not that the remarkable clause "in the midst of the week he shall cause the sacrifice and oblation to cease," were added, I admit that the natural interpretation would be, that he would do this personally, and that we might look for something which he would himself accomplish during the whole period of seven years. That clause, however, looks as if some remarkable event were to occur in the middle of that period; for the fact that he would cause the sacrifice and oblation to cease—that is, would bring the rites of the temple to a close—shows that what is meant by "confirming the covenant" is different from the ordinary worship under the ancient economy. No *Jew* would think of expressing himself thus, or would see how it was practicable to "confirm the covenant" at the same time that all his sacrifices were to cease. The confirming of the covenant, therefore, during that "one week," must be consistent with some work or event that would cause the sacrifice and oblation to cease in the middle of that period. (*b*) The true fulfilment, it seems to me, is to be found in the bearing of the work of the Saviour on the Hebrew people—the ancient covenant people of God—for about the period of seven years after he entered on his work. Then the particular relation of his work to the Jewish people ceased. It may not be practicable to make out the *exact* time of "seven years" in reference to this, and it may be admitted that this would not be understood from the prophecy before the things occurred; but still there are a number of circumstances which will show that this interpretation is not only plausible, but that it has in its very nature strong probability in its favour. They are such as these: (1.) The ministry of the Saviour himself was wholly among the Jews, and his work was what would, in their common language, be spoken of as "confirming the covenant;" that is, it would be strengthening the principles of religion, bringing the Divine promises to bear on the mind, and leading men to God, &c. (2.) This same work was continued by the apostles as they laboured among the Jews. They endeavoured to do the same thing that their Lord and Master had done, with all the additional sanctions, now derived from his life and death. The whole tendency of their ministry would have been properly expressed in this language: that they endeavoured to "confirm the covenant" with the Hebrew people; that is, to bring them to just views of the character of their natural covenant with God; to show them how it was confirmed in the Messiah; to establish the ancient promises; and to bring to bear upon them

the sanctions of their law as it was now fulfilled, and ratified, and enlarged through the Messiah. Had the Saviour himself succeeded in this, or had his apostles, it would have been, in fact, only "confirming the ancient covenant" — the covenant made with Abraham, Isaac, and Jacob; the covenant established under Moses, and ratified by so many laws and customs among the people. The whole bearing of the Saviour's instructions, and of his followers, was to carry out and fulfil the real design of that ancient institution—to show its true nature and meaning, and to impress it on the hearts of men. (3.) This was continued for *about* the period here referred to; at least for a period so long that it could properly be represented in round numbers as "one week," or seven years. The Saviour's own ministry continued about half that time; and then the apostles prosecuted the same work, labouring with the Jews for about the other portion, before they turned their attention to the Gentiles, and before the purpose to endeavour to bring in the Jewish people was abandoned. They remained in Jerusalem; they preached in the synagogues; they observed the rites of the temple service; they directed their first attention everywhere to the Hebrew people; they had not yet learned that they were to turn away from the "covenant people," and to go to the Gentiles. It was a slow process by which they were led to this. It required a miracle to convince Peter of it, and to show him that it was right to go to Cornelius (Acts x.), as a representative of the Gentile people, and it required another miracle to convert Saul of Tarsus, "the apostle of the Gentiles," and to prepare him for the work of carrying the gospel to the heathen world, and a succession of severe persecutions was demanded to induce the apostles to leave Jerusalem, and to go abroad upon the face of the earth to convey the message of salvation. Their first work was among the Jewish people, and they would have remained among them if they had not been driven away by these persecutions, and been thus constrained to go to other lands. It is true that it cannot be shown that this was a period of exactly "half a week," or three years and a half after the ascension of the Saviour, but, in a prophecy of this nature, it was a period that might, in round numbers, be well expressed by that; or the whole might be properly described by "seventy weeks," or four hundred and ninety years, and the last portion after the appearing of the Messiah as *one* of these weeks. There has been much needless anxiety to make out the exact time to a month or a day in regard to this prophecy—not remembering its general design, and not reflecting how uncertain are all the questions in ancient chronology. Compare the sensible remarks of Calvin on ver. 25. (4.) *When* this occurred; *when* the apostles turned away from the Hebrew people, and gave themselves to their labours among the Gentiles, the work of "confirming the covenant" with those to whom the promises had been made, and to whom the law was given, ceased. They were regarded as "broken off" and left, and the hope of success was in the Gentile world. See the reasoning of the apostle Paul in Rom. xi. Jerusalem was given up soon after to destruction, and the whole work, as contemplated in this prophecy, ceased. The object for which the city and temple were rebuilt was accomplished, and here was a proper termination of the *prophecy*. It was not necessary, indeed, that these should be *at once* destroyed, but they were henceforth regarded as having fulfilled the work designed, and as being now left to ruin. The ruin did not at once occur, but the sacrifices thenceforward offered were without meaning, and the train of events was constantly preparing that would sweep away city and temple together. I suppose, therefore, that this last "one week" embraced the period from the beginning of the ministry of the Saviour to that when the direct and exclusive efforts to bring the principles of his religion to bear on the Hebrew people, as carrying out the design of the covenant made by God with their fathers, and confirmed with so many promises, ceased, and the great effort was commenced to

evangelize the heathen world. Then was the proper close of the seventy weeks; what is added is merely a statement of the winding up of the whole affair in the destruction of the city and temple. That occurred, indeed, some years after; but at this period all that was material in regard to that city had taken place, and consequently that was all that was necessary to specify as to the proper termination of the design of rebuilding the city and the temple. ¶ *And in the midst of the week.* The word here rendered "in the midst"—דְּצִי־—means, properly, half, the half part, Exod. xxiv. 6; Numb. xii. 12; then the middle, or the midst, Judg. xvi. 3. The Vulgate renders it, *in dimidio;* the Greek. ἐν τῷ ἡμίσει. Hengstenberg, "the half." So Lengerke, *die Hälfte;* Luther, *mitten.* The natural and obvious interpretation is that which is expressed in our translation, and that will convey the essential idea in the original. It refers to something which was to occur at about the middle portion of this time, or when about half of this period was elapsed, or to something which it would require half of the "one week," or seven years, to accomplish. The meaning of the passage is fully met by the supposition that it refers to the Lord Jesus and his work, and that the exact thing that was intended by the prophecy was his death, or his being "cut off," and thus causing the sacrifice and oblation to cease. Whatever difficulties there may be about the *precise* time of our Lord's ministry, and whether he celebrated three passovers or four after he entered on his public work, it is agreed on all hands that it lasted about three years and a half—the time referred to here. Though a few have supposed that a longer period was occupied, yet the general belief of the church has coincided in that, and there are few points in history better settled. On the supposition that this pertains to the death of the Lord Jesus, and that it was the design of the prophecy here to refer to the effects of that death, this is the very language which would have been used. If the period of "a week" were for any purpose mentioned, then it would be indispensable to suppose that there would be an allusion to the important event—in fact, the *great* event which was to occur in the middle of that period, when the ends of the types and ceremonies of the Hebrew people would be accomplished, and a sacrifice made for the sins of the whole world. ¶ *He shall cause the sacrifice and the oblation to cease.* The word "*he*," in this place, refers to the Messiah, if the interpretation of the former part of the verse is correct, for there can be no doubt that it is the same person who is mentioned in the phrase "*he* shall confirm the covenant with many." The words "sacrifice" and "oblation" refer to the offerings made in the temple. The former word more properly denotes *bloody* offerings ; the latter *offerings* of any kind—whether of flour, fruits, grain, &c. See these words explained in the Notes on Isa. i. 11, 13. The word rendered "cease" (וְהִשְׁבִּית) means, properly, *to rest* (whence the word *Sabbath*), and then in Hiphil, to cause to rest, or to cause to cease. It conveys the idea of *putting an end to*—as, for example, *war*, Psa. xlvi. 9; *contention*, Prov. xviii. 18; *exultation*, Isa. xvi. 10.— Gesenius. The literal signification here would be met by the supposition that an end would be made of these sacrifices, and this would occur either by their being made wholly to cease to be offered at that time, or by the fact that the object of their appointment was accomplished, and that henceforward they would be useless and would die away. As a matter of fact, so far as the Divine intention in the appointment of these sacrifices and offerings was concerned, they *ceased* at the death of Christ—in the middle of the "week." Then the great sacrifice which they had adumbrated was offered. Then they ceased to have any significancy, no reason existing for their longer continuance. Then, as they never had had any efficacy in themselves, they ceased also to have any propriety as *types*—for the thing which they had prefigured had been accomplished. Then, too, began a series of events and influences which led to their abolition,

for soon they were interrupted by the Romans, and the temple and the altars were swept away to be rebuilt no more. The death of Christ was, in fact, the thing which made them to cease, and the fact that the great atonement has been made, and that there is now no further need of those offerings, is the only philosophical reason which can be given why the Jews have never been able again to rebuild the temple, and why for eighteen hundred years they have found no place where they could again offer a bloody sacrifice. The "sacrifice and the oblation" were made, as the result of the coming of the Messiah, to "cease" *for ever*, and no power of man will be able to restore them again in Jerusalem. Comp. Gibbon's account of the attempt of Julian to rebuild the temple at Jerusalem : *Dec. and Fall*, ii. 35–37. ¶ *And for the overspreading of abominations he shall make it desolate.* The marginal reading here is very different, showing clearly the perplexity of the translators : "Upon the battlements shall be the idols of the desolator." There is great variety, also, in the ancient versions in rendering this passage. The Latin Vulgate is, "And there shall be in the temple the abomination of desolation." The Greek, "And upon the temple shall be an abomination of desolations." The Syriac, "And upon the extremities of the abomination shall rest desolation." The Arabic, "And over the sanctuary shall there be the abomination of ruin." Luther renders it, "And upon the wings shall stand the abomination of desolation." Lengerke and Hengstenberg render it, "And upon the summit of abomination comes the destroyer." Prof. Stuart, "And the water shall be over a winged fowl of abominations." These different translations show that there is great obscurity in the original, and perhaps exclude the hope of being able entirely to free the passage from all difficulties. An examination of the *words*, however, may perhaps enable us to form a judgment of its meaning. The *literal* and *obvious* sense of the original, as I understand it, is, "And upon the wing of the abominations one causing desolation"—וְעַל כְּנַף שִׁקּוּצִים מְשֹׁמֵם. The word rendered *overspreading* (כְּנַף) means, properly, *a wing;* so called as *covering,* or because it *covers*—from כָּנַף, to cover, to hide. Then it denotes anything having a resemblance to a wing, as an extremity, a corner, as (*a*) of a garment, the skirt, or flap, 1 Sam. xxiv. 4 (5), 11 (12); Numb. xv. 38, and hence, as the outer garment was used by the Orientals to wrap themselves in at night, the word is used for the extremity or border of a bed-covering, Deut. xxii. 30 (xxiii. 1); Ruth iii. 9. (*b*) It is applied to land, or to the earth—as the earth is compared with a garment spread out, Isa. xxiv. 16; Job xxxvii. 3; xxxviii. 13. (*c*) It is used to denote the highest point, or a battlement, a pinnacle— as having a resemblance to a wing spread out. So the word πτερύγιον is used in Matt. iv. 5. See Notes on that passage. It would seem most probable.that the allusion by the word as applied to a building would not be, as supposed by Gesenius (*Lex.*), and by Hengstenberg and Lengerke, to the *pinnacle* or *summit,* but to some roof, porch, or piazza that had a resemblance to the wings of a bird as spread out— a use of the word that would be very natural and obvious. The extended porch that Solomon built on the eastern side of the temple would, not improbably, have, to one standing on the opposite Mount of Olives, much the appearance of the wings of a bird spread out. Nothing certain can be determined about the allusion here from the use of this *word,* but the *connection* would lead us to suppose that the reference was to something pertaining to the city or temple, for the whole prophecy has a reference to the city and temple, and it is natural to suppose that in its close there would be an allusion to it. The use of the word "*wing*" here would lead to the supposition that what is said would pertain to something in connection with the temple having a resemblance to the wings of a bird, and the word "upon" (עַל) would lead us to suppose that what was to occur would be somehow *upon* that. The word rendered

abominations (שִׁקּוּצִים) means *abominable things,* things to be held in detestation, as things unclean, filthy garments, &c., and then idols, as things that are to be held in abhorrence. The word שִׁקּוּץ *shik-kootz,* is rendered *abomination* in Deut. xxix. 17; 1 Kings xi. 5, 7; 2 Kings xxiii. 13, 24; Isa. lxvi. 3; Jer. iv. 1; vii. 30; xiii. 27; xxxii. 34; Ezek. v. 11; vii. 20; xx. 7, 8, 30; Dan. ix. 27; xi. 31; xii. 11; Hos. ix. 10; Zech. ix. 7; *abominable idols* in 2 Chron. xv. 8 (in the margin *abominations*); *detestable* in Jer. xvi. 18; Ezek. xi. 18, 21; xxxvii. 23; and *abominable filth* in Nah. iii. 6. It does not occur elsewhere. In most of these places it is applied to *idols,* and the current usage would lead us so to apply it, if there were nothing in the connection to demand a different interpretation. It *might* refer to anything that was held in abomination, or that was detestable and offensive. The *word* is one that might be used of an idol god, or of anything that would pollute or defile, or that was from any cause offensive. It is not used in the Old Testament with reference to a *banner* or *military standard,* but there can be no doubt that it might be so applied as denoting the standard of a foe—of a heathen—planted on any part of the temple—a thing which would be particularly detestable and abominable in the sight of the Jews. The word rendered "he shall make *it* desolate"— מְשֹׁמֵם—is "he making desolate;" that is, *a desolator.* It is a Poel participle from שָׁמֵם—to be astonished, to be laid waste; and then, in an active sense, to lay waste, to make desolate.—Gesenius. The same word, and the same phrase, occur in ch. xi. 31: "And they shall place the abomination that maketh desolate," or, as it is in the margin, *astonisheth.* There, also, the expression is used in connection with "taking away the daily sacrifices." The word would be more properly rendered in this place *desolator,* referring to some one who would produce desolation. There is great abruptness in the entire expression, and it is evident that it was not the intention to give so clear a prediction in this that it could be fully understood beforehand. The other portions of the prophecy respecting the building of the city, and the coming of the Messiah, and the work that he would accomplish, are much more clear, and their meaning could have been made out with much more certainty. But, in reference to this, it would seem, perhaps, that all that was designed was to throw out suggestions—fragments of thought, that would rather hint at the subject than give any continuous idea. Perhaps a much more *abrupt* method of translation than that which attempts to express it in a continuous grammatical construction capable of being parsed easily, would better express the state of the mind of the speaker, and the language which he uses, than the ordinary versions. The Masoretic pointing, also, may be disregarded, and then the real idea would be better expressed by some such translation as the following :—" He shall cause the sacrifice and the offering to cease. And—upon the wing—the porch of the temple—abominations ! And a desolator !" That is, after the ceasing of the sacrifice and the oblation, the mind is fixed upon the temple where they had been offered. The first thing that arrests the eye is some portion of the temple, here denoted by the word *wing*. The next is something abominable or detestable—an object to be hated and loathed in the very temple itself. The next is a *desolator*— one who had come to carry desolation to that very temple. Whether the "abomination" is connected with the " desolator" or not is not intimated by the language. It might or might not be. The angel uses language as these objects strike the eye, and he expresses himself in this abrupt manner as the eye rests on one or the other. The question then arises, What does this mean ? Or what is to be regarded as the proper fulfilment ? It seems to me that there can be no doubt that there is a reference to the Roman standard or banners planted on some part of the temple, or to the Roman army, or to some idols set up by the Romans— objects of abomination to the Jews— as attracting the eye of the angel in

the distant future, and as indicating the close of the series of events here referred to in the prophecy. The reasons for this opinion are, summarily, the following :—(*a*) The *place* or *order* in which the passage stands in the prophecy. It is *after* the coming of the Messiah ; *after* the proper cessation of the sacrifice and oblation, and at the close of the whole series of events— the termination of the whole design about rebuilding the city and the temple. (*b*) The *language* is such as would properly represent that. Nothing could be more appropriate, in the common estimation of the Jews, than to speak of such an object as a Roman military standard planted in any part of the temple, as an *abomination ;* and no word would better denote the character of the Roman conqueror than the word *desolator*—for the effect of his coming was to lay the whole city and temple in ruins. (*c*) The language of the Saviour in his reference to this would seem to demand such an interpretation, Matt. xxiv. 15 : "When ye, therefore, shall see the abomination of desolation spoken of by Daniel the prophet stand in the holy place," &c. There can be no reasonable doubt that the Saviour refers to this passage in Daniel (see Notes on Matt. xxiv. 15), or that events occurred in the attack on Jerusalem and the temple that would fully correspond with the language used here. Josephus, for instance, says, that when the city was taken, the Romans brought their ensigns into the temple, and placed them over the eastern gate, and sacrificed to them there. " And now the Romans," says he, " upon the flight of the seditious into the city, and upon the burning of the holy house itself, and all the buildings round about it, brought their ensigns into the temple, and set them over against its eastern gate ; and there they did offer sacrifices to them, and there did they make Titus *Imperator* with the greatest acclamations of joy." —*Jewish Wars*, b. vi. ch. vi. § 1. This fact fully accords with the meaning of the language as above explained, and the reference to it was demanded in order that the purpose of the prophecy should be complete. Its proper termination is the destruction of the city and temple—as its beginning is the order to rebuild them. ¶ *Even until the consummation.* Until the completion—וְעַד־כָּלָה. That is, the series of events in the prophecy shall in fact reach to the completion of everything pertaining to the city and temple. The whole purpose in regard to that shall be completed. The design for which it is to be rebuilt shall be consummated; the sacrifices to be offered there shall be finished, and they shall be no longer efficacious or proper; the whole civil and religious polity connected with the city and temple shall pass away. ¶ *And that determined.* וְנֶחֱרָצָה. See this word explained in the Notes on vers. 24, 26. See also Notes on Isa. x. 23. There seems to be an allusion in the word here to its former use, as denoting that this is the fulfilment of the determination in regard to the city and temple. The idea is, that that which was determined, or decided on, to wit, with reference to the closing scenes of the city and temple, would be accomplished. ¶ *Shall be poured.* תִּתַּךְ The word here used means to pour, to pour out, to overflow—as rain, water, curses, anger, &c. It may be properly applied to calamity or desolation, as these things may be represented as *poured down* upon a people, in the manner of a storm. Compare 2 Sam. xxi. 10; Exod. ix. 33; Psa. xi. 6; Ezek. xxxviii. 22; 2 Chron. xxxiv. 21; xii. 7; Jer. vii. 20; xlii. 18; xliv. 6. ¶ *Upon the desolate.* Marg., *desolator.* The Hebrew word (שֹׁמֵם) is the same, though in another form (*Kal* instead of *Poel*) which is used in the previous part of the verse, and rendered "he shall make it desolate," but which is proposed above to be rendered *desolator.* The verb שָׁמֵם is an intransitive verb, and means, in *Kal,* the form used here, to be astonished or amazed; then "to be laid waste, to be made desolate" (Gesenius); and the meaning in this place, therefore, is that which is desolate or laid waste—the wasted, the perishing, the solitary. The reference is to Jerusalem viewed as desolate or reduced to ruins. The

angel perhaps contemplates it, as he is speaking, in ruins or as desolate, and he sees this also as the termination of the entire series of predictions, and, in view of the whole, speaks of Jerusalem appropriately as *the desolate.* Though it would be rebuilt, yet it would be again reduced to desolation, for the purpose of the rebuilding—the coming of the Messiah—would be accomplished. As the prophecy *finds* Jerusalem a scene of ruins, so it *leaves* it, and the last word *in* the prophecy, therefore, is appropriately the word *desolate.* The intermediate state indeed between the condition of the city as seen at first and at the close is glorious —for it embraces the whole work of the Messiah; but the beginning is a scene of ruins, and so is the close. The sum of the whole in the latter part of the verse may be expressed in a free paraphrase: "He, the Messiah, shall cause the sacrifice and oblation to cease," by having fulfilled in his own death the design of the ancient offerings, thus rendering them now useless, and upon the outspreading—upon the temple regarded as spread out, or some wing or portico, there are seen abominable things—idolatrous ensigns, and the worship of foreigners. A desolator is there, also, come to spread destruction—a foreign army or leader. And this shall continue even to the end of the whole matter—the end of the events contemplated by the prophecy—the end of the city and the temple. And that which is determined on—the destruction decreed—shall be poured out like a tempest on the city doomed to desolation—desolate as surveyed at the beginning of the prophecy—desolate at the close, and therefore appropriately called "*the desolate.*"

After this protracted examination of the meaning of this prophecy, all the remark which it seems proper to make is, that this prediction could have been the result only of inspiration. There is the clearest evidence that the prophecy was recorded long before the time of the Messiah, and it is manifest that it could not have been the result of any natural sagacity. There is not the slightest proof that it was uttered as late as the coming of Christ, and there is nothing better determined in relation to any ancient matter than that it was recorded long before the birth of the Lord Jesus. But it is equally clear that it could have been the result of no mere natural sagacity. How could such events have been foreseen except by Him who knows all things? How could the order have been determined? How could the time have been fixed? How could it have been anticipated that the Messiah, the Prince, would be cut off? How could it have been known that he would cause the sacrifice and oblation to cease? How could it have been ascertained that the period during which he would be engaged in this would be one week—or about seven years? How could it be predicted that a remarkable event would occur in the middle of that period that would in fact cause the sacrifice and oblation ultimately to cease? And how could it be conjectured that a foreign prince would come, and plant the standard of abomination in the holy city, and sweep all away —laying the city and the temple in ruins, and bringing the whole polity to an end? These things lie beyond the range of natural sagacity, and if they are fairly implied in this prophecy, they demonstrate that this portion of the book is from God.

CHAPTER X.

ANALYSIS OF THE CHAPTER.

This chapter introduces the last revelation made to Daniel, and is *merely* introductory to the disclosures made in the two following chapters. The whole extends to the time of the coming of the Messiah, embracing a detail of the principal historical events that would occur, and closes with some

fearful allusions to the ultimate results of human conduct in the day of judgment, and to the great principles on which God governs the world. The contents of this introductory chapter are as follows :—(*a*) The statement of the time when the revelation occurred, ver. 1. This was in the third year of Cyrus king of Persia, subsequently, therefore, to the visions in the previous chapters, and after the order had been given by Cyrus for the restoration of the Jews, Ezra i. 1. (*b*) The particular period when this occurred was when Daniel was observing a fast that continued through three weeks, vers. 2, 3. This was at the passover, the first month in their ecclesiastical year, and the fast was observed by Daniel, evidently, on account of the sins and the calamities of his people. (*c*) The place where this occurred, ver. 4. He was by the side of the river Hiddekel or Tigris. Why he was there he does not say. But it is to be remembered that he seems to have been employed on some occasions in other parts of the empire than Babylon ; and one of his former visions occurred on the banks of a river that flowed into the Tigris —the river Ulai. See Notes on ch. viii. 2. Indeed, it would appear that the banks of rivers were not unfrequently the places to which the prophets resorted, or where they were favoured with their visions. They were retired places, and were on many accounts favourable for devotion. Comp. Ezek. i. 1 ; Acts xvi. 13. See also Rev. xxii. 1, 2. (*d*) While there, engaged in his devotions, Daniel saw a man, who suddenly appeared to him, clothed in linen, and girded with a belt of gold. Those who were with him fled astonished, and left him alone to contemplate the vision, and to receive the communication which this glorious stranger had to make to him.

CHAPTER X.

I N the third year of Cyrus king of Persia, a thing was revealed

The effect of this vision on himself, however, was wholly to overcome him, to prostrate him to the earth, and to render him insensible, until the angel touched him, and raised him up, vers. 4-10. In all this there is nothing unnatural. The effect is such as would be produced in any case in similar circumstances, and it has a striking resemblance to what occurred to Saul of Tarsus on his way to Damascus (Acts ix. 3, 4; xxii. 7-9; and to ·John in the visions of Patmos, Rev. i. 10-17. (e) He who had thus appeared to Daniel proceeded to state to him the design for which he had come, vers. 11-14. The prayer of Daniel, he said, had been heard the first day in which he had given himself to these solemn acts of devotion. He had himself been commissioned at that time to come to Daniel, and to disclose the events which were to occur. During a period of twenty-one days, however, in which Daniel had been engaged in this season of devotion, he had been withstood by "the prince of the kingdom of Persia," and had been detained until Michael, one of the chief princes, had interposed to release him, and he had now come, at last, to make known to Daniel what would occur to his people in the latter days. The nature of this detention will, of course, be considered in the Notes on ver. 13. (f) Daniel then (vers. 15-17) describes the effect which this vision had on him, rendering him unable to converse with him who had thus appeared to him. (g) The heavenly messenger then touched him, and bade him be of good courage and be strong (vers. 18, 19), and then said that he would return and fight with the prince

unto Daniel, whose name was called Belteshazzar; and the thing was true, but the time appointed was

of Persia, after having stated that which was "noted in the Scripture of truth," vers. 20, 21.

1. *In the third year of Cyrus, king of Persia.* In regard to Cyrus, see Notes on Isa. xli. 2. In ch. i. 21, it is said that "Daniel continued even unto the first year of king Cyrus." But it is not necessarily implied in that passage that he *died* then. It may mean only that he continued in authority, and was employed, in various ways, as a public officer, until that time. See Notes on that passage. For anything that appears, he may have lived several years after, though, for causes now unknown, he may have retired from the court after the accession of Cyrus. This vision may have occurred when he was no longer a public officer, though the whole narrative leads us to suppose that he had not lost his interest in the affairs of the Jewish people. He may have retired on account of age, though his declining years would be naturally devoted to the welfare of his people, and he would embrace any opportunity which he might have of doing them good. ¶ *A thing was revealed unto Daniel.* A revelation was made to him. The occasion on which it was done is stated in the next verse. It was when he was earnestly engaged in prayer for his people, and when his mind was deeply anxious in regard to their condition. ¶ *Whose name was called Belteshazzar.* See Notes on ch. i. 7. The name Belteshazzar was probably that by which he was known in Babylon, and as this prophecy was perhaps published in his own time, the use of this name would serve to identify the author. The name *Daniel* would have been sufficient to give it currency and authority among his own countrymen. ¶ *And the thing* was *true.* That is, it would be certainly accomplished. This expresses the deep conviction of the writer that what was revealed in this vision would certainly come to pass. In his own mind there was no

long: [1] and he understood the
thing, and had understanding of
the vision.

1 *great.*

2 In those days I Daniel was
mourning three [2] full weeks.

2 *weeks of days.*

doubt that it would be so, though the time extended through many years, and though it could not be expected that it would be complete until long after his own death. Perhaps the declaration here is designed to bring the weight of his own authority and his well-known character to pledge his own word, that what is here said would be accomplished; or, as we should say, to stake his veracity as a prophet and a man, on the fulfilment of what he had affirmed. Such an assertion *might* be of great use in consoling the minds of the Jews in the troubles that were to come upon their nation. ¶ *But the time appointed was long.* Marg., *great.* There is considerable variety in the translation and interpretation of this passage. The Latin Vulgate renders it, *fortitudo magna.* The Greek, "And the power was great." The Syriac, "And the discourse was apprehended with great effort, but he understood the vision." Luther, "And it was of great matters." Lengerke, "And the misery (*Elend*) is great;" that is, the distress of the people. Bertholdt renders it, "Whose contents pertained to great wars." This variety of interpretation arises from the word rendered in our version "the time appointed"— אבצ.

This word properly means an army, host, as going forth to war; then the host of angels, of the stars, and hence God is so often called "Jehovah of hosts." Then the word means warfare, military service, a hard service, a season of affliction or calamity. See Notes on Job vii. 1. It seems to me that this is the meaning here, and that Gesenius (*Lex.*) has correctly expressed the idea: "And true is the edict, and *relates to long warfare;* that is, to many calamities to be endured." It was not a thing to be soon accomplished, nor did it pertain to peaceful and easy times, but it had reference to the calamities, the evils, and the hardships of wars— wars attended with the evils to which they are usually incident, and which were to be conducted on a great scale.

This interpretation will accord with the details in the following chapters. ¶ *And he understood the thing,* &c. This seems to be said in contradistinction to what had occurred on some other occasions when the meaning of the vision which he saw was concealed from him. Of this he says he had full understanding. The prophecy was, in fact, more clearly expressed than had been usual in the revelations made to Daniel, for this is almost entirely a historical narrative, and there could be little doubt as to its meaning.

2. *In those days I Daniel was mourning.* I was afflicting myself; that is, he had set apart this time as an extraordinary fast. He was sad and troubled. He does not say on what account he was thus troubled, but there can be little doubt that it was on account of his people. This was two years after the order had been given by Cyrus for the restoration of the Hebrew people to their country, but it is not improbable that they met with many embarrassments in their efforts to return, and possibly there may have sprung up in Babylon some difficulties on the subject that greatly affected the mind of Daniel. The difficulties attending such an enterprise as that of restoring a captured people to their country, when the march lay across a vast desert, would at any time have been such as to have made an extraordinary season of prayer and fasting proper. ¶ *Three full weeks.* Marg., *weeks of days.* Heb., "Three sevens of days." He does not say whether he had designedly set apart that time to be occupied as a season of fasting, or whether he had, under the influence of deep feeling, continued his fast from day to day until it reached that period. Either supposition will accord with the circumstances of the case, and either would have justified such an act at any time, for it would be undoubtedly proper to designate a time of extraordinary devotion, or, under the influence of deep feeling, of domestic trouble, of national affliction, to continue

3 I ate no¹ pleasant bread, neither came flesh nor wine in my mouth, neither did I anoint myself at all, till three whole weeks were fulfilled.

1 *bread of desires.*

4 And in the four and twentieth day of the first month, as I was by the side of the great river, which *is* Hiddekel;

5 Then I lifted up mine eyes,

---

such religious exercises from day to day.

3. *I ate no pleasant bread.* Marg., *bread of desires.* So the Hebrew. The meaning is, that he abstained from ordinary food, and partook of that only which was coarse and disagreeable. ¶ *Neither came flesh nor wine in my mouth.* That is, he lived on bread or vegetables. It is not to be inferred from this that Daniel ordinarily made use of wine, for it would seem from ch. i. that that was not his custom. What would appear from this passage would be, that he practised on this occasion the most rigid abstinence. ¶ *Neither did I anoint myself.* The use of unguents was common in the East (see Notes on Matt. vi. 17), and Daniel here says that he abstained during these three weeks from that which he ordinarily observed as promoting his personal comfort. He gave himself up to a course of life which would be expressive of deep grief. Nature prompts to this when the mind is overwhelmed with sorrow. Not only do we become indifferent to our food, but it requires an effort *not* to be indifferent to our dress, and to our personal appearance.

4. *And in the four and twentieth day of the first month.* At the close of his season of fasting. Though he had not set apart this season of fasting with any view or expectation that it would be followed by such a result, yet there was a propriety that an occasion like this should be selected as that on which the communication which follows should be made to his mind; for (*a*) his mind was in a prepared state by this extraordinary season of devotion for such a communication; and (*b*) his attention during that period had been turned towards the condition of his people, and it was a fit opportunity to impart to him these extraordinary views of what would occur to them in future days. It may be added, that we shall be more likely to receive

Divine communications to our souls at the close of seasons of sincere and prolonged devotion than at other times, and that, though we may set apart such seasons for different purposes, the Spirit of God may take occasion from them to impart to us clear and elevated views of Divine truth, and of the Divine government. A man is in a better state to obtain such views, and is more likely to obtain them, in such circumstances than he is in others, and he who desires to understand God and his ways should wait upon him with intense and prolonged devotion. The *time* here specified is the "first month"—the month Nisan, answering to a part of our month April. This was the month in which the Passover was celebrated, and was a time, therefore, which a Jew would be likely to select as a season of extraordinary devotion. It was, for some reason, very common for the prophets to record *the very day* on which the visions which they saw appeared to them, or on which Divine communications were made to them. This was often of importance, because it served to determine the time when a prophecy was fulfilled. ¶ *I was by the side of the great river, which* is *Hiddekel.* That is, the Tigris. The Syriac renders it the Euphrates. The name in the Scriptures, however, denotes the Tigris. *Why* Daniel was there he does not say. He was often away from Babylon (comp. Notes on ch. viii. 2), and he may have been now among some of his people who resided near the Tigris. Possibly he may at that time have ceased to reside at the court in Babylon, and have taken up his residence in some place on the Tigris. See Notes on ver. 1.

5. *Then I lifted up mine eyes, and looked,* &c. While he was engaged in devotion. What is here said would lead us to suppose that he had been occupied in deep thought and meditation, perhaps with his eyes fixed on

DANIEL II.

N

and looked, and, behold, ¹ a certain man clothed in linen, whose loins *were* girded with fine gold of Uphaz.

1 *one.*

6 His body *ᵃ* also *was* like the beryl, and his face as the appearance of lightning, and his eyes as

a Rev. 1. 13-17.

the ground. ¶ *Behold, a certain man clothed in linen.* One who had the form and appearance of a man.

[To the same extent that the prophetic beasts find their types in the conventional forms of the Assyrian divinities, it is probable that the "certain man clothed in linen, whose loins were girded with fine gold of Uphaz," has reference to the gorgeous kingly and sacerdotal costume shown in the annexed engraving. This figure forms a tablet or slab, taken from one of the chambers at Nimroud, and represents the Assyrian monarch in his twofold character of king and priest. It is "one of the most carefully sculptured and best preserved in the palace, and is included in the collection sent to England." The king has one hand on the hilt of his sword, and with the other grasps a wand, or staff.]

The subsequent disclosures showed that he was an angel, but when angels have appeared on earth they have commonly assumed the human form. The margin is, "*one.*" So also is the Hebrew "one man." From ch. xii. 6, it would seem that two other such beings appeared in the course of the

vision, but either one only was manifest now to Daniel, or his attention was particularly directed to him. The *name* of this celestial messenger is not given, but all the circumstances of the case lead us to suppose that it was the same who had appeared to him on the banks of the Ulai (ch. viii. 16), and the same who had made the revelation of the seventy weeks, ch. ix. 21, *seq.* Linen was the common raiment of priests, because it was supposed to be more pure than wool, Exod. xxviii. 42; Lev. vi. 10; xvi. 4, 23; 1 Sam. ii. 18. It was also worn by prophets, Jer. xiii. 1, and is represented as the raiment of angels, Rev. xv. 6. The nature of the raiment would suggest the idea at once that this person thus appearing was one sustaining a saintly character. ¶ *Whose loins* were *girded with fine gold of Uphaz.* With a girdle made of fine gold; that is, probably, it was made of something in which fine gold was interwoven, so as to give it the appearance of pure gold. It was customary in the East, as it is now, to wear a girdle around the loins. See Notes on Matt. v. 38-41. These girdles are often made of rich material, and are highly ornamented. Compare Notes on Rev. i. 13. Nothing is known of Uphaz, unless, as Gesenius supposes, the word is a corruption of Ophir, made by a change of a single letter—ז for ר. Ophir was celebrated for its gold, but its situation is unknown. See Notes on Job xxii. 24.

6. *His body also* was *like the beryl.* There is a very striking resemblance between the description here given and that of the Saviour as he appeared to John in Patmos, Rev. i. 13-16. See Notes on that passage. It contains, however, no description of the appearance of the *body. Beryl* is "a mineral of great hardness, occurring in green and bluish-green six-sided prisms. It is identical with the emerald, except that the latter has a purer and richer colour."—Dana, in Webster's *Dic.* The Hebrew word here used is תַּרְשִׁישׁ

lamps of fire, and his arms and his feet like in colour to polished brass, and the voice of his words like the voice of a multitude.

7 And I Daniel alone saw the vision: for the men that were with me saw not the vision; but a great quaking fell upon them, so that they fled to hide themselves.

8 Therefore I was left alone, and

Tarshish, Tartessus, and properly refers to a country supposed to be on the south of Spain, a place where this mineral was probably found. This was situated between the mouths of the river Bætis, or Guadalquivir, and was a flourishing mart of the Phœnicians, Gen. x. 4; Psa. lxxii. 10; Isa. xxiii. 1, 6, 10, &c.—Gesenius. The name was given to this gem because it was brought from that place. The true meaning of the word, as applied to a gem, is supposed to be the chrysolite, that is, the topaz of the moderns. "Tarshish, the chrysolite," says Rosenmüller (*Mineralogy and Botany of the Bible,* pp. 38, 39), "is a crystalline precious stone of the quartz kind, of a glassy fracture. The prevailing colour is yellowish-green, and pistachiogreen of every variety and degree of shade, but always with a yellow and gold lustre. It is completely diaphanous, and has a strong double refraction. Most commonly the chrysolite is found solid and in grains, or in angular pieces. The Hebrew word *Tarshish* denotes the south of Spain, the Tartessus of the Greeks and Romans, a place to which the Phœnicians traded even in the earliest ages. Probably the Phœnicians first brought the chrysolite from Spain to Syria, and it was on that account called *Tarshish stone.*" ¶ *And his face as the appearance of lightning.* Bright, shining. In Rev. i. 16 it is, "And his countenance was as the sun shineth in his strength." See Notes on that passage. ¶ *And his eyes as lamps of fire.* Keen, penetrating. So in Rev. i. 14: "His eyes were as a flame of fire." ¶ *And his arms and his feet like in colour to polished brass.* So in Rev. i. 15: "And his feet like unto fine brass, as if they burned in a furnace." See Notes on that passage. The meaning is, that they were bright—like burnished metal. The Hebrew here is, "like the *eye* of brass;" then, as the word *eye* comes to denote the *face* or *countenance,* the

meaning is, "like the face or appearance of brass." Compare Exod. x. 5, 15; Numb. xxii. 5, 11. It is easy to conceive of the appearance which one would make whose arms and feet resembled burnished brass. ¶ *And the voice of his words like the voice of a multitude.* A multitude of people—loud and strong. So in Rev. i. 15: "And his voice as the sound of many waters."

7. *And I Daniel alone saw the vision.* That is, he only saw it distinctly. The others who were with him appear to have seen or heard something which alarmed them, and they fled. Who those men were, or why they were with him, he does not say. They may have been his own countrymen, engaged with him in the act of devotion, or they may have been Babylonians occupied in the public service; but whoever they were, or whatever was the reason why they were there, they became alarmed and fled. The case was somewhat different with the companions of Saul of Tarsus when the Saviour appeared to him on his way to Damascus. These saw the light; they all fell to the earth together, but Saul only heard the voice of him that spake. Acts xxii. 9.

8. *Therefore I was left alone, and saw this great vision.* That is, I distinctly saw it, or contemplated it. He perceived, doubtless, that it was a heavenly vision; and as he had often been favoured with similar manifestations, he remained to receive the communication which probably he understood was to be made. ¶ *And there remained no strength in me.* He was completely overcome. A similar effect was produced on John when he was in Patmos: "And when I saw him I fell at his feet as dead," Rev. i. 17. That he should be overcome, and his strength taken away, was not an unnatural effect; and what occurred to Daniel and John may demonstrate that there *may* be such views of the Divine character and glory now as to prostrate our phy-

saw this great vision, and there remained no strength in me: for my ¹comeliness was turned in me into corruption, and I retained no strength.

9 Yet heard I the voice of his words: and when I heard the voice of his words, then was I in a deep sleep on my face, and my face toward the ground.

10 ¶ And, behold, an hand touched me, which ² set me upon my knees and *upon* the palms of my hands:

11 And he said unto me, O Daniel, a man ³ greatly beloved, understand the words that I speak unto thee, and stand ⁴ upright : for unto thee am I now sent. And when he had spoken this word unto me, I stood trembling.

12 Then said he unto me, Fear not, Daniel ; for from the first day that thou didst set thine heart to

1 or, *vigour.*   2 *moved.*   3 *of desires.*   4 *upon thy standing.*

---

sical powers. It is certain that such visions as those which appeared to Daniel and John would have this effect ; and, though we are not to expect that they will now be vouchsafed to men, no one can doubt that there *may* be such views of God, and heaven, and eternal realities presented to the eye of faith and hope ; such joy in the evidence of pardoned sin ; such a change from a sense of condemnation to the peace resulting from forgiveness, that the powers of the body may be prostrated, and sink from exhaustion. Indeed, it is not much of the revelation of the Divine character that in our present state we can bear. ¶ *For my comeliness.* Marg., *vigour.* Heb., הוד *hŏdh.* The word means, properly, majesty or splendour ; then beauty or brightness, as of the complexion. The meaning here is, that his "*bright complexion*" (Gesenius, *Lex.*) was changed upon him ; that is, that he turned pale. ¶ *Into corruption.* The phrase here used means literally "into destruction." The sense is, that by the change that came over him, his beauty—his bright or florid complexion was completely *destroyed.* He became deadly pale.

9. *Yet heard I the voice of his words.* What the angel said when he appeared to him Daniel has not recorded. He says (ver. 6) that the voice of his words was "like the voice of a multitude." It is probable that those who were with him had heard that voice, and hearing it, and being struck with the remarkable character of the vision, they had suddenly fled in alarm. Daniel heard more distinctly what he said, though it does not yet appear that he had heard anything more than the *sound* of his voice. ¶ *And when I heard the voice of his words, then was I in a deep sleep on my face.* Comp. Notes on ch. viii. 18. Lengerke renders this, "I *sank* into a deep sleep," &c. This is undoubtedly the meaning, that when he heard this voice he was overcome, and sank prostrate and senseless upon the earth. The sense of the Hebrew may be thus expressed : "I became (הָיִיתִי) oppressed with sleep," &c.

10. *And, behold, an hand touched me.* The hand of the angel. Comp. ch. viii. 18. ¶ *Which set me upon my knees and* upon *the palms of my hands.* Not "upright," as in ch. viii. 18. That is, he had not strength given him at once to stand erect, but he was partially raised up and enabled to move, though in a feeble and tottering manner. The word here used (נוֹעַ) means to move to and fro ; to waver ; to vacillate ; and the sense here, as expressed by Gesenius (*Lex.*) is, "lo, a hand touched me, and caused me to reel (*i.e.*, to stand reeling and trembling) upon my knees and hands." He was gradually restored to strength.

11. *And he said unto me, O Daniel, a man greatly beloved.* That is, in heaven. Marg., as in Heb., *of desires.* See Notes on ch. ix. 23. ¶ *Understand the words that I speak unto thee.* That is, attend to them, implying that he would be able to understand them. ¶ *And stand upright.* Marg., as in Heb., *upon thy standing.* That is, stand erect. See Notes on ch. viii. 18.

12. *Then said he unto me, Fear not.*

understand, and to chasten thyself before thy God, thy words were heard, ^a and I am come for thy words.

13 But the prince of the kingdom of Persia withstood me one and twenty days: but, lo, Michael, ¹ one of the chief princes, came to help me; and I remained there with the kings of Persia.

a Acts 10. 30, 31.

1 or, *the first.* Jude 9; Rev. 12. 7.

Be not alarmed at my presence; do not fear that your devotions are not accepted, and that your prayers are not heard. ¶ *For from the first day that thou didst set thine heart to understand.* That is, by a season of extraordinary devotion. Daniel had devoted three full weeks to such a service (vers. 2, 3), and it would seem from this that one object which he had in view was to make inquiry about the future condition of his people, or to learn what was his own duty in the present circumstances, or what methods he might use to secure the return of his countrymen to their own land. The circumstances of the case were such as to make either of these inquiries proper; and the angel now affirms that, from the first day when he entered on these investigations, he was despatched to come to him, and to assure him that his prayer was heard. The reason why he had not sooner arrived, and why Daniel was left to continue his prayers so long without any answer being returned, is stated in the following verses. Comp. Notes on ch. ix. 23. ¶ *And to chasten thyself before thy God.* That is, by fasting and humiliation. Literally, *to afflict thyself.* ¶ *Thy words were heard.* In heaven. Another proof that prayer is at once heard, though the answer may be long delayed. The instance before us shows that the answer to prayer may *seem* to be delayed, from causes unknown to us, though the prayer ascends at once to heaven, and God *designs* to answer it. In this case, it was deferred by the detention of the messenger on the way (ver. 13); in other cases it may be from a different cause; but it should never be set down as a proof that prayer is not heard, and that it will not be answered, because the answer is not granted at once. Weeks, or months, or years may elapse before the Divine purpose shall be made known, though, so to speak, the messenger may be on his way to us. Something may prevent the answer being borne to us; some "prince of the kingdom of Persia" may withstand the messenger; some cause which we may not know may hinder the immediate answer of our prayer, either in our own hearts, or in outward events which cannot at once be controlled without a miracle, or in the feelings and views of our friends whom we seek to have converted and saved; but the purpose to answer the prayer may have been simultaneous with its being offered, and a train of measures may have been commenced at once to bring about the result, though many weeks or months of delay, of anxiety, of tears, may elapse before we attain the object we desired. Daniel would have been cheered in his days of fasting and service if he had known that an angel was *on his way* to him to comfort him, and to communicate to him an answer from God; often—if not *always*—in our days of deepest anxiety and trouble; when our prayers seem not to penetrate the skies; when we meet with no response; when the thing for which we pray seems to be withheld; when our friends remain unconverted; when irreligion abounds and prevails; when we seem to be doing no good, and when calamity presses upon us, if we saw the arrangement which God was already making to answer the prayer, and could see the messenger on the way, our hearts would exult, and our tears would cease to flow. And why, in our days of trouble and anxiety, should we not believe that it *is* so; and that God, even though the delay may seem to be long, will yet show himself to be a hearer and an answerer of prayer?

13. *But the prince of the kingdom of Persia.* In explaining this very difficult verse, it may be proper (1) to

consider the literal sense of the words; (2) to deduce the fair meaning of the passage as thus explained; and (3) to notice the practical truths taught.

The word rendered *prince*—שַׂר *săr*— means, properly, a leader, commander, chief, as of troops, Gen. xxi. 22; of a king's body-guard, Gen. xxxvii. 36; of cup-bearers, Gen. xli. 9; of a prison, Gen. xxxix. 21, 22; of a flock, Gen. xlvii. 6. Then it means a prince, a noble, a chief in the state, Gen. xii. 15. In Dan. viii. 25, in the phrase "Prince of princes," it refers to God. So far as the *word* is concerned in the phrase "prince of the kingdom of Persia," it might refer to a prince ruling over that kingdom, or to a prime minister of the state; but the language also is such that it is applicable to an angelic being supposed to preside over a state, or to influence its counsels. If this idea is admitted; if it is believed that angels *do* thus preside over particular states, this language would properly express that fact. Gesenius (*Lex.*) explains it in this passage as denoting the "chiefs, princes, and angels; *i.e.*, the archangels acting as patrons and advocates of particular nations before God." That this is the proper meaning here as deduced from the words is apparent, for (*a*) it is an angel that is speaking, and it would seem most natural to suppose that he had encountered one of his own rank; (*b*) the mention of Michael who came to his aid—a name which, as we shall see, properly denotes an angel, leads to the same conclusion; (*c*) it accords, also, with the prevailing belief on the subject. Undoubtedly, one who takes into view all the circumstances referred to in this passage would most naturally understand this of an angelic being, having some kind of jurisdiction over the kingdom of Persia. What was the *character* of this "prince," however, whether he was a good or bad angel, is not intimated by the language. It is only implied that he had a chieftainship, or some species of guardian care over that kingdom—watching over its interests and directing its affairs. As he offered resistance, however, to this heavenly messenger on his way to Daniel, as it was necessary to counteract his plans, and as the aid of Michael was required to overcome his opposition, the fair construction is, that he belonged to the class of evil angels. ¶ *Withstood me.* Heb., "stood over against me." Vulgate, *restitit mihi.* The fair meaning is, that he resisted or opposed him; that he stood over against him, and delayed him on his way to Daniel. In what manner he did this is not stated. The most obvious interpretation is, that, in order to answer the prayers of Daniel in respect to his people, it was necessary that some arrangement should be made in reference to the kingdom of Persia —influencing the government to be favourable to the restoration of the Jews to their own land; or removing some obstacles to such return—obstacles which had given Daniel such disquietude, and which had been thrown in his way by the presiding angel of that kingdom. ¶ *One and twenty days.* During the whole time in which Daniel was engaged in fasting and prayer (vers. 2, 3). The angel had been sent forth to make arrangements to secure the answer to his prayer when he began to pray, but had been delayed during all that time by the opposition which he had met with in Persia. That is, it required all that time to overcome the obstacles existing there to the accomplishment of these purposes, and to make those arrangements which were necessary to secure the result. Meantime, Daniel, not knowing that these arrangements were in a process of completion, or that an angel was employed to secure the answer to his prayers, yet strong in faith, was suffered to continue his supplications with no intimation that his prayers were heard, or that he would be answered. How many arrangements may there be in progress designed to answer our prayers of which we know nothing! How many agents may be employed to bring about an answer! What mighty obstacles may be in a process of removal, and what changes may be made, and what influences exerted, while we are suffered to pray, and fast, and weep, amidst many discouragements, and many trials of our faith and patience!

For a much longer period than Daniel was engaged in his devotions, may we be required often now to pray before the arrangements in the course of Providence shall be so far complete that we shall receive an answer to our supplications, for the things to be done may extend far into future months or years. ¶ *But, lo, Michael, one of the chief princes.* Marg., *the first.* That is, the first in rank of the "princes," or the angels. In other words, "Michael, the archangel." The proper meaning of this name (מִיכָאֵל) is, "Who as God," and is a name given, undoubtedly, from some resemblance to God. The exact reason *why* it is given is not anywhere stated; but may it not be this—that one looking on the majesty and glory of the chief of the angels would instinctively ask, "Who, after all, is like God? Even this lofty angel, with all his glory, cannot be compared to the high and lofty One." Whatever may have been the reason of the appellation, however, the name in the Scriptures has a definite application, and is given to the chief one of the angels. Comp. Notes on Jude 9. The word *Michael*, as a proper name, occurs several times in the Scriptures, Nu. xiii. 13 ; 1 Ch. v. 13 ; vi. 40; vii. 3; viii. 16 ; xii. 20 ; xxvii. 18 ; 2 Chron. xxi. 2 ; Ezra viii. 8. It is used as applicable to an angel or archangel in the following places : Dan. x. 13, 21; xii. 1; Jude 9 ; Rev. xii. 7. Little more is known of him than (*a*) that he occupied the rank which entitled him to be called an archangel ; and (*b*) that he sustained, in the time of Daniel, the relation of patron of Israel before God (ch. x. 21). That an *angel* is referred to here is manifest ; for, (1.) It occurs in the account of transactions conducted by an angel. (2.) The use of the word elsewhere leads to this supposition. (3.) What is said to have been done is the appropriate work of an angel. This is apparent, because Gabriel, the speaker, says that what was done was beyond *his* power to accomplish. He was effectually resisted and thwarted by the counsels of Persia, until one of higher wisdom and rank than himself came to his aid. He could, therefore, have been no less than an angel, and was clearly a being of a higher rank than Gabriel himself. (4.) The phrase "one of the chief princes" sustains this interpretation. It implies that he was one of those who held an exalted rank among those who are called "princes," and if this word in this connection denotes *angels*, then Michael was an angel, and one of the most exalted of the angels. This accords with the appellation given to him by Jude — "the archangel." ¶ *Came to help me.* He does not state in what way this was done, but it is fairly implied that it was by securing better counsels at the court of Persia —counsels more favourable to the Hebrews, and different from those which would have been carried out under the auspices of him who is called "the prince of Persia." There is nothing in the passage to forbid the supposition that it was by so influencing the mind of the king and his ministers as to dispose them to favour the return of the Jews, or to afford them facilities to rebuild their temple, or to remove some of the obstacles which would tend to prevent their restoration. ¶ *And I remained there with the kings of Persia.* The *kings* of Persia here, in the plural, must mean the *rulers.* There was properly but one *king* of that nation, though the name may have been given to subordinate rulers, or perhaps to those who *had been* kings in their own country, and whose countries had been subdued by the Persian arms, and who now resided, with more or less authority, at the Persian court. The phrase "I remained there" has been variously translated. The Vulgate renders it as in our version. The Greek, "And I left him [to wit, Michael] there with the prince of the kingdom of Persia." The Syriac, "And I was hindered there against the prince of the Persians." Luther, "Then obtained I the victory with the kings in Persia." Lengerke, "Then obtained I the ascendency (Vorrang) among the kings of Persia." That is, as he explains it, " I obtained the victory ; I secured this result that my counsel in behalf of the Jewish people prevailed," p. 503. The same explanation is given by Geier,

Gesenius, De Wette, Hävernick. The word יָתַר (*Yáthar*) properly means, to hang out and over ; to be redundant ; to remain or be left ; to be over and above ; to excel, &c. Hence the notion in Niphal, of excelling others, of getting the ascendency, of obtaining a victory. This is, undoubtedly, the meaning here, for he was not *left* with the kings of Persia ; he did not *remain* there. The true idea is, that by the help of Michael, who came to his aid, he was enabled so far to influence the Persian counsels against the purposes of him who is called the "prince of Persia," as to secure the favours for the Hebrew people which Daniel sought by prayer ; and having done this, he came at once to him. The only delay in the case was that which was caused by the purposes of the Persian court, and by the difficulty of securing such arrangements there as to favour the Hebrew people, and to facilitate their return to their own country. Having done this, he came at once to Daniel to announce the long series of events which would follow pertaining to his people, and in reference to which his mind had been so much affected during his protracted period of devotion.

Such is the explanation of the literal meaning of this difficult passage. Now, in reference to the second point suggested as necessary to its proper interpretation — its real meaning — the exact truth taught in it, the following remarks may be made :—(1.) There was early a prevailing opinion that special angels had the charge of individuals, as their guardians ; and the same idea existed respecting nations, that their affairs were assigned to particular celestial beings. This notion among the Hebrews was found in *this* form—that they were *angels*, or *created* beings of exalted rank who thus presided over the affairs of men. Among the Greeks, and other heathen nations, the form which it took was, that they were *gods* or tutelary divinities, and hence each people, each class, each family, each house, had its own god. The Hebrews never approximated to this opinion so far as to suppose that these beings were divine, or that they occupied the place of the supreme God—JEHOVAH — who was peculiarly their covenant God, and who was the only true God. They did admit the supposition, however, that there might be guardian angels of their own nation, and the same idea seems to have prevailed among them in regard to other nations. This is clearly the idea in the passage before us, that while Michael was, in a peculiar sense, intrusted with the affairs of the Hebrew people, there were intelligent invisible beings of angelic rank who presided over other nations, and who influenced their counsels. It does not appear by any means that it was supposed that in all cases these were *good* beings, for the counsels of the nations were too often malignant and evil to admit of this supposition. In the case before us, it is evidently supposed that the influence of the presiding angel of Persia was adverse to that which was right, and such as should be counteracted by one who came from heaven. Comp. Notes on Eph. ii. 2. (2.) No one can demonstrate that this is *not* so. The existence of wicked angels is no more incredible in itself than the existence of wicked men, and that they should influence nations and rulers is in itself no more improbable than that distinguished statesmen should. There may be, indeed, no foundation for the opinion that particular angels are *assigned* to particular individuals or nations as peculiar *guardians ;* but it may be true, notwithstanding, that some one of these fallen spirits—for if there are *any* such beings at all, they are numerous—may have special influence over a particular individual or nation. If it be said that we know too little about this to enable us to make any positive statements in *favour* of this opinion, it should also be said that we know too little to enable us to make any positive statements *against* it ; and for aught any one can prove, it *may* be so. No one has a right to assume that it is not so ; no one can demonstrate that it is not so. It may be said further, that things look *as if* this were so. There are many influences on nations and individuals ; many things that occur that can be most easily accounted for on the supposition that there is such an agency from some invisible quarter. If we admit the reality of such influence, and such interpositions, the things which occur are more easily explained than if we deny it. There are measures taken ; plans proposed ; influences exerted; schemes adopted— there are things from an unseen quarter to give prosperity, or to thwart the best laid plans, that cannot be well explained without the supposition of such an interference ; things which perplex all philosophers and all historians in accounting for them ; things which cannot be anticipated or explained on any known principles of human nature. If we admit the reality of the influence of invisible beings, as in the case before us, the solution becomes comparatively easy; at least we find phenomena just such as we should expect on such a supposition. (3.) It may be added, also, in regard to the particular case before us (a) that the counsels *against* the Jews to prevent their return to their own land, and to embarrass them, were such as we should anticipate on the supposition that an evil angel—an enemy of God and his people—had influenced the Persian rulers; and (b) that the changes wrought *in* those counsels in favour of the Jews, facilitating their return to their own land, were such as we should expect to find on the supposition that those counsels and plans were overruled and changed by the interposition say of Gabriel and Michael. And similar events often happen. There are such changes in the counsels of nations, and in the minds of rulers, as *would* occur on the supposition that superior beings were engaged in thwarting evil plans, and influencing those who have the power to do right. In reference to the Jews in their exile, there had been a long series of acts of opposition and oppression pursued by the governments of the East, *as if* under the direction of some malignant spirit; then a series of acts in their favour followed, *as if* the change had been brought about by the interposition of some benignant angel. These facts are the historical basis on which the representation is here made.

In reference to the third point suggested pertaining to this passage—the practical truths taught that may be of use to us—it may be remarked that the *great* truth is, that the answer to prayer is often delayed, not by any indisposition on the part of God to answer it, and not by any purpose *not* to answer it, and not by the mere intention of trying our faith, but *by the necessary arrangements to bring it about.* It is of such a nature that it *cannot* be answered at once. It requires *time* to make important changes ; to influence the minds of men ; to remove obstacles; to raise up friends ; to put in operation agencies that shall secure the thing desired. There is some obstacle to be overcome. There is some plan of evil to be checked and stayed. There is some agency to be used which is not now in existence, and which is to be created. The opposition of the "prince of Persia" could not be overcome at once, and it was necessary to bring in the agency of a higher power—that of Michael—to effect the change. This could not be done in a moment, a day, or a week, and hence the long delay of three "full weeks" before Daniel had an assurance that his prayers would be answered. So it often happens now. We pray for the conversion of a child; yet there may be obstacles to his conversion, unseen by us, which are to be patiently removed, and perhaps by a foreign influence, before it can be done. Satan may have already secured a control over his heart, which is to be broken gradually, before the prayer shall be answered. We pray for the removal of the evils of intemperance, of slavery, of superstition, of idolatry; yet these may be so interlocked with the customs of a country, with the interests of men, and with the laws, that they cannot be at once eradicated except by miracle, and the answer to the prayer seems to be long delayed. We pray for the universal spread of the gospel of Christ; yet how many obstacles are to be overcome, and how many arrangements made, before this prayer can be fully answered; and how many tears are to be shed, and perils encountered, and lives sacrificed, before the prayer of the church shall be

14 Now I am come to make thee understand what shall befall thy people in the latter *a* days : for *b* yet the vision *is* for *many* days.

15 And when he had spoken such words unto me, I set my face toward the ground, and I became dumb.

16 And, behold, *one* like the

a Gen. 49. 1; 2 Tim. 3. 1.
b ch. 8. 26; Hab. 2. 3.

similitude of the sons of men touched *c* my lips : then I opened my mouth and spake, and said unto him that stood before me, O my lord, by the vision my sorrows are turned upon me, and I have retained no strength.*d*

17 For how can ¹ the servant of this my lord talk with this my lord?

c Isa. 6. 7; Jer. 1. 9.
d ver. 8.   1 or, *this servant of.*

---

fully answered, and the earth shall be filled with the knowledge of the Lord. The *duty*, then, which is taught, is that of patience, of perseverance, of faith in God, of a firm belief that he is true to all his promises, and that he is a hearer of prayer—though the blessing seems long delayed.

14. *Now I am come to make thee understand*, &c. After these long delays, and after the arrangements have been made necessary to bring about the objects sought by your prayers. ¶ *In the latter days.* In future times—extending down to the last period of the world. See Notes on Isa. ii. 2. ¶ *For yet the vision* is *for* many *days.* Extends far into future time. It is probable that the prayer of Daniel referred more particularly to what he desired should soon occur—the restoration of the people to their own land; the angel informs him that the disclosures which he was to make covered a much more extended period, and embraced more important events. So it is often. The answer to prayer often includes much more than we asked for, and the abundant blessings that are conferred, beyond what we supplicate, are vastly beyond a compensation for the delay.

15. *And when he had spoken such words*, &c. Daniel was naturally overcome by the communication which had been made to him. The manner in which the prayer was answered seems to have been entirely different from what he had expected. The presence of a heavenly being; the majesty of his appearance; the assurance that he gave that he had come to answer his prayer; and the fact that he had important revelations to make respecting

the future, overcame him, and he laid his face upon the ground in silence. Is there any one of us who would *not* be awed into profound silence if a heavenly messenger should stand before us to disclose what was to occur to us, to our families, to our friends, to our country, in far-distant years ?

16. *And, behold,* one *like the similitude of the sons of men touched my lips.* In the form of a man. The reference here is undoubtedly to Gabriel appearing to Daniel in human form. Why he does not *name* him is unknown ; nor is there any intimation whether he changed his form as he now approached the prophet. It would seem not improbable that, seeing the effect of his presence and his words on Daniel, he laid aside some of the manifestations of awe and majesty in which he had at first appeared to him, and approached him as a man, and placed his hands on his lips—as a sign that he should speak, or as imparting power to him to speak. See Notes on Isa. vi. 6, 7. ¶ *I opened my mouth, and spake.* His fear was removed, and he was now able to address the heavenly messenger. ¶ *O my lord.* A title of respectful address, but without indicating the rank of him to whom it is applied. ¶ *By the vision my sorrows are turned upon me.* The word rendered *sorrows* (צִירִים) means, properly, *writhings, throes, pains,* as of a woman in travail, Isa. xiii. 8; xxi. 3; 1 Sam. iv. 19; and then *any* deep pain or anguish. Here it refers to *terror* or *fright,* as so great as to prostrate the strength of Daniel. The word rendered *are turned* (נֶהֶפְכוּ—from הָפַךְ)

for as for me, straightway there remained no strength in me, neither is there breath left in me.

18 Then there came again and touched me *one* like the appearance of a man, and he strengthened me,

19 And said, O man greatly beloved, fear not; peace *be* unto thee; be strong, yea, be strong. And when he had spoken unto me, I was strengthened, and said, Let my lord speak; for *a* thou hast strengthened me.

20 Then said he, Knowest thou wherefore I come unto thee? and

a 2 Cor. 12. 9.

---

means, in Niphal, to turn one's self about, to turn back. The same phrase which is here used occurs also in 1 Sam. iv. 19, "her pains turned upon her;" that is, came upon her. Perhaps *we* should express the idea by saying that they *rolled* upon us, or over us—like the surges of the ocean.

17. *For how can the servant of this my lord.* Acknowledging his humble and lowly condition and rank in the presence of an angel—a messenger now sent from heaven. ¶ *Neither is there breath left in me.* That is, he was utterly overcome and prostrate. He felt that he was incapable of speaking in the presence of one who had descended from God.

18. *Then there came again and touched me,* &c. The same one is here referred to doubtless who is mentioned in ver. 16—the angel. He came to him again in this condescending and familiar manner in order to allay his fears, and to prepare him to receive his communications with entire calmness.

19. *And said, O man greatly beloved.* See Notes on ch. ix. 23. ¶ *Fear not.* Neither at my presence, nor at what I have to say. There was nothing in the visitation of an angel that could be a ground of dread to a good man; there was nothing in what he had to communicate that could be a reasonable cause of alarm. ¶ *Be strong, yea, be strong.* These are words of encouragement such as we address to those who are timid and fearful. We exhort them not to yield; to make a vigorous effort to meet danger, difficulty, or trial. ¶ *Let my lord speak.* That is, I am now prepared to receive what you have to communicate. ¶ *For thou hast strengthened me.* By your encouraging words, and by the kindness of your manner.

20. *Then said he, Knowest thou*

wherefore I come unto thee? This was known by what the angel had said in ver. 14. He seems to have called his attention to it, and to have proposed the question, because Daniel had been so overcome by his fright that it might be doubtful whether he had understood him distinctly when he had told him the object of his coming. He therefore proposes the question here; and as the silence of Daniel seems to have been construed as a declaration that he *did* understand the purpose of the visit, he proceeds to unfold fully the purport of his message. ¶ *And now will I return.* That is, evidently, after he had made known to him the message which he came to deliver. He cannot mean that he would *then* leave Daniel, and return immediately to Persia, for he proceeds at length (ch. xi., xii.) to deliver his message to him, and to state what would occur in the world in future times. ¶ *To fight with the prince of Persia.* In ver. 13, he says that he had had a contest with that "prince," and that in consequence of that he had been delayed on his journey to Daniel. By the interposition of Michael, the affairs of Persia had been so arranged that the opposition to what was desired by Daniel had been in part removed—so far, at least, as to make it certain that his prayers would be answered. See Notes on that verse. But still it would seem that the difficulty was not entirely overcome, and that it would be desirable for him to return, and to complete the arrangements which had been commenced. There were still causes in existence in Persia which might tend to frustrate all these plans unless they were counteracted, and his presence might still be necessary there to secure the safe return of the exiles to their own land, and the means renow will I return to fight with the prince *a* of Persia: and when I am

a ver 13.

quired to rebuild the city and temple. The simple meaning of this is, that it would be necessary to exert a farther influence at the Persian court in order to bring about the object desired; and this fact is expressed in language derived from the belief that angelic beings, good and bad, have much to do in controlling the minds of men. ¶ *And when I am gone forth.* Literally, "and I go forth." The meaning seems to be, that he would return to Persia, and would so direct affairs there that the welfare of the Jews would be promoted, and that protection would be extended to them. This, he says, he would continue as long as it was necessary, for when *he* should have gone forth, the king of Greece would come, and the affairs of Persia would be put on a new footing, but on such a footing as not to require *his* presence—for the government would be of itself favourable to the Jews. The sense is, that up to the time when this "king of Grecia" should come, there would be a state of things in the Persian court that would demand the presence of some being from heaven—exerting some constant influence to prevent an outbreak against the Jews, and to secure their peace and prosperity; but that when the "king of Grecia" should come, he would himself favour their cause, and render the presence of the angel unnecessary. No one can prove that this is *not* a correct representation, or that the favour shown to the Jews at the Persian court during all the time of the rebuilding of the city and the temple, was not to be traced to some presiding influence from above, or that that was not put forth in connection with the ministration of an angelic being. Indeed, it is in accordance with all the teachings of the Bible that the disposition of kings and princes to show favour to the people of God, like all else that is good in this world, is to be traced to an influence from above; and it is not contrary to any of the laws of analogy, or anything with which we are ac-

gone forth, lo, the prince of Grecia shall come.

21 But I will show thee that

quainted pertaining to the spiritual world, to suppose that angelic interposition may be employed in any case in bringing about that which is good ¶ *Lo, the prince of Grecia shall come* Hebrew, *Javan*—יָוָן. There can be no doubt that Greece is intended. The word properly denotes Ionia (derived from this word), "the name of which province," says Gesenius, "as being adjacent to the East, and better known, was extended so as to comprehend the whole of Greece, as is expressly said by Greek writers themselves."—*Lex.* By the "prince of Greece" here, there can be no doubt that there is reference to Alexander the Great, who conquered Persia. See ch. xi. 1–4. The meaning here is, that when he should come, and conquer Persia, the opposition which the Hebrews had encountered from that country would cease, and there would then be no need of the interposition of the angel at the Persian court. The matter of fact was, that the Hebrews were favoured by Alexander the Great, and that whatever there was in the Persian or Chaldean power which they had had reason to dread was then brought to an end, for all those Eastern governments were absorbed in the empire of Alexander—the Macedonian monarchy.

21. *But I will show thee that which is noted in the scripture of truth.* The word *noted* here means *written*, or *recorded.* The *scripture of truth* means the *true writing*, and the reference is doubtless to the Divine purposes or decrees in this matter—for (*a*) there is no other writing where these things were then found; (*b*) the angel came to make known what could be known in no other way, and therefore what was not yet found in any book to which man had access; (*c*) this language accords with common representations in the Scriptures respecting future events. They are described as written down in a book that is in the hands of God, in which are recorded

which is noted in the scripture of truth: and *there is* none that

1 *strengtheneth himself.*

holdeth[1] with me in these things, but Michael [a] your prince.

a ver. 13.

all future events—the names of those that shall be saved—and all the deeds of men. Comp. Deut. xxxii. 34; Mal. iii. 16; Ps. cxxxix. 16; Rev. v. 1. The representation is figurative, of course; and the meaning is, that, in the view of the Divine mind, all future events are as certain as if they were actually recorded as history, or as if they were now all written down. The angel came that he might unfold a portion of that volume, and disclose the contents of its secret pages; that is, describe an important series of events of great interest to the Jewish people and to the world at large. ¶ *And there is* none *that holdeth with me in these things.* Marg., *strengtheneth himself.* So the Hebrew. The idea is, that there was none that rendered aid in this matter, or that stood by him, and would accomplish the designs which he was meditating in their behalf pertaining to Persia. The angel saw that there were powerful influences against the interests of the Hebrew people at work in the court of Persia; that it was necessary that they should be counteracted; that unless this were done, fearful calamities would come upon the Jewish people, and they would be subjected to great embarrassments in their efforts to rebuild their city and temple, and he says that there was no one whose aid could be permanently and certainly relied on but that of Michael. He himself was to return to the court of Persia to endeavour to counteract the influence of the "prince of Persia," but, as in the former case when on his way to Daniel (ver. 13), he would not have been able to counteract the machinations of that prince if it had not been for the interposition of Michael, so he felt now that reliance was still to be placed on his assistance in the matter. ¶ *But Michael your prince.* See Notes on ver. 13. The patron, or guardian of your people, and of their interests. The idea intended to be conveyed here undoubtedly is, that Michael was a guardian angel for the

Jewish people; that he had special charge of their affairs; that his interposition might be depended on in the time of trouble and danger, and that, under him, their interests would be safe. No one can prove that this is *not* so; and as on earth some of the most important favours that we enjoy are conferred by the instrumentality of others; as we are often defended when in danger by them; as we are counselled and directed by them; as God raises up for the orphan, and the widow, and the insane, and the sorrowful, and the feeble, those of wealth, and power, and learning, who can better guard their interests than they could themselves, and as these relations are often sustained, and these favours conferred by those who are invisible to the recipients, so it gives, in a higher sense, a new beauty to the arrangements of the universe to suppose that this benevolent office is often undertaken and discharged by angelic beings. Thus they may defend us from danger; ward off the designs of our enemies; defeat their machinations, and save us from numberless evils that would otherwise come upon us. This view receives additional confirmation, if it be admitted that there are *evil* angels, and that they seek the ruin of mankind. They are malignant; they tempt the race of man; they have power far superior to our own; they can set in operation a train of evil influences which we can neither foresee nor counteract; and they can excite the minds of wicked men to do us injury in a way which we cannot anticipate, and against which we cannot defend ourselves. In these circumstances, any one can perceive that there is concinnity and propriety in the supposition that there are good beings of a higher order who feel an interest in the welfare of man, and who come to us, on their benevolent errand, to defend us from danger, and to aid us in our efforts to escape from the perils of our fallen condition, and to reach the kingdom of heaven.

CHAPTER XI.

ANALYSIS OF THE CHAPTER.

This chapter contains a portion of those things which the angel said were written in "the scripture of truth," and which he came to disclose to Daniel. The revelation also embraces the twelfth chapter, and the two comprise the last recorded communication that was made to Daniel. The revelation which is made in these chapters not only embraces a large portion of history of interest to the Jewish people of ancient times, and designed to give instruction as to the important events that would pertain to their nation, but also, in its progress, alludes to important *periods* in the future as marking decisive eras in the world's history, and contains hints as to what would occur down to the end of all things.

The chapter before us embraces the following definitely marked periods:—

I. The succession of kings in Persia to the time of a mighty king who should arouse all the strength of his kingdom to make war on Greece—referring doubtless to Xerxes, vers. 1, 2. Of those kings in Persia there would be three—three so prominent as to deserve notice in the rapid glance at future events—Cambyses, Smerdis, and Darius Hystaspis.

II. After this succession of kings, one would stand up or appear who would be characterized as ruling "with great dominion," and "according to his will," ver. 3. The dominion evidently would pass into his hand, and he would be distinguished from all that went before him. There can be no doubt, from the connection, and from what is said in ver. 4, that the reference here is to Alexander the Great.

III. The state of the empire after the death of this mighty king, ver. 4. His kingdom would be broken, and would be divided into four parts—referring doubtless to the division of the empire of Alexander after his death.

IV. The history then proceeds to notice the events that would pertain to *two* of these portions of the empire —the conflicts between the king of the south, and the king of the north—or between Egypt and Syria, vers. 5–19. This portion of the history embraces, in detail, an account of the policy, the negotiations, and the wars of Antiochus the Great, till the time of his death. These kingdoms are particularly referred to, probably because their conflicts would affect the holy land, and pertain ultimately to the history of religion, and its establishment and triumph in the world. In the notice of these two sovereignties, there is considerable detail—so much so that the principal events could have been readily anticipated by those who were in possession of the writings of Daniel. The destiny of the other two portions of the empire of Alexander did not particularly affect the history of religion, or pertain to the holy land, and therefore they are not introduced. In a particular manner, the history of Antiochus the Great is traced with great minuteness in this portion of the prophecy, because his doings had a special bearing on the Jewish nation, and were connected with the progress of religion. The commentary on this portion of the chapter will show that the leading events are traced *as* accurately as would be a summary of the history made out *after* the transactions had occurred.

V. A brief reference to the successor of Antiochus the Great, Seleucus IV., ver. 20. As he occupied the throne, however, but for a short period, and as his doings did not particularly affect the condition of the Hebrew people, or the interests of religion, and his

CHAPTER XI.

ALSO I, in the first ^a year of Darius the Mede, *even* I stood

a ch. 9. 1.

reign was, in every respect, unimportant, it is passed over with only a slight notice.

VI. The life and acts of Antiochus Epiphanes, vers. 21–45. There can be no doubt that this portion of the chapter refers to Antiochus, and it contains a full detail of his character and of his doings. The account here, though without naming him, is just such as would have been given by one who should have written *after* the events had occurred, and there is no more difficulty in applying the description in this chapter to him now than there would have been in such a historical narrative. The revelation is made, evidently, to prepare the Jewish people for these fearful events, and these heavy trials, in their history; and also to assure them that more glorious results would follow, and that deliverance would succeed these calamities. In the troubles which Antiochus would bring upon the Hebrew people, it was important that they should have before them a record containing the great outlines of what would occur, and the assurance of ultimate triumph—just as it is important for us now in the trials which we have reason to anticipate in this life, to have before us in the Bible the permanent record that we shall yet find deliverance. In the twelfth chapter, therefore, the angel directs the mind onward to brighter times, and assures Daniel that there would be a day of rejoicing.

1. *Also I.* I the angel. He alludes here to what he had done on a former occasion to promote the interests of the Hebrew people, and to secure those arrangements which were necessary

to confirm and to strengthen him.
2 And now will I show ^a thee

a Amos 3. 7.

for their welfare—particularly in the favourable disposition of Darius the Mede towards them. ¶ *In the first year of Darius the Mede.* See Notes on ch. v. 31. He does not here state the things contemplated or done by Darius in which he had confirmed or strengthened him, but there can be no reasonable doubt that it was the purpose which he had conceived to restore the Jews to their own land, and to give them permission to rebuild their city and temple. Comp. ch. ix. 1. It was in that year that Daniel offered his solemn prayer, as recorded in ch. ix.; in that year that, according to the time predicted by Jeremiah (see Dan. ix. 2), the captivity would terminate; and in that year that an influence from above led the mind of the Persian king to contemplate the restoration of the captive people. Cyrus was, indeed, the one through whom the edict for their return was promulgated; but as he reigned under his uncle Cyaxares or Darius, and as Cyaxares was the source of authority, it is evident that *his* mind must have been influenced to grant this favour, and it is to this that the angel here refers. ¶ *I stood to confirm and to strengthen him.* Comp. Notes on ch. x. 13. It would seem that the mind of Darius was not wholly decided; that there were adverse influences bearing on it: that there were probably counsellors of his realm who advised against the proposed measures, and the angel here says that *he* stood by him, and confirmed him in his purpose, and secured the execution of his benevolent plan. Who can prove that an angel may not exert an influence on the heart of kings? And what class of men is there who, when they *intend* to do good and right, are more likely to have their purposes changed by evil counsellors than kings; and who are there that more need a heavenly influence to confirm their design to do right?

2. *And now will I show thee the truth.* That is, the truth about events that are to occur in the future, and which

the truth. Behold, there shall stand up yet three kings in Persia;

and the fourth shall be far richer than *they* all: and by his strength

will accord with what is written in "the scripture of truth," chap. x. 21. ¶ *Behold, there shall stand up yet three kings in Persia.* The phrase "stand up," means that there would *be* so many kings in Persia; that is, there would be three *before* the fourth which he mentions. The same Hebrew word here rendered *stand up* (עָמַד) occurs in vers. 3, 4, 6–8, 14–16 (twice), 17, 20, 21, 25, 31; also in ch. xii. 1, 13. In ver. 8 it is rendered *continue;* in ver. 15, *withstand;* in the other cases, *stand up,* or simply *stand.* Gesenius says it is a word used particularly of a new prince, as in Dan. viii. 23; xi. 2, 3, 20. He does not say that there would be none afterwards, but he evidently designs to touch on the great and leading events respecting the Persian empire, so far as they would affect the Hebrew people, and so far as they would constitute prominent points in the history of the world. He does not, therefore, go into all the details respecting the history, nor does he mention all the kings that would reign. The prominent, the material points, would be the reign of those three kings; then the reign of the fourth, or Xerxes, as his mad expedition to Greece would lay the real foundation for the invasion of Persia by Alexander, and the overthrow of the Persian empire; then the life and conquests of Alexander, and then the wars consequent on the division of his empire at his death. The "three kings" here referred to were Cambyses, Smerdis, and Darius Hystaspis. As this communication was made in the third year of Cyrus (ch. x. 1), these would be the next in order; and by the fourth is undoubtedly meant Xerxes. There were several kings of Persia *after* Xerxes, as Artaxerxes Longimanus, Darius Nothus, Artaxerxes Mnemon, Ochus, and Darius Codomanus, but these are not enumerated because the real ground of the invasion of Alexander, the thing which connected him with the affairs of Persia, did not oc-

cur in their reign, but it was the invasion of Greece by Xerxes. ¶ *And the fourth shall be far richer than* they *all.* That is, Xerxes—for he was the fourth in order, and the description here agrees entirely with him. He would of course inherit the wealth accumulated by these kings, and it is here implied that he would increase that wealth, or that, in some way, he would possess more than they all combined. The *wealth* of this king is here mentioned probably because the magnificence and glory of an Oriental monarch was estimated in a considerable degree by his possessions, and because his riches enabled him to accomplish his expedition into Greece. Some idea of the treasures of Xerxes may be obtained by considering, (*a*) That Cyrus had collected a vast amount of wealth by the conquest of Lydia, and the subjugation of Crœsus, its rich king, by the conquest of Asia Minor, of Armenia, and of Babylon—for it is said respecting him, "I will give thee the treasures of darkness, and hidden riches of secret places," Isa. xlv. 3: see Notes on that passage. (*b*) That Cambyses increased that wealth which he inherited from Cyrus by his victories, and by his plundering the temples wherever he came. A single case occurring in his conquests may illustrate the amount of wealth which was accumulated. On his return from Thebes, in Egypt, he caused all the temples in that city to be pillaged and burnt to the ground. But he saved from the flames gold to the amount of three hundred talents, and silver to the amount of two thousand and five hundred talents. He is also said to have carried away the famous circle of gold that encompassed the tomb of king Ozymandias, being three hundred and sixty-five cubits in circumference, on which were represented all the motions of the several constellations.—*Universal History,* iv. 140. (*c*) This was further increased by the conquests of Darius Hystaspis, and by his heavy taxes on the people. So burdensome were these taxes, that he was called

through his riches he shall stir up all against the realm of Grecia.

3 And a mighty king shall stand up, that shall rule with great do-

by the Persians, ὁ κάπηλος —the "merchant," or "hoarder." One of the first acts of Darius was to divide his kingdom into provinces for the purpose of raising tribute. "During the reign of Cyrus, and indeed of Cambyses, there were no specific tributes; but presents were made to the sovereign. On account of these and similar innovations, the Persians call Darius a merchant, Cambyses a despot, but Cyrus a parent."—Herodotus, b. iii. lxxxix. A full account of the taxation of the kingdom, and the amount of the revenue under Darius, may be seen in Herodotus, b. iii. xc.–xcvi. The sum of the tribute under Darius, according to Herodotus, was fourteen thousand five hundred and sixty talents. Besides this sum received from regular taxation, Herodotus enumerates a great amount of gold and silver, and other valuable things, which Darius was accustomed to receive annually from the Ethiopians, from the people of Colchis, from the Arabians, and from India. All this vast wealth was inherited by Xerxes, the son and successor of Darius, and the "fourth king" here referred to. Xerxes was full four years in making provision for his celebrated expedition into Greece. Of the amount of his forces, and his preparation, a full account may be seen in Herodotus, b. vii. Of his *wealth* Justin makes this remark: *Si regem spectes, divitias, non ducem, laudes: quarum tanta copia in regno ejus fuit, ut cum flumina multitudine consumerentur, opes tamen regiæ superessent.* — *Hist.* ii. 10. Comp. Diod. Sic. x. c. 3; Pliny, *Hist. Nat.* xxiii. 10; Æl. xiii. 3; Herod. iii. 96; vii. 27–29. In the city of Celænæ, Herodotus says, there lived a man named Pythius, son of Atys, a native of Lydia, who entertained Xerxes and all his army with great magnificence, and who farther engaged to supply the king with money for the war. Xerxes on this was induced to inquire of his Persian attendants who this Pythius was, and what were the resources which enabled him to make these

offers. "It is the same," they replied, "who presented your father Darius with a plane-tree and a vine of gold, and who, next to yourself, is the richest of mankind."—Herod. vii. 27.

¶ *And by his strength through his riches he shall stir up all against the realm of Grecia.* That is, all his kingdom. He was enabled to do this by his great wealth—collecting and equipping, probably, the largest army that was ever assembled. The expedition of Xerxes against Greece is too well known to need to be detailed here, and no one can fail to see the applicability of this description to that invasion. Four years were spent in preparing for this expedition, and the forces that constituted the army were gathered out of all parts of the vast empire of Xerxes, embracing, as was then supposed, all the habitable world except Greece. According to Justin, the army was composed of seven hundred thousand of his own, and three hundred thousand auxiliaries. Diodorus Siculus makes it to be about three hundred thousand men; Prideaux, from Herodotus and others, computes it to have amounted, putting all his forces by sea and land together, to two millions six hundred and forty-one thousand six hundred and ten men; and he adds that the servants, eunuchs, suttlers, and such persons as followed the camp, made as many more, so that the whole number that followed Xerxes could not have been less than *five millions.*—*Connexions*, pt. i. b. iv. vol. i. p. 410. Grotius reckons his forces at five millions two hundred and eighty-two thousand. These immense numbers justify the expression here, and show with what propriety it is applied to the hosts of Xerxes. On the supposition that this was written *after* the event, and that it was *history* instead of *prophecy*, this would be the very language which would be employed.

3. *And a mighty king shall stand up.* So far as the *language* here is concerned, it is not said whether this would be in Persia, as a successor of the "fourth king" (ver. 2), or whether

minion, and do according to his will.

4 And when he shall stand up,

his kingdom ^a shall be broken, and shall be divided toward the four

it would be in some other part of the world. The next verse, however, shows that the reference is to Alexander the Great—for to no other one is it applicable. There were several monarchs of Persia, indeed, that succeeded Xerxes before the kingdom was invaded and subdued by Alexander (see Notes on ver. 2), and these are here entirely passed over without being alluded to. It must be admitted, that one who should have read this prophecy before the events had occurred would have inferred naturally that this "mighty king that should stand up" would appear immediately *after* the "fourth," and probably that he would be his successor in the realm; but it may be remarked, (*a*) that the *language* here is not inconsistent with the facts in the case—it being literally true that such a "mighty king" did "stand up" who "ruled with great dominion, and according to his will;" (*b*) that there was no necessity in the prophetic history of referring to the acts of these intermediate kings of Persia, since they did not contribute at all to the result—it being well known that the reason alleged by Alexander for his invasion of the Persian empire was not anything which *they* had done, but the wrongs sustained by Greece in consequence of the invasion by Xerxes and his predecessor. The real *succession* of events in the case was that last invasion of Greece by Xerxes, and the consequent invasion of the Persian empire by Alexander. It was these transactions which the angel evidently meant to connect together, and hence all that was intermediate was omitted. Thus Alexander, in his letter to Darius, says: "Your ancestors entered into Macedonia, and the other parts of Greece, and did us damage, when they had received no affront from us as the cause of it; and now I, created general of the Grecians, provoked by you, and desirous of avenging the injury done by the Persians, have passed over into Asia." —Arrian, *Exped. Alex.* i. 2. ¶ *That shall rule with great dominion.* That

shall have a wide and extended empire. The *language* here would apply to any of the monarchs of Persia that succeeded Xerxes, but it would be more strictly applicable to Alexander the Great than to any prince of ancient or modern times. The whole world, except Greece, was supposed to be subject to the power of Persia; and it was one of the leading and avowed purposes of Darius and Xerxes in invading Greece, by adding that to their empire, to have the earth under their control. When, therefore, Alexander had conquered Persia, it was supposed that *he* had subdued the world; nor was it an unnatural feeling that, having done this, he, whose sole principle of action was ambition, should sit down and weep because there were no more worlds to conquer. In fact, he then swayed a sceptre more extended and mighty than any before him had done, and it is with peculiar propriety that the language here is used in regard to him. ¶ *And do according to his will.* Would be an arbitrary prince. This also was true of the Persian kings, and of Oriental despots generally; but it was eminently so of Alexander—who, in subduing kingdoms, conquering mighty armies, controlling the millions under his sway, laying the foundations of cities, and newly arranging the boundaries of empires, seemed to consult only his own will, and felt that everything was to be subordinate to it. It is said that this passage was shown to Alexander by the high-priest of the Jews, and that these prophecies did much to conciliate his favour towards the Hebrew people.

4. *And when he shall stand up.* In the might and power of his kingdom. When his power shall be fully established. I understand this, with Rosenmüller and Hävernick, as meaning, when he shall be at the height of his authority and power, then his kingdom would be broken up. The reference is, undoubtedly, to the sudden death of Alexander; and the sense

winds of heaven; and not to his posterity, nor according to his dominion which he ruled: for his

is, that his empire would not *gradually* diminish and decay, but that some event would occur, the effect of which would be to rend it into four parts. ¶ *His kingdom shall be broken.* To wit, by his death. The language is such as is properly applicable to this, and indeed implies this, for it is said that it would not be "to his posterity" —an event which might be naturally expected to occur; or, in other words, the allusion to his posterity is such language as would be employed on the supposition that the reference here is to his death. ¶ *And shall be divided toward the four winds of heaven.* Into four parts. For the remarkable fulfilment of this prediction, see the Notes on ch. viii. 8. ¶ *And not to his posterity.* See also the Notes on ch. viii. 8. ¶ *Nor according to his dominion which he ruled.* This was literally true of the division of the empire. No one of his successors ever obtained as wide a dominion as he did himself. ¶ *For his kingdom shall be plucked up.* By his death. This does not naturally mean that it would be by *conquest*, for it is said that it would be "divided towards the four winds of heaven"— language which is not properly expressive of conquest. All that is implied is met by the supposition, that at his decease the kingdom which had been founded by him, and which had been sustained by his valour and political wisdom, would fall to pieces. ¶ *Even for others beside those.* That is, to others beside those to whom it should be at first divided. Literally, *exclusively*, or *to the exclusion of*—מִלְּבַד.

The word *those* refers to his posterity; and the meaning is, that the process of division would not stop with them, or that the four portions of the empire, as thus divided, would not remain in their hands, or pass to their posterity. There would be other changes and other divisions; and it was not to be expected that just four, and no more, empires would grow out of the one which had been founded, or that when

kingdom shall be plucked up, even for others beside those.

5 ¶ And the king of the south

that one should be divided into four parts, that partition would always continue. There would be other divisions, and other princes besides those who first obtained the empire would come in, and the process of division would ultimately be carried much farther. It is unnecessary to say that this occurred in the empire founded by Alexander. It was, soon after his death, separated into four parts, but at no distant period this arrangement was broken up, and all traces of the empire, as established by him, or as divided among his four successors, wholly disappeared.

5. *And the king of the south.* The angel here leaves the general history of the empire, and confines himself, in his predictions, to two parts of it— the kingdom of the south, and the kingdom of the north; or the kingdoms to the north and the south of Palestine—that of Syria and that of Egypt; or that of the Seleucidæ, and that of the Ptolemies. The reason why he does this is not stated, but it is, doubtless, because the events pertaining to these kingdoms would particularly affect the Jewish people, and be properly connected with sacred history. Comp. Notes on chap. viii. 7, 8. The "king of the south" here is, undoubtedly, the king of Egypt. This part of the empire was obtained by Ptolemy, and was in the hands of his successors until Egypt was subdued by the Romans. Between the kingdoms of Egypt and Syria long and bloody wars prevailed, and the prospective history of these wars it is the design of the angel here to trace. As the remainder of the chapter refers to these two dynasties, till the death of the great persecutor, Antiochus Epiphanes, and as the events referred to were very important in history, and as introductory to what was to follow in the world, it may be useful here, in order to a clear exposition of the whole chapter, to present a list of these two lines of princes. It is necessary only to premise, that the death of Alexan-

shall be strong, and *one* of his princes; and he shall be strong above him, and have dominion; his dominion *shall be* a great dominion.

der the Great occurred B.C. 323; that of his brother, Philip Aridæus, B.C. 316; that of his son, Alexander Ægus, by Roxana, B.C. 309; and that a short time after this (about B.C. 306), the chief Macedonian governors and princes assumed the royal title. The following list of the succession of the Seleucidæ and the Ptolemies—or the kings of the north and the south—of Syria and Egypt, is copied from Elliott *on the Apocalypse,* iv. 123 :—

The Ptolemies.	The Seleucidæ.
B.C.	B.C.
323 Ptolemy Soter, son of Ptolemy Lagus, governor of Egypt.	323 Seleucus Nicator, governor of Babylon.
	312 ————— recovers Babylon, and the Æra of the Seleucidæ begins.
306 ————— takes the title of king of Egypt.	
284 Ptolemy Philadelphus. (It was under him that the Septuagint Greek translation of the Old Testament was made.)	
	280 Antiochus Soter.
	261 Antiochus Theus.
246 Ptolemy Euergetes.	246 Seleucus Callinicus.
	226 Seleucus Ceraunus.
	225 Antiochus the Great.
221 Ptolemy Philopator.	
204 Ptolemy Epiphanes.	
	187 Seleucus Philopator.
180 Ptolemy Philometor.	
	175 Antiochus Epiphanes.
	164 Antiochus Eupator, of whom the *Romans* assume the guardianship.

" After this, fourteen more *Syrian* kings reigned, in reigns of short and uncertain power, till Syria was occupied and formed into a Roman province under Pompey, at which time the era of the Seleucidæ properly ends; and six more *Egyptian* princes, to the death of Ptolemy Auletes, who dying B.C. 51, left his kingdom and children to Roman guardianship—one of these children being the *Cleopatra* so famous in the histories of Cæsar and Anthony." —Elliott, *ut supra.* ¶ *Shall be strong.* This is in accordance with the well-known fact. One of the most powerful of those monarchies, if not *the* most powerful, was Egypt. ¶ *And* one of *his princes; and he shall be strong above him.* The meaning of this passage is, that there would be "one of his princes," that is, of the princes of Alexander, who would be more mighty than **the** one who obtained Egypt, or the south, and that he would have a more extended dominion. The reference is, doubtless, to Seleucus Nicator, or the conqueror. In the division of the empire he obtained Syria, Babylonia, Media, Susiana, Armenia, a part of Cappadocia, and Cilicia, and his kingdom stretched from the Hellespont to the Indus. See Notes on ch. viii. 8. Comp. Arrian, *Exp. Alex.* vii. 22; Appian, p. 618; and Lengerke, *in loc.* The proper translation of this passage probably would be, "And the king of the south shall be mighty. But from among his princes [the princes of Alexander] also there shall be [one] who shall be mightier than he, and he shall reign, and his dominion shall be a great dominion." It was of these two dominions that the angel spake, and hence follows, through the remainder of the chapter, the history pertaining to them and their successors.

6 And in the end of years they shall ¹ join themselves together; for the king's daughter of the south shall come to the king of the north to make an ² agreement: but she shall not retain the power of the

1 *associate.*

2 *rights.*

Seleucus Nicator reigned from B.C. 312 to B.C. 280—or thirty-two years. In his time lived Berosus and Megasthenes, referred to in the Introduction to ch. iv.

6. *And in the end of years.* In the future periods of the history of these two kingdoms. The event here referred to did not occur during the lives of these two kings, Seleucus Nicator and Ptolemy Soter, but in the reign of their successors, Ptolemy Philadelphus and Antiochus Theos or Theus. The phrase "the end of years" would well denote such a future period. The Vulgate renders it, "after the end of years;" that is, after many years have elapsed. The meaning is "after a certain course or lapse of years." The word *end* in Daniel (קֵץ) often seems to refer to a time when a predicted event would be fulfilled, whether near or remote; whether it would be really the *end* or *termination* of an empire or of the world, or whether it would be succeeded by other events. It would be the end of that matter—of the thing predicted; and in this sense the word seems to be employed here. Compare chap. viii. 17, ver. 13 of this chapter (margin), and ch. xii. 13. ¶ *They shall join themselves together*. Marg., *associate.* The meaning is, that there would be an alliance formed, or an attempt made, to unite the two kingdoms more closely by a marriage between different persons of the royal families. The word "they" refers to the two sovereigns of Egypt and Syria—the south and the north. ¶ *For the king's daughter of the south shall come to the king of the north to make an agreement.* Marg., *rights.* The Hebrew word properly means rectitudes or rights (in the plural מֵישָׁרִים) ; but here it seems to be used in the sense of *peace*, or an alliance. The act of making peace was regarded as an act of *justice*, or doing *right*, and hence the word came to be used in the sense of making an alliance

or compact. This idea we should now express by saying that the design was "to make things right or straight"— as if they were wrong and crooked before, giving occasion to discord, and misunderstanding, and wars. The intention now was to establish peace on a permanent basis. The compact here referred to was one formed between Berenice, the daughter of Ptolemy Philadelphus, king of Egypt, and Antiochus Theos, king of Syria. Ptolemy, in order to bring a war in which he was engaged to an end, and to restore peace, gave his daughter in marriage to Antiochus, in hopes of establishing a permanent peace and alliance between the two kingdoms. One of the conditions of this alliance was, that Antiochus should divorce his former wife Laodice, and that the children of that former wife should be excluded from the succession to the throne. In this way Ptolemy hoped that the kingdom of Syria might become ultimately attached to that of Egypt, if there should be children by the marriage of Berenice with Antiochus. Ptolemy, however, died two years after this marriage was consummated, and Antiochus restored again his former wife Laodice, and put away Berenice, but was himself murdered by Laodice, who feared the fickleness of her husband. The officers of the court of Syria then planned the death of Berenice and her children, but she fled with them to Daphné, and was there put to death, with her children.—Appian, c. lxv.; Lengerke, *in loc.* She was put to death by poison. See Gill, *in loc.* ¶ *But she shall not retain the power of the arm.* The word *retain* here is the same as in ch. x. 8, "I retained no strength." The word *arm* is a word of frequent use in the Old Testament, both in the singular and plural, to denote *strength, power,* whether of an individual or an army. So Job xxii. 8, "A man of *arm,*" that is, *strength;* Gen. xlix. 24, "The arms [power] of his hands were made strong by the God

arm; neither shall he stand, nor his arm: but she shall be given up, and they that brought her, and¹ he that begat her, and he that strengthened her in *these* times.

1 or, *whom she brought forth.*

7 But out of a branch of her roots shall *one* stand up in his estate,² which shall come with an army, and shall enter into the fortress of the king of the north,

2 *place,* or, *office,* ver. 20.

of Jacob." Comp. Isa. li. 9, and lxii. 8. It is frequently used in this chapter in the sense of *strength,* or *power.* See vers. 15, 22, 31. This alliance was formed with the hope that the succession might be in her. She was, however, as stated above, with her children, put to death. While queen of Syria, she, of course, had power, and had the prospect of succeeding to the supreme authority. ¶ *Neither shall he stand.* The king of the south; to wit, Egypt. That is, he would not prosper in his ambitious purpose of bringing Syria, by this marriage alliance, under his control. ¶ *Nor his arm.* What he regarded as his strength, and in which he placed reliance, as one does on his arm in accomplishing any design. The word "arm" here is used in the sense of *help,* or *alliance;* that is, that on which he depended for the stability of his empire. ¶ *But she shall be given up.* That is, she shall be given up to death, to wit, by the command of Laodice. ¶ *And they that brought her.* That is, those who conducted her to Daphné; or those who came with her into Syria, and who were her attendants and friends. Of course they would be surrendered or delivered up when she was put to death. ¶ *And he that begat her.* Marg., "or, *whom she brought forth.*" The margin expresses the sense more correctly. The Latin Vulgate is, *adolescentes ejus.* The Greek, ἡ νεάνις. So the Syriac. The Hebrew (וְהַיֹּלְדָהּ) will admit of this construction. The article in the word has the force of a relative, and is connected with the suffix, giving it a relative signification. See Ewald, as quoted by Lengerke, *in loc.* According to the present pointing, indeed, the literal meaning would be, "and he who begat her;" but this pointing is not authoritative. Dathe, Bertholdt, Dereser, De Wette, and Rosenmüller suppose that the reading

should be וְהַיֹּלְדָהּ. Then the sense would be, "her child," or "her offspring." Lengerke and Ewald, however, suppose that this idea is implied in the present reading of the text, and that no change is necessary. The obvious meaning is, that she and her child, or her offspring, would be thus surrendered. The matter of fact was, that her little son was slain with her. See Prideaux's *Connexions,* iii. 120. ¶ *And he that strengthened her in these times.* It is not known who is here referred to. Doubtless, on such an occasion, she would have some one who would be a confidential counsellor or adviser, and, whoever that was, he would be likely to be cut off with her.

7. *But out of a branch of her roots.* Comp. Notes on Isa. xi. 1. The meaning is, that as a branch or shoot springs up from a tree that is decayed and fallen, so there would spring up some one of her family who would come to avenge her. That is, a person is indicated who would be of a common stock with her; or, in other words, if taken strictly, a brother. The phrase "branch of her roots" is somewhat peculiar. The words "her roots" must refer to her family; that from which she sprang. We speak thus of the root or *stem* of a family or house; and the meaning here is, not that one of her *descendants,* or one that should *spring from her,* would thus come, but a branch of the same family; a branch springing from the same root or stem. The fact in the case—a fact to which there is undoubted reference here—is, that her revenge was undertaken by Ptolemy Euergetes, her brother. As soon as he heard of the calamities that had come upon her, he hastened with a great force out of Egypt to defend and rescue her. But it was in vain. She and her son were cut off before he could arrive for her help, but, in con-

and shall deal against them, and shall prevail :

8 And shall also carry captives into Egypt their gods, with their princes, *and* with [1] their precious vessels of silver and of gold ; and

1 *vessels of their desire.* 2 or, *war.*

he shall continue *more* years than the king of the north.

9 So the king of the south shall come into *his* kingdom, and shall return into his own land.

10 But his sons shall [2] be stirred up, and shall assemble a multitude

---

nection with an army which had come from Asia Minor for the same purpose, he undertook to avenge her death. He made himself master not only of Syria and Cilicia, but passed over the Euphrates, and brought all under subjection to him as far as the river Tigris. Having done this, he marched back to Egypt, taking with him vast treasures. See Prideaux, *Con.* iii. 120, 121. ¶ *Shall* one *stand up.* Shall one arise. See Notes, ver. 2. That is, there shall *be* one who shall appear for that purpose. ¶ *In his estate.* Marg., *place,* or *office.* The word בֵּן

means, properly, stand, station, place; then base, pedestal. Comp. vers. 20, 21, 38. See also Gen. xl. 13: "Within three days shall Pharaoh restore thee to *thy place.*" And again, Gen. xli. 13, "to my *office.*" Here it means, in his place or stead. That is, he would take the place which his father would naturally occupy—the place of protector, or defender, or avenger. Ptolemy Philadelphus, her father, in fact died before she was put to death ; and his death was the cause of the calamities that came upon her, for as long as he lived his power would be dreaded. But .when he was dead, Ptolemy Euergetes stood up in his place as her defender and avenger. ¶ *Which shall come with an army.* As Ptolemy Euergetes did. See above. He came out of Egypt as soon as he heard of these calamities, to defend her. ¶ *And shall enter into the fortress of the king of the north.* His strongholds. In fact, he overran Syria and Cilicia, and extended his ravages to the Euphrates and the Tigris. Polybius (*Hist.* 1. 5) says that he entered into the fortified cities of Syria, and took them. In the passage before us, the singular—*fortress*—is put for the plural. ¶ *And shall deal against them.* Shall *act* against them. Literally,

"shall do against them." ¶. *And shall prevail.* Shall overcome, or subdue them. As seen above, he took possession of no small part of the kingdom of Syria. He was recalled home by a sedition in Egypt; and had it not been for this (Justin says), he would have made himself master of the whole kingdom of Seleucus.

8. *And shall also carry captives into Egypt their gods,* &c. That is, their idols. Jerome (*in loc.*) says that Ptolemy took with him, on his return, forty thousand talents of silver, a vast number of precious vessels of gold, and images to the number of two thousand four hundred, among which were many of the Egyptian idols, which Cambyses, on his conquering Egypt, had carried into Persia. These Ptolemy restored to the temple to which they belonged, and by this much endeared himself to his people. It was on account of the service which he thus rendered to his country that he was called Euergetes, that is, the Benefactor.—Prideaux, iii. 121. In 1631, an inscription on an ancient marble in honour of this action of Euergetes was published by Allatius : *Sacris quæ ab Egypto Persæ abstulerant receptis, ac cum reliquâ congestâ gazâ in Egyptum relatis.* — Wintle. ¶ *And he shall continue* more *years than the king of the north.* Ptolemy Euergetes survived Seleucus about four years.—Prideaux, iii. 122. He reigned twenty-five years.

9. *So the king of the south shall come into* his *kingdom.* That is, into the kingdom of the north, or the kingdom of Syria. This verse seems to be a summary of what had been said about his invading Syria. He would come, on account of the wrongs done to his sister, into the kingdom of the north, and would then return again to his own land.

10. *But his sons shall be stirred up.*

of great forces: and *one* shall certainly come, and overflow,[a] and pass through; then shall he [1]return, and be stirred up, *even* to his fortress.[b]

11 And the king of the south shall be moved with choler, and shall come forth and fight with him, *even* with the king of the north: and he shall set forth a

1 *be stirred up again.*   *b* ver. 7.

Marg., "*or, war.*" The Hebrew word (יִתְגָּרוּ—from גָּרָה) means, to be rough; then, in Piel, to excite, stir up; and then, in Hithpa, to excite one's self, to be stirred up to anger, to make war upon, &c. Here it means, according to Gesenius (*Lex.*), that they would be excited or angry. The reference here, according to Lengerke, Maurer, Gill, and others, is to the son of the king of the north, Seleucus Callinicus. He was killed, according to Justin (lib. xxvii. c. 3), by a fall from his horse. The war with Egypt was continued by his two sons, Seleucus Ceraunus and Antiochus the Great, until the death of the former, when it was prosecuted by Antiochus alone. See Prideaux, iii. 136. Seleucus Ceraunus succeeded his father—assuming the name of Ceraunus, or the Thunderer; but, dying soon, he left the crown to his brother, Antiochus the Great, then only fifteen years of age, by whom the war with Egypt was successfully prosecuted. ¶ *And shall assemble a multitude of great forces.* Against Egypt. In such a war they would naturally summon to their aid all the forces which they could command. ¶ *And one shall certainly come.* There is a change here in the Hebrew from the plural to the singular number, as is indicated in our translation by the insertion of the word *one*. The fact was, that the war was prosecuted by Antiochus the Great alone. Seleucus died in the third year of his reign, in Phrygia; being slain, according to one report (Jerome), through the treachery of Nicanor and Apaturius, or, according to another, was poisoned. See Prideaux, iii. 137. Antiochus succeeded to the empire, and prosecuted the war. This was done for the purpose of recovering Syria from the dominion of Ptolemy of Egypt, and was conducted with various degrees of suc-

cess, until the whole was brought under the control of Antiochus. See Prideaux, *Con.* iii. 138, *seq.* ¶ *And overflow.* Like a torrent. ¶ *And pass through.* Through the land—not the land of Egypt, but every part of Syria. ¶ *Then shall he return.* Marg., *be stirred up again.* The margin is the more correct rendering—the Hebrew word being the same as that which is used in the first part of the verse. The idea would seem to be, that he would be aroused or stirred up after a defeat, and would on the second expedition enter into the strongholds or fortresses of the land. This was literally true. Ptolemy marched into Syria with an army of seventy thousand foot, five thousand horse, and seventy-three elephants, and was met by Antiochus with an army of sixty-two thousand foot, six thousand horse, and one hundred and two elephants. In a great battle, Antiochus was defeated, and returned to Antioch (Prideaux, *Con.* iii. 151–153); but the following year he again rallied his forces, and invaded Syria, took Gaza and the other strongholds, and subdued the whole country of Syria (including Palestine) to himself.—Prideaux, *Con.* iii. 176, 177. ¶ *Even to his fortress.* The singular for the plural; perhaps using the word "fortress" by way of eminence, as denoting his *strongest* fortress, and, therefore, including all the others.

11. *And the king of the south shall be moved with choler.* With anger. That is, that his provinces were invaded, and his strongholds taken—referring particularly to the invasion of Syria and Palestine as mentioned in the previous verse, and the attempt to wrest them out of the hands of the king of Egypt. Nothing would be more natural than that this should occur. ¶ *And shall come forth and fight with him,* even *with the king of the north.* There were frequent

great multitude; but *a* the multitude shall be given into his hand.

12 *And* when he hath taken

a Psa. 33. 16; Eccl. 9. 11, 12.

away the multitude, his heart shall
be lifted up; and he shall cast
down *many* ten thousands: but he
shall not be strengthened *by it.*

and almost constant wars between
these two kingdoms. Yet the reference here is to Ptolemy Philopator,
who succeeded Ptolemy Euergetes in
Egypt, and who was exasperated at
the conduct of Antiochus in invading
Syria and Palestine. He assembled
an army, and marched with it to Raphia, where he met Antiochus, and a
battle was fought. ¶ *And he shall set
forth a great multitude.* This army of
Ptolemy, according to Polybius, ch. 86,
was led through Arabia Petræa, and
consisted of seventy thousand infantry,
and five thousand cavalry, and seventy-
three elephants. The army of Antiochus consisted of sixty-two thousand
foot, six thousand horse, and a hundred and two elephants. — Prideaux,
Con. iii. 151. ¶ *But the multitude
shall be given into his hand.* That is,
the multitude of the army of Antiochus. In the battle that was fought
at Raphia, Ptolemy gained the victory.
Ten thousand of the army of Antiochus were slain, four thousand taken
prisoners, and with the remainder of
his forces Antiochus retreated to Antioch.—Prideaux, iii. 152, 153. Perhaps also the expression "the multitude shall be given into his hand" may
refer not only to the army, and his
victory over it, but to the fact that
the inhabitants of Cœlo-Syria and Palestine would hasten to submit themselves to him. After this great battle
at Raphia, and the retreat of Antiochus, we are told that the cities of
Cœlo-Syria and Palestine vied with
each other in submitting themselves to
Ptolemy. They had been long under
the government of Egypt, and preferred that to the government of Antiochus. They had submitted to Antiochus only by force, and that force
now being removed, they returned
readily to the authority of their old
masters. Had Ptolemy possessed energy and capacity for government, it
would have been easy to have retained
the control over these countries.

12. And *when he hath taken away*

the multitude. When he has subdued
them. Lengerke, however, renders
this, "And the multitude shall lift
themselves up," supposing it to refer
to the fact that the people as well as
the king would be excited. But the
more natural interpretation is that in
our common version, and the same
sense of the word (אָשָׂא) occurs in Amos
iv. 2. ¶ *His heart shall be lifted up.*
That is, he will be proud and self-con-
fident. The reference is to the effect
which would be produced on him after
his defeat of Antiochus. He was a
man naturally indolent and effeminate
—a most profligate and vicious prince.
—Prideaux, *Con.* iii. 146. The effect
of such a victory would be to lift him
up with pride. ¶ *And he shall cast
down many ten thousands.* Or, rather,
the meaning is, "he *has* cast down
many myriads." The object seems to
be to give a reason why his heart was
lifted up. The fact that he had been
thus successful is the reason which is
assigned, and this effect of a great
victory has not been uncommon in the
world. ¶ *But he shall not be strengthened by it.* He was wholly given up
to luxury, sloth, and voluptuousness,
and returned immediately after his
victory into Egypt, and surrendered
himself up to the enjoyment of his
pleasures. The consequence was, that
he, by his conduct, excited some of his
people to rebellion, and greatly weakened himself in the affections and confidence of the rest. After the victory,
he concluded a truce with Antiochus;
and the result was, that his people,
who expected much more from him,
and supposed that he would have prosecuted the war, became dissatisfied
with his conduct, and broke out into
rebellion. As a matter of fact, he was
less strong in the confidence and affections of his people, and would have
been less able to wage a war, after his
triumph over Antiochus than he was
before. See Prideaux, *Con.* iii. 155,
seq.

13 For the king of the north shall return, and shall set forth a multitude greater than the former, and shall certainly come ¹ after certain years with a great army and with much riches.

14 And in those times there shall many stand up against the king of the south: also the ² robbers of thy people shall exalt themselves

1 *at the end of times, even years:* ch. 4. 16; 12. 7.
2 *children of robbers.*

---

13. *For the king of the north shall return.* That is, he shall come again into the regions of Cœlo-Syria and Palestine, to recover them if possible from the power of the Egyptian king. ¶ *And shall set forth a multitude greater than the former.* Than he had in the former war when he was defeated. The fact was, that Antiochus, in this expedition, brought with him the forces with which he had successfully invaded the East, and the army had been raised for that purpose, and was much larger than that with which he had formerly attacked Ptolemy. See Prideaux, iii. 163–165. ¶ *And shall certainly come after certain years with a great army.* This occurred B.C. 203, fourteen years after the former war.—Prideaux, iii. 19. ¶ *With much riches.* Obtained in his conquests in Parthia and other portions of the East. See Prideaux, *ut supra.* The *history* of Antiochus corresponds precisely with the statement here.

14. *And in those times there shall many stand up against the king of the south.* Against the king of Egypt. That is, not only Antiochus the Great, who was always opposed to him, and who was constantly waging war with him, but also others with whom he would be particularly involved, or who would be opposed to him. The reference is especially to Philip, king of Macedon, and to Agathocles, who excited a rebellion against him in Egypt. See Jerome on Dan. xi.; Polybius, xv. 20; Lengerke, *in loc.;* and Prideaux, iii. 198. Antiochus and Philip of Macedon entered into an agreement to invade the dominions of Ptolemy Epiphanes, and to divide them between themselves. At the same time a treasonable plot was laid against the life of Ptolemy by Scopas the Ætolian (Polyb. xvii.), who had under his command the army of the Egyptians, and who designed to take advantage of the

youth of the king, and seize upon the throne. This project was defeated by the vigilance of Aristomenes, the prime minister.—Prideaux, iii. 181. See also the account of the conspiracy of Agathocles, and his sister Agathoclea, against Ptolemy, when an infant, in Prideaux, iii. 168, *seq.* These facts fully accord with what is said in the passage before us. ¶ *Also the robbers of thy people shall exalt themselves.* The angel here turns to Daniel, and states what would be done in these circumstances by his own people—the Jews. It is to be remembered that, in these times, they were alternately under the dominion of the Egyptian and the Syrian monarchs—of Ptolemy and of Antiochus. The principal seat of the wars between Syria and Egypt was Palestine — the border land between them and Judea, therefore, often changed masters. Ptolemy Philopator had subdued Cœlo-Syria and Palestine, and Ptolemy Epiphanes came into possession of them when he ascended the throne. But the angel now says that a portion of his people would take occasion, from the weakness of the youthful monarch of Egypt, and the conspiracies in his own kingdom, and the foreign combinations against him, to attempt to throw off his authority, and to become independent. That part of the people who would attempt to do this is designated in the common translation as "the robbers of thy people." This, however, is scarcely a correct version, and does not properly indicate the persons that would be engaged in the plot. The marginal reading is, *children of robbers.* The Latin Vulgate, *filii quoque prævaricatorum populi tui.* The Greek renders it οἱ υἱοὶ τῶν λοιμῶν τοῦ λαοῦ σοῦ —" the sons of the pests of thy people." Lengerke renders it, " the most powerful people of thy nation"—*die gewaltsamsten Leute deines Volkes.* The Hebrew

to establish the vision; but they shall fall.[a]

15 So the king of the north shall come, and cast up a mount, and take the [1] most fenced cities; and

a Rev 17. 17.

the arms of the south shall not withstand, neither [2] his chosen people, neither *shall there be any* strength to withstand.

1 *city of munitions.* 2 *the people of his choices.*

---

word (פָּרִיץ) means, properly, *rending, ravenous*—as of wild beasts, Isa. xxxv. 9; and then *violent, rapacious; an oppressor, robber.*—Gesenius, *Lex.* The reference here seems to be to the mighty ones of the nation; the chiefs, or rulers —but a name is given them that would properly denote their character for oppression and rapacity. It would seem —what is indeed probable from the circumstances of the case — that the nation was not only subject to this foreign authority, but that those who were placed over it, under that foreign authority, and who were probably mainly of their own people, were also themselves tyrannical and oppressive in their character. These subordinate rulers, however, preferred the authority of Antiochus to that of Ptolemy, and on the occasion of his return from the conquests of Cœlo-Syria and Samaria, they met him, and professed submission to him.—Josephus, *Ant.* b. xii. ch. iii. § 3. "The Jews," says Josephus,' "of their own accord, went over to him, and received him into the city [Jerusalem], and gave plentiful provision to his army, and to his elephants, and readily assisted him when he besieged the garrison which was in the citadel of Jerusalem." On this occasion, Josephus says that Antiochus bestowed many favours on the Jews; wrote letters to the generals of his armies commending their conduct; published a decree respecting the piety of the Jewish people, and sent an epistle to Ptolemy, stating what he had done for them, and what he desired should be further done. See these statements and letters in Josephus, *ut supra.* ¶ *To establish the vision.* That is, to bring to pass what is seen in the vision, and what had been predicted in regard to the Hebrew people. Their conduct in this matter shall have an important bearing on the fulfilment of the prophecy pertaining

to that people—shall be one of the links in the chain of events securing its accomplishment. The angel does not say that it was a part of their *design* to "establish the vision," but that that would be the *result* of what they did. No doubt their conduct in this matter had a great influence on the series of events that contributed to the accomplishment of that prediction. Lengerke supposes that the "vision" here refers to that spoken of in ch. ix. 24. ¶ *But they shall fall.* They shall not succeed in the object which they have in view. Their conduct in the affair will indeed promote the fulfilment of the "vision," but it will not secure the ends which *they* have in view— perhaps their own aggrandizement; or the favour of Antiochus towards themselves; or the permanent separation of the nation from the Egyptian rule, or the hope that their country might become independent altogether. As a matter of fact, Antiochus subsequently, on his return from Egypt (B.C. 198), took Jerusalem, and slew many of the party of Ptolemy, who had given themselves up to him, though he showed particular favour to those who had adhered to the observance of their own law, and could not be prevailed on by the king of Egypt to apostatize from it.—Prideaux, iii. 198; Jos. *Ant.* b. xii. ch. v. § 3.

15. *So the king of the north.* Antiochus the Great. ¶ *Shall come.* Shall come again into these provinces. This occurred after he had vanquished the army of the Egyptians at Paneas. He then took Sidon and Patara, and made himself master of the whole country. —Prideaux, iii. 198. This happened B.C. 198. Scopas, a general of Ptolemy, had been sent by him into Cœlo-Syria and Palestine, with a view of subjecting those countries again to Egyptian rule. He was met by Antiochus at Paneas, near the sources of the Jordan, and defeated, and fled with ten thousand men to Sidon, where he

16 But he that cometh against him shall do according to his own will, and none shall stand before him; and he shall stand in ¹ the glorious land, which by his hand shall be consumed.

¹ *the land of ornament,* or, *goodly land,* vers. 41, 45.

fortified himself, but from whence he was expelled by Antiochus. ¶ *And cast up a mount.* A fortification. That is, he shall so entrench himself that he cannot be dislodged. The reference does not seem to be to any particular fortification, but to the general fact that he would so entrench or fortify himself that he would make his conquests secure. ¶ *And take the most fenced cities.* Marg., *city of munitions.* Heb., "city of fortifications." The singular is used here in a collective sense; or perhaps there is allusion particularly to Sidon, where Scopas entrenched himself, making it as strong as possible. ¶ *And the arms of the south shall not withstand.* Shall not be able to resist him, or to dislodge him. The power of the Egyptian forces shall not be sufficient to remove him from his entrenchments. The Hebrew is, "shall not *stand;*" that is, shall not stand against him, or maintain their position in his advances. The word *arms* (זְרֹעוֹת) is used here in the sense of *heroes, warriors, commanders,* as in Ezek. xxx. 22, 24, 25. ¶ *Neither his chosen people.* Marg., "the people of his choices." Those whom he had selected or chosen to carry on the war —referring, perhaps, to the fact that he would deem it necessary to employ picked men, or to send the choicest of his forces in order to withstand Antiochus. Such an occurrence is in every way probable. To illustrate this, it is only necessary to say that the Egyptians sent three of their most distinguished generals, with a select army, to deliver Sidon—Eropus, Menocles, and Damoxenus.—Lengerke, *in loc.* ¶ *Neither* shall there be any *strength to withstand.* No forces which the Egyptians can employ. In other words, Antiochus would carry all before him. This is in strict accordance with the history. When Scopas was defeated by Antiochus at Paneas, near the sources of the Jordan, he fled and

entrenched himself in Sidon. There he was followed and besieged by Antiochus. The king of Egypt sent the three generals above named, with a choice army, to endeavour to deliver Scopas, but they were unable. Scopas was obliged to surrender, in consequence of famine, and the chosen forces returned to Egypt.

16. *But he that cometh against him shall do according to his own will.* That is, Antiochus, who " came against" Scopas, the Egyptian general, sent out by Ptolemy. The idea is, that Antiochus would be entirely successful in the countries of Cœlo-Syria and Palestine. As a matter of fact, as stated above, he drove Scopas out of those regions, and compelled him to take refuge in Sidon, and then besieged him, and compelled him to surrender. ¶ *And none shall stand before him.* That is, neither the forces that Scopas had under his command, nor the choice and select armies sent out from Egypt for his rescue, under Eropus, Menocles, and Damoxenus. ¶ *And he shall stand in the glorious land.* Marg., "*the land of ornament,* or, *goodly land.*" The Hebrew word צְבִי means, properly, *splendour, beauty,* and was given to the holy land, or Palestine, on account of its beauty, as being a land of beauty or fertility. Compare Ezek. xx. 6, 15; xxvi. 12; Jer. iii. 19, and Dan. xi. 45. The meaning here is, that he would obtain possession of the land of Israel, and that no one would be able to stand against him. By the defeat of Scopas, and of the forces sent to aid him when entrenched in Sidon, this was accomplished. ¶ *Which by his hand shall be consumed.* As would be natural when his invading army should pass through it. The angel does not seem to refer to any *wanton* destruction of the land, but only to what would necessarily occur in its invasion, and in securing provision for the wants of an

17 He shall also set his face ^ato enter with the strength of his

army. As a matter of fact, Antiochus did many things to conciliate the favour of the Jews, and granted to them many privileges. See Josephus, *Ant.* b. xii. ch. iii. § 3. But, according to Josephus, these favours were granted subsequently to the wars with Scopas, and as a compensation for the injuries which their country had suffered in the wars which had been waged between him and Scopas within their borders. The following language of Josephus respecting the effect of these wars will justify and explain what is here said by the angel: "Now it happened that, in the reign of Antiochus the Great, who ruled over all Asia, the Jews, as well as the inhabitants of Cœlo-Syria, suffered greatly, and their land was sorely harassed; for while he was at war with Ptolemy Philopator, and with his son who was called *Epiphanes,* it fell out that these nations were equally sufferers, both when he was beaten, and when he beat the others; so that they were like to a ship in a storm, which is tossed by the waves on both sides; and just thus were they in their situation in the middle between Antiochus's prosperity and its change to adversity."—*Ant.* b. xii. ch. iii. § 3. When Antiochus was successful against Scopas, however, the Jews "went over to him," says Josephus, "of their own accord," and received him into Jerusalem; and as a consequence of the aid which they rendered him, he granted them the favours and privileges mentioned by Josephus. The immediate consequence of the wars, however, was extended desolation; and it is this to which the passage before us refers. Lengerke, however, supposes that the meaning of the passage is, that the whole land would be subdued under him. The Hebrew word rendered " shall be consumed"—כָּלָה—means, properly, *to be completed, finished, closed;* then to be *consumed, wasted, spent, destroyed;* Gen. xxi. 15 ; 1 Kings xvii. 16; Jer. xvi. 4; Ezek. v. 13. The destruction

whole kingdom, and ¹upright ones with him; thus shall he do: and

caused by invading and conflicting armies in a land would answer to all that is properly implied in the use of the word.

17. *He shall also set his face.* Antiochus. That is, he shall resolve or determine. To set one's face in any direction is to determine to go there. The meaning here is, that Antiochus, flushed with success, and resolved to push his conquests to the utmost, would make use of all the forces at his disposal to overcome the Egyptians, and to bring them into subjection to his sway. He had driven Scopas from Cœlo-Syria, and from Sidon; had subjected the land of Palestine to his control; and now nothing seemed to prevent his extending his conquests to the utmost limits of his ambition. The reference here is to a *purpose* of Antiochus to wage war with Egypt, and to invade it. From that purpose, however, he was turned, as we shall see, by his wars in Asia Minor; and he endeavoured, as stated in the subsequent part of the verse, if not to subdue Egypt and to bring it under his control, at least to neutralize it so that it would not interfere with his wars with the Romans. If his attention had not been diverted, however, by more promising or more brilliant prospects in another direction, he would undoubtedly have made an immediate descent on Egypt itself. ¶ *With the strength of his whole kingdom.* Summoning all the forces of his empire. This would seem to be necessary in invading Egypt, and in the purpose to dethrone and humble his great rival. The armies which he had employed had been sufficient to drive Scopas out of Palestine, and to subdue that country; but obviously stronger forces would be necessary in carrying the war into Egypt, and attempting a foreign conquest. ¶ *And upright ones with him.* Marg., "or, *much uprightness, or, equal conditions.*" The Hebrew word here used (יְשָׁרִים) means, properly, *straight, right;* then that which is straight or

he shall give him the daughter of
women, ¹corrupting her: but she

shall not stand *on his side,* neither
be for him.   1 *to corrupt.*

upright—applied to persons, denoting
their righteousness or integrity, Job i.
1, 8; Psal. xi. 7. By way of eminence
it is applied to the Jewish people, as
being a righteous or upright people—
the people of God—and is language
which a Hebrew would naturally apply
to his own nation. In this sense it is
undoubtedly used here, to denote not
the *pious* portion, but the nation as
such; and the meaning is, that, in addition to those whom he could muster
from his own kingdom, Antiochus
would expect to be accompanied with
large numbers of the Hebrews—the
" upright" people—in his invasion of
Egypt. This he might anticipate from
two causes, (*a*) the fact that they had
already rendered him so much aid, and
showed themselves so friendly, as stated
by Josephus in the passage referred to
above; and (*b*) from the benefits which
he had granted to them, which furnished a reasonable presumption that
they would not withhold their aid in
his further attempts to subdue Egypt.
The Jews might hope at least that if
Egypt were subjected to the Syrian.
sceptre, their own country, lying between the two, would be at peace, and
that they would no more be harassed
by its being made the seat of wars—
the battle-field of two great contending
powers. It was not without reason,
therefore, that Antiochus anticipated
that in his invasion of Egypt he would
be accompanied and assisted by not a
few of the Hebrew people. As this is the
natural and obvious meaning of the
passage, and accords entirely with the
sense of the Hebrew word, it is unnecessary to attempt to prove that the
marginal reading is not correct. ¶ *Thus
shall he do.* That is, in the manner
which is immediately specified. He
shall adopt the policy there stated—by
giving his daughter in marriage with
an Egyptian prince—to accomplish
the ends which he has in view. The
reference here is to another stroke of
policy, made necessary by his new wars
with the Romans, and by the diversion
of his forces, in consequence, in a new
direction. The *natural* step, after the

defeat of the Egyptian armies in Palestine, would have been to carry his
conquests at once into Egypt, and this
he appears to have contemplated. But,
in the meantime, he became engaged
in wars in another quarter—with the
Romans; and, as Ptolemy in such circumstances would be likely to unite
with the Romans against Antiochus,
in order to bind the Egyptians to himself, and to neutralize them in these
wars, this alliance was proposed and
formed by which he connected his own
family with the royal family in Egypt
by marriage. ¶ *And he shall give
him.* Give to Ptolemy. Antiochus
would seek to form a matrimonial alliance that would, for the time at least,
secure the neutrality or the friendship
of the Egyptians. ¶ *The daughter of
women.* The reference here is undoubtedly to his own daughter, Cleopatra.
The historical facts in the case, as
stated by Lengerke (*in loc.*), are these:
—After Antiochus had subdued Cœlo-
Syria and Palestine, he became involved in wars with the Romans in
Asia Minor, in order to extend the
kingdom of Syria to the limits which
it had in the time of Seleucus Nicator.
In order to carry on his designs in that
quarter, however, it became necessary
to secure the neutrality or the co-operation of Egypt, for Ptolemy would naturally, in such circumstances, favour
the Romans in their wars with Antiochus. Antiochus, therefore, negotiated
a marriage between his daughter Cleopatra and Ptolemy Epiphanes, the son
of Ptolemy Philopator, then thirteen
years of age. The valuable consideration in the view of Ptolemy in this
marriage was, that, as a dowry, Cœlo-
Syria, Samaria, Judea, and Phœnicia
were given to her.—Josephus, *Ant.*
b. xii. ch. 4, § 1. This agreement or
contract of marriage was entered into
immediately after the defeat of Scopas,
B.C. 197. The contract was, that the
marriage should take place as soon as
the parties were of suitable age, and
that Cœlo-Syria and Palestine should
be given as a dowry. The marriage
took place B.C. 193, when Antiochus

18 After this shall he turn his face unto the isles, and shall take many: but a prince for [1] his own

1 *him.*

was making preparation for his wars with the Romans.—Jahn, *Heb. Commonwealth*, ch. ix. § 89, p. 246. In this way the neutrality of the king of Egypt was secured, while Antiochus prosecuted his work against the Romans. The appellation here bestowed on Cleopatra—*daughter of women*—seems to have been given to her by way of eminence, as an heiress to the crown, or a princess, or as the principal one among the women of the land. There can be no doubt of its reference to her. ¶ *Corrupting her.* Marg., as in Hebrew, *to corrupt.* There has been some doubt, however, in regard to the word *her*, in this place, whether it refers to Cleopatra or to the kingdom of Egypt. Rosenmüller, Prideaux, J. D. Michaelis, Bertholdt, Dereser, and others, refer it to Cleopatra, and suppose that it means that Antiochus had instilled into her mind evil principles, in order that she might betray her husband, and that thus, by the aid of her arts, he might obtain possession of Egypt. On the other hand, Lengerke, Maurer, De Wette, Hävernick, Elliott (*Apocalypse*, iv. 130), and others, suppose that the reference is to Egypt, and that the meaning is, that Antiochus was disposed to enter into this alliance with a view of influencing the Egyptian government not to unite with the Romans and oppose him; that is, that it was on his part an artful device to turn away the Egyptian government from its true interest, and to accomplish his own purposes. The latter agrees best with the connection, though the Hebrew will admit of either construction. As a matter of fact, *both* these objects seem to have been aimed at—for it was equally true that in this way he sought to turn away the Egyptian government and kingdom from its true interests, and that in making use of his daughter to carry out this project, it was expected that she would employ artifice to influence her future husband. This arrangement was the more necessary, as, in consequence of the fame which the Romans had acquired in overcoming Hannibal,

the Egyptians had applied to them for protection and aid in their wars with Antiochus, and offered them, as a consideration, the guardianship of young Ptolemy. This offer the Romans accepted with joy, and sent M. Æmilius Lepidus to Alexandria as guardian of the young king of Egypt.—Polybius, xv. 20; Appian, *Syriac.* i. 1; Livy, xxxi. 14; xxxiii. 19; Justin, xxx. 2, 3; xxxi. 1. The whole was, on the part of Antiochus, a stroke of policy; and it could not be accomplished without that which has been found necessary in political devices—the employment of bribery or corruption. It accords well with the character of Antiochus to suppose that he would not hesitate to instil into the mind of his daughter all his own views of policy. ¶ *But she shall not stand* on his side, *neither be for him.* That is, she would become attached to her husband, and would favour his interests rather than the crafty designs of her father. On this passage, Jerome remarks: "Antiochus, desirous not only of possessing Syria, Cilicia, and Lycia, and the other provinces which belonged to Ptolemy, but of extending also his own sceptre over Egypt itself, betrothed his own daughter Cleopatra to Ptolemy, and promised to give as a dowry Cœlo-Syria and Judea. But he could not obtain possession of Egypt in this way, because Ptolemy Epiphanes, perceiving his design, acted with caution, and because Cleopatra favoured the purposes of her husband rather than those of her father." So Jahn (*Heb. Commonwealth*, p. 246) says:—"He indulged the hope that when his daughter became queen of Egypt, she would bring the kingdom under his influence; but she proved more faithful to her husband than to her father."

18. *After this shall he turn his face unto the isles.* The islands of the Mediterranean, particularly those in the neighbourhood of and constituting a part of Greece. This he did in his wars with the Romans, for the Roman power then comprehended that part of the world, and it was the design of

behalf shall cause [1] the reproach offered by him to cease; without his own reproach he shall cause *it* to turn upon him.   1 *his reproach.*

Antiochus, as already remarked, to extend the limits of his empire as far as it was at the time of Seleucus Nicator. This occurred after the defeat of Scopas, for, having given his daughter in marriage to Ptolemy, he supposed that he had guarded himself from any interference in his wars with the Romans from the Egyptians, and sent two of his sons with an army by land to Sardis, and he himself with a great fleet sailed at the same time into the Ægean Sea, and took many of the islands in that sea. The war which was waged between Antiochus and the Romans lasted for three years, and ended in the defeat of Antiochus, and in the subjugation of the Syrian kingdom to the Roman power, though, when it became a Roman province, it continued to be governed by its own kings. In this war, Hannibal, general of the Carthaginians, was desirous that Antiochus should unite with him in carrying his arms into Italy, with the hope that together they would be able to overcome the Romans; but Antiochus preferred to confine his operations to Asia Minor and the maritime parts of Greece; and the consequence of this, and of the luxury and indolence into which he sank, was his ultimate overthrow. Comp. Jahn's *Heb. Commonwealth*, pp. 246–249. ¶ *And shall take many.* Many of those islands; many portions of the maritime country of Asia Minor and Greece. As a matter of fact, during this war which he waged, he became possessed of Ephesus, Ætolia, the island of Eubœa, where, in the year 191 B.C. he married Eubia, a young lady of great beauty, and gave himself up for a long time to festivity and amusements—and then entrenched himself strongly at the pass of Thermopylæ. Afterwards, when driven from that stronghold, he sailed to the Thracian Chersonesus, and fortified Sestos, Abydos, and other places, and, in fact, during these military expeditions, obtained the mastery of no inconsiderable part of the maritime portions of Greece. The prophecy was strictly fulfilled, that he should "take many" of those places. ¶ *But a prince for his own behalf.* A Roman prince, or a leader of the Roman armies. The reference is to Lucius Cornelius Scipio, called Scipio Asiaticus, in contradistinction from Publius Cornelius Scipio, called Africanus, from his conquest over Hannibal and the Carthaginians. The Scipio here referred to received the name *Asiaticus*, on account of his victories in the East, and particularly in this war with Antiochus. He was a brother of Scipio Africanus, and had accompanied him in his expedition into Spain and Africa. After his return he was rewarded with the consulship for his services to the state, and was empowered to attack Antiochus, who had declared war against the Romans. In this war he was prosperous, and succeeded in retrieving the honour of the Roman name, and in wiping off the reproach which the Roman armies had suffered from the conquests of Antiochus. When it is said that he would do this *"for his own behalf,"* the meaning is, doubtless, that he would engage in the enterprise for his own glory, or to secure fame for himself. It was not the love of justice, or the love of country, but it was to secure for himself a public triumph— perhaps hoping, by subduing Antiochus, to obtain one equal to that which his brother had received after his wars with Hannibal. The motive here ascribed to this "prince" was so common in the leaders of the Roman armies, and has been so generally prevalent among mankind, that there can be no hesitation in supposing that it was accurately ascribed to this conqueror, Scipio, and that the enterprise in which he embarked in opposing Antiochus was primarily "on his own behalf." ¶ *Shall cause the reproach offered by him to cease.* The reproach offered by Antiochus to the Roman power. The margin is, *"his reproach."* The reference is to the disgrace brought on the Roman armies by the conquests of Antiochus. Antiochus had seemed to mock that power; he had engaged in war with the conquerors of nations;

19 Then he shall turn his face toward the fort of his own land:

a Psa. 37. 36.

but he shall stumble and fall, and not *a* be found.

20 Then shall stand up in his

he had gained victories, and thus appeared to insult the majesty of the Roman name. All this was turned back again, or caused to cease, by the victories of Scipio. ¶ *Without his own reproach.* Without any reproach to himself—any discomfiture—any imputation of want of skill or valour. That is, he would so conduct the war as to secure an untarnished reputation. This was in all respects true of Scipio. ¶ *He shall cause* it *to turn upon him.* The reproach or shame which he seemed to cast upon the Romans would return upon himself. This occurred in the successive defeats of Antiochus in several engagements by water and by land, and in his final and complete overthrow at the battle of Magnesia (B.C. 190) by Scipio. After being several times overcome by the Romans, and vainly sueing for peace, "Antiochus lost all presence of mind, and withdrew his garrisons from all the cities on the Hellespont, and, in his precipitate flight, left all his military stores behind him. He renewed his attempts to enter into negotiations for peace, but when he was required to relinquish all his possessions west of the Taurus, and defray the expenses of the war, he resolved to try his fortune once more in a battle by land. Antiochus brought into the field seventy thousand infantry, twelve thousand cavalry, and a great number of camels, elephants, and chariots armed with scythes. To these the Romans could oppose but thirty thousand men, and yet they gained a decisive victory. The Romans lost only three hundred and twenty-five men; while, of the forces of Antiochus, fifty thousand infantry, four thousand cavalry, and fifteen elephants were left dead on the field, fifteen hundred men were made prisoners, and the king himself with great difficulty made his escape to Sardis. He now humbly sued for peace, and it was granted on the terms with which he had formerly refused compliance—that he should

surrender all his possessions west of the Taurus, and that he should defray the expenses of the war. He further obligated himself to keep no elephants, and not more than twelve ships. To secure the performance of these conditions, the Romans required him to deliver up twelve hostages of their own selection, among whom was his son Antiochus, afterwards surnamed Epiphanes."—Jahn's *Hebrew Commonwealth*, pp. 248, 249.

19. *Then he shall turn his face toward the fort of his own land.* The strong fortifications of his own land—for the Hebrew word is in the plural. This he would do, of course, for protection. He would cease his attempts at conquest, and endeavour to find security in his own fortresses. As a matter of fact, after this defeat, Antiochus, in order to replenish his exhausted coffers, and to find the means of meeting the claims of the Romans, went into certain provinces of his empire. He attempted no other foreign wars, but sought security in his own dominions. ¶ *But he shall stumble and fall, and not be found.* He died in an attempt to plunder the temple of Elymaïs. In this he provoked the people to an insurrection, and was slain, together with the soldiers who were with him. What was his *motive* for plundering that temple is uncertain, whether it was to meet the demands of the Romans, or whether it was avarice (Justin, xxxiii. 2); but it was in this way that he "stumbled and fell," and passed away.—Jerome, *Com. in loc.*; Diod. Sic., *Fragmenta*, xxvi. 30, 49; Justin, xxxii. 2; Strabo, p. 744. The prophecy respecting him terminates here, and the particulars specified are as minute and accurate as if it had been written *after* the event. Indeed, the whole account is just such as one would prepare now who should undertake to express in a brief compass the principal events in the life of Antiochus the Great.

20. *Then shall stand up in his estate.*

DANIEL II.

P

estate,[1] a [2]raiser of taxes *in the glory* of the kingdom: but within

few days he shall be destroyed, neither in [3]anger, nor in battle.

1 or, *place*, ver. 7.
2 *one that causeth an exacter to pass over.*

3 *angers.*

Marg., "or, *place*." The word used — קֵן — means, properly, *a stand, station, place* (see Notes on verse 7), and the idea here is simply that he would be succeeded in the kingdom by such an one. His successor would have the character and destiny which the prophecy proceeds to specify. ¶ *A raiser of taxes.* One who shall be mainly characterized for this; that is, whose government would be distinguished eminently by his efforts to wring money out of the people. The Hebrew word נֹגֵשׂ means, properly, to urge, to drive, to impel, and it is then applied to one who urges or presses a debtor, or who exacts tribute of a people. The word is used with reference to *money* exactions in Deut. xv. 2, 3: "Every creditor that lendeth aught unto his neighbour, he shall not *exact* it of his neighbour or of his brother. Of a foreigner thou mayest *exact* it again." So in 2 Kings xxiii. 35, Jehoiakim taxed the land "to give the money according to the commandment of Pharaoh: he *exacted* the silver and the gold of the people of the land." In Zech. ix. 8—"And no *oppressor* shall pass through them any more"—the same word is used. Here it denotes one who would be mainly characterized by his extorting tribute of his people, or using means to obtain money. ¶ In *the glory of the kingdom.* The word "*in*" here is supplied by our translators. Lengerke renders it, "who shall suffer the tax-gatherer (eintreiber) to go through the glory of the kingdom." This is evidently the meaning. He would lay the richest and most productive parts of his kingdom under contribution. This might be either to pay a debt contracted by a former monarch; or to carry on war; or to obtain the means of luxurious indulgence; or for purposes of magnificence and display. ¶ *But within few days.* A comparatively brief period. Comp. Gen. xxvii. 44; xxix. 20. It is impossible from this to determine

the precise period which he would live, but the language would leave the impression that his would be a short reign. ¶ *He shall be destroyed.* Heb., *shall be broken.* That is, his power shall be broken; he shall cease to reign. It would not be certainly inferred from this that he would be put to death, or would die at that time, but that his reign then would come to an end, though it might be in some peaceful way. ¶ *Neither in anger.* Heb., *angers.* Not in any tumult or excitement, or by any rage of his subjects. This would certainly imply that his death would be a peaceful death. ¶ *Nor in battle.* As many kings fell. The description would indicate a reign of peace, and one whose end would be peace, but who would have but a brief reign. The reference here is, undoubtedly, to Seleucus Philopator, the eldest son of Antiochus the Great, and his immediate successor. The fulfilment of the prediction is seen in the following facts in regard to him: (*a*) As an exactor of tribute. He was bound to pay the tribute which his father had agreed to pay to the Romans. This tribute amounted to a thousand talents annually, and consequently made it necessary for him to apply his energies to the raising of that sum. The Jewish talent of silver was equal to about 1505 dollars of our money [about £339], and, consequently, this thousand talents, of the Jewish talent of silver here referred to, was equal to about a million and a half of dollars. The Greek talent of silver was worth 1055 dollars of our money [about £238], and, if this was the talent, the sum would be about a million dollars. To raise this, in addition to the ordinary expenses of the government, would require an effort, and, as this was continued from year to year, and as Seleucus was known for little else, it was not unnatural that he should be characterized as the "raiser of taxes." (*b*) Especially would this be true in the estimation of the Jews,

21 And in his [1] estate shall stand up a vile person, to whom they shall not give the honour of the kingdom: but he shall come in peaceably, and obtain the kingdom by flatteries.　　　1 or, *place*, ver. 7.

---

for no small part of these taxes, or this revenue, was derived from Palestine. Seleucus, taking advantage of the disturbances in Egypt, had reunited to the Syrian crown the provinces of Cœlo-Syria and Palestine, which his father Antiochus the Great had given in dowry to his daughter Cleopatra, who was married to Ptolemy Epiphanes. — Jahn, *Heb. Commonwealth*, p. 255. In the year 176 B.C., Simon, a Benjamite, who became governor of the temple at Jerusalem, the farmer of the revenues of the Egyptian kings, attempted to make some innovations, which were steadily resisted by the high-priest Onias III. Simon, in anger, went to Apollonius, governor of Cœlo-Syria under Seleucus, and informed him of the great treasures contained in the temple. "The king," says Jahn (*Heb. Commonwealth*, p. 255), "though a friend to the Jews, and though he had regularly made disbursements, according to the directions of his father, towards sustaining the expenses of the sacrifices at Jerusalem, determined to apply to his own use the treasures of the temple; for the annual payment of one thousand talents to the Romans had reduced his finances to a very low ebb. With the design, therefore, of replenishing his exhausted treasury, he sent Heliodorus to Jerusalem to plunder the temple." Comp. Appian, *Syriac.* xlv. 60–65. See also Prideaux, *Con.* iii. 208; 2 Macc. iii. Besides this, the necessity of raising so much revenue would give him the character of a "raiser of taxes." (*c*) This was done in what might properly be termed "the glory of his kingdom," or in what would, in the language of an Hebrew, be so called—Cœlo-Syria and Palestine. To the eye of a Hebrew this was the glory of all lands, and the Jewish writers were accustomed to designate it by some such appellation. Comp. Notes on ver. 16. (*d*) His reign continued but a short time—answering to what is here said, that it would be for a "few days." In fact,

he reigned but eleven or twelve years, and that, compared with the long reign of Antiochus his father—thirty-seven years—was a brief period. (*e*) The manner of his death. He did not fall in battle, nor was he cut off in a popular tumult. He was, in fact, poisoned. In the eleventh year of his reign, he sent his only son Demetrius as hostage to Rome, and released his brother Antiochus, who had resided twelve years in that city. As the heir to the crown was now out of the way, Heliodorus sought to raise himself to the royal dignity, and for this purpose he destroyed the king by poison. He attached a large party to his interests, and finally gained over those who were in favour of submitting to the king of Egypt. Antiochus Epiphanes received notice of these transactions while he was at Athens on his return from Rome. He applied himself to Eumenes, king of Pergamos, whom, with his brother Attalus, he easily induced to espouse his cause, and they, with the help of a part of the Syrians, deprived Heliodorus of his usurped authority. Thus, in the year 175 B. C., Antiochus Epiphanes quietly ascended the throne, while the lawful heir, Demetrius, was absent at Rome. — Appian, *Syriac.* xlv. 60–65 ; Jahn, *Heb. Commonwealth*, ch. ix. § 91. The remainder of this chapter is occupied with a detail of the crimes, the cruelties, and the oppressions of Antiochus Epiphanes, or Antiochus IV.

21. *And in his estate.* In his place. Notes on vers. 7, 20. ¶ *Shall stand up a vile person.* There shall succeed to the throne. The reference here is to Antiochus Epiphanes, who reigned from B.C. 175 to B.C. 163. The epithet "*vile*" here given him was one which his subsequent history showed was eminently appropriate to him in all respects, as a man and as a prince. The Hebrew word rendered "vile"— נִבְזֶה—properly means one despised or held in contempt, Isa. xlix. 7; Psa.

xxii. 6 (7). The meaning here is, that he was one who deserved to be despised, and who would be held in contempt—a man of a low, base, contemptible character. Vulg., *despectus;* Gr. ἐξου-δενώθη; Luther, *ein ungeachteter.* Never were terms better applied to a man than these to Antiochus Epiphanes—both before and after his ascension to the throne. The manner of his seizing upon the crown is stated above. He was surnamed Epiphanes (᾽Επιφανής), *the Illustrious,* because, if we believe Appian, he vindicated the claims of the royal family against the usurpations of the foreigner Heliodorus. He also bore the name Θεός, *God,* which is still seen upon his coins. But by his subjects he was called Epimanes (᾽Επι-μανής), *the Insane,* instead of *Epiphanes* —a name which he much more richly deserved. The following statement from Jahn (*Heb. Commonwealth,* ch. x. § 92) will show with what propriety the term "*vile*" was applied to him: "He often lounged like a mere idler about the streets of Antioch, attended by two or three servants, and not deigning to look at the nobles; would talk with goldsmiths and other mechanics in their workshops, engage in idle and trifling conversation with the lowest of the people, and mingle in the society of foreigners and men of the vilest character. He was not ashamed to go into the dissipated circles of the young, to drink and carouse with them, and to assist their merriment by singing songs and playing on his flute. He often appeared in the public baths among the common people, engaging in every kind of foolish jest, without the least regard to the dignity of his station and character. Not unfrequently he was seen drunk in the streets, when he would throw his money about, and practise various other fooleries equally extravagant. He would parade the streets of his capital in a long robe, and with a garland of roses upon his head: and if any attempted to pass by or to follow him, he would pelt them with stones, which he carried concealed under his garments," &c. See also Appian in *Syriacis,* xlv. 70 – 75 ; Eusebius in *Chronicon;* Athenæus, lib. v. p. 193 ;

x. p. 438 ; Livy, xli. 20 ; Diod. Sic. *Frag.* xxvi. 65 ; xxxi. 7, 8 ; Prideaux, *Con.* iii. 212 – 214 ; 1 Macc. i. 9. ¶ *To whom they shall not give the honour of the kingdom.* That is, the people. Or, in other words, it should not be conferred on him by any law or act of the nation, or in any regular succession or claim. The true heir to the crown was Demetrius, who was absent at Rome. On him the crown would have regularly devolved ; but in his absence it was obtained by Antiochus by arts which he practised, and not by any voluntary grant of the nation. ¶ *But he shall come in peaceably.* Quietly ; without war or force ; by art rather than by arms. Gesenius (*Lex.*) renders the phrase here used "in the midst of security ;" that is, unexpectedly, suddenly. The idea seems to be, that he would do it when the nation was not expecting it, or apprehending it ; when they would be taken off their guard, and he would "steal a march upon them." All this accorded with fact. The nation seemed not to have anticipated that Antiochus would attempt to ascend the throne on the death of his brother. But he quietly left Rome—while Demetrius, his nephew, the true heir to the crown, remained there ; came to Athens, and learned what was the state of things in Syria, where Heliodorus had usurped the authority ; made an agreement with the king of Pergamos to aid him, and, by the assistance of a part of the Syrians who were opposed to the usurper Heliodorus, deprived him of the authority, and himself took possession of the crown. No one seemed to suspect that this was his aim, or to doubt that his object was to remove an usurper that his nephew might be placed on the throne. ¶ *And obtain the kingdom by flatteries.* חֲלַקְלַקּוֹת—*lubricitates, blanditiæ.* "The word," says Elliott (*Apoc.* iv. 133), "has a double sense, being applied both to the slipperiness of a path, and the slipperiness or flattering and deceit of the tongue." In the former sense it occurs in Psa. xxxv. 6, "Let their way be dark and slippery ;" in the latter, its originating verb, Prov. ii. 16. vii. 5, "The stranger that flattereth or dis-

22 And [a] with the arms of a flood shall they be overflown from before him, and shall be broken; yea, also the prince of the covenant.

a ver. 10. Fulfilled, 170 B.C.

23 And after the league *made* with him he shall work deceitfully: [b] for he shall come up, and shall become strong with a small people.

b ch. 8. 25.

---

sembleth with his words;" and Prov. xxix. 5, " A man that flattereth [or dissembleth to] his neighbour." In this latter sense the verbal seems to be used both here and in the verses (32, 34) below: " arts of dissimulation."—Gesenius. The probable meaning here is, that he would obtain the throne by acts of dissembling, and by promises of rewards and offices. Such promises he would probably make to Eumenes, king of Pergamos, and to the Syrian nobles and people who espoused his cause. It would not be difficult to secure the aid of multitudes in this way, and the character of Antiochus was just such as to permit him to use any of these arts to accomplish his ends. Perhaps, also, he might hold out the hope of aid from the Romans, with whom he had long lived. It was no uncommon thing for an usurper to make his way by flattering certain classes of a people, and by promises of largesses, of offices, and of the removal of oppressive burdens. Comp. Prideaux, *Con.* iii. 212. See also the case of Absalom in 2 Sam. xv. 1–6

22. *And with the arms of a flood.* The reference here is to some mighty invasion of some country by Antiochus, which would sweep everything before him. There seems to be some confusion of metaphor in the phrase, " the *arms* of a flood." The idea in the mind of the writer appears to have been this: He saw an invasion of some country by hosts of men under the command of Antiochus. This it was not unnatural to compare with an *inundation of waters* spreading over a land. See Isa. viii. 8. Nor was it altogether unnatural to speak of an inundation as having *arms* extending far and near; sweeping everything to itself, or carrying it away. Thus we speak of an arm of the sea, an arm of a river, &c. In this manner the inundation—the invasion—seemed to

spread itself out like waters, sweeping all away. ¶ *Shall they be overflown from before him.* The prophet does not specify *who* they would be that would thus be overthrown. Some have supposed that the reference is to the Hebrews, but the more correct interpretation is that which refers it to Egypt, See Notes on ver. 25. As a matter of fact, the forces of Heliodorus, the forces of the Hebrews, and the forces of the Egyptians, were alike broken and scattered before him. The eye of the prophet, however, seems rather here to be on the invasion of Egypt, which was one of the earliest and most prominent acts of Antiochus, and into the history of which the prophet goes most into detail. ¶ *Yea, also the prince of the covenant.* He also shall be broken and overcome. There has been some diversity of opinion as to who is meant by " the prince of the covenant" here. Many suppose that it is the high priest of the Jews, as being the chief prince or ruler under the " covenant" which God made with them, or among the " covenant" people. But this appellation is not elsewhere given to the Jewish high priest, nor is it such as could with much propriety be applied to him. The reference is rather to the king of Egypt, with whom a covenant or compact had been made by Antiochus the Great, and who was supposed to be united, therefore, to the Syrians by a solemn treaty. See Lengerke, *in loc.* So Elliott, *Apoc.* iv. 133.

23. *And after the league* made *with him.* A treaty of peace and concord. The great subject of contention between the kings of Syria and Egypt was the possession of Cœlo-Syria and Palestine. This they often endeavoured to settle by conquest, as each of them claimed that in the original partition of the empire of Alexander this portion of the empire fell to him.

self; and often they endeavoured to settle it by treaty. Consequently this region was constantly passing from one to the other, and was also the seat of frequent wars. The "league" here referred to seems to have been that respecting this country—the successive promises which had been made to the king of Egypt that Cœlo-Syria and Palestine should be made over to him. These provinces had been secured to Ptolemy Lagus by the treaty made 301 B.C., and they had been again pledged by Antiochus the Great, in dowry, when his daughter Cleopatra should be made queen of Egypt.—Jahn, *Heb. Commonwealth*, p. 260. Antiochus Epiphanes, however, was by no means disposed to confirm this grant, and hence the wars in which he was involved with the Egyptians. ¶ *He shall work deceitfully.* In reference to the covenant or treaty above referred to. He shall endeavour to evade its claims; he shall refuse to comply with its conditions; he shall not deliver up the provinces according to the terms of the compact. The history accords exactly with this, for he did not intend to comply with the terms of the treaty, but sought every means to evade it, and finally waged a succession of bloody wars with Egypt. In reference to the terms of this treaty, and to secure their respective interests, both parties sent ambassadors to Rome to urge their claims before the Roman Senate.—Polybius, *Legat.* § 78, 82 ; Jerome, *Com. in loc.* As soon as Ptolemy Philometor had reached his fourteenth year, he was solemnly invested with the government; and ambassadors from all surrounding countries came to congratulate him on his accession to the throne. " On this occasion Antiochus sent to Egypt Apollonius, the son of Mnestheus, apparently to congratulate the king on his coronation, but with the real intention of sounding the purposes of the Egyptian court. When Apollonius, on his return, informed Antiochus that he was viewed as an enemy by the Egyptians, he immediately sailed to Joppa to survey his frontiers towards Egypt, and to put them in a state of defence."—Jahn, *Heb. Commonwealth,*

p. 260 ; 2 Macc. iv. 21. The purpose of Antiochus was undoubtedly not to surrender Cœlo-Syria and Palestine according to the treaties which had been made ; and yet he designed to secure them if possible without an open rupture, and hence his arts of diplomacy, or his efforts to evade compliance with the terms of the compact. Even when he had invaded Egypt, and had obtained possession of the king, Ptolemy Philometor, he still "pretended that he had come to Egypt solely for the good of king Ptolemy, to set the affairs of his kingdom in order for him; and Ptolemy found it expedient to act as though he really thought him his friend. But he must have seen," says Jahn, "that Antiochus, with all his professions of friendship, was not unmindful of spoil, for he plundered Egypt in every quarter."—*Heb. Commonwealth*, p. 263. ¶ *For he shall come up.* Come upon Egypt. The result would be war. Rather than surrender the provinces according to the treaty, he would ultimately invade Egypt, and carry war into its borders. ¶ *And shall become strong with a small people.* The meaning of this seems to be, that at first his own forces would be small; that he would go up in such a way as not to excite suspicion, but that, either by an increase of his forces there, by uniting himself to confederates, by alluring the people by the promise of rewards, or by gradually taking one town after another and adding them to his dominions, he would become strong. Jahn (*Heb. Commonwealth,* p. 263) says, "*with a small body of troops* he made himself master of Memphis, and of all Egypt as far as Alexandria, almost without striking a blow." Compare Diod. Sic. xxvi. 75, 77; Jos. *Ant.* xii. 5, 2. The fact in the case was, that Antiochus pretended in his invasion of Egypt to be the friend of the Egyptian king, and that he came to aid him, and to settle him firmly on the throne. By degrees, however, he became possessed of one town after another, and subdued one place after another, until he finally became possessed of the king himself, and had him entirely in his power.

24 He shall enter [1] peaceably even upon the fattest places of the province; and he shall do *that* which his fathers have not done, nor his fathers' fathers; he shall scatter among them the prey, and spoil, and riches; *yea*, and he shall forecast [2] his devices against the strong holds, even for a time.

25 And he shall stir up his power

[1] or, *into the peaceable and fat.*

[2] *think his thoughts.*

24. *He shall enter peaceably even upon the fattest places of the province.* The margin is, " or, *into the peaceable and fat.*" The version in the text, however, is the more correct, and the sense is, that he would do this *unexpectedly* (Lengerke, *unvermuthet*); he would make gradual and artful approaches until he had seized upon the best portions of the land. Comp. Gen. xxvii. 28, 39. The history is, that he went there with different professions than those of conquest, and one after another he took possession of the principal towns of Egypt. In his first invasion of that country, Diodorus Siculus and Josephus both say that Antiochus "availed himself of a mean artifice," without specifying what it was. Jahn says that probably it was that he pretended to come as the friend of Ptolemy. It was to this that the allusion is here, when it is said that he would "enter *peaceably*"—that is, with some pretence of peace or friendship, or with some false and flattering art. Josephus (*Ant.* xii. ch. v. § 2) says of Antiochus, that "he came with great forces to Pelusium, and circumvented Ptolemy Philometor *by treachery*, and seized upon Egypt." The fact stated by Diodorus and Josephus, that he took possession of Memphis and of all Egypt, as far as Alexandria, fully illustrates what is said here, that he would " enter upon the fattest places of the province." These were the most choice and fertile portions of Egypt." ¶ *And he shall do* that *which his fathers have not done, nor his fathers' fathers.* Which none of his predecessors have been able to do; to wit, in the conquest of Egypt. No one of them had it so completely in his possession; no one obtained from it so much spoil. There can be no doubt that such was the fact. The wars of his predecessors with the Egyptians had been mostly waged in Cœlo-Syria and Palestine, for the possession of these provinces. Antiochus Epiphanes, however, at first took Pelusium, the key of Egypt, and then invaded Egypt itself, seized upon its strongest places, and made the king a captive.—Jahn, *Heb. Commonwealth*, p. 263. Comp. 1 Macc. i. 16. ¶ *He shall scatter among them the prey,* &c. Among his followers. He shall reward them with the spoils of Egypt. Comp. 1 Macc. i. 19 : "Thus they got the strong cities in the land of Egypt, and he took the spoils thereof. ¶ *And he shall forecast his devices.* Marg., "*think his thoughts.*" The margin is in accordance with the Hebrew. The meaning is, that he would form plans, or that this would be his aim. He would direct the war against the strongly-fortified places of Egypt. ¶ *Against the strongholds.* Antiochus took possession of Pelusium, the key of Egypt ; he seized upon Memphis, and he then laid siege to Alexandria, supposing that if that were reduced, the whole country would be his.—Jos. *Ant.* b. xii. ch. v. § 2. ¶ *Even for a time.* Josephus (*ut sup.*) says that he was driven from Alexandria, and out of all Egypt, by the threatenings of the Romans, commanding him to let that country alone. There were other reasons also which, combined with this, induced him to retire from that country. He was greatly enraged by the effect which a report of his death had produced in Judea. It was said that all the Jews rejoiced at that report, and rose in rebellion ; and he therefore resolved to inflict revenge on them, and left Egypt, and went to Jerusalem, and subdued it either by storm or by stratagem.

25. *And he shall stir up his power and his courage against the king of the south with a great army.* This must refer to a subsequent invasion of Egypt by Antiochus. In the course of his reign he four times invaded that country with various degrees of success. In

and his courage against the king of the south with a great army; and the king of the south shall be stirred up to battle with a very great and mighty army; but he shall not stand: for they shall forecast devices against him.

26 Yea, they that feed of the portion of his meat shall destroy him, and his army shall overflow; and many shall fall down slain.

27 And both these kings' [1] hearts *shall be* to do mischief, and they

1 *their hearts.*

---

the first, he took Pelusium, and having placed a garrison there, retired into winter-quarters to Tyre. In the second, above referred to, he took Memphis and laid siege to Alexandria. The third invasion here referred to was after he had taken Jerusalem, and was caused by the fact that, as Ptolemy Philometor was in the hands of Antiochus, the Egyptians had raised Ptolemy Physcon (*the Gross*) to the throne. This prince assumed the name of Euergetes II. The pretended object of Antiochus in this invasion (B.C. 168) was to support the claims of Ptolemy Philometor against the usurpation of his brother, but his real purpose was to subject the whole country to his own power. He defeated the Alexandrians by sea near Pelusium, and then drew up his land forces before the city of Alexandria. Ptolemy Physcon sent an embassy to Rome to solicit the protection of the Senate, and at the same time entered into negotiations of peace with Antiochus. The proposals were rejected; but when Antiochus perceived that the conquest of Alexandria would be difficult, he retired to Memphis, and pretended to deliver up the kingdom to Ptolemy Philometor, and having left a strong garrison at Pelusium, he returned to Antioch. This invasion is thus described by the author of the book of Maccabees (1 Macc. i. 17); "Wherefore he entered Egypt with a great multitude, with chariots, and elephants, and horsemen, and a great navy."—Porphyry, as quoted by Scaliger; Polybius, *Legat.*, §§ 81, 82, 84; Livy, xliv. 19; xlv. 11; Justin, xxxiv. 2; Prideaux, *Con.* iii. 232–235. ¶ *And the king of the south.* Ptolemy Physcon, king of Egypt. ¶ *Shall be stirred up to battle with a very great and mighty army.* To oppose Antiochus. ¶ *But he shall not stand.* He shall not be able to resist him. His navy was defeated; Antiochus still held possession

of Memphis, and laid siege to Alexandria. ¶ *For they shall forecast devices against him.* Heb., "shall think thoughts" (see Notes on ver. 24); that is, they shall form plans against him to defeat him. The reference here is to the invading forces, that they would form sagacious plans for the overthrow of the king of Egypt.

26. *Yea, they that feed of the portion of his meat shall destroy him.* They of his own family; they who are nourished at his table; they who are his cabinet counsellors, and professed and confidential friends. The meaning is, that they would prove treacherous and unfaithful. This is by no means improbable. Antiochus was powerful, and had seized upon Pelusium, and upon Memphis, and upon the fairest portions of Egypt. He was also in possession of the person of the lawful king, and had a fair prospect of subduing the whole country. In these circumstances, nothing would be more natural than that the very inmates of the palace—the persons around the reigning king—should begin to doubt whether he could hold out, and should be disposed to make terms with the invader. ¶ *And his army shall overflow.* The connection here requires us to understand this of the army of the king of Egypt. The meaning seems to be, that his forces would be great, and would spread themselves out like overflowing waters, but that notwithstanding this many of them would be slain. ¶ *And many shall fall down slain.* In battle. Notwithstanding the army would be numerous, and would, as it were, spread over the land, still it would not be sufficient to keep out the invaders, but many of them would fall in the field. The account in 1 Macc. i. 18 is, that "Ptolemy was afraid of him [Antiochus] and fled; *and many were wounded to death.*"

27. *And both these kings' hearts* shall

shall speak lies at one table; but it shall not prosper: *a*for yet the end *shall be* at the time appointed.

a vers. 29, 35, 40; ch. 8. 19.

be *to do mischief*. Marg., *their hearts*. The meaning is, that their hearts were set on some evil or unjust purpose. The reference here is, evidently, to Antiochus and Ptolemy Philometor, and the time alluded to is when Ptolemy was in the possession of Antiochus, and when they were together forming their plans. Antiochus invaded the country under pretence of aiding Ptolemy and establishing him in the government, and for the same reason, under pretence of protecting him, he had him now in his possession. At first, also, it would seem that Ptolemy coincided with his plans, or was so far deceived by the acts of Antiochus as to believe in his friendship, and to unite with him in his schemes, for it is expressly said by the historians, as quoted above, that when Antiochus left Egypt, leaving Ptolemy at Memphis, and a strong garrison in Pelusium, Ptolemy began to see through his crafty designs, and to act accordingly. Until that time, however, he seems to have regarded the professions of Antiochus as sincere, and to have entered fully into his plans. To that fact there is allusion here; and the meaning is, that they were forming united schemes of evil— of conquests, and robbery, and oppression. The guiding spirit in this was undoubtedly Antiochus, but Ptolemy seems to have concurred in it. ¶ *And they shall speak lies at one table*. At the same table. Ptolemy was a captive, and was entirely in the possession of Antiochus, but it was a matter of policy with the latter to hide from him as far as possible the fact that he was a prisoner, and to treat him as a king. It is to be presumed, therefore, that he would do so, and that they would be seated at the same table; that is, that Ptolemy would be treated outwardly with the respect due to a king. In this familiar condition—in this state of apparently respectful and confidential intercourse — they would form their plans. Yet the devices of both would

28 Then shall he return into his land with great riches; and his heart *shall be* against the holy covenant; and he shall do *exploits*, and return to his own land.

be *false*—or would be, in fact, *speaking lies*. Antiochus would be acting perfidiously throughout, endeavouring to impose on Ptolemy, and making promises, and giving assurances, which he knew to be false; and Ptolemy would be equally acting a deceitful part —entering into engagements which, perhaps, he did not intend to keep, and which would, at any rate, be soon violated. It is impossible now to know *how* he came into the hands of Antiochus—whether he surrendered himself in war; or whether he was persuaded to do it by the arts of his courtiers; or whether he was really deceived by Antiochus and supposed that he was his friend, and that his protection was necessary. On any of these suppositions it cannot be supposed that he would be very likely to be sincere in his transactions with Antiochus. ¶ *But it shall not prosper*. The scheme concocted, whatever it was, would not be successful. The plan of Antiochus was to obtain possession of the whole of Egypt, but in this he failed; and so far as Ptolemy entered into the scheme proposed by Antiochus, on pretence for the good of his country, it also failed. Whatever the purpose was, it was soon broken up by the fact that Antiochus left Egypt, and made war on Jerusalem. ¶ *For yet the end* shall be *at the time appointed*. See ver. 29. The end—the result—shall not be now, and in the manner contemplated by these two kings. It shall be at the time "appointed," to wit, by God, and in another manner. The whole case shall issue differently from what they design, and at the time which an overruling Providence has designated. The *reason* implied here why they could not carry out their design was, that there was an "appointed time" when these affairs were to be determined, and that no purposes of theirs could be allowed to frustrate the higher counsels of the Most High.

28. *Then shall he return into his*

29 At the time appointed he shall return, and come toward the south: but it shall not be as the former, or as the latter.

land with great riches. Enriched with the spoils of Egypt. Having taken Memphis, and the fairest portions of Egypt, he would, of course, carry great wealth to his own country on his return. Thus it is said in 1 Macc. i. 19: "Thus they got the strong cities in the land of Egypt, and he took the spoils thereof." The meaning here is, that he would *set out* to return to his own land. As a matter of fact, on his way he would pause to bring desolation on Jerusalem, as is intimated in the subsequent part of the verse. ¶ *And his heart* shall be *against the holy covenant.* The words "holy covenant" are a technical expression to denote the Jewish institutions. The Hebrew people were called the "covenant people," as being a people with whom God had entered into covenant. All their privileges were regarded as the result of that covenant, and hence the word came to be applied to all the institutions of the nation. When it is said that his heart was against that covenant, the meaning is, that he was enraged against it ; and determined to bring calamity upon the place and people connected with it. The reason of this was the following: When he was in Egypt, a report was spread abroad that he was dead. In consequence of this rumour, Jason took the opportunity of recovering the office of high-priest from his brother Menelaus, and with a thousand men took Jerusalem, drove Menelaus into the castle, and slew many whom he took for his enemies. Antiochus, hearing of this, supposed that all the Jews had revolted, and determined to inflict summary chastisement on them on his way to his own land. See Jahn, *Hebrew Commonwealth,* p. 263. ¶ *And he shall do* exploits, *and return to his own land.* The word "exploits" is supplied by the translators. The Hebrew is, simply, "he shall do;" that is, he shall accomplish the purpose of his heart on the covenant people. In this expedition he took Jerusalem, whether by storm or by stratagem is not quite certain. Diodorus Siculus, and the author of the second book of Macca-

bees, and Josephus (*Jewish Wars,* i. 1, 2, and vi. 10, 1), say that it was by storm. The account which he gives in his *Antiquities* (b. xii. ch. v. § 3) is, that he took it by stratagem, but the statement in the *Jewish Wars* is much more probable, for Antiochus plundered the city, slew eighty thousand persons, men, women, and children, took forty thousand prisoners, and sold as many into slavery, 2 Macc. v. 5, 6, 11–14. As if this were not enough, under the guidance of the high-priest Menelaus, he went into the sanctuary, uttering blasphemous language, took away all the gold and silver vessels he could find there, the golden table, altar, and candlestick, and all the great vessels, and that he might leave nothing behind, searched the subterranean vaults, and in this manner collected eighteen hundred talents of gold. He then sacrificed swine on the altar, boiled a piece of the flesh, and sprinkled the whole temple with the broth, 2 Macc. v. 15–21; 1 Macc. i. 21–28; Diodorus Sic. xxxiv. 1 ; Jahn, *Hebrew Commonwealth,* p. 264.

29. *At the time appointed.* In the purposes of God. See Notes on ver. 27. That is, at the time when God shall design to accomplish his own purposes in regard to him. The idea is, that there was a definite period in the Divine Mind in which all this was to be done, and that when this should occur Antiochus would return again to invade Egypt. ¶ *He shall return, and come toward the south.* With an intention of invading Egypt. The occasion of this invasion was, that after the departure of Antiochus, leaving Ptolemy in possession of Egypt, or having professedly given up the kingdom to him, Ptolemy suspected the designs of Antiochus, and came to an agreement with his brother Physcon, that they should share the government between them, and resist Antiochus with their united power. To do this, they hired mercenary troops from Greece. Antiochus, learning this, openly threw off the mask, and pre-

30 ¶ For the ships[a] of Chittim shall come against him; therefore he shall be grieved, and return, and have indignation against the

a Nu. 24. 24.

holy covenant: so shall he do; [1] he shall even return, and have intelligence with them that forsake the holy covenant.

1 Fulfilled, 168, 169, B.C.

pared to invade Egypt again, B.C. 167. He sent his fleet to Cyprus to secure possession of that island, and led his army towards Egypt to subdue the two brothers, designing to annex the whole country to his dominions. ¶ *But it shall not be as the former, or as the latter.* At the first invasion or the second. In these he was successful; in this he would not be. The reason of his want of success is stated in the following verse—that by the aid which the two brothers had obtained from abroad, as expressed in the next verse, they would be able to oppose him.

30. *For the ships of Chittim shall come against him.* The word rendered *Chittim*—כִּתִּים—according to Gesenius, properly means *Cyprians,* so called from a celebrated Phœnician colony in the island of Cyprus. In a wider acceptation the name came to comprehend the islands and coasts of the Mediterranean Sea, especially the northern parts, and therefore stands for the islands and coasts of Greece and the Ægean Sea. See Gesenius, *Lex.*, and comp. Josephus, *Ant.* b. i. ch. vi. 1. The Egyptian government had called in the aid of the Romans, and Antiochus, therefore, was threatened with a war with the Romans if he did not abandon his enterprise against Egypt. The reference in the passage before us is to the embassage which the Romans sent to Antiochus in Egypt, requiring him to desist from his enterprise against Egypt. "When he had arrived at Leusine, about four miles from Alexandria, he met Caius Popilius Lænas, Caius Decimius, and Caius Hostilius, ambassadors, whom the Roman Senate had sent to him at the earnest request of Ptolemy Physcon. They were instructed to assure Antiochus that he must leave the kingdom of Egypt and the island of Cyprus in peace, or expect a war with the Romans. When Antiochus said that he would lay the

affair before his council, Popilius, the head of the legation, with his staff drew a circle about the king in the sand on which they stood, and exclaimed, 'Before you leave that circle, you must give me an answer which I can report to the Senate.' Antiochus was confounded, but on a little reflection, he said he would do whatever the Senate required."— Jahn, *Heb. Commonwealth,* pp. 265, 266; Polyb. *Legat.* §§ 90, 92; Livy, xliv. 14, 29; 41–46; xlv. 10, 12. These ambassadors came by the way of Greece, and in Grecian vessels, and their coming might properly be described as "ships from Chittim." They went from Rome to Brundusium, and then passed over to the Grecian shore, and from thence by the way of Chalcis, Delos, and Rhodes, to Alexandria.—Prideaux, iii. 237. ¶ *Therefore he shall be grieved.* The word here used—כָּאָה—means, properly, to become faint-hearted; to be frightened; to be dejected, sad, humbled, Job xxx. 8; Ezek. xiii. 22; Psa. cix. 16. The meaning here is, that he became dispirited, dejected, cast down, and abandoned his purpose. He saw that it would be vain to attempt to contend with the Romans, and he was constrained reluctantly to relinquish his enterprise. ¶ *And return.* Set out to return to his own land. ¶ *And have indignation against the holy covenant.* See Notes on ver. 28. That is, he would be filled with wrath against Jerusalem and the Jews. Polybius says that he left Egypt in great anger, because he was compelled by the Romans to abandon his designs. In this condition he was, of course, in a state of mind to become irritated against any other people, and, if an occasion should be given, would seek to vent his wrath in some other direction. This habitual state of feeling towards Jerusalem and the Jews would make him ready to seize upon the slightest pretext to

31 And arms shall stand on his part, and they shall pollute the sanctuary of strength, and shall take away the daily *sacrifice*, and they shall place the abomination that maketh [1] desolate. 1 or, *astonisheth.*

wreak his vengeance on the holy land. What was the immediate occasion of his taking this opportunity to attack Jerusalem is not certainly known, but in his marching back through Palestine, he detached from his army twenty-two thousand men, under the command of Apollonius, and sent them to Jerusalem to destroy it.—Prideaux, iii. 239; Jahn, *Heb. Commonwealth,* p. 266. Apollonius arrived before Jerusalem B. C. 167, just two years after the city had been taken by Antiochus himself. ¶ *So shall he do.* That is, in the manner described in this and the following verses. ¶ *He shall even return.* On his way to his own land. ¶ *And have intelligence with them that forsake the holy covenant.* Have an understanding with them; that is, with a portion of the nation—with those who were disposed to cast off the religion of their fathers. There was a considerable part of the nation that was inclined to do this, and to introduce the customs of the Greeks (comp. Jahn, *Heb. Commonwealth,* pp. 258–260); and it was natural that Antiochus should seek to have an understanding with them, and to make use of them in accomplishing his designs. It was very probably at the solicitation of this infidel and disaffected party of the Hebrew people that Antiochus had interfered in their affairs at all. Comp. 1 Macc. i. 11–15.

31. *And arms shall stand on his part.* Up to this verse there is a general agreement among commentators, that the reference is to Antiochus Epiphanes. From this verse, however, to the end of the chapter, there is no little diversity of opinion. One portion suppose that the description of Antiochus and his deeds continues still to be the design of the prophet ; another, that the Romans are here introduced, and that a part of the predictions in the remainder of this chapter are yet to be fulfilled ; another, as Jerome, and most of the Christian fathers, suppose that the reference is to Antiochus as the type of Antichrist, and that the description passes from the type to the antitype. In this last class are found Bishop Newton, Gill, Calvin, Prideaux, Wintle, Elliott (*Apocalypse,* iv. 137, *seq.*), and others ; in the former, Grotius, Lengerke, Bertholdt, Maurer, &c. In this same class is found the name of Porphyry—who maintained that the whole referred to Antiochus, and that the allusion was so clear as to prove that this portion of the book was written *after* the events had occurred. The reason suggested for the change in the supposed reference, as alleged by Bishop Newton *on the Prophecies,* p. 296, is, substantially, that what follows can be applied only in part to Antiochus. Whether this portion of the chapter can be shown to refer to him, we shall be able to determine as we proceed. Nothing can be clearer than the allusion up to this point. The word rendered *arms,* in the verse before us

(זְרֹעִים — sing. זְרֹיעַ), means, properly, the arm — especially the lower arm below the elbow ; and then comes to denote strength, might, power ; and thence is applied to a military force, or an army. See ver. 15. Such is undoubtedly the meaning here, and the reference is to the military force which Antiochus would employ to wreak his vengeance on the Jews—particularly by the instrumentality of Apollonius. Others would apply this to the Romans, and suppose that they are introduced here ; but this construction is forced and unnatural, for (*a*) the reference in the previous verses was, undoubtedly, to Antiochus, and the narrative seems to proceed as if there were no change. (*b*) There is nothing in the statement which does not agree with what was done by Antiochus. As a matter of fact, as attested by all history, he detached Apollonius with twenty-two thousand men, on his mortified return to his own land, to attack and lay waste Jerusalem, and Apollonius did all that is here said would be done. Bishop Newton concedes (p. 294) that " this interpretation might be admitted, if the other parts were equally applicable to Antiochus; but," says he, "the difficulty, or rather impossibility of applying them to Antiochus, or any of the Syrian kings, his successors, obliges us to look out for another interpretation." Accordingly, he says that Jerome and the Christians of his time contend that these things apply to Antichrist; and he himself adopts the view proposed by Sir Isaac Newton, that it refers to the Romans, and that the allusion is to the fact that, at the very time when Antiochus retreated out of Egypt, the Romans conquered Macedonia, "putting an end to the reign of Daniel's third beast," and that the prophet here leaves off the description of the actions of the Greeks, and commences a description of those of the Romans in Greece. As, however, all that is *here* said is strictly applicable to what was done by Antiochus, such an interpretation is unnecessary. ¶ *And they shall pollute the sanctuary of strength.* The "sanctuary *of strength*" seems to refer to the fortifications or defences that had been set up to protect Jerusalem, or the temple. At various points the temple was defended in this manner, not only by the walls of the city, but by fortifications erected within, and so as to prevent an army from approaching the temple, even if they should penetrate the outer wall. Comp. 1 Macc. i. 36. The temple itself might thus be regarded as fortified, or as a place of strength—and, as a matter of fact, when Titus ultimately destroyed the city, the chief difficulty was to obtain possession of the temple—a place that held out to the last. When it is said that they would "*pollute* the sanctuary of strength," the reference is to what was done by Apollonius, at the command of Antiochus, to profane the temple, and to put an end to the sacrifices and worship there. Comp. 1 Macc. i. 29, 37–49; Jos. *Ant.* b. xii. ch. v. § 4. The account in the book of Maccabees is as follows: "Thus they shed innocent blood on every side of the sanctuary and defiled it, insomuch that the inhabitants of Jerusalem fled because of them, wherefore the city was made a habitation of strangers,

and became strange to those who were born in her, and her own children left her. Her sanctuary was laid waste like a wilderness, and her feasts were turned into mourning, her sabbaths into reproach, her honour into contempt. As had been her glory, so was her dishonour increased, and her excellency was turned into mourning. Moreover, king Antiochus wrote to his whole kingdom that all should be one people, and every one should leave his laws; so all the heathen agreed, according to the commandment of the king. Yea, many Israelites consented to his religion, and sacrificed unto idols, and profaned the Sabbath. For the king had sent letters by messengers unto Jerusalem and the cities of Judah, that they should follow the strange laws of the land, and forbid burnt-offerings, and sacrifices, and drink-offerings, in the temple; and that they should profane the sabbaths and festival days, and pollute the sanctuary and holy people; set up altars, and groves, and chapels of idols, and sacrifice swine's flesh and unclean beasts; that they should also leave their children uncircumcised, and make their souls abominable with all manner of uncleanness and profanation, to the end they might forget the law, and change all the ordinances." ¶ *And shall take away the daily* sacrifice. That is, shall forbid it, and so pollute the temple and the altar as to prevent its being offered. See the quotation above. This occurred in the month of June, B.C. 167. See Jahn, *Heb. Commonwealth*, p. 267. ¶ *And they shall place the abomination that maketh desolate.* Marg., or, *astonisheth.* The Hebrew word מְשֹׁמֵם

will bear either interpretation, though the usage of the word is in favour of the translation in the text. The passage will also admit of this translation —"the abomination of desolation *of him* who makes desolate," or of *the desolater.* See Gesenius, *Lex.* 3. The idea is, that somehow the thing here referred to would be connected with the *desolation*, or the laying waste of the city and temple; and the sense is not materially varied whether we regard it as "the abomination that makes

32 And such as do wickedly against the covenant shall he [1] corrupt by flatteries: but the people that do know their God shall be strong, and do *exploits*.

1 or, *cause to dissemble.*

33 And they that understand among the people shall instruct many; yet they shall fall by the sword, and by flame, by captivity, and by spoil, *many* days.

desolate," that is, that *indicates* the desolation, or, "the abomination *of the desolater*," that is, of him who has laid the city and temple waste. On the meaning of the phrase "abomination of desolation," see Notes on ch. ix. 27. The reference here is, undoubtedly, to something that Antiochus set up in the temple that was an indication of desolation, or the result of his having laid the temple in ruins. The very expression occurs in 1 Macc. i. 54: "Now, the fifteenth day of the month Casleu, in the hundred and forty-fifth year, they set up *the abomination of desolation* upon the altar, and builded idol-altars throughout the cities of Judah on every side." This would seem, from ver. 59, to have been an idol-altar erected *over* or *upon* the altar of burnt-offerings. "They did sacrifice upon the idol-altar, which was upon the altar of God." "At this time an old man, by the name of Athenæus, was sent to Jerusalem to instruct the Jews in the Greek religion, and compel them to an observance of its rites. He dedicated the temple to Jupiter Olympius; and on the altar of Jehovah he placed a smaller altar, to be used in sacrificing to the heathen god."—Jahn, *Heb. Commonwealth*, pp. 267, 268. The reference here is, probably, to this altar, as being in itself and in the situation where it was located an "abominable" thing in the eyes of the Hebrews, and as being placed there by *a desolater*, or *waster*. The same *language* which is here used is applied in ch. ix. 27, and in the New Testament, with great propriety to what the Romans set up in the temple as an indication of its conquest and profanation; but that fact does not make it certain that it is so to be understood *here*, for it is as applicable to what Antiochus did as it is to what was done by the Romans. See Notes on ch. ix. 27.

32. *And such as do wickedly against the covenant*. That is, among the Jews.

They who apostatized, and who became willing to receive the religion of foreigners. - There *was* such a party in Jerusalem, and it was numerous. See Jahn, *Heb. Commonwealth*, pp. 258, 259. Comp. 1 Macc. i. 52: "Then many of the people were gathered unto them, to wit, every one that forsook the law; and so they committed evils in the land." ¶ *Shall he corrupt by flatteries*. By flattering promises of his favour, of office, of national prosperity, &c. See Notes on ver. 21. The margin is, "or, *cause to dissemble*." The meaning of the Hebrew word חָנֵף is, rather, *to profane, to pollute, to defile;* and the idea here is, that he would cause them to become defiled; that is, that he would seduce them to impiety and apostasy. ¶ *But the people that do know their God*. They who adhere to the service and worship of the true God, and who are incapable of being seduced to apostasy and sin. The reference here is, undoubtedly, to Judas Maccabeus and his followers— a full account of whose doings is to be found in the books of the Maccabees. See also Prideaux, *Con.* iii. 245, *seq.*, and Jahn, *Heb. Commonwealth*, pp. 268, *seq.* ¶ *Shall be strong*. Shall evince great valour, and shall show great vigour in opposing him. ¶ *And do* exploits. The word "*exploits*," as in ver. 28, is supplied by the translators, but not improperly. The meaning is, that they would show great prowess, and perform illustrious deeds in battle. See Prideaux, *Con.* iii. pp. 262, 263.

33. *And they that understand among the people*. Among the Hebrew people. The allusion is to such as, in those times of so general corruption and apostasy, should have a proper understanding of the law of God and the nature of religion. There were such in the days of Judas Maccabeus, and it is reasonable to suppose that they would endeavour to inculcate just

34 Now when they shall fall, they shall be holpen with a little help : but many shall cleave to them with flatteries.

views among the people. ¶ *Shall instruct many.* In the nature of religion; in their duty to their country and to God. See Prideaux, *Con.* iii. 265. ¶ *Yet they shall fall by the sword.* They shall not be immediately nor always successful. Their final triumph would be only after many of them had fallen in battle, or been made captives. Mattathias, the father of Judas Maccabeus, who began the opposition to Antiochus (1 Macc. ii. 1), having summoned to his standard as many as he could induce to follow him, retired for security to the mountains. He was pursued, and refusing to fight on the Sabbath, his enemies came upon him, and slew many of his followers, 1 Macc. ii. 14–37. The author of the book of Maccabees (1 Macc. ii. 38) says of this : "So they rose up against them in battle on the sabbath, and they slew them, with their wives and children, and their cattle, to the number of a thousand people." ¶ *And by flame.* By fire. That is, probably, their dwellings would be fired, and they would perish in the flames, or in caves where they fled for shelter, or by being cast into heated caldrons of brass. See 2 Macc. vi. 11 : "And others that had run together into caves near by" (when Antiochus endeavoured to enforce on them the observance of heathen laws and customs), "to keep the sabbath-day secretly, being discovered to Philip, were all burnt together, because they made a conscience to help themselves for the honour of the most sacred day." 2 Macc. vii. 3–5 : "Then the king, being in a rage, commanded pans and caldrons to be made hot : which forthwith being heated, he commanded to cut out the tongue of him that spake first, and to cut off the utmost parts of his body, the rest of his brethren and his mother looking on. Now when he was thus maimed in all his members, he commanded him, being yet alive, to be brought to the fire, and to be fried in the pan," &c. ¶ *By captivity.* 1 Macc. i. 32 : "But the women and children took they captive." See also 2 Macc. v. 24. ¶ *And*

by spoil. By plunder, to wit, of the temple and city. See 1 Macc. i. 20–24. ¶ Many *days.* Heb., *days.* The time is not specified, but the idea is that it would be for a considerable period. Josephus says it was three years.— *Ant.* b. xii. ch. vii. §§ 6, 7 ; 1 Macc. i. 59 ; iv. 54 ; 2 Macc. x. 1–7.

34. *Now when they shall fall, they shall be holpen with a little help.* By small accessions to their forces. The armies of the Maccabees were never *very* numerous ; but the idea here is, that when they should be persecuted, there would be accessions ·to their forces, so that they would be able to prosecute the war. At first the numbers were very few who took up arms, and undertook to defend the institutions of religion, but their numbers increased until they were finally victorious. Those who first banded together, when the calamities came upon the nation, were Mattathias and his few followers, and this is the little help that is here referred to. See 1 Macc. ii. ¶ *But many shall cleave to them.* As was the case under Judas Maccabeus, when the forces were so far increased as to be able to contend successfully with Antiochus. ¶ *With flatteries.* Perhaps with flattering hopes of spoil or honour ; that is, that they would not unite sincerely with the defenders of the true religion, but would be actuated by prospect of plunder or reward. For the meaning of the word, see Notes on ver. 21. The sense here is not that Judas would flatter them, or would secure their co-operation by flatteries, but that this would be what they would propose to their own minds, and what would influence them. Comp. 1 Macc. v. 55–57 : "Now what time as Judas and Jonathan were in the land of Galaad, and Simon his brother in Galilee before Ptolemais, Joseph the son of Zacharias, and Azarias, captains of the garrisons, heard of the valiant acts and warlike deeds which they had done. Wherefore they said, Let us also get us a name, and go fight against the heathen round about us." Comp. 2 Macc. xii. 40 ; xiii. 21.

35 And *some* of them of understanding shall fall, to ª try ¹ them,
and to purge, and to make *them*
white, *even* to the time of the end:

a 2 Chron. 32. 31.   1 or, *by them.*

There can be no doubt that many
might join them from these motives.
Such an event would be likely to occur
anywhere, when one was successful,
and where there was a prospect of
spoils or of fame in uniting with a
victorious leader of an army.

35. *And* some *of them of understanding shall fall.* Some of those who
have a correct understanding of religion, and who have joined the army
from pure motives. The idea seems
to be that on some occasion they would
meet with a temporary defeat, in order
that the sincerity of the others might
be tested, or that it might be seen who
adhered to the cause from principle,
and who from selfish purposes. If
they should not always be successful;
if they should be temporarily defeated;
if some of the most eminent among
them should fall among the slain; and
if the cause should at any time look
dark, this would serve to try the sincerity of the remainder of the army,
and would be likely to *thin it off* of
those who had joined it only from
mercenary motives. ¶ *To try them.*
Marg., "or, *by them.*" So the Hebrew—בָּהֶם. The meaning perhaps is,
that it would be *by* them, as it were,
that the army would be tried. As
they would fall in battle, and as the
cause would seem to be doubtful, this
would test the fidelity of others. The
word *try* here (צָרַף) means, properly, *to
melt, to smelt*—as metals; then to prove
any one; and then to purify. ¶ *And
to purge.* To purify; to test the army
and to make it pure. ¶ *And to make*
them *white.* To wit, by thus allowing those who had joined the army
from mercenary motives to withdraw.
Comp. 2 Macc. xii. 39–41. ¶ *Even
to the time of the end.* The end
of the war or the conflict. There
would be an end of these persecutions
and trials, and this process had reference to that, or tended to bring it
about. The act of freeing the army

because *it is* yet for a time ap-
pointed.ᵇ

36 And the king shall do according to his will; and ᶜ he shall

b Hab. 2. 3.   *c* Isa. 14. 13, 14; Rev. 13, 5. 6.

from false friends—from those who had
joined it from mercenary motives,
would have a tendency to accomplish
the result in the best way possible, and
in the speediest manner. ¶ *Because* it
is *yet for a time appointed.* See Notes
on ver. 27. This seems to be designed
for an assurance that the calamity
would come to an end, or that there
was a limit beyond which it could not
pass. Thus it would be an encouragement to those who were engaged in the
struggle, for they would see that success
must ultimately crown their labours.

36. *And the king shall do according
to his will.* Shall be absolute and supreme, and shall accomplish his purposes. This refers, it seems to me,
beyond question, to Antiochus Epiphanes, and was exactly fulfilled in
him. He accomplished his purposes
in regard to the city and temple in the
most arbitrary manner, and was, in
every respect, an absolute despot. It
should be said, however, here, that
most Christian interpreters suppose
that the allusion here to Antiochus
ceases, and that henceforward it refers
to Antichrist. So Jerome, Gill, Bp.
Newton, and others; and so Jerome
says many of the Jews understood it.
The only reason alleged for this is, that
there are things affirmed here of the
"king" which could not be true of
Antiochus. But, in opposition to this,
it may be observed (*a*) that the allusion
in the previous verses is undoubtedly
to Antiochus Epiphanes. (*b*) There is
no indication of any *change*, for the
prophetic narrative seems to proceed
as if the allusion to the same person
continued. (*c*) The word "*king*" is
not a word to be applied to Antichrist,
it being nowhere used of him. (*d*) Such
a transition, without any more decided
marks of it, would not be in accordance with the usual method in the prophetic writings, leaving a plain prediction in the very midst of the description, and passing on at once to a
representation of one who would arise

exalt himself, and magnify himself above every god, and shall speak marvellous things against the God of gods, and shall prosper till the in-

dignation be accomplished: for that that is determined *a* shall be done.

37 Neither shall he regard the

after many hundred years, and of whom the former could be considered as in no way the type. The most obvious and honest way, therefore, of interpreting this is, to refer it to Antiochus, and perhaps we shall find that the difficulty of applying it to him is not insuperable. ¶ *And he shall exalt himself.* No one can doubt that *this* will agree with Antiochus Epiphanes—a proud, haughty, absolute, and stern monarch, the purpose of whose reign was to exalt himself, and to extend the limits of his empire. ¶ *And magnify himself above every god.* That is, by directing what gods should or should not be worshipped; attempting to displace the claim of all those who were worshipped as gods at his pleasure, and establishing the worship of other gods in their place. Thus he assumed the right to determine what god should be worshipped in Jerusalem, abolishing the worship of Jehovah, and setting up that of Jupiter Olympius in the stead; and so throughout his whole dominion, by a proclamation, he forbade the worship of any god but his, 1. Macc. i. 44–51; Jos. *Ant.* b. xii. ch. v. §§ 4, 5. One who assumes or claims the right to forbid the adoration of any particular god, and to order divine homage to be rendered to any one which he chooses, exalts himself *above* the gods, as he in this way denies the right which *they* must be supposed to claim to prescribe their own worship. ¶ *And shall speak marvellous things.* The Hebrew word נִפְלָאֹות would properly denote things wonderful, or fitted to excite astonishment; things that are unusual and extraordinary: and the meaning here is, that the things spoken would be so impious and atrocious—so amazing and wonderful for their wickedness, as to produce amazement. ¶ *Against the God of gods.* The true God, Jehovah; he is supreme, and is superior to all that is called God, or that is worshipped as such. Nothing could be better descrip-

tive of Antiochus than this; nothing was ever more strikingly fulfilled than this was in him. ¶ *And shall prosper till the indignation be accomplished.* Referring still to the fact that there was an appointed time during which this was to continue. That time might well be called a time of "indignation," for the Lord seemed to be angry against his temple and people, and suffered this heathen king to pour out *his* wrath without measure against the temple, the city, and the whole land. ¶ *For that that is determined shall be done.* What is purposed in regard to the city and temple, and to all other things, must be accomplished. Comp. ch. x. 21. The angel here states a general truth—that all that God has ordained will come to pass. The application of this truth here is, that the series of events must be suffered to run on, and that it could not be expected that they would be arrested until all that had been determined in the Divine mind should be effected. They who would suffer, therefore, in those times must wait with patience until the Divine purposes should be brought about, and when the period should arrive, the calamities would cease.

37. *Neither shall he regard the God of his fathers.* The god that his fathers or ancestors had worshipped. That is, he would not be bound or restrained by the religion of his own land, or by any of the usual laws of religion. He would worship any God that he pleased, or none as he pleased. The usual restraints that bind men—the restraints derived from the religion of their ancestors—would in this case be of no avail. See Notes on ver. 36. This was in all respects true of Antiochus. At his pleasure he worshipped the gods commonly adored in his country, or the gods worshipped by the Greeks and Romans, or no gods. And, in a special manner, instead of honouring the god of his fathers, and causing the image of that god to be placed in the temple at Jerusalem, as it might have been

God of his fathers, nor the desire
of women, nor regard any god: for

he shall magnify himself above
all. [a]

a 2 Thess. 2. 4.

supposed he would, he caused the altar
of Jupiter Olympius to be set up there,
and his worship to be celebrated there.
In fact, as Antiochus had been edu-
cated abroad, and had passed his early
life in foreign countries, he had never
paid much respect to the religion of
his own land. The attempt to introduce a foreign religion into Judea was
an attempt to introduce the religion of
the Greeks (Jahn, *Heb. Commonwealth*,
p. 267); and in no instance did he endeavour to force upon them the peculiar religion of his own nation. In his
private feelings, therefore, and in his
public acts, it might be said of Antiochus, that he was characterized in an
eminent degree by a want of regard for
the faith of his ancestors. The language used here by the angel is that
which would properly denote great infidelity and impiety. ¶ *Nor the desire of women.* The phrase "the desire
of women" is in itself ambiguous, and
may either mean what *they* desire, that
is, what is agreeable to them, or what
they commonly seek, and for which
they would plead; or it may mean *his
own* desire—that is, that he would not
be restrained by the desire of women,
by any regard for women, for honourable matrimony, or by irregular passion. The phrase here is probably to
be taken in the former sense, as this
best suits the connection. There has
been great variety in the interpretation of this expression. Some have
maintained that it cannot be applicable
to Antiochus at all, since he was a man
eminently licentious and under the influence of abandoned women. Jerome,
in loc., J. D. Michaelis, Dereser, Gesenius, and Lengerke suppose that this
means that he would not regard the
beautiful statue of the goddess Venus
whose temple was in Elymaïs, which
he plundered. Stäudlin and Dathe,
that he would not regard the weeping
or tears of women—that is, that he
would be cruel. Bertholdt, that he
would not spare little children, the object of a mother's love—that is, that
he would be a cruel tyrant. Jerome
renders it, *Et erit in concupiscentiis*

fœminarum, and explains it of un-
bridled lust, and applies it principally
to Antiochus. Elliott, strangely it
seems to me (*Apocalypse*, iv. 152), interprets it as referring to that which
was so much the object of desire among
the *Hebrew* women—the Messiah, the
promised seed of the woman; and he
says that he had found this opinion
hinted at by Faber *on the Prophecies*
(Ed. 5), i. 380–385. Others expound
it as signifying that he would not regard honourable matrimony, but would
be given to unlawful pleasures. It
may not be practicable to determine
with certainty the meaning of the expression, but it seems to me that the
design of the whole is to set forth the
impiety and hard-heartedness of Antiochus. He would not regard the gods
of his fathers; that is, he would not be
controlled by any of the principles of
the religion in which he had been edu-
cated, but would set them all at defi-
ance, and would do as he pleased; and,
in like manner, he would be unaffected
by the influences derived from the female character—would disregard the
objects that were nearest to their hearts,
their sentiments of kindness and compassion; their pleadings and their tears;
he would be a cruel tyrant, alike regardless of all the restraints derived
from heaven and earth—the best influences from above and from below.
It is not necessary to say that this
agrees exactly with the character of
Antiochus. He was sensual and corrupt, and given to licentious indulgence, and was incapable of honourable and pure love, and was a stranger
to all those bland and pure affections
produced by intercourse with refined
and enlightened females. If one wishes
to describe a high state of tyranny and
depravity in a man, it cannot be done
better than by saying that he disre-
gards whatever is attractive and interesting to a virtuous female mind.
¶ *Nor regard any god.* Any religious restraints whatever—the laws of
any god worshipped in his own land
or elsewhere—in heaven or on earth.
That is, he would be utterly irreligious

38 But ¹in his ²estate shall he honour the God of ³forces; and a god whom his fathers knew not

1 *as for the Almighty God, in his seat, he shall honour, yea, he shall honour a god,* &c.
2 *or, stead.*

shall he honour with gold, and silver, and with precious stones, and ⁴pleasant things.

3 *Mauzzim, or, gods protectors, or, munitions.*
4 *things desired;* Isa. 44. 9.

in heart, and where it conflicted with his purposes would set at nought every consideration derived from reverence to God. This harmonizes well with the previous declaration about women. The two commonly go together. He that is unrestrained by the attractive virtues of the female mind and character; he that has no regard for the sympathies and kindnesses that interest virtuous females; he that sees nothing lovely in what commonly engages their thoughts ; and he that throws himself beyond the restraints of their society, and the effects of their conversation, is commonly a man who cuts himself loose from all religion, and is at the same time a despiser of virtuous females and of God. No one will expect piety towards God to be found in a bosom that sees nothing to interest him in the sympathies and virtues of the female mind; and the character of a woman-hater and a hater of God will uniformly be found united in the same person. Such a person was Antiochus Epiphanes ; and such men have often been found in the world. ¶ *For he shall magnify himself above all.* Above all the restraints of religion, and all those derived from the intercourse of virtuous social life—setting at nought all the restraints that usually bind men. Comp. Notes on ch. viii. 10, 11.

38. *But in his estate.* The marginal reading here is, " *As for the Almighty God, in his seat he shall honour, yea, he shall honour a god,*" &c. The more correct rendering, however, is that in the text, and the reference is to some god which he would honour, or for which he would show respect. The rendering proposed by Lengerke is the true rendering, " But the god of forces [firm places, fastnesses—*der Vesten*] he shall honour in their foundation " [*auf seinem Gestelle*]. The Vulgate renders this, " But the god Maozim shall he honour in his place." So also the Greek. The phrase "in his estate"

—עַל־כַּנּוֹ—means, properly, "upon his base," or foundation. It occurs in vers. 20, 21, where it is applied to a monarch who would succeed another —occupying the same place, or the same seat or throne. See Notes on ver. 2. Here it seems to mean that he would honour the god referred to in the place which he occupied, or, as it were, on his own throne, or in his own temple. The margin is, " or *stead;*" but the idea is not that he would honour this god *instead* of another, but that he would do it in his own place. If, however, as Gesenius and De Wette suppose, the sense is, " in his place, or stead," the correct interpretation is, that he would honour this "god of forces," in the stead of honouring the god of his fathers, or any other god. The general idea is clear, that he would show disrespect or contempt for all other gods, and pay his devotions to this god alone. ¶ *Shall he honour.* Pay respect to ; worship ; obey. This would be *his* god. He would show no respect to the god of his fathers, nor to any of the idols usually worshipped, but would honour *this* god exclusively. ¶ *The God of forces.* Marg., *Mauzzim,* or *gods protectors;* or, *munitions.* Heb., מָעֻזִּים *Mauzzim;* Latin Vulg., *Maozim;* Gr., Μαωζεὶμ ; Syriac, "the strong God ;" Luther, *Mausim;* Lengerke, *der Vesten* —fastnesses, fortresses. The Hebrew word מָעוֹז means, properly, a strong or fortified place, a fortress ; and Gesenius (*Lex.*) supposes that the reference here is to " the god of fortresses, a deity of the Syrians obtruded upon the Jews, perhaps *Mars.*" So also Grotius, C. B. Michaelis, Stäudlin, Bertholdt, and Winer. Dereser, Hävernick, and Lengerke explain it as referring to the Jupiter Capitolinus that Antiochus had learned to worship by his long residence in Rome, and whose worship he transferred to his own country. There has been no little speculation as to the meaning of this passage, and as to the god here referred to ; but it would seem that the general idea is plain. It is, that the only god which he would acknowledge would be *force,* or *power,* or *dominion.* He would set at nought the worship of the god of his fathers, and all the usual obligations and restraints of religion ; he would discard and despise all the pleadings of humanity and kindness, as if they were the weaknesses of women, and he would depend solely on force. He would, as it were, adore only the "god of force," and carry his purposes, not by right, or by the claims of religion, but by arms. The meaning is not, I apprehend, that he would formally set up this "god of forces," and adore him, but that this would be, in fact, the *only* god that he would practically acknowledge. In selecting such a god as would properly represent his feelings he would choose such an one as would denote *force* or *dominion.* Such a god would be the god of war, or the Roman Jupiter, who, as being supreme, and ruling the world by his mere power, would be a fit representative of the prevailing purpose of the monarch. The general sentiment is, that all obligations of religion, and justice, and compassion, would be disregarded, and he would carry his purposes by mere power, with the idea, perhaps, included, as seems to be implied in the remainder of the verse, that he would set up and adore such a foreign god as would be a suitable representation of this purpose. It is hardly necessary to say that this was eminently true of Antiochus Epiphanes ; and it may be equally said to be true of all the great heroes and conquerors of the world. Mars, the god of war, was thus adored openly in ancient times, and the devotion of heroes and conquerors to that idol god, though less open and formal, has not been less real by the heroes and conquerors of modern times ; and, as we say now of an avaricious or covetous man that he is a worshipper of mammon, though he in fact formally worships no god, and has no altar, so it might be affirmed of Antiochus, and

may be of heroes and conquerors in general, that the only god that is honoured is the god of war, of power, of force ; and that setting at nought all the obligations of religion, and of worship of the true God, they pay their devotions to this god alone. , Next to mammon, the god that is most adored in this world is the "god of force"— this *Mauzzim* that Antiochus so faithfully served. In illustration of the fact that seems here to be implied, that he would introduce such a god as would be a fit representative of this purpose of his life, it may be remarked that, when in Rome, where Antiochus spent his early years, he had learned to worship the Jupiter of the Capitol, and that he endeavoured to introduce the worship of that foreign god into Syria. Of this *fact* there can be no doubt. It was one of the characteristics of Antiochus that he imitated the manners and customs of the Romans to a ridiculous extent (Diod. Sic. *Frag.* xxvi. 65) ; and it was a fact that he sent rich gifts to Rome in honour of the Jupiter worshipped there (Livy, lxii. 6), and that he purposed to erect a magnificent temple in honour of Jupiter Capitolinus in Antioch—Livy, xli. 20. This temple, however, was not completed. It will be remembered, also, that he caused an altar to Jupiter to be erected over the altar of burnt-sacrifice in Jerusalem. It should be added, that they who apply this to Antichrist, or the Pope, refer it to idol or image worship. Elliott (*Apocalypse,* iv. 153) supposes that it relates to the homage paid to the saints and martyrs under the Papacy, and says that an appellation answering to the word *Mahuzzim* was actually given to the departed martyrs and saints under the Papal apostasy. Thus he remarks : "As to what is said of the wilful king's honouring the god *Mahuzzim* (a god whom his fathers knew not) in place of his ancestors' god, and the true God, it seems to me to have been well and consistently explained, by a reference to those *saints,* and their *relics* and *images,* which the apostasy from its first development regarded and worshipped as the *Mahuzzim,* or *fortresses* of the places where they were depo-

39 Thus shall he do in the ¹ most strong holds with a strange god, whom he shall acknowledge *and*

1 *fortresses of munitions.*

increase with glory: and he shall cause them to rule over many, and shall divide the land for ² gain.

2 *a price.*

---

sited."—*Apoc.* iv. 157. But all this appears forced and unnatural; and if it be not supposed that it was designed to refer to Antichrist or the Papacy, no application of the *language* can be found so obvious and appropriate as that which supposes that it refers to Antiochus, and to his reliance on *force* rather than on justice and right. ¶ *And a god whom his fathers knew not.* This foreign god, Jupiter, whom he had learned to worship at Rome. ¶ *Shall he honour with gold, and silver, and with precious stones,* &c. That is, he shall lavish these things on building a temple for him, or on his image. This accords with the account which Livy gives (xli. 20) of the temple which he commenced at Antioch in honour of Jupiter. Livy says that, although in his conduct he was profligate, and although in many things it was supposed that he was deranged—"Quidam haud dubie insanire aiebant"—yet that in two respects he was distinguished for having a noble mind—for his worship of the gods, and for his favour towards cities in adorning them : " In duabus tamen magnis honestisque rebus vere regius erat animus, in urbium donis, et deorum cultu." He then adds, in words that are all the commentary which we need on the passage before us: " Magnificentiæ vero in deos vel Jovis Olympii templum Athenis, unum in terris inchoatum pro magnitudine dei, potest testis esse. Sed et Delon aris insignibus statuarumque copia exornavit ; et Antiochiæ Jovis capitolini magnificum templum, non laqueatum auro tantum, sed parietibus totis lamina inauratum, et alia multa in aliis locis pollicita, quia perbreve tempus regni ejus fuit, non perfecit." ¶ *And pleasant things.* Marg., *things desired.* That is, with ornaments, or statuary, or perhaps pictures. Comp. Notes on Isa. ii. 16. He meant that the temple should be beautified and adorned in the highest degree. This temple, Livy says, he did not live to finish.

39. *Thus shall he do in the most strong holds.* Marg., *fortresses of munitions.* The reference is to strongly fortified places ; to those places which had been made strong for purposes of defence. The idea is, that he would carry on his purposes against these places, as it were, under the auspices of this strange god. It was a fact, that in his wars Antiochus came into possession of the strong places, or the fortified towns of the nations which he attacked—Jerusalem, Sidon, Pelusium, Memphis — then among the strongest places in the world. ¶ *With a strange god.* A foreign god whom his fathers did not acknowledge; that is, according to the supposition above, and according to the fact, with the god whom he had adored at Rome, and whose worship he was ambitious to transfer to his own empire—the Jupiter of the Capitol. He seemed to be acting under the auspices of this foreign god. ¶ *Whom he shall acknowledge.* By building temples and altars to him. ¶ *And increase with glory.* That is, with honour. He would seem to *increase* or extend his dominion in the world, by introducing his worship in his own country and in the lands which he would conquer. Before, his dominion appeared to be only at Rome; Antiochus sought that it might be extended farther, over his own kingdom, and over the countries that he would conquer. ¶ *And he shall cause them to rule over many.* That is, the foreign gods. Mention had been made before of only one god ; but the introduction of the worship of Jupiter would be naturally connected with that of the other gods of Rome, and they are, therefore, referred to in this manner. The conquests of Antiochus would seem to be a setting up of the dominion of these gods over the lands which he subdued. ¶ *And shall divide the land for gain.* Marg., *a price.* The reference here is, probably, to the Holy Land, and the idea is that it would be partitioned out among his followers for

40 And at the time of the end shall the king of the south push at him: and the king of the north shall come against him like a

a price, or with a view to gain; that is, perhaps, that it would be "farmed out" for the purpose of raising revenue, and that with this view, as often occurred, it would be set up for sale to the highest bidder. This was a common way of raising revenue, by "farming out" a conquered province; that is, by disposing of the privilege of raising a revenue in it to the one who would offer most for it, and the consequence was, that it gave rise to vast rapacity in extorting funds from the people. Comp. 1 Macc. iii. 35, 36, where, speaking of Lysias, whom Antiochus had "set to oversee the affairs of the king from the river Euphrates unto the borders of Egypt," it is said of Antiochus that he " gave him [Lysias] charge of all things that he would have done, as also concerning them that dwelt in Judea and Jerusalem : to wit, that he should send an army against them, to destroy and root out the strength of Israel, and the remnant of Jerusalem, and to take away their memorial from that place ; and that he should place strangers in all their quarters, *and divide their land by lot.*"

40. *And at the time of the end.* See ver. 35. The "time of the end" must properly denote the end or consummation of the series of events under consideration, or the matter in hand, and properly and obviously means here the end or consummation of the transactions which had been referred to in the previous part of the vision. It is equivalent to what we should say by expressing it thus : "at the winding up of the affair." In ch. xii. 4, 9, 13, the word "end," however, obviously refers to *another* close or consummation—the end or consummation of the affairs that reach far into the future—the final dispensation of things in this world. It has been held by many that this could not be understood as referring to Antiochus, because what is here stated did not occur in the close of his reign. Perhaps at first sight the most obvious interpretation of what is said in this and the

subsequent verses to the end of the chapter would be, that, after the series of events referred to in the previous verses ; after Antiochus had invaded Egypt, and had been driven thence by the fear of the Romans, he would, in the close of his reign, again attack that country, and bring it, and Libya, and Æthiopia into subjection (ver. 43) ; and that when there, tidings out of the north should compel him to abandon the expedition and return again to his own land. Porphyry (see Jerome, *in loc.*) says that this was so, and that Antiochus actually invaded Egypt in the "eleventh year of his reign," which was the year before he died ; and he maintains, therefore, that all this had a literal application to Antiochus, and that *being* so literally true, it must have been written *after* the events had occurred. Unfortunately the fifteen books of Porphyry are lost, and we have only the fragments of his works preserved which are to be found in the Commentary of Jerome on the book of Daniel. The statement of Porphyry, referred to by Jerome, is contrary to the otherwise universal testimony of history about the last days of Antiochus, and there are such improbabilities in the statement as to leave the general impression that Porphyry in this respect falsified history in order to make it appear that this must have been written *after* the events referred to. If the statement of Porphyry were correct, there would be no difficulty in applying this to Antiochus. The common belief, however, in regard to Antiochus is, that he did *not* invade Egypt after the series of events referred to above, and after he had been required to retire by the authority of the Roman ambassadors, as stated in the Notes on ver. 30. This belief accords also with all the probabilities of the case. Under these circumstances, many commentators have supposed that this portion of the chapter (vers. 40–45) could not refer to Antiochus, and they have applied it to Antichrist, or to the Roman power. Yet how forced and unnatural such an

whirlwind, *a* with chariots, and with horsemen, and with many

a Zech. 9. 14.

ships; and he shall enter into the countries, and shall overflow and pass over.

application must be, any one can perceive by examining Newton *on the Prophecies,* pp. 308–315. The obvious, and perhaps it may be added the *honest,* application of the passage must be to Antiochus. This is that which would occur to any reader of the prophecy; this is that which he would obviously hold to be the true application; and this is that only which would occur to any one, unless it were deemed necessary to *bend* the prophecy to accommodate it to the *history.* Honesty and fairness, it seems to me, require that we should understand this as referring to the series of events which had been described in the previous portion of the chapter, and as designed to state the ultimate issue or close of the whole. There will be no difficulty in this if we may regard these verses (40–45) as containing a recapitulation, or a summing up of the series of events, with a statement of the manner in which they would close. If so interpreted all will be clear. It will then be a general statement of what would occur in regard to this remarkable transaction that would so materially affect the interests of religion in Judea, and be such an important chapter in the history of the world. This summing up, moreover, would give occasion to mention some circumstances in regard to the conquests of Antiochus which could not so well be introduced in the narrative itself, and to present, in few words, a summary of all that would occur, and to state the manner in which all would be terminated. Such a summing up, or recapitulation, is not uncommon, and in this way the impression of the whole would be more distinct. With this view, the phrase "and at the time of the end" (ver. 40) would refer, not so much to the "time of the end" of the reign of Antiochus, but to the "time of the end" of *the whole series* of the transactions referred to by the angel as recorded "in the scripture of truth" (ch. x. 21), from the time of Darius the Mede (ch. xi. 1)

to the close of the reign of Antiochus —a series of events embracing a period of some three hundred and fifty years. Viewed in reference to this long period, the whole reign of Antiochus, which was only eleven years, might be regarded as "the time of the end." It was, indeed, the most disastrous portion of the whole period, and in this chapter it occupies more space than all that went before it—for it was to be the time of the peculiar and dreadful trial of the Hebrew people, but it was "*the end*" of the matter—the winding up of the series—the closing of the events on which the eye of the angel was fixed, and which were so important to be known beforehand. In these verses, therefore (40–45) he sums up what would occur in what he here calls appropriately "the time of the end"—the period when the predicted termination of this series of important events should arrive—to wit, in the brief and eventful reign of Antiochus. ¶ *Shall the king of the south.* The king of Egypt. See vers. 5, 6, 9. ¶ *Push at him.* As in the wars referred to in the previous verse—in endeavouring to expel him from Cœlo-Syria and Palestine, and from Egypt itself, vers. 25, 29, 30. See Notes on those verses. ¶ *And the king of the north shall come against him.* The king of Syria—Antiochus. Against the king of Egypt. He shall repeatedly invade his lands. See the Notes above. ¶ *Like a whirlwind.* As if he would sweep everything before him. This he did when he invaded Egypt; when he seized on Memphis, and the best portion of the land of Egypt, and when he obtained possession of the person of Ptolemy. See Notes on vers. 25–27. ¶ *With chariots, and with horsemen, and with many ships.* All this literally occurred in the successive invasions of Egypt by Antiochus. See the Notes above. ¶ *And he shall enter into the countries.* Into Cœlo-Syria, Palestine, Egypt, and the adjacent lands. ¶ *And shall overflow and pass over.* Like a flood he shall

41 He shall enter also into the glorious ¹land,ᵃ and many *countries* shall be overthrown; but these

1 *land of delight*, or *ornament*, or *goodly land*.

shall escape out of his hand, *even* Edom, ᵇ and Moab, and the chief of the children of Ammon.

a vers. 16, 45.   *b* Isa. 11. 14, 15.

spread his armies over these countries. See Notes on ver. 22.

41. *He shall enter also into the glorious land.* Marg., *land of delight*, or *ornament*, or *goodly land.* The Hebrew is, "land of ornament;" that is, of beauty, to wit, Palestine, or the Holy Land. The same word is used in ver. 16. See Notes on that place. As to the *fact* that he would invade that land, see Notes on vers. 28, 31–33. ¶ *And many* countries *shall be overthrown.* The word *countries* here is supplied by the translators. The Hebrew word רִבּוֹת may denote "many things," and might refer to cities, dwellings, institutions, &c. The meaning is, that he would produce wide devastation, which was true of Antiochus, when, either personally or by his generals, he invaded the land of Palestine. See the Notes above. ¶ *But these shall escape out of his hand,* &c. Intent on his work in Palestine, and having enough there to occupy his attention, the neighbouring lands of Edom, Moab, and Ammon shall not be molested by him. The wrath of Antiochus was particularly against the Jews, and it is not a little remarkable that no mention is made of his invading these adjacent countries. The route which he pursued was to Egypt, along the shores of the Mediterranean, and though he turned from his course to wreak his vengeance on the Jews, yet it does not appear that he carried his arms farther from the main line of his march. Antiochus was principally engaged with the Egyptians and the Romans; he was also engaged with the Jews, for Palestine had been the battle-field—the main place and object of contention between the king of Syria and the king of Egypt. Moab, and Edom, and Ammon were comparatively remote from the scene of conflict, and were left unmolested. It would seem most probable, also, that these nations were friendly to Anti-

ochus, and were in alliance with him, or at least it is certain that they were hostile to the Jews, which, for the purposes of Antiochus, amounted to the same thing. Judas Maccabeus is represented as engaged with them in war, and consequently they must have either been in alliance with Antiochus, or in some other way promoting his interests. See 1 Macc. iv. 61; v. 3, 6–9. These countries were, therefore, in fact, secure from the invasions of Antiochus, and so far the prophecy was literally fulfilled. It may be added (*a*), that no occurrence *since* that time has taken place to which the prophecy can with propriety be applied; and (*b*), that no natural sagacity could have foreseen this, and that, therefore, if the prediction was uttered *before* the days of Antiochus, it must have been the result of Divine inspiration. As to the former of these remarks (*a*), if any one is desirous of seeing how forced and unnatural must be any attempt to apply this to any other times than those of Antiochus, he has only to consult Bishop Newton *on the Prophecies* (pp. 311–313), who explains it as referring to the Ottoman empire, and to the fact that though the Turks have been able to take Jerusalem, they have never been able to subdue the Arabians, the Moabites, or the Ammonites. Aleppo, Damascus, and Gaza, says he, were forced to submit, but these other places "escaped out of the hands" of the Turks. As to the other remark (*b*), if one, writing *after* the events, had intended to give a brief and striking view of what Antiochus did, he could not find better language to express it than to say in the words of the passage before us, "He shall enter also into the glorious land, and many *countries* shall be overthrown; but these shall escape out of his hand, *even* Edom, and Moab, and the chief of the children of Ammon." But it is clear that there is no natural sagacity by which this could

42 He shall ¹ stretch forth his hand also upon the countries; and the land of Egypt shall not escape.

43 But he shall have power

¹ *send forth.*

over the treasures of gold and of silver, and over all the precious things of Egypt; and the Libyans and the Ethiopians *shall be* at his steps.

---

be foreseen. There was nothing in the character of those nations, or in the nature of the case, which would lead one to anticipate it—for the presumption would be, that if a desolating war were waged on Palestine by a cruel conqueror, his ravages would be extended to the neighbouring countries also.

42. *He shall stretch forth his hand also upon the countries.* Marg., *send forth.* Significant of war and conquest. The idea is, that he would be an invader of foreign lands—a characteristic which it is not necessary to show appertained to Antiochus. ¶ *And the land of Egypt shall not escape.* Moab and Edom, and the land of Ammon would escape, but Egypt would not. We have seen in the exposition of this chapter (Notes on vers. 25–28) that he, in fact, subdued Memphis and the best portions of Egypt, and even obtained possession of the person of the king.

43. *But he shall have power over the treasures of gold and of silver.* See Notes on ver. 28. Having seized upon the most important places in Egypt, and having possession of the person of the king, he would, of course, have the wealth of Egypt at his disposal, and would return to his land laden with spoils. ¶ *And over all the precious things of Egypt.* The rich lands, the public buildings, the contents of the royal palace, the works of art, and the monuments, and books, and implements of war. All these would, of course, be at the disposal of the conqueror. ¶ *And the Libyans.* The word *Libyans*, in the Hebrew Scriptures, is everywhere joined with the Egyptians and Ethiopians. They are supposed to have been a people of Egyptian origin, and their country bordered on Egypt in the west. See Tanner's *Ancient Atlas.* A conquest of Egypt was almost in itself a conquest of Libya. ¶ *And the Ethiopians.* Heb., *Cushites*—כּוּשִׁים. On the general meaning of the word *Cush* or *Ethiopia* in the Scriptures, see Notes on Isa xi.

11. The reference here, undoubtedly, is to the African Cush or Ethiopia, which bounded Egypt on the south. This country comprehended not only Ethiopia above Syene and the Cataracts, but likewise Thebais or Upper Egypt. A subjugation of Egypt would be, in fact, almost a conquest of this land. ¶ Shall be *at his steps.* Gesenius renders this, "in his company." The word means properly *step*, or *walk.* Comp. Psa. xxxvii. 23 ; Prov. xx. 24. The Vulgate renders this, "And he shall pass also through Libya and Ethiopia." The Greek, "and he shall have power over all the secret treasures of gold and of silver, and over all the desirable things of Egypt, and of the Libyans, and of the Ethiopians, in their strongholds." Lengerke renders it, "And the Libyans and Ethiopians shall follow his steps." The proper sense of the Hebrew would be, that they accompanied him ; that they marched with him or followed him ; and the phrase would be applicable either to those who were allies, or who were led captive. The more probable idea would be that they were allies, or were associated with him, than that they were captives. I do not know that there are any distinct historical facts which show the truth of what is here predicted respecting Antiochus, but it cannot be considered as improbable that the prophecy was fulfilled ; for (*a*), as already observed, these nations, naturally allied to Egypt as being a part of the same people, bounded Egypt on the west and on the south ; (*b*) in the days of Ezekiel (Ezekiel xxx. 4, 5), we find that they were actually confederated with Egypt in a "league," and that the calamity which fell upon Egypt, also fell directly upon Ethiopia and Libya ; and (*c*) the possession of Egypt, therefore, would be naturally followed with the subjugation of these places, or it might be presumed that they would seek the alliance and friendship of one who had subdued it.

44 But tidings out of the east and out of the north shall trouble him: therefore he shall go forth with great fury to destroy, and utterly to make away many.

45 And he shall plant the taber-

44. *But tidings out of the east and out of the north shall trouble him.* Shall disturb him, or alarm him. That is, he will hear something from those quarters that will disarrange all his other plans, or that will summon him forth in his last and final expedition— on that expedition in which "he will come to his end" (ver. 45), or which will be the end of this series of historical events. The reference here is to the winding up of this series of transactions, and, according to the view taken on ver. 40 (see Notes on that place), it is not necessary to suppose that this would happen immediately after what is stated in ver. 43, but it is rather to be regarded as a statement of what would occur *in the end,* or of the manner in which the person here referred to would finally come to an end, or in which these events would be closed. As a matter of fact, Antiochus, as will be seen in the Notes on ver. 45, was called forth in a warlike expedition by tidings or reports from Parthia and Armenia — regions lying to the east and the north, and it was in this expedition that he lost his life, and that this series of historical events was closed. Lengerke says, Antiochus assembled an army to take vengeance on the Jews, who, after the close of the unfortunate campaign in Egypt, rose up, under the Maccabees, against Antiochus, 1 Macc. iii. 10, *seq.* Then the intelligence that the Parthians in the east, and the Armenians in the north, had armed themselves for war against him, alarmed him. So Tacitus (*Hist.* v. 8) says [Antiochus Judæis], *Demere superstitionem et mores Græcorum dare adnixus, quominus teterrimam gentem in melius mutaret, Parthorum bello prohibitus est, nam ea tempestate Arsaces defecerat.* In the year 147 B.C., Antiochus went on the expedition to Persia and Armenia, on the return from which he died. The occasions for this were these : (*a*) Artaxias, the king of Armenia, who was his vassal, had revolted from him, and (*b*) he sought to replenish his exhausted treasury, that he might wage the war with Judas Maccabeus. See 1 Macc. iii. 27–37 ; Jos. *Ant.* b. xii. ch. vii. § 2 ; Appian, *Syriac.* xlvi. 80 ; Porphyry, in Jerome, *in loc.* ¶ *Therefore he shall go forth with great fury to destroy,* &c. Great fury at the revolt of Artaxias, and especially at this juncture when he was waging war with the Jews ; and great fury at the Jews, with a determination to obtain the means utterly to destroy them. 1 Macc. iii. 27 : "Now when king Antiochus heard these things [the successes of Judas Maccabeus], he was full of indignation." In every way his wrath was kindled. He was enraged against the Jews on account of their success ; he was enraged against Artaxias for revolting from him ; he was enraged because his treasury was exhausted, and he had not the means of prosecuting the war. In this mood of mind he crossed the Euphrates (1 Macc. iii. 37) to prosecute the war in the East, and, as it is said here, "utterly to make away many." Everything conspired to kindle his fury, and in this state of mind, he went forth on his last expedition to the East. Nothing, in fact, could better describe the state of mind of Antiochus than the language here used by the angel to Daniel. 45. *And he shall plant the tabernacles of his palace.* The royal tents ; the military tents of himself and his court. Oriental princes, when they went forth even in war, marched in great state, with a large retinue of the officers of their court, and often with their wives and concubines, and with all the appliances of luxury. Comp. the account of the invasion of Greece by Xerxes, or of the camp of Darius, as taken by Alexander the Great. The military stations of Antiochus, therefore, in this march, would be, for a time, the residence of the court, and would be distinguished for as great a degree of royal luxury as the circumstances would allow. At the same time, they would consist of *tabernacles* or *tents,* as those stations were not designed to be permanent. The meaning is, that

nacles of his palace between the seas in the [1] glorious holy moun-

tain; yet [a] he shall come to his end, and none shall help him.

1 or, *goodly*; Heb. *mountain of delight of holiness.*

a 2 Thess. 2. 8.

the royal temporary residence in this expedition, and previous to the close —the end of the whole matter, that is, the death of Antiochus—would be in the mountain here referred to. ¶ *Between the seas.* That is, between some seas in the "east," or "north"—for it was by tidings from the east and north that he would be disturbed and summoned forth, ver. 44. We are, therefore, most naturally to look for this place in one of those quarters. The *fact* was, that he had two objects in view—the one was to put down the revolt in Armenia, and the other to replenish his exhausted treasury from Persia. The former would be naturally that which he would first endeavour to accomplish, for if he suffered the revolt to proceed, it might increase to such an extent that it would be impossible to subdue it. Besides, he would not be likely to go to Persia when there was a formidable insurrection in his rear, by which he might be harassed either *in* Persia, or on his return. It is most probable, therefore, that he would first quell the rebellion in Armenia on his way to Persia, and that the place here referred to where he would pitch his royal tent, and where he would end his days, would be some mountain where he would encamp before he reached the confines of Persia. There have been various conjectures as to the place here denoted by the phrase "between the seas," and much speculation has been employed to determine the precise location. Jerome renders it, "And he shall pitch his tent in Apadno between the seas"—regarding the word which our translators have rendered *his palaces* (אַפַּדְנוֹ) as a proper name denoting a place. So the Greek, ἐφαδανῷ. The Syriac renders it, "in a plain, between the sea and the mountain." Theodoret takes it for a place near Jerusalem; Jerome says it was near Nicopolis, which was formerly called Emmaus, where the mountainous parts of Judea began to rise, and that it lay between the Dead Sea

on the east, and the Mediterranean on the west, where he supposes that Antichrist will pitch his tent; Porphyry and Calmet place it between the two rivers, the Tigris and Euphrates—the latter supposing it means "Padan of two rivers," that is, some place in Mesopotamia; and Dr. Goodwin supposes that the British Isles are intended, "which so eminently stand 'between the seas.'" Prof. Stuart understands this of the Mediterranean Sea, and that the idea is, that the encampment of Antiochus was in some situation between this sea and Jerusalem, mentioned here as "the holy and beautiful mountain." So far as the *phrase* here used—"between the seas"—is concerned, there can be no difficulty. It might be applied to any place lying between two sheets of water, as the country between the Dead Sea and the Mediterranean, or the Dead Sea, and Persian Gulf; or the Caspian and Euxine Seas; or the Caspian Sea and the Persian Gulf, for there is nothing in the *language* to determine the exact locality. There is no reason for taking the word אַפַּדְנוֹ (*apadno*) as a proper name—the literal meaning of it being *tent* or *tabernacle;* and the simple idea in the passage is, that the transaction here referred to—the event which would close this series, and which would constitute the "end" of these affairs — would occur in some mountainous region situated between two seas or bodies of water. *Any such place*, so far as the meaning of the word is concerned, would correspond with this prophecy. ¶ *In the glorious holy mountain.* That is, this would occur (*a*) in a mountain, or in a mountainous region; and (*b*) it would be a mountain to which the appellation here used—"glorious holy"—would be properly given. The most obvious application of this phrase, it cannot be doubted, would be Jerusalem, as being the "holy mountain," or "the mountain of holiness," and as the place which the word "glorious" (צְבִי) would most naturally suggest. Comp. vers. 16, 41. Bertholdt and Dereser propose a change in the text here, and understand it as signifying that "he would pitch his tent between a sea and a mountain, and would seize upon a temple (קֹדֶשׁ) there." But there is no authority for so changing the text. Rosenmüller, whom Lengerke follows, renders it, "between some sea and the glorious holy mountain;" Lengerke supposes that the meaning is, that Antiochus, on his return from Egypt, and *before* he went to Persia, "pitched his tents in that region, somewhere along the coasts of the Mediterranean, for the purpose of chastising the Jews," and that this is the reference here. But this, as well as the proposed reading of Dereser and Bertholdt, is a forced interpretation. Gesenius (*Lex.*) supposes that the phrase means, "mount of holy beauty," *i.e.*, Mount Sion. There are some things which are clear, and which the honest principles of interpretation demand in this passage, such as the following: (*a*) What is here stated was to occur *after* the rumour from the east and the north (ver. 44) should call forth the person here referred to on this expedition. (*b*) It would not be long before his "end,"—before the close of the series, and would be connected with that; or would be the place where that would occur. (*c*) It would be on some mountainous region, to which the appellation "glorious holy" might with propriety be applied. The only question of difficulty is, whether it is necessary to interpret this of Jerusalem, or whether it may be applied to some other mountainous region where it may be supposed Antiochus "pitched his tents" on his last expedition to the East, and near the close of his life. Jerome renders this, *Supermontem inclytum et sanctum;* the Greek, "on the holy mountain Sabaein"—σαβαεὶν. The Syriac, "in a plain, between a sea and a mountain, and shall preserve his sanctuary." The *literal* meaning of the passage may be thus expressed, "on a mountain of beauty that is holy or sacred." The essential things are, (*a*) that it would be on a mountain,

or in a mountainous region; (*b*) that this mountain would be celebrated or distinguished for *beauty*—צְבִי—that is, for the beauty of its situation, or the beauty of its scenery, or the beauty of its structures—or that it should be *regarded* as beautiful; (*c*) that it would be held as sacred or holy—קֹדֶשׁ—that is, as sacred to religion, or regarded as a holy place, or a place of worship. Now it is true that this language *might* be applied to Mount Sion, for *that* was a mountain; it was distinguished for beauty, or was so regarded by those who dwelt there (comp. Psa. xlviii. 2); and it was holy, as being the place where the worship of God was celebrated. But it is also true, that, so far as the language is concerned, it might be applied to any other mountain or mountainous region that was distinguished for beauty, and that was regarded as sacred, or in any way consecrated to religion. I see no objection, therefore, to the supposition, that this may be understood of some mountain or elevated spot which was held as sacred to religion, or where a temple was reared for worship, and hence it *may* have referred to some mountain, in the vicinity of some temple dedicated to idol worship, where Antiochus would pitch his tent for the purpose of rapine and plunder. ¶ *Yet he shall come to his end.* Evidently in the expedition referred to, and in the vicinity referred to. Though he had gone full of wrath; and though he was preparing to wreak his vengeance on the people of God; and though he had every prospect of success in the enterprise, yet he would come to an end there, or would die. This would be the end of his career, and would be at the same time the end of that series of calamities that the angel predicted. The assurance is more than once given (vers. 27, 35); that there was an "appointed" time during which these troubles would continue, or that there would be an "end" of them at the appointed time, and the design was, that when these inflictions came upon the Jews they should be permitted to comfort themselves with the assurance that they would have a termination—that is, that the institutions of religion in their land would not be utterly overthrown. ¶ *And none shall help him.* None shall save his life; none shall rescue him out of his danger. That is, he would certainly die, and his plans of evil would thus be brought to a close.

The question now is, whether this can be applied to the closing scenes in the life of Antiochus Epiphanes. The materials for writing the life of Antiochus are indeed scanty, but there is little doubt as to the place and manner of his death. According to all the accounts, he received intelligence of the success of the Jewish arms under Judas Maccabeus, and the overthrow of the Syrians, at Elymaïs or Persepolis (2 Macc. ix. 2), in Persia; and as he was detained there by an insurrection of the people, occasioned by his robbing the celebrated Temple of Diana (Jos. *Ant.* b. xii. ch. ix. § 1), in which his father, Antiochus the Great, lost his life; his vexation was almost beyond endurance. He set out on his return with a determination to make every possible effort to exterminate the Jews; but during his journey he was attacked by a disease, in which he suffered excessive pain, and was tormented by the bitterest anguish of conscience, on account of his sacrilege and other crimes. He finally died at Tabæ in Paratacene, on the frontiers of Persia and Babylon, in the year 163 B.C, after a reign of eleven years. See the account of his wretched death in 2 Macc. ix.; Jos. *Antiq.* b. xii. ch. ix.; § 1; Prideaux, *Con.* iii. pp. 272, 273; Polybius in *Excerpta Valesii de Virtutibus et Vitiis,* xxxi., and Appian, *Syriac.* xlvi. 80. Now this account agrees substantially with the prediction in the passage before us in the following respects:—(*a*) The circumstances which called him forth. It was on account of "tidings" or rumours out of the east and north that he went on this last expedition. (*b*) The place specified where the last scenes would occur, "between the seas." Any one has only to look on a map of the Eastern hemisphere to see that the ancient Persepolis, the capital of Persia, where the rumour of the success of the Jews

reached him which induced him to return, is "between the seas"—the Caspian Sea and the Persian Gulf—lying not far from midway between the two. (*c*) The "glorious holy mountain," or, as the interpretation above proposed would render it, "the mountain of beauty," sacred to religion or to worship. (1.) The whole region was mountainous. (2.) It is not unlikely that a temple would be raised on a mountain or elevated place, for this was the almost universal custom among the ancients, and it may be assumed as not improbable, that the temple of Diana, at Elymaïs, or Persepolis, which Antiochus robbed, and where he "pitched his tent," was on such a place. Such a place would be regarded as "holy," and would be spoken of as "an ornament," or as beautiful, for this was the language which the Hebrews were accustomed to apply to a place of worship. I suppose, therefore, that the reference is here to the closing scene in the life of Antiochus, and that the account in the prophecy agrees in the most striking manner with the facts of history, and consequently that it is not necessary to look to any other events for a fulfilment, or to suppose that it has any secondary and ultimate reference to what would occur in far-distant years.

In view of this exposition, we may see the force of the opinion maintained by Porphyry, that this portion of the book of Daniel must have been written *after* the events occurred. He could not but see, as any one can now, the surprising accuracy of the statements of the chapter, and their applicability to the events of history as they had actually occurred; and seeing this, there was but one of two courses to be taken—either to admit the inspiration of the book, or to maintain that it was written *after* the events. He chose the latter alternative; and, so far as can be judged from the few fragments which we have of his work in the commentary of Jerome on this book, he did it solely on the ground of the *accuracy* of the description. He referred to no external evidence; he adduced no historical proofs that the book was written subsequent to the events; but he maintained simply that an account so minute and exact could not have been written *before* the events, and that the very accuracy of the alleged predictions, and their entire agreement with history, was full demonstration that they were written *after*. The testimony of Porphyry, therefore, may be allowed to be a sufficient proof of the correspondence of this portion of the book of Daniel with the facts of history; and if the book was written before the age of Antiochus Epiphanes, the evidence is clear of its inspiration, for no man will seriously maintain that these historic events could be drawn out, with so much particularity of detail, by any natural skill, three hundred and seventy years before they occurred, as must have been the case if written by Daniel. Human sagacity does not extend its vision thus far into the future with the power of foretelling the fates of kingdoms, and giving in detail the lives and fortunes of individual men. Either the infidel must dispose of the testimony that Daniel lived and wrote at the time alleged, or, as an honest man, he should admit that he was inspired.

CHAPTER XII.

ANALYSIS OF THE CHAPTER.

There are several general remarks which may be made respecting this, the closing chapter of the book of Daniel.

I. It is a part, or a continuation of the general prophecy or vision which was commenced in ch. x., and which embraces the whole of the eleventh chapter. Except for the *length* of the prophecy there should have been no division whatever, and it should be read as a continuous whole; or if a division were desirable, that which was made by Cardinal Hugo in the 13th century, and which occurs in our translation of the Bible, is one of the most unhappy. On every account, and for every reason, the division should have been at the close of the fourth verse of this chapter, and the first four verses should have been attached to the pre-

vious portion. That the beginning of this chapter is a continuation of the address of the angel to Daniel, is plain from a mere glance. The address ends at ver. 4; and then commences a colloquy between two angels who appear in the vision, designed to cast further light on what had been said. It will contribute to a right understanding of this chapter to remember, that it is a part of the one vision or prophecy which was commenced in ch. x., and that the whole three chapters (x., xi., xii.) should be read together. If ch. xi., therefore, refers to the historical events connected with the reign of Antiochus, and the troubles under him, it would seem to be plain that this does also, and that the angel meant to designate the time when these troubles would close, and the indications by which it might be known that they were about to come to an end.

II. At the same time that this is true, it must also be admitted that the *language* which is used is such as is applicable to other events, and that it supposed that there was a belief in the doctrines to which that language would be naturally applied. It is not such language as would have been originally employed to describe the historical transactions respecting the persecutions under Antiochus, nor unless the doctrines which are obviously conveyed by that language were understood and believed. I refer here to the statements respecting the resurrection of the dead and of the future state. This language is found particularly in ver. 2, 3: "And many of them that sleep in the dust of the earth shall awake, some to everlasting life, and some to shame and everlasting contempt. And they that be wise shall shine as the brightness of the firmament; and they that turn many to righteousness, as the stars for ever and ever." This language is appropriate to express such doctrines as the following: (*a*) that of the resurrection of the dead—or a being raised up out of the dust of the earth; (*b*) that of retribution *after* the resurrection: a part being raised to everlasting life, and a part to everlasting shame; (*c*) that of the eternity of future retribution, or the eternity of rewards and punishments: awaking to *everlasting* life, and to *everlasting* shame; (*d*) that of the high honours and rewards of those who would be engaged in doing good, or of that portion of mankind who would be instrumental in turning the wicked from the paths of sin: "they that turn many to righteousness, as the stars for ever and ever." It is impossible to conceive that this language would have been used unless these doctrines were known and believed, and unless it be supposed that they were so familiar that it would be readily understood. Whatever may have been the particular thing to which it was applied by the angel, it is such language as could have been intelligible only where there was a belief of these doctrines, and it may, therefore, be set down as an indication of a prevalent belief in the time of Daniel on these subjects. Such would be understood now if the same language were used by us, to whatever we might apply it, for it would not be employed unless there was a belief of the truth of the doctrines which it is naturally adapted to convey.

III. If the angel intended, therefore, primarily to refer to events that would occur in the time of Antiochus —to the arousing of many to defend their country, as if called from the dust of the earth, or to their being summoned by Judas Maccabeus from caves and fastnesses, and to the honour to which many of them might be raised, and the shame and con-tempt which would await others, it seems difficult to doubt that the mind of the speaker, at the same time, glanced onward to higher doctrines, and that it was the intention of the angel to bring into view far-distant events, of which these occurrences might be regarded as an emblem, and that he meant to advert to what would literally occur in the time of the Maccabees as a beautiful and striking illustration of more momentous and glorious scenes when the earth should give up its dead, and when the final judgment should occur. On these scenes, perhaps, the mind of the angel ultimately rested, and a prominent part of the design of the entire vision may have been to bring them into view, and to direct the thoughts of the pious onward, far beyond the troubles and the triumphs in the days of the Maccabees, to the time when the dead should arise, and when the retributions of eternity should occur. It was no uncommon thing among the prophets to allow the eye to glance from one object to another lying in the same range of vision, or having such points of resemblance that the one would suggest the other; and it often happened, that a description which commenced with some natural event terminated in some more important spiritual truth, to which that event had a resemblance, and which it was adapted to suggest. Comp. Intro. to Isaiah, § VII. 3. (3) (4) (5). Three things occur often in such a case: (1) language is employed in speaking of what is to take place, which is derived from the secondary and remote event, and which naturally suggests that; (2) ideas are intermingled in the description which are appropriate to the secondary event only, and which should be understood as applicable to that; and

(3) the description which was *commenced* with reference to one event or class of events, often passes over entirely, and *terminates* on the secondary and ultimate events. This point will be more particularly examined on the Notes on the chapter.

IV. The contents of the chapter are as follows:—

(1.) The concluding statement of what would occur at the time referred to in the previous chapter, ver. 1–3. This statement embraces many particulars : that Michael, the guardian angel, would stand up in behalf of the people; that there would be great trouble, such as there had not been since the time when the nation began to exist; that there would be deliverance for all whose names were recorded in the book; that there would be an awakening of those who slept in the dust—some coming to life and honour, and some to shame and dishonour; and that distinguished glory would await those who turned many to righteousness.

(2.) At this stage of the matter, all having been disclosed that the angel purposed to reveal, Daniel is commanded to shut and seal the book; yet with the encouragement held out that more would yet be known on the subject, ver. 4. The matter was evidently involved still in mystery, and there were many points on which it could not but be desired that there should be fuller information—points relating to the time when these things would happen, and a more particular account of the full meaning of what had been predicted, &c. On these points it is clear that many questions might be asked, and it is probable that the mind of Daniel would be left still in perplexity in regard to them. To meet this state of mind, the angel says to Daniel that "many would run to

and fro, and that knowledge would be increased;" that is, that by intercourse with one another in future times; by spreading abroad the knowledge already obtained ; by diffusing information, and by careful inquiry, those of coming ages would obtain much clearer views on these points; or, in other words, that time, and the intercourse of individuals and nations, would clear up the obscurities of prophecy.

(3.) In this state of perplexity, Daniel looked and saw two other personages standing on the two sides of the river, and between them and the angel who had conversed with Daniel a colloquy or conversation ensues, respecting the time necessary to accomplish these things, ver. 5–7. They are introduced as interested in the inquiry as to the *time* of the continuance of these things—that is, how long it would be to the end of these wonders. These were evidently angels also, and they are represented (*a*) as ignorant of the future—a circumstance which we must suppose to exist among the angels; and (*b*) as feeling a deep interest in the transactions which were to occur, and the period when it might be expected they would have their completion. To this natural inquiry, the angel who had conversed with Daniel gives a solemn answer (ver. 7), that the period would be "a time, and times, and an half ;" and that all these things would be accomplished, when he to whom reference was made had finished his purpose of scattering the holy people.

(4.) Daniel, perplexed and overwhelmed with these strange predictions, hearing what was said about the time, but not understanding it, asks with intense interest when the end of these things should be, ver. 8. He had heard the reply of the angel, but it conveyed no idea to his mind. He was deeply solicitous to look into the

CHAPTER XII.

AND at that time shall *a* Michael stand up, the great prince

future, and to ascertain *when* these events would end, and *what* would be their termination. The answer to his anxious, earnest inquiry, is contained in vers. 9–13, and embraces several points—giving some further information, but still evidently designed to leave the matter obscure in many respects. (*a*) The matter was sealed up, and his question could not be definitely answered, ver. 9. When the time of the end should come, it is implied the matter would be clearer, and might be understood, but that all had been communicated substantially that could be. (*b*) A statement is made (ver. 10) of the general result of the trials on two classes of persons: the things that would occur would tend to make the righteous more holy, but the wicked would continue to do wickedly, notwithstanding all these heavy judgments. The latter too would, when these events took place, fail to understand their design; but the former would obtain a just view of them, and would be made wiser by them. Time, to the one class, would disclose the meaning of the Divine dealings, and they would comprehend them; to the other they would still be dark and unintelligible. (*c*) A statement is, however, made as to the *time* when these things would be accomplished, but still so obscure as to induce the angel himself to say to Daniel that he must go his way till the end should be, vers. 11–13. Two periods of time are mentioned, both different from the one in ver. 7. In one of them (ver. 11) it is said that from the time when the daily sacrifice should be taken away, and the abomination that maketh desolate should be set up, would be a

which standeth for the children of thy people; and *b* there shall be a

a ch. 10. 13, 21; Jude 9.   *b* Matt. 24. 21.

thousand two hundred and ninety days. In the other (ver. 12) it is said that he would be blessed or happy who should reach a certain period mentioned—a thousand three hundred and thirty-five days. What these different periods of time refer to will of course be the subject of inquiry in the Notes on the chapter. (*d*) The whole closes, therefore (ver. 13), with a direction to Daniel that, for the present, he should go his way. Nothing additional would be disclosed. Time would reveal more; time would explain all. Meanwhile there is an assurance given that, as for himself, he would have "rest," and would "stand in his lot at the end of the days." This seems to be a gracious assurance to him that he had nothing to fear from these troubles personally, and that whatever should come, he would have peace, and would occupy the position in future times which was due to him. His lot would be happy and peaceful; his name would be honoured; his salvation would be secured. It seems to be implied that, with this pledge, he ought to allow his mind to be calm, and not suffer himself to be distressed because he could not penetrate the future, and foresee all that was to occur; and the truth, therefore, with which the book closes is, that, having security about our own personal salvation—or having no ground of solicitude respecting that— or having that matter made safe—we should calmly commit all events to God, with the firm conviction that in his own time his purposes will be accomplished, and that being then understood, he will be seen to be worthy of confidence and praise.

1. *And at that time.* At the period

time of trouble, such as never was
since there was a nation *even* to
that same time: and at that time

a Jer. 30. 7; Rom. 11. 26.

thy *a* people shall be delivered,
every one that shall be found
written *b* in the book.

b Rev. 13. 8.

referred to in the preceding chapter.
The fair construction of the passage
demands this interpretation, and if
that refers to Antiochus Epiphanes,
then what is here said must also; and
we are to look for the direct and immediate fulfilment of this prediction in
something that occurred under him,
however it may be supposed to have
an ultimate reference to other and more
remote events. The phrase "at that
time," however, does not limit what is
here said to any one part of his life, or
to his death, but to the general period
referred to in the time of his reign.
That reign was but eleven years, and
the fulfilment must be found somewhere during that period. ¶ *Shall
Michael.* On the meaning of this word,
and the being here referred to, see
Notes on ch. x. 13. ¶ *Stand up.* That
is, he shall interpose; he shall come
forth to render aid. This does not
mean necessarily that he would *visibly*
appear, but that he would *in fact* interpose. In the time of great distress
and trouble, there would be super-
natural or angelic aid rendered to the
people of God. No man can prove
that this would not be so, nor is there
any inherent improbability in the supposition that good angels may be employed to render assistance in the time
of trouble. Comp. Notes on ch. x. 13.
¶ *The great prince which standeth for
the children of thy people.* See Notes
as above on ch. x. 13. The meaning
is, that he had the affairs of the Hebrew people, or the people of God, especially under his protection, or he was
appointed to watch over them. This
doctrine is in accordance with the notions that prevailed at that time; and
no one can demonstrate that it is not
true. There is no authority for applying this to the Messiah, as many have
done, for the term *Michael* is not elsewhere given to him, and all that the
language fairly conveys is met by the
other supposition. The simple meaning
is, that he who was the guardian angel
of that nation, or who was appointed

to watch over its interests, would at
that time of great trouble interpose
and render aid. ¶ *And there shall be
a time of trouble.* Under Antiochus
Epiphanes. See Notes on ch. xi.
21–45. Comp. the books of the Maccabees, *passim.* ¶ *Such as never was
since there was a nation* even *to that
same time.* This *might* be construed
with reference to the Jewish nation, as
meaning that the trouble would be
greater than any that had occurred
during its history. But it may also
be taken, as our translators understand
it, in a more general sense, as referring
to any or all nations. In either sense
it can hardly be considered as the
language of hyperbole. The troubles
that came upon the land under the
persecutions of Antiochus probably
surpassed any that the Hebrew nation
ever experienced, nor could it be shown
that, for the same period of time, they
were surpassed among any other people.
The Saviour has employed this language
as adapted to express the intensity of
the trials which would be brought upon
the Jews by the Romans (Matt. xxiv.
21), but he does not say that as used
in Daniel it had reference originally
to that event. It was language appropriate to express the thought which
he wished to convey, and he, therefore,
so employed it. ¶ *And at that time.*
When these troubles are at their height.
¶ *Thy people shall be delivered.* To
wit, by the valour and virtues of the
Maccabees. See the accounts in the
books of the Maccabees. Comp. Prideaux, *Con.* iii. 257, *seq.* ¶ *Every
one that shall be found written in the
book.* Whose names are enrolled; that
is, enrolled as among the living. The
idea is, that a register was made of the
names of those who were to be spared,
to wit, by God, or by the angel, and
that all whose names were so recorded
would be preserved. Those not so enrolled would be cut off under the persecutions of Antiochus. The language
here does not refer to the book of eternal
life or salvation, nor is it implied that

2 And many of them that sleep in the dust of the earth shall awake, some to everlasting life, [a] and some to [b] shame *and* everlasting contempt.

a Matt. 25. 46.   *b* Isa. 66. 24.

they who would thus be preserved would necessarily be saved, but to their preservation from death and persecution, *as if* their names were recorded in a book, or were enrolled. We frequently meet with similar ideas in the Scriptures. The idea is, of course, poetical, but it expresses with sufficient clearness the thought that there was a Divine purpose in regard to them, and that there was a definite number whom God designed to keep alive, and that these would be delivered from those troubles, while many others would be cut off. Comp. Notes on ch. x. 21.

2. *And many of them.* The natural and obvious meaning of the word *many* (רַבִּים) here is, that a large portion of the persons referred to would thus awake, but not all. So we should understand it if applied to other things, as in such expressions as these— "many of the people," "many of the houses in a city," "many of the trees in a forest," "many of the rivers in a country," &c. In the Scriptures, however, it is undeniable that the word is sometimes used to denote the whole considered *as* constituted of many, as in Rom. v. 15, 16, 19. In these passages no one can well doubt that the word *many* is used to denote *all,* considered as composed of the "*many*" that make up the human race, or the "*many*" offences that man has committed. So if it were to be used respecting those who were to come forth from the caves and fastnesses where they had been driven by persecution, or those who sleep in their graves, and who will come forth in a general resurrection, it *might* be used of them considered as the many, and it might be said "the many" or "the multitude" comes forth. Not a few interpreters, therefore, have understood this in the sense of *all,* considered as referring to a multitude, or as suggesting the idea of a multitude, or keeping up the idea that there would be great numbers. If this is the proper interpretation, the word "many" was

used instead of the word "all" to suggest to the mind the idea that there would be a *multitude,* or that there would be a *great number.* Some, as Lengerke, apply it to all the Israelites who "were not written in the book" (ver. 1), that is, to a resurrection of all the Israelites who had died; some, as Porphyry, a coming forth of the multitudes out of the caves and fastnesses who had been driven there by persecution; and some, as Rosenmüller and Hävernick, understand it as meaning *all,* as in Rom. v. 15, 19. The sum of all that can be said in regard to the meaning of the word, it seems to me, is, that it is so far ambiguous that it *might* be applied (*a*) to "*many*" considered as a large portion of a number of persons or things; (*b*) or, in an absolute sense, to the whole of any number of persons or things considered as a multitude or great number. As used here in the visions of the future, it would seem to denote that the eye of the angel was fixed on a great multitude rising from the dust of the earth, without any particular or distinct reference to the question whether all arose. There would be a vast or general resurrection from the dust; so much so that the mind would be interested mainly in the contemplation of the *great hosts* who would thus come forth. Thus understood, the language might, of itself, apply either to a general arousing of the Hebrew people in the time of the Maccabees, or to a general resurrection of the dead in the last day. ¶ *That sleep.* This expression is one that denotes either natural sleep, or anything that resembles sleep. In the latter sense it is often used to denote death, and especially the death of the pious—who calmly slumber in their graves in the hope of awaking in the morning of the resurrection. See Notes on 1 Thess. iv. 14. It cannot be denied that it might be applied to those who, for any cause, were inactive, or whose energies were not aroused—as we often employ the word sleep or slumber—and that it might be thus used of those who seemed to slumber in the midst of the persecutions which raged, and the wrongs that were committed by Antiochus; but it would be most natural to understand it of those who were *dead*, and this idea would be particularly suggested in the connection in which it stands here. ¶ *In the dust of the earth.* Heb., "In the ground, or earth of dust"—אַדְמַת־עָפָר. The language denotes the ground or earth considered as composed of dust, and would naturally refer to those who are dead and buried—considered as sleeping there with the hope of awaking in the resurrection. ¶ *Shall awake.* This is language appropriate to those who are asleep, and to the dead considered as being asleep. It might, indeed, be applied to an arousing from a state of lethargy and inaction, but its most obvious, and its full meaning, would be to apply it to the resurrection of the dead, considered as an awaking to life of those who were slumbering in their graves. ¶ *Some.* One portion of them. The relative number is not designated, but it is implied that there would be two classes. They would not all rise to the same destiny, or the same lot. ¶ *To everlasting life.* So that they would live for ever. This stands in contrast with their "sleeping in the dust of the earth," or their being dead, and it implies that that state would not occur in regard to them again. Once they slept in the dust of the earth; now they would live for ever, or would die no more. Whether in this world or in another is not here said, and there is nothing in the passage which would enable one to determine this. The single idea is that of living for ever, or never dying again. This is language which *must* have been derived from the doctrine of the resurrection of the dead, and of the future state, and which must imply the belief of that doctrine in whatever sense it may be used here. It is such as in subsequent times was employed by the sacred writers to denote the future state, and the rewards of the righteous. The most common term employed in the New Testament, perhaps, to describe true religion, is

life, and the usual phrase to denote the condition of the righteous after the resurrection is *eternal* or *everlasting life.* Comp. Matt. xxv. 46. This language, then, would most naturally be referred to that state, and covers all the subsequent revelations respecting the condition of the blessed. ¶ *And some to shame.* Another portion in such a way that they shall have only shame or dishonour. The Hebrew word means *reproach, scorn, contumely;* and it may be applied to the reproach which one casts on another, Job xvi. 10; Psa. xxxix. 8 (9); lxxix. 12; or to the reproach which rests on any one, Josh. v. 9; Isa. liv. 4. Here the word means the reproach or dishonour which would rest on them for their sins, their misconduct, their evil deeds. The word itself would apply to any persons who were subjected to disgrace for their former misconduct. If it be understood here as having a reference to those who would be aroused from their apathy, and summoned from their retreats in the times of the Maccabees, the meaning is, that they would be called forth to public shame on account of their apostasy, and their conformity to heathen customs; if it be interpreted as applying to the resurrection of the dead, it means that the wicked would rise to reproach and shame before the universe for their folly and vileness. As a matter of fact, one of the bitterest ingredients in the doom of the wicked will be the shame and confusion with which they will be overwhelmed in the great day on account of the sins and follies of their course in this world. ¶ And *everlasting contempt.* The word "everlasting" in this place is the same which in the former part of the verse is applied to the other portion that would awake, and like that properly denotes eternal; as in Matt. xxv. 46, the word translated "everlasting" [punishment] is the same which is rendered "eternal" [life], and means that which is to endure forever. So the Greek here, where the same word occurs, as in Matt. xxv. 46—"some to everlasting life," εἰς ζωὴν αἰώνιον, "and some to everlasting contempt," εἰς αἰσχύνην αἰώνιον—is one which would denote a strict and proper eternity.

3 And they that be [1] wise shall
shine [a] as the brightness of the
firmament; and they that turn

many to righteousness, as the [b] stars
for ever and ever.

1 or, *teachers*.   *a* Matt.13.43.   *b* 1 Cor.15.41,42.

The word "contempt" (דְּרָאוֹן) means,
properly, *a repulse;* and then *aversion,
abhorrence*. The meaning here is aversion or abhorrence—the feeling with
which we turn away from that which
is loathsome, disgusting, or hateful.
Then it denotes the state of mind with
which we contemplate the vile and the
abandoned; and in this respect expresses the emotion with which the
wicked will be viewed on the final trial.
The word *everlasting* completes the
image, meaning that this feeling of
loathing and abhorrence would continue for ever. In a subordinate sense
this language *might* be used to denote
the feelings with which cowards, in-
grates, and apostates are regarded on
earth; but it cannot be doubted that it
will receive its most perfect fulfilment
in the future world—in that aversion
with which the lost will be viewed by
all holy beings in the world to come.

3. *And they that be wise.* This is the
language which, in the Scriptures, is
employed to denote the pious, or those
who serve God and keep his commandments. See the book of Proverbs,
passim. True religion is wisdom, and
sin is folly, and they who live for God
and for heaven are the truly wise. The
meaning is, that they have chosen the
path which true wisdom suggests as
that in which man should walk, while
all the ways of sin are ways of folly.
The language here used is expressive
of a general truth, applicable in itself
to all the righteous at all times, and
nothing can be inferred from the term
employed as to what was designed by
the angel. ¶ *Shall shine as the brightness of the firmament.* As the sky
above us. The image is that of the
sky at night, thick set with bright and
beautiful stars. No comparison could
be more striking. The meaning would
seem to be, that each one of the righteous will be like a bright and beautiful
star, and that, in their numbers, and
order, and harmony, they would re-
semble the heavenly constellations at
night. Nothing can be more sublime
than to look on the heavens in a clear

night, and to think of the number and
the order of the stars above us as an
emblem of the righteous in the heavenly
world. The word rendered *firmament*
means, properly, *expanse,* or that which
is spread out, and it is applied to the
sky as it *appears* to be spread out above
us. ¶ *And they that turn many to
righteousness*. Referring to those who
would be instrumental in converting
men to the worship of the true God,
and to the ways of religion. This is
very general language, and might be
applied to any persons who have been
the means of bringing sinners to the
knowledge of the truth. It would
apply in an eminent degree to ministers
of the gospel who were successful in
their work, and to missionaries among
the heathen. From the mere language,
however, nothing certain can be argued
as to the original reference as used by
the angel, and it seems to have been his
intention to employ language so general
that it might be applied to *all*, of all
ages and countries, who would be instrumental in turning men to God.
¶ *As the stars*. As the stars that are
distinguished by their size and lustre
in the firmament. In the former part
of the verse, when speaking of those
who were "wise," the design seems to
be to compare them to the sky as it
appears, set over with innumerable
stars, and in their numbers and group-
ings constituting great beauty; in this
member of the sentence the design
seems to be to compare those who are
eminent in converting men, to the particular beautiful and bright stars that
strike us as we look on the heavens—
those more distinguished in size and
splendour, and that seem to lead on
the others. The meaning is, that amidst
the hosts of the saved they will be conspicuous, or they will be honoured in
proportion to their toils, their sacrifices, and their success. ¶ *For ever
and ever*. To all eternity. This
refers to those who shall turn many
to righteousness; and the meaning is,
that they shall continue thus to be distinguished and honoured to all eternity.

4 But thou, O Daniel, shut *a* up the words, and seal the book, *even* to the time of the end ; many shall run to and fro, and knowledge shall be increased.

a Rev. 10. 4.

4. *But thou, O Daniel, shut up the words.* To wit, by sealing them up, or by closing the book, and writing no more in it. The meaning is, that all has been communicated which it was intended to communicate. The angel had no more to say, and the volume might be sealed up. ¶ *And seal the book.* This would seem to have been not an unusual custom in closing a prophecy, either by affixing a seal to it that should be designed to confirm it as the prophet's work—as we seal a deed, a will, or a contract ; or to secure the volume, as we seal a letter. Comp. Notes on chap. viii. 26 ; Isa. viii. 16. ¶ *Even to the time of the end.* That is, the period when all these things shall be accomplished. Then (*a*) the truth of the prediction now carefully sealed up will be seen and acknowledged ; (*b*) and then, also, it may be expected that there will be clearer knowledge on all these subjects, for the facts will throw increased light on the meaning and the bearing of the predictions. ¶ *Many shall run to and fro.* Shall pass up and down in the world, or shall go from place to place. The reference is clearly to those who should thus go to impart knowledge ; to give information ; to call the attention of men to great and important matters. The *language* is applicable to any methods of imparting important knowledge, and it refers to a time when this would be the characteristic of the age. There is nothing else to which it can be so well applied as to the labours of Christian missionaries, and ministers of the gospel, and others who, in the cause of Christian truth, go about to rouse the attention of men to the great subjects of religion ; and the natural application of the language is to refer it to the times when the gospel would be preached to the world at large. ¶ *And knowledge shall be increased.* To wit, by this method. The angel seems to mean that in this way there would be an advance in knowledge on all the subjects of reli-

gion, and particularly on the points to which he had referred. This would be one of the characteristics of these times, and this would be the means by which it would be accomplished. Our own age has furnished a good *illustration* of the meaning of this language, and it will be still more fully and strikingly illustrated as the time approaches when the knowledge of the Lord shall fill the whole world.

Having thus gone through with an exposition of these, the closing words of the vision (vers. 1-4), it seems proper that we should endeavour to ascertain the meaning of the angel in what is here said, and the bearing of this more particularly on what he had said before. With this view, therefore, several remarks may be made here. (1.) It seems clear that there was in some respects, and for some purpose, a *primary* reference to Antiochus, and to the fact that in his times there would be a great rousing up of the friends of God and of religion, *as if* from their graves. (*a*) The connection demands it. If the close of the last chapter refers to Antiochus, then it cannot be denied that this does also, for it is introduced in immediate connection with that, and as referring to that time: "And at that time." (*b*) The facts referred to would require the same interpretation. Thus it is said that it would be a time of trouble, such as there had never been since the nation existed—a state of things which clearly refers to the calamities which would be brought upon them by the persecutions of Antiochus Epiphanes. (*c*) This interpretation seems to be in accordance with the purpose of the angel to give the assurance that these troubles would come to an end, and that in the time of the greatest calamity, when everything seemed tending to ruin, God would interpose, and would secure the people, and would cause his own worship to be restored. Porphyry then, it appears to me, was so far right as to apply this to the times of Antiochus, and to the events that occurred under the Maccabees. "Then," says he, "those who, as it were, sleep in the dust of the earth, and are pressed down with the weight of evils, and, as it were, hid in sepulchres of misery, shall rise from the dust of the earth to unexpected victory, and shall raise their heads from the ground—the observers of the law rising to everlasting life, and the violators of it to eternal shame." He also refers to the history, in which it is said that, in the times of the persecutions, many of the Jews fled to the desert, and hid themselves in caves and caverns, and that after the victories of the Maccabees they came forth, and that this was metaphorically (μεταφορικῶς) called a resurrection of the dead.—Jerome, *in loc.* According to this interpretation, the meaning would be, that there would be a general uprising of the people ; a general arousing of them from their lethargy, or summoning them from their retreats and hiding-places, *as if* the dead, good and bad, should arise from their dust.

(2.) This *language,* however, is derived from the doctrine of the literal resurrection of the dead. It implies the belief of that doctrine. It is such language as would be used only where that doctrine was known and believed. It would convey no proper idea *unless* it were known and believed. The passage, then, may be adduced as full proof that the doctrine of the resurrection of the dead, both of the just and the unjust, was understood and believed in the time of Daniel. No one can reasonably doubt this. Such language is *not* used in countries where the doctrine of the resurrection of the dead is not believed, and where used, as it is in Christian lands, is full proof, even when employed for illustration, that the doctrine of the resurrection is a common article of belief. Compare Notes on Isa. xxvi. 19. This language is not found in the Greek and Latin classic writers ; nor in heathen writings in modern times ; nor is it found in the earlier Hebrew Scriptures ; nor is it used by infidels even for illustration ; and the proof, therefore, is clear that as employed in the time of Daniel

the doctrine of the resurrection of the dead was known and believed. If so, it marks an important fact in the progress of theological opinion and knowledge in his times. How it came to be known is not intimated here, nor explained elsewhere, but of the fact no one can have any reasonable doubt. Even now, so clear and accurate is the language, that if we wish to ·express the doctrine of the resurrection of the dead, we cannot do it better than by employing the language of the angel in addressing Daniel. (See Editor's Preface to volume on Job.)

(3.) The *full* meaning of the language is not met by the events that occurred in the times of the Maccabees. As figurative, or, as Porphyry says, *metaphorical,* it might be used to describe those events. But what then occurred would not come up to the proper and complete meaning of the prediction. That is, if nothing *more* was intended, we should feel that the event fell far short of the full import of the language ; of the ideas which it was fitted to convey; and of the hopes which it was adapted to inspire. If that was all, then this lofty language would not have been used. There was nothing in the *facts* that adequately corresponded with it. In the obvious and literal sense, there was nothing which could be called a resurrection to "*everlasting* life;" nothing that could be called an awaking to "*everlasting* shame and contempt." There was nothing which would justify literally the language " they shall shine as the brightness of the firmament, and as the stars *for ever and ever.*" The language naturally has a higher signification than this, and even when employed for illustration, that higher signification should be recognized and would be suggested to the mind.

(4.) The passage looks onward to a higher and more important event than any that occurred in the times of the Maccabees—to the general resurrection of the dead, of the just and the unjust, and to the final glory of the righteous. The order of thought in the mind of the angel would seem to have been this : he designed primarily to furnish to Daniel an assur-

5 ¶ Then I Daniel looked, and, behold, there stood other two, the one on this side of the ¹ bank of the river, and the other on that side of the bank of the river.

1 *lip.*

ance that deliverance would come in the time of the severe troubles which were to overwhelm the nation, and that the nation would ultimately be safe. In doing this his mind almost unconsciously glanced forward to a final deliverance from death and the grave, and he expressed the thought which he designed to convey in the well-known and familiar language used to describe the resurrection. Commencing the description in this manner, by the laws of prophetic suggestion (comp. Intro. to Isa. § VII. III.), the mind finally rested on the ultimate event, and that which *began* with the deliverance in the times of the Maccabees, *ended* in the full contemplation of the resurrection of the dead, and the scenes beyond the last judgment.

(5.) If it be asked what would be the *pertinency* or the *propriety* of this language, if this be the correct interpretation, or what would be its bearing on the design of the angel, it may be replied: (*a*) that the assurance was in this way conveyed that *these* troubles under Antiochus would cease—an assurance as definite and distinct as though all that was said had been confined to that; (*b*) that a much more important, and more cheering *general* truth was thus brought to view, that ultimately the people of God would emerge from all trouble, and would stand before God in glory—a truth of great value then, and at all times ; (*c*) that this truth was of so universal a nature that it might be applied in *all* times of trouble—that when the church was assailed ; when the people of God were persecuted ; when they were driven away from their temples of worship, and when the rites of religion were suspended ; when the zeal of many should grow cold, and the pious should be disheartened, they might look on to brighter times. There was to be an end of all these troubles. There was to be a winding up of these affairs. All the dead were to be raised from their graves, the good and the bad, and

thus the righteous would triumph, and would shine like the brightness of the firmament, and the wicked would be overwhelmed with shame and contempt.

(6.) From all this it follows that this passage may be used to prove the doctrine of the resurrection of the dead, and the doctrine of eternal retribution. Not, indeed, the primary thing in the use of the language as applied by the angel, it is, nevertheless, based on the *truth* and the *belief* of these doctrines, and the mind of the angel ultimately rested on these great truths as adapted to awe the wicked, and to give consolation to the people of God in times of trouble. Thus Daniel was directed to some of the most glorious truths that would be established and inculcated by the coming of the Messiah, and long before he appeared had a glimpse of the great doctrine which he came to teach respecting the ultimate destiny of man.

5. *Then I Daniel looked.* My attention was attracted in a new direction. Hitherto, it would seem, it had been fixed on the angel, and on what he was saying. The angel now informed him that he had closed his communication, and Daniel was now attracted by a new heavenly vision. ¶ *And, behold, there stood other two.* Two other angels. The connection requires us to understand this of angels, though they are not expressly called so. ¶ *The one on this side of the bank of the river.* Marg., as in Heb., *lip.* The word is used to denote the bank of the river from its resemblance to a lip. The river referred to here is the Hiddekel or Tigris, Notes on ch. x. 4. These angels stood on each side of the river, though it does not appear that there was any special significancy in that fact. It perhaps contributed merely to the majesty and solemnity of the vision. The names of these angels are not mentioned, and their appearing is merely an indication of the interest which they take in the affairs of men, and in the Divine purposes and doings. They came here as if they had been deeply interested lis-

6 And *one* said to the man clothed in linen, which *was* [1] upon the waters of the river, How long *shall it be to* the end of these wonders? 1 or, *from above.* a Rev. 10. 5–7.

7 And I heard the man clothed in linen, which *was* upon the waters of the river, when he[a] held up his right hand and his left hand unto heaven, and sware by him that

---

teners to what the angel had been saying, and for the purpose of making inquiry as to the final result of all these wonderful events. The angel which had been addressing Daniel stood *over* the river, ver. 6.

6. *And* one *said.* One of these angels. It would seem that, though before unseen by Daniel, they had been present, and had listened with deep interest to the communication respecting the future which the angel had made to him. Feeling a deep concern in the issue of these wonderful events—thus evincing the interest which we are taught to believe the heavenly beings take in human affairs (see Notes on 1 Pet. i. 12)—one of them now addressed him who had been endowed with so much ability to disclose the future, as to the termination of these events. Such an inquiry was natural, and accords with what we should suppose an angel would make on an occasion like this. ¶ *To the man clothed in linen.* The angel. Notes on ch. x. 5. ¶ *Which* was *upon the waters of the river.* Marg., *from above.* So the Hebrew. The meaning is, the man seemed to stand *over* the river. Comp. ch. viii. 16. Lengerke supposes that by this was intimated the fact that the Divine control was over the waters as well as over the land— in other words, over the whole earth. ¶ *How long* shall it be to *the end of these wonders?* Nothing had been said on this point that could determine it. The angel had detailed a succession of remarkable events which must, from the nature of the case, extend far into future years; he had repeatedly spoken of an end, and had declared that that series of events would terminate, and had thus given the assurance to Daniel that these troubles would be succeeded by brighter and happier times, but he had said nothing by which it could be determined when this would be. It was natural to start this inquiry, and as well for the sake of Daniel as himself, the angel here puts the question when this would be.

7. *And I heard the man,* &c. That is, he replied to the question at once, and in a most solemn manner, as if he were communicating a great and momentous truth respecting the future. ¶ *When he held up his right hand and his left hand unto heaven.* Towards heaven; as if appealing to heaven for the sincerity and truth of what he was about to utter. The act of swearing or taking an oath was often accompanied with the lifting up of the hand to heaven, usually the right hand (comp. Gen. xiv. 22; Exod. vi. 8; Deut. xxxii. 40; Ezek. xx. 5; Rev. x. 5); but here the angel stretched *both* hands towards heaven, as if he were about to make the affirmation in the most solemn manner conceivable. ¶ *And sware by him that liveth for ever.* By the eternal God. That is, he appealed to him: he made the solemn asseveration in his presence; he called him to witness to the truth of what he said. The occasion; the manner; the posture of the angel; the appeal to the Eternal One—all give great sublimity to this transaction, and all imply that the answer was to be one of great consequence in regard to future times. ¶ *That* it shall be *for a time, times, and an half.* Marg., or, *a part.* The word חֵצִי means, properly, *half, the half part,* that which is *divided* (חָצָה —to divide), *s.c.,* in the middle. The word "*times*" means *two* times, for it is dual in its form, and the expression means three times, or periods, and a half. See the meaning of the language fully considered and explained in the Notes on ch. vii. 24–28. (See Editor's Essay on Year-day Principle, prefixed to vol. on Revelation.) ¶ *And when he shall have accomplished.* When he shall have finished his purpose in the matter; when he shall have done all that he could do. ¶ *To scatter the*

liveth for ever, that *it shall be* for a time, times, and [1] an half; and

1 or, *a part.*

power. All that constituted the power —their armies, means of defence, &c.

The word rendered *power* (יָד) means, properly, *hand,* but it is sometimes used to denote *a part* of a thing—as a portion that we take up by the hand—a handful; that is, a part of a thing taken up at once in dividing,—Gesenius, *Lex.* See Jer. vi. 3; 2 Kings xi. 7; Gen. xlvii. 24. In accordance with this, Gesenius, Lengerke, and De Wette suppose that the reference here is to the scattering of a *portion* or *part* of the Hebrew people in other lands, and to the hope that they would be restored again to their own country ; and that the meaning of the angel is, that when these dispersions were ended, all this would have been accomplished. The word has also the sense of *power, might, strength* (Ges., *Lex.*), the hand being regarded as the seat of strength, Isa. xxviii. 2 ; Job xxvii. 11 ; Psa. lxxvi. 5 (6). Thus employed, it may denote whatever *constituted* their strength ; and then the idea in the passage before us is, that all this would be *scattered.* When that should have been done ; when that dispersion should have been ended ; when these scattered forces and people should have been again restored, then all this that was predicted would be accomplished, and these troubles cease. This would be in the period designated by the "time, and times, and an half." If it refers to Antiochus, it means that the scattered forces and people of the Hebrews would be rallied under the Maccabees, and that on their return victory would crown their efforts, and the land would be again at peace. If it has a higher and an ultimate signification, it would seem to imply that when the scattered Hebrew people should be gathered into the Christian church—when their dispersions and their wanderings should come to an end by their returning to the Messiah, and, under him, to the true God, then the series of predictions will have received their complete fulfilment—for then religion will triumph

when he shall have accomplished to scatter the power of the holy people, all these *things* shall be finished.

in the world, and the kingdom of God be set up over all the nations, agreeably to Rom. xi. 15–25. In reference, then, to the *meaning* of the passage as used by the angel here, the following remarks may be made: (1.) It *had* an applicability to the times of Antiochus, and to the duration of the calamities that would come upon the Hebrew people under his reign. If there had been nothing further intended than this, - the mere language employed would have found a literal fulfilment in these events, and there can be no reasonable doubt that the primary reference of the angel was to them. See this point fully considered and illustrated in the Notes on ch. vii. 24–28. (2.) Yet there are circumstances which lead us to suppose that, at the same time, and by the laws of prophetic suggestion (see Intro. to Isa. § VII. III.), more important events were also referred to, and were designed to be connected with this statement. Those circumstances are (*a*) the manner in which the angel introduces the subject—by a solemn appeal, with outstretched arms, to heaven. This would look as if he regarded the answer as of momentous importance, and as if he were contemplating vast movements in the future. (*b*) The fact that the language here had a. *settled meaning* —referring, as used elsewhere, to future events deeply affecting the welfare of the world. The language is so couched, indeed, that it *would* express the fact in regard to the duration of the troubles under Antiochus ; but it was also of such a nature that in its higher signification it would describe the duration of more momentous transactions, and would designate a period when the true religion would begin its universal reign ; when the evils of a vast Antichristian power would come to an end, and when the kingdom of the saints would be set up in the world. See the Notes on ch. vii. 24–28. (3.) The full meaning of the language would then seem to be, that the angel designed to include *all* in the future to which those

8 And I heard, but I understood not; then said I, O my Lord, what *shall be* the end of these *things?*

9 And he said, Go thy way,

Daniel; for the words *are* closed up and sealed till the time of the end.

10 Many shall be purified, and

---

words, as intended by the Divine Spirit, would be applicable. The period designated by the phrase, "a time, and times, and an half," was most momentous. *In* that time the troubles introduced by Antiochus would end, and a state of peace and prosperity would succeed; and *in* that time, also, far greater troubles and woes—those connected with a most fearful apostasy from the true religion, and the setting up of a kingdom of oppression and wrong over the people of God, of which the oppressions and wrongs under Antiochus would be but an emblem, would also come to an end, and there would be a state of peace—a reign of righteousness—a prevalence of religion—and a far-diffused happiness in the world, at which the joy at the dedication of the temple, and the triumphs over Antiochus, would be but a symbol. The ultimate reference, therefore, I suppose, is to the downfall of that great Antichristian power, the Papacy, and the spread and triumphs of the true religion subsequent to that, and consequent on that in the world. These were events that justified the solemn asseveration of the angel, and that made it proper for him, in referring to them, to stretch out both his hands in this sublime manner to heaven.

8. *And I heard, but I understood not.* He understood not the full significance of the language employed— "a time, and times, and an half." This would make it probable that there was something more intended than merely three years and a half as the period of the continuation of these troubles. Daniel saw, apparently from the manner of the angel, as well as from the terms which he used, that there was something mystical and unusual in those terms, and he says, therefore, that he could not understand their full import. ¶ *Then said I, O my Lord.* A term of civil address. The language is such as would be used by an inferior when respectfully addressing one of superior rank. It is

not a term that is peculiarly appropriate to God, or that implies a Divine nature, but is here given to the angel as an appellation of respect, or as denoting one of superior rank. ¶ *What shall be the end of these* things? Indicating great anxiety to know what was to be the termination of these wonders. The "end" had been often referred to in the communication of the angel, and now he had used an enigmatical expression as referring to it, and Daniel asks, with great emphasis, when the end *was* to be.

9. *And he said, Go thy way, Daniel.* That is, make no further inquiries. All has been disclosed that is to be. At the close of his communication (ver. 4), he had told Daniel to shut up, and seal the book, for his revelations were ended. He here repeats substantially the same thing, and he assures him that no more could be imparted on the subject. ¶ *For the words* are *closed up and sealed till the time of the end.* He had finished his communication, and had directed Daniel to close up the record which he made of it, and to affix a seal to the volume, ver. 4. He regarded the whole, therefore, as closed and sealed, until the "end" should come. The events themselves would unfold the meaning of the prediction more fully, and would confirm its truth by their exact correspondence with it. Yet, though the revelation was closed, and all that the angel had designed to say had been said, he does, in the subsequent verses, throw out some suggestions as to the *time,* or as to some important events which were to mark the termination of the wonders referred to. They are bare hints, however, the meaning of which was to be reserved till the time when the predictions would be accomplished, and they are not of such a nature that they can be supposed to have furnished any additional light to Daniel, or to have done anything to relieve the perplexity of his mind in the case.

10. *Many shall be purified.* In fu-

made white, and tried; but ^a the wicked shall do wickedly: and

a Rev. 22. 11.

ture times. That is, as the connection would seem to require, there will be a system introduced by which many will become purified, and made holy. Daniel might hope and expect that under the arrangements which God would make, many of the human race would be cleansed from sin. To what *he* would apply this we cannot determine, but it is a great truth of immense importance in regard to the human family, that, before the "end," or the consummation, "*many*" will be made holy. ¶ *And made white.* White is the emblem of innocence or purity, and hence the term is so often applied to the righteous. "They have washed their robes, and made them *white* in the blood of the Lamb," "they shall walk before me in *white*," &c. Hence the angels are represented as appearing in white raiment. The meaning here is, that many on the earth would be made *holy* before the end would come. The mind of Daniel was thus directed onward to one of the most glorious truths pertaining to future times—that multitudes of the human race would be redeemed, and would be prepared for a holy heaven. ¶ *And tried.* Tried as in a furnace; that is, they will be subjected to persecutions, and to various other forms of suffering, that will test the strength of their faith, and the nature of their religion. This language, also, is of a general character, and would in itself apply to the times of Antiochus, but it is also fitted to describe what would occur in other ages. Perhaps the meaning is, that it would be *a prominent thing* in the future, in introducing the triumphs of religion; and in preparing the people of God for heaven, that they would be subjected to various forms of trial. There have been facts enough of this kind in the history of the church to justify this description, and to show that it would be a marked feature in spreading religion on the earth, that its friends would be persecuted. ¶ *But the wicked shall do wickedly.* They will continue to do wickedly. Not-

none of the wicked shall understand; but the wise shall understand.

withstanding all the judgments that will come upon men; notwithstanding all that will be done to purify the people of God, and, notwithstanding the fact that "*many*" will be of a different character—will be "purified and made white, and tried," yet it will be a truth still, that there will be wicked men upon the earth, and that they will act out their nature. This remark seems to have been thrown in by the angel to prevent the impression which Daniel might possibly get from what was said, not only that the true religion would generally prevail, but that wickedness would *wholly* cease in the earth. Such a time, perhaps, we are not authorized to look for; while we may hope and believe that there will be a period when the worship of God will pervade the world, and will supersede all other forms of worship, yet we have no reason to expect that every individual of the human family at any one time will be converted, and that none of the remains of the apostasy will be seen on the earth. There will be wicked men still, and they will act out their nature, despite all that is done to save them, and despite the fact that religion will have the ascendency in the hearts and lives of the great mass of mankind. For an illustration of this, see Notes on Rev. ix. 20, 21, and xx. 7. ¶ *And none of the wicked shall understand.* This, also, is a general declaration. It means, that none of the wicked would understand the import of these prophecies, or the true nature of religion. Their depravity of heart would prevent it; their purpose to lead a wicked life would so cloud their understandings, and pervert their moral judgments, that they would have no correct appreciation of the government of God, and the nature of the Divine plans and dispensations. Comp. Notes on 1 Cor. ii. 14. The fact here asserted has been always true, and always will be, that sin prevents a clear perception of Divine truth, and that wicked men have no appropriate views of the plans and

11 And from the time *that* the daily *sacrifice* shall be taken away,

1 *to set up the abomination.*

and ¹ the abomination that ² maketh desolate set up, *there shall be* a

2 or, *astonisheth.*

purposes of God. To comprehend religion aright a man needs a pure heart; and no one under the influence of depraved feelings, and corrupt propensities and appetites, can expect to have a just appreciation of that which is good. Doubtless it will be found to be true in the days of millennial glory, when the true religion shall spread over the world, and when the earth shall be filled with light, that there will be wicked men who will have no correct understanding of the nature of religion, and whose minds will be blind to all the evidences of the truth of revelation which shall be diffused around them. No man, unless he is converted, has any proper conception of the beauty of religion. ¶ *But the wise shall understand.* They who serve God and love him, and who, therefore, come under the denomination of the truly *wise.* Notes on ver. 3. The meaning is, that religion—the love of God and a pure heart—will qualify them to perceive the import of Divine truth; to appreciate what is revealed, and to obtain a just view of passing events—or to "understand the signs of the times." Humble and sincere piety—a heart and mind made pure and clear by the influence of Divine truth—is the best preparation for understanding the works and ways of God. Comp. Notes on 1 Cor. ii. 9–12, 14, 15.

11. *And from the time.* Though the angel had said (vers. 4, 9) that his communication was closed, and that he imparted all that he was *commissioned* to communicate to Daniel, yet, as it would seem, in reply to the earnest request of Daniel, he volunteers an additional statement, in regard to certain important *periods* that were to occur in the future. The language, however, is *very* obscure; and it would appear, from ver. 13, that the angel scarcely expected that Daniel would understand it. The statement relates to certain *periods* that would succeed the time when the daily sacrifice would be taken away. Two such periods are mentioned as marking important epochs

in the future. ¶ That *the daily* sacrifice *shall be taken away.* This is the point of reckoning—the *terminus a quo.* The "taking away of the daily, sacrifice" refers, undoubtedly, to some act, or some state of things, by which it would be made to cease; by which the daily offerings at Jerusalem would be either temporarily suspended or totally abolished. See Notes on ch. viii. 11; ix. 27; xi. 31. The *language* here is applicable to either of two events :— to the act of Antiochus, causing the daily sacrifice to cease in Jerusalem (ch. viii. 11; xi. 31), or to the final closing of those sacrifices by the death of the Messiah as the great offering to whom they referred, and the destruction of the temple and the altar by the Romans, ch. ix. 27. The view taken in the interpretation of this passage will depend on the question to *which* of these there is allusion here by the angel, or whether there is an allusion to *both.* The *language* evidently is applicable to both, and might be employed with reference to either. ¶ *And the abomination that maketh desolate set up.* See these words explained in the Notes on ch. viii. 13; ix. 27; xi. 31. The same remark may be made here which was made respecting the previous expression—that the *language* is applicable to two quite distinct events, and events which were separated by a long interval of time : to the act of Antiochus in setting up an image of Jupiter in the temple, and to a similar act on the part of the Romans when the temple was finally destroyed. The view which is taken of the *time* referred to here will depend on the question which of these is to be regarded as the *stand-point* or the *terminus a quo,* or whether the language is *designedly* so used that an important epoch was to occur in *both* cases within a specified period *after* these events. On these points there has been great diversity of opinion. ¶ There shall be *a thousand two hundred and ninety days.* If this is to be taken literally, it would be three years and two hun-

thousand two hundred and ninety days.

12 Blessed *is* he that waiteth, and cometh to the thousand three

dred and ten days, reckoning the year at 360 days, and is thirty days more than the three years and a half referred to in ver. 7. Prof. Stuart, who supposes that the time is to be taken literally, and that the passage refers exclusively to Antiochus Epiphanes, explains the application of the language in the following manner: "Antiochus took away the daily sacrifice as is here declared. This was in the latter part of May, B.C. 168. Profane history does not indeed give us the *day*, but it designates the year and the season. As we have already seen [compare the extract copied from Prof. Stuart on ch. vii. 24–28], about three and a half years elapsed, after the temple worship was entirely broken up, before Judas Maccabeus expurgated the temple and restored its rites. The *terminus ad quem* is not mentioned in the verse now before us; but still it is plainly implied. The end of the 1290 days must, of course, be marked by some signal event, just as the commencement of them is so marked. And as the *suppression* of the temple rites constitutes the definitive mark of the commencement, so it would seem plain that the *restoration* of the same rites must mark the conclusion of the period which is designated. The 'time of the end,' *i.e.*, the period at the close of which the persecutions of Antiochus would cease, is distinctly adverted to in ch. vii. 25; xi. 30–35; and xii. 7. The nature of the case, in the verse before us, shows that the same period is tacitly referred to in the words of the speaker. No doubt remains that his march [the march of Antiochus] from Antioch to Egypt, for hostile purposes, was in the spring of the year 168 B.C. He was delayed for some time on this march by ambassadors from Egypt, who met him in Cœlo-Syria. Very naturally, therefore, we may conclude that he arrived opposite Jerusalem in the latter part of May, and that there and then he commissioned Apollonius to rifle and profane the temple. The exact time from the period when this was done, down to the time of the expurga-

tion, seems to have been, and is designated as being, 1290 days."—*Hints on Prophecy*, pp. 94, 95. It is evident, however, that there is here no clear making out of the exact time by any historical records, though it is in itself not improbable. Still the great difficulty is, that in the supposition that the "time, and times, and an half" refers to Antiochus, as denoting the period of his persecutions, thus limiting it to three years and a half—a period which can be made out without material difficulty (comp. Notes on ch. vii. 24–28)—that *another* time or period should be mentioned here of *thirty* days more, concerning which there is no corresponding event in the historical facts, or at least none that can now be demonstrated to have occurred. See the remarks at the close of the next verses.

12. *Blessed* is *he that waiteth.* This indicates a patient expectation of an event that was to occur, and the happy state of him who would reach it. The angel refers to another period different from the "time, and times, and an half," and different also from the twelve hundred and ninety days. He speaks of *this* as the consummation—as the desirable time; and pronounces him blessed who shall be permitted to see it. The idea here is, that of one looking out for this as a happy period, and that he would be regarded as a happy man who should live in that age. ¶ *And cometh to.* Literally, "touches." That is, whose life would reach to that time; or who would not be cut off before that period. ¶ *The thousand three hundred and five and thirty days.* The *article* is not used in the original, and its insertion here seems to make the period more distinct and definite than it is necessarily in the Hebrew. There is much apparent abruptness in all these expressions; and what the angel says in these closing and additional communications has much the appearance of a fragmentary character —of hints, or detached and unexplained thoughts thrown out on which he was not *disposed* to enlarge, and which, for

hundred and five and thirty days.

13 But go thou thy way till the end *be*, for [1] thou shalt rest, and stand in thy lot at the end of the days.   1 or, *and*.

---

some reason, he was not inclined to explain. In respect to this period of 1335 days, it seems to stand by itself. Nothing is said of the time when it would occur; no intimation is given of its commencement, as in the former cases—the *terminus a quo;* and nothing is said of its characteristics further than that he would be blessed who should be permitted to see it—implying that it would be, on some accounts, a happy period.

13. *But go thou thy way till the end* be. See vers. 4, 9. The meaning is, that nothing more would be communicated, and that he must wait for the disclosures of future times. When that should occur which is here called *"the end,"* he would understand this more fully and perfectly. The language implies, also, that *he* would be present at the development which is here called *"the end;"* and that then *he* would comprehend clearly what was meant by these revelations. This is such language as would be used on the supposition that the reference was to far-distant times, and to the scenes of the resurrection and the final judgment, when Daniel would be present. Comp. Notes on vers. 2, 3. ¶ *For thou shalt rest.* Rest now; and perhaps the meaning is, shalt enjoy a long season of repose before the consummation shall occur. In ver. 2, he had spoken of those who *"sleep* in the dust of the earth;" and the allusion here would seem to be the same as applied to Daniel. The period referred to was far distant. Important events were to intervene. The affairs of the world were to move on for ages before the "end" should come. There would be scenes of revolution, commotion, and tumult—momentous changes before that consummation would be reached. But during that long interval Daniel would "rest." He would quietly and calmly *"sleep* in the dust of the earth"—in the grave. He would be agitated by none of these troubles—disturbed by none of these changes; for he would peacefully

slumber in the hope of being awaked in the resurrection. This also is such language as would be employed by one who believed in the doctrine of the resurrection, and who meant to say that he with whom he was conversing would repose in the tomb while the affairs of the world would move on in the long period that would intervene between the time when he was then speaking and the "end" or consummation of all things—the final resurrection. I do not see that it is possible to explain the language on any other supposition than this. The word rendered "shalt rest"—תָּנוּחַ—would be well applied to the *rest* in the grave. So it is used in Job iii. 13, "Then had I been *at rest;"* Job iii. 17, "There the weary be *at rest."* ¶ *And stand in thy lot.* In thy place. The language is derived from the lot or portion which falls to one—as when a lot is cast, or anything is determined by lot. Comp. Judg. i. 3; Isa. lvii. 6; Psa. cxxv. 3; xvi. 5. Gesenius (*Lex.*) renders this, "And arise to thy lot in the end of days; *i.e.,* in the Messiah's kingdom." Comp. Rev. xx. 6. The meaning is, that he need have no apprehension for himself as to the future. That was not now indeed disclosed to him; and the subject was left in designed obscurity. He would "rest," perhaps a long time, in the grave. But in the far-distant future he would occupy his appropriate place; he would rise from his rest; he would appear again on the stage of action; he would have the lot and rank which properly belonged to him. What idea this would convey to the mind of Daniel it is impossible now to determine, for he gives no statement on that point; but it is clear that it is such language as would be appropriately used by one who believed in the doctrine of the resurrection of the dead, and who meant to direct the mind onward to those far-distant and glorious scenes when the dead would all arise, and when each one of the righteous would stand up in his appropriate place or lot.   ¶ *At the end of the days.* After the close of the periods referred to, when the consummation of all things should take place. It is impossible not to regard this as applicable to *a* resurrection from the dead; and there is every reason to suppose that Daniel would so understand it, for (*a*) if it be interpreted as referring to the close of the persecutions of Antiochus Epiphanes, it must be so understood. This prophecy was uttered about 534 years B.C. The death of Antiochus occurred 164 B.C. The *interval* between the prophecy and that event was, therefore, 370 years. It is impossible to believe that it was *meant* by the angel that Daniel would continue to live during all that time, so that he should then "stand in his lot," not having died; or that he *did* continue to live during all that period, and that at the end of it he "stood in his lot," or occupied the post of distinction and honour which is referred to in this language. But if this *had* been the meaning, it would have implied that he would, at that time, rise from the dead. (*b*) If it be referred, as Gesenius explains it, to the times of the Messiah, the same thing would follow—for that time was still more remote; and, if it be supposed that Daniel understood it as relating to those times, it must also be admitted that *he* believed that there would be a resurrection, and that he would then appear in his proper place. (*c*) There is only one other supposition, and that directly involves the idea that the allusion is to the general resurrection, as referred to in ver. 3, and that Daniel would have part in that. This is admitted by Lengerke, by Maurer, and even by Bertholdt, to be the meaning, though he applies it to the reign of the Messiah. No other interpretation, therefore, can be ·affixed to this than that it implies the doctrine of the resurrection of the dead, and that the mind of Daniel was directed onward to that. With this great and glorious doctrine the book appropriately closes. The hope of such a resurrection was fitted to soothe the mind of Daniel in view of all the troubles which he then experienced,

and of all the darkness which rested on the future; for what we most want in the troubles and in the darkness of the present life is the assurance that, after having "rested" in the grave—in the calm sleep of the·righteous—we shall "awake" in the morning of the resurrection, and shall "stand in our lot"—or in our appropriate place, as the acknowledged children of God, "at the end of days"—when time shall be no more, and when the consummation of all things shall have arrived.

In reference to the application of this prophecy, the following general remarks may be made:—

I. One class of interpreters explain it literally as applicable to Antiochus Epiphanes. Of this class is Prof. Stuart, who supposes that its reference to Antiochus can be shown in the following manner :—" The place which this passage occupies shows that the *terminus a quo*, or period from which the days designated are to be reckoned, is the same as that to which reference is made in the previous verse. This, as we have already seen, is the period when Antiochus, by his military agent Apollonius, took possession of Jerusalem, and put a stop to the temple worship there. The author of the first book of Maccabees, who is allowed by all to deserve credit as an historian, after describing the capture of Jerusalem by the agent of Antiochus (in the year 145 of the Seleucidæ—168 B.C.), and setting before the reader the widespread devastation which ensued, adds, respecting the invaders: 'They shed innocent blood around the sanctuary, and defiled the holy place; and the inhabitants of Jerusalem fled away: the sanctuary thereof was made desolate; her feasts were turned into mourning, her sabbaths into reproach, and her honour into disgrace;' 1 Macc. i. 37–39. To the period when this state of things commenced we must look, then, in order to find the date from which the 1335 days are to be reckoned. Supposing now that Apollonius captured Jerusalem in the latter part of May, B.C. 168, the 1335 days would expire about the middle of February, in the year B.C. 164. Did any event take place at this period which would naturally call forth the congratulations of the prophet, as addressed in the text before us to the Jewish people?

"History enables us to answer this question. Late in the year 165 B.C., or at least very early in the year 164 B.C., Antiochus Epiphanes, learning that there were great insurrections and disturbances in Armenia and Persia, hastened thither with a portion of his armies, while the other portion was commissioned against Palestine. He was victorious for a time; but being led by cupidity to seek for the treasures that were laid up in the temple of the Persian Diana at Elymaïs, he undertook to rifle them. The inhabitants of the place, however, rose *en masse* and drove him out of the city; after which he fled to Ecbatana. There he heard of the total discomfiture by Judas Maccabeus of his troops in Palestine, which were led on by Nicanor and Timotheus. In the rage occasioned by this disappointment, he uttered the most horrid blasphemies against the God of the Jews, and threatened to make Jerusalem the burying-place of the nation. Immediately he directed his course toward Judea; and designing to pass through Babylon, he made all possible haste in his journey. In the meantime he had a fall from his chariot which injured him; and soon after, being seized with a mortal sickness in his bowels (probably the cholera), he died at Tabæ, in the mountainous country, near the confines of Babylonia and Persia. Report stated, even in ancient times, that Antiochus was greatly distressed on his death-bed by the sacrilege which he had committed.

"Thus perished the most bitter and bloody enemy which ever rose up against the Jewish nation and their worship. By following the series of events, it is easy to see that his death took place some time in February of the year 164 B.C. Assuming that the commencement or *terminus a quo* of the 1335 days is the same as that of the 1290 days, it is plain that they terminate at the period when the death

of Antiochus is said to have taken place. 'It was long before the commencement of the spring,' says Frœlich, ' that Antiochus passed the Euphrates, and made his attack on Elymaïs:' so that no more probable time can be fixed upon for his death than at the expiration of the 1335 days; *i.e.*, some time in February of 164 B.C.   No wonder that the angel pronounced those of the pious and believing Jews to be *blessed* who lived to see such a day of deliverance."—*Hints on Prophecy,* pp. 95–97.

There are, however, serious and obvious difficulties in regard to this view, and to the supposition that this is all that is intended here—objections and difficulties of so much force that most Christian interpreters have supposed that something further was intended. Among these difficulties and objections are the following:—

(*a*) The air of *mystery* which is thrown over the whole matter by the angel, as if he were reluctant to make the communication; as if something more was meant than the words expressed; as if he shrank from disclosing all that he knew, or that might be said. If it referred to Antiochus alone, it is difficult to see why so much mystery was made of it, and why he was so unwilling to allude further to the subject — *as if* it were something that did not pertain to the matter in hand.

(*b*) The *detached* and *fragmentary* character of what is here said. It stands aside from the main communication. It is uttered after all that the angel had intended to reveal had been said. It is brought out at the earnest request of Daniel, and then only in *hints,* and in enigmatical language, and in such a manner that it would convey no distinct conception to his mind. This would seem to imply that it referred to something else than the main point that had been under consideration.

(*c*) The difference of *time* specified here by the angel. This relates to two points:—

1. To what would occur *after* the " closing of the daily sacrifice, and the setting up of the abomination of deso-

lation." The angel *now* says that what he here refers to would extend to a period of twelve hundred and *ninety* days. But in the accounts before given, the time specified had uniformly been "a time, and times, and half a time;" that is, three years and a half, or twelve hundred and *sixty* days—differing from this by thirty days. Why should this thirty days have been added here if it referred to the time when the sanctuary would be cleansed, and the temple worship restored? Professor Stuart (*Hints on Prophecy*, pp. 93, 94) supposes that it was in order that the *exact* period might be mentioned. But this is liable to objections. For (*a*) the period of three and a half years was sufficiently exact; (*b*) there was no danger of mistake on the subject, and no such error had been made as to require correction; (*c*) this was not of sufficient importance to justify the manifest anxiety of the angel in the case, or to furnish any answer to the inquiries of Daniel, since so small an item of information would not relieve the mind of Daniel. The allusion, then, would *seem* to be something else than what had been referred to by the "three and a half years."

2. But there is a greater difficulty in regard to the other period—the 1335 days; for (*a*) that stands wholly *detached* from what had been said. (*b*) The *beginning* of that period—the *terminus a quo*—is not specified. It is true that Prof. Stuart (*Hints on Prophecy*, p. 95) supposes that this must be the same as that mentioned in the previous verse, but this is not apparent in the communication. It is an isolated statement, and would *seem* to refer to some momentous and important period in the future which would be characterized as a glorious or "blessed" period in the world's history, or of such a nature that he ought to regard himself as peculiarly happy who should be permitted to live then. Now it is true that with much probability this may be shown, as Prof. Stuart has done in the passage quoted above, to accord well with the time when Antiochus died, as that was an important event, and

would be so regarded by those pious Jews who would be permitted to live to that time; but it is true also that the *main* thing for rejoicing was the conquest of Judas Maccabeus and the cleansing of the sanctuary, and that the death of Antiochus does not seem to meet the fulness of what is said here. If that were all, it is not easily conceivable why the angel should have made so much a mystery of it, or why he should have been so reluctant to impart what he knew. The whole matter, therefore, appears to have a higher importance than the mere death of Antiochus and the delivery of the Jews from his persecutions.

II. Another class, and it may be said Christian interpreters generally, have supposed that there was here a reference to some higher and more important events in the far-distant future. But it is scarcely needful to say, that the opinions entertained have been almost as numerous as the writers on the prophecies, and that the judgment of the world has not settled down on any one particular method of the application. It would not be profitable to state the opinions which have been advanced; still less to attempt to refute them—most of them being fanciful conjectures. These may be seen detailed in great variety in Poole's *Synopsis*. It is not commonly pretended that these opinions are based on any exact interpretation of the words, or on any certain mode of determining their correctness, and those who hold them admit that it must be reserved to future years—to their fulfilment—to understand the exact meaning of the prophecy. Thus Prideaux, who supposes that this passage refers to Antiochus, frankly says: "Many things may be said for the probable solving of this difficulty [the fact that the angel here refers to an additional thirty days above the three years and a half, which he says can neither be applied to Antiochus nor to Antichrist], but I shall offer none of them. Those that shall live to see the extirpation of Antichrist, which will be at the end of those years, will best be able to unfold these matters, it being of the nature of these prophecies not thoroughly to be understood till they are thoroughly fulfilled."—Vol. iii. 283, 284. So Bishop Newton, who supposes that the setting up of the abomination of desolation here refers to the Mahometans invading and devastating Christendom, and that the religion of Mahomet will prevail in the East for the space of 1260 years, and then a great revolution—"perhaps the restoration of the Jews, perhaps the destruction of Antichrist" —indicated by the 1290 years, will occur; and that this will be succeeded by another still more glorious event— perhaps "the conversion of the Gentiles, and the beginning of the millennium, or reign of the saints on the earth"—indicated by the 1335 years —says, notwithstanding, "What is the precise time of their beginning, and consequently of their ending, as well as what are the great and signal events which will take place at the end of each period, we can only conjecture; time alone can with certainty discover."—*Prophecies*, p. 321. These expressions indicate the *common* feeling of those who understand these statements as referring to future events; and the reasonings of those who have attempted to make a more specific application have been such as to demonstrate the wisdom of this modesty, and to make us wish that it had been imitated by all. At all events, such speculations on this subject have been so wild and unfounded; so at variance with all just rules of interpretation; so much the fruit of mere fancy, and so incapable of solid support by reasoning, as to admonish us that no more conjectures should be added to the number.

III. The sum of all that it seems to me can be said on the matter is this :—

(1.) That it is probable, for the reasons above stated, that the angel referred to *other* events than the persecutions and the death of Antiochus, for if that was all, the additional information which he gave by the specification of the period of 1260 days, and 1290 days, and 1335 days, was quite too meagre to be worthy of a formal and solemn revelation from

God. In other words, if this was all, there was no correspondence between the importance of the events and the solemn manner in which the terms of the communication were made. There was no such *importance* in these three periods as to make these separate disclosures necessary. If this were all, the statements were such indeed as might be made by a *weak man* attaching importance to trifles, but not such as would be made by an *inspired angel* professing to communicate great and momentous truths.

(2.) Either by design, or because the language which he would employ to designate higher events happened to be such as would note those periods also, the angel employed terms which, in the main, would be applicable to what would occur under the persecutions of Antiochus, while, at the same time, his eye was on more important and momentous events in the far-distant future. Thus the three years and a half would apply with sufficient accuracy to the time between the taking away of the daily sacrifice, and the expurgation of the temple by Judas Maccabeus, and then, also, it so happens that the *thirteen hundred and thirty-five* days would designate with sufficient accuracy the death of Antiochus, but there is nothing in the history to which the period of *twelve hundred and ninety* days could with particular propriety be applied, and there is no reason in the history why reference should have been made to that.

(3.) The angel had his eye on three great and important epochs lying apparently far in the future, and constituting important periods in the history of the church and the world. These were, respectively, composed of 1260, 1290, and 1335 prophetic days, that is, years. Whether they had the same beginning or point of reckoning—*termini a quo*— and whether they would, as far as they would respectively extend, cover the same space of time, he does not intimate with any certainty, and, of course, if this is the correct view it would be impossible now to determine, and the development is to be left to the times specified. One of them, the 1260 years, or the three years and a half, we can fix, we think, by applying it to the Papacy. See Notes on ch. vii. 24–28. But in determining even this, it was necessary to wait until the time and course of events should disclose its meaning; and in reference to the other two periods, doubtless still future, it may be necessary now to wait until events, still to occur, shall disclose what was intended by the angel. The first has been made clear by history: there can be no doubt that the others in the same manner will be made equally clear. That this is the true interpretation, and that this is the view which the angel desired to convey to the mind of Daniel, seems to be clear from such expressions as these occurring in the prophecy: " Seal the book *to the time of the end*," ver. 4; "many shall run to and fro, *and knowledge shall be increased*," ver. 4; "the words are closed up and sealed *till the time of the end*," ver. 9; "many shall be made *white*," ver. 10; "the wise *shall understand*," ver. 10; "go thou thy way *till the end be*," ver. 13. This language seems to imply that these things could not then be understood, but that when the events to which they refer should take place they would be plain to all.

(4.) Two of those events or periods —the 1290 days and the 1335 days— seem to lie still in the future, and the full understanding of the prediction is to be reserved for developments yet to be made in the history of the world. Whether it be by the conversion of the Jews and the Gentiles, respectively, as Bishop Newton supposes, it would be vain to conjecture, and time must determine. That such *periods*—marked and important periods—*are* to occur in the future, or in some era now commenced but not yet completed, I am constrained to believe; and that it will be possible, in time to come, to determine what they are, seems to me to be *as* undoubted. But where there is nothing certain to be the basis of calculation, it is idle to add other conjectures to those already made, and it is wiser to leave the matter, as much of the predictions respecting the future must of necessity be left to time and to events to make them clear.

Let me add, in the conclusion of the exposition of this remarkable book :—

(*a*) That the mind of Daniel is left at the close of all the Divine communications to him looking into the far-distant future, ver. 13. His attention is directed onward. Fragments of great truths had been thrown out, with little apparent connection, by the angel; hints of momentous import had been suggested respecting great doctrines to be made clearer in future ages. A time was to occur, perhaps in the far-distant future, when the dead were to be raised; when all that slept in the dust of the earth should awake; when the righteous should shine as the brightness of the firmament, and when he himself should "stand in his lot"— sharing the joys of the blessed, and occupying the position which would be appropriate to him. With this cheering prospect the communications of the angel to him are closed. Nothing could be better fitted to comfort his heart in a land of exile: nothing better fitted to elevate his thoughts.

(*b*) In the same manner it is proper that *we* should look *onward*. All the revelations of God terminate in this manner; all are designed and adapted to direct the mind to far-distant and most glorious scenes in the future. We have all that Daniel had; and we have what Daniel had not—the clear revelation of the gospel. In that gospel are stated in a still more clear manner those glorious truths respecting the future which are fitted to cheer us in time of trouble, to elevate our minds amidst the low scenes of earth, and to comfort and sustain us on the bed of death. With much more distinctness than Daniel saw them, we are permitted to contemplate the truths respecting the resurrection of the dead, the scenes of the final judgment, and the future happiness of the righteous. We have now knowledge of the resurrection of the Redeemer, and, through him, the assurance that all his people will be raised up to honour and glory; and though, in reference to the resurrection of the dead, and the future glory of the righteous, there is much that is still obscure, yet there is all that is necessary to inspire us with hope, and to stimulate us to endeavour to obtain the crown of life.

(c) It is not improper, therefore, to close the exposition of this book with the expression of a wish that what was promised to Daniel may occur to us who read his words—that "we may stand in our lot at the end of days;" that when all the scenes of earth shall have passed away in regard to us, and the end of the world itself shall have come, it may be our happy portion to occupy a place among the redeemed, and to stand accepted before God. To ourselves, if we are truly righteous through our Redeemer, we may apply the promise made to Daniel; and for his readers the author can express no higher wish than that this lot may be theirs. If the exposition of this book shall be so blessed as to confirm any in the belief of the great truths of revelation, and lead their minds to a more confirmed hope in regard to these future glorious scenes; if by dwelling on the firm piety, the consummate wisdom, and the steady confidence in God evinced by this remarkable man, their souls shall be more established in the pursuit of the same piety, wisdom, and confidence in God; and if it shall lead the minds of any to contemplate with a more steady and enlightened faith the scenes which are yet to occur on our earth, when the saints shall reign, or in heaven, when all the children of God shall be gathered there from all lands, the great object of these studies will have been accomplished, and the labour which has been bestowed upon it will not have been in vain. To these high and holy purposes I now consecrate these reflections on the book of Daniel, with an earnest prayer that He, from whom all blessings come, may be pleased so to accept this exposition of one of the portions of his revealed truth, as to make it the means of promoting the interests of truth and piety in the world; with a grateful sense of his goodness in allowing me to complete it, and with thankfulness that I have been permitted for so many hours, in the preparation of this work, to contemplate the lofty integrity, the profound wisdom, the stern and unyielding virtue, and the humble piety of this distinguished saint and eminent statesman of ancient times. He is under a good influence, and he is likely to have his own piety quickened, and his own purposes of unflinching integrity and faithfulness, and of humble devotion to God strengthened, who studies the writings and the character of the prophet Daniel.

APPENDIX.

The books of Maccabees are the titles of certain Jewish histories, containing principally the details of the heroic exploits of the family of that name. The first book contains a lucid and authentic history of the undertakings of Antiochus Epiphanes against the Jews, from the year B.C. 175 to the death of Simon Maccabeus B.C. 135. This history is confessedly of great value. It is on the whole entitled to credit, chronologically accurate, and advantageously distinguished above all other historical productions of this period. It is the second book in order of time. Of the author nothing is known; but he must have been a Palestinian Jew, who wrote some considerable time after the death of Simon Maccabeus, and even of Hyrcanus, and made use of several written, although chiefly of traditionary, sources of information. At the same time, it is not impossible that the author was present at several of the events which he so graphically describes.

The second book of Maccabees is a work of very inferior character to the first. It is an abridgment of a more ancient work, written by a Jew named Jason, who lived at Cyrene in Africa, comprising the principal transactions of the Jews which occurred during the reigns of Seleucus IV., Antiochus Epiphanes, and Antiochus Eupator. It partly goes over the same ground with the first book, but commences ten or twelve years earlier, and embraces in all a period of fifteen years. It does not appear that the author of either saw the other's work. This history supplies some blanks in the first book, but the letters prefixed to it contradict some of the facts recorded in the body of the work, and are not considered genuine. A different account, too, is given of the place and manner of the death of Antiochus Epiphanes from that contained in the first book.—*Kitto Abridged.*

FIRST BOOK OF THE MACCABEES.

CHAP. I.

14 *Antiochus gave leave to set up the fashions of the Gentiles in Jerusalem, 22 and spoiled it, and the temple in it, 57 and set up therein the abomination of desolation, 63 and slew those that did circumcise their children.*

AND it happened, after that Alexander son of Philip, the Macedonian, who came out of the land of Chettiim, had smitten Darius king of the Persians and Medes, that he reigned in his stead, the first over Greece,

2 And made many wars, and won many strong holds, and slew the kings of the earth,

3 And went through to the ends of the earth, and took spoils of many nations, insomuch that the earth was quiet before him; whereupon he was exalted, and his heart was lifted up.

4 And he gathered a mighty strong host, and ruled over countries, and nations, and kings, who became tributaries unto him.

5 And after these things he fell sick, and perceived that he should die.

6 Wherefore he called his servants, such as were honourable, and had been brought up with him from his youth, and parted his kingdom among them, while he was yet alive.

7 So Alexander reigned twelve years, and *then* died.

8 And his servants bare rule every one in his place.

9 And after his death they all put crowns *upon themselves;* so did their sons after them many years: and evils were multiplied in the earth.

10 And there came out of them a wicked root, Antiochus *surnamed* Epiphanes, son of Antiochus the king, who had been an hostage at Rome, and he reigned in the hundred and thirty and seventh year of the kingdom of the Greeks.

11 In those days went there out of Israel wicked men, who persuaded many, saying, Let us go and make a covenant with the heathen that are round about us: for since we departed from them we have had much sorrow.

12 So this device pleased them well.

13 Then certain of the people were so forward herein, that they went to the king, who gave them licence to do after the ordinances of the heathen:

14 Whereupon they built a place of exercise at Jerusalem according to the customs of the heathen:

15 And made themselves uncircumcised, and forsook the holy covenant, and joined themselves to the heathen, and were sold to do mischief.

16 Now when the kingdom was established before Antiochus, he thought to reign over Egypt, that he might have the dominion of two realms.

17 Wherefore he entered into Egypt with a great multitude, with chariots, and elephants, and horsemen, and a great navy,

18 And made war against Ptolemee king of Egypt: but Ptolemee was afraid of him, and fled; and many were wounded to death.

19 Thus they got the strong cities in the land of Egypt, and he took the spoils thereof.

20 And after that Antiochus had smitten Egypt, he returned again in the hundred forty and third year, and went up against Israel and Jerusalem with a great multitude,

21 And entered proudly into the sanctuary, and took away the golden altar, and the candlestick of light, and all the vessels thereof,

22 And the table of the shewbread, and the pouring vessels, and the vials, and the censers of gold, and the veil, and the crowns, and the golden ornaments that were before the temple, all which he pulled off.

23 He took also the silver and the gold, and the precious vessels: also he took the hidden treasures which he found.

24 And when he had taken all away, he went into his own land, having made a great massacre, and spoken very proudly.

25 And there was great mourning in Israel, in every place where they were;

26 So that the princes and elders mourned, the virgins and young men were made feeble, and the beauty of women was changed.

27 Every bridegroom took up lamentation, and she that sat in the marriage chamber was in heaviness.

28 The land also was moved for the inhabitants thereof, and all the house of Jacob was covered with confusion.

29 And after two years fully expired the king sent his chief collector of tribute unto the cities of Judah, who came unto Jerusalem with a great multitude,

30 And spake peaceable words unto them, but *all was* deceit: for when they had given him credence, he fell suddenly upon the city, and smote it very sore, and destroyed much people of Israel.

31 And when he had taken the spoils of the city, he set it on fire, and pulled down the houses and walls thereof on every side.

32 But the women and children took they captive, and possessed the cattle.

33 Then builded they the city of David with a great and strong wall, *and* with mighty towers, and made it a strong hold for them.

34 And they put therein a sinful nation, wicked men, and fortified *themselves* therein.

35 They stored it also with armour and victuals, and when they had gathered together the spoils of Jerusalem, they laid them up there, and so they became a sore snare:

36 For it was a place to lie in wait against the sanctuary, and an evil adversary to Israel.

37 Thus they shed innocent blood on every side of the sanctuary, and defiled it:

38 Insomuch that the inhabitants of Jerusalem fled because of them: whereupon *the city* was made an habitation of strangers, and became strange to those that were born in her; and her own children left her.

39 Her sanctuary was laid waste like a wilderness, her feasts were turned into mourning, her sabbaths into reproach, her honour into contempt.

40 As had been her glory, so was her dishonour increased, and her excellency was turned into mourning.

41 Moreover king Antiochus wrote to his whole kingdom, that all should be one people,

42 And every one should leave his laws: so all the heathen agreed according to the commandment of the king.

43 Yea, many also of the Israelites consented to his religion, and sacrificed unto idols, and profaned the sabbath.

44 For the king had sent letters by messengers unto Jerusalem and the cities of Judah, that they should follow the strange laws of the land,

45 And forbid burnt-offerings, and sacrifice, and drink-offerings, in the temple; and that they should profane the sabbaths and festival days:

46 And pollute the sanctuary and holy people:

47 Set up altars, and groves, and chapels of idols, and sacrifice swine's flesh, and unclean beasts:

48 That they should also leave their children uncircumcised, and make their souls abominable with all manner of uncleanness and profanation:

49 To the end they might forget the law, and change all the ordinances.

50 And whosoever would not do according to the commandment of the king, *he said*, he should die.

51 In the selfsame manner wrote he to his whole kingdom, and appointed overseers over all the people, commanding the cities of Judah to sacrifice, city by city.

52 Then many of the people were gathered unto them, to wit, every one that forsook the law; and so they committed evils in the land;

53 And drove the Israelites into secret places, even wheresoever they could flee for succour.

54 Now the fifteenth day of *the month* Casleu, in the hundred forty and fifth year, they set up the abomination of desolation upon the altar, and builded idol altars throughout the cities of Juda on every side;

55 And burnt incense at the doors of their houses, and in the streets.

56 And when they had rent in pieces the books of the law which they found, they burnt them with fire.

57 And wheresoever was found with any the book of the testament, or if any consented to the law, the king's commandment was, that they should put him to death.

58 Thus did they by their authority unto the Israelites every month, to as many as were found in the cities.

59 Now the five and twentieth day of the month they did sacrifice upon the idol altar, which was upon the altar of God.

60 At which time according to the commandment they put to death certain women,

that had caused their children to be circumcised.

61 And they hanged the infants about their necks, and rifled their houses, and slew them that had circumcised them.

62 Howbeit many in Israel were fully resolved and confirmed in themselves not to eat any unclean thing.

63 Wherefore they chose rather to die, that they might not be defiled with meats, and that they might not profane the holy covenant: so then they died.

64 And there was very great wrath upon Israel.

CHAP. II.

6 *Mattathias lamenteth the case of Jerusalem.* 24 *He slayeth a Jew that did sacrifice to idols in his presence, and the king's messenger also.* 34 *He and his are assailed upon the sabbath, and make no resistance.* 50 *He dieth, and instructeth his sons;* 66 *and maketh their brother Judas Maccabeus general.*

IN those days arose Mattathias *the son* of John, *the son* of Simeon, a priest of the sons of Joarib, from Jerusalem, and dwelt in Modin.

2 And he had five sons, Joannan, called Caddis:

3 Simon, called Thassi:

4 Judas, who was called Maccabeus:

5 Eleazar, called Avaran: and Jonathan, whose surname was Apphus.

6 And when he saw the blasphemies that were committed in Juda and Jerusalem,

7 He said, Woe is me! wherefore was I born to see this misery of my people, and of the holy city, and to dwell there, when it was delivered into the hand of the enemy, and the sanctuary into the hand of strangers?

8 Her temple is become as a man without glory.

9 Her glorious vessels are carried away into captivity, her infants are slain in the streets, her young men with the sword of the enemy.

10 What nation hath not had a part in *her* kingdom, and gotten of her spoils?

11 All her ornaments are taken away; of a free woman she is become a bondslave.

12 And, behold, our sanctuary, even our beauty and our glory, is laid waste, and the Gentiles have profaned it.

13 To what end therefore shall we live any longer?

14 Then Mattathias and his sons rent their clothes, and put on sackcloth, and mourned very sore.

15 In the mean while the king's officers, such as compelled the people to revolt, came into the city Modin, to make them sacrifice.

16 And when many of Israel came unto them, Mattathias also and his sons came together.

17 Then answered the king's officers, and said to Mattathias on this wise, Thou art a ruler, and an honourable and great man in this city, and strengthened with sons and brethren :

18 Now therefore come thou first, and fulfil the king's commandment, like as all the heathen have done, yea, and the men of Judah also, and such as remain at Jerusalem: so shalt thou and thy house be in the number of the king's friends, and thou and thy children shall be honoured with silver and gold, and many rewards.

19 Then Mattathias answered and spake with a loud voice, Though all the nations that are under the king's dominion obey him, and fall away every one from the religion of their fathers, and give consent to his commandments:

20 Yet will I and my sons and my brethren walk in the covenant of our fathers.

21 God forbid that we should forsake the law and the ordinances.

22 We will not hearken to the king's words, to go from our religion, either on the right hand, or the left.

23 Now when he had left speaking these words, there came one of the Jews in the sight of all to sacrifice on the altar which was at Modin, according to the king's commandment.

24 Which thing when Mattathias saw, he was inflamed with zeal, and his reins trembled, neither could he forbear to show his anger according to judgment: wherefore he ran, and slew him upon the altar.

25 Also the king's commissioner, who compelled men to sacrifice, he killed at that time, and the altar he pulled down.

26 Thus dealt he zealously for the law of God, like as Phinees did unto Zambri the son of Salom.

27 And Mattathias cried throughout the city with a loud voice, saying, Whosoever is zealous of the law, and maintaineth the covenant, let him follow me.

28 So he and his sons fled into the mountains, and left all that ever they had in the city.

29 Then many that sought after justice and judgment went down into the wilderness, to dwell there:

30 Both they, and their children, and their wives, and their cattle; because afflictions increased sore upon them.

31 Now when it was told the king's servants, and the host that was at Jerusalem, in the city of David, that certain men, who had broken the king's commandment, were gone down into the secret places in the wilderness,

32 They pursued after them a great number, and having overtaken them, they camped against them, and made war against them on the sabbath day.

33 And they said unto them, Let that which ye have done hitherto suffice; come forth, and do according to the commandment of the king, and ye shall live.

34 But they said, We will not come forth, neither will we do the king's commandment, to profane the sabbath day.

35 So then they gave them the battle with all speed.

36 Howbeit they answered them not, neither cast they a stone at them, nor stopped the places where they lay hid;

37 But said, Let us die all in our innocency: heaven and earth shall testify for us, that ye put us to death wrongfully.

38 So they rose up against them in battle on the sabbath, and they slew them, with their wives and children, and their cattle, to the number of a thousand people.

39 Now when Mattathias and his friends understood hereof, they mourned for them right sore.

40 And one of them said to another, If we all do as our brethren have done, and fight not for our lives and laws against the heathen, they will now quickly root us out of the earth.

41 At that time therefore they decreed, saying, Whosoever shall come to make battle with us on the sabbath day, we will fight against him; neither will we die all, as our brethren that were murdered in the secret places.

42 Then came there unto him a company of Assideans, who were mighty men of Israel, even all such as were voluntarily devoted unto the law.

43 Also all they that fled for persecution joined themselves unto them, and were a stay unto them.

44 So they joined their forces, and smote sinful men in their anger, and wicked men in their wrath: but the rest fled to the heathen for succour.

45 Then Mattathias and his friends went round about, and pulled down the altars:

46 And what children soever they found within the coast of Israel uncircumcised, those they circumcised valiantly.

47 They pursued also after the proud men, and the work prospered in their hand.

48 So they recovered the law out of the hand of the Gentiles, and out of the hand of kings, neither suffered they the sinner to triumph.

49 Now when the time drew near that Mattathias should die, he said unto his sons, Now hath pride and rebuke gotten strength, and the time of destruction, and the wrath of indignation:

50 Now therefore, my sons, be ye zealous for the law, and give your lives for the covenant of your fathers.

51 Call to remembrance what acts our fathers did in their time; so shall ye receive great honour and an everlasting name.

52 Was not Abraham found faithful in temptation, and it was imputed unto him for righteousness?

53 Joseph in the time of his distress kept the commandment, and was made lord of Egypt.

54 Phinees our father in being zealous and fervent obtained the covenant of an everlasting priesthood.

55 Jesus for fulfilling the word was made a judge in Israel.

56 Caleb for bearing witness before the congregation received the heritage of the land.

57 David for being merciful possessed the throne of an everlasting kingdom.

58 Elias for being zealous and fervent for the law was taken up into heaven.

59 Ananias, Azarias, and Misael, by believing were saved out of the flame.

60 Daniel for his innocency was delivered from the mouth of lions.

61 And thus consider ye throughout all ages, that none that put their trust in him shall be overcome.

62 Fear not then the words of a sinful man: for his glory shall be dung and worms.

63 To-day he shall be lifted up, and to-morrow he shall not be found, because he is returned into his dust, and his thought is come to nothing.

64 Wherefore, ye my sons, be valiant, and shew yourselves men in the behalf of the law; for by it shall ye obtain glory.

65 And, behold, I know that your brother Simon is a man of counsel, give ear unto him alway: he shall be a father unto you.

66 As for Judas Maccabeus, he hath been mighty and strong, even from his youth up: let him be your captain, and fight the battle of the people.

67 Take also unto you all those that observe the law, and avenge ye the wrong of your people.

68 Recompense fully the heathen, and take heed to the commandments of the law.

69 So he blessed them, and was gathered to his fathers.

70 And he died in the hundred forty and sixth year, and his sons buried him in the sepulchres of his fathers at Modin, and all Israel made great lamentation for him.

CHAP. III.

1 *The valour and fame of Judas Maccabeus.* 10 *He overthroweth the forces of Samaria and Syria.* 27 *Antiochus sendeth a great power against him.* 44 *He and his fall to fasting and prayer,* 58 *and are encouraged.*

THEN his son Judas, called Maccabeus, rose up in his stead.

2 And all his brethren helped him, and so did all they that held with his father, and, they fought with cheerfulness the battle of Israel.

3 So he gat his people great honour, and put on a breastplate as a giant, and girt his warlike harness about him, and he made battles, protecting the host with his sword.

4 In his acts he was like a lion, and like a lion's whelp roaring for his prey.

5 For he pursued the wicked, and sought them out, and burnt up those that vexed his people.

6 Wherefore the wicked shrunk for fear of him, and all the workers of iniquity were troubled, because salvation prospered in his hand.

7 He grieved also many kings, and made Jacob glad with his acts, and his memorial is blessed for ever.

8 Moreover he went through the cities of Juda, destroying the ungodly out of them, and turning away wrath from Israel:

9 So that he was renowned unto the utmost part of the earth, and he received unto him such as were ready to perish.

10 Then Apollonius gathered the Gentiles together, and a great host out of Samaria, to fight against Israel.

11 Which thing when Judas perceived, he went forth to meet him, and so he smote him, and slew him: many also fell down slain, but the rest fled.

12 Wherefore Judas took their spoils, and Apollonius' sword also, and therewith he fought all his life long.

13 Now when Seron, a prince of the army of Syria, heard say that Judas had gathered unto him a multitude and company of the faithful to go out with him to war;

14 He said, I will get me a name and honour in the kingdom; for I will go fight with Judas and them that are with him, who despise the king's commandment.

15 So he made him ready to go up, and there went with him a mighty host of the ungodly to help him, and to be avenged of the children of Israel.

16 And when he came near to the going up of Bethhoron, Judas went forth to meet him with a small company:

17 Who, when they saw the host coming to meet them, said unto Judas, How shall we be able, being so few, to fight against so great a multitude *and* so strong, seeing we are ready to faint with fasting all this day?

18 Unto whom Judas answered, It is no hard matter for many to be shut up in the hands of a few; and with *the God of* heaven it is all one, to deliver with a great multitude, or a small company:

19 For the victory of battle standeth not in the multitude of an host; but strength cometh from heaven.

20 They come against us in much pride and iniquity to destroy us, and our wives and children, and to spoil us:

21 But we fight for our lives and our laws.

22 Wherefore the Lord himself will overthrow them before our face: and as for you, be ye not afraid of them.

23 Now as soon as he had left off speaking, he leapt suddenly upon them, and so Seron and his host was overthrown before him.

24 And they pursued them from the going down of Bethhoron unto the plain, where were slain about eight hundred men of them; and the residue fled into the land of the Philistines.

25 Then began the fear of Judas and his brethren, and an exceeding great dread, to fall upon the nations round about them:

26 Insomuch as his fame came unto the king, and all nations talked of the battles of Judas.

27 Now when king Antiochus heard these things, he was full of indignation: wherefore he sent and gathered together all the forces of his realm, *even* a very strong army.

28 He opened also his treasure, and gave his soldiers pay for a year, commanding them to be ready whensoever he should need them.

29 Nevertheless, when he saw that the money of his treasures failed, and that the tributes in the country were small, because of the dissension and plague, which he had brought upon the land in taking away the laws which had been of old time;

30 He feared that he should not be able to bear the charges any longer, nor to have such gifts to give so liberally as he did before: for he had abounded above the kings that were before him.

31 Wherefore, being greatly perplexed in his mind, he determined to go into Persia, there to take the tributes of the countries, and to gather much money.

32 So he left Lysias, a nobleman, and one of the blood royal, to oversee the affairs of the king from the river Euphrates unto the borders of Egypt:

33 And to bring up his son Antiochus, until he came again.

34 Moreover he delivered unto him the half of his forces, and the elephants, and gave him charge of all things that he would have done, as also concerning them that dwelt in Juda and Jerusalem:

35 *To wit*, that he should send an army against them, to destroy and root out the strength of Israel, and the remnant of Jerusalem, and to take away their memorial from that place;

36 And that he should place strangers in all their quarters, and divide their land by lot.

37 So the king took the half of the forces that remained, and departed from Antioch, his royal city, the hundred forty and seventh year; and having passed the river Euphrates, he went through the high countries.

38 Then Lysias chose Ptolemee the *son* of Dorymenes, and Nicanor, and Gorgias, mighty men of the king's friends:

39 And with them he sent forty thousand footmen, and seven thousand horsemen, to go into the land of Juda, and to destroy it, as the king commanded.

40 So they went forth with all their power, and came and pitched by Emmaus in the plain country.

41 And the merchants of the country, hearing the fame of them, took silver and gold very much, with servants, and came into the camp to buy the children of Israel for slaves: a power also of Syria and of the land of the Philistines joined themselves unto them.

42 Now when Judas and his brethren saw that miseries were multiplied, and that the forces did encamp themselves in their borders; for they knew how the king had given commandment to destroy the people, and utterly abolish them;

43 They said one to another, Let us restore the decayed estate of our people, and let us fight for our people and the sanctuary.

44 Then was the congregation gathered together, that they might be ready for battle, and that they might pray, and ask mercy and compassion.

45 Now Jerusalem lay void as a wilderness, there was none of her children that went in or

out: the sanctuary also was trodden down, and aliens kept the strong hold; the heathen had their habitation in that place; and joy was taken from Jacob, and the pipe with the harp ceased.

46 Wherefore the Israelites assembled themselves together, and came to Maspha, over against Jerusalem; for in Maspha was the place where they prayed aforetime in Israel.

47 Then they fasted that day, and put on sackcloth, and cast ashes upon their heads, and rent their clothes,

48 And laid open the book of the law, wherein the heathen had sought to paint the likeness of their images.

49 They brought also the priests' garments, and the firstfruits, and the tithes: and the Nazarites they stirred up, who had accomplished their days.

50 Then cried they with a loud voice toward heaven, saying, What shall we do with these, and whither shall we carry them away?

51 For thy sanctuary is trodden down and profaned, and thy priests are in heaviness, and brought low.

52 And, lo, the heathen are assembled together against us to destroy us: what things they imagine against us, thou knowest.

53 How shall we be able to stand against them, except thou, O God, be our help?

54 Then sounded they with trumpets, and cried with a loud voice.

55 And after this Judas ordained captains over the people, *even* captains over thousands, and over hundreds, and over fifties, and over tens.

56 But as for such as were building houses, or had betrothed wives, or were planting vineyards, or were fearful, those he commanded that they should return, every man to his own house, according to the law.

57 So the camp removed, and pitched upon the south side of Emmaus.

58 And Judas said, Arm yourselves, and be valiant men, and see that ye be in readiness against the morning, that ye may fight with these nations, that are assembled together against us to destroy us and our sanctuary:

59 For it is better for us to die in battle, than to behold the calamities of our people and our sanctuary.

60 Nevertheless, as the will *of God* is in heaven, so let him do.

CHAP. IV.

6 *Judas defeateth the plot,* 14 *and forces of Gorgias,* 23 *and spoileth their tents,* 34 *and overthroweth Lysias.* 45 *He pulleth down the altar which the heathen had profaned, and setteth up a new:* 60 *and maketh a wall about Sion.*

THEN took Gorgias five thousand footmen, and a thousand of the best horsemen and removed out of the camp by night;

2 To the end he might rush in upon the camp of the Jews, and smite them suddenly. And the men of the fortress were his guides.

3 Now when Judas heard thereof, he himself removed, and the valiant men with him, that he might smite the king's army which was at Emmaus,

4 While as yet the forces were dispersed from the camp.

5 In the mean season came Gorgias by night into the camp of Judas: and when he found no man there, he sought them in the mountains: for said he, These fellows flee from us.

6 But as soon as it was day, Judas shewed himself in the plain with three thousand men, who nevertheless had neither armour nor swords to their minds.

7 And they saw the camp of the heathen, that it was strong and well harnessed, and compassed round about with horsemen; and these were expert of war.

8 Then said Judas to the men that were with him, Fear ye not their multitude, neither be ye afraid of their assault.

9 Remember how our fathers were delivered in the Red sea, when Pharaoh pursued them with an army.

10 Now therefore let us cry unto heaven, if peradventure the Lord will have mercy upon us, and remember the covenant of our fathers, and destroy this host before our face this day:

11 That so all the heathen may know that there is one who delivereth and saveth Israel.

12 Then the strangers lifted up their eyes, and saw them coming over against them.

13 Wherefore they went out of the camp to battle; but they that were with Judas sounded their trumpets.

14 So they joined battle, and the heathen being discomfited fled into the plain.

15 Howbeit all the hindmost of them were slain with the sword: for they pursued them unto Gazera, and unto the plains of Idumea, and Azotus, and Jamnia, so that there were slain of them upon a three thousand men.

16 This done, Judas returned again with his host from pursuing them,

17 And said to the people, Be not greedy of the spoils, inasmuch as there is a battle before us,

18 And Gorgias and his host are here by us

in the mountain: but stand ye now against our enemies, and overcome them, and after this ye may boldly take the spoils.

19 As Judas was yet speaking these words, there appeared a part of them looking out of the mountain:

20 Who when they perceived that the Jews had put their host to flight, and were burning the tents; for the smoke that was seen declared what was done:

21 When therefore they perceived these things, they were sore afraid, and seeing also the host of Judas in the plain ready to fight,

22 They fled every one into the land of strangers.

23 Then Judas returned to spoil the tents, where they got much gold, and silver, and blue silk, and purple of the sea, and great riches.

24 After this they went home, and sung a song of thanksgiving, and praised the Lord in heaven: because it is good, because his mercy *endureth* for ever.

25 Thus Israel had a great deliverance that day.

26 Now all the strangers that had escaped came and told Lysias what had happened:

27 Who, when he heard thereof, was confounded and discouraged, because neither such things as he would were done unto Israel, nor such things as the king commanded him were come to pass.

28 The next year therefore following Lysias gathered together threescore thousand choice men *of foot*, and five thousand horsemen, that he might subdue them.

29 So they came into Idumea, and pitched their tents at Bethsura, and Judas met them with ten thousand men.

30 And when he saw that mighty army, he prayed and said, Blessed art thou, O Saviour of Israel, who didst quell the violence of the mighty man by the hand of thy servant David, and gavest the host of strangers into the hands of Jonathan the son of Saul, and his armour-bearer;

31 Shut up this army in the hand of thy people Israel, and let them be confounded in their power and horsemen:

32 Make them to be of no courage, and cause the boldness of their strength to fall away, and let them quake at their destruction:

33 Cast them down with the sword of them that love thee, and let all those that know thy name praise thee with thanksgiving.

34 So they joined battle; and there were slain of the host of Lysias about five thousand men, even before them were they slain.

35 Now when Lysias saw his army put to flight, and the manliness of Judas' soldiers, and how they were ready either to live or die valiantly, he went into Antiochia, and gathered together a company of strangers, and having made his army greater than it was, he purposed to come again into Judea.

36 Then said Judas and his brethren, Behold, our enemies are discomfited: let us go up to cleanse and dedicate the sanctuary.

37 Upon this all the host assembled themselves together, and went up into mount Sion.

38 And when they saw the sanctuary desolate, and the altar profaned, and the gates burned up, and shrubs growing in the courts as in a forest, or in one of the mountains, yea, and the priests' chambers pulled down;

39 They rent their clothes, and made great lamentation, and cast ashes upon their heads,

40 And fell down flat to the ground upon their faces, and blew an alarm with the trumpets, and cried toward heaven.

41 Then Judas appointed certain men to fight against those that were in the fortress, until he had cleansed the sanctuary.

42 So he chose priests of blameless conversation, such as had pleasure in the law:

43 Who cleansed the sanctuary, and bare out the defiled stones into an unclean place.

44 And when as they consulted what to do with the altar of burnt-offerings, which was profaned;

45 They thought it best to pull it down, lest it should be a reproach to them, because the heathen had defiled it: wherefore they pulled it down,

46 And laid up the stones in the mountain of the temple in a convenient place, until there should come a prophet to shew what should be done with them.

47 Then they took whole stones according to the law, and built a new altar according to the former;

48 And made up the sanctuary, and the things that were within the temple, and hallowed the courts.

49 They made also new holy vessels, and into the temple they brought the candlestick, and the altar of burnt-offerings, and of incense, and the table.

50 And upon the altar they burned incense, and the lamps that were upon the candlestick they lighted, that they might give light in the temple.

51 Furthermore they set the loaves upon the table, and spread out the veils, and finished all the works which they had begun to make.

52 Now on the five and twentieth day of the ninth month, which *is called* the month Casleu,

in the hundred forty and eighth year, they rose up betimes in the morning,

53 And offered sacrifice according to the law upon the new altar of burnt-offerings, which they had made.

54 Look, at what time and what day the heathen had profaned it, even in that was it dedicated with songs, and citherns, and harps, and cymbals.

55 Then all the people fell upon their faces, worshipping and praising the God of heaven, who had given them good success.

56 And so they kept the dedication of the altar eight days, and offered burnt-offerings with gladness, and sacrificed the sacrifice of deliverance and praise.

57 They decked also the forefront of the temple with crowns of gold, and with shields; and the gates and the chambers they renewed, and hanged doors upon them.

58 Thus was there very great gladness among the people, for that the reproach of the heathen was put away.

59 Moreover Judas and his brethren with the whole congregation of Israel ordained, that the days of the dedication of the altar should be kept in their season from year to year by the space of eight days, from the five and twentieth day of the month Casleu, with mirth and gladness.

60 At that time also they builded up the mount Sion with high walls and strong towers round about, lest the Gentiles should come and tread it down, as they had done before.

61 And they set there a garrison to keep it, and fortified Bethsura to preserve it; that the people might have a defence against Idumea.

CHAP. V.

3 Judas smiteth the children of Esau, Bean, and Ammon. 17 Simon is sent into Galilee. 25 The exploits of Judas in Galaad. 51 He destroyeth Ephron, for denying him to pass through it. 56 Divers, that in Judas' absence would fight with their enemies, are slain.

NOW when the nations round about heard that the altar was built, and the sanctuary renewed as before, it displeased them very much.

2 Wherefore they thought to destroy the generation of Jacob that was among them, and thereupon they began to slay and destroy the people.

3 Then Judas fought against the children of Esau in Idumea at Arabattine, because they besieged Israel: and he gave them a great overthrow, and abated their courage, and took their spoils.

4 Also he remembered the injury of the children of Bean, who had been a snare and an offence unto the people, in that they lay in wait for them in the ways.

5 He shut them up therefore in the towers, and encamped against them, and destroyed them utterly, and burned the towers of that *place* with fire, and all that were therein.

6 Afterward he passed over to the children of Ammon, where he found a mighty power, and much people, with Timotheus their captain.

7 So he fought many battles with them, till at length they were discomfited before him; and he smote them.

8 And when he had taken Jazar, with the towns belonging thereto, he returned into Judea.

9 Then the heathen that were at Galaad assembled themselves together against the Israelites that were in their quarters, to destroy them; but they fled to the fortress of Dathema,

10 And sent letters unto Judas and his brethren, The heathen that are round about us are assembled together against us to destroy us:

11 And they are preparing to come and take the fortress whereunto we are fled, Timotheus being captain of their host.

12 Come now therefore, and deliver us from their hands, for many of us are slain:

13 Yea, all our brethren that were in the places of Tobie are put to death: their wives and their children also they have carried away captives, and borne away their stuff; and they have destroyed there about a thousand men.

14 While these letters were yet reading, behold, there came other messengers from Galilee with their clothes rent, who reported on this wise,

15 And said, They of Ptolemais, and of Tyrus, and Sidon, and all Galilee of the Gentiles, are assembled together against us to consume us.

16 Now when Judas and the people heard these words, there assembled a great congregation together, to consult what they should do for their brethren, that were in trouble, and assaulted of them.

17 Then said Judas unto Simon his brother, Choose thee out men, and go and deliver thy brethren that are in Galilee, for I and Jonathan my brother will go into the country of Galaad.

18 So he left Joseph the *son* of Zacharias, and Azarias, captains of the people, with the remnant of the host in Judea to keep it.

19 Unto whom he gave commandment, saying, Take ye the charge of this people, and see that ye make not war against the heathen until the time that we come again.

20 Now unto Simon were given three thousand men to go into Galilee, and unto Judas eight thousand men for the country of Galaad.

21 Then went Simon into Galilee, where he fought many battles with the heathen, so that the heathen were discomfited by him.

22 And he pursued them unto the gate of Ptolemais; and there were slain of the heathen about three thousand men, whose spoils he took.

23 And those that were in Galilee, and in Arbattis, with their wives and their children, and all that they had, took he away *with him,* and brought them into Judea with great joy.

24 Judas Maccabeus also and his brother Jonathan went over Jordan, and travelled three days' journey in the wilderness,

25 Where they met with the Nabathites, who came unto them in a peaceable manner, and told them every thing that had happened to their brethren in the land of Galaad:

26 And how that many of them were shut up in Bosora, and Bosor, and Alema, Casphor, Maked, and Carnaim; all these cities are strong and great:

27 And that they were shut up in the rest of the cities of the country of Galaad, and that against to-morrow they had appointed to bring their host against the forts, and to take them, and to destroy them all in one day.

28 Hereupon Judas and his host turned suddenly by the way of the wilderness unto Bosora; and when he had won the city, he slew all the males with the edge of the sword, and took all their spoils, and burned the city with fire.

29 From whence he removed by night, and went till he came to the fortress.

30 And betimes in the morning they looked up, and, behold, there was an innumerable people bearing ladders and other engines of war, to take the fortress: for they assaulted them.

31 When Judas therefore saw that the battle was begun, and that the cry of the city went up to heaven, with trumpets, and a great sound,

32 He said unto his host, Fight this day for your brethren.

33 So he went forth behind them in three companies, who sounded their trumpets, and cried with prayer.

34 Then the host of Timotheus, knowing that it was Maccabeus, fled from him: wherefore he smote them with a great slaughter; so that

there were killed of them that day about eight thousand men.

35 This done, Judas turned aside to Maspha; and after he had assaulted it, he took it, and slew all the males therein, and received the spoils thereof, and burnt it with fire.

36 From thence went he, and took Casphon, Magad, Bosor, and the other cities of the country of Galaad.

37 After these things gathered Timotheus another host, and encamped against Raphon beyond the brook.

38 So Judas sent *men* to espy the host, who brought him word, saying, All the heathen that be round about us are assembled unto them, even a very great host.

39 He hath also hired the Arabians to help them, and they have pitched their tents beyond the brook, ready to come and fight against thee. Upon this Judas went to meet them.

40 Then Timotheus said unto the captains of his host, When Judas and his host come near the brook, if he pass over first unto us, we shall not be able to withstand him; for he will mightily prevail against us:

41 But if he be afraid, and camp beyond the river, we shall go over unto him, and prevail against him.

42 So when Judas came near the brook, he caused the scribes of the people to remain by the brook: unto whom he gave commandment, saying, Suffer no man to remain in the camp, but let all come to the battle.

43 So he went first over unto them, and all the people after him: then all the heathen, being discomfited before him, cast away their weapons, and fled unto the temple that was at Carnaim.

44 But they took the city, and burned the temple with all that were therein. Thus was Carnaim subdued, neither could they stand any longer before Judas.

45 Then Judas gathered together all the Israelites that were in the country of Galaad, from the least unto the greatest, even their wives, and their children, and their stuff, a very great host, to the end they might come into the land of Judea.

46 Now when they came unto Ephron, (this was a great city in the way as they should go, very well fortified) they could not turn from it, either on the right hand or the left, but must needs pass through the midst of it.

47 Then they of the city shut them out, and stopped up the gates with stones.

48 Whereupon Judas sent unto them in peaceable manner, saying, Let us pass through your land to go into our own country, and none

shall do you any hurt; we will only pass through on foot: howbeit they would not open unto him.

49 Wherefore Judas commanded a proclamation to be made throughout the host, that every man should pitch his tent in the place where he was.

50 So the soldiers pitched, and assaulted the city all that day and all that night, till at the length the city was delivered into his hands:

51 Who then slew all the males with the edge of the sword, and rased the city, and took the spoils thereof, and passed through the city over them that were slain.

52 After this went they over Jordan into the great plain before Bethsan.

53 And Judas gathered together those that came behind, and exhorted the people all the way through, till they came into the land of Judea.

54 So they went up to mount Sion with joy and gladness, where they offered burnt-offerings, because not one of them were slain until they had returned in peace.

55 Now what time as Judas and Jonathan were in the land of Galaad, and Simon his brother in Galilee before Ptolemais,

56 Joseph the *son* of Zacharias, and Azarias, captains of the garrisons, heard of the valiant acts and warlike deeds which they had done.

57 Wherefore they said, Let us also get us a name, and go fight against the heathen that are round about us.

58 So when they had given charge unto the garrison that was with them, they went toward Jamnia.

59 Then came Gorgias and his men out of the city to fight against them.

60 And so it was, that Joseph and Azarias were put to flight, and pursued unto the borders of Judea: and there were slain that day of the people of Israel about two thousand men.

61 Thus was there a great overthrow among the children of Israel, because they were not obedient unto Judas and his brethren, but thought to do some valiant act.

62 Moreover these men came not of the seed of those, by whose hand deliverance was given unto Israel.

63 Howbeit the man Judas and his brethren were greatly renowned in the sight of all Israel, and of all the heathen, wheresoever their name was heard of;

64 Insomuch as the people assembled unto them with joyful acclamations.

65 Afterward went Judas forth with his brethren, and fought against the children of Esau in the land toward the south, where he

DANIEL II.

smote Hebron, and the towns thereof, and pulled down the fortress of it, and burned the towers thereof round about.

66 From thence he removed to go into the land of the Philistines, and passed through Samaria.

67 At that time certain priests, desirous to shew their valour, were slain in battle, for that they went out to fight unadvisedly.

68 So Judas turned to Azotus in the land of the Philistines, and when he had pulled down their altars, and burned their carved images with fire, and spoiled their cities, he returned into the land of Judea.

CHAP. VI.

8 Antiochus dieth, 12 *and confesseth that he is plagued for the wrong done to Jerusalem.* 20 *Judas besiegeth those in the tower at Jerusalem.* 28 *They procure Antiochus the younger to come into Judea.* 51 *He besiegeth Sion,* 60 *and maketh peace with Israel;* 62 *yet overthroweth the wall of Sion.*

ABOUT that time king Antiochus travelling through the high countries heard say, that Elymais in the country of Persia was a city greatly renowned for riches, silver, and gold;

2 And that there was in it a very rich temple, wherein were coverings of gold, and breastplates, and shields, which Alexander, *son* of Philip, the Macedonian king, who reigned first among the Grecians, had left there.

3 Wherefore he came and sought to take the city, and to spoil it; but he was not able, because they of the city, having had warning thereof,

4 Rose up against him in battle: so he fled, and departed thence with great heaviness, and returned to Babylon.

5 Moreover there came one who brought him tidings into Persia, that the armies, which went against the land of Judea, were put to flight:

6 And that Lysias, who went forth first with a great power, was driven away of the Jews; and that they were made strong by the armour, and power, and store of spoils, which they had gotten of the armies, whom they had destroyed:

7 Also that they had pulled down the abomination, which he had set up upon the altar in Jerusalem, and that they had compassed about the sanctuary with high walls, as before, and his city Bethsura.

8 Now when the king heard these words, he was astonished and sore moved: whereupon he laid him down upon his bed, and fell sick for grief, because it had not befallen him as he looked for.

9 And there he continued many days: for

his grief was ever more and more, and he made account that he should die.

10 Wherefore he called for all his friends, and said unto them, The sleep is gone from mine eyes, and my heart faileth for very care.

11 And I thought with myself, Into what tribulation am I come, and how great a flood *of misery* is it, wherein now I am! for I was bountiful and beloved in my power.

12 But now I remember the evils that I did at Jerusalem, and that I took all the vessels of gold and silver that were therein, and sent to destroy the inhabitants of Judea without a cause.

13 I perceive therefore that for this cause these troubles are come upon me, and, behold, I perish through great grief in a strange land.

14 Then called he for Philip, one of his friends, whom he made ruler over all his realm,

15 And gave him the crown, and his robe, and his signet, to the end he should bring up his son Antiochus, and nourish him up for the kingdom.

16 So king Antiochus died there in the hundred forty and ninth year.

17 Now when Lysias knew that the king was dead, he set up Antiochus his son, whom he had brought up being young, to reign in his stead, and his name he called Eupator.

18 About this time they that were in the tower shut up the Israelites round about the sanctuary, and sought always their hurt, and the strengthening of the heathen.

19 Wherefore Judas, purposing to destroy them, called all the people together to besiege them.

20 So they came together, and besieged them in the hundred and fiftieth year, and he made mounts for shot against them, and *other* engines.

21 Howbeit certain of them that were besieged got forth, unto whom some ungodly men of Israel joined themselves:

22 And they went unto the king, and said, How long will it be ere thou execute judgment, and avenge our brethren?

23 We have been willing to serve thy father, and to do as he would have us, and to obey his commandments;

24 For which cause they of our nation besiege the tower, and are alienated from us: moreover as many of us as they could light on they slew, and spoiled our inheritance.

25 Neither have they stretched out their hand against us only, but also against all their borders.

26 And, behold, this day are they besieging the tower at Jerusalem, to take it: the sanctuary also and Bethsura have they fortified.

27 Wherefore if thou dost not prevent them quickly, they will do greater things than these, neither shalt thou be able to rule them.

28 Now when the king heard this, he was angry, and gathered together all his friends, and the captains of his army, and those that had charge of the horse.

29 There came also unto him from other kingdoms, and from isles of the sea, bands of hired soldiers.

30 So that the number of his army was an hundred thousand footmen, and twenty thousand horsemen, and two and thirty elephants exercised in battle.

31 These went through Idumea, and pitched against Bethsura, which they assaulted many days, making engines of war; but they *of Bethsura* came out, and burned them with fire, and fought valiantly.

32 Upon this Judas removed from the tower, and pitched in Bathzacharias, over against the king's camp.

33 Then the king rising very early marched fiercely with his host toward Bathzacharias, where his armies made them ready to battle, and sounded the trumpets.

34 And to the end they might provoke the elephants to fight, they showed them the blood of grapes and mulberries.

35 Moreover they divided the beasts among the armies, and for every elephant they appointed a thousand men, armed with coats of mail, and with helmets of brass on their heads; and beside this, for every beast were ordained five hundred horsemen of the best.

36 These were ready at every occasion: wheresoever the beast was, and whithersoever the beast went, they went also, neither departed they from him.

37 And upon the beasts were there strong towers of wood, which covered every one of them, and were girt fast unto them with devices: there were also upon every one two and thirty strong men, that fought upon them, beside the Indian that ruled him.

38 As for the remnant of the horsemen, they set them on this side and that side at the two parts of the host, giving them signs what to do, and being harnessed all over amidst the ranks.

39 Now when the sun shone upon the shields of gold and brass, the mountains glistered therewith, and shined like lamps of fire.

40 So part of the king's army being spread upon the high mountains, and part on the valleys below, they marched on safely and in order.

41 Wherefore all that heard the noise of their multitude, and the marching of the company,

and the rattling of the harness, were moved: for the army was very great and mighty.

42 Then Judas and his host drew near, and entered into battle, and there were slain of the king's army six hundred men.

43 ¶ Eleazar also, *surnamed* Savaran, perceiving that one of the beasts, armed with royal harness, was higher than all the rest, and supposing that the king was upon him,

44 Put himself in jeopardy, to the end he might deliver his people, and get him a perpetual name:

45 Wherefore he ran upon him courageously through the midst of the battle, slaying on the right hand and on the left, so that they were divided from him on both sides.

46 Which done, he crept under the elephant, and thrust him under, and slew him: whereupon the elephant fell down upon him, and there he died.

47 Howbeit *the rest of the Jews* seeing the strength of the king, and the violence of his forces, turned away from them.

48 ¶ Then the king's army went up to Jerusalem to meet them, and the king pitched his tents against Judea, and against mount Sion.

49 But with them that were in Bethsura he made peace: for they came out of the city, because they had no victuals there to endure the siege, it being a year of rest to the land.

50 So the king took Bethsura, and set a garrison there to keep it.

51 As for the sanctuary, he besieged it many days: and set there artillery with engines and instruments to cast fire and stones, and pieces to cast darts and slings.

52 Whereupon they also made engines against their engines, and held them battle a long season.

53 Yet at the last, their vessels being without victuals, (for that it was the seventh year, and they in Judea, that were delivered from the Gentiles, had eaten up the residue of the store;)

54 There were but a few left in the sanctuary, because the famine did so prevail against them, that they were fain to disperse themselves, every man to his own place.

55 At that time Lysias heard say, that Philip, whom Antiochus the king, whiles he lived, had appointed to bring up his son Antiochus, that he might be king,

56 Was returned out of Persia and Media, and the king's host also that went with him, and that he sought to take unto him the ruling of the affairs.

57 Wherefore he went in all haste, and said to the king and the captains of the host and the company, We decay daily, and our victuals are but small, and the place we lay siege unto is strong, and the affairs of the kingdom lie upon us;

58 Now therefore let us be friends with these men, and make peace with them, and with all their nation;

59 And covenant with them, that they shall live after their laws, as they did before: for they are therefore displeased, and have done all these things, because we abolished their laws.

60 So the king and the princes were content: wherefore he sent unto them to make peace; and they accepted thereof.

61 Also the king and the princes made an oath unto them: whereupon they went out of the strong hold.

62 Then the king entered into mount Sion; but when he saw the strength of the place, he brake his oath that he had made, and gave commandment to pull down the wall round about.

63 Afterward departed he in all haste, and returned unto Antiochia, where he found Philip to be master of the city: so he fought against him, and took the city by force.

SECOND BOOK OF THE MACCABEES.

CHAP. I.

1 *A letter of the Jews from Jerusalem to them of Egypt, to thank God for the death of Antiochus.* 19 *Of the fire that was hid in the pit.* 24 *The prayer of Neemias.*

THE brethren, the Jews that be at Jerusalem and in the land of Judea, wish unto the brethren, the Jews that are throughout Egypt, health and peace:

2 God be gracious unto you, and remember his covenant that he made with Abraham, Isaac, and Jacob, his faithful servants;

3 And give you all an heart to serve him, and to do his will, with a good courage and a willing mind;

4 And open your hearts in his law and commandments, and send you peace,

5 And hear your prayers, and be at one with you, and never forsake you in time of trouble.

6 And now we be here praying for you.

7 What time as Demetrius reigned, in the hundred threescore and ninth year, we the Jews wrote unto you in the extremity of trouble that came upon us in those years, from the time that Jason and his company revolted from the holy land and kingdom,

8 And burned the porch, and shed innocent blood: then we prayed unto the Lord, and were heard; we offered also sacrifices and fine flour, and lighted the lamps, and set forth the loaves.

9 And now see that ye keep the feast of tabernacles in the month Casleu.

10 In the hundred fourscore and eighth year, the people that were at Jerusalem and in Judea, and the council, and Judas, sent greeting and health unto Aristobulus, king Ptolemeus' master, who was of the stock of the anointed priests, and to the Jews that were in Egypt:

11 Insomuch as God hath delivered us from great perils, we thank him highly, as having been in battle against a king.

12 For he cast them out that fought within the holy city.

13 For when the leader was come into Persia, and the army with him that seemed invincible, they were slain in the temple of Nanea by the deceit of Nanea's priests.

14 For Antiochus, as though he would marry her, came into the place, and his friends that were with him, to receive money in name of a dowry.

15 Which when the priests of Nanea had set forth, and he was entered with a small company into the compass of the temple, they shut the temple as soon as Antiochus was come in:

16 And opening a privy door of the roof, they threw stones like thunderbolts, and struck down the captain, hewed them in pieces, smote off their heads, and cast them to those that were without.

17 Blessed be our God in all things, who hath delivered up the ungodly.

18 Therefore whereas we are now purposed to keep the purification of the temple upon the five and twentieth day of *the month* Casleu, we thought it necessary to certify you thereof, that ye also might keep *it, as the feast* of the tabernacles, and of the fire, *which was given us* when Neemias offered sacrifice, after that he had builded the temple and the altar.

19 For when our fathers were led into Persia, the priests that were then devout took the fire of the altar privily, and hid it in an hollow place of a pit without water, where they kept *it* sure, so that the place was unknown to all men.

20 Now after many years, when it pleased God, Neemias, being sent from the king of Persia, did send of the posterity of those priests that had hid it to the fire: but when they told us they found no fire, but thick water;

21 Then commanded he them to draw it up, and to bring it; and when the sacrifices were laid on, Neemias commanded the priests to sprinkle the wood and the things laid thereupon with the water.

22 When this was done, and the time came that the sun shone, which afore was hid in the cloud, there was a great fire kindled, so that every man marvelled.

23 And the priests made a prayer whilst the sacrifice was consuming, *I say,* both the priests, and all *the rest,* Jonathan beginning, and the rest answering thereunto, as Neemias did.

24 And the prayer was after this manner; O Lord, Lord God, Creator of all things, who art fearful and strong, and righteous, and merciful, and the only and gracious King,

25 The only giver of all things, the only just, almighty, and everlasting, thou that deliverest Israel from all trouble, and didst choose the fathers, and sanctify them:

26 Receive the sacrifice for thy whole people Israel, and preserve thine own portion, and sanctify it.

27 Gather those together that are scattered from us, deliver them that serve among the heathen, look upon them that are despised and abhorred, and let the heathen know that thou art our God.

28 Punish them that oppress us, and with pride do us wrong.

29 Plant thy people again in thy holy place, as Moses hath spoken.

30 And the priests sung psalms of thanksgiving.

31 Now when the sacrifice was consumed, Neemias commanded the water that was left to be poured on the great stones.

32 When this was done, there was kindled a flame: but it was consumed by the light that shined from the altar.

33 So when this matter was known, it was told the king of Persia, that in the place, where the priests that were led away had hid the fire, there appeared water, and that Neemias had purified the sacrifices therewith.

34 Then the king, inclosing the place, made it holy, after he had tried the matter.

35 And the king took many gifts, and bestowed thereof on those whom he would gratify.

36 And Neemias called this thing Naphthar, which is as much as to say, a cleansing: but many men call it Nephi.

CHAP. II.

1 *What Jeremy the prophet did.* 5 *How he hid the tabernacle, the ark, and the altar.* 15 *What Neemias and Judas wrote.* 20 *What Jason wrote in five books: 25 and how those were abridged by the author of this book.*

IT is also found in the records, that Jeremy the prophet commanded them that were carried away to take of the fire, as it hath been signified:

2 And how that the prophet, having given them the law, charged them not to forget the commandments of the Lord, and that they should not err in their minds, when they see images of silver and gold, with their ornaments.

3 And with other such speeches exhorted he them, that the law should not depart from their hearts.

4 It was also contained in the same writing, that the prophet, being warned of God, commanded the tabernacle and the ark to go with him, as he went forth into the mountain, where Moses climbed up, and saw the heritage of God.

5 And when Jeremy came thither, he found an hollow cave, wherein he laid the tabernacle, and the ark, and the altar of incense, and so stopped the door.

6 And some of those that followed him came to mark the way, but they could not find it.

7 Which when Jeremy perceived, he blamed them, saying, As for that place, it shall be unknown until the time that God gather his people again together, and receive them unto mercy.

8 Then shall the Lord shew them these things, and the glory of the Lord shall appear, and the cloud also, as it was shewed under Moses, and as when Solomon desired that the place might be honourably sanctified.

9 It was also declared, that he being wise offered the sacrifice of dedication, and of the finishing of the temple.

10 And as when Moses prayed unto the Lord, the fire came down from heaven, and consumed the sacrifices; even so prayed Solomon also, and the fire came down from heaven, and consumed the burnt-offerings.

11 And Moses said, Because the sin-offering was not to be eaten, it was consumed.

12 So Solomon kept those eight days.

13 The same things also were reported in the writings and commentaries of Neemias; and how he founding a library gathered together the acts of the kings, and the prophets, and of David, and the epistles of the kings concerning the holy gifts.

14 In like manner also Judas gathered together all those things that were lost by reason of the war we had, and they remain with us.

15 Wherefore if ye have need thereof, send some to fetch them unto you.

16 Whereas we then are about to celebrate the purification, we have written unto you, and ye shall do well, if ye keep the same days.

17 We hope also, that the God, that delivered all his people, and gave them all an heritage, and the kingdom, and the priesthood, and the sanctuary,

18 As he promised in the law, will shortly have mercy upon us, and gather us together out of every land under heaven into the holy place: for he hath delivered us out of great troubles, and hath purified the place.

19 Now as concerning Judas Maccabeus, and his brethren, and the purification of the great temple, and the dedication of the altar,

20 And the wars against Antiochus Epiphanes, and Eupator his son,

21 And the manifest signs that came from heaven unto those that behaved themselves manfully to their honour for Judaism: so that, being but a few, they overcame the whole country, and chased barbarous multitudes,

22 And recovered again the temple renowned all the world over, and freed the city, and up-

held the laws which were going down, the Lord being gracious unto them with all favour:

23 *All these things, I say*, being declared by Jason of Cyrene in five books, we will assay to abridge in one volume.

24 For considering the infinite number, and the difficulty which they find that desire to look into the narrations of the story, for the variety of the matter,

25 We have been careful, that they that will read may have delight, and that they that are desirous to commit to memory might have ease, and that all into whose hands it comes might have profit.

26 Therefore to us, that have taken upon us this painful labour of abridging, it was not easy, but a matter of sweat and watching;

27 Even as it is no ease unto him that prepareth a banquet, and seeketh the benefit of others: yet for the pleasuring of many we will undertake gladly this great pains;

28 Leaving to the author the exact handling of every particular, and labouring to follow the rules of an abridgement.

29 For as the master builder of a new house must care for the whole building; but he that undertaketh to set it out, and paint it, must seek out fit things for the adorning thereof: even so I think it is with us.

30 To stand upon every point, and go over things at large, and to be curious in particulars, belongeth to the first author of the story:

31 But to use brevity, and avoid much labouring of the work, is to be granted to him that will make an abridgement.

32 Here then will we begin the story: only adding thus much to that which hath been said, that it is a foolish thing to make a long prologue, and to be short in the story itself.

CHAP. III.

1 *Of the honour done to the temple by the kings of the Gentiles.* 4 *Simon uttereth what treasures are in the temple.* 7 *Heliodorus is sent to take them away.* 24 *He is stricken of God, and healed at the prayer of Onias.*

NOW when the holy city was inhabited with all peace, and the laws were kept very well, because of the godliness of Onias the high priest, and his hatred of wickedness,

2 It came to pass that even the kings themselves did honour the place, and magnify the temple with their best gifts;

3 Insomuch that Seleucus king of Asia of his own revenues bare all the costs belonging to the service of the sacrifices.

4 But one Simon of the tribe of Benjamin, who was made governor of the temple, fell out with the high priest about disorder in the city.

5 And when he could not overcome Onias, he gat him to Apollonius *the son* of Thraseas, who then was governor of Celosyria and Phenice,

6 And told him that the treasury in Jerusalem was full of infinite sums of money, so that the multitude of their riches, which did not pertain to the account of the sacrifices, was innumerable, and that it was possible to bring all into the king's hand.

7 Now when Apollonius came to the king, and had showed him of the money whereof he was told, the king chose out Heliodorus his treasurer, and sent him with a commandment to bring him the foresaid money.

8 So forthwith Heliodorus took his journey, under a colour of visiting the cities of Celosyria and Phenice, but indeed to fulfil the king's purpose.

9 And when he was come to Jerusalem, and had been courteously received of the high priest of the city, he told him what intelligence was given of the money, and declared wherefore he came, and asked if these things were so indeed.

10 Then the high priest told him that there was such money laid up for the relief of widows and fatherless children:

11 And that some of it belonged to Hircanus son of Tobias, a man of great dignity, and not as that wicked Simon had misinformed: the sum whereof in all was four hundred talents of silver, and two hundred of gold:

12 And that it was altogether impossible that such wrongs should be done unto them, that had committed it to the holiness of the place, and to the majesty and inviolable sanctity of the temple, honoured over all the world.

13 But Heliodorus, because of the king's commandment given him, said, That in any wise it must be brought into the king's treasury.

14 So at the day which he appointed he entered in to order this matter: wherefore there was no small agony throughout the whole city.

15 But the priests, prostrating themselves before the altar in their priests' vestments, called unto heaven upon him that made a law concerning things given to be kept, that they should safely be preserved for such as had committed them to be kept.

16 Then whoso had looked the high priest in the face, it would have wounded his heart: for his countenance and the changing of his colour declared the inward agony of his mind.

17 For the man was so compassed with fear and horror of the body, that it was manifest to

them that looked upon him, what sorrow he had now in his heart.

18 Others ran flocking out of their houses to the general supplication, because the place was like to come into contempt.

19 And the women, girt with sackcloth under their breasts, abounded in the streets, and the virgins that were kept in ran, some to the gates, and some to the walls, and others looked out of the windows.

20 And all, holding their hands toward heaven, made supplication.

21 Then it would have pitied a man to see the falling down of the multitude of all sorts, and the fear of the high priest, being in such an agony.

22 They then called upon the Almighty Lord to keep the things committed of trust safe and sure for those that had committed them.

23 Nevertheless Heliodorus executed that which was decreed.

24 Now as he was there present himself with his guard about the treasury, the Lord of spirits, and the Prince of all power, caused a great apparition, so that all that presumed to come in with him were astonished at the power of God, and fainted, and were sore afraid.

25 For there appeared unto them an horse with a terrible rider upon him, and adorned with a very fair covering, and he ran fiercely, and smote at Heliodorus with his forefeet, and it seemed that he that sat upon the horse had complete harness of gold.

26 Moreover two other young men appeared before him, notable in strength, excellent in beauty, and comely in apparel, who stood by him on either side, and scourged him continually, and gave him many sore stripes.

27 And Heliodorus fell suddenly unto the ground, and was compassed with great darkness: but they that were with him took him up, and put him into a litter.

28 Thus him, that lately came with a great train and with all his guard into the said treasury, they carried out, being unable to help himself with his weapons: and manifestly they acknowledged the power of God:

29 For he by the hand of God was cast down, and lay speechless without all hope of life.

30 But they praised the Lord, that had miraculously honoured his own place ; for the temple, which a little afore was full of fear and trouble, when the Almighty Lord appeared, was filled with joy and gladness.

31 Then straightway certain of Heliodorus' friends prayed Onias, that he would call upon the most High to grant him his life, who lay ready to give up the ghost.

32 So the high priest, suspecting lest the king should misconceive that some treachery had been done to Heliodorus by the Jews, offered a sacrifice for the health of the man.

33 Now as the high priest was making an atonement, the same young men in the same clothing appeared and stood beside Heliodorus, saying, Give Onias the high priest great thanks, insomuch as for his sake the Lord hath granted thee life:

34 And seeing that thou hast been scourged from heaven, declare unto all men the mighty power of God. And when they had spoken these words, they appeared no more.

35 So Heliodorus, after he had offered sacrifice unto the Lord, and made great vows unto him that had saved his life, and saluted Onias, returned with his host to the king.

36 Then testified he to all men the works of the great God, which he had seen with his eyes.

37 And when the king asked Heliodorus, who might be a fit man to be sent yet once again to Jerusalem, he said,

38 If thou hast any enemy or traitor, send him thither, and thou shalt receive him well scourged, if he escape with his life: for in that place, no doubt, there is an especial power of God.

39 For he that dwelleth in heaven hath his eye on that place, and defendeth it; and he beateth and destroyeth them that come to hurt it.

40 And the things concerning Heliodorus, and the keeping of the treasury, fell out on this sort.

CHAP. IV.

1 *Simon slandereth Onias.* 7 *Jason, by corrupting the king, obtaineth the office of the high priest.* 24 *Menelaus getteth the same from Jason by the like corruption.* 34 *Andronicus traitorously murdereth Onias.* 36 *The king being informed thereof, causeth Andronicus to be put to death.* 39 *The wickedness of Lysimachus, by the instigation of Menelaus.*

THIS Simon now, of whom we spake afore, having been a bewrayer of the money, and of his country, slandered Onias, as if he had terrified Heliodorus, and been the worker of these evils.

2 Thus was he bold to call him a traitor, that had deserved well of the city, and tendered his own nation, and was so zealous of the laws.

3 But when their hatred went so far, that by one of Simon's faction murders were committed,

4 Onias seeing the danger of this contention, and that Apollonius, as being the governor of

Celosyria and Phenice, did rage, and increase Simon's malice,

5 He went to the king, not to be an accuser of his countrymen, but seeking the good of all, both publick and private:

6 For he saw that it was impossible that the state should continue quiet, and Simon leave his folly, unless the king did look thereunto.

7 But after the death of Seleucus, when Antiochus, called Epiphanes, took the kingdom, Jason the brother of Onias laboured underhand to be high priest,

8 Promising unto the king by intercession three hundred and threescore talents of silver, and of another revenue eighty talents:

9 Beside this, he promised to assign an hundred and fifty more, if he might have licence to set him up a place for exercise, and for the training up of youth in the fashions of the heathen, and to write them of Jerusalem *by the name of* Antiochians.

10 Which when the king had granted, and he had gotten into his hand the rule, he forthwith brought his own nation to the Greekish fashion.

11 And the royal privileges granted of special favour to the Jews by the means of John the father of Eupolemus, who went ambassador to Rome for amity and aid, he took away; and putting down the governments which were according to the law, he brought up new customs against the law:

12 For he built gladly a place of exercise under the tower itself, and brought the chief young men under his subjection, and made them wear a hat.

13 Now such was the height of Greek fashions, and increase of heathenish manners, through the exceeding profaneness of Jason, that ungodly wretch, and no high priest;

14 That the priests had no courage to serve any more at the altar, but despising the temple, and neglecting the sacrifices, hastened to be partakers of the unlawful allowance in the place of exercise, after the game of Discus called them forth;

15 Not setting by the honours of their fathers, but liking the glory of the Grecians best of all.

16 By reason whereof sore calamity came upon them: for they had them to be their enemies and avengers, whose custom they followed so earnestly, and unto whom they desired to be like in all things.

17 For it is not a light thing to do wickedly against the laws of God: but the time following shall declare these things.

18 Now when the game that was used every

fifth year was kept at Tyrus, the king being present,

19 This ungracious Jason sent special messengers from Jerusalem, who were Antiochians, to carry three hundred drachms of silver to the sacrifice of Hercules, which even the bearers thereof thought fit not to bestow upon the sacrifice, because it was not convenient, but to be reserved for other charges.

20 This money then, in regard of the sender, was appointed to Hercules' sacrifice; but because of the bearers thereof, it was employed to the making of gallies.

21 Now when Apollonius the *son* of Menestheus was sent into Egypt for the coronation of king *Ptolemeus* Philometor, Antiochus, understanding him not to be well affected to his affairs, provided for his own safety: whereupon he came to Joppe, and from thence to Jerusalem:

22 Where he was honourably received of Jason, and of the city, and was brought in with torch light, and with great shoutings: and so afterward went with his host unto Phenice.

23 Three years afterward Jason sent Menelaus, the aforesaid Simon's brother, to bear the money unto the king, and to put him in mind of certain necessary matters.

24 But he being brought to the presence of the king, when he had magnified him for the glorious appearance of his power, got the priesthood to himself, offering more than Jason by three hundred talents of silver.

25 So he came with the king's mandate, bringing nothing worthy the high priesthood, but having the fury of a cruel tyrant, and the rage of a savage beast.

26 Then Jason, who had undermined his own brother, being undermined by another, was compelled to flee into the country of the Ammonites.

27 So Menelaus got the principality: but as for the money that he had promised unto the king, he took no good order for it, albeit Sostratus the ruler of the castle required it:

28 For unto him appertained the gathering of the customs. Wherefore they were both called before the king.

29 Now Menelaus left his brother Lysimachus in his stead in the priesthood; and Sostratus *left* Crates, who was governor of the Cyprians.

30 While those things were in doing, they of Tarsus and Mallos made insurrection, because they were given to the king's concubine, called Antiochis.

31 Then came the king in all haste to appease matters, leaving Andronicus, a man in authority, for his deputy.

32 Now Menelaus, supposing that he had gotten a convenient time, stole certain vessels of gold out of the temple, and gave some of them to Andronicus, and some he sold into Tyrus and the cities round about.

33 Which when Onias knew of a surety, he reproved him, and withdrew himself into a sanctuary at Daphne, that lieth by Antiochia.

34 Wherefore Menelaus, taking Andronicus apart, prayed him to get Onias into his hands; who being persuaded thereunto, and coming to Onias in deceit, gave him his right hand with oaths; and though he were suspected *by him*, yet persuaded he him to come forth of the sanctuary: whom forthwith he shut up without regard of justice.

35 For the which cause not only the Jews, but many also of other nations, took great indignation, and were much grieved for the unjust murder of the man.

36 And when the king was come again from the places about Cilicia, the Jews that were in the city, and certain of the Greeks that abhorred the fact also, complained because Onias was slain without cause.

37 Therefore Antiochus was heartily sorry, and moved to pity, and wept, because of the sober and modest behaviour of him that was dead.

38 And being kindled with anger, forthwith he took away Andronicus his purple, and rent off his clothes, and leading him through the whole city unto that very place, where he had committed impiety against Onias, there slew he the cursed murderer. Thus the Lord rewarded him his punishment, as he had deserved.

39 Now when many sacrileges had been committed in the city by Lysimachus with the consent of Menelaus, and the bruit thereof was spread abroad, the multitude gathered themselves together against Lysimachus, many vessels of gold being already carried away.

40 Whereupon the common people rising, and being filled with rage, Lysimachus armed about three thousand men, and began first to offer violence; one Auranus being the leader, a man far gone in years, and no less in folly.

41 They then seeing the attempt of Lysimachus, some of them caught stones, some clubs, others taking handfuls of dust, that was next at hand, cast them all together upon Lysimachus, and those that set upon them.

42 Thus many of them they wounded, and some they struck to the ground, and all *of them* they forced to flee: but as for the churchrobber himself, him they killed beside the treasury.

43 Of these matters therefore there was an accusation laid against Menelaus.

44 Now when the king came to Tyrus, three men that were sent from the senate pleaded the cause before him:

45 But Menelaus, being now convicted, promised Ptolemee the *son* of Dorymenes to give him much money, if he would pacify the king toward him.

46 Whereupon Ptolemee taking the king aside into a certain gallery, as it were to take the air, brought him to be of another mind:

47 Insomuch that he discharged Menelaus from the accusations, who notwithstanding was cause of all the mischief: and those poor men, who, if they had told their cause, yea, before the Scythians, should have been judged innocent, them he condemned to death.

48 Thus they that followed the matter for the city, and for the people, and for the holy vessels, did soon suffer unjust punishment.

49 Wherefore even they of Tyrus, moved with hatred of that wicked deed, caused them to be honourably buried.

50 And so through the covetousness of them that were of power Menelaus remained still in authority, increasing in malice, and being a great traitor to the citizens.

CHAP. V.

2 Of the signs and tokens seen in Jerusalem. 6 Of the end and wickedness of Jason. 11 The pursuit of Antiochus against the Jews. 15 The spoiling of the temple. 27 Maccabeus fleeth into the wilderness.

ABOUT the same time Antiochus prepared his second voyage into Egypt:

2 And then it happened, that through all the city, for the space almost of forty days, there were seen horsemen running in the air, in cloth of gold, and armed with lances, like a band of soldiers,

3 And troops of horsemen in array, encountering and running one against another, with shaking of shields, and multitude of pikes, and drawing of swords, and casting of darts, and glittering of golden ornaments, and harness of all sorts.

4 Wherefore every man prayed that that apparition might turn to good.

5 Now when there was gone forth a false rumour, as though Antiochus had been dead, Jason took at the least a thousand men, and suddenly made an assault upon the city; and they that were upon the walls being put back, and the city at length taken, Menelaus fled into the castle.

6 But Jason slew his own citizens without mercy, not considering that to get the day of

them of his own nation would be a most unhappy day for him; but thinking they had been *his* enemies, and not *his* countrymen, whom he conquered.

7 Howbeit for all this he obtained not the principality, but at the last received shame for the reward of his treason, and fled again into the country of the Ammonites.

8 In the end therefore he had an unhappy return, being accused before Aretas the king of the Arabians, fleeing from city to city, pursued of all men, hated as a forsaker of the laws, and being had in abomination as an open enemy of his country and countrymen, he was cast out into Egypt.

9 Thus he that had driven many out of their country perished in a strange land, retiring to the Lacedemonians, and thinking *there* to find succour by reason of his kindred:

10 And he that had cast out many unburied had none to mourn for him, nor any solemn funerals at all, nor sepulchre with his fathers.

11 Now when this that was done came to the king's ear, he thought that Judea had revolted: whereupon removing out of Egypt in a furious mind, he took the city by force of arms,

12 And commanded his men of war not to spare such as they met, and to slay such as went up upon the houses.

13 Thus there was killing of young and old, making away of men, women, and children, slaying of virgins and infants.

14 And there were destroyed within the space of three whole days fourscore thousand, whereof forty thousand were slain in the conflict; and no fewer sold than slain.

15 Yet was he not content with this, but presumed to go into the most holy temple of all the world; Menelaus, that traitor to the laws, and to his own country, being his guide:

16 And taking the holy vessels with polluted hands, and with profane hands pulling down the things that were dedicated by other kings to the augmentation and glory and honour of the place, he gave them away.

17 And so haughty was Antiochus in mind, that he considered not that the Lord was angry for a while for the sins of them that dwelt in the city, and therefore his eye was not upon the place.

18 For had they not been formerly wrapped in many sins, this man, as soon as he had come, had forthwith been scourged, and put back from his presumption, as Heliodorus was, whom Seleucus the king sent to view the treasury.

19 Nevertheless God did not choose the people for the place's sake, but the place for the people's sake.

20 And therefore the place itself, that was partaker with them of the adversity that happened to the nation, did afterward communicate in the benefits sent from the Lord: and as it was forsaken in the wrath of the Almighty, so again, the great Lord being reconciled, it was set up with all glory.

21 So when Antiochus had carried out of the temple a thousand and eight hundred talents, he departed in all haste unto Antiochia, weening in his pride to make the land navigable, and the sea passable by foot: such was the haughtiness of his mind.

22 And he left governors to vex the nation: at Jerusalem, Philip, for his country a Phrygian, and for manners more barbarous than he that set him there;

23 And at Garizim, Andronicus; and besides, Menelaus, who worse than all the rest bare an heavy hand over the citizens, having a malicious mind against his countrymen the Jews.

24 He sent also that detestable ringleader Apollonius with an army of two and twenty thousand, commanding him to slay all those that were in their best age, and to sell the women and the younger sort:

25 Who coming to Jerusalem, and pretending peace, did forbear till the holy day of the sabbath, when taking the Jews keeping holy day, he commanded his men to arm themselves.

26 And so he slew all them that were gone to the celebrating of the sabbath, and running through the city with weapons slew great multitudes.

27 But Judas Maccabeus with nine others, or thereabout, withdrew himself into the wilderness, and lived in the mountains after the manner of beasts, with his company, who fed on herbs continually, lest they should be partakers of the pollution.

CHAP. VI.

1 *The Jews are compelled to leave the law of God.* 4 *The temple is defiled.* 8 *Cruelty upon the people and the women.* 12 *An exhortation to bear affliction, by the example of the valiant courage of Eleazarus, cruelly tortured.*

NOT long after this the king sent an old man of Athens to compel the Jews to depart from the laws of their fathers, and not to live after the laws of God:

2 And to pollute also the temple in Jerusalem, and to call it the temple of Jupiter Olympius; and that in Garizim, of Jupiter the Defender of strangers, as they did desire that dwelt in the place.

3 The coming in of this mischief was sore and grievous to the people:

4 For the temple was filled with riot and revelling by the Gentiles, who dallied with harlots, and had to do with women within the circuit of the holy places, and besides that brought in things that were not lawful.

5 The altar also was filled with profane things, which the law forbiddeth.

6 Neither was it lawful for a man to keep sabbath days or ancient feasts, or to profess himself at all to be a Jew.

7 And in the day of the king's birth every month they were brought by bitter constraint to eat of the sacrifices; and when the feast of Bacchus was kept, the Jews were compelled to go in procession to Bacchus, carrying ivy.

8 Moreover there went out a decree to the neighbour cities of the heathen, by the suggestion of Ptolemee, against the Jews, that they should observe the same fashions, and be partakers of their sacrifices:

9 And whoso would not conform themselves to the manners of the Gentiles should be put to death. Then might a man have seen the present misery.

10 For there were two women brought, who had circumcised their children; whom when they had openly led round about the city, the babes hanging at their breasts, they cast them down headlong from the wall.

11 And others, that had run together into caves near by, to keep the sabbath day secretly, being discovered to Philip, were all burnt together, because they made a conscience to help themselves for the honour of the most sacred day.

12 Now I beseech those that read this book, that they be not discouraged for these calamities, but that they judge those punishments not to be for destruction, but for a chastening of our nation.

13 For it is a token of his great goodness, when wicked doers are not suffered any long time, but forthwith punished.

14 For not as with other nations, whom the Lord patiently forbeareth to punish, till they be come to the fulness of their sins, so dealeth he with us.

15 Lest that, being come to the height of sin, afterwards he should take vengeance of us.

16 And therefore he never withdraweth his mercy from us: and though he punish with adversity, yet doth he never forsake his people.

17 But let this that we have spoken be for a warning unto us. And now will we come to the declaring of the matter in few words.

18 Eleazar, one of the principal scribes, an aged man, and of a well favoured countenance, was constrained to open his mouth, and to eat swine's flesh.

19 But he, choosing rather to die gloriously, than to live stained with such an abomination, spit it forth, and came of his own accord to the torment,

20 As it behoved them to come, that are resolute to stand out against such things, as are not lawful for love of life to be tasted.

21 But they that had the charge of that wicked feast, for the old acquaintance they had with the man, taking him aside, besought him to bring flesh of his own provision, such as was lawful for him to use, and make as if he did eat of the flesh taken from the sacrifice commanded by the king;

22 That in so doing he might be delivered from death, and for the old friendship with them find favour.

23 But he began to consider discreetly, and as became his age, and the excellency of his ancient years, and the honour of his gray head, whereunto he was come, and his most honest education from a child, or rather the holy law made and given by God: therefore he answered accordingly, and willed them straightways to send him to the grave.

24 For it becometh not our age, said he, in any wise to dissemble, whereby many young persons might think that Eleazar, being fourscore years old and ten, were now gone to a strange religion;

25 And so they through mine hypocrisy, and desire to live a little time and a moment longer, should be deceived by me, and I get a stain to mine old age, and make it abominable.

26 For though for the present time I should be delivered from the punishment of men: yet should I not escape the hand of the Almighty, neither alive, nor dead.

27 Wherefore now, manfully changing this life, I will shew myself such an one as mine age requireth,

28 And leave a notable example to such as be young to die willingly and courageously for the honourable and holy laws. And when he had said these words, immediately he went to the torment:

29 They that led him changing the good will they bare him a little before into hatred, because the foresaid speeches proceeded, as they thought, from a desperate mind.

30 But when he was ready to die with stripes, he groaned, and said, It is manifest unto the Lord, that hath the holy knowledge, that whereas I might have been delivered from death, I now endure sore pains in body by being beaten: but in soul am well content to suffer these things, because I fear him.

31 And thus this man died, leaving his death

for an example of a noble courage, and a memorial of virtue, not only unto young men, but unto all his nation.

CHAP. VII.

The constancy and cruel death of seven brethren and their mother in one day, because they would not eat swine's flesh at the king's commandment.

IT came to pass also, that seven brethren with their mother were taken, and compelled by the king against the law to taste swine's flesh, and were tormented with scourges and whips.

2 But one of them that spake first said thus, What wouldest thou ask or learn of us? we are ready to die, rather than to transgress the laws of our fathers.

3 Then the king, being in a rage, commanded pans and chaldrons to be made hot:

4 Which forthwith being heated, he commanded to cut out the tongue of him that spake first, and to cut off the utmost parts of his body, the rest of his brethren and his mother looking on.

5 Now when he was thus maimed in all his members, he commanded him being yet alive to be brought to the fire, and to be fried in the pan: and as the vapour of the pan was for a good space dispersed, they exhorted one another with the mother to die manfully, saying thus,

6 The Lord God looketh upon us, and in truth hath comfort in us, as Moses in his song, which witnessed to their faces, declared, saying, And he shall be comforted in his servants.

7 So when the first was dead after this manner, they brought the second to make him a mocking stock: and when they had pulled off the skin of his head with the hair, they asked him, Wilt thou eat, before thou be punished throughout every member of thy body?

8 But he answered in his own language, and said, No. Wherefore he also received the next torment in order, as the former did.

9 And when he was at the last gasp, he said, Thou like a fury takest us out of this present life, but the King of the world shall raise us up, who have died for his laws, unto everlasting life.

10 After him was the third made a mocking stock: and when he was required, he put out his tongue, and that right soon, holding forth his hands manfully,

11 And said courageously, These I had from heaven; and for his laws I despise them; and from him I hope to receive them again.

12 Insomuch that the king, and they that were with him, marvelled at the young man's courage, for that he nothing regarded the pains.

13 Now when this man was dead also, they tormented and mangled the fourth in like manner.

14 So when he was ready to die he said thus, It is good, being put to death by men, to look for hope from God to be raised up again by him: as for thee, thou shalt have no resurrection to life.

15 Afterward they brought the fifth also, and mangled him.

16 Then looked he unto the king, and said, Thou hast power over men, thou art corruptible, thou doest what thou wilt; yet think not that our nation is forsaken of God;

17 But abide a while, and behold his great power, how he will torment thee and thy seed.

18 After him also they brought the sixth, who being ready to die said, Be not deceived without cause: for we suffer these things for ourselves, having sinned against our God: therefore marvellous things are done *unto us*.

19 But think not thou, that takest in hand to strive against God, that thou shalt escape unpunished.

20 But the mother was marvellous above all, and worthy of honourable memory: for when she saw her seven sons slain within the space of one day, she bare it with a good courage, because of the hope that she had in the Lord.

21 Yea, she exhorted every one of them in her own language, filled with courageous spirits; and stirring up her womanish thoughts with a manly stomach, she said unto them,

22 I cannot tell how ye came into my womb; for I neither gave you breath nor life, neither was it I that formed the members of every one of you;

23 But doubtless the Creator of the world, who formed the generation of man, and found out the beginning of all things, will also of his own mercy give you breath and life again, as ye now regard not your own selves for his laws' sake.

24 Now Antiochus, thinking himself despised, and suspecting it to be a reproachful speech, whilst the youngest was yet alive, did not only exhort him by words, but also assured him with oaths, that he would make him both a rich and a happy man, if he would turn from the laws of his fathers; and that also he would take him for his friend, and trust him with affairs.

25 But when the young man would in no case hearken unto him, the king called his mother, and exhorted her that she would counsel the young man to save his life.

26 And when he had exhorted her with many

words, she promised him that she would counsel her son.

27 But she bowing herself toward him, laughing the cruel tyrant to scorn, spake in her country language on this manner; O my son, have pity upon me that bare thee nine months in my womb, and gave thee suck three years, and nourished thee, and brought thee up unto this age, and endured the troubles of education.

28 I beseech thee, my son, look upon the heaven and the earth, and all that is therein, and consider that God made them of things that were not; and so was mankind made likewise.

29 Fear not this tormentor, but, being worthy of thy brethren, take thy death, that I may receive thee again in mercy with thy brethren.

30 Whiles she was yet speaking these words, the young man said, Whom wait ye for? I will not obey the king's commandment: but I will obey the commandment of the law that was given unto our fathers by Moses.

31 And thou, that hast been the author of all mischief against the Hebrews, shalt not escape the hands of God.

32 For we suffer because of our sins.

33 And though the living Lord be angry with us a little while for our chastening and correction, yet shall he be at one again with his servants.

34 But thou, O godless man, and of all other most wicked, be not lifted up without a cause, nor puffed up with uncertain hopes, lifting up thy hand against the servants of God:

35 For thou hast not yet escaped the judgment of Almighty God, who seeth all things.

36 For our brethren, who now have suffered a short pain, are dead under God's covenant of everlasting life: but thou, through the judgment of God, shalt receive just punishment for thy pride.

37 But I, as my brethren, offer up my body and life for the laws of our fathers, beseeching God that he would speedily be merciful unto our nation; and that thou by torments and plagues mayest confess, that he alone is God;

38 And that in me and my brethren the wrath of the Almighty, which is justly brought upon all our nation, may cease.

39 Then the king, being in a rage, handled him worse than all the rest, and took it grievously that he was mocked.

40 So this man died undefiled, and put his whole trust in the Lord.

41 Last of all after the sons the mother died.

42 Let this be enough now to have spoken concerning the idolatrous feasts, and the extreme tortures.

CHAP. VIII.

1 *Judas gathereth an host.* 9 *Nicanor is sent against him: who presumeth to make much money of his prisoners.* 16 *Judas encourageth his men, and putteth Nicanor to flight,* 28 *and divideth the spoils.* 30 *Other enemies are also defeated,* 35 *and Nicanor fleeth with grief to Antioch.*

THEN Judas Maccabeus, and they that were with him, went privily into the towns, and called their kinsfolks together, and took unto them all such as continued in the Jews' religion, and assembled about six thousand men.

2 And they called upon the Lord, that he would look upon the people that was trodden down of all; and also pity the temple profaned of ungodly men;

3 And that he would have compassion upon the city, sore defaced, and ready to be made even with the ground; and hear the blood that cried unto him,

4 And remember the wicked slaughter of harmless infants, and the blasphemies committed against his name; and that he would shew his hatred against the wicked.

5 Now when Maccabeus had his company about him, he could not be withstood by the heathen: for the wrath of the Lord was turned into mercy.

6 Therefore he came at unawares, and burnt up towns and cities, and got into his hands the most commodious places, and overcame and put to flight no small number of his enemies.

7 But specially took he advantage of the night for such privy attempts, insomuch that the bruit of his manliness was spread every where.

8 So when Philip saw that this man increased by little and little, and that things prospered with him still more and more, he wrote unto Ptolemeus, the governor of Celosyria and Phenice, to yield more aid to the king's affairs.

9 Then forthwith choosing Nicanor the son of Patroclus, one of his special friends, he sent him with no fewer than twenty thousand of all nations under him, to root out the whole generation of the Jews; and with him he joined also Gorgias a captain, who in matters of war had great experience.

10 So Nicanor undertook to make so much money of the captive Jews, as should defray the tribute of two thousand talents, which the king was to pay to the Romans.

11 Wherefore immediately he sent to the cities upon the sea coast, proclaiming a sale of the captive Jews, and promising that they should have fourscore and ten bodies for one

talent, not expecting the vengeance that was to follow upon him from the Almighty God.

12 Now when word was brought unto Judas of Nicanor's coming, and he had imparted unto those that were with him that the army was at hand,

13 They that were fearful, and distrusted the justice of God, fled, and conveyed themselves away.

14 Others sold all that they had left, and withal besought the Lord to deliver them, being sold by the wicked Nicanor before they met together:

15 And if not for their own sakes, yet for the covenants he had made with their fathers, and for his holy and glorious name's sake, by which they were called.

16 So Maccabeus called his men together unto the number of six thousand, and exhorted them not to be stricken with terror of the enemy, nor to fear the great multitude of the heathen, who came wrongfully against them; but to fight manfully,

17 And to set before their eyes the injury that they had unjustly done to the holy place, and the cruel handling of the city, whereof they made a mockery, and also the taking away of the government of their forefathers:

18 For they, said he, trust in their weapons and boldness; but our confidence is in the Almighty God, who at a beck can cast down both them that come against us, and also all the world.

19 Moreover he recounted unto them what helps their forefathers had found, and how they were delivered, when under Sennacherib an hundred fourscore and five thousand perished.

20 And he told them of the battle that they had in Babylon with the Galatians,' how they came but eight thousand in all to the business, with four thousand Macedonians, and that the Macedonians being perplexed, the eight thousand destroyed an hundred and twenty thousand because of the help that they had from heaven, and so received a great booty.

21 Thus when he had made them bold with these words, and ready to die for the laws and the country, he divided his army into four parts.

22 And joined with himself his own brethren, leaders of each band, *to wit*, Simon, and Joseph, and Jonathan, giving each one fifteen hundred men.

23 Also *he appointed* Eleazar to read the holy book: and when he had given them this watchword, The help of God; himself leading the first band, he joined battle with Nicanor.

24 And by the help of the Almighty, they slew above nine thousand of their enemies, and wounded and maimed the most part of Nicanor's host, and so put all to flight;

25 And took their money that came to buy them, and pursued them far: but lacking time they returned:

26 For it was the day before the sabbath, and therefore they would no longer pursue them.

27 So when they had gathered their armour together, and spoiled their enemies, they occupied themselves about the sabbath, yielding exceeding praise and thanks to the Lord, who had preserved them unto that day, which was the beginning of mercy distilling upon them.

28 And after the sabbath, when they had given part of the spoils to the maimed, and the widows, and orphans, the residue they divided among themselves and their servants.

29 When this was done, and they had made a common supplication, they besought the merciful Lord to be reconciled with his servants for ever.

30 Moreover of those that were with Timotheus and Bacchides, who fought against them, they slew above twenty thousand, and very easily got high and strong holds, and divided among themselves many spoils more, and made the maimed, orphans, widows, yea, and the aged also, equal in spoils with themselves.

31 And when they had gathered their armour together, they laid them up all carefully in convenient places, and the remnant of the spoils they brought to Jerusalem.

32 They slew also Philarches, that wicked person, who was with Timotheus, and had annoyed the Jews many ways.

33 Furthermore at such time as they kept the feast for the victory in their country they burnt Callisthenes, that had set fire upon the holy gates, who had fled into a little house; and so he received a reward meet for his wickedness.

34 As for that most ungracious Nicanor, who had brought a thousand merchants to buy the Jews,

35 He was through the help of the Lord brought down by them, of whom he made least account; and putting off his glorious apparel, and discharging his company, he came like a fugitive servant through the midland unto Antioch, having very great dishonour, for that his host was destroyed.

36 Thus he, that took upon him to make good to the Romans their tribute by means of the captives in Jerusalem, told abroad, that the Jews had God to fight for them, and therefore they could not be hurt, because they followed the laws that he gave them.

CHAP. IX.

1 *Antiochus is chased from Persepolis.* 5 *He is stricken with a sore disease,* 14 *and promiseth to become a Jew.* 28 *He dieth miserably.*

ABOUT that time came Antiochus with dishonour out of the country of Persia.

2 For he had entered the *city* called Persepolis, and went about to rob the temple, and to hold the city; whereupon the multitude running to defend themselves with their weapons put them to flight; and so it happened, that Antiochus being put to flight of the inhabitants returned with shame.

3 Now when he came to Ecbatane, news was brought him what had happened unto Nicanor and Timotheus.

4 Then swelling with anger, he thought to avenge upon the Jews the disgrace done unto him by those that made him flee. Therefore commanded he his chariotman to drive without ceasing, and to dispatch the journey, the judgment of God now following him. For he had spoken proudly in this sort, That he would come to Jerusalem, and make it a common burying-place of the Jews.

5 But the Lord Almighty, the God of Israel, smote him with an incurable and invisible plague: for as soon as he had spoken these words, a pain of the bowels that was remediless came upon him, and sore torments of the inner parts;

6 And that most justly: for he had tormented other men's bowels with many and strange torments.

7 Howbeit he nothing at all ceased from his bragging, but still was filled with pride, breathing out fire in his rage against the Jews, and commanding to haste the journey: but it came to pass that he fell down from his chariot, carried violently; so that having a sore fall, all the members of his body were much pained.

8 And thus he that a little afore thought he might command the waves of the sea, (so proud was he beyond the condition of man) and weigh the high mountains in a balance, was now cast on the ground, and carried in an horselitter, showing forth unto all the manifest power of God.

9 So that the worms rose up out of the body of this wicked man, and whiles he lived in sorrow and pain, his flesh fell away, and the filthiness of his smell was noisome to all his army.

10 And the man, that thought a little afore he could reach to the stars of heaven, no man could endure to carry for his intolerable stink.

11 Here therefore, being plagued, he began to leave off his great pride, and to come to the knowledge *of himself* by the scourge of God, his pain increasing every moment.

12 And when he himself could not abide his own smell, he said these words, It is meet to be subject unto God, and that a man that is mortal should not proudly think of himself, as if he were God.

13 This wicked person vowed also unto the Lord, who now no more would have mercy upon him, saying thus,

14 That the holy city (to the which he was going in haste, to lay it even with the ground, and to make it a common burying-place,) he would set at liberty:

15 And as touching the Jews, whom he had judged not worthy so much as to be buried, but to be cast out with their children to be devoured of the fowls and wild beasts, he would make them all equals to the citizens of Athens:

16 And the holy temple, which before he had spoiled, he would garnish with goodly gifts, and restore all the holy vessels with many more, and out of his own revenue defray the charges belonging to the sacrifices:

17 Yea, and that also he would become a Jew himself, and go through all the world that was inhabited, and declare the power of God.

18 But for all this his pains would not cease: for the just judgment of God was come upon him: therefore despairing of his health, he wrote unto the Jews the letter underwritten, containing the form of a supplication, after this manner:

19 Antiochus, king and governor, to the good Jews his citizens wisheth much joy, health, and prosperity:

20 If ye and your children fare well, and your affairs be to your contentment, I give very great thanks to God, having my hope in heaven.

21 As for me, I was weak, or else I would have remembered kindly your honour and good will. Returning out of Persia, and being taken with a grievous disease, I thought it necessary to care for the common safety of all:

22 Not distrusting mine health, but having great hope to escape this sickness.

23 But considering that even my father, at what time he led an army into the high countries, appointed a successor,

24 To the end that, if any thing fell out contrary to expectation, or if any tidings were brought that were grievous, they of the land, knowing to whom the state was left, might not be troubled:

25 Again, considering how that the princes that are borderers and neighbours unto my

kingdom wait for opportunities, and expect what shall be the event, I have appointed my son Antiochus king, whom I often committed and commended unto many of you, when I went up into the high provinces; to whom I have written as followeth:

26 Therefore I pray and request you to remember the benefits that I have done unto you generally, and in special, and that every man will be still faithful to me and my son.

27 For I am persuaded that he understanding my mind will favourably and graciously yield to your desires.

28 Thus the murderer and blasphemer having suffered most grievously, as he entreated other men, so died he a miserable death in a strange country in the mountains.

29 And Philip, that was brought up with him, carried away his body, who also fearing the son of Antiochus went into Egypt to Ptolemeus Philometor.

CHAP. X.

1 *Judas recovereth the city, and purifieth the temple.* 14 *Gorgias vexeth the Jews.* 16 *Judas winneth their holds.* 29 *Timotheus and his men are discomfited.* 35 *Gazara is taken, and Timotheus slain.*

NOW Maccabeus and his company, the Lord guiding them, recovered the temple and the city:

2 But the altars which the heathen had built in the open street, and also the chapels, they pulled down.

3 And having cleansed the temple they made another altar, and striking stones they took fire out of them, and offered a sacrifice after two years, and set forth incense, and lights, and shewbread.

4 When that was done, they fell flat down, and besought the Lord that they might come no more into such troubles; but if they sinned any more against him, that he himself would chasten them with mercy, and that they might not be delivered unto the blasphemous and barbarous nations.

5 Now upon the same day that the strangers profaned the temple, on the very same day it was cleansed again, even the five and twentieth day of the same month, which is Casleu.

6 And they kept eight days with gladness, as in the feast of the tabernacles, remembering that not long afore they had held the feast of the tabernacles, when as they wandered in the mountains and dens like beasts.

7 Therefore they bare branches, and fair boughs, and palms also, and sang psalms unto him that had given them good success in cleansing his place.

8 They ordained also by a common statute and decree, That every year those days should be kept of the whole nation of the Jews.

9 And this was the end of Antiochus, called Epiphanes.

10 Now will we declare the acts of Antiochus Eupator, who was the son of this wicked man, gathering briefly the calamities of the wars.

11 So when he was come to the crown, he set one Lysias over the affairs of his realm, and *appointed him* chief governor of Celosyria and Phenice.

12 For Ptolemeus, that was called Macron, choosing rather to do justice unto the Jews for the wrong that had been done unto them, endeavoured to continue peace with them.

13 Whereupon being accused of *the king's* friends before Eupator, and called traitor at every word, because he had left Cyprus, that Philometor had committed unto him, and departed to Antiochus Epiphanes, and seeing that he was in no honourable place, he was so discouraged, that he poisoned himself and died.

14 But when Gorgias was governor of the holds, he hired soldiers, and nourished war continually with the Jews:

15 And therewithal the Idumeans, having gotten into their hands the most commodious holds, kept the Jews occupied, and receiving those that were banished from Jerusalem, they went about to nourish war.

16 Then they that were with Maccabeus made supplication, and besought God that he would be their helper; and so they ran with violence upon the strong holds of the Idumeans,

17 And assaulting them strongly, they won the holds, and kept off all that fought upon the wall, and slew all that fell into their hands, and killed no fewer than twenty thousand.

18 And because certain, who were no less than nine thousand, were fled together into two very strong castles, having all manner of things convenient to *sustain* the siege,

19 Maccabeus left Simon and Joseph, and Zaccheus also, and them that were with him, who were enough to besiege them, and departed himself unto those places which more needed his help.

20 Now they that were with Simon, being led with covetousness, were persuaded for money through certain of those that were in the castle, and took seventy thousand drachms, and let some of them escape.

21 But when it was told Maccabeus what was done, he called the governors of the people together, and accused those men, that they had sold

their brethren for money, and set their enemies free to fight against them.

22 So he slew those that were found traitors, and immediately took the two castles.

23 And having good success with his weapons in all things he took in hand, he slew in the two holds more than twenty thousand.

24 Now Timotheus, whom the Jews had overcome before, when he had gathered a great multitude of foreign forces, and horses out of Asia not a few, came as though he would take Jewry by force of arms.

25 But when he drew near, they that were with Maccabeus turned themselves to pray unto God, and sprinkled earth upon their heads, and girded their loins with sackcloth,

26 And fell down at the foot of the altar, and besought him to be merciful to them, and to be an enemy to their enemies, and an adversary to their adversaries, as the law declareth.

27 So after the prayer they took their weapons, and went on further from the city: and when they drew near to their enemies, they kept ,y themselves.

28 Now the sun being newly risen, they joined both together; the one part having together with their virtue their refuge also unto the Lord for a pledge of their success and victory: the other side making their rage leader of their battle.

29 But when the battle waxed strong, there appeared unto the enemies from heaven five comely men upon horses, with bridles of gold, and two of them led the Jews,

30 And took Maccabeus betwixt them, and DANIEL II.

covered him on every side with their weapons, and kept him safe, but shot arrows and lightnings against the enemies: so that being confounded with blindness, and full of trouble, they were killed.

31 And there were slain *of footmen* twenty thousand and five hundred, and six hundred horsemen.

32 As for Timotheus himself, he fled into a very strong hold, called Gazara, where Chereas was governor.

33 But they that were with Maccabeus laid siege against the fortress courageously four days.

34 And they that were within, trusting to the strength of the place, blasphemed exceedingly, and uttered wicked words.

35 Nevertheless upon the fifth day early twenty young men of Maccabeus' company, inflamed with anger because of the blasphemies, assaulted the wall manly, and with a fierce courage killed all that they met withal.

36 Others likewise ascending after them, whiles they were busied with them that were within, burnt the towers, and kindling fires, burnt the blasphemers alive; and others broke open the gates, and, having received in the rest of the army, took the city,

37 And killed Timotheus, that was hid in a certain pit, and Chereas his brother, with Apollophanes.

38 When this was done, they praised the Lord with psalms and thanksgiving, who had done so great things for Israel, and given them the victory.

U

HISTORICAL SYNCHRONISMS,

AND

THE EMPIRES OF PROPHECY.

The historical portions of the Book of DANIEL make extensive reference to the principal ancient nations of the East; and the prophecies are universally interpreted as Divine predictions concerning the great monarchies that were to succeed in order, after the Chaldæo-Babylonian empire had passed away. It is desirable, therefore, to state in few words, what were the condition and circumstances of the countries in the time of the prophet, and in what order of succession the several empires arose, to what extent they attained, and how they merged the one into the other, until Rome, the last and greatest, absorbed the most valuable states and kingdoms which had appertained to the nations that preceded her.

When Daniel was chief minister in the court of Nebuchadnezzar (B.C. 560), that monarch had founded the Chaldæo-Babylonian empire, by the conquest of Nineveh, and the subjugation of Phœnicia, Syria, Judah, and other countries of the East. At this time, Babylon was the centre of a monarchy that claimed superiority of place and power over every other kingdom then existent. The extensive rule and absolute authority of Nebuchadnezzar, are expressively stated in Daniel ii. 37, 38; and iii. 22; and in other passages.

The kingdom of Israel had ceased for nearly a century and a half, and its people had been transplanted into Media. The Assyrian monarch, Esarhaddon, about 711 B.C. established in Samaria colonies from Babylon and neighbouring countries, and these people, afterwards known as Samaritans, were regarded with bitter animosity by the Jews, at the end of the Captivity, on account of their idolatrous practices, and their erection of a rival temple on Mount Gerizim.

Judah had been subjected by Nebuchadnezzar, who had carried the people captive to Babylon, and destroyed the temple in Jerusalem. To this event, the pathetic lamentation in the 137th Psalm refers.

Media, a country of ten tribes, of which the chief was the Magians, had become great in arms, and had aided Nebuchadnezzar in the overthrow of Nineveh. Astyages, the successor of the warlike Cyaxares, was dethroned by Cyrus in the time of Belshazzar. At an earlier period, Media was a country of nomadic people, unpossessed of much political importance.

Egypt, a few years before the coming of Daniel to Babylon, was under the government of Pharaoh-Necho, an enterprising sovereign, who endeavoured to connect the Mediterranean and Red Seas by a canal, but abandoned the undertaking after a loss of 120,000 men.

Greece was rejoicing in the wise legislation of Solon.

Rome was under the rule of the first Tarquin, by whom the walls of the city were built of stone, also the Cloacæ and Circus Maximus, and the foundations of the Capitol laid.

In Magna Græcia, or Southern Italy, the city of Sybaris, on the Bay of Tarentum, was in its prosperity. This city, which was then a seat of luxury, became afterwards a centre of effeminate and sensual pleasures, and its name passed into a proverb as a synonyme for immorality.

Asia Minor was governed by the rich Lydian king, Crœsus, whose name has also become a proverb for wealth.

Cyrus having dethroned Astyages, 559 B.C., and thus become master of Media, next directed his power against Babylon, at that time subject to Belshazzar, and by its conquest laid the foundation of the Persian empire, which gradually comprehended Media, Persia proper, Assyria, Babylonia, Asia Minor, Syria, Phœnicia, and Palestine. Cambyses, the successor of Cyrus, besieged and took Memphis, and added Egypt, Libya, and Cyrene, to the empire. Darius I. was unsuccessful in an expedition against Scythia, but rendered Macedonia and Thrace tributaries, and also the countries north of the Indus. The Persians were led into quarrels with the Greeks on account of the loss of Macedonia, and their after-history is a record of continual wars between the two peoples, which eventually resulted in the destruction of the Persian monarchy. The Greeks obtained decisive victories at Marathon, Thermopylæ, Salamis, Platæa, and Mycale, in the time of Xerxes; and the overthrow of Darius by Alexander of Macedon, known in history as Alexander the Great, put an end to the Persian empire, which thereafter became part of the great Macedonian monarchy. The royal palaces of Persia were at Babylon, Susa, and Ecbatana; and the mausoleum of the kings at Persepolis. The reference of the prophetic beasts to the preceding empires, and those which follow, is discussed in the notes of our author.

Macedonia, the nucleus of Alexander's empire, goes back to about 800 B.C. Its early history records continual wars with the Persians and Illyrians. It became subject to Persia, but was set free by the battle and victory of Platæa. After many vicissitudes it came under the government of Philip of Macedon, whose son and successor Alexander, overthrew Darius III. at Arbela, and by the subjugation of Persia, laid the foundation of the Macedonian empire, B.C. 333. This vast monarchy included Media, Persia, Thrace, Macedonia, Greece, Syria, Phœnicia, Palestine, Egypt, and provinces beyond the Indus to the river Hyphasis. Still seeking fresh conquests, Alexander arrived in Babylon, where he died either by poison, or intemperate excess, B.C. 323. His dominions were then dismembered, and partitioned amongst his generals and his family, who, for twenty-two years were in deadly contest with each other, before their several claims were adjusted.

The Roman empire, about 200 B.C. had become the dictator of all the nations from the Atlantic to the Euphrates. Passing through many vicissitudes, sometimes subject to internal strife and the war of factions, at others, enlarging the boundaries of her rule and consolidating her power, she 'at length reached the age of Augustus, under whom she extended her sway over the principal countries of the then known world. Her possessions in Europe were Spain, Gaul, Britain, Rhœtia, Vindelicia, Noricum, Pannonia, Illyria, Greece, Thrace, Mœsia, and Daria; in Asia, Asia Minor, Syria, Phœnicia, Palestine, the north-eastern coasts of the Black Sea, Armenia, Mesopotamia, and Assyria; and in Africa, Egypt and the whole of the northern coast. After Augustus, and to the reign of Vitellius, Rome was subject to the arbitrary will of tyrants, noticeable for little beyond their vices and luxurious effeminacy. From Vitellius to Antoninus she enjoyed a period of happiness and prosperity; but from Commodus to Diocletian the power was in the hands of a military despotism. The Roman spirit became thoroughly enervated by luxury and vicious indulgence, and the empire gradually tottered to its fall. The removal of the seat of government from Rome to Constantinople by Constantine, hastened on the crisis, and the subsequent divisions of the empire divided and weakened its power. The German tribes began to make bolder incursions, and effected permanent settlements. At length, A.D. 476, the Western empire, of which Rome was the capital, fell under the power of the Heruli. The Eastern empire survived for centuries, and after many alternations of grandeur and declension, finally terminated A.D. 1453, when the Ottoman power became triumphant. The Gothic kingdoms which arose out of the ruins of the Roman empire are considered to be pointed at in Daniel vii. 20, and denoted by the ten horns of the fourth beast.

On the ruins of the Western empire, arose the temporal power of the Papacy. The barbarian conquerors of Rome, not less superstitious than ferocious and cruel, submitted themselves to the designs of an ambitious hierarchy, which sought to establish an universal empire, on the basis of an infallible spiritual authority. To effect this, the Roman church threw aside the simplicity of the Gospel system, and amalgamated with Truth the various forms of idolatry, which prevailed amongst the peoples over whom she sought to lay her rule. Following out this line of policy, she at length succeeded in her designs, and secured an absolute and arbitrary power, both in temporal and spiritual matters; but every step in her advance to this point degraded her more and more as a church of Christ; and when her ambitious views were at length realized, she had reached the bad eminence in idolatry and all wickedness that identifies her with the Antichrist of prophecy.